The UK's Leading Dealer F...

RODERICK RICHARDSON

Numismatist

(Specialist in English Hammered - Early Milled Coins)

For appointments in London or my latest circular, please contact me at
Old Granary Antiques Centre, Kings Staithe Lane,
King's Lynn, Norfolk, England PE 30 ILZ
Tel: (+44) 1553 670833
Email: **roderickrichardson@yahoo.co.uk**
Check out my website: **roderickrichardson.com**

WORLD & ANCIENT COIN AUCTIONS
Always Accepting Consignments of High Quality British Coins

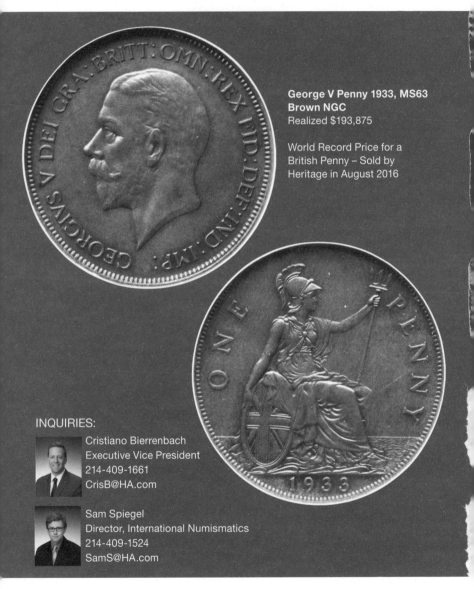

George V Penny 1933, MS63 Brown NGC
Realized $193,875

World Record Price for a British Penny – Sold by Heritage in August 2016

INQUIRIES:

Cristiano Bierrenbach
Executive Vice President
214-409-1661
CrisB@HA.com

Sam Spiegel
Director, International Numismatics
214-409-1524
SamS@HA.com

DALLAS | NEW YORK | BEVERLY HILLS | SAN FRANCISCO | CHICAGO | PALM BEACH
PARIS | GENEVA | AMSTERDAM | HONG KONG

Always Accepting Quality Consignments in 40 Categories
Immediate Cash Advances Available
1 Million+ Online Bidder-Members

HERITAGE
AUCTIONS
THE WORLD'S LARGEST NUMISMATIC AUCTIONEER

43118

MORTON
& EDEN

Consultants to Sotheby's

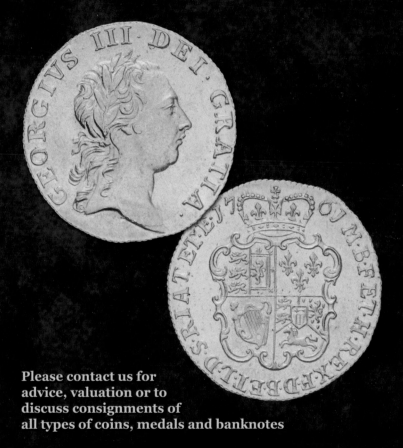

Please contact us for
advice, valuation or to
discuss consignments of
all types of coins, medals and banknotes

Sample auction catalogues are availabe on request

Nash House
St George Street
London W1S 2FQ

+44 (0) 207 493 5344
info @mortonandeden.com
www.mortonandeden.com

Daruma

DARUMA
BUYING AND SELLING
WORLD NUMISMATIC
SILVER AND GOLD COINS

Daruma INTERNATIONAL GALLERIES Nihon Coin Auction

2-16-32-701 Takanawa , Minato-ku , Tokyo 108-0074 , JAPAN
Tel:(81)3-3447-5567 FAX:(81)3-3449-3344 E-mail:sales@darumacoins.co.jp

www.darumacoins.co.jp

1839 G.BRITAIN 5SOV
W&R-278 UNA AND THE LION
PF 66 ULTRA CAMEO
2797484-001
NUMISMATIC GUARANTY CORPORATION NGC®

NGC
Terms & Descriptions - www.NGCcoin.com/terms - 1-800-NGC-COIN
The Official Grading
Service of the PNG

The world coins you can trust.
GUARANTEED

Every NGC world coin is backed by our comprehensive guarantee so you can buy and sell with confidence. That's why we've graded more world coins than any other grading company, and how we've become the largest and most trusted grading company in the world. NGC — the name you can trust. Guaranteed. NGCcoin.com

30 YEARS NGC®
FOUNDED 1987

NGCcoin.com | Europe@NGCcoin.com   North America | Europe | Asia

NUMIS·OR

Consign & Sell your coin collections with Numisor of Switzerland

- 40 years of numismatic experience
- A proven track record in volume bullion sales
- Close relationship with many major Swiss banks
- Extensive worldwide client list
- Member of many prestigious numismatic societies
- Partnership with David Feldman, renowned international stamp auctioneers

For those clients that are looking to sell their collections, we offer a variety of opportunities:
- **Bi-annual public auctions** for high quality coins
- **Monthly online auctions** for vendors looking to receive auction proceeds within a short period of time
- **Direct purchase** of your coins for those who desire the certitude of an immediate cash offer

Contact us today !

NUMIS·OR

4, Rue des Barques
1207 Geneva, Switzerland
Tel: +41 (0)22 735 92 55
Email: info@numisor.ch

www.numisor.ch

Member of:

K.B. COINS

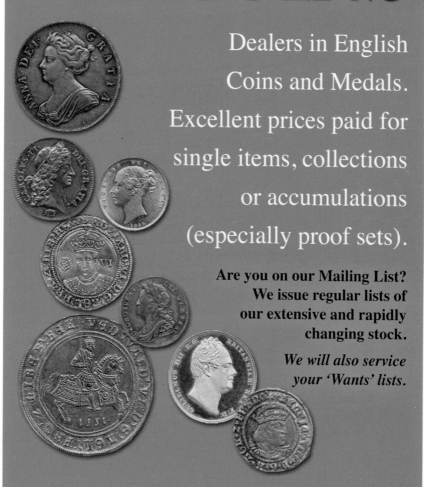

Dealers in English
Coins and Medals.
Excellent prices paid for
single items, collections
or accumulations
(especially proof sets).

**Are you on our Mailing List?
We issue regular lists of
our extensive and rapidly
changing stock.**

*We will also service
your 'Wants' lists.*

*Visit our online store
www.kbcoins.com*

K.B. COINS
PO Box 499
Stevenage
Herts SG1 9JT
*Tel: 01438 312661
Fax: 01438 311990*

COIN, MEDAL & BANKNOTE FAIRS

THE LONDON COIN FAIR

HOLIDAY INN
London, Bloomsbury, Coram Street, WC1N 1HT
2017 dates:
4th February, 3rd June, 2nd September, 4th November
9.30 am - 4.00 pm – Closes at 5.00pm
Admission £5, Concession £3

MIDLAND COIN FAIR

NATIONAL MOTORCYCLE MUSEUM
Bickenhill, Birmingham, B92 0EJ
(Opposite the NEC on the M42/A45 Junction)

2017 dates:
8th January, 12th February, 12th March, 9th April,
14th May, 11th June, 9th July, 13th August, 10th September,
8th October, 12th November, 10th December
9.30am - 3.00pm – Closes at 4.00pm
Admission £2

For more information please contact:
Lu Veissid, Hobsley House, Frodesley, Shrewsbury SY5 7HD
Email: l.veissid@btinternet.com

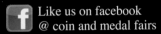 Like us on facebook
@ coin and medal fairs

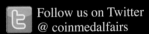 Follow us on Twitter
@ coinmedalfairs

www.coinfairs.co.uk

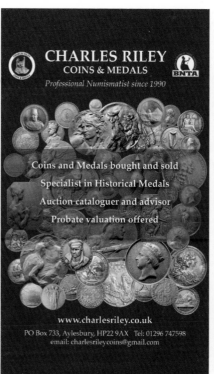

CHARLES RILEY
COINS & MEDALS
Professional Numismatist since 1990

BNTA

Coins and Medals bought and sold

Specialist in Historical Medals

Auction cataloguer and advisor

Probate valuation offered

www.charlesriley.co.uk

PO Box 733, Aylesbury, HP22 9AX Tel: 01296 747598
email: charlesrileycoins@gmail.com

Peter Nichols
Cabinet Makers
Coin, Medal & Collector's Cabinets

A range of mahogany coin & medal cabinets handmade in England.

Bespoke cabinets & boxes designed & made to order.

Supplier to leading international museums and collectors.

www.coincabinets.com

Email: orders@coincabinets.com
For a full descriptive leaflet please contact:
The Workshop +44 (0) 115 922 4149

ABC Coins and Tokens

We stock a large selection of Scottish coins,
tokens & communion tokens & also offer a wide range of
hammered & milled British & World coins,
tokens and numismatic books.

British & Colonial
Coins & Tokens
P.O. Box 52, Alnwick,
Northumberland NE66 1YE
United Kingdom

Website: www.abccoinsandtokens.com
E-mail: d-stuart@d-stuart.demon.co.uk
Telephone: 01665 603851

SELLING YOUR COINS & BANKNOTES?

Warwick and Warwick have an expanding requirement for coin and banknote collections, British and worldwide and for coins and notes of individual value. Our customer base is increasing dramatically and we need an ever larger supply of quality material to keep pace with demand. The market has never been stronger and if you are considering the sale of your collection, now is the time to act.

FREE VALUATIONS

We will provide a free, professional and without obligation valuation of your collection. Either we will make you a fair, binding private treaty offer, or we will recommend inclusion of your property in our next specialist public auction.

FREE TRANSPORTATION

We can arrange insured transportation of your collection to our Warwick offices completely free of charge. If you decline our offer, we ask you to cover the return carriage costs only.

FREE VISITS

Visits by our valuers are possible anywhere in the country or abroad, usually within 48 hours, in order to value larger collections. Please telephone for details.

ADVISORY DAYS

We are staging a series of advisory days and will be visiting all areas of England, Scotland, Wales and Ireland during the coming months. Please visit our website or telephone for further details.

EXCELLENT PRICES

Because of the strength of our customer base we are in a position to offer prices that we feel sure will exceed your expectations.

ACT NOW

Telephone or email Richard Beale today with details of your property.

Warwick & Warwick Ltd.
Auctioneers and Valuers
Chalon House, Scar Bank, Millers Road,
Warwick CV34 5DB
Tel: 01926 499031 Fax: 01926 491906
E-mail: richard.beale@warwickandwarwick.com
www.warwickandwarwick.com

Warwick & Warwick

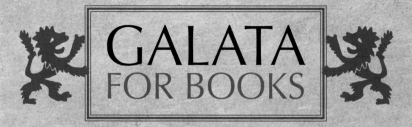

GALATA
FOR BOOKS

We have the largest selection of numismatic books for sale in the UK.

Our website features many thousands of new and second-hand numismatic books on the following subjects:

- Ancient Greek, Roman and Byzantine coins
- Celtic, British hammered and milled coins
- World coins, general and specialist catalogues
- Tokens and medals, weights and banknotes, history, archaeology, and treasure hunting
- Periodicals and off-prints
- Auction catalogues.

Browse through our stock by category, or search for a specific item by title, author or key words. Almost all items are illustrated to make finding the things you want easy.

- We publish several standard reference works and guides for the beginner
- We also sell coins, tokens and medals
- We buy books - single items and whole libraries

www.galata.co.uk

Galata, The Old White Lion, Market Street,
Llanfyllin, Powys, SY22 5BX, Wales.
Telephone: 01691 648 765

COLIN COOKE

P.O. Box 602, Altrincham WA14 5UN
Telephone: 0161 927 9524   Fax: 0161 927 9540
website: www.colincooke.com   email: coins@colincooke.com

Complimentary List available on request

www.colincooke.com

Colin Cooke Coins is founded on long-established traditions of honesty, integrity and
accurate grading of merchandise, always dedicated to total customer satisfaction.

**WILLIAM MACKAY
NUMISMATICS**

SPECIALIST
SUPPORT FOR
COLLECTORS
AND
NUMISMATISTS

British Hammered Coins
Acquisition and Disposal
Research and Cataloguing

Tel: 01763 849386
Mob: 07753 576692
E: wm@williammackaynumismatics.com

williammackaynumismatics.com

Sold for:
£14,520

Timeline
Auctions

Inc. Gregory's **Est.1858**

We are accepting single entries and collections of
Anglo-Saxon coins & antiquities

www.timelineauctions.com

Contact:
+44 [0]1277 815121
enquiries@timelineauctions.com

Follow us on:
f /TimeLineAuctions
t @TimeLineAuction

AIAΔ

BNTA

Dealers who display this symbol are Members of the

British Numismatic Trade Association

Buy in confidence from members of the British Numismatic Trade Association—an association formed to promote the very highest standards of professionalism in all matters involving members of the public in the sale or purchase of numismatic items.

For a free Membership Directory please send a stamped addressed envelope to:
General Secretary, BNTA, 3 Unwin Mansions, Queen's Club Gardens, London W14 9TH
Telephone: 07799 662181 Email: secretary@bnta.net

The BNTA will be organising the following event:

COINEX 2017—22–23 September, 2017 at The Ballroom, Millennium Hotel, London Mayfair, 44 Grosvenor Square, London W1K 2HP

BNTA MEMBERS IN COUNTY ORDER

LONDON AREA
*A.H. Baldwin & Sons Ltd · www.baldwin.co.uk
*ArtAncient Ltd · www.artancient.com
ATS Bullion Ltd · www.atsbullion.com
Beaver Coin Room · www.beaverhotel.co.uk
Jon Blyth · www.jonblyth.com
Bonhams incorporating Glendining's
  · www.bonhams.com
Arthur Bryant Coins Ltd · www.bryantcoins.com
Keith Chapman · www.anglosaxoncoins.com
*Classical Numismatic Group Inc / Seaby Coins
  · www.cngcoins.com
*Philip Cohen Numismatics · www.coinheritage.co.uk
Coin Invest Direct.com · www.coininvestdirect.com
Andre de Clermont · www.declermont.com
*Dix Noonan Webb · www.dnw.co.uk
Christopher Eimer · www.christophereimer.co.uk

Harrow Coin & Stamp Centre
*Knightsbridge Coins
C. J. Martin (Coins) Ltd · www.antiquities.co.uk
Nigel Mills · www.nigelmills.net
Morton & Eden Ltd · www.mortonandeden.com
Moruzzi Ltd · www.moruzzi.co.uk
Numismatica Ars Classica · www.arsclassicacoins.com
Physical Gold Ltd · www.physicalgold.co.uk
Predecimal.com incorporating
Rotographic Publications · www.predecimal.com
Roma Numismatics Ltd · www.romanumismatics.com
Simmons Gallery · www.simmonsgallery.co.uk
*Sovereign Rarities Ltd
*Spink & Son Ltd · www.spink.com
Surena Ancient Art & Numismatic
The London Coin Company Ltd
  · www.thelondoncoincompany.com

The BNTA is a member of the International Numismatic Commission.

NORTH AMERICAN SPECIALISTS IN
BRITISH COINS, TOKENS, AND MEDALS

Davissons
Ltd.

- High quality print catalogs
- Bi-monthly E-Auctions on a simple to use website
- Transactions in Pounds or Dollars

www.davcoin.com

Allan, Marnie, & Lief Davisson
PO Box 323
Cold Spring, MN 56320 USA
(001) 320-685-3835
info@davcoin.com

drake sterling
numismatics
BUYING and SELLING

GOLD SOVEREIGNS | COLONIAL COINS | WORLD GOLD COINS

www.drakesterling.co.uk

info@drakesterling.co.uk

+44 (0) 20 7097 1781

FREE UK POST & PACKING
ON ALL BOOKS

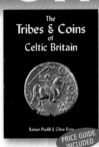

The Tribes & Coins of Celtic Britain

The Celts left no written records and the only historical accounts we have of them derive mainly from Roman writers.

As little as 30 years ago many mysteries – and misconceptions – still existed as to the Celtic tribes of Britain and their kings. But thanks to metal detecting finds and the Celtic Coin Index, far more is now known. In this book *Rainer Pudill* draws on his own experience as a collector – and this new knowledge – to present the latest thinking and facts on the Celts and their coins. Includes over 300 illustrations.

The contents include: **The Celtic Pantheon • Mercenaries & The First Celtic Coins • Iron Bars & Ring Money • Caesar's Expeditions To Britain • The Celtic Tribes Of Britain & Early Celtic Coinage • Pedigree • The British Policy Of Augustus & His Successors • The Coinages Of Cunobelin • Epaticcus • The Coinage Of Verica • The Invasion Of Britain • Resistance & Rebellion Against The Roman Occupation • The Final Celtic Coins Of Britain • The 'Conquest Of The Rest' • Time Line.**

250mm x 190mm, 84 pages, £16.50

A History of Medieval Coinage in England

by Richard Kelleher

This book is an excellent reference guide to identifying medieval coins with a comprehensive listing of mints, moneyers and denominations for all English and Irish coins struck between 1066 and 1489.

It provides an illustrated guide to the coinage of medieval England from the Norman Conquest of 1066 to the reign of the first Tudor king, Henry VII. While providing guidance on identification this book also places coinage in its historical context and gives insight into how coins were manufactured, used in circulation and lost or buried in a hoard. It is illustrated by more than 530 colour photographs, as well as 125 distribution maps, tables and images of places and people which help bring to life the medieval world in which coins were used and lost.

A4, 224 pages, £25.00

A History of Roman Coinage in Britain

by Sam Moorhead

If you have a Roman coin that you want to identify look no further. If you want to delve deeper into the coin, emperor, history and particular period, this book is an excellent starting point for further and deeper research. With over 1600 colour photographs this is the only book on Roman Coins you will ever need!

Written by Sam Moorhead of the British Museum, this book provides a chronological overview of Roman coinage from the Republican period (300BC) to the early 5th century, with an emphasis on Roman coinage used in Britain.

The text provides an introduction to the history of each period and then outlines the coinage (denominations, mints, contemporary copies etc.), using Portable Antiquities Scheme and British Museum coins as illustrations. Throughout, indications are made of the numbers and distribution of particular Roman coin finds in Britain. There are also over 30 distribution maps.

A4, 224 pages, £25.00

Ancient British Coins (ABC)

Never before have so many ancient British coins been so easy to identify, so easy to study, so easy to enjoy. ABC catalogues 999 iron age coins, including 418 new types not shown by Van Arsdell in 1989. The book describes and dates them, gives up to six references for each, estimates their rarity and shows every coin twice actual size, so that its distinctive differences can be seen at a glance. Contains 4000 superb coin photos, plus 500 other illustrations, diagrams, tables and maps.

Hardback Cover, A4
256 pages, £75.00

Medieval English Groats

This is the definitive reference work on English Groats. Written *by Ivan Buck*, it covers the groat from its introduction in the reign of Edward I (1272-1307) right up to the end of the Tudors in the early 17th century. Essential reading – this work helps to identify the various types of groat and the major varieties. There are over 400 colour illustrations in the text and a number of scarce and rare coins are illustrated for the first time. In many cases the information provided can be applied to the parallel series of half groats.

A4, 68 pages, £16.50

Visit our website to order online and to see our full range of over 50 books
www.greenlightpublishing.co.uk ☎ orders 01376 521900

   Greenlight Publishing, 119 Newland Street, Witham, Essex CM8 1WF PayPal

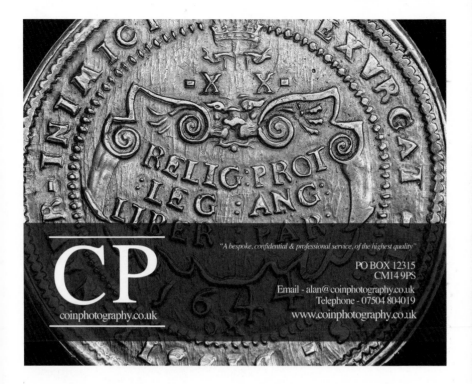

"A bespoke, confidential & professional service, of the highest quality"

CP
coinphotography.co.uk

PO BOX 12315
CM14 9PS
Email - alan@coinphotography.co.uk
Telephone - 07504 804019
www.coinphotography.co.uk

Ancient &
Gothic
(Chris Belton)
ESTABLISHED 1977

ROMAN • CELTIC
ANGLO-SAXON • ENGLISH HAMMERED

For sale & wanted.
Bi-monthly mail order catalogues.
Hundreds of coins & antiquities, each listing completely different from the last two.

SCARCE ROMAN EMPERORS
INTERESTING & UNUSUAL REVERSES SCARCE ENGLISH KINGS
GOOD ANGLO-SAXON SECTION

Also plenty of English hammered & Roman coins under £20

Please write or phone for our latest catalogue (free)
Ancient & Gothic, P.O. Box 5390, Bournemouth BH7 6XR
Tel: +44 (0)1202 431721

BY APPOINTMENT TO
HER MAJESTY THE QUEEN
MEDALLISTS & PHILATELISTS
SPINK & SON LTD , LONDON

BY APPOINTMENT TO
H.R.H. THE DUKE OF EDINBURGH
MEDALLISTS
SPINK & SON LTD : LONDON

SPINK

LONDON
1666

THE GLOBAL COLLECTABLES
AUCTION HOUSE

STAMPS | COINS | BANKNOTES | MEDALS | BONDS & SHARES | AUTOGRAPHS | BOOKS | WINES

LONDON
69 Southampton Row
Bloomsbury
London
WC1B 4ET
concierge@spink.com
Tel: +44 (0)20 7563 4000
Fax: +44 (0)20 7563 4066

NEW YORK
145 W. 57th St.
18th Floor,
New York, NY
10019
usa@spink.com
Tel: +1 212 262 8400
Fax: +1 212 262 8484

HONG KONG
4/F & 5/F
Hua Fu Commercial Building
111 Queen's Road West
Hong Kong
china@spink.com
Tel:+852 3952 3000
Fax: +852 3952 3038

SINGAPORE
Registered at:
50 Raffles Place
#17-01 Singapore Land Tower
Singapore 048623
singapore@spink.com
Tel. +852 3952 3000
Fax +852 3952 3038

LUGANO
Via Balestra 7
6901
Lugano
switzerland@spink.com
Tel: +41 91 911 62 00
Fax: +41 91 922 20 52

WWW.SPINK.COM

The British Numismatic Society

The Society was founded in 1903 and was the world's first organisation devoted to the study of coins, tokens, jettons, medals and paper money of the British Isles and the Commonwealth and other territories that have been subject to British rule.

The Society has around 550 members from around the world and includes collectors, dealers and specialists from leading museums and institutions, aged from under 18 to over 80. Meetings take place regularly in London, nine times per year with an additional meeting now held in New York in January.

There has never been a better time to join the British Numismatic Society as we are currently running a special reduced rate for the first two years of membership of £15 per annum (normally £32). If you are under the age of 25 or in full-time study there is a further reduction to only £10 per annum.

To find out more about the B.N.S. or to apply to become a member visit our website.

Promoting the study of British numismatics since 1903

www.britnumsoc.org

Inc. Gregory's **Est.1858**

Auction Venue:
The Swedenborg Hall
20-21 Bloomsbury Way
London WC1A 2TH

Since our founding TimeLine has sold ancient art and collectibles to collectors around the world. We have enabled thousands of buyers to experience the joy of collecting through our beautiful catalogues, viewing days and our rostrum auctions in central London. Our catalogues feature many unique pieces from fascinating ancient civilisations, including Egypt, Greece, Rome, Asia and Europe.

Follow us on:

f /TimeLineAuctions
t @TimeLineAuction

AIAΔ

BNTA

THE ART LOSS ■ REGISTER™
www.artloss.com

Enquiries:
+44 (0) 1277 815121
+44 (0) 1708 225689 fax
info@timelineauctions.com
www.timelineauctions.com

TimeLine Auctions Limited
The Court House
363 Main Road
Harwich, Essex
CO12 4DN, UK

Standard Catalogue of British Coins
Part One

COINS OF ENGLAND

AND
THE UNITED KINGDOM
Pre-Decimal Issues

52nd Edition

SPINK

LONDON

A Catalogue of the Coins of Great Britain
and Ireland
first published 1929

Standard Catalogue of British Coins
Coins of England and the United Kingdom
52nd edition, 2017

© Spink & Son Ltd, 2016
69 Southampton Row, Bloomsbury
London WC1B 4ET

Typeset by Design to Print UK Ltd,
9 & 10 Riverview Business Park, Forest Row, East Sussex RH18 5DW
www.designtoprintuk.com
Printed and bound in Malta
by Gutenberg Press Ltd.

The contents of this catalogue, including the numbering system and illustrations,
are protected by copyright.

All rights are reserved. No part of this publication may be reproduced,
stored in a retrieval system, or transmitted, in any form or by any
means, electronic, mechanical, photocopying, recording or otherwise,
without the prior permission of Spink & Son Ltd.

ISBN 978-1-907427-98-5

CONTENTS

Page

ACKNOWLEDGEMENTS AND ABBREVIATIONS iv
FOREWORD AND MARKET TRENDS v
INTRODUCTION vi
A BEGINNERS GUIDE TO COIN COLLECTING vii
SOME NUMISMATIC TERMS EXPLAINED xii
CELTIC COINAGE c. 150 B.C-40 A.D.
    Introduction, Grading, References xiv
    Imported Coinage, Dynastic and Later Uninscribed Coinage, Atrebates and Regni,
    Cantii, Trinovantes, Catuvellauni, Durotriges, Dobunni, Corieltauvi, Iceni 1
ROMAN BRITAIN 43-411 A.D. 46
ENGLISH HAMMERED COINAGE c. 600-1662 82
EARLY ANGLO SAXON c. 600-775
    Thrymsas, Sceattas, Kings of Northumbria, Archbishops of York 84
MIDDLE ANGLO SAXON c. 780-973
    Kings of Kent, Archbishops of Canterbury, Kings of Mercia,
    Kings of East Anglia 106
VIKING COINAGES c. 885-954 115
KINGS OF WESSEX 786-959, AND ALL ENGLAND FROM 959 121
LATE ANGLO SAXON 973-1066
    Eadgar, Edward the Martyr, Aethelred II, Cnut, Harold I, Harthacnut,
    Edward the Confessor, Harold II 132
NORMAN KINGS 1066-1154
    William I, William II, Henry I, Stephen, Civil War and the Anarchy 149
PLANTAGENET KINGS 1154-1399
    Henry II, Richard I, John, Henry III, Edward I, Edward II, Edward III, Richard II 161
HOUSE OF LANCASTER 1399-1461
    Henry IV, Henry V, Henry VI, first reign 197
HOUSE OF YORK 1461-1485
    Edward IV, Henry VI, restored, Edward IV, second reign, Edward IV or V,
    Richard III 213
HOUSE OF TUDOR 1485-1603
    Henry VII, Henry VIII, Edward VI, Mary, Philip and Mary, Elizabeth I 227
HOUSE OF STUART, THE COMMONWEALTH, AND THE HOUSE OF ORANGE
1603-1714
    James I, Charles I, The Commonwealth, Oliver Cromwell, Charles II,
    James II, William and Mary, William III, Anne 272
HOUSE OF HANOVER 1714-1901
    George I, George II, George III, George IV, William IV, Victoria 399
HOUSE OF SAXE-COBURG-GOTHA 1901-1910
    Edward VII 493
HOUSE OF WINDSOR 1910-
    George V, Edward VIII, George VI, Elizabeth II 499
APPENDICES:
    A Select Numismatic Bibliography 529
    Latin or Foreign Legends on English Coins 532
    Numismatic Clubs and Societies 534
    Mintmarks and other symbols 535
ALPHABETICAL INDEX OF RULERS AND COIN ISSUES 538

ACKNOWLEDGEMENTS

We wish to acknowledge the valuable contributions of the following to this edition.

Richard Abdy *(The British Museum)*
Tony Abramson
Dr Martin Allen *(Fitzwilliam Museum)*
Keith Bayford, K.B. Coins
Joe Bispham
Jon Blyth
James Booth
Ron Churchill
Nigel Clark
Chris Comber
Barrie Cook *(The British Museum)*
Geoff Cope
Simon Cope
Jonathan Cope
Dave Craddock
Joe Cribb *(The British Museum)*
Mike Cuddeford
Paul Davies
Charles Davis
Paul Dawson
Tim Everson
Stephen Fass
David Fletcher
Michael Freeman
Glen Gittoes
Megan Gooch
Eric Green
Dave Greenhalgh
David Guest
Peter Hendra

Steve Hill
Dr John Hulett
Peter Jackson
Richard Kelleher *(The British Museum)*
Geoff Kitchen
Ian Leins *(The British Museum)*
Joe Linzalone
Stewart Lyon
William MacKay
Nigel Mills
Graeme Monk
Neil Paisley *(Colin Cooke Coins)*
Rob Pearce
Gary Poole
Nigel Prevost
Mark Rasmussen
The Schneider Family
Dr Irving Schneider
May Sinclair
Peter D Spencer
Bob Thomas
Andrew Wayne
Tim Webb-Ware
Walter Wilkinson
Barry Williams
Gareth Williams *(The British Museum)*
Antony Wilson
Paul & Bente R. Withers
Peter Woodhead

Museums/Institutions
The Trustees of the British Museum, London
The Fitzwilliam Museum, Cambridge

Photography
Richard Hodges
Paul & Bente R. Withers
Wioletta Madaj

ABBREVIATIONS

Archb.	Archbishop	laur.	laureate
Æ	bronze	mm.	mintmark
Ꞧ	silver	mon.	monogram
N	gold	O., obv.	obverse
Bp.	Bishop	p.	new penny, pence
BV	bullion value	pl	plume
cuir.	cuirassed	quat.	quatrefoil
d.	penny, pence	qtr.	quarter
diad.	diademed	rad.	radiate
dr.	draped	R., rev.	reverse
ex.	exergue	r.	right
grs.	grains	s.	shillings
hd.	headstg.	stg.	standing
i.c.	inner circle	trun.	truncation
illus.	illustration	var.	variety
l.	left	wt.	weight

FOREWORD

Welcome to the 52nd edition of Coins of England and the United Kingdom.

The choice of the 1817 sovereign of George III on the cover this year celebrates the bicentenary of the first issue of the 'modern' sovereign that is still produced today. The original sovereign, first produced in 1489 during the reign of Henry VII, was a different coin altogether, minted in 23ct gold instead of 22ct and at 15.55g almost twice the weight of the modern sovereign.

3,235,239 sovereigns and a very small quantity of proof sovereigns were minted in 1817 as part of a proposed range of new gold coins, following a substantial reorganisation of the Royal Mint by William Wellesley Pole, then Master of the Mint. The twenty shilling full sovereign carried a face value of £1, with both the obverse and reverse by Benedetto Pistrucci.

On the obverse, George III wears a 'crown' of laurel leaves, hence it is described as a laureate head, tied at the back with a ribbon and formed into a bow. The image of St George slaying the dragon graces the reverse, with Pistrucci's initials on the ground, just under the broken shaft of St George's spear. Below it, on the buckle of the garter, are William Wellesley Pole's initials, WWP. Both sets of initials are incuse. The image sits inside an inscribed garter, Honi Soit Qui Mal Y Pense, meaning "Shame On Him Who Thinks Evil of It" - this is the motto of the Order of the Garter, the highest order of chivalry in the UK.

High grade examples of the coin are always sought by collectors, but price is determined more often by historic interest than by rarity value.

2016 saw the first four sales of The Academic Collection of Lord Stewartby take place at Spink. Highlights from the third sale in September included lot 998, a rare very fine well struck Mary Sovereign dated 1553 which realised £50,400; lot 1018, a third coinage very rare, almost extremely fine James I Rose-Ryal which realised £45,600; and lot 1038, a good very fine and very rare (only four examples known from this reverse die) Charles I Triple Unite dated 1642 which realised £43,200.

It is not often that a collection comes on the market containing some of the most exquisite coins from Edward III to Charles II and each monarch in between, but in March Spink had the privilege of offering the Dr Paul Broughton Collection of English Hammered Gold Coins for sale. The best collection of its type to be offered in London for some years, it saw some of the highest grossing hammer prices for Tudor Coins seen for some time, including a good extremely fine, extremely rare Charles I, Oxford, Triple Unite dated 1643 - one of only three known examples, and an exceptionally rare example of a coin in a private collection with a Royal provenance – which realised £126,000; and an extremely fine, very rare James I, second coinage, Spur Ryal which realised £84,000.

As always, thanks are due to those who have contacted us with corrections for this catalogue – the input of all who use this reference work is essential in keeping it as accurate and interesting as possible. As I am new to the role as Editor here this year I would especially appreciate any feedback or suggestions from users for next year's edition, and look forward to working with you all in the future.

Emma Howard
Editor, Coins of England

INTRODUCTION

Arrangement

The arrangement of this catalogue is not completely uniform, but generally it is divided into metals (gold, silver, copper, etc) under each reign, then into coinages, denominations and varieties. In the Celtic section the uninscribed coins are listed before the dynastic coins; under Charles II all the hammered coins precede the milled coinage; the reign of George III is divided into coins issued up to 1816 and the new coinage from 1816 to the end of the reign; and under Elizabeth II the decimal issues are separated from the pre-decimal *(£.s.d.)* coinages and listed in a separate volume of the SCBC since 2015.

Every major coin type is listed though not every variety. We have endeavoured to give rather more coverage to the varieties of relatively common coins, such as the pennies of Edward I, II and III, than to the very much rarer coins of, for instance, King Offa of Mercia.

Values

The values given represent the range of retail prices at which coins are being offered for sale at the time of going to press and **not** the price which a dealer will pay for those coins. These prices are based on our knowledge of the numismatic market, the current demand for particular coins, recent auction sale prices and, in those cases where certain coins have not appeared for sale for some years, our estimation of what they would be likely to sell at today, bearing in mind their rarity and appeal in relation to somewhat similar coins where a current value is known. Values are given for two grades of preservation from the Celtic period onwards and three to four grades of preservation for coins of the 17th to the 20th century.

Collectors normally require coins in the best condition they can afford and, except in the case of a really rare coin, a piece that is considerably worn is not wanted and has little value. The values given in the catalogue are for the exact state of preservation stated at the head of each column and bearing in mind that a score of identical coins in varying states of wear could be lined up in descending order from mint condition (FDC, *fleur de coin*), through very fine (VF) to *poor* state. It will be realized that only in certain instances will the values given apply to particular coins. A 'fine' (F) coin may be worth anything between one quarter and a half of the price quoted for a 'very fine' (VF); on the other hand, a piece in really mint condition will be valued substantially higher than the price quoted for 'extremely fine' (EF). The designation BV has been adopted for coins whose value on the market has yet to exceed its bullion value. Purchasing sovereigns, catalogued as BV, will attract a dealers' premium.

We emphasize again that the purpose of this catalogue is to give a general value for a particular class of coin in a specified state of preservation, and also to give the collector an idea of the range and value of coins in the English series. The value of any particular piece depends on three things:

Its exact design, legend, mintmark or date.

Its exact state of preservation; this is of prime importance.

The demand for it in the market at any given time.

Some minor varieties are much scarcer than others and, as the number of coins issued varies considerably from year to year, coins of certain dates and mintmarks are rarer and of more value than other pieces of similar type. The prices given for any type are for the commonest variety, mintmark or date of that type.

The Scope

Coin collecting, numismatics, is a fascinating hobby. It requires very little physical exertion and only as much mental effort as one wishes or is able to put into it at any time. There is vast scope and boundless ramifications and byways encompassing not only things historical and geographical, but also touching on economics, metallurgy, heraldry, literature, the fine arts, politics, military history and many other disciplines. This catalogue is solely concerned with British coinage from its earliest times right up to date. From the start the beginner should appreciate that the coinage of our own nation may be seen as a small but very important part of the whole story of world currency.

The first coins, made of electrum, a natural alloy of gold and silver, were issued in western Asia Minor (Lydia) in the later seventh century B.C. Over the next century or so coinage of gold and silver spread across the Aegean to mainland Greece, southwards to the eastern Mediterranean lands and eventually westward to the Greek colonies in southern Italy, Sicily (Magna Graecia) and beyond. The coins of the Greeks are noted for their beautiful, sometimes exquisite craftsmanship, with many of the coin types depicting the patron deities of their cities. Coins of Philip II of Macedon (359-336 B.C.), father of Alexander the Great, circulated amongst the Celtic peoples of the Danubian Basin and were widely copied through central Europe and by the Gauls in France. Gold Gaulish staters were reaching Britain around the beginning of the first century B.C. and the earliest gold to be struck in the island must have been produced shortly afterwards. Although their types and designs copy the Apollo head and racing charioteer of Philip II's gold coins, they are stylistically much removed from the original representation and very individually Celtic in concept.

The coins of the Romans cover some seven centuries and include an enormous number of different types that were current throughout a major part of the civilized world from Spain to Syria and from the Rhine in the north to the Sudan in the south. The Roman province of Britain was part of this vast empire for four hundred years from AD 43 until the early fifth century. Innumerable Roman coins have been recovered from sites in this country, most being made of brass or bronze. Many of these are quite inexpensive and very collectable. In recent years many hoards of gold and silver coins have been found, usually by use of metal detectors.

Following the revival of commerce after the Dark Ages, coinage in Western Europe was virtually restricted to silver until the thirteenth century, though gold was still being minted in Byzantium and in the Islamic world. In the Middle Ages many European cities had their own distinctive coinage and money was issued not only by the kings but also by nobles, bishops and abbots. From the time of the later Crusades gold returned to the West, and the artistic developments of the Renaissance in the fifteenth century brought improved portraiture and new minting techniques.

Large silver crown-size thalers were first minted at Joachimsthal in Bohemia early in the sixteenth century. The substantial shipments of silver coming to Europe from the mines of Spanish America over the next couple of centuries led to a fine series of larger coins being issued by the European states and cities. The larger size allowed greater artistic freedom in the designs and the portraits on the coins.

Both Germany and Italy became unified nation states during the later nineteenth century, thereby substantially reducing the number of mints and coin types. Balancing the reduction in European minting authorities were the new coins that were issued by the independent states of South and Central America. Since the 1950s many new nations have established their independence and their coinage provides a large field for the collector of modern coins.

It can be seen that the scope for the collector is truly vast, but besides the general run of official coinage there is also the large series of token coins—small change unofficially produced to supplement the inadequate supply of authorized currency. These tokens were issued by merchants, innkeepers and manufacturers in many towns and villages in the seventeenth, eighteenth and nineteenth centuries and many collectors specialize in their local issues.

Some coins have designs of a commemorative nature; an example being the Royal Wedding crown of 1981, but there are also large numbers of commemorative medals which, though never intended for use as coinage, are sometimes confused with coins because they are metal objects of a similar shape and sometimes a similar size to coins. This is another interesting field for collectors as these medals often have excellent portraits of famous men or women, or they may commemorate important events or scientific discoveries. Other metallic objects of coin-like appearance that can be confusing for the beginner are reckoning counters, advertising tickets, various other tickets and passes, and items such as brass coin weights.

Minting processes

From the time of the earliest Greek coins in the late seventh century BC to about the middle of the sixteenth century AD, coins were made by hand. The method of manufacture was simple. The obverse and reverse designs were engraved or punched into the prepared ends of two bars of bronze or iron, shaped or tapered to the diameter of the required coin. The obverse die, known as the *pile*, was usually spiked so that it could be anchored firmly into a block of wood or metal. The reverse die, the *trussel*, was held by hand or grasped by tongs.

The coin was struck by placing a metal blank between the two dies and striking the trussel with a hammer. Thus, all coinage struck by this method is known as 'hammered'. Some dies are known to have been hinged so there would be an exact register between the upper and lower die. Usually a 'pair of dies' consisted of one obverse die (normally the more difficult to make because it had the finer detail, such as the ruler's portrait) and two reverse dies. This was because the shaft of iron bearing the reverse design eventually split under the constant hammering; two reverse dies were usually needed to last out the life of the obverse die.

Some time toward the middle of the sixteenth century, experiments, first in Germany and later in France, resulted in the manufacture of coins by machinery.

The term 'milled', which is applied to all machine-made coins, comes from the type of machinery used – the mill and screw press. With this machinery the obverse die was fixed as the lower die and the reverse die brought down into contact with the blank by heavy vertical pressure applied by a screw or worm-drive connected to a cross bar with heavy weights at each end. These weights usually had long leather thongs attached which allowed a more powerful force to be applied by the operators who revolved the arms of the press. New blanks were placed on the lower die and the struck coins were removed by hand. The screw press brought more pressure to bear on the blanks and this pressure was evenly applied, producing a far better and sharper coin.

Various attempts were made during the reigns of Elizabeth I and Charles I to introduce this type of machinery with its vastly superior products. Unfortunately problems associated with the manufacture of blanks to a uniform weight greatly reduced the rate of striking and the hand manufacture of coins continued until the Restoration in 1660, when Charles II brought to London from Holland the Roettiers brothers and their improved screw press.

The first English coins made for circulation by this new method were the silver crowns of 1662, which bore an inscription on the edge, DECVS ET TVTAMEN, 'an ornament and a safeguard', a reference to the fact that the new coins could not be clipped, a crime made easy by the thin and often badly struck hammered coins.

The mill and screw press was used until new steam-powered machinery made by Boulton and Watt was installed in the new mint on Tower Hill in London. This machinery had been used most successfully by Boulton to strike the large 'cartwheel' two- and one- penny pieces of 1797 and other coins, including 'overstriking' Spanish *eight-reale* pieces into Bank of England 'dollars' since the old Mint presses were not able to exert sufficient power to do this. This new machinery was first used at the Mint to strike the 'new coinage' halfcrowns of 1816, and it operated at a far greater speed than the old type of mill and screw presses and achieved a greater sharpness of design.

The very latest coining presses now operating at the Royal Mint at Llantrisant in South Wales, are capable of striking at a rate of up to 800 coins a minute.

Condition

One of the more difficult problems for the beginner is to assess accurately the condition of a coin. A common fault among collectors is to overgrade and, consequently, to overvalue their coins.

Most dealers will gladly spare a few minutes to help new collectors. Many dealers issue price lists with illustrations, enabling collectors to see exactly what the coins look like and how they have been graded.

Coins cannot always be graded according to precise rules. Hammered coins often look weak or worn on the high parts of the portrait and the tops of the letters; this can be due to weak striking or worn dies and is not always attributable to wear through long use in circulation. Milled coins usually leave the Mint sharply struck so that genuine wear is easier to detect. However a x5 or x10 magnifying glass is essential, especially when grading coins of Edward VII and George V where the relief is very low on the portraits and some skill is required to distinguish between an uncirculated coin and one in EF condition.

The condition or grade of preservation of a coin is usually of greater importance than its rarity. By this we mean that a common coin in superb condition is often more desirable and more highly priced than a rarity in poor condition. Coins that have been pierced or mounted as a piece of jewellery generally have little interest to collectors.

One must also be on the lookout for coins that have been 'plugged', i.e. that have been pierced at some time and have had the hole filled in, sometimes with the missing design or letters re-engraved.

Badly cleaned coins will often display a complexity of fine interlaced lines and such coins have a greatly reduced value. It is also known for coins to be tooled or re-engraved on the high parts of the hair, in order to 'increase' the grade of coin and its value. In general it is better to have a slightly more worn coin than a better example with such damage.

In recent years professional grading services have come to exert considerable influence over the grading of coins and the subsequent prices they can command. Whilst such services can provide an accurate way to grade coins, and is well -suited to milled and machine made issues, the resulting grading remains an opinion with grading of hammered and ancient requiring different considerations to milled and machine made coins. Associated with professional grading is the practise of sealing the coin within a clear plastic container, colloquially referred to as slabbing. Whilst now a well-established practise in the US market it has had less impact in the UK where collectors prefer to handle a coin which allows for closer examination of the surfaces and the edges, a necessity for a milled coin with an inscribed edge which once enscapulated cannot be examined.

Cleaning coins

Speaking generally, *do not* clean coins. More coins are ruined by injudicious cleaning than through any other cause, and a badly cleaned coin loses much of its value. A nicely toned piece is usually considered desirable. Really dirty gold and silver can, however, be carefully washed in soap and water. Copper coins should never be cleaned or washed, they may be lightly brushed with a brush that is not too harsh.

Buying and selling coins

Exchanging coins with other collectors, searching around the antique shops, telling your relatives and friends that you are interested in coins, or even trying to find your own with a metal detector, are all ways of adding to your collection. However, the time will come when the serious collector needs to acquire specific coins or requires advice on the authenticity or value of a coin.

At this point an expert is needed, and the services of a reputable coin dealer or independent numismatic consultant are necessary. There are now a large number of coin dealers in the UK, many of whom belong to the B.N.T.A. (The British Numismatic Trade Association) or the I.A.P.N. (The International Association of Professional Numismatists) and a glance through the 'yellow pages' under 'coin dealer' or 'numismatist' will often provide local information. Many dealers publish their own lists of coins. Studying these lists is a good way for a collector to learn about coins and to classify and catalogue their own collections.

In recent years the internet has made it very much easier to locate, view and acquire coins online not just in the United Kingdom but worldwide. Many dealers now offer lists of stock online. It has also revolutionised the availability of coins at auction with printed catalogues supplemented by online catalogues and the increasing use of online bidding making the need to attend an auction on the day less critical than it once was. As a result buying and selling at auction has grown as a way to add to and dispose of collections. In buying at auction it is always advisable to examine the coin before deciding to bid and it should be borne in mind that the description given will only be as good as the expertise of the person describing the coin. It is still possible to find and acquire bargains at auction, but the chance of doing so is perhaps less these days than it once was. It should also be pointed out that auction houses charge the buyer a premium on the hammer price, generally at 20%, on which, in the United Kingdom , VAT is applicable with the total price paid generally hammer price plus 24%. Coins disposed of at auction will be subject to a vendor's commission charge made by the auction house which can be up to 15% of the price realised. An active market for buying and selling coins exists also on e-bay, however in general items offered here should be treated with caution with the onus on checking the veracity of the coin very much with the bidder.

The Standard Catalogue of Coins of England and the UK has been published since 1929. It serves as a price guide for all coin collectors. Spink also publish books on many aspects of English, Greek, Roman and Byzantine coins and on British tokens which serve as a valuable source of information for coin collectors. Our books are available directly from Spink, selected high street booksellers and online outlets such as Amazon.

Numismatic Clubs and Societies

There are over thirty numismatic societies and clubs in the British Isles. Joining one is the best way to meet fellow enthusiasts, learn about your coins and other series in a friendly and informative way. For details and contacts for a club or society near you see Appendix IV, page 534 or online, www.coinclubs.org.uk. The British Association of Numismatic Societies (BANS), which acts as the national body for all Societies, holds two weekend meetings each year with a range of speakers in convivial surroundings.

Useful suggestions

Security and insurance. The careful collector should not keep valuable coins at home unless they are insured and have adequate protection. Local police and insurance companies will give advice on what precautions may be necessary.

Most insurance companies will accept a valuation based on *The Standard Catalogue.* It is usually possible to have the amount added to a householder's contents policy but particularly valuable individual coins may have to be separately listed. A 'Fire, Burglary and Theft' policy will cover loss only from the insured's address, but an 'All Risks' policy will usually cover accidental damage and loss anywhere within the U.K.

Until recently most high street banks offered safe-deposit boxes which formed a useful way for holding a collection in a secure environment. However in recent years many high street banks have stopped providing such services. The alternative is to acquire and install a safe at your home where coins can be stored. There are many options available here and most insurance companies will offer reduced premiums for coins securely stored at the home.

Keeping a record. All collectors are advised to have an up-to-date record of their collection and, if possible, photographs of the more important and more easily identifiable coins. This should be kept in a separate place from the collection so that a list and photographs can be given to the police should loss occur. Note the price paid, from whom purchased, the date of acquisition and the condition of the coin.

Storage and handling. New collectors should get into the habit of handling coins by the edge. This is especially important as far as highly polished proof coins are concerned.

Collectors may initially keep their coins in paper or plastic envelopes housed in boxes, albums or special containers. Many collectors will eventually wish to own a hardwood coin cabinet in which the collection can be properly arranged and displayed. If a home-made cabinet is being constructed avoid using oak and cedar wood; mahogany, walnut and rosewood are ideal. It is important that coins are not kept in a humid atmosphere; especial care must be taken with copper and bronze coins which are very susceptible to damp or condensation which may result in a green verdigris forming on them.

From beginner to numismatist

The new collector can best advance to becoming an experienced numismatist by examining as many coins as possible, noting their distinctive features and by learning to use the many books of reference that are available. It will be an advantage to join a local numismatic society, as this will provide an opportunity for meeting other enthusiasts and obtaining advice from more experienced collectors. Most societies have a varied programme of lectures, exhibitions and occasional auctions of members' duplicates.

Those who become members of one or both of the national societies, the Royal Numismatic Society and the British Numismatic Society, receive an annual journal containing authoritative papers and have access to the societies' library and programme of lectures.

Many museums have coin collections available for study, although they may not always be displayed, and a number of museum curators are qualified numismatists.

SOME NUMISMATIC TERMS EXPLAINED

Obverse	That side of the coin which normally shows the monarch's head or name.
Reverse	The side opposite to the obverse, the 'Tails'.
Blank	The coin as a blank piece of metal, i.e. before it is struck.
Flan	The whole piece of metal after striking.
Type	The main, central design.
Legend	The inscription. Coins lacking a legend are called 'mute' or anepigraphic.
Field	That flat part of the coin between the main design and the inscription or edge.
Exergue	That part of the coin below the main design, usually separated by a horizontal line, and normally occupied by the date.
Die	The block of metal, with design cut into it, which actually impresses the coin blank with the design.
Die variety	Coin showing slight variation of design.
Mule	A coin with the current type on one side and the previous (and usually obsolete) type on the other side, or a piece struck from two dies that are not normally used together.
Graining or reeding	The crenellations around the edge of the coin, commonly known as 'milling'.
Proof	Carefully struck coin from special dies with a mirror-like or matt surface. (In this country 'Proof' is not a term used to describe the state of preservation, but the method of striking.)
Hammered	Refers to the old craft method of striking a coin between dies hammered by hand.
Milled	Coins struck by dies worked in a coining press. The presses were hand powered from 1560-1800, powered by steam from 1790 and by electricity from 1895.

The Celtic or Ancient British issues are amongst the most interesting and varied of all British coins. They are our earliest coins and are the product of a society that left no historical sources of its own. It is therefore often difficult to be specific about for whom, when or where they were produced. Despite only being used for approximately a hundred and fifty years they do provide a rich variety of designs and types in gold, silver and bronze. Collectors looking for a theme to concentrate on may find the coins of one tribe, an individual ruler or a particular phase in the coinage interesting.

SPINK

LONDON
1666

ALSO AVAILABLE FROM SPINK

COINS OF SCOTLAND, IRELAND AND THE ISLANDS INCLUDING ANGLO-GALLIC COINS.

3rd edition, 2015

Featuring a new section on Anglo-Gallic coins with valuations.

Price: £40 + postage

To order your copy, please contact the Spink Books Department:
Tel: +44 (0)20 7563 4046 | Email: books@spink.com
SPINK LONDON | 69 Southampton Row | Bloomsbury | London | WC1B4ET
LONDON | NEW YORK | HONG KONG | SINGAPORE | LUGANO

#SPINK_AUCTIONS   WWW.SPINK.COM   WWW.SPINKBOOKS.COM

CELTIC COINAGE EXPLAINED

Grading Celtic Coins

The majority of Celtic coins were struck by hand, sometimes resulting in a loss of definition through weak striking. In addition, the design on the dies was often bigger than the blank flan employed, resulting in the loss of some of the design. Coins with full legends are generally more valuable than examples with incomplete legends. Bronze coins in good condition (VF or better) and especially toned examples attract a premium. Factors that detract from a coin's value are chips, scratches and verdigris on bronze coins. It is important to take into account these factors as well as the amount of wear on a coin when assessing its grade.

	Cunobelin Bronze Unit	Epaticcus Silver Unit	Cunobelin Gold Stater
Fine			
Very Fine			

Plated Coins

Plated gold staters, quarter staters and silver units are recorded for many known types. They vary considerably in the quality of their production and are usually priced at around a quarter of the substantive types value. Their exact purpose or relation to the type they copy is not fully understood.

References and Select Bibliography.

M   Mack, R.P. (1975), 3rd edition, The Coinage of Ancient Britain.
V   Van Arsdell, R.D. (1989), Celtic Coinage of Britain.
BMC   Hobbs, R. (1996), British Iron Age Coins in the British Museum.
R   Rudd, C. (2010), ABC.

de Jersey, P. (1996), Celtic Coinage in Britain. *A good general introduction to the series.*
Nash, D. (1987), Coinage in the Celtic World. *Sets the coinage in its social context.*

The layout of the following list is derived from the standard works by Van Arsdell and the British Museum Catalogue by Richard Hobbs. References are made to these works where possible, in the case of the last work it should be noted that the British Museum collection is not exhaustive, and therefore should not be used to assess the rarity of a coin. More detailed information than that given here can be gained from these works.

IMPORTED COINAGE

The earliest coins to circulate in Britain were made in northern Gaul (Belgica) and imported into the south-east of England from around 150 B.C. onwards. They were principally the product of two tribal groups in this region, the Ambiani and Suessiones. In Britain these types are known as Gallo-Belgic A to F. The first type Gallo-Belgic A is ultimately derived from the Macedonian gold staters (M) of Philip II (359-336 B.C.)

The reasons why they were imported are not fully understood. However, the context for their importation is one of close social, political and economic ties between Britain and Gaul. Within this cross-channel relationship they undoubtedly had various functions, such as payment for military service or mercenaries, in exchanges between the elite of each society: in cementing alliances for example, or as gifts in a system of exchange.

GALLO-BELGIC ISSUES

| | 2 | 4 | 5 | 7 | | |

					F	VF
					£	£
From c.150 B.C. – c.50 B.C.						
1	**Gold Stater.** Gallo-Belgic (Ambiani). Good copy of Macedonian stater, large flan. Laureate head of Apollo r. R. Horse l. *M. 1; V. 10. (1)*				1750	8500
2	Similar, but head and horse l. *M. 3; V. 12. (1)*				1100	5500
3	B. (Ambiani). Somewhat similar to 1, but small flan and 'defaced' *obv.* die. R. Horse r. *M. 5; V. 30. (3)*				550	2250
4	— Similar, but with lyre between horse's legs. *M. 7; V. 33. (3)*				575	2500
5	C. (Ambiani), *Stater.* Disintegrated Apollo head. R. horse. *M. 26; V. 44. (5)*				275	1000
6	**Gold Quarter Stater.** Gallo-Belgic A. Similar to 1. *M. 2; V .15. (2)*				300	1000
7	— Similar to 2. *M. 4; V. 20. (2)*				275	850
8	B. Similar to 3. *M. 6; V. 35. (4)*				300	950
9	— Similar. R. Two horses l. with lyre between legs. *M. 8; V. 37. (4)*				200	525
10	D. Portions of Apollo head R. A mixture of stars, crescents, pellets, zig-zag lines; often referred to as 'Geometric' types (See also British 'O', S. 46.). *M. 37, 39, 41, 41a, 42; V. 65/7/9/146. (6)*				80	185

From *c.*50 B.C.

11

		F £	VF £
11	**Gold Stater.** Gallo-Belgic E. (Ambiani). Blank obv. ℞. Disjointed curved horse r., pellet below, zig-zag in exergue. *M. 27; V. 52, 54. (7)*	175	400
12	F. (Suessiones). Devolved Apollo head r. ℞. Disjointed horse r. With triple-tail. *M. 34a; V. 85. (8)*	575	2000
13	Xc. Blank except for VE monogram at edge of coin, ℞. S below horse r. *M. 82; V. 87-1. (9)*	300	1000

Armorican (Channel Islands and N.W. Gaul, *c.*75-50 B.C.)

14	**Billon Stater.** Class I. Head r. ℞. Horse, boar below, remains of driver with Victory above, lash ends in or two loops, or 'gate'. *(12)*	35	160
15	— Class II. Head r. ℞. Horse, boar below, remains of Victory only, lash ends in small cross of four pellets. *(13)*	30	150
16	— Class III. Head r., anchor-shaped nose. ℞. Somewhat similar to Class I. *(14)*	30	150
17	— Class IV. Head r. ℞. Horse with reins, lyre shape below, driver holds vertical pole, lash ends in three prongs. *(15)*	35	160
18	— Class V. Head r. ℞. Similar to last, lash ends in long cross with four pellets. *(16)*	45	200
19	— Class VI. Head r. ℞. Horse, boar below, lash ends in 'ladder' *(17)*	50	225
20	**Billon Quarter Stater.** Similar types to above. *(18)*	45	185

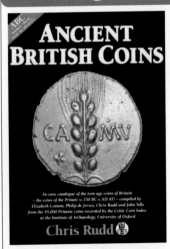

Three good Celtic coin books

ANCIENT BRITISH COINS

An easy catalogue of the iron age coins of Britain – the coins of the Pritani (c.150 BC–c.AD 45) – compiled by Elizabeth Cottam, Philip de Jersey, Chris Rudd and John Sills from the 45,000 Pritanic coins recorded by the Celtic Coin Index at the Institute of Archaeology, University of Oxford

Chris Rudd

A new introduction to Ancient British coins c.120 BC–AD 45. *"A perfect starting point. Profusely illustrated is an understatement"* says Professor Vincent Megaw. 56 pages, 300 coin photos. £10 + p&p.

The first-ever catalogue of Lincolnshire's first silver coins, struck by the Corieltavi c.60 BC–AD 10. *"Superbly illustrated"* says Dr John Sills. 80 pages, 230 coin drawings. £15 + p&p.

Never before have so many Ancient British coins been so easy to identify. *ABC* catalogues 999 coins, including 418 new types not shown by Van Arsdell in 1989. *"A great book"* says Prof. Sir Barry Cunliffe. 256 pages, 2000 twice-size coin photos. £75 + p&p.

  liz@celticcoins.com **Chris Rudd**

CELTIC COINS STRUCK IN BRITAIN

Coin production in Britain began at the very end of the second century B.C. with the cast potin coinage of Kent (Nos 62-64). Inspired by Gaulish issues and ultimately derived from the potin coins of Massalia (Marseilles) in southern Gaul, the precise function and period of use of this coinage is not fully understood. The domestic production of gold coins started around 70 B.C., these issues are traditionally known as British A-P and are derived from imported Gallo-Belgic issues. Broadly contemporary with these issues are quarter staters, silver units, and bronze units. Recent work by John Sills has further enhanced our understanding of this crucial early period with the identification of two new British staters (Insular Belgic C or Kentish A and the Ingoldisthorpe type) and their related quarters and a Westerham quarter stater. The Insular Belgic C or Kentish A type derived from Gallo-Belgic C now becomes the first British stater.

EARLY UNINSCRIBED COINAGE FROM c.65 BC

20A   20B

		F £	VF £
20A	**Gold Stater.** Insuler Belgic C/Kentish A type. Devolved Apollo head r. R. Disjointed horse r, a rosette behind or in front, or both. *M. —; V. —; BMC —*	575	2250
20B	Ingoldisthorpe type. Similar to last, as illustration. *M.—; V.—; BMC—* ..	475	1750

21   22   23   24

21	British A. Westerham type. Devolved Apollo head r. R. Disjointed horse l. large pellet below. *M. 28, 29; V. 200, 202; BMC 1-32 (19)*	275	575
22	B. Chute type. Similar to 9 but crab-like object below horse. *M. 32; V. 1205; BMC 35-76. (20)*	175	425
23	C. Yarmouth type. Similar to 9 but star-like object in front of horse. *M. 31; V. 1220; BMC 78-85. (21)*	725	2500
24	D. Cheriton type. Similar to Chute type but with large crescent face. *M. 33; V. 1215; BMC 86-128. (22)*	225	625
25	E. Waldingfield type. Annulet and pellet below horse. *M. 48; V. 1462; BMC — —. (23)*	475	1650

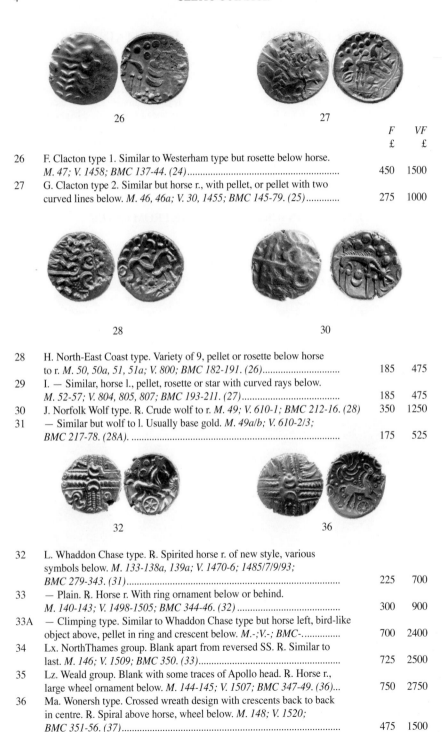

26

27

		F £	VF £

26 F. Clacton type 1. Similar to Westerham type but rosette below horse.
M. 47; V. 1458; BMC 137-44. (24) 450 1500

27 G. Clacton type 2. Similar but horse r., with pellet, or pellet with two
curved lines below. M. 46, 46a; V. 30, 1455; BMC 145-79. (25) 275 1000

28

30

28 H. North-East Coast type. Variety of 9, pellet or rosette below horse
to r. M. 50, 50a, 51, 51a; V. 800; BMC 182-191. (26) 185 475

29 I. — Similar, horse l., pellet, rosette or star with curved rays below.
M. 52-57; V. 804, 805, 807; BMC 193-211. (27) 185 475

30 J. Norfolk Wolf type. Ṛ. Crude wolf to r. M. 49; V. 610-1; BMC 212-16. (28) 350 1250

31 — Similar but wolf to l. Usually base gold. M. 49a/b; V. 610-2/3;
BMC 217-78. (28A). 175 525

32

36

32 L. Whaddon Chase type. Ṛ. Spirited horse r. of new style, various
symbols below. M. 133-138a, 139a; V. 1470-6; 1485/7/9/93;
BMC 279-343. (31) 225 700

33 — Plain. Ṛ. Horse r. With ring ornament below or behind.
M. 140-143; V. 1498-1505; BMC 344-46. (32) 300 900

33A — Climping type. Similar to Whaddon Chase type but horse left, bird-like
object above, pellet in ring and crescent below. M.-;V.-; BMC-. 700 2400

34 Lx. NorthThames group. Blank apart from reversed SS. Ṛ. Similar to
last. M. 146; V. 1509; BMC 350. (33) 725 2500

35 Lz. Weald group. Blank with some traces of Apollo head. Ṛ. Horse r.,
large wheel ornament below. M. 144-145; V. 1507; BMC 347-49. (36)... 750 2750

36 Ma. Wonersh type. Crossed wreath design with crescents back to back
in centre. Ṛ. Spiral above horse, wheel below. M. 148; V. 1520;
BMC 351-56. (37).. 475 1500

37 38

		F £	VF £
37	Mb. Savernake Forest type. Similar but *obv.* plain or almost blank. *M. 62; V. 1526; BMC 361-64*	175	500
38	Qa. British 'Remic' type. Crude laureate head. R. Triple-tailed horse, wheel below. *M. 58, 60, 61; V. 210-214; BMC 445-58. (41)*	225	700
39	Qb. — Similar, but *obv.* blank. *M. 59; V. 216; BMC 461-76. (42)*	200	550
39A	**Gold Quarter Stater.** Insular Belgic C/Kentish A type. Similar to Gallo-Belgic D, but with rosette in field on obverse. *M. —; V.—; BMC—*	250	850
39B	Ingoldisthorpe type. Similar to last but with sperm-like objects in field. *M.—; V.—; BMC—*	300	975
39C	British A. Westerham type. Similar to last but of cruder style, or with L-shapes in field on rev. *M.—; V.—; BMC—*	225	750
40	British D. Cheriton type. Similar to Stater, large crescent face. R. Cross motif with pellets. *M. —; V. 143 var; BMC 129-136*	250	800
41	F/G. Clacton type. Plain, traces of pattern. R. Ornamental cross with pellets. *M. 35; V. 1460; BMC 180-1. (43A)*	125	400
42	H. Crescent design and pellets. R. Horse r. *M. —; V. —; BMC 192*	125	400

43 44 45

43	Lx. N.Thames group. Floral pattern on wreath. R. Horse l. or r. *M. 76; V. 234; BMC 365-370. (44)*	150	525
44	Ly. N.Kent group. Blank. R. Horse l. or r. *M. 78; V. 158; BMC 371-3. (45)*	120	350
45	Lz. Weald group. Spiral design on wreath. R. Horse l. or r. *M. 77; V. 250; BMC 548-50. (46)*	150	450

46 47 48

46	O. Geometric type. Unintelligible patterns (some blank on obv.). *M. 40, 43-45; V. 143, 1225/27/29; BMC 410-32. (49)*	80	225
47	P. Trophy type. Blank. R. Trophy design. *M. 36, 38; V. 145-7; BMC 435-44. (50)*	110	300
48	Qc. British 'Remic' type. Head or wreath pattern. R. Triple-tailed horse, l. or r. *M. 63-67; 69-75; V. 220-32, 36, 42-6, 56; BMC 478-546. (51)*	135	400
49	Xd. Head l. of good style, horned serpent behind ear. R. Horse l. *M. 79; V. 78; BMC 571-575. (11)*	325	950

51

53

		F £	VF £
50	**Silver Unit** Lx. Head l.or r. R. Horse l. or r. *M. 280, 435, 436, 438, 441; V. 80, 1546, 1549, 1555; BMC 376-382. (53)*	90	325
51	— Head l. R. Stag r. with long horns. *M. 437; V. 1552; BMC 383-7. (54)*	90	325
52	— **Silver Half Unit.** Two horses or two beasts. *M. 272, 442, 443, 445; V. 474, 1626, 1643, 1948; BMC 389-400. (55)*	80	300
53	Lz. Danebury group. Head r. with hair of long curves. R. Horse l., flower above. *M. 88; V. 262; BMC 580-82*	125	450

54

54A

		F £	VF £
54	— Helmeted head r. R. Horse r. wheel below. *M. 89; V. 264; BMC 583 -592. (58)*	90	350
54A	Cruciform pattern with ornaments in angles. R. Horse l., ear of corn between legs, crescents and pellets above, *M.—; V.—; BMC—*	125	475
55	— **Silver Quarter Unit.** As last. *M. 90; V. 268; BMC 642-43. (59)*	50	175

56

61

		F £	VF £
56	— Head r. R. Horse r. star above, wheel below. *M. –; V. 280; BMC 595-601*	75	250
57	— Head l., pellet in ring in front. R. Horse l. or r. *M. –; V. 284; BMC 610-630*	50	175
58	— Serpent looking back. R. Horse l. *M. –; V. 286; BMC 631-33*	90	325
59	— **Silver Quarter Unit.** Cross pattern. R. Two-tailed horse. *M. 119; V. 482; BMC 654-56. (56C). (Formerly attributed to Verica)*	40	135
60	**Bronze Unit.** Lx. Winged horse l. R. Winged horse l. *M. 446; V. 1629; BMC 401 (78)*	60	250
61	Chichester Cock type. Head r. R. Head r. surmounted by cock. *M. –; V. – BMC 657-59*	70	275

POTIN, c.120-100 BC
(Cast copper/tin alloy, mainly Kent)

62

		F	VF
		£	£
62	**Unit.** Thurrock type.Head l. R. Bull butting l. or r. *M. —; V. 1402-42; BMC 660-666. (84A)*	20	60

63   64

63	Class I type. Crude head. R. Lines representing bull *(Allen types A-L.)* M. 9-22a; V. 104, 106, 108, 112, 114, 115, 117, 119, 120, 122, 123, 125, 127, 129, 131, 133; BMC 667-714. (83)...................................	25	85
64	Class II type. Smaller flan, large central pellet. *(Allen types M-P.)* M. 23-25; V. 135-39; BMC 715-23. (84)	20	70

Timeline Auctions
Inc. Gregory's **Est.1858**

We are accepting single entries and collections
of Celtic coins & antiquities

www.timelineauctions.com

+44 [0]1277 815121

enquiries@timelineauctions.com

Follow us on:

f /TimeLineAuctions

t @TimeLineAuction

AIAD

BNTA

CELTIC DYNASTIC AND LATER UNINSCRIBED COINAGE

From Julius Caesar's expeditions to Britain in 55/54 B.C. and his conquest of Gaul in 52 B.C. to the Claudian invasion in 43 A.D., southern Britain was increasingly drawn into the orbit of the Roman world. This process is reflected not only in the coins but also in what we know about their issuers and the tribes they ruled. Latin legends begin to appear for the first time and increasingly accompany objects and designs drawn from the classical world. A lot of what we know about the Celtic tribes and their rulers, beyond just their names on coins, is drawn from contemporary and slightly later Roman historical sources. A great deal however is still uncertain and almost all attributions to either tribes or historically attested individuals have to be seen as tentative.

The coin producing tribes of Britain can be divided into two groups, those of the core and those of the periphery. The tribes of the core, the Atrebates/Regni, Trinovantes/Catuvellauni and Cantii, by virtue of their geographical location controlled contact with the Roman world. Unlike the tribes of the periphery they widely employed Latin legends, classical designs and used bronze coinage in addition to gold and silver.

Following the Roman invasion of 43 A.D. it is likely that some coinage continued to be produced for a short time. However in 61 A.D. with the death of King Prasutagus and the suppression of the Boudiccan revolt that followed, it is likely that Celtic coinage came to an end.

TRIBAL/MINT MAP

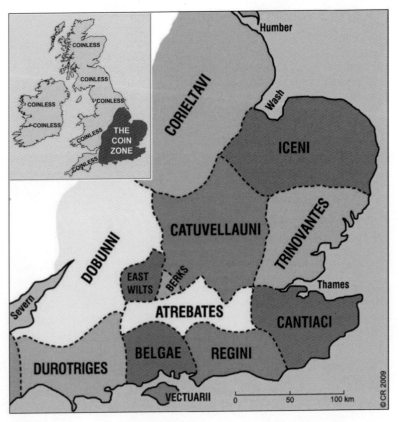

ATREBATES AND REGNI

The joint tribal area of these two groups corresponds roughly with Berkshire and Sussex and parts of northern and eastern Hampshire. The Atrebatic portion being in the north of this region with its main centre at Calleva (Silchester). The Regni occupying the southern part of the region centred around Chichester.

COMMIUS
(Mid to Late 1st Century B.C.)

The first inscribed staters to appear in Britain, closely resemble British Q staters (no.38) and are inscribed 'COMMIOS'. Staters and silver units with an inscribed 'E' are also thought to be related. Traditionally this Commius was thought to be the Gaulish chieftain who Caesar refers to in De Bello Gallico, as firstly serving him in his expeditions to Britain and finally fleeing to Britain c.50 B.C. This attribution does however present chronological problems, and the appearance of a few early staters reading 'COM COMMIOS' suggests that the Commius who issued coins is more likely to have been the son of Caesar's Commius.

65

		F £	VF £
65	**Gold Stater.** Devolved Apollo head r. ℞. COMMIOS around triple tailed horse r., wheel below. *M. 92; V. 350; BMC 724-29. (85)*	275	900

66

67

66	Similar, but 'E' symbol above horse instead of legend. *M. —;V. 352. BMC 730*	350	1050
67	**Gold Quarter Stater.** Blank except for digamma. ℞. Horse l. *M. 83; V. 353-5; BMC —. (10)*	150	375

69

69	**Silver Unit.** Head l. ℞. Horse l. Mostly with 'E' symbol above. *M. —;V. 355; BMC 731-58. (57)*	40	150

70

70	**Silver Minim.** Similar to Unit. *M. —; V. 358-5; BMC 759-60*	35	120

TINCOMARUS or TINCOMMIUS
(Late 1st Century B.C. – Early 1st Century A.D.)

Successor to Commius and on his coins styled as 'COM.F' (son of Commius). Early coins of the reign like his predecessors are very obiviously Celtic in their style. However later coins exhibit an increasing tendancy towards Roman designs. Indeed Tincommius is recorded as a suppliant king of the Roman emperor Augustus (Res Gestae, xxxii), finally fleeing to Rome in the early 1st century A.D. The discovery of the Alton Hoard in 1996 brought to light gold staters with the new legend TINCOMARVS.

72

73

		F £	VF £
71	**Gold Stater.** *Celtic style.* Devolved Apollo head r. R. TINC COMM. F. around horse. *M. 93; V. 362; BMC —. (86)*	700	2500
72	Similar but legend reads TINCOMARVS. *M. 94; V. 363; BMC 761-765. (86)*	475	1750
73	**Gold Quarter Stater.** Spiral with pellet centre. R. Horse r. T above. *M. 81; V. 366; BMC 781-797. (46)*	125	350

74

75

74	TINCOM, zig-zag ornament below. R. Horse l. *M. 95; V. 365; BMC 798-810. (87)*	150	425
75	**Gold Stater.** *Classical style.* TINC(O) on a sunk tablet. R. Horseman with javelin r. often with CF in field. *M. 96-98; V. 375-76; BMC 765-769. (88)*	425	1500

76

77

76	COM.(F). on a sunk tablet. R. Horseman with javelin r. TIN in field *M. 100; V. 385; BMC 770-774. (88)*	350	1250
77	**Gold Quarter Stater.** TINC on a tablet, C above, A or B below. R. Winged head (Medusa?) facing. *M. 97; V. 378; BMC 811-826. (89)*	375	1350
78	TIN on tablet. R. Boar l. *M. 99; V. 379; BMC 827-837. (90)*	125	350

79

83

		F £	VF £
79	COMF on tablet. R. Horse r. TIN around. *M. 101; V. 387;* *BMC 838-841. (90)*	135	425
80	— R. Horse l. TIC around. *M. 102; V. 388; BMC 842-851. (90)*	135	425
81	COM on tablet. R. Horse l. T above. *M. 103; V. 389; BMC 852-3. (90)*	150	475
82	COMF on tablet. R. Horse r. TINC around. *M. 104; V. 390;* *BMC 854-879. (90)*	135	425
83	**Silver Unit.** Laureate head r. TINCOM in front, V behind. R. Eagle stg. on snake. *M. 105; V. 397; BMC 880-905. (91)*	40	180
84	Laureate head l. R. Bull l. TINC around. *M. 106; V. 396;* *BMC 906-910. (91A)*	45	200
85	Laureate head r. R. Bull r. TIN(C) around. *M. —; V. 381;* *BMC 911-925. (92B)*	40	185
86	Facing head. R. Bull l. TINC around. *M. —; V. 370; BMC 926-29 (92)*	45	200

87

91

87	TINC in angles of cross, R. Lion l. *M. —; V. 372; BMC 930-45. (93B)*	45	200
88	Star. R. Boy riding dolphin r. TINC in field. *M. —; V. 371;* *BMC 946-977. (93C)*	35	175
89	TINC around pellet. R. Lion l. *M. 106a; V. 382; BMC 978-80. (93)*	45	200
90	Head l. TINCOMMIVS in front. R. Horse l. lyre above. *M. 131b; V. 473;* *BMC —. (92C) (Formerly attributed to Verica)*	50	225
91	**Silver Minim.** CF within two interlinked squares. R. Boar? r. TINC. *M. 118;* *V. 383-1; BMC 981-82. (94)*	35	125
92	As above but CO. R. Bull r. TI. *M. —; V. 383-5; BMC —*	40	135
93	C inside box, box above and below. R. Bull r. TIN. *M. —; V. 383-7;* *BMC 983*	40	135
94	Cross, T? in angles. R. uncertain object. *M. 120; V. 483; BMC 984-85.* *(Formerly attributed to Verica)*	35	125

Chris Rudd is the only dealer who deals only in Celtic coins

For a free catalogue ask liz@celticcoins.com
Chris Rudd, PO Box 222, Aylsham, Norfolk NR11 6TY. *Tel* 01263 735007

EPPILLUS

(Later 1st Century B.C. – Early 1st Century A.D.)

His reign is likely to have coincided with that of Tincommius's. Eppillus also claimed to be a son of Commius. Two coinages appear in his name, one for Kent and one minted at Calleva (Silchester, Hants.) in the northern part of the territory of the Atrebates and Regni. The coins of Calleva conform to the southern denominational structure of gold and silver with fractions of each, whilst the Kentish series is distinctly tri-metallic, replacing the silver minim with bronze. A joint coinage was issued by Eppillus and Verica. It is not understood if Eppillus held both territories simultaneously.

COINAGE STRUCK AT CALLEVA

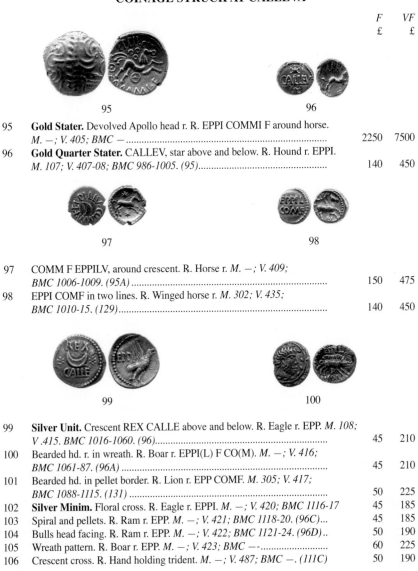

		F £	VF £
95	**Gold Stater.** Devolved Apollo head r. R. EPPI COMMI F around horse. *M. —; V. 405; BMC —*	2250	7500
96	**Gold Quarter Stater.** CALLEV, star above and below. R. Hound r. EPPI. *M. 107; V. 407-08; BMC 986-1005. (95)*................................	140	450
97	COMM F EPPILV, around crescent. R. Horse r. *M. —; V. 409; BMC 1006-1009. (95A)*	150	475
98	EPPI COMF in two lines. R. Winged horse r. *M. 302; V. 435; BMC 1010-15. (129)*...	140	450
99	**Silver Unit.** Crescent REX CALLE above and below. R. Eagle r. EPP. *M. 108; V .415. BMC 1016-1060. (96)*................................	45	210
100	Bearded hd. r. in wreath. R. Boar r. EPPI(L) F CO(M). *M. —; V. 416; BMC 1061-87. (96A)*	45	210
101	Bearded hd. in pellet border. R. Lion r. EPP COMF. *M. 305; V. 417; BMC 1088-1115. (131)*	50	225
102	**Silver Minim.** Floral cross. R. Eagle r. EPPI. *M. —; V. 420; BMC 1116-17*	45	185
103	Spiral and pellets. R. Ram r. EPP. *M. —; V. 421; BMC 1118-20. (96C)*...	45	185
104	Bulls head facing. R. Ram r. EPP. *M. —; V. 422; BMC 1121-24. (96D)*..	50	190
105	Wreath pattern. R. Boar r. EPP. *M. —; V. 423; BMC —-*..........................	60	225
106	Crescent cross. R. Hand holding trident. *M. —; V. 487; BMC —. (111C)*	50	190

KENTISH TYPES

107

		F £	VF £
107	**Gold Stater.** COMF within wreath. R. Horseman l. EPPILLVS above. M. 300; V. 430; BMC 1125-26. (127)	2250	7500
108	Victory holding wreath l., within wreath. R. Horseman r. holding carnyx, F EPPI COM below. M. 301; V. 431; BMC 1127-28. (128)	2750	10500
109	**Gold Quarter Stater.** Crossed wreaths, EPPI in angles. R. Horse l. M. 303; V. 436; BMC 1129. (130)	475	1500
110	COMF in pellet border. R. Horse r. EPPI. M. 304; V. 437; BMC 1130-31. (130)	425	1350
111	**Silver Unit.** Head l. EPPIL in field. R. Horseman holding carnyx, EPPILL. M. 306; V. 441; BMC 1132. (131)	275	950
112	**Bronze Unit.** Bow cross, EPPI COMF around. R. Eagle facing. M. 309; V. 450; BMC 1137-38. (134)	45	240
113	Bull r., EPPI COF around. R. eagle facing. M. 310; V. 451; BMC 1139-41. (134)	45	240
114	Head l., EPPI in front. R. Victory l. holding wreath and standard. M. 311; V. 452; BMC 1142. (133)	50	250
115	Bearded hd. r., EPPI CF. R. Biga r. CF. M. 312; V. 453; BMC —	60	300

JOINT TYPES OF EPPILUS AND VERICA

		F £	VF £
116	**Silver Unit.** Head l. CO VIR in front. R. Victory, EP. M. 307; V. 442; BMC 1133-34. (132)	350	1250

117

		F £	VF £
117	Head r. VIR CO in front. R. Capricorn l. EPPI COMF. M. 308/a; V. 443; BMC 1135-36. (132)	175	625

Chris Rudd offers you six all-Celtic auctions a year. Nobody else does

For a free catalogue ask liz@celticcoins.com
Chris Rudd, PO Box 222, Aylsham, Norfolk NR11 6TY. *Tel* 01263 735007

VERICA
(*c*.10.-*c*.40 A.D.)

The exact details of Verica's succession and relationship to Eppillus and Tincommius are not fully understood. However by c.10 A.D. it seems likely that Verica was the sole ruler of the southern region. His close contact with Rome, both political and economic, seen in the increasing use of classical designs on his coins, culminated in his flight to Rome in c.42 A.D. to seek assistance from Claudius.

			F £	VF £
118	**Gold Stater.** COM:F on tablet. R. Horseman r. holding spear, VIR below.			
	M. 109; V. 460; BMC 1143-44. (97)		350	1200
119	COM.F. on tablet, pellet in ring ornament above and below. R.			
	Similar to last. *M.121; 461; BMC 1146-53. (97)*		350	1200

120   121

120	COM.F on tablet. R. Horseman r. holding spear, VIR above, REX below.			
	M. 121 var; V. 500; BMC 1155-58. (98)		300	900
121	Vine-leaf dividing VI RI. R. Horseman r. with shield and spear. COF in			
	field. *M. 125; V. 520-1; BMC 1159-73. (99)*		325	950
122	Similar, reads VE RI. *M. 125; V. 520-5/7; BMC 1174-76. (99)*		350	1100
123	**Gold Quarter Stater.** COMF on tablet. R. Horse l. VIR. *M. 111; V. 465;*		150	475
	BMC 1177-78. (100)			

124

124	COMF on tablet, pellet in ring ornament above and below R. Horse			
	r. VI. *M. 112; V. 466; BMC 1179-1206. (100)*		135	375
125	COMF on tablet, pellet border. R. Horse r. VI above. *M. 113; V. 467;*		135	375
	BMC 1207-16. (100)			

126   128

126	COM FILI. in two lines, scroll in between. R. Horse r. VIR(I) above.			
	M. 114; V. 468; BMC 1217-22. (100)		150	475
127	VERI COMF, crescent above, star below. R. Horse r. REX below.			
	M. 122; V. 501; BMC 1223-36. (101)		150	475
128	VERI beneath vine-leaf. R. Horseman r. with sword and shield,			
	FRX in field. *M. 124; V. 525; BMC 1237-38. (102)*		375	1350
129	COM, horseman r. R. Seated figure, VERICA around. *M. 126; V. 526;*		525	1850
	BMC 1239. (103)			
130	Similar to last. R. Laureate bust r., VIRI in front. *M. 127; V. 527;*		500	1750
	BMC 1240. (103)			

	F	VF
	£	£

131 **Silver Unit.** COMF, crescent and or pellet in ring above and below. R. Boar r. VI(RI) below. *M. 115; V. 470/72; BMC 1241-1331. (104)*...................... 45 175

132

133

132 VERICA COMMI F around pellet in ring. R. Lion r. REX below. *M. 123; V. 505; BMC 1332-1359. (105)*.. 45 175

133 COMMI F, horseman with shield r. R. VERI CA, mounted warrior with spear r. *M. 128; V. 530; BMC 1360-92. (106)* 45 175

134

137

134 Two cornucopiae, COMMI F. R. Figure seated r. VERICA. *M. 129; V. 531; BMC 1393-1419. (107)*.. 40 165

135 Bust r. VIRI. R. Figure seated l. *M. 130; V. 532; BMC 1420. (108)* 100 450

136 Naked figure l. R. Laureate bust r., COMMI F. *M. 131; V. 533; BMC 1421-49. (108)*.. 40 165

137 VERICA REX, bull r. R. Figure stg. l., COMMI F. *M. —; V. 506; BMC 1450-84. (108B)* 40 165

138 COMF, in tablet and scroll. R. Eagle facing, VI RI. *M. —; V. 471; BMC 1485-1505. (104A)* 40 150

139 VIRIC across field, ornaments above and below. R. Pegasus r., star design below. *M. —; V. —; BMC —. (104B)* 75 350

140 Head r. Verica. R. COMMI F., eagle l. *M. 131A; V. 534; BMC —. (108A)* 90 400

141 **Silver Minim.** COF in tablet, R. Facing head (Medusa?), VE below. *M. —; V. 384; BMC 1506.(94A). (Formerly attributed to Tincommius)*.............. 40 160

142 Head r. R. Horse r., VIRICO. *M. 116; V. 480; BMC —. (109)* 40 160

143 Pellet and ring pattern. R. Lion r. VIR. *M. 120a/c; V. 484; BMC 1514-17. (109)*.. 35 135

144 VIRIC reversed. R. Boar r. *M. —; V. 485; BMC 1518* 35 135

145 Cross. R. Trident. *M. —; V. 486-1; BMC —*... 40 160

146 Uncertain. R. Boar r. *M. 120b; V. 510-1; BMC —. (109)* 30 120

147 Crescent cross. R. Boar r. *M. —; V. 510-5; BMC 1521-23. (109)* 35 140

148 VIR VAR in tablets. R. Winged horse r. CO. *M. 120d; V. 511; BMC 1507-12. (109)*.. 35 140

149

150

149 Vine-leaf, CFO. R. Horse r. VERI CA. *M. —; V. 550; BMC 1524-25* 35 140

150 CF in torc. R. Head r. VERIC. *M. 132; V. 551; BMC 1526-33. (111A)*.... 30 135

		F	VF
		£	£
151	Altar, CF, R. Bulls head facing, VERICA. *M. 120e; V. 552;*		
	BMC 1534-37. (109)..	50	200
152	Temple, CF. R. Bull r, VER REX. *M. —; V. 553; BMC 1538-41*............	30	135

153   154

		F	VF
153	Cornucopia, VER COM. R. Lion r. *M. —; V. 554; BMC 1542*	35	150
154	Two cornucopiae. R. Eagle l. *M. —; V. 555; BMC 1543-58*.....................	30	100
155	Floral pattern, CF. R. Lion r. *M.—; V. 556; BMC 1559-63. (111E)*.........	35	140
156	Sphinx r., CF, R. dog curled up, VERI. *M. —; V. 557; BMC 1564-68.*		
	(109B)	30	135
157	VERI. R. Urn, COMMI F. *M. —; V. 559; BMC* —-	40	160
158	A in star. R. Bird r. *M. 316; V. 561; BMC 1569-71*	45	175
159	Urn, Rex. R. Eagle r., VERRICA COMMI F. *M. —; V. 563;*		
	BMC 1572-78. (109C)..	30	110
160	VIR inside tablet. R. Boars head r. *M. 117; V. 564; BMC 1579-81. (109A)*	30	130
161	Cross. R. bull l. *M. —; V. —; BMC 1582*...	35	150
162	Boars head r., CF, R. Eagle, VE. *M. —; V. —; BMC 1583-86*.................	30	120
163	Head r, COMM IF., R. Sphinx, R VE. *M. —; V. —; BMC 1587-89*.........	35	150
164	A in tablet. R. Boar r. VI CO. *M. —; V. —; BMC 1590*............................	50	200
	The two following coins are possibly issues of Epatticus.		
165	Bull r. R. Eagle with snake l. *M. —; V. 512; BMC 2366-70*....................	35	150
166	Bust r. R. dog r. *M. —; V. 558; BMC 2371-74*...	40	160

CANTII

The Cantii, who gave their name to Kent, occupied a similar area to that of the modern county.
Caesar considered this most civilised part of Britain and the early production of potin units
in Kent can be seen as indicative of this. A number of Kentish rulers for whom we have coins,
appear to be dynasts from the two neighbouring kingdoms, who were involved in struggles to
acquire territory. Eppillus (see Atrebates and Regni) produced coins specifically for circulation
in Kent and like those of Cunobelin they circulated widely.

EARLY UNINSCRIBED

		F	VF
167	**Gold Stater.** Ly. Blank. R. Horse l. numerous ring ornaments in field.		
	M. 293; V. 142; BMC 2472. (34)	675	2750
168	Blank. R. Horse r. numerous ornaments in field. *M. 294; V. 157;*		
	BMC— (34)..	675	2750

169   170

		F	VF
169	Lz. Blank. R. Horse l., box with cross hatching below. *M. 84, 292;*		
	V. 150, 144; BMC 2466-68. (35)..	725	3000
170	**Gold Quarter Stater.** Ly. Blank. R. Horse r., pentagram below. *M. 285;*		
	V. 163; BMC 2473-74. (45)..	135	400

171 173 176

		F	VF
		£	£
171	Blank. Ŗ. Horse r., 'V' shape above. *M. 284; V. 170; BMC 2475-77. (45)*	130	375
172	Lz. Blank. Ŗ. Horse l., 'V' shape above. *M. 85; V. 151; BMC 2469-70. (47)*	110	300
173	**Silver Unit.** Curved star. Ŗ. Horse r. Pentagram below. *M. 272a; V. 164; BMC—. (56)*	125	375
174	Serpent torc. Ŗ. Horse r., box with cross hatching below. *cf Mossop 8; BMC 2478*	160	550
175	**Silver Half Unit.** Spiral of three arms. Ŗ. Horse l. *M. —; V. —; BMC 2479*	75	275
176	**Bronze Unit.** Various animal types, Ŗ. Various animal types. *M. 295-96, 316a-d; V. 154/167; BMC 2480-91. (80/141-44)*	50	225

INSCRIBED

DUBNOVELLAUNUS
(Late 1st Century B.C.)

Likely to be the same Dubnovellaunus recorded on coins in Essex (see Trinovantes / Catuvellauni). The two coinages share the same denominational structure and have some stylistic similarities. It has been suggested that Dubnovellaunus is the British king of that name mentioned along with Tincommius as a client king in the Res Gestae of the Roman emperor Augustus.

177 180

177	**Gold Stater.** Blank. Ŗ. Horse r., bucranium above, serpent like object below, DUBNOV[ELLAUNUS] or similar around. *M. 282; V. 169; BMC 2492-96. (118)*	325	950
178	— Ŗ. Horse r., but without bucranium and with wheel below. *M. 283; V. 176; BMC 2497-98. (118)*	425	1350
179	**Silver Unit.** Winged animal r. R. Horse l., DVBNO. *M. 286; V. 171; BMC 2499-2501. (119)*	125	400
180	Winged animal l. Ŗ. Seated fig. l., holding hammer, DVBNO. *M. 287; V. 178; BMC 2502-03. (119)*	130	425
181	**Bronze Unit.** Horse r. Ŗ. Lion l., DVBN. *M. 290; V. 166; BMC 2504-06. (122).*	60	250
182	Boar l., DVBNO. Ŗ. Horseman r. *M. 291; V. 181; BMC 2507-08. (121).*	60	250
183	Boar r., DVBNO. Ŗ. Eagle facing. *M. 289; V. 180; BMC 2509-10. (121)*	55	225

VOSENOS
(Late 1st Century B.C./ Early 1st Century A.D.)

Little is known of this ruler who issued coins in a characteristically Kentish style similar to those of Dubnovellaunus.

		F £	VF £
184	**Gold Stater.** Blank. R. Horse l., bucranium above, serpent like object below., [VOSE]NOS. *M. 297; V. 184; BMC 2511-12. (123)*	2000	6500

185

185	**Gold Quarter Stater.** Blank. R. Horse r., VOSI below. *M. 298; V. 185; BMC 2514-15. (124)*	450	1500
186	**Silver Unit.** Horse and griffin. R. Horse r., retrograde legend. *M. 299a; V. 186; BMC —. (125)*	175	650

"SA" or "SAM"
(Late 1st Century B.C./ Early 1st Century A.D.)

An historically unattested individual whose coins are stylistically associated with those of Dubnovellaunus and Vosenos. His coins have been predominantly found in north Kent

187	**Silver Unit.** Head l., R. Horse l., SA below. *M. —; V. —; BMC —*	200	700
187A	**Bronze Unit.** Boar l., R. Horse l., SA below. *M. 299; V. 187; BMC 2516-19. (126)*	70	250

187B

187B	Horse l., SAM below. R. Horse l., SAM below. *M. —; V. —; BMC —*	75	300

AMMINUS
(Early 1st Century A.D.)

Issued a coinage stylistically distinct from other Kentish types and with strong affinities to those of Cunobelin. Indeed it has been suggested that he is the Adminius recorded by Suetonius, as a son of Cunobelin. The enigmatic legend DVN or DVNO may be an unknown mint site.

189

188	**Silver Unit.** Plant, AMMINUS around. R. Winged horse r., DVN. *M. 313; V. 192; BMC 2522-23. (136)*	125	475
189	(Last year 190). A in wreath. R. Capricorn r., S AM (I). *M. 314; V. 194; BMC 2520-21. (137)*	110	425
190	**Bronze Unit.** (Last year 189). AM in wreath. R. Horse r., DVNO. *M. —; V. 193; BMC — —*	60	250
191	Head r. R. Hippocamp r., AM. *M. 315; V. 195; BMC 2524. (139)*	70	300

TRINOVANTES AND CATUVELLAUNI

Occupying the broad area of Essex, southern Suffolk, Bedfordshire, Buckinghamshire, Hertfordshire, parts of Oxfordshire, Cambridgeshire and Northamptonshire, they are likely to have been two separate tribes for most of their history. The Trinovantes were originally located in the eastern half of this area, with their main centre at Camulodunum (Colchester). The original Catuvellauni heartland was further west, with their main centre at Verulamium (St.Albans). The whole area eventually came under the control of Cunobelin at the end of the period.

TRINOVANTES

ADDEDOMAROS
(Late 1st Century B.C.)

Unknown to history, he appears to have been a contemporary of Tasciovanus. The design of his staters is based on the Whaddon Chase type (No.32) which circulated widely in this region.

200

		F £	VF £
200	**Gold Stater.** Crossed wreath. R. Horse r., wheel below, AθθIIDOM above. *M. 266; V. 1605; BMC 2390-94. (148)*	300	1000

201   202

201	Six armed spiral. R. Horse r., cornucopia below, AθθIIDOM above. *M. 267; V. 1620; BMC 2396-2404. (148)*	250	800
202	Two opposed crescents. R. Horse r., branch below, spiral or wheel above, AθθDIIDOM. *M. 268; V. 1635; BMC 2405-2415. (149)*..............	325	1100

203   204

203	**Gold Quarter Stater.** Circular flower pattern. R. Horse r. *M. 271; V. 1608; BMC 2416. (44)*	165	475
204	Cross shaped flower pattern. R. Horse r. *M. 270; V. 1623; BMC 2417-21. (44)*..	150	350
205	Two opposed crescents. R. Horse r., AθθDIIDOM around. *M. 269; V. 1638; BMC 2422-24. (150)*..	200	650
206	**Bronze Unit.** Head l. R. Horse l. *M. 274; V. 1615/46 BMC 2450-60. (77)*	35	130

DUBNOVELLAUNUS

(Late 1st Century B.C./ Early 1st Century A.D.)

Dubnovellaunus is likely to have been the successor to Addedomaros, with whom his coins are stylistically related. It is not clear if he was the same Dubnovellaunus who also issued coins in Kent (see Cantii) or if he is the same Dumnobeallaunos mentioned in the Res Gestae of the emperor Augustus c.AD14.

207   208

		F £	VF £
207	**Gold Stater.** Two crescents on wreath. Ṛ. Horse l., leaf below, pellet in ring, DVBNOVAIIAVNOS above. *M. 275; V. 1650; BMC 2425-40. (152)*.....	325	1050
208	**Gold Quarter Stater.** Similar. *M. 276; V. 1660; BMC 2442. (153)*	150	450

210

209	**Silver Unit**. Head l., DVBNO. Ṛ. Winged horse r., lattice box below. *M. 288; V. 165; BMC 2443-44. (120)*......................	130	400
210	Head l., legend ?, Ṛ. Horse l. DVB[NOV]. *M. 278; V. 1667; BMC 2445. (154)*......................	125	375
211	**Bronze Unit.** Head l., Ṛ. Horse l., DVBNO above. *M. 281; V. 1669; BMC 2446-48. (154)*......................	45	170
212	Head r., Ṛ. Horse l. *M. 277; V. 1665; BMC 2461-65. (154)*	45	170

DIRAS

(Late 1st Century B.C./ Early 1st Century A.D.)

An historically unattested ruler, responsible for a gold stater related stylistically to Dubnovellaunus's.

213	**Gold Stater.** Blank. Ṛ. Horse r., DIRAS? above, yoke like object above. *M. 279; V. 162; BMC 2449. (151)*	2250	7500

Six times a year Liz's List offers you nice rare Celtic coins at nice low prices - all under £1,000 including gold coins

For a free catalogue ask liz@celticcoins.com
Chris Rudd, PO Box 222, Aylsham, Norfolk NR11 6TY. *Tel* 01263 735007

CATUVELLAUNI

TASCIOVANUS
(Late 1st Century B.C./ Early 1st Century A.D.)

The early gold coins of Tasciovanus, like those of his contemporary Addedomaros, are based on the Whaddon Chase stater. Verulamium (St. Albans) appears to have been his principal mint, appearing as VER or VERL on the coinage. Staters and quarter staters inscribed CAM (Camulodunum/ Colchester) are known and perhaps suggest brief or weak control of the territory to the east. The later coins of Tasciovanus use increasingly Romanised designs. The adoption of the title RICON, perhaps a Celtic equivalent to the Latin REX (King), can be seen as a parallel move to that of his contemporary Tincommius to the south.

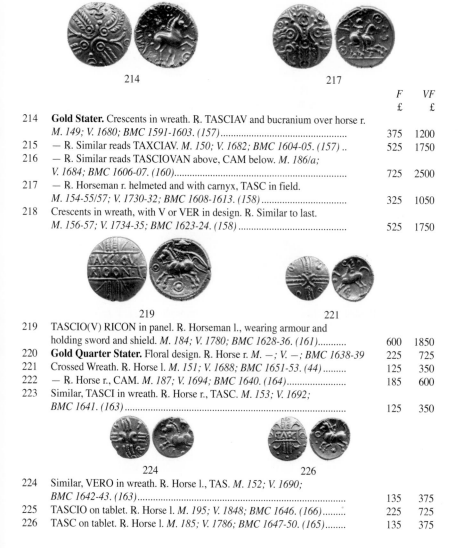

214   217

		F £	VF £
214	**Gold Stater.** Crescents in wreath. R. TASCIAV and bucranium over horse r. M. 149; V. 1680; BMC 1591-1603. (157)	375	1200
215	— R. Similar reads TAXCIAV. M. 150; V. 1682; BMC 1604-05. (157)	525	1750
216	— R. Similar reads TASCIOVAN above, CAM below. M. 186/a; V. 1684; BMC 1606-07. (160)	725	2500
217	— R. Horseman r. helmeted and with carnyx, TASC in field. M. 154-55/57; V. 1730-32; BMC 1608-1613. (158)	325	1050
218	Crescents in wreath, with V or VER in design. R. Similar to last. M. 156-57; V. 1734-35; BMC 1623-24. (158)	525	1750

219   221

219	TASCIO(V) RICON in panel. R. Horseman l., wearing armour and holding sword and shield. M. 184; V. 1780; BMC 1628-36. (161)	600	1850
220	**Gold Quarter Stater.** Floral design. R. Horse r. M. —; V. —; BMC 1638-39	225	725
221	Crossed Wreath. R. Horse l. M. 151; V. 1688; BMC 1651-53. (44)	125	350
222	— R. Horse r., CAM. M. 187; V. 1694; BMC 1640. (164)	185	600
223	Similar, TASCI in wreath. R. Horse r., TASC. M. 153; V. 1692; BMC 1641. (163)	125	350

224   226

224	Similar, VERO in wreath. R. Horse l., TAS. M. 152; V. 1690; BMC 1642-43. (163)	135	375
225	TASCIO on tablet. R. Horse l. M. 195; V. 1848; BMC 1646. (166)	225	725
226	TASC on tablet. R. Horse l. M. 185; V. 1786; BMC 1647-50. (165)	135	375

		F £	VF £
227	**Silver Unit.** Head l. R. Horse r. *M. —; V. 1698; BMC 1654*	65	225
228	Cross and box. R. Horse r., VER in front. *M. —; V. —; BMC 1655*.........	65	250
229	Cross and crescent. R. Horse l., TASCI. *M. —; V. —; BMC 1665-57*	65	225
230	Bearded head l. R. Horseman r., TASCIO. *M. 158; V. 1745; BMC 1667-68. (167)*	75	325
231	Winged horse l., TAS. R. Griffin r., within circle of pellets. *M. 159; V. 1790; BMC 1660. (168)*........................	70	275
232	Eagle stg. l., TASCIA. R. Griffin r. *M. 160; V. 1792; BMC 1658-59. (169)*	75	300
233	VER in beaded circle. R. Horse r., TASCIA. *M. 161; V. 1699; BMC 1670-73. (170)*..	70	300
234	— R. Naked horseman. *M. 162; V. 1747; BMC 1674-76. (171)*	70	300

235   238

235	Laureate hd. r., TASCIA. R. Bull l. *M. 163; V. 1794; BMC 1681-82. (172)*	70	300
236	Cross and box, VERL. R. Boar r. TAS. *M. 164; V. 1796; BMC 1661-62. (173)*..	70	275
237	TASC in panel. R. Winged horse l. *M. 165; V. 1798; BMC 1664-65. (174)*	65	260
238	— R. Horseman l., carrying long shield. *M. 166; V. 1800; BMC 1677-79. (174)*..	70	300
239	Two crescents. R. Winged griffin, VIR. *M. —; V. —; BMC 1666*	75	325
240	Head r., TAS?. R. Horseman r. *M. —; V. —; BMC 1669*	75	325

241

| 241 | **Bronze Double Unit.** Head r., TASCIA, VA. R. Horseman r. *M. 178; V. 1818; BMC 1685-87. (190)*.. | 85 | 300 |

242

242	**Bronze Unit.** Two heads in profile, one bearded. R. Ram l., TASC. *M. 167; V. 1705; BMC 1711-13. (178)*........................	30	135
243	Bearded head r. VER(L). R. Horse l., VIIR or VER. *M. 168; V. 1707; BMC 1714-21. (179)*..	25	135
244	Bearded head r. R. Horse l., TAS. *M. 169; V. 1709; BMC 1722-23. (179)*	30	135
245	Head r., TASC. R. Winged horse l., VER. *M. 170; V. 1711; BMC 1688-89. (180)*..	25	125
246	— R. Horseman r., holding carnyx, VIR. *M. 171; V. 1750; BMC 1724-27. (182)*..	25	125

247

		F £	VF £
247	VERLAMIO between rays of star. R. Bull l. *M. 172; V. 1808; BMC 1745-51. (183)*	25	120
248	Similar without legend. R. Bull r. *M. 174; V. 1810; BMC 1752-55. (185)*	30	135
249	Similar. R. Horse l., TASCI. *M. 175; V. 1812; BMC 1709-10. (186)*	30	135
250	Head r., TASCIO. R. Lion r., TA SCI. *M. 176; V. 1814; BMC 1736-38. (188)*	25	125
251	Head r. R. Figure std. l., VER below. *M. 177; V. 1816; BMC 1739-44. (189)*	30	135
252	Cross and Crescents. R. Boar r., VER. *M. 179; V. 1713; BMC 1702-05. (191)*	25	130
253	Laureate head r. R. Horse l., VIR. *M. 180; V. 1820; BMC 1706-08. (192)*	25	130
254	Raised band across centre, VER or VERL below. R. Horse grazing r. *M. 183a; V. 1717; BMC —. (193)*	35	150
255	**Bronze Fractional Unit.** Animal r. R. Sphinx l. *M. 181; V. 1824; BMC 1760-61. (198)*	30	135
256	Head l., VER. R. Goat r. *M. 182; V. 1715; BMC 1765-68. (199)*	25	125
257	Head r. R. Boar r, *M. 183; V. 1826; BMC 1762-64. (199)*	25	130
258	Head l. R. Animal with curved tail. *M. 183b, c; V. 1822; BMC 1759. (200)*	30	135

ASSOCIATES OF TASCIOVANUS

(Early 1st Century A.D.)

Towards the end of his reign, a number of joint issues bearing his name and the name of either Sego or Dias appear. In addition coins similar in style to those of Tasciovanus appear with either the name Andoco or Rues. It has been suggested that these issues belong to a period of struggle following the death of Tasciovanus and are all rival contestants for the throne. Another theory is that they are associates or sub-kings of Tasciovanus responsible for areas within the wider territory.

SEGO

259

| 259 | **Gold Stater.** TASCIO in tablet, annulets above. R. Horseman with carnyx r., SEGO. *M. 194; V. 1845; BMC 1625-27. (162)* | 1350 | 5250 |

260

		F £	VF £
260	**Silver Unit.** SEGO on panel. R. Horseman r. *M. 196; V. 1851;* *BMC 1684. (176)*	375	1450
261	**Bronze Unit.** Star shaped pattern. R. Winged sphinx l., SEGO. *M. 173; V. 1855;* *BMC 1690. (184)*	110	450

ANDOCO

262

262	**Gold Stater.** Crescents in wreath. R. Bucranium over horse r., AND below. *M. 197; V. 1860; BMC 2011-14. (202)*	725	2250
263	**Gold Quarter Stater.** Crossed wreaths, ANDO in angles. R. Horse l. *M. 198;* *V. 1863; BMC 2015-17. (203)*...	200	650

264

| 264 | **Silver Unit.** Bearded head l. R. Winged horse l., ANDOC. *M. 199; V. 1868;*
BMC 2018. (204) .... | 110 | 375 |

265

265	**Bronze Unit.** Head r., ANDOCO. R. Horse r., ANDOCO. *M. 200; V. 1871;* *BMC 2019-20. (205)*..	40	200
266	Head r., TAS ANDO. R. Horse r. *M. 175a; V. 1873; BMC —. (187)*	50	250

DIAS

267   268

267	**Silver Unit.** Saltire over cross within square. R. Boar r., TASC DIAS. *M. —; V. —; BMC 1663. (173A)*..	90	275
268	DIAS CO, in star. R. Horse l., VIR. *M. 188; V. 1877; BMC 1683. (177).*	95	300

269

		F £	VF £

269 **Bronze Unit.** Bearded head r., DIAS TASC. R. Centaur r., playing pan pipes.
M. 192; V. 1882; BMC 1728-35. (197) 40 225

RUES

270 **Bronze Unit.** Lion r., RVII. R. Eagle. *M. 189; V. 1890; BMC 1691. (194)* 35 180
271 — R. Similar reads RVE. *M. 189; V. 1890-3; BMC 1692. (194)* 30 165

272 273

272 Bearded head r., RVIIS. R. Horseman r., VIR. *M. 190; V. 1892;*
BMC 1698-1701. (195) 30 165
273 RVIIS on tablet. R. Winged sphinx l. *M. 191; V. 1895;*
BMC 1693-97. (196) 30 165
274 **Bronze Fractional Unit.** Annulet within square with curved sides. R.
Eagle l.,RVII. *M. 193; V. 1903; BMC 1756-58. (201)* 35 180

CUNOBELIN
(Early 1st Century A.D. to *c.*40 A.D.)

Styled as son of Tasciovanus on some of his coins, Cunobelin appears to have ruled over the unified territories of the Trinovantes and Catuvellauni, with additional territory in Kent. His aggressive policy of expansion that involved members of his family eventually lead to Roman concern over the extent of his power. Following his death just prior to 43 AD, the emperor Claudius took the decision to invade Britain.

During his long reign an extensive issue of gold, silver and bronze coins used ever increasingly Romanised designs. It has been estimated from a study of known dies that around one million of his gold corn ear staters were produced. His main centre and mint was at Camulodunum (Colchester) appearing as the mint signature CAMV. The names SOLIDV and AGR appear on a few coins associated with Cunobelin and are likely to represent personal names.

280 281

280 **Gold Stater.** Biga type. CAMVL on panel. R. Two horses l., wheel below,
CVNOBELIN. *M. 201; V. 1910; BMC 1769-71. (207)* 725 2250
281 Linear type. Corn ear dividing CA MV. R. Horse r., branch above.,
CVN. *M. 210; V. 1925; BMC 1772-76. (208)* 325 850

		F £	VF £

282   — Similar, privy mark 'x' above a letter in *obv.* legend. *M. 210a;*
VA 1925-3/5; BMC 1777-81. (208).. 375   1100

283

285

283   Wild type. Corn ear dividing CA MV. Ŗ. Horse r., branch above.,
CVN(O). *M. 211/2; V. 1931/33; BMC 1784-92/1804-08. (208)*.............. 300   800

284   — Similar, heart shaped object between horses forelegs. *M. 211 var;*
V. 1931-3; BMC 1793. (208).. 550   2000

285   — Similar, privy mark pellet or pellet triangle above a letter(s) in *obv.*
legend. *M. —; V. 1931-5/7/9; BMC 1797-1803. (208)* 325   950

286

288

286   Plastic type. Corn ear dividing CA MV. Ŗ. Horse r., branch above.,
CVNO. *M. 203/13; V. 2010-1/3/5; BMC 1809-11/15-23. (208)*.............. 300   800

287   — Similar, 'B' in front of horse. *M. —; V. 2010-7; BMC 1813. (208)*..... 525   1850

289

290

288   Classic type. Corn ear dividing CA MV. Ŗ. Horse r., branch above.,
CVNO. *M. 206-07; V. 2025/27; BMC 1827-31/33. (208)* 375   1050

289   — Similar, horse l., lis like object above. *M. 208; V. 2029;*
BMC 1834-35. (209).. 600   2000

290   **Gold Quarter Stater.** Biga type. Similar to 280. *M. 202; V. 1913;*
BMC 1836/A. (210).. 225   750

292

296

292   Linear type. Similar to 281. *M. 209; V. 1927; BMC 1837-42. (211)*........ 140   350

293   Wild type. Similar to 283. *M. —; V. 1935; BMC 1843-44. (211)*.............. 140   350

294   Plastic type. Similar to 286. *M. 204; V. 2015; BMC 1846-48. (211)*........ 135   325

295   — Similar but corn ear dividing CAM CVN. *M. 205; V. 2017;*
BMC 1845. (212) 165   475

296   Classic type. Similar to 288. *M. —; V. 2038; BMC —. (211)* 175   550

299

		F £	VF £
299	**Silver Unit.** Two bull headed serpents, inter twined. R. Horse l., CVNO. *M. 214; V. 1947; BMC 1856. (213)*	90	475
300	Curled serpent inside wheel. R. Winged horse l., CVN. *M. —; V. —; BMC 1857*	90	475
301	CVN on panel R. Dog l., (C)M. *M. 255; V. 1949; BMC 1858-59. (228)*.	80	375
302	CVNO BELI on two panels. R. CVN below horseman r. *M. 216/7; V. 1951/53; BMC 1862. (215)*	75	325
303	Head l., CAMVL. R. CVNO beneath Victory std. r. *M. 215; V. 2045; BMV 1863-65. (214)*	80	350

304   305

304	Two leaves dividing CVN. R. Horseman r., CAM. *M. 218; V. 2047; BMC 1866-67. (216)*	75	325
305	Flower dividing CAMV. R. CVNO below horse r. *M. 219; V. 2049; BMC1867A. (217)*	85	425
306	CVNO on panel. R. CAMV on panel below griffin. *M. 234; V. 2051; BMC 1868-69. (218)*	80	375
307	CAMVL on panel. R. CVNO below centaur l. carrying palm. *M. 234a; V. 1918; BMC —. (219)*	80	375
308	CAMVL on panel. R. Figure seated l. holding wine amphora, CVNOBE. *M. —; V. —; BMC —. (219A)*	75	325
309	Plant, CVNOBELINVS. R. Figure stg. r. holding club and thunderbolt dividing CA MV. *M. —; V .—; BMC 1897. (219B)*	85	425
310	Laur. hd. r., CVNOBELINVS. R. Winged horse springing l., CAMV below. *M. —; V. —; BMC —. (219C)*	85	425
311	CVNO on panel, wreath around. R. Winged horse r., TASC F. *M. 235; V. 2053; BMC 1870. (220)*	85	400

312   313

312	Head r., CVNOBELINI. R. Horse r., TASCIO. *M. 236; V. 2055; BMC 1871-73. (221)*	70	300
313	Winged bust r., CVNO. R. Sphinx std. l., TASCIO. *M. 237; V. 2057; BMC 1874-78. (222)*	60	240

314 316 318

		F £	VF £
314	Draped female fig. r., TASCIIOVAN. ℞. Figure std. r. playing lyre, tree behind. *M. 238; V. 2059; BMC 1879-82. (223)*	70	300
315	Figure stg. l., holding club and lionskin., CVNO. ℞. Female rider r., TASCIOVA. *M. 239; V. 2061; BMC 1884-85. (224)*	70	275
316	Female head r., CVNOBELINVS. ℞. Victory r., TASCIO(VAN). *M. —; V. —; BMC 1883. (224A)*	75	300
317	Fig. r. carrying dead animal, CVNOBELINVS. ℞. Fig. stg. holding bow, dog at side, TASCIIOVANI. *M. 240; V. 2063; BMC 1886-88. (225)*	75	325
318	CVNO on panel, horn above, dolphin below. ℞. Fig. stg. r. altar behind. *M. 241/41a; V. 2065; BMC 1889-90. (226)*	85	425
319	CVN on panel. ℞. Fig. holding club walking r., CVN. *M. 254; V. 2067; BMC 1891-92. (227)*	80	400
320	CVN in wreath. ℞. CAM, dog? trampling on serpent r. *M. 256; V. 2069; BMC 1893. (229)*	90	475
321	Winged horse l., CVN. ℞. Std. fig. r. *M. 258; V. 2071; BMC 1896. (230)*	85	425
322	CVNO in angles of cross. ℞. Capricorn r., CVNO. *M. —; V. —; BMC 1898*	80	400

BRONZE

		F £	VF £
323	**Bronze Unit.** Head l., CVNO. ℞. Boar l., branch above. *M. 220; V. 1969; BMC—. (232)*	35	130
324	CVNOB ELINI in two panels. ℞. Victory std. l., TASC. *M. 221; V. 1971; BMC 1921-27. (233)*	25	110
325	Winged horse l., CAM. ℞. Winged Victory stg l., CVN. *M. 222; V. 1973; BMC 1938-43. (234)*	30	120

326

		F £	VF £
326	Bearded head facing ℞. Boar l., CVN. *M.223; V.1963; BMC 1904-05. (235)*	35	125
327	Ram-headed animal coiled up in double ornamental circle. ℞. Animal l., CAM. *M. 224; V. 1965; BMC —. (236)*	35	125
328	Griffin r., CAMV. ℞. Horse r., CVN. *M. 225; V. 2081; BMC 1909-12. (237)*	30	120
329	Bearded head l., CAMV. ℞. CVN or CVNO below horse l. *M. 226, 229; V. 2085/2131; BMC 1900-01. (238)*	30	120
330	Laureate head r., CVNO. ℞. CVN below bull butting l. *M. 227; V. 2083; BMC 1902-03. (239)*	35	125
331	Crude head r., CVN. ℞. Figure stg. l., CVN. *M. 228; V. 2135; BMC —. (240)*	35	135

332

		F £	VF £
332	CAMVL / ODVNO in two panels. R. CVNO beneath sphinx crouching l. *M. 230; V. 1977; BMC 1928-30. (241)*	30	120
333	Winged horse l., CAMV. R. Victory stg. r. divides CV NO. *M. 231; V. 1979; BMC 1931-34. (242)*	30	120
334	Victory walking r. R. CVN below, horseman r. *M. 232; V. 1981; BMC 1935. (243)*	35	135
335	Head l., CAM. R. CVNO below eagle. *M. 233; V. 2087; BMC −. (244)*	35	135

336 337

336	Head l., CVNOBELINI. R. Centaur r., TASCIOVANI.F. *M. 242; V. 2089; BMC 1968-71. (245)*	25	100
337	Helmeted bust r. R. TASCIIOVANII above, sow stg. r., F below. *M. 243; V. 2091; BMC 1956-60. (246)*	25	100
338	Horseman galloping r. holding dart and shield, CVNOB. R. Warrior stg. l., TASCIIOVANTIS. *M. 244; V. 2093; BMC 1961-67. (247)*	25	100

339 340

339	Helmeted bust l., CVOBELINVS REX. R. TASC FIL below boar l., std. on haunches. *M. 245; V. 1983; BMC 1952-55. (248)*	30	120
340	Bare head r., CVNOBELINVS REX. R. TASC below bull butting r. *M. 246; V. 2095; BMC 1944-51. (249)*	25	110
341	Bare head l., CVNO. R. TASC below bull stg. r. *M. 247; V. 1985; BMC −. (250)*	35	125

342 343

342	Head l., CVNOBELIN. R. Metal worker std. r. holding hammer, working on a vase, TASCIO. *M. 248; V. 2097; BMC 1972-83. (251)*	30	120
343	Winged horse r., CVNO. R. Victory r. sacrificing bull, TASCI. *M. 249; V. 2099; BMC 1913-19. (252)*	25	95
344	CVNO on panel within wreath. R. CAMV below horse, prancing r. *M. 250; V. 2101; BMC 1987-90. (253)*	30	120

345   346

		F £	VF £

345   Bearded head of Jupiter Ammon l., CVNOBELIN. ℞. CAM below
horseman galloping r. *M. 251; V. 2103; BMC 1984-86. (254)*   35   125

346   Janus head, CVNO below. ℞. CAMV on panel below, sow std. r.
beneath a tree. *M. 252; V. 2105; BMC 1998-2003. (255)*........................   30   125

347

347   Bearded head of Jupiter Ammon r., CVNOB. ℞. CAM on panel below
lion crouched r. *M. 253; V. 2107; BMC 1991-97. (256)*...........................   30   125

348   Sphinx r., CVNO. ℞. Fig stg. l. divides CA M. *M. 260; V. 2109;
BMC 2004-09. (257)*..   30   125

349   Horse r. ℞. CVN below horseman r. *M. 261; V. 1987; BMC 1936-47. (258)*   35   135

350   Animal l. looking back. ℞. CVN below horse l. *M. 233a; V. 1967;
BMC— . (259)*...   35   125

350A   Ship, CVN below. ℞. Fig. r. dividing S E. *M. —; V. 1989; BMC 2010....*   135   675

"SOLIDV"

351

351   **Silver Unit.** SOLIDV in centre of looped circle. ℞, Stg. fig. l., CVNO.
M. 259; V. 2073; BMC 1894-95. (231)..   325   1000

"AGR"

352   353

352   **Gold Quarter Stater**. Corn ear dividing CAM CVN. ℞. Horse r., branch
above., AGR below *M. —; V. —; BMC 1854*   350   1250

353   — ℞. Horse r., branch above., cross and A below. *M. —; V. —;
BMC 1855*...   375   1350

354

	F	VF
	£	£

354 **Silver Unit.** AGR inside wreath. Ṛ. Female dog r., AGR below. *M. —; V. —;*
BMC 1899 .... 250 900

EPATICCUS
(1st Half 1st Century A.D.)

Epaticcus, styled as a son of Tasciovanus on his coins, was most probably a brother of Cunobelin.
The corn ear employed on his staters is similar to that of his brother's produced at Colchester. His
coins appear in northern Atrebatic territory and conform to the area's denominational structure.
It seems likely that Epaticcus's coinage reflects an incursion into Atrebatic territory by the
Trinovantian/Catuvellaunian dynasty.

355

355 **Gold Stater.** Corn ear dividing TAS CIF. Ṛ. Horseman r., with spear and
shield. EPATI. *M. 262; V. 575; BMC 2021-23. (112)* 950 3500

356   357

356 **Silver Unit.** Head of Hercules r., EPAT(I). Ṛ. Eagle stg. on snake.
M. 263; V. 580; BMC 2024-2268/2270-76. (113) 30 110
357 Victory seated r. TASCIOV. Ṛ. Boar r., EPAT. *M. 263a; V. 581;*
BMC 2294-2328. (114) 35 135

358

358 Bearded head l., TASCIO. Ṛ. EPATI below lion r. *M. —; V. 582;*
BMC 2329 .... 95 425
359 EPATI inside panel. Ṛ. Lion r. *M. —; V. 583; BMC 2330. (114A)* 90 400

360   361

360 **Silver Minim.** EPATI. Ṛ. Boars head r., TA. *M. 264; V. 585; BMC 2331-46.*
(115) 30 125
361 TA inside star. Ṛ. Winged horse r., EPA below. *M. —; V. 560;*
BMC 2351-57. (116) 30 135
362 Helmeted head r. Ṛ. Horse r., E below. *M. —; V. —; BMC 2358-63* 30 135
363 EPATI. Ṛ. Winged horse r., cross below. *M. —; V .—; BMC 2365* 35 150

CARATACUS
(1st Half 1st Century A.D.)

Coins inscribed CARA have been traditionally associated with the historically attested son of Cunobelin, Caratacus the leader of British resistance against Rome. His coins appear in the same area as those of Epaticcus and he may have been his successor.

364   364A

		F £	VF £
364	**Silver Unit.** Head of Hercules r., CARA. R. Eagle stg. on snake. *M. 265; V. 593; BMC 2376-84. (117)*	125	450
364A	**Silver Minim.** CARA around pellet in ring. R. Winged horse r. *M. —; V. 595; BMC 2385-89. (117A)*	85	300

DUROTRIGES
(Mid 1st Century B.C. to Mid 1st Century A.D.)

The Durotriges inhabited West Hampshire, Dorset and adjoining parts of Somerset and Wiltshire. Their coinage is one of the most distinctive in Britain due to its rapid debasement. The disappearance of precious metals from the coinage should perhaps be linked to the declining trade between the south-west and western Gaul, following the Roman conquest of the Gaul. Hengistbury Head is the probable mint site of the cast bronzes. Coins inscribed CRAB have been traditionally associated with the tribe.

UNINSCRIBED

365	**Silver Stater.** White Gold type. Derived from Westerham stater (no. 21). *M. 317; V. 1235, 52, 54, 55; BMC 2525-2731. (60)*	110	350

366   368

366	Silver type. Similar. *M. 317; V. 1235, 52, 54, 55; BMC 2525-2731. (60)*	45	150
367	Billon type. Similar. *M. 317; V. 1235, 52, 54, 55; BMC 2525-2731. (60)*	20	65
368	**Silver Quarter Stater.** Geometric type. Crescent design. R. Zig-zag pattern. *M. 319; V. 1242/29; BMC 2734-79. (61). Quality of metal varies, obv. almost blank on later issues*	25	90

369

371

		F £	VF £
369	Starfish type. Spiral. R. Zig-zag pattern. *M. 320; V. 1270; BMC 2780-81 (61A)*	50	225
370	Hampshire Thin Flan type. Crude head of lines and pellets. R. Stylised horse l. *M. 321; V. 1280; BMC 2782-87. (62)*	75	350
371	**Bronze Stater.** Struck Bronze type. Similar to No.365-67. *M. 318; V. 1290; BMC 2790-2859. (81)*	20	50

372

372	Cast Bronze type. Many varities, as illustration. *M. 322-70; V. 1322-70; BMC 2860-2936. (82)*	25	125

INSCRIBED

"CRAB"

373

373	**Silver Unit.** CRAB in angles of cross. R. Eagle. *M. 371; V. 1285; BMC 2788. (145)*	225	750
373A	**Silver Minim.** CRAB on tablet. R. Star shape. *M. 372; V. 1286; BMC 2789. (146)*	125	375

Chris Rudd gives you a double your money back guarantee of authenticity. Nobody else does

For peace of mind talk to liz@celticcoins.com
Chris Rudd, PO Box 222, Aylsham, Norfolk NR11 6TY. *Tel* 01263 735007

DOBUNNI

(Mid 1st Century B.C. to Mid 1st Century A.D.)

Dobunnic territory stretched over Gloucestershire, Hereford and Worcester and into parts of Somerset, Wiltshire and Gwent. The earliest Dobunnic coins are developed from the British Q stater, and have the distinctive tree-like motif of the tribe on the obverse. The inscribed coinage is difficult to arrange chronologically and it may be that some of the rulers named held different parts of the territory simultaneously.

UNINSCRIBED

374

374 (variant)

375

		F £	VF £
374	**Gold Stater.** Plain except for tree-like object. R. Triple tailed horse r., wheel below. *M. 374; V. 1005; BMC 2937-40. (43)*	700	2750
375	**Gold Quarter Stater.** Plain with traces of wreath pattern. R. Horse r. *M. 68; V. 1010-3; BMC 2942-46. (52)*	175	475
376	Wreath pattern. R. Horse l., pellet in ring motifs in field. *M. 74; V. 1015; BMC 2949. (51)*	175	500

377

378

377	**Silver Unit.** Allen types A-F/I-J. Regular series. Head r. R. Triple tailed horse l. or r. *M. 374a, b/75/76, 378a-384; V. 1020/45/49/74/78/95/1135/1137; BMC 2950-3011. (63-64). Style becomes progressively more abstract, from-*	40	160
378	Allen types L-O. Irregular series. Similar to last. *M. 377-384d; V. 1170-85; BMC 3012-22. (63-64)*	45	175

INSCRIBED

The following types are not arranged chronologically.

ANTED

379

379	**Gold Stater.** Dobunnic emblem. R. ANTED or ANTEDRIG over triple tailed horse r., wheel below. *M. 385-86; V. 1062-69; BMC 3023-3031. (260)*	475	1650

	F	VF
	£	£

380 **Silver Unit.** Crude head r. R̥. ANTED over horse. *M. 387; V. 1082; BMC 3032-38. (261)* 35 140

EISV

381  382

381 **Gold Stater.** Dobunnic emblem. R̥. EISV or EISVRIG over triple tailed horse r., wheel below. *M. 388; V. 1105; BMC 3039-42. (262)* 525 1850

382 **Silver Unit.** Crude head r. R̥. Horse l., EISV. *M. 389; V. 1110; BMC 3043-55. (263)* 35 130

INAM or INARA

383 **Gold Stater.** Dobunnic emblem. R̥. INAM or INARA over triple tailed horse r., wheel below. *M. 390; V. 1140; BMC 3056. (264)* 1200 4500

CATTI

384

384 **Gold Stater.** Dobunnic emblem. R̥. CATTI over triple tailed horse r., wheel below. *M. 391; V. 1130; BMC 3057-60. (265)* 425 1500

COMUX

385 **Gold Stater.** Dobunnic emblem. R̥. COMVX retrograde, over triple tailed horse r., wheel below. *M. 392; V. 1092; BMC 3061-63. (266)* 1250 4750

CORIO

386  387

386 **Gold Stater.** Dobunnic emblem. R̥. CORIO over triple tailed horse r., wheel below. *M. 393; V. 1035; BMC 3064-3133. (267)* 425 1500

387 **Gold Quarter Stater.** COR in centre. R̥. Horse r., without legend. *M. 394; V. 1039; BMC 3134. (268)* 375 1350

BODVOC

388

389

		F £	VF £
388	**Gold Stater.** BODVOC across field. R. Horse r., without legend. *M. 395; V. 1052; BMC 3135-42. (269)*	825	3000
389	**Silver Unit.** Head l., BODVOC. R. Horse r., without legend. *M. 396; V. 1057; BMC 3143-45. (270)*	125	400

CORIELTAUVI

The Corieltauvi, formerly known as the Coritani, occupied Lincolnshire and adjoining parts of Yorkshire, Northamptonshire, Leicestershire and Nottinghamshire. The earliest staters, the South Ferriby type, are developed from Gallo-Belgic C staters, and are associated with the silver Boar/ Horse types. The distinctive dish shaped scyphate coinages have no parallels in Britain and stand apart from the main series. The later inscribed issues present a complex system of inscriptions. It has been suggested that some of the later inscriptions refer to pairs of names, possibly joint rulers or moneyers and rulers.

EARLY UNINSCRIBED
(Mid to Late 1st Century B.C.)

390

393

390	**Gold Stater.** South Ferriby type. Crude laureate head. R. Disjointed horse l., rosette or star below, anchor shape and pellets above. *M. 449-50; V. 809-815/19; BMC 3146-3179. (30)*	185	425
391	Wheel type. Similar, but wheel below horse. *M. 449c; V. 817; BMC 3180*	425	1350
392	Kite type. Similar to 390, but diamond shape containing pellets above, spiral below horse. *M. 447; V. 825; BMC 3181-84. (29)*	210	650
393	Domino type. Similar to last, but with rectangle containing pellets. *M. 448; V. 829; BMC 3185-86. (29)*	200	525

394

395

	F	VF
	£	£

394   Trefoil type. Trefoil with central rosette of seven pellets. R. Similar to 390. *M. 450a; V. 821; BMC* —. *(30A)*   1250   5250

395   North Lincolnshire Scyphate type. Stylised boar r. or l. R. Large S symbol with pellets and rings in field. *M.* —; *V.* —; *BMC 3187-93*   200   525

* chipped or cracked specimens are often encountered and are worth less

396

396   **Silver Unit.** Boar/Horse type I. Boar r., large pellet and ring motif above, reversed S below. R. Horse l. or r., pellet in ring above. *M. 405-06, 451; V. 855-60, 864, 867; BMC 3194-3214. (66)*   45   225

397   Boar Horse type II. Vestiges of boar on obv. R. Horse l. or r. *M. 410, 452-53; V. 875-877; BMC 3214-27. (68)*   30   110

398

399

398   Boar Horse type III. Blank. R. Horse l.or r. *M. 453-54; V. 884-77; BMC 3228-35. (69)*   20   70

399   **Silver Fractional Unit.** Similar to 396-97. *M. 406a, 451a; V. 862/66; BMC 3236-3250. (67)*   25   80

400   Similar to 398. *M.* —; *V. 877-81; BMC 3251-55. (70/71)*   20   70

401   Pattern/Horse. Flower pattern. R. Horse l. *M.* —; *V.* —; *BMC 3256-57...*   65   300

Timeline
Auctions
Inc. Gregory's **Est.1858**

We are accepting single entries
& collections of Celtic coins & antiquities

www.timelineauctions.com

INSCRIBED
(Early to Mid 1st Century A.D.)
The following types are not arranged chronologically.

AVN COST

402   403

		F £	VF £
402	**Gold Stater.** Crude wreath design. R. Disjointed horse l., AVN COST. *M. 457;V. 910; BMC 3258. (286)*	325	1350
403	**Silver Unit.** Remains of wreath or blank. R. AVN COST, horse l. *M. 458;* *V. 914; BMC 3261-66. (287)*..	25	90
403A	**Silver Unit.** Inscription between three lines. R. Horse l. AVN. *M. -; V-; BMC-.*	75	200
404	**Silver Fractional Unit.** Similar. *M. —; l V. 918; BMC 3267-68. (288)* ..	30	85

ESVP RASV

405

405	**Gold Stater.** Crude wreath design. R. Disjointed horse l., IISVP RASV. *M. 456b; V. 920; BMC 3269. (289)*	300	1100
406	**Silver Unit.** Similar. *M. 456c; V. 924; BMC 3272-73. (290)*	35	140

VEP

407

407	**Gold Stater.** Blank or with traces of wreath. R. Disjointed horse l., VEP. *M. —; V. 905; BMC 3274-75. (296)*	375	1500
408	**Silver Unit.** Blank or with traces of wreath. R. VEP, horse r. *M. —; V. 963;* *BMC 3277-82. (297)*..	30	110
409	**Silver Half Unit.** Similar. *M. 464b; V. 967; BMC 3283-3295. (298)*	25	95

VEP CORF

410

412

	F £	VF £
410 **Gold Stater.** Crude wreath design. R. Disjointed horse l., VEP CORF. M. 459, 460; V. 930/40/60; BMC 3296-3304. (291)	250	800
411 **Silver Unit.** Similar. M. 460b/464; V. 934/50; BMC 3305-14. (292)	30	110
412 Similar but VEPOC (M)ES, pellet in ring below horse. M. —; V. 955; BMC —. (294)	35	125
413 **Silver Half Unit.** Similar. M. 464a; V. 938/58; BMC 3316-24. (293/95)	30	85

DVMNO TIGIR SENO

414

415

414 **Gold Stater.** DVMN(OC) across wreath. R. Horse l., TIGIR SENO. M. 461; V. 972; BMC 3325-27. (299)	525	2000
415 **Silver Unit.** DVMNOC in two lines. R. Horse r., TIGIR SENO. M. 462; V. 974; BMC 3328-29. (300)	110	425

VOLISIOS DVMNOCOVEROS

416

416 **Gold Stater.** VOLISIOS between three lines in wreath. R. Horse r. or l., DVMNOCOVEROS. M. 463/a; V. 978-80; BMC 3330-3336. (301)	275	950
417 **Silver Unit.** Similar. R. Horse r., DVMNOCO. M. 463a; V. 980; BMC 3339. (302)	125	500
418 **Silver Half Unit.** Similar. M. 465; V. 984; BMC 3340-41. (303)	65	225

VOLISIOS DVMNOVELLAUNOS

419

		F £	VF £
419	**Gold Stater.** VOLISIOS between three lines in wreath. R. Horse r. or l., DVMNOVELAVNOS. *M. 466; V .988; BMC 3342-43. (304)*	325	1350
420	**Silver Half Unit.** As last but DVMNOVE. *M. 467; V. 992; BMC 3344-46. (305)*	90	350

VOLISIOS CARTIVEL

		F £	VF £
420A	**Gold Stater.** VOLISIOS between three lines in wreath. R. Horse l. CARTILLAVNOS. *M-; VA 933; BMC -*	950	4000
421	**Silver Half Unit.** VOLISIOS between three lines in wreath. R. Horse r., CARTILEV. *M. 468; V. 994; BMC 3347-48. (306)*	185	700

IAT ISO E

		F £	VF £
422	**Silver Unit.** IAT ISO (retrograde)on tablet, rosettes above and below. R. Horse r., E above. *M. 416; V. 998; BMC 3349-51. (284)*	95	400

CAT

		F £	VF £
422A	**Silver Unit.** Boar r., pellet ring above, CAT above. R. Horse r. *M. —; V. —; BMC 3352*	175	650

LAT ISON

423

		F £	VF £
423	**Gold Stater.** LAT ISO(N) in two lines retrograde. R. Horse r., ISO in box above, N below. *M. —; V. —; BMC —. Only recorded as an AE/AV plated core, as illustrated.*	*Extremely rare*	

ICENI

The Iceni, centred on Norfolk but also occupying neighbouring parts of Suffolk and Cambridgeshire, are well attested in the post conquest period as the tribe who under Boudicca revolted against Roman rule. Their earliest coins are likely to have been the British J staters, Norfolk Wolf type (no.30/31), replaced around the mid first century B.C. by the Snettisham, Freckenham and Irstead type gold staters and quarter staters. Contemporary with these are silver Boar/Horse and Face/Horse units and fractions. The introduction of legends around the beginning of the millennia led to the adoption of a new obverse design of back to back crescents. The continuation of the coinage after the Roman invasion is attested by the coins of King Prasutagus. Some of the Face/Horse units (no.434) have been attributed to Queen Boudicca but this attribution is uncertain.

EARLY UNINSCRIBED
(Mid to Late 1st Century B.C.)

424

		F	VF
		£	£
424	**Gold Stater.** Snettisham type. Blank or with traces of pellet cross. R. Horse r., serpent like pellet in ring motif above. *M. —; V.—; BMC 3353-59....*	575	2000
425	Similar. Blank or with three short curved lines. R. Horse r., symbol above more degraded. *M. —; V. —; BMC 3360-83*	350	1250

426   427

426	Freckenham type. Two opposed crescents with stars or pellets in field. R. Horse r., various symbols in field. *M. 397/99; V. 620; BMC 3384-89. (38)*	275	900
427	Similar. Blank or with traces of pellet cross. R. Horse r., wheel or arch containing pellets above. *M. 400; V. 624; BMC 3390-95. (40)*	300	1000

428

428	Similar. Trefoil on cross design. R. Similar. *M. 401-03; V. 626; BMC 3396-3419. (39)*	250	825

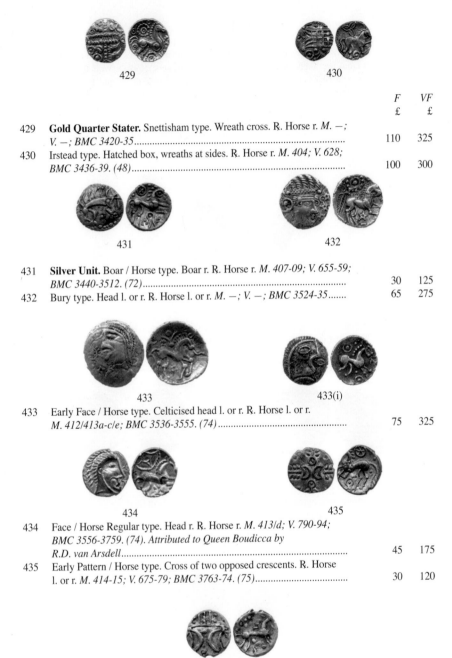

429

430

	F £	VF £
429 **Gold Quarter Stater.** Snettisham type. Wreath cross. ℞. Horse r. *M. —; V. —; BMC 3420-35*	110	325
430 Irstead type. Hatched box, wreaths at sides. ℞. Horse r. *M. 404; V. 628; BMC 3436-39. (48)*	100	300

431

432

431 **Silver Unit.** Boar / Horse type. Boar r. ℞. Horse r. *M. 407-09; V. 655-59; BMC 3440-3512. (72)*	30	125
432 Bury type. Head l. or r. ℞. Horse l. or r. *M. —; V. —; BMC 3524-35*	65	275

433

433(i)

433 Early Face / Horse type. Celticised head l. or r. ℞. Horse l. or r. *M. 412/413a-c/e; BMC 3536-3555. (74)*	75	325

434

435

434 Face / Horse Regular type. Head r. ℞. Horse r. *M. 413/d; V. 790-94; BMC 3556-3759. (74). Attributed to Queen Boudicca by R.D. van Arsdell*	45	175
435 Early Pattern / Horse type. Cross of two opposed crescents. ℞. Horse l. or r. *M. 414-15; V. 675-79; BMC 3763-74. (75)*	30	120

436

436 ECEN symbol type. Two opposed crescents. ℞. Horse r. *M. 429; V. 752; BMC 4297-4325*	25	75

	F £	VF £

437 **Silver Half Unit.** Boar / Horse type. Similar to 431. *M. 411; V. 661; BMC 3513-20. (73)* 25 75

438 **Silver Fractional Unit.** Early Pattern / Horse type. Similar to 435. *M. 417/a; V. 681-83; BMC 3775-89. (76/A)* 25 75

INSCRIBED
(Early to Mid 1st Century A.D.)
The following types are not arranged chronologically.

CAN DVRO

439

439 **Silver Unit.** Boar. R. Horse r., CAN(S) above, DVRO below. *M. 434; V. 663; BMC 3521-23. (271)* 75 325

ANTED

440

440 **Gold Stater.** Triple crescent design. R. Horse r., ANTED monongram below. *M. 418; V. 705; BMC 3790. (272)* 525 1750

441

441 **Silver Unit.** Two opposed crescents. R. Horse r., ANTED. *M. 419-21; V. 710-11/15; BMC 3791-4025. (273)* 25 80

442 **Silver Fractional Unit.** Similar to last. *M. 422; V. 720; BMC 4028-31. (274)* 25 85

Why sell your Celtic coins in London when you can do better in Aylsham?

For a free valuation ask liz@celticcoins.com
Chris Rudd, PO Box 222, Aylsham, Norfolk NR11 6TY. *Tel* 01263 735007

ECEN

443

		F £	VF £
443	**Gold Stater.** Triple crescent design. R. Horse r., ECEN below. *M. —; V. 725;* *BMC 4032.*	725	2250
443A	**Silver Unit.** Two opposed crescents. R, Horse r., ECEN. *M. 424; V. 730;* *BMC 4033-4215. (275)*	25	85
443B	**Silver Half Unit.** Similar to last. *M. 431; V. 736; BMC 4216-17. (276)* .	20	70

EDN

| 444 | **Silver Unit.** Two opposed crescents. R, Horse r., ED, E, EI or EDN. *M. 423,*
425b; V. 734/40; BMC 4219-81. (277) .... | 25 | 80 |

ECE

| 444A | **Gold Stater** Triple crescent design R. Horse r., ECE. *M. — ; V. — ;* ..... | 850 | 3000 |

445

| 445 | **Silver Unit.** Two opposed crescents. R, Horse r., ECE. *M. 425-28; V. 761-66;*
BMC 4348-4538. (278-80) .... | 20 | 75 |

SAENU

| 446 | **Silver Unit.** Two opposed crescents. R. Horse r., SAENV. *M. 433; V. 770;*
BMC 4540-57. (281) .... | 30 | 120 |

AESU

447

| 447 | **Silver Unit.** Two opposed crescents. R. Horse r., AESV. *M. 432; V. 775;*
BMC 4558-72. (282) .... | 30 | 120 |

ALE SCA

| 448 | **Silver Unit.** Boar r., ALE. R. Horse r., SCA. *M. 469; V. 996; BMC 4576* | 135 | 575 |

AEDIC SIA

		F	VF
		£	£
449	**Silver Unit.** AEDIC in two lines. R. Horse r., SIA? below. *M.—; V.—;* BMC 4581	200	750

PRASUTAGUS

450

450 **Silver Unit.** Romanised head l., SUB RII PRASTO. R. Rearing horse r., ESICO FECIT. *M. 434a; V. 780; BMC 4577-80. (283)* 475 2000
This legend translates as "Under King Prasto, Esico made me", giving the name of both King and moneyer.

Three good Celtic coin books

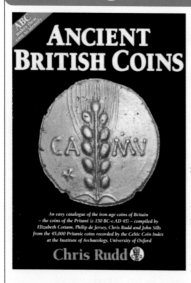

ANCIENT BRITISH COINS

An easy catalogue of the iron age coins of Britain – the coins of the Pritani (c.150 BC-c.AD 45) – compiled by Elizabeth Cottam, Philip de Jersey, Chris Rudd and John Sills from the 45,000 Pritanic coins recorded by the Celtic Coin Index at the Institute of Archaeology, University of Oxford

Chris Rudd

A new introduction to Ancient British coins c.120 BC-AD 45. *"A perfect starting point. Profusely illustrated is an understatement"* says Professor Vincent Megaw. 56 pages, 300 coin photos. £10 + p&p.

The first-ever catalogue of Lincolnshire's first silver coins, struck by the Corieltavi c.60 BC-AD 10. *"Superbly illustrated"* says Dr John Sills. 80 pages, 230 coin drawings. £15 + p&p.

Never before have so many Ancient British coins been so easy to identify. *ABC* catalogues 999 coins, including 418 new types not shown by Van Arsdell in 1989. *"A great book"* says Prof. Sir Barry Cunliffe. 256 pages, 2000 twice-size coin photos. £75 + p&p.

  liz@celticcoins.com **Chris Rudd**

ROMAN BRITAIN

The systematic conquest of Britain by the Romans began in A.D. 43 when the Emperor Claudius (41-54), anxious to enhance his military reputation, authorized an invasion in which he personally participated, albeit in a purely symbolic role. The initial military contact between the two cultures had taken place almost a century before when Julius Caesar, during the course of his conquest of Celtic Gaul, led expeditions to the island in 55 and 54 B.C. Although no actual Roman occupation of Britain resulted from Caesar's reconnoitring campaigns, commercial intercourse was certainly accelerated, as evidenced by the 'Romanization' of the British Celtic coinage in the final decades of its production.

The Claudian conquest, commencing in A.D. 43, brought about a complete change in the nature of the currency circulating in Britain and ushered in a period lasting more than three and a half centuries during which Roman coinage was the only official medium of exchange. Local copies of the money brought with them by the four legions of the invasion army began to appear at a very early stage, the most popular type for imitation being the well-known Claudian copper as with reverse type fighting Minerva. Some of these copies are well-executed and of a style not much inferior to the prototype, suggesting that their local minting may have been officially sanctioned by the Roman government in order to make good a shortage of currency in the newly-conquered territory. Other examples are of much poorer style and execution and are frequently well below the normal weight of a Claudian as (usually between 10 and 11 grams). These copies must have been issued unofficially and provide evidence of the huge demand for this type of currency in a population which had never before experienced the benefits of having base metal coins available for small everyday transactions. In the decades that followed, the boundaries of the Roman province of Britannia were continually pushed further north and west until, under the celebrated Flavian governor Gnaeus Julius Agricola, the Roman army even penetrated to northern Scotland (A.D. 83/4). A few years later, under Trajan, the northern frontier was established along the Tyne-Solway line, a barrier made permanent by the construction of Hadrian's Wall following the emperor's visit to the province in 122. For a brief period in the mid-2nd century the frontier was temporarily advanced to the Forth-Clyde line with the building of the Antonine Wall, though this seems to have been abandoned early in the reign of Marcus Aurelius (ca. 163) when the Hadrianic barrier was re-commissioned and became the permanent frontier. The security thus provided to the now-peaceful province in the south facilitated urban expansion and the development of commerce. The new prosperity brought a flood of Roman coinage into the island-province and it was no longer necessary for shortages to be made good by large scale local imitation.

Until the mid-3rd century the production of Roman coinage remained the prerogative of the mint in the capital, with only occasional issues from provincial centres to serve short-term local needs. But with the deepening political and economic crisis in the third quarter of the century there was a dramatic decentralization of minting operations, with permanent establishments being set up in many important cities in the western as well as the eastern provinces. Britain, however, still remained without an official mint at this time and in the dark days of the 270s, when the separatist Gallic Empire to which Britain belonged was close to collapse, large scale production of imitative antoniniani (commonly called 'barbarous radiates') occurred in the province. The integrity and prestige of the Empire was, to some extent, restored by a rapid succession of Illyrian 'soldier emperors', until the situation was finally stabilized by Diocletian (A.D. 284-305) who established the tetrarchy system under which governmental responsibility was shared by four rulers. By the end of the 3rd century Britain had been reorganized into a civil diocese of four provinces: it had already been subdivided into Britannia Superior and Britannia Inferior almost a hundred years before, under Septimius Severus or Caracalla.

It was left to the colourful and enigmatic usurper Carausius (A.D. 287-293) to establish mints in Britain. It was, of course, vital for him to do so as his dominion was mostly confined to the island-province. Londinium (London) was his principal mint, with a secondary establishment at a place usually signing itself 'C' (probably Camulodunum, modern Colchester). After the downfall of Carausius' murderer and successor Allectus (293-296) Britain was restored to the central government, an event commemorated by the celebrated gold medallion of Constantius I showing the Caesar riding alongside the Thames approaching the gateway of the city of Londinium. At this point the mysterious 'C' mint disappears from the picture. Londinium, on the other hand, retained its status as an official mint under Diocletian's tetrarchy and its successors down to A.D. 325, when it was closed by Constantine the Great who regarded it as superfluous to his needs. In nearly four decades of existence as a Roman mint Londinium had produced a varied and extensive coinage in the names of almost all the emperors, empresses and Caesars of the period. It was destined never again to be active during Roman times, unless the extremely rare gold and silver issues of the late 4th century usurper Magnus Maximus, signed AVG, AVGOB and AVGPS, are correctly attributed to Londinium under its late Roman name of Augusta.

The termination of Roman rule in the British provinces is traditionally dated to A.D. 410 when the emperor Honorius, in response to an appeal for aid from his British subjects, told them to arrange for their own defence as best they might ('Rescript of Honorius'). In reality, the end probably came quite gradually. As the machinery of government ground to a halt and the soldiers stopped receiving their pay there would have been a steady drift of population away from the semi-ruinous cities and military installations to the countryside, where they could better provide for themselves through farming. Under these conditions the need for coinage would have been drastically reduced, as a primitive economy based on barter would largely have replaced the complex monetary economy of the late Roman period. In any case the supply of coinage from the Continent would now have dried up. The few monetary transactions which still took place were made with worn-out coins from earlier periods augmented by local imitations, production of which in Britain had resumed in the mid-4th century. Such was the pitiful end of the long tradition of Roman coinage in the remote island-province of Britannia. More than two centuries of 'Dark Ages' were to elapse before England's new rulers, the Anglo-Saxons, commenced the issue of gold thrymsas, the designs of many of which were based on late Roman types.

As Rome's Imperial coinage provided the currency needs of this country over a period of almost four centuries no representative collection of British coins is complete without some examples of these important issues. The following listing is divided into four categories: 1. Regular Roman issues, all of which would have been legal tender in Britain after A.D. 43; 2. Issues with types referring specifically to the province of Britannia, usually in commemoration of military campaigns in the north; 3. Official Roman coinage struck in Britain; 4. Imitations of Roman coins produced in Britain, all but possibly some of the earliest being of unofficial origin. The reference 'R.R.C.' is to the listing of the type in Michael Crawford's *Roman Republican Coinage* (Cambridge, 1974); and 'R.I.C.' to *The Roman Imperial Coinage* (London, 1923-1994, in ten volumes).

For more detailed collectors' information on Roman coinage, including a more comprehensive listing of types, the reader is referred to *Roman Coins and their Values Volumes 1, 2 and 3* by David R. Sear. A complete catalogue of silver issues may be found in the 5 volumes of *Roman Silver Coins* (H.A. Seaby and C.E. King) which provides a quick and convenient reference and is especially aimed at the collector. Gilbert Askew's *The Coinage of Roman Britain* (2nd edition) concentrates on those issues which are particularly associated with the Roman province of Britannia, but does not provide valuations. More recent works on this subject include R. Reece's *Coinage in Roman Britain* and *The Coinage of Roman Britain*, and also David R. Sear's *The History and Coinage of the Roman Imperators, 49—27 BC* which is devoted to the vital two decades of transition from Republic to Empire.

The standard works on the coinages of the Roman Republic and the Roman Empire have already been mentioned *(Roman Republican Coinage and Roman Imperial Coinage)*. These monumental publications are essential to the advanced collector and student and their importance cannot be overstated. The British Museum Catalogues (3 volumes of Republican, 6 volumes of Imperial recently reprinted by SPINK) are also vital. They contain superb interpretive material in their introductions and are very fully illustrated. A similar work is Anne S. Robertson's *Roman Imperial Coins in the Hunter Coin Cabinet*, in 5 volumes (volume 4 is especially important for the later 3rd century coinage). For more general reading we may recommend J.P.C. Kent and M. & A. Hirmer's *Roman Coins*, undoubtedly the most lavishly illustrated book on the subject; C.H.V. Sutherland's *Roman Coins;* and R.A.G. Carson's *Coins of the Roman Empire*. Finally, for a most useful single-volume work on interpretation and background information, we would suggest A *Dictionary of Ancient Roman Coins* by John Melville Jones.

1. REGULAR ROMAN ISSUES

A token selection of the types of Roman coins which might be found on Romano-British archaeological sites. Many of the rarer emperors and empresses have been omitted and the types listed often represent only one of hundreds of variant forms which might be encountered.

		F £	VF £
451	**THE REPUBLIC: P. Aelius Paetus** (moneyer), 138 B.C. Æ *denarius.* Helmeted hd. of Roma r. Rev. The Dioscuri galloping r. R.R.C. 233/1 ... *Although dating from long before the Roman conquest many Republican* *coins circulated well into the Imperial period and found their way to Britain* *where they are often represented in early hoards.*	38	110
452	**L. Thorius Balbus** (moneyer), 105 B.C. Æ denarius. Hd. of Juno Sospita r., clad in goat's skin. Rev. Bull charging r. *R.R.C. 316/1.*	40	120
453	**Q. Antonius Balbus** (moneyer), 83-82 B.C. Æ *denarius.* Laur. hd. of Jupiter r. Rev. Victory in quadriga r. *R.R.C. 364/1.*	40	120

454

455B

454	**C. Calpurnius Piso** (moneyer), 67 B.C. Æ *denarius.* Laur. hd. of Apollo r. Rev. Horseman galloping r., holding palm-branch. *R.R.C. 408/1a.*	40	120
455	**Mn. Acilius Glabrio** (moneyer), 49 B.C. Æ *denarius.* Laur. hd. of Salus r. Rev. Valetudo stg. l., holding snake and resting on column. *R.R.C. 442/1.*	38	110
455A	**Pompey the Great** (imperator) 49-48 BC. Æ *denarius.* Diademed head of Numa r. Rev. MAGN PRO COS. Prow of galley r. *R.R.C. 446/1.*	180	450
455B	**Scipio** (imperator) 47-46 BC, Æ *denarius.* Laureate head of Jupiter r. Rev. SCIPIO IMP. Elephant r. *R.R.C. 459/1.*	100	250
455C	**Pompey Junior** (imperator) 46-45 BC. Æ *denarius.* Helmeted head of Roma r. Rev. CN MAGNVS IMP. Hispania stg r presenting palm branch to Pompeian soldier. *RRC 469/1a.*	130	320
455D	**Sextus Pompey** (imperator) 45-36 BC. Æ *denarius.* Bare head of Pompey. Rev. Neptune stg l between brothers Anapias and Amphinomus. *R.R.C. 511/3a.*	340	850
455E	**Julius Caesar** (dictator), visited Britain 55 and 54 B.C., died 44 B.C. Æ *aureus.* Veiled head of Vesta r. Rev. A. HIRTIVS PR. Jug between lituus and axe. *R.R.C.* *466/1.*	1100	2800

456

456B

456	Æ *denarius.* CAESAR. Elephant r. Rev. Priestly emblems. *R.R.C. 443/1.*	200	500
456A	— Wreathed hd. of Caesar r. Rev. P. SEPVLLIVS MACER. Venus stg. l., holding Victory and sceptre. *R.R.C. 480/9.*	650	1600
456B	Head of Venus. Rev CAESAR. Aeneas l bearing his father Anchises on shoulder. *R.R.C. 458/1.*	130	300

456F

	F £	VF £

456C Head of Venus r. Rev. CAESAR. Trophy of Gallic arms between seated captives. *R.R.C. 468/1* 140 320

456D **Brutus** (imperator) 42 BC. Æ *denarius*. Head of Apollo r. Rev. BRVTVS IMP. Trophy. *R.R.C. 506/2.* 225 550

456E **Cassius** (imperator) 42 BC. Æ *denarius*. Head of Libertas. Rev. LENTVLVS SPINT. Jug and lituus. *R.R.C. 500/3* 160 400

456F **Ahenobarbus** (imperator) 41-40 BC. Æ *denarius*. Bare head r. Rev. CN DOMITIVS IMP. Prow of galley r, surmounted by trophy. *R.R.C. 519/2.* 340 850

457 **Mark Antony** (triumvir), died 30 B.C. Æ *denarius*. Galley r. Rev. LEG. II. Legionary eagle between two standards. *R.R.C. 544/14.* 110 280

457A Head of Antony r. Rev. CAESAR DIC. Head of Caesar r. *R.R.C. 488/2.* 340 900

457B Bare head of Antony. Rev. CAESAR IMP PONT III VIR RPC. Bare head of Octavian. *R.R.C. 517/2.* 240 575

457C **Cleopatra VII** 34 BC Æ *denarius*. Bust of Cleopatra r. Rev. ANTONI ARMENIA DEVICTA. Head of Antony r. *R.R.C. 543/1.* 2800 6500

458   459

458 **Octavian** (triumvir), named Augustus 27 B.C. Æ *denarius*. Bare hd. of Octavian r. Rev. IMP. CAESAR. Trophy set on prow. *R.I.C. 265a* 160 400

458A **THE EMPIRE: Augustus,** 27 B.C.-A.D. 14. Æ *aureus*. Rev. IMP XII ACT. Apollo stg r, holding lyre. *R.I.C. 192a.* 1600 4000

459 Æ *denarius*. Rev. C. L. CAESARES AVGVSTI F COS DESIG PRINC IVVENT. The emperor's grandsons, Gaius and Lucius, stg. facing, with spears and shields. *R.I.C. 207* 100 240

Almost all the coins in the Roman Imperial series have a head or bust of the emperor, empress or prince as their obverse type. Therefore, in most instances only the reverses will be described in the following listings.

459A — Rev IMP X. Bull butting r. *R.I.C. 167a.* 150 400

460 Æ *as*. ROM. ET AVG. The altar of Lugdunum. *R.I.C. 230.* 75 180

460A Æ *quadrans*. Obv. Anvil. Rev. Moneyers' inscription around large S. C. *R.I.C. 443* 22 50

461 **Augustus and Agrippa,** general and designated heir of Augustus, died 12 B.C. Æ *dupondius*. Obv. Their hds. back to back. Rev. COL. NEM. Crocodile r., chained to palm-branch. *R.I.C. 159.* 100 240
See also no. 468.

461A **Gaius Caesar,** 17 BC, grandson of Augustus. Æ *denarius*. Rev. AVGVST. Candelabrum within floral wreath. *R.I.C. 539* 380 1100

464

		F	VF
		£	£
462	**Divus Augustus,** deified A.D. 14. Æ as. PROVIDENT S. C. Large altar. *R.I.C. 81.*	75	180
463	**Tiberius,** A.D. 14-37. *N aureus.* PONTIF MAXIM. Livia (?) seated r., holding sceptre and branch. *R.I.C. 29.*	950	2400
464	*R denarius.* Similar. *R.I.C. 30.*	140	350
	This type is commonly referred to as the 'Tribute Penny' of the Bible (Matthew 22, 17-21).		
464A	Æ *sestertius.* Tiberius seated l. Rev Inscription around large S. C. *R.I.C. 48.*	300	800
464B	Æ *as.* Inscription around large S. C. *R.I.C. 44*	75	180
465	**Livia,** wife of Augustus, mother of Tiberius. Æ *dupondius.* Obv. Veiled bust of Livia as Pietas r. Rev. Inscription of Drusus Caesar around large S. C. *R.I.C. 43.*	160	400
466	**Drusus,** son of Tiberius. Æ *as.* Inscription around large S. C. *R.I.C. 45.*	80	200
466A	**Caligula,** A.D. 37-41. *N aureus.* Rev. SPQR/PP/OBCS in three lines within oak wreath. R.I.C. 27.	3500	8500
466B	*R denarius,* SPQR/PP/OBCS in three lines within oak wreath, *R.I.C. 28.*	650	1875
466C	Æ *sestertius.* Rev. ADLOCVT COH. Caligula stg l on platform, haranguing soldiers. *R.I.C. 40.*	375	1050

467

| 467 | Æ *as.* VESTA S. C. Vesta seated l. *R.I.C. 38.* .... | 100 | 320 |

468

| 468 | **Agrippa,** grandfather of Caligula, died 12 B.C. Æ *as.* S. C. Neptune stg. l., holding dolphin and trident. *R.I.C. 58.* .... | 85 | 230 |
| | *See also no. 461 and under Category 4.* | | |

		F £	VF £

469 **Germanicus,** father of Caligula, brother of Claudius, died A.D. 19. Æ *as.*
Inscription of Caligula around large S. C. *R.I.C. 35.* 80 200

470 **Agrippina Senior,** mother of Caligula, died A.D. 33. Æ *sestertius.* S.P.Q.R.
MEMORIAE AGRIPPINAE. Carpentum drawn l. by two mules. *R.I.C. 55.* 480 1600

470A **Claudius,** A.D. 41-54, initiated the conquest of Britain by his invasion in
A.D. 43. *N aureus* Rev. EX SC/OBCIVES/SERVATOS in three lines within
oak wreath. *R.I.C. 15.* 1750 4500

470B *R denarius.* PACI AVGVSTAE, winged Nemesis advancing r, snake at feet.
R.I.C. 52. .... 425 1100

470C Æ *sestertius.* Rev. SPES AVGVSTA SC. Spes walking l, holding flower.
R.I.C. 115. (see also no 744) 260 700

471   474

471 Æ *as.* LIBERTAS AVGVSTA S. C. Libertas stg. r., holding pileus.
R.I.C. 113. .... 75 200

471A Æ *quadrans.* Obv. Hand holding scales. Rev. Inscription around large
S. C. *R.I.C. 85.* 22 48
See also under Categories 2 and 4.

472 **Nero Claudius Drusus,** father of Claudius, died 9 B.C. Æ *sestertius.*
TI. CLAVDIVS CAESAR AVG. P. M. TR .P. IMP. P. P. S. C. Claudius seated
l. on curule chair amidst arms. *R.I.C. 109.* 260 950
See also under Category 4.

473 **Antonia,** mother of Claudius, died A.D. 37. Æ *dupondius.* TI. CLAVDIVS
CAESAR AVG P.M. TR. P. IMP. S. C. Claudius stg. l., holding simpulum.
R.I.C. 92. .... 120 340
See also under Category 4.

474 **Nero,** 54-68, emperor at the time of Queen Boudicca's rebellion in Britain.
N aureus. SALVS. Salus seated l. *R.I.C. 66.* 1000 2750

475 *R denarius.* IVPPITER CVSTOS. Jupiter seated l. *R.I.C. 53.* 140 400

476 Æ *sestertius.* ROMA S. C. Roma seated l., holding Victory and parazonium.
R.I.C. 274. .... 300 1000

476A Æ *as.* S. C. Victory hovering l., holding shield inscribed S. P. Q. R. *R.I.C. 312.* 85 230

476B **Civil Wars** (Gaul). *R denarius.* Clasped hands. Rev. FIDES PRAETOR
IANORUM. Clasped r hands. R.I.C. 121. .... 290 780

476C **Galba,** 68-69. *N aureus.* Rev. SPQR/OB CS in two lines within oak
wreath. *R.I.C. 164.* 2400 6000

477 *R denarius.* S.P.Q.R. / OB / C.S. within oak-wreath. *R.I.C. 167.* 185 475

477A **Otho,** 69. *N aureus.* Rev. SECVRITAS PR. Securitas stg l, holding wreath
and sceptre. *R.I.C. 7.* 4000 10000

478 *R denarius.* SECVRITAS P. R. Securitas stg. l. *R.I.C. 10.* 320 860

478A **Vitellius,** 69. *N aureus.* Rev. CONCORDIA PR. Concordia seated l, holding
patera and cornucopiae. *R.I.C. 72.* 2600 6500

		F £	VF £
479	Æ denarius. CONCORDIA P. R. Concordia seated l. *R.I.C. 90*...............	185	450
480	**Vespasian,** 69-79, commanded Legio II in the Claudian invasion of Britain (43) and appointed Agricola to governorship of the province in 77/8. Aʋ *aureus*. ANNONA AVG. Annona seated l. *R.I.C. 131a.*	850	2250

481

		F £	VF £
481	Æ *denarius.* VICTORIA AVGVSTI. Victory advancing r., crowning standard. *R.I.C. 52.*...	42	100
481A	Æ *sestertius.* Rev. JVDAEA CAPTA SC. Palm tree with standing Jewish captive r and female captive seated r. *R.I.C. 424*...................................	475	1250
481B	Æ *dupondius.* FELICITAS PVBLICA S. C. Felicitas stg. l. *R.I.C. 554*...	55	140
481C	**Titus,** 79-81 (Caesar 69-79). Aʋ *aureus.* Rev. TRP VIIII IMP XIIII COS VII PP. Venus stg r resting on column. *R.I.C. 9.*	1200	3000
482	Æ *denarius.* TR. P. IX. IMP. XV. COS. VIII. P. P. Thunderbolt on throne. *R.I.C. 23a.*..	85	220
482A	**Julia Titi,** daughter of Titus and mistress of Domitian. Æ *denarius.* Rev. VENVS AVGVST. Venus stg r resting on column. *R.I.C. 56.*..................	340	850
482B	**Domitian,** 81-96 (Caesar 69-81), recalled Agricola in 83/4 and abandoned the conquest of northern Scotland (ca. 87). Aʋ *aureus.* Rev. GERMANICVS COS XV. Minerva stg l holding spear. *R.I.C. 163.*..	1100	2800

483   485

		F £	VF £
483	Æ *denarius.* IMP. XIX. COS. XIIII. CENS. P. P. P. Minerva stg. l., resting on spear. *R.I.C. 140.*.............................	46	140
483A	Æ *sestertius.* Rev. IOVI VICTORI SC. Jupiter seated l, holding Victory and sceptre. *R.I.C. 358.*..	160	425
484	Æ *dupondius.* VIRTVTI AVGVSTI S. C. Virtus stg. r. *R.I.C. 393*...........	45	130
484A	Æ *as.* MONETA AVGVSTI S. C. Moneta stg. l. *R.I.C. 354b.*	45	130
484B	**Domitia,** wife of Domitian. Æ *denarius.* Rev CONCORDIA AVGVST. Peacock stg r. *R.I.C. 212.*...	575	1550
484C	**Nerva,** 96-98. Aʋ *aureus.* Rev. CONCORDIA EXERCITVVM. Clasped r hands. *R.I.C. 14.*...	2000	4750
485	Æ *denarius.* AEQVITAS AVGVST. Aequitas stg. l. *R.I.C. 13.*	85	220
485A	Æ *as.* LIBERTAS PVBLICA S. C. Libertas stg. l. *R.I.C. 86.*....................	75	220
486	**Trajan,** 98-117, established the northern frontier in Britain along the Tyne-Solway line (ca. 100). Aʋ *aureus.* P. M. TR. P. COS. VI. P. P. S. P. Q. R. Genius stg. l., holding patera and corn-ears. *R.I.C. 347.*	1000	2600

487   489

	F £	VF £
487 Æ *denarius*. COS. V. P. P. S. P. Q. R. OPTIMO PRINC. Military trophy. R.I.C. 147.	40	115
488 Æ *sestertius*. S. P. Q. R. OPTIMO PRINCIPI S. C. Spes walking l., holding flower. R.I.C. 519.	90	340
488A Æ *dupondius*. SENATVS POPVLVSQVE ROMANVS S. C. Emperor advancing between two trophies. R.I.C. 676.	65	140
489 **Hadrian,** 117-138, visited Britain in 122 and initiated the construction of a fortified frontier line (Hadrian's Wall). Æ *aureus*. HISPANIA. Hispania reclining l. R.I.C. 305.	1200	3250
490 Æ *denarius*. P. M. TR. P. COS. III. Roma stg. l., holding Victory and spear. R.I.C. 76.	45	130
491 Æ *sestertius*. COS. III. S. C. Neptune stg. r., holding dolphin and trident, foot on prow. R.I.C. 632.	95	360
491A Æ *as*. FELICITATI AVG COS. III. P. P. S. C. Galley travelling l. over waves. R.I.C. 719.	60	150
See also under Category 2.		
492 **Sabina,** wife of Hadrian. Æ *denarius*. IVNONI REGINAE. Juno stg. l. R.I.C. 395a.	65	160
493 **Aelius Caesar,** heir of Hadrian, 136-138. Æ *denarius*. CONCORD. TR. POT. COS. II. Concordia seated l. R.I.C. 436.	115	285
493A Æ *as*. TR. POT. COS. II. S. C. Spes walking l., holding flower. R.I.C. 1067.	75	190
494 **Antoninus Pius,** 138-161, ordered the expansion of the Roman province to include southern Scotland and constructed the Antonine Wall on the Forth-Clyde line (beginning ca. 143). An uprising in northern Britain in the 150s resulting in a permanent withdrawal to the Hadrianic frontier early in the next reign. Æ *aureus*. COS. IIII. Togate emperor stg. l., holding globe. R.I.C. 233b.	950	2400
495 Æ *denarius*. PIETATI AVG. COS. IIII. Pietas stg. l. between two children, holding two more in her arms. R.I.C. 313c.	36	100

496

	F £	VF £
496 Æ *sestertius*. SALVS AVG. S. C. Salus stg. l. at altar, feeding snake. R.I.C. 635.	70	240
496A Æ *dupondius*. TR. POT. XX. COS. IIII. S. C. Providentia stg. l., pointing at globe at her feet and holding sceptre. R.I.C. 2025.	35	90
See also under Categories 2 and 3.		

	F £	VF £

497   **Antoninus Pius and Marcus Aurelius Caesar**. Ɍ *denarius*. Obv. Laur. hd. of Antoninus Pius r. Rev. AVRELIVS CAESAR AVG PII F. COS. Bare hd. of young Marcus Aurelius r. *R.I.C. 417a.*   100   240

498   501

498   **Divus Antoninus Pius,** deified 161. Ɍ *denarius*. CONSECRATIO. Four-storeyed crematorium of Antoninus Pius. *R.I.C. 436.*   38   100

499   **Diva Faustina Senior,** wife of Antoninus Pius, deified 141. Ɍ *denarius*. AETERNITAS. Aeternitas stg. l., holding globe and billowing veil. *R.I.C. 351.*   32   90

499A Æ *sestertius*. AVGVSTA S. C. Ceres stg. l., holding two torches. *R.I.C. 1120.*   55   170

500   **Marcus Aurelius,** 161-180 (Caesar 139-161), re-established Hadrian's Wall as the permanent northern frontier of the province, ca. 163. *N aureus*. PROV. DEOR. TR. P. XV. COS. III. Providentia stg. l., holding globe and cornucopiae. *R.I.C. 19.*   1100   2600

501   Ɍ *denarius*. PIETAS AVG. Priestly emblems. *R.I.C. 424a.*   40   110

501A — SALVTI AVG. COS. III. Salus stg. l. at altar, feeding snake. *R.I.C. 222.*   36   100

502   Æ *sestertius*. CONCORD. AVGVSTOR. TR. P. XVI. COS. III. S. C. Marcus Aurelius and Lucius Verus stg. face to face, clasping hands. *R.I.C. 826..*   90   400

502A Æ *as*. HONOS TR. POT. II. COS. II. S. C. Honos stg. r. *R.I.C. 1271a.* ..   40   120

503   **Divus Marcus Aurelius,** deified 180. Ɍ *denarius*. CONSECRATIO. Eagle stg. r. on altar. *R.I.C. 272.*   38   100

504   506A

504   **Faustina Junior,** daughter of Antoninus Pius, wife of Marcus Aurelius. Ɍ *denarius*. FECVNDITAS. Fecunditas stg. r., holding sceptre and child. *R.I.C. 677.*   32   90

504A Æ *sestertius*. HILARITAS S. C. Hilaritas stg. l. *R.I.C. 1642.*   60   220

505   **Diva Faustina Junior,** deified 175. Æ *as*. S. C. Crescent and seven stars. *R.I.C. 1714.*   40   120

506   **Lucius Verus,** 161-169. Ɍ *denarius*. PAX TR. P. VI. IMP. IIII. COS. II. Pax stg. l. *R.I.C. 561.*   60   150

506A Æ *dupondius*. TR. P. IIII. IMP. II. COS. II. S. C. Mars stg. r., resting on spear and shield. *R.I.C. 1387.*   50   160

507   **Lucilla,** daughter of Marcus Aurelius, wife of Lucius Verus. Ɍ *denarius*. IVNONI LVCINAE. Juno stg. l., holding child in swaddling clothes. *R.I.C. 771*   45   120

507A Æ *sestertius*. PIETAS S. C. Pietas stg. l., altar at feet. *R.I.C. 1756.*   65   240

	F £	VF £

508 **Commodus,** 177-192 (Caesar 175-177), major warfare on the British frontier early in the reign; situation restored by Ulpius Marcellus in 184/5, followed by unrest in the British legions. Æ *denarius.* LIB. AVG. IIII. TR. P. VI. IMP. IIII. COS. III. P. P. Liberalitas stg. l. *R.I.C. 22.* ... 46 125

509

511

509 Æ *sestertius.* IOVI VICTORI IMP. III. COS. II. P. P. S. C. Jupiter seated l. *R.I.C. 1612.* ... 75 330
509A Æ *as.* ANN. AVG. TR. P. VII. IMP. IIII. COS. III. P. P. S. C. Annona stg. l., modius at feet. *R.I.C. 339 (See also under Category 2.)* ... 35 90
510 **Crispina,** wife of Commodus. Æ *denarius.* CONCORDIA. Clasped hands. *R.I.C. 279.* ... 46 125
511 **Pertinax,** January-March 193, formerly governor of Britain, ca. 185-7. Æ *denarius.* PROVID. DEOR. COS. II. Providentia stg l., reaching up to star. *R.I.C. 11a.* ... 340 850

512

513

514A

512 **Didius Julianus,** March-June 193. Æ *denarius.* CONCORD MILIT. Concordia Militum stg. l., holding standards. *R.I.C. 1.* ... 675 1550
513 **Clodius Albinus,** 195-197 (Caesar 193-195), governor of Britain (from 191/2) at the time of his imperial proclamation by his troops. Æ *denarius.* MINER. PACIF. COS. II. Minerva stg. l. *R.I.C. 7.* ... 85 200
513A — FIDES LEGION. COS. II. Clasped hands holding legionary eagle. *R.I.C. 20b.* 100 240
514 **Septimius Severus,** 193-211, restored the frontier forts in northern Britain following the downfall of Clodius Albinus; later repaired Hadrian's Wall, and spent the years 208-11 in Britain campaigning in Scotland; divided Britannia into two provinces, Superior and Inferior; died at York, February 211. Æ *denarius.* VIRT AVGG. Roma stg. l., holding Victory, spear and shield. *R.I.C. 171a.* 26 65
514A — P.M. TR. P. XVIII. COS. III. P. P. Jupiter stg. l. between two children. *R.I.C. 240 (See also under Category 2.)* ... 26 65
515 **Julia Domna,** wife of Septimius Severus, mother of Caracalla and Geta, accompanied her husband and sons on the British expedition, 208-211, and probably resided in London during the northern campaigns. Æ *denarius.* VENERI VICTR. Venus stg. r., resting on column. *R.I.C. 536.* ... 24 60
515A — VESTA. Vesta stg. l., holding palladium and sceptre. *R.I.C. 390.* ... 24 60

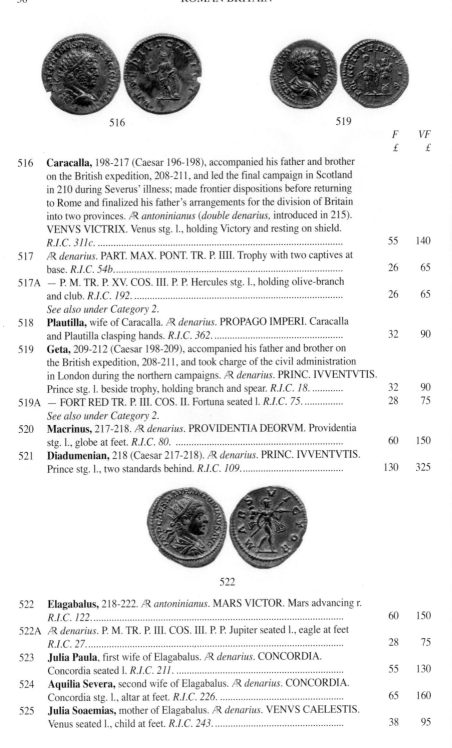

516

519

		F £	VF £

516 **Caracalla,** 198-217 (Caesar 196-198), accompanied his father and brother on the British expedition, 208-211, and led the final campaign in Scotland in 210 during Severus' illness; made frontier dispositions before returning to Rome and finalized his father's arrangements for the division of Britain into two provinces. Æ *antoninianus* (*double denarius,* introduced in 215). VENVS VICTRIX. Venus stg. l., holding Victory and resting on shield. *R.I.C. 311c.* 55 140

517 Æ *denarius.* PART. MAX. PONT. TR. P. IIII. Trophy with two captives at base. *R.I.C. 54b.* 26 65

517A — P. M. TR. P. XV. COS. III. P. P. Hercules stg. l., holding olive-branch and club. *R.I.C. 192.* 26 65
See also under Category 2.

518 **Plautilla,** wife of Caracalla. Æ *denarius.* PROPAGO IMPERI. Caracalla and Plautilla clasping hands. *R.I.C. 362.* 32 90

519 **Geta,** 209-212 (Caesar 198-209), accompanied his father and brother on the British expedition, 208-211, and took charge of the civil administration in London during the northern campaigns. Æ *denarius.* PRINC. IVVENTVTIS. Prince stg. l. beside trophy, holding branch and spear. *R.I.C. 18.* 32 90

519A — FORT RED TR. P. III. COS. II. Fortuna seated l. *R.I.C. 75.* 28 75
See also under Category 2.

520 **Macrinus,** 217-218. Æ *denarius.* PROVIDENTIA DEORVM. Providentia stg. l., globe at feet. *R.I.C. 80.* 60 150

521 **Diadumenian,** 218 (Caesar 217-218). Æ *denarius.* PRINC. IVVENTVTIS. Prince stg. l., two standards behind. *R.I.C. 109.* 130 325

522

522 **Elagabalus,** 218-222. Æ *antoninianus.* MARS VICTOR. Mars advancing r. *R.I.C. 122.* 60 150

522A Æ *denarius.* P. M. TR. P. III. COS. III. P. P. Jupiter seated l., eagle at feet *R.I.C. 27.* 28 75

523 **Julia Paula,** first wife of Elagabalus. Æ *denarius.* CONCORDIA. Concordia seated l. *R.I.C. 211.* 55 130

524 **Aquilia Severa,** second wife of Elagabalus. Æ *denarius.* CONCORDIA. Concordia stg. l., altar at feet. *R.I.C. 226.* 65 160

525 **Julia Soaemias,** mother of Elagabalus. Æ *denarius.* VENVS CAELESTIS. Venus seated l., child at feet. *R.I.C. 243.* 38 95

		F £	*VF* £

526 **Julia Maesa,** grandmother of Elagabalus and Severus Alexander. Æ
denarius. SAECVLI FELICITAS. Felicitas stg. l., altar at feet. *R.I.C. 271.*   30   80
527 **Severus Alexander,** 222-235 (Caesar 221-222). Æ *denarius.*
PAX AETERNA AVG. Pax stg. l. *R.I.C. 165.*   28   65
527A — P. M. TR. P. XIII. COS. III. P. P. Sol advancing l., holding whip. *R.I.C. 123.*   28   65

528

528 Æ *sestertius.* MARS VLTOR S. C. Mars advancing r., with spear and shield.
R.I.C. 635.   40   120
529 **Orbiana,** wife of Severus Alexander. Æ *denarius.* CONCORDIA AVGG.
Concordia seated l. *R.I.C. 319.*   80   200

530   531A

530 **Julia Mamaea,** mother of Severus Alexander. Æ *denarius.* VESTA.
Vesta stg. l. *R.I.C. 362.*   24   60
530A Æ *sestertius.* FELICITAS PVBLICA S. C. Felicitas stg. facing, hd. l.,
resting on column. *R.I.C. 676.*   36   100
531 **Maximinus I,** 235-238. Æ *denarius.* PAX AVGVSTI. Pax stg. l. *R.I.C. 12.*   30   70
531A Æ *sestertius.* SALVS AVGVSTI S. C. Salus seated l., feeding snake arising
from altar. *R.I.C. 85.*   38   110
532 **Maximus Caesar,** son of Maximinus I. Æ *denarius.* PRINC IVVENTVTIS.
Prince stg. l., two standards behind. *R.I.C. 3.*   65   190
533 **Gordian I Africanus,** March-April 238, governor of Britannia Inferior
late in the reign of Caracalla. Æ *denarius.* P. M. TR. P. COS. P. P. Togate
emperor stg. l. *R.I.C. 1.*   475   1150
534 **Gordian II Africanus,** March-April 238. Æ *denarius.* VIRTVS AVGG.
Virtus stg. l., with shield and spear. *R.I.C. 3.*   475   1150
535 **Balbinus,** April-July 238. Æ *antoninianus.* FIDES MVTVA AVGG.
Clasped hands. *R.I.C. 11.*   100   230
535A Æ *denarius.* PROVIDENTIA DEORVM. Providentia stg. l., globe at feet. *R.I.C. 7.*   80   210
536 **Pupienus,** April-July 238. Æ *antoninianus.* AMOR MVTVVS AVGG.
Clasped hands. *R.I.C. 9a.*   100   230
536A Æ *denarius.* PAX PVBLICA. Pax seated l. *R.I.C. 4.*   75   200

537   539

		F	VF
		£	£
537	**Gordian III,** 238-244 (Caesar 238). Æ *antoninianus*. LAETITIA AVG. N. Laetitia stg. l. *R.I.C. 86.*	20	45
538	Æ *denarius*. DIANA LVCIFERA. Diana stg. r., holding torch. *R.I.C. 127.*	20	45
538A	Æ *sestertius*. AETERNITATI AVG. S.C. Sol stg. l., holding globe. *R.I.C. 297a.*	32	85
539	**Philip I,** 244-249. Æ *antoninianus*. ROMAE AETERNAE. Roma seated l. *R.I.C. 65.*	20	45
539A	Æ *sestertius*. SECVRIT. ORBIS S. C. Securitas seated l. *R.I.C. 190.*	34	95
540	**Otacilia Severa,** wife of Philip I. Æ *antoninianus*. PIETAS AVGVSTAE. Pietas stg. l. *R.I.C. 125c.*	20	45
540A	Æ *sestertius*. CONCORDIA AVGG. S. C. Concordia seated l. *R.I.C. 203a.*	34	95
541	**Philip II,** 247-249 (Caesar 244-247). Æ *antoninianus*. PRINCIPI IVVENT. Prince stg. l., holding globe and spear. *R.I.C. 218d.*	22	55
541A	Æ *sestertius*. PAX AETERNA S. C. Pax stg. l. *R.I.C. 268c.*	34	95

542   543

542	**Trajan Decius,** 249-251. Æ *antoninianus*. DACIA. Dacia stg. l., holding staff with ass's hd. *R.I.C. 12b.*	22	50
542A	Æ *sestertius*. PANNONIAE S. C. The two Pannoniae stg., each holding standard. *R.I.C. 124a.*	40	110
543	**Herennia Etruscilla,** wife of Trajan Decius. Æ *antoninianus*. PVDICITIA AVG. Pudicitia stg. l. *R.I.C. 58b.*	24	55
544	**Herennius Etruscus,** 251 (Caesar 250-251). Æ *antoninianus*. PIETAS AVGG. Mercury stg. l., holding purse and caduceus. *R.I.C. 142b.*	32	80
545	**Hostilian,** 251 (Caesar 251). Æ *antoninianus*. PRINCIPI IVVENTVTIS. Apollo seated l., holding branch. *R.I.C. 180.*	50	120
546	**Trebonianus Gallus,** 251-253. Æ *antoninianus*. FELICITAS PVBLICA. Felicitas stg. l., resting on column. *R.I.C. 34A.*	20	45
546A	Æ *sestertius*. SALVS AVGG S. C. Salus stg. r., feeding snake held in her arms. *R.I.C. 121a.*	45	120
547	**Volusian,** 251-253 (Caesar 251). Æ *antoninianus*. VIRTVS AVGG. Virtus stg. l. *R.I.C. 186.*	22	50
548	**Aemilian,** 253. Æ *antoninianus*. PACI AVG. Pax stg. l., resting on column. *R.I.C. 8.*	85	200
549	**Valerian,** 253-260. Billon antoninianus. FIDES MILITVM. Fides stg. r., holding two standards. *R.I.C. 241.*	15	34

	F £	VF £
550 **Diva Mariniana,** wife of Valerian, deified 253. Billon *antoninianus*. CONSECRATIO. Empress seated on peacock flying r. *R.I.C. 6*.	55	140
551 **Gallienus,** 253-268, during whose reign Rome temporarily lost control over Britain when Postumus rebelled and established the independent Gallic Empire in 260. Billon *antoninianus*. VIRT GALLIENI AVG. Emperor advancing r., captive at feet. *R.I.C. 54*.	12	28

552

552 — DIANAE CONS. AVG. Doe l. *R.I.C. 176*.	10	24
552A — SOLI INVICTO. Sol stg. l., holding globe. *R.I.C. 658*.	10	22
553 **Salonina,** wife of Gallienus. Billon *antoninianus*. VENVS FELIX. Venus seated l., child at feet. *R.I.C. 7*.	10	24
553A — IVNONI CONS. AVG. Doe l. *R.I.C. 16*.	10	24
554 **Valerian Junior,** son of Gallienus, Caesar 256-258. Billon *antoninianus*. IOVI CRESCENTI. Infant Jupiter seated on goat r. *R.I.C. 13*.	22	50
555 **Divus Valerian Junior,** deified 258. Billon *antoninianus*. CONSECRATIO. Large altar. *R.I.C. 24*.	20	45
556 **Saloninus,** 260 (Caesar 258-260). Billon *antoninianus*. PIETAS AVG. Priestly emblems. *R.I.C. 9*.	20	45
557 **Macrianus,** usurper in the East, 260-261. Billon *antoninianus*. SOL. INVICTO. Sol stg. l., holding globe. *R.I.C. 12*.	50	120
558 **Quietus,** usurper in the East, 260-261. Billon *antoninianus*. INDVLGENTIAE AVG. Indulgentia seated l. *R.I.C. 5*.	50	120

559

559 **Postumus,** usurper in the West, 260-268, founder of the 'Gallic Empire' which temporarily detached Britain from the rule of the central government, a state of affairs which continued until Aurelian's defeat of Tetricus in 273. Billon *antoninianus*. HERC. DEVSONIENSI. Hercules stg. r. *R.I.C. 64*.	14	35
560 — MONETA AVG. Moneta stg. l. *R.I.C. 75*.	12	30
560A Æ *sestertius*. FIDES MILITVM. Fides stg. l., holding two standards. *R.I.C. 128*.	65	185
561 **Laelianus,** usurper in the West, 268. Billon *antoninianus*. VICTORIA AVG. Victory advancing r. *R.I.C. 9*.	350	875
562 **Marius,** usurper in the West, 268. Billon *antoninianus*. CONCORDIA MILITVM. Clasped hands. *R.I.C. 7*.	95	240

		F £	VF £
563	**Victorinus**, usurper in the West, 268-270. Billon *antoninianus*. INVICTVS. Sol advancing l. *R.I.C. 114*.	10	25
564	**Tetricus,** usurper in the West, 270-273, defeated by Aurelian, thus ending the 'Gallic Empire' and the isolation of Britain from the authority of Rome. Billon *antoninianus*. LAETITIA AVGG. Laetitia stg. l. *R.I.C. 87*.	10	25
	See also under Category 4.		
565	**Tetricus Junior,** son of Tetricus, Caesar 270-273. Billon *antoninianus*. SPES PVBLICA. Spes walking l., holding flower *R.I.C. 272*.	10	25
	See also under Category 4.		
566	**Claudius II Gothicus,** 268-270. Billon *antoninianus*. IOVI STATORI. Jupiter stg. r. *R.I.C. 52*.	10	25
567	**Divus Claudius II,** deified 270. Billon *antoninianus*. CONSECRATIO. Large altar. *R.I.C. 261*	10	25
	See also under Category 4.		
568	**Quintillus,** 270. Billon *antoninianus*. DIANA LVCIF. Diana stg. r., holding torch. *R.I.C. 49*.	26	70
569	**Aurelian,** 270-275, restored Britain to the rule of the central government through his defeat of Tetricus in 273; possibly began construction of the chain of 'Saxon Shore' forts on the eastern and southern coastlines. Billon *antoninianus*. ORIENS AVG. Sol stg. l. between two captives. *R.I.C. 63*.	14	35
569A	— RESTITVT. ORBIS. Female stg. r., presenting wreath to emperor stg. l. *R.I.C. 399*.	14	35
570	**Aurelian and Vabalathus,** ruler of Palmyra 267-272 and usurper in the East from 271. Billon *antoninianus*. Obv. Laur. bust of Vabalathus r. Rev. Rad. bust of Aurelian r. *R.I.C. 381*	38	100

571   574A

571	**Severina,** wife of Aurelian. Billon *antoninianus*. PROVIDEN. DEOR. Concordia (or Fides) Militum stg. r., facing Sol stg. l. *R.I.C. 9*.	22	55
572	**Tacitus,** 275-276. Billon *antoninianus*. SECVRIT. PERP. Securitas stg. l., leaning on column. *R.I.C. 163*.	22	55
573	**Florian,** 276. Billon *antoninianus*. LAETITIA FVND. Laetitia stg. l. *R.I.C. 34*.	40	100
574	**Probus,** 276-282, suppressed governor's revolt in Britain and lifted restrictions on viticulture in Britain and Gaul. Billon *antoninianus*. ADVENTVS PROBI AVG. Emperor on horseback l., captive seated before. *R.I.C. 160*.	14	35
574A	— VICTORIA GERM. Trophy between two captives. *R.I.C. 222*	16	45
574B	**Proculus** (usurper 280-281) Billon *antoninianus*. VICTORIA AVG. Female figure stg l.	12500	36000
575	**Carus,** 282-283. Billon *antoninianus*. PAX EXERCITI. Pax stg. l., holding olive-branch and standard. *R.I.C. 75*.	24	60

| | F | VF |
| | £ | £ |

576 **Divus Carus,** deified 283. Billon *antoninianus*. CONSECRATIO. Eagle
facing, hd. l. *R.I.C. 28.*.. 26 65

577 **Carinus,** 283-285 (Caesar 282-283). Billon *antoninianus*. SAECVLI
FELICITAS. Emperor stg. r. *R.I.C. 214.* 22 55

578 **Magnia Urbica,** wife of Carinus. Billon *antoninianus*. VENVS VICTRIX.
Venus stg. l., holding helmet, shield at feet. *R.I.C. 343.*......................... 70 170

579 **Numerian,** 283-284 (Caesar 282-283). Billon *antoninianus*. CLEMENTIA
TEMP. Emperor stg. r., receiving globe from Jupiter stg. l. *R.I.C. 463....* 24 60

580 **Diocletian,** 284-305. Æ *argenteus*. VIRTVS MILITVM. The four tetrarchs
sacrificing before gateway of military camp. *R.I.C. 27a (Rome).* 130 260

581 Billon *antoninianus*. IOVI CONSERVAT AVGG. Jupiter stg. l. *R.I.C. 162.* 12 30

582 Æ *follis*. GENIO POPVLI ROMANI. Genius stg. l. R.I.C. 14a *(Alexandria)*. 14 35

582A — (post-abdication coinage, after 305). PROVIDENTIA DEORVM QVIES
AVGG. Quies and Providentia stg. facing each other. *R.I.C. 676a (Treveri).* 28 75
See also under Category 3.

583 **Maximian,** 286-305 and 306-308, failed in his attempts to suppress the
usurpation of Carausius in Britain. Æ *argenteus*. VICTORIA SARMAT. The
four tetrarchs sacrificing before gateway of military camp. *R.I.C. 37b (Rome).* 120 240

584

584 Billon *antoninianus*. SALVS AVGG. Salus stg. r., feeding snake held in
her arms. *R.I.C. 417.* 12 28

585 Æ *follis*. SAC. MON. VRB. AVGG. ET CAESS. NN. Moneta stg. l.
R.I.C. 105b (Rome)... 14 35

585A — (second reign). CONSERVATORES VRB SVAE. Roma seated in
hexastyle temple. *R.I.C. 84b (Ticinum).* 14 35
See also under Category 3.
[For coins of the usurpers Carausius and Allectus see under Category 3]

586 **Constantius I,** 305-306 (Caesar 293-305), invaded Britain 296 and defeated
the usurper Allectus, thus restoring the island to the rule of the central government;
Britain now divided into four provinces and the northern frontier defences
reconstructed; died at York, July 306. Æ *argenteus*. PROVIDENTIA AVGG.
The four tetrarchs sacrificing before gateway of military camp. *R.I.C. 11a (Rome).* 140 280

587

587 Æ *follis*. GENIO POPVLI ROMANI. Genius stg. l. *R.I.C. 26a (Aquileia).* 14 35

| | F | VF |
| | £ | £ |

587A — SALVIS AVGG. ET CAESS. FEL. KART. Carthage stg. l., holding
fruits. *R.I.C. 30a (Carthage).* 15 40
See also under Category 3.

588   593

588   **Galerius,** 305-311 (Caesar 293-305). Æ argenteus. VIRTVS MILITVM.
The four tetrarchs sacrificing before gateway of military camp.
R.I.C. 15b (Ticinum). 130 260
588A — XC / VI in wreath. *R.I.C. 16b (Carthage).* 190 425
589   Æ *follis.* GENIO AVGG ET CAESARVM NN. Genius stg. l. *R.I.C. 11b
(Cyzicus).* 14 35
589A — GENIO IMPERATORIS. Genius stg. l. *R.I.C. 101a (Alexandria)* 12 30
See also under Category 3.
590   **Galeria Valeria,** wife of Galerius. Æ *follis.* VENERI VICTRICI. Venus
stg. l. *R.I.C. 110 (Alexandria).* 36 90
591   **Severus II,** 306-307 (Caesar 305-306). Æ *follis.* FIDES MILITVM. Fides
seated l. *R.I.C. 73 (Ticinum).* 36 90
See also under Category 3.
592   **Maximinus II,** 310-313 (Caesar 305-310). Æ *follis.* GENIO CAESARIS.
Genius stg. l. *R.I.C. 64 (Alexandria).* 12 30
592A — GENIO POP. ROM. Genius stg. l. *R.I.C. 845a (Treveri).* 10 25
See also under Category 3.
593   **Maxentius,** 306-312 (Caesar 306). Æ *follis.* CONSERV. VRB. SVAE.
Roma seated in hexastyle temple. *R.I.C. 210 (Rome).* 14 35
594   **Romulus,** son of Maxentius, deified 309. Æ *quarter follis.* AETERNAE
MEMORIAE. Temple with domed roof. *R.I.C. 58 (Ostia).* 65 170
595   **Licinius,** 308-324. Æ *follis.* GENIO AVGVSTI. Genius stg. l. *R.I.C. 198b
(Siscia).* 10 25
595A   Æ 3. IOVI CONSERVATORI AVGG. Jupiter stg. l. *R.I.C. 24 (Nicomedia).* 10 25
See also under Category 3.
596   **Licinius Junior,** son of Licinius, Caesar 317-324. Æ 3. CAESARVM
NOSTRORVM around wreath containing VOT. / V. *R.I.C. 92 (Thessalonica).* 10 25
597   **Constantine I, the Great,** 307-337 (Caesar 306-307), campaigned with
his father Constantius I against the Picts in northern Britain, summer 306,
and proclaimed emperor by the legions at York on Constantius' death
in July; closed the London mint early in 325 ending almost four decades
of operation. Æ *follis.* GENIO POP ROM. Genius stg. l. *R.I.C. 719b
(Treveri).* 14 35
598   — SOLI INVICTO COMITI. Sol stg. l. *R.I.C. 307 (Lugdunum).* 9 22
598A   Æ 3. PROVIDENTIAE AVGG. Gateway of military camp. *R.I.C. 153
(Thessalonica)* 7 18

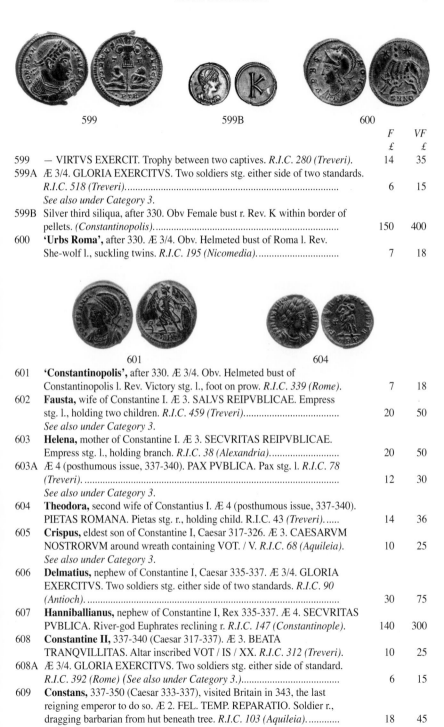

599 599B 600

	F	VF
	£	£

599 — VIRTVS EXERCIT. Trophy between two captives. *R.I.C. 280 (Treveri).* 14 35

599A Æ 3/4. GLORIA EXERCITVS. Two soldiers stg. either side of two standards.
R.I.C. 518 (Treveri)................. 6 15
See also under Category 3.

599B Silver third siliqua, after 330. Obv Female bust r. Rev. K within border of
pellets. *(Constantinopolis).*......... 150 400

600 **'Urbs Roma',** after 330. Æ 3/4. Obv. Helmeted bust of Roma l. Rev.
She-wolf l., suckling twins. *R.I.C. 195 (Nicomedia).*............. 7 18

601 604

601 **'Constantinopolis',** after 330. Æ 3/4. Obv. Helmeted bust of
Constantinopolis l. Rev. Victory stg. l., foot on prow. *R.I.C. 339 (Rome).* 7 18

602 **Fausta,** wife of Constantine I. Æ 3. SALVS REIPVBLICAE. Empress
stg. l., holding two children. *R.I.C. 459 (Treveri).*.................... 20 50
See also under Category 3.

603 **Helena,** mother of Constantine I. Æ 3. SECVRITAS REIPVBLICAE.
Empress stg. l., holding branch. *R.I.C. 38 (Alexandria).*............ 20 50

603A Æ 4 (posthumous issue, 337-340). PAX PVBLICA. Pax stg. l. *R.I.C. 78
(Treveri).* 12 30
See also under Category 3.

604 **Theodora,** second wife of Constantius I. Æ 4 (posthumous issue, 337-340).
PIETAS ROMANA. Pietas stg. r., holding child. R.I.C. 43 *(Treveri)......* 14 36

605 **Crispus,** eldest son of Constantine I, Caesar 317-326. Æ 3. CAESARVM
NOSTRORVM around wreath containing VOT. / V. *R.I.C. 68 (Aquileia).* 10 25
See also under Category 3.

606 **Delmatius,** nephew of Constantine I, Caesar 335-337. Æ 3/4. GLORIA
EXERCITVS. Two soldiers stg. either side of two standards. *R.I.C. 90
(Antioch).* 30 75

607 **Hanniballianus,** nephew of Constantine I, Rex 335-337. Æ 4. SECVRITAS
PVBLICA. River-god Euphrates reclining r. *R.I.C. 147 (Constantinople).* 140 300

608 **Constantine II,** 337-340 (Caesar 317-337). Æ 3. BEATA
TRANQVILLITAS. Altar inscribed VOT / IS / XX. *R.I.C. 312 (Treveri).* 10 25

608A Æ 3/4. GLORIA EXERCITVS. Two soldiers stg. either side of standard.
R.I.C. 392 (Rome) (See also under Category 3.)..................... 6 15

609 **Constans,** 337-350 (Caesar 333-337), visited Britain in 343, the last
reigning emperor to do so. Æ 2. FEL. TEMP. REPARATIO. Soldier r.,
dragging barbarian from hut beneath tree. *R.I.C. 103 (Aquileia).*............. 18 45

609A   611B

		F £	*VF* £
609A	— FEL. TEMP. REPARATIO. Emperor stg. l. on galley steered by Victory. *R.I.C. 219 (Treveri)*...	18	45
609B	Æ 4. VICTORIAE DD. AVGG. Q. NN. Two Victories stg. face to face. *R.I.C. 195 (Treveri)*...	6	15
610	**Constantius II,** 337-361 (Caesar 324-337). Æ 3/4. GLORIA EXERCITVS. Two soldiers stg. either side of two standards. *R.I.C. 85 (Cyzicus)*..........	6	15
611	Æ *siliqua*. VOTIS / XXX. / MVLTIS / XXXX. in wreath. *R.I.C. 207 (Arelate)*.	60	160
611A	Æ 2. FEL. TEMP. REPARATIO. Emperor stg. l. on galley. *R.I.C. 218 (Treveri)*..	18	45
611B	Æ 3. FEL. TEMP. REPARATIO. Soldier advancing l., spearing fallen horseman. *R.I.C. 189 (Lugdunum)*...	6	15

See also under Categories 3 and 4.

612   616

612	**Magnentius,** usurper in the West, 350-353, temporarily detached Britain from the rule of the legitimate Constantinian dynasty. Æ 1. SALVS DD. NN. AVG. ET CAES. *Chi-Rho* Christian monogram between Alpha and Omega. *R.I.C. 34 (Ambianum)*...	120	280
612A	Æ 2. FELICITAS REIPVBLICAE. Emperor stg. l., holding Victory and labarum. *R.I.C. 264 (Treveri)*......................................	24	60
	See also under Category 4.		
613	**Decentius,** brother of Magnentius, Caesar 351-353. Æ 2. VICTORIAE DD. NN. AVG. ET CAE. Two Victories supporting between them shield inscribed VOT. / V. / MVLT. / X. *R.I.C. 146 (Lugdunum).*	32	75
	See also under Category 4.		
614	**Vetranio,** 'usurper' in the Balkans, 350. Æ 2. CONCORDIA MILITVM. Emperor stg. l., holding two labara. *R.I.C. 281 (Siscia)*...........................	65	160
615	**Constantius Gallus,** Caesar under Constantius II, 351-354. Æ 2. FEL. TEMP. REPARATIO. Soldier advancing l., spearing fallen horseman. *R.I.C. 94 (Cyzicus)*...	18	45
615A	**Julian II,** 360-363 (Caesar 355-360). Æ *miliarense*. Rev. VIRTVS EXERCITVM. Soldier stg l, holding spear and resting on shield. *R.I.C. 290. (Arelate)*	380	975
616	Æ *siliqua*. VOT. / X. / MVLT. / XX. in wreath. *R.I.C. 309 (Arelate).*	60	160

		F £	VF £
617	Æ 1. SECVRITAS REIPVB. Bull stg. r. *R.I.C. 411 (Siscia)*. .... *Beware of recent forgeries.*	50	150
617A	Æ 3. VOT. / X. / MVLT. / XX. in wreath. *R.I.C. 108 (Sirmium)*.............	10	25
618	**Jovian,** 363-364. Æ 3. VOT. / V. / MVLT. / X. in wreath. *R.I.C. 426 (Siscia)*.	16	45

619   620

619 **Valentinian I,** 364-375 (in the West), during whose reign the Roman province of Britannia was devastated by the simultaneous attack of hordes of invaders on several fronts (the 'Barbarian Conspiracy'); order eventually restored by Count Theodosius, father of the future emperor . *Ν solidus.* RESTITVTOR REIPVBLICAE. Emperor stg. r., holding standard and Victory. *R.I.C. 2b (Antioch)*. 240 550

619A *Ɑ miliarense.* Rev. VICTORIA AVGVSTORVM. Victory stg r, inscribing shield. *R.I.C. 24a. (Trier)*.............................. 360 950

619B *Ɑ siliqua.* Rev. VRBS ROMA. Roma seated l. *R.I.C. 27a (Trier)*.......... 65 170

619C Æ 3. GLORIA ROMANORVM. Emperor advancing r., dragging barbarian and holding labarum. *R.I.C. 14a (Siscia)*. 7 18

619D — SECVRITAS REIPVBLICAE. Victory advancing l. *R.I.C. 32a (Treveri)*. 7 18

619E **Valens,** 364-378 (in the East). *Ν solidus.* Rev. RESTITVTOR REIPVBLICAE. Valens stg , holding labarum and Victory. *R.I.C. 2d (Antioch)* 240 550

619F *Ɑ miliarense.* Rev. VIRTVS EXERCITVS. Valens stg, holding standard. *R.I.C. 26c (Trier)* 340 900

620 *Ɑ siliqua.* VRBS ROMA. Roma seated l. *R.I.C. 27e (Treveri)*. 65 170

620A Æ 3. SECVRITAS REIPVBLICAE. Victory advancing l. *R.I.C. 42b (Constantinople)*. 7 18

621 **Procopius,** usurper in the East, 365-366. Æ 3. REPARATIO FEL. TEMP. Emperor stg. r., holding standard and shield. *R.I.C. 17a (Constantinople)*. 55 140

621A **Gratian,** 367-383 (in the West), overthrown by Magnus Maximus who had been proclaimed emperor by the army in Britain. *Ν solidus.* Rev. VICTORIA AVGG. Two Emperors enthroned holding globe, Victory behind. *R.I.C. 17g (Trier)* 260 650

621B *Ɑ miliarense.* Rev. VIRTVS EXERCITVS. Gratian stg, holding standard. *R.I.C. 40 .(Lugdunum)*.. 360 950

622 *Ɑ siliqua.* VRBS ROMA. Roma seated l. *R.I.C. 27f (Treveri)*............... 65 170

622A **Valentinian II,** 375-392 (in the West). *Ν solidus.* Rev. VICTORIA AVGG. Two Emperors enthroned holding globe, Victory behind. *R.I.C. 34b (Thessalonica)* 300 700

622B *Ɑ miliarense.* Rev. GLORIA ROMANORVM. Valentinian stg , holding standard. *R.I.C. 40 (lugdunum)* 375 980

622C *Ɑ siliqua.* Rev. VIRTVS ROMANORVM. Roma seated l. *R.I.C. 43a. (Lugdunum)*.. 70 180

623 Æ 2. REPARATIO REIPVB. Emperor stg. l., raising kneeling female figure. *R.I.C. 20c (Arelate)*.. 14 36

623A Æ 4. SALVS REIPVBLICAE. Victory advancing l., dragging barbarian. *R.I.C. 20a (Alexandria)*. 7 18

	F	VF
	£	£

623B **Theodosius I,** the Great, 379-395 (in the East), son of the Count Theodosius who had cleared Britain of barbarian invaders in the reign of Valentinian I; the Emperor Theodosiua twice restored Britain to the rule of the central government, by his defeat of the usurpers Magnus Maximus (in 388) and Eugenius (in 394).
N solidus. Rev. CONCORDIA AUGGG. Constantinopolis seated, holding sceptre and shield. *R.I.C. 71a (Constantinople)* 280 700
623C Æ *miliarense.* Rev. VIRTUS EXERCITUS. Theodosius stg , holding standard.
R.I.C. 53c (Trier) 380 1000
624 Æ *siliqua.* CONCORDIA AVGGG. Constantinopolis enthroned facing, foot on prow. *R.I.C. 55a (Treveri)* 65 170

624A

624A — VIRTVS ROMANORVM. Roma enthroned facing. *R.I.C (Aquileia) 28d.* 65 170
624B Æ 2. VIRTVS EXERCIT. Emperor stg. r., foot on captive, holding labarum and globe. *R.I.C. 24b (Heraclea)* 18 45
625 **Aelia Flaccilla,** wife of Theodosius I. Æ 2. SALVS REIPVBLICAE. Victory seated r., inscribing Christian monogram on shield set on cippus.
R.I.C. 81 (Constantinople) 28 70
625A **Magnus Maximus,** usurper in the West, 383-388, proclaimed emperor by the army in Britain, invaded Gaul, and overthrew the legitimate western emperor Gratian; possibly reopened the London mint for a brief issue of precious metal coinage (Rudyard Kipling presented a rather fanciful version of his career in "Puck of Pook's Hill"). *N solidus.* Rev. RESTITVTOR REPVBLICAE.
Maximus stg, holding labarum and Victory. *R.I.C. 76 (Trier)* 900 2400
625B Æ *miliarense.* Rev. VIRTVS EXERCITVS. Maximus stg, holding labarum.
R.I.C. 82 (Trier) 725 1800

326   627

626 Æ *siliqua.* VIRTVS ROMANORVM. Roma enthroned facing. *R.I.C. 84b (Treveri)*
(See also under Category 3.) 75 200
626A **Flavius Victor,** son of Magnus Maximus, co-emperor 387-388. Æ *siliqua.*
VIRTVS ROMANORVM. Roma seated facing on throne. *R.I.C. 84d (Treveri)* 280 650
627 Æ 4. SPES ROMANORVM. Gateway of military camp. *RIC 55b (Aquileia).* 50 120
627A **Eugenius,** usurper in the West, 392-394, recognized in Britain until his defeat by Theodosius the Great. *N solidus.* VICTORIA AUGG. Two emperors enthroned facing holding globe. *R.I.C. 28 (Treveri)* 2800 7600
627B Æ *miliarense.* Rev. VIRTVS EXERCITVS. Eugenius stg, holding standard.
R.I.C. 105 (Trier) 1600 4000

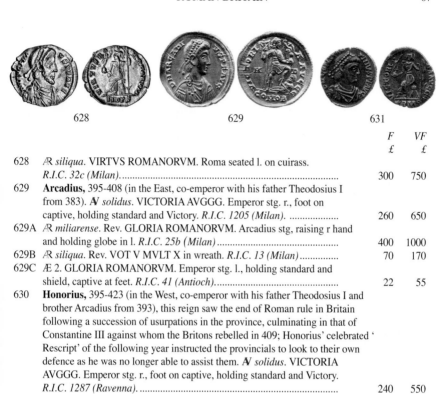

628   629   631

	F	VF
	£	£

628   Æ *siliqua.* VIRTVS ROMANORVM. Roma seated l. on cuirass.
      R.I.C. 32c (Milan). 300   750

629   **Arcadius,** 395-408 (in the East, co-emperor with his father Theodosius I
      from 383). *N solidus.* VICTORIA AVGGG. Emperor stg. r., foot on
      captive, holding standard and Victory. *R.I.C. 1205 (Milan).* 260   650

629A Æ *miliarense.* Rev. GLORIA ROMANORVM. Arcadius stg, raising r hand
      and holding globe in l. *R.I.C. 25b (Milan)* 400   1000

629B Æ *siliqua.* Rev. VOT V MVLT X in wreath. *R.I.C. 13 (Milan)* 70   170

629C Æ 2. GLORIA ROMANORVM. Emperor stg. l., holding standard and
      shield, captive at feet. *R.I.C. 41 (Antioch).* 22   55

630   **Honorius,** 395-423 (in the West, co-emperor with his father Theodosius I and
      brother Arcadius from 393), this reign saw the end of Roman rule in Britain
      following a succession of usurpations in the province, culminating in that of
      Constantine III against whom the Britons rebelled in 409; Honorius' celebrated '
      Rescript' of the following year instructed the provincials to look to their own
      defence as he was no longer able to assist them. *N solidus.* VICTORIA
      AVGGG. Emperor stg. r., foot on captive, holding standard and Victory.
      R.I.C. 1287 (Ravenna). 240   550

630A Æ *miliarense.* Rev. VIRTVS EXERCITVS *(Rome)* 425   1100

630B Æ *siliqua.* VIRTVS ROMANORVM. Roma seated l. on cuirass.
      R.I.C. 1228 (Milan) 65   170

631   **Constantine III,** usurper in the West, 407-411, proclaimed emperor by the
      army in Britain, but his authority rejected by the Romano-Britons two years
      later, thus effectively ending 366 years of Roman rule in Britain. Æ *siliqua.*
      VICTORIA AVGGG. Roma enthroned l. *R.I.C. 1532 (Treveri)* 200   450

632   **Valentinian III,** 425-455 (in the West), during whose reign the Saxon
      conquest of the former Roman province commenced, following the final
      unsuccessful appeal of the Romano-Britons for help addressed to the general
      Aetius in 446. *N solidus.* VICTORIA AVGGG. Emperor stg. facing, foot
      on human-headed serpent. *R.I.C. 2010 (Ravenna).* 250   600

632A Æ 4. VOT. PVB. Gateway of military camp. *R.I.C. 2123 (Rome).* 30   85

Inc. Gregory's **Est.1858**

We are accepting single entries
and collections of Roman coins & antiquities

www.timelineauctions.com

Sold for:
£17,360
(World Record Price)

2. ISSUES WITH TYPES REFERRING SPECIFICALLY
TO THE PROVINCE OF BRITANNIA

Struck in Rome, unless otherwise indicated. These usually commemorate military operations in the northern frontier region of the province or beyond.

633

635

	F £	VF £
633 **Claudius,** A.D. 41-54. AV aureus, celebrating the early stages of the Roman conquest of Britain which commenced in A.D. 43. DE BRITANN on architrave of triumphal arch. *R.I.C. 33.*	2400	5300
634 Æ *denarius.* Similar. *R.I.C. 34.*	600	1500
634A Æ *didrachm* of Caesarea in Cappadocia. DE BRITANNIS. Emperor in triumphal quadriga r. *R.I.C. 122.*	500	1350
635 **Hadrian,** 117-138. Æ as, commemorating the restoration of order in the province following a serious uprising (or invasion) in the north, probably early in the governorship of Q. Pompeius Falco (118-122). BRITANNIA PONT. MAX. TR. POT. COS. III. S. C. Britannia seated facing on rock. *R.I.C. 577a.*	300	750
636 Æ *sestertius,* commemorating Hadrian's visit to the province in 122, when he planned and initiated the construction of the northern frontier system which bears his name. ADVENTVI AVG. BRITANNIAE S.C. Emperor and Britannia stg. either side of altar. *R.I.C. 882.*	6000	19000

638A

637 — BRITANNIA S. C. Britannia seated facing, foot resting on rock. *R.I.C. 845.*	6500	21000
637A Æ *dupondius* or as. *Similar. R.I.C. 846.*	550	1600
638 Æ *sestertius,* commemorating Hadrian's attention to the legionary garrison strength of the province, principally his transfer of *VI Victrix* from Germany in 122. EXERC. BRITANNICVS S. C. Emperor on horseback r., addressing gathering of troops. *R.I.C. 912.*	6000	19000
638A — EXERC. BRITANNICVS S.C. Emperor stg. r. on tribunal, addressing gathering of troops. *R.I.C. 913.*	6000	19000

	F £	VF £

639 **Antoninus Pius,** 138-161. Æ *aureus,* commemorating the conquests in Scotland by the governor Q. Lollius Urbicus (138/9-142/3) at which time construction of the Antonine Wall was begun. BRITAN. IMPERATOR II. Victory stg. l. on globe. *R.I.C. 113* 1800 4200

640

640 Æ *sestertius.* BRITANNIA S. C. Britannia seated l. on rock, holding standard. *R.I.C. 742.* 800 2000

641 — BRITAN. IMPERATOR II. S. C. Helmeted Britannia seated l., foot on rock. *R.I.C. 743* 800 2000

642 — BRITAN. IMPERATOR II. S. C. Britannia seated l. on globe above waves, holding standard. *R.I.C. 744.* 900 2400

643 — BRITAN. IMPERATOR II. S. C. Victory stg. l. on globe. *R.I.C. 719.* 280 675

643A — BRITANNIA IMPERATOR II. S. C. Britannia seated l. on rock, holding standard. *R.I.C. 745.* 800 2000

644 Æ *as.* IMPERATOR II. S. C. Victory hovering l., holding shield inscribed BRI / TAN. *R.I.C. 732.* 140 325

645 Æ *dupondius,* commemorating the quelling of a serious uprising in the north, ca. 154/5, necessitating the evacuation of the recently constructed Antonine Wall in Scotland. BRITANNIA COS. IIII. S. C. Britannia seated l. on rock, shield and vexillum in background. *R.I.C. 930.* 200 500

646 Æ *as.* Similar. *R.I.C. 934.* 120 325

Many specimens of this type are carelessly struck on inadequate flans. Moreover, they have been found in significant quantities on Romano-British sites, notably in Coventina's Well at Carrawburgh fort on Hadrian's Wall, raising the interesting possibility that they may have been issued from a temporary mint in Britain. The style of the engraving is quite regular, indicating that even if locally produced these coins would have been struck from normal Roman dies brought to Britain especially for this purpose. See under Category 3.

647 **Commodus,** 177-192. Æ *sestertius,* commemorating the victories in Scotland of the governor Ulpius Marcellus in 184/5. These were in retribution for a major barbarian invasion several years earlier resulting in serious damage to Hadrian's Wall, which had been temporarily overrun, and the defeat and death of an unknown governor. BRITT. P. M. TR. P. VIIII. IMP. VII. COS. IIII. P. P. S. C. Britannia stg. l., holding curved sword and helmet. *R.I.C. 437.* 5500 17000

648

		F £	VF £

648 — VICT. BRIT. P. M. TR. P. VIIII. (or X.) IMP. VII. COS. IIII. P. P. S. C.
Victory seated r., about to inscribe shield. *R.I.C. 440, 452*....................... 200 550

649

649 **Septimius Severus,** 193-211. *N aureus,* commemorating the success of
the punitive Roman campaigns in Scotland during 209 and 210 culminating
in the illness and death of Severus at York in Feb. 211. VICTORIAE BRIT.
Victory advancing l. *R.I.C. 334.* 2500 6250
650 — VICTORIAE BRIT. Victory advancing r., leading child by hand.
R.I.C. 302... 2750 6500
651 Æ *denarius.* VICTORIAE BRIT. Victory advancing r. *R.I.C. 332.* 60 130
651A — VICTORIAE BRIT. Victory stg. facing beside palm-tree with shield
attached. *R.I.C. 336.*... 65 140
651B — VICTORIAE BRIT. Victory stg. l. *R.I.C. 333.*.................................... 60 130
651C — VICTORIAE BRIT. Victory seated l., holding shield. *R.I.C. 335.*....... 60 130

652

652 Æ *sestertius.* VICTORIAE BRITTANNICAE S. C. Two Victories placing
shield on palm-tree with captives at base. *R.I.C. 818.*............................... 450 1400
653 — P. M. TR. P. XVIII. COS. III. P. P. S. C. Similar. *R.I.C. 796.* 275 650
654 Æ *dupondius.* VICT. BRIT. P. M. TR. P. XIX. COS. III. P. P. S. C. Victory
stg. r. between two captives, holding vexillum. *R.I.C. 809.* 160 400
655 Æ *as.* VICTORIAE BRITTANNICAE S. C. Similar. *R.I.C. 837a*........... 175 425

		F	VF
		£	£
656	Billon *tetradrachm* of Alexandria in Egypt. NEIKH KATA BRET. Nike flying l. *Milne 2726.*	925	2250
657	**Caracalla,** 198-217. *N aureus,* commemorating the victories achieved by the Romans in Scotland during the campaigns led jointly by Severus and Caracalla in 209, and by Caracalla alone the following year during his father's illness. VICTORIAE BRIT. Victory seated l., holding shield. *R.I.C. 174.*	2600	6500

658   659A

658	*R denarius.* VICTORIAE BRIT. Victory advancing l. *R.I.C. 231.*	60	130
658A	— VICTORIAE BRIT. Victory advancing r., holding trophy. *R.I.C. 231A.*	60	130
659	*Æ sestertius.* VICTORIAE BRITTANNICAE S. C. Victory stg. r., erecting trophy to r. of which Britannia stands facing, captive at feet. *R.I.C. 464.*	375	950
659A	— VICT. BRIT. TR. P. XIIII. COS. III. S.C. Similar. *Cf. R.I.C. 483c.*	325	850
660	*Æ dupondius.* VICTORIAE BRITTANNICAE S. C. Victory stg. r., inscribing shield set on palm-tree. *R.I.C. 467*..............	150	380
661	*Æ as.* VICT. BRIT. TR. P. XIIII. COS. III. S. C. Similar. *R.I.C. 490*.......	140	350
662	**Geta,** 209-212. *R denarius,* commemorating the victories achieved by his father and brother in Scotland in 209-10 while he and his mother were resident in London. VICTORIAE BRIT. Victory stg. l. *R.I.C. 92*............	65	140
662A	— VICTORIAE BRIT. Victory advancing r. *R.I.C. 91.*	65	140

663

663	*Æ sestertius.* VICTORIAE BRITTANNICAE S. C. Victory seated r., inscribing shield set on knee. *R.I.C. 166.*	450	1300
663A	— VICT. BRIT. TR. P. III. COS. II. S. C. Similar. *R.I.C. 172b.*	380	1000
664	*Æ as.* VICTORIAE BRITTANNICAE S. C. Victory seated l., balancing shield on knee. *R.I.C. 191a*..............	160	425
665	Billon *tetradrachm* of Alexandria in Egypt. NEIKH KATA BRETAN. Nike advancing l. *B.M.C. (Alexandria) 1481.*	1000	2500

3. OFFICIAL ROMAN COINAGE STRUCK IN BRITAIN

The London mint, and the associated 'C' mint (new research indicates that this was a secondary mint that operated initially in North London and subsequently moved around the country with Carausius), were created by the usurper Carausius soon after his seizure of Britain in 287. Prior to this, in the mid-2nd century, there may have been minting of 'Britannia' asses of Antoninus Pius in the province using dies brought from Rome, though this has not been firmly established. After the downfall of the rebel British regime in 296 the minting establishment in London (though not the subsidiary mint) was retained by the tetrarchal government and the succeeding Constantinian administration. Early in 325, however, Constantine the Great closed the London mint after almost four decades of operation. A possible brief revival under the usurper Magnus Maximus has been postulated for gold and silver coins marked 'AVG', 'AVGOB' and 'AVGPS', though the attribution has not received universal acceptance.

	F	VF
	£	£

666 **Antoninus Pius,** 138-161. Æ *as*, struck in northern Britain (?) in 155. BRITANNIA COS. IIII. S. C. Britannia seated l. on rock, shield and vexillum in background. *R.I.C. 930.*.. 160 450

Many poorly struck examples of this type have been found on Romano-British sites, notably at Brocolitia (Carrawburgh) fort on Hadrian's Wall in Northumberland, where no fewer than 327 specimens were discovered in the great votive deposit in the well which formed part of the shrine of the water-nymph Coventina. There appears to be a very real possibility that many of these 'Britannia' asses had been issued from a temporary mint in Britain, most likely situated in the north. The dies, however, are quite regular, and would thus have been brought from Rome to the island province for the express purpose of supplementing the money supply at a time of crisis.

667 **Carausius,** usurper in Britain and northwestern Gaul, A.D. 287-293. Nʹ *aureus*, London. CONSERVAT. AVG. Jupiter stg. l., eagle at feet, ML in ex. *R.I.C. 1.* 18000 46000

667A Ɑʀ *denarius* ADVENTVS AUG. Emperor riding l, captive before horse. *R.I.C. 1068.*.. 1400 3200

667B — CONCORDIA AVG. Clasped hands. RSR. *R.I.C. 545.*....................... 975 2300

668 — EXPECTATE VENI. Britannia stg. r. and emperor l., clasping hands, RSR in ex. *R.I.C. 555.*.. 1300 3000

669   672A

669 — RENOVAT. ROMANO. She-wolf r., suckling twins, RSR in ex. *R.I.C. 571.*.. 1100 2600

669A — Rev. VIRTVS AVG. Lion walking l. RSR in exergue. *R.I.C. 591.*....... 1500 3500

669B — Rev. VOTO PVBLICO, MVLTIS XX IMP in altar. RSR below. *R.I.C. 595.* 1200 2700

670 Billon *antoninianus,* London. COMES AVG. Victory stg. l., S—P in field, ML in ex. *R.I.C. 14.* 95 260

670A — HILARITAS AVG. Hilaritas stg. l., B—E in field, MLXXI in ex. *R.I.C. 41.* 70 180

671 — LAETITIA AVG. Laetitia stg. l., F—O in field, ML in ex. *R.I.C. 50.*.. 55 140

		F £	VF £
671A	— LEG. II. AVG. Capricorn l., ML in ex. *R.I.C. 58*...............................	140	360
	Legio II Augusta was stationed at Isca (Caerleon in South Wales).		
672	— LEG. XX. V. V. Boar stg. r. *R.I.C. 82.*	150	380
	Legio XX Valeria Victrix was stationed at Deva (Chester in the northwest Midlands).		
672A	— PAX AVG. Pax stg. l., F—O in field, ML in ex. *R.I.C. 101.*	45	120
673	— Similar, but without mint mark. *R.I.C. 880.*	40	110
673A	— PROVIDENT. AVG. Providentia stg. l., B—E in field, MLXXI in ex. *R.I.C. 149.*..	55	140
674	— SALVS AVGGG. Salus stg. r., feeding snake held in her arms, S—P in field, ML in ex. *R.I.C. 164.*...	70	180
	The reverse legends with triple-ending (AVGGG.) presumably are subsequent to Carausius' recognition by Diocletian and Maximian in 289 following the failure of the latter's attempt to dislodge the usurper from his island stronghold.		
674A	— TEMPORVM FELICITAS. Felicitas stg. l., B—E in field, ML in ex. *R.I.C. 172.*..	55	140
675	— VIRTVS AVGGG. Mars (or Virtus) stg. r., holding spear and shield, S—P in field, MLXXI in ex. *R.I.C. 183.*	70	180
676	Billon *antoninianus,* Colchester (?). CONCORDIA MILIT. Emperor stg. r. and Concordia l., clasping hands, C in ex. *R.I.C. 205.*	120	325
676A	— EXPECTATE VENI. Britannia stg. r. and emperor l., clasping hands, MSC in ex. *R.I.C. 216.*...	180	475
677	— FELICITAS AVG. Galley with mast and rowers, CXXI in ex. *R.I.C. 221.*	160	425
677A	— FORTVNA RAEDVX. Fortuna seated l., SPC in ex. *R.I.C. 237.*	90	240
678	— LAETITIA AVG. Laetitia stg. l., globe at feet, S—P in field, C in ex. *R.I.C. 255.*..	55	140
678A	—-MONETA AVG. Moneta stg. l., CXXI in ex. *R.I.C. 287.*	60	150
679	— ORIENS AVG. Sol stg. l., C in ex. *R.I.C. 293.*...................................	70	170
679A	— PAX AVGGG. Pax stg. l., S—P in field, MC in ex. *R.I.C. 335.*..........	50	120

680

680	— PROVID. AVG. Providentia stg. l., S—P in field, C in ex. *R.I.C. 353.*	55	140

Timeline Auctions
Inc. Gregory's Est.1858

Proud sponsor of the Wildwinds project

WILDWINDS
WWW.WILDWINDS.COM

ONLINE REFERENCE, ATTRIBUTION & VALUATION SITE
FOR ANCIENT GREEK, ROMAN & BYZANTINE COINS

	F	VF
	£	£

680A — SALVS AVG. Salus stg. l. at altar, feeding snake, S—C in field,
C in ex. *R.I.C. 396.* 70 180

681 — SPES PVBLICA. Spes walking l., holding flower, S—P in field,
C in ex. *R.I.C. 413.* 80 200

681A — VICTORIA AVG. Victory advancing l., captive at feet, MC in ex. *R.I.C. 429.* 85 220

682 **Carausius, Diocletian and Maximian,** after 289. Billon *antoninianus,*
Colchester (?). Obv. CARAVSIVS ET FRATRES SVI. Conjoined busts
of the three emperors l. Rev. PAX AVGGG. Pax stg. l., S—P in field,
C in ex. *R.I.C. 1.* 1600 4200

682A   684A

682A — MONETA AVGGG. Moneta stg. l., S—P in field, C in ex. *R.I.C.* —.. 1800 4500
*See also nos. 693-4 and 698-700 as well as regular Carausian types with
the triple-ending 'AVGGG.' on reverse.*

683 **Allectus,** usurper in Britain, 293-296. *N aureus,* London. ORIENS AVG.
Sol stg. l. between two captives, ML in ex. *R.I.C. 4*................................. 25000 60000

684 Æ *antoninianus,* London. LAETITIA AVG. Laetitia stg. l., S—A in field,
MSL in ex. *R.I.C. 22.*.. 65 160

684A — PAX AVG. Pax stg. l., S—A in field, ML in ex. *R.I.C. 28.* 55 150

685 — PROVID. AVG. Providentia stg. l., holding globe and cornucopiae,
S—P in field, ML in ex. *R.I.C. 36.* 70 175

685A — SALVS AVG. Salus stg. r., feeding snake held in her arms, S—A in
field, MSL in ex. *R.I.C. 42.*.. 75 200

686 — TEMPOR. FELICITAS. Felicitas stg. l., S—A in field, ML in ex. *R.I.C. 47.* 65 170

686A — VICTORIA AVG. Victory advancing l., S—P in field, ML in ex. *R.I.C. 48.* 85 225

687 Æ *antoninianus,* Colchester (?). AEQVITAS AVG. Aequitas stg. l., S—P
in field, C in ex. *R.I.C. 63.*... 65 170

687A — FIDES MILITVM. Fides stg. l., holding two standards, S—P in field,
C in ex. *R.I.C. 69.* 85 200

688A

688 — LAETITIA AVG. Laetitia stg. l., S—P in field, CL in ex. *R.I.C. 79.* ... 70 190
*This form of mint mark has given rise to the alternative identification of
this mint as Clausentum (Bitterne, Hants.)*

688A — MONETA AVG. Moneta stg. l., S—P in field, C in ex. *R.I.C. 82.* 65 170

		F	VF
		£	£

689 — PAX AVG. Pax stg. l., S—P in field, C in ex. *R.I.C. 86.* 55 150
689A — PROVIDENTIA AVG. Providentia stg. l., globe at feet, S—P in field,
C in ex. *R.I.C. 111.*... 60 160
690 — TEMPORVM FELIC. Felicitas stg. l., S—P in field, CL in ex. *R.I.C. 117.* 65 170
690A — VIRTVS AVG. Mars stg. r., holding spear and shield, S—P in field,
C in ex. *R.I.C. 121.*... 75 200
691 Æ *'quinarius',* London. VIRTVS AVG. Galley l., QL in ex. *R.I.C. 55....* 50 130
*An experimental denomination issued only during this reign, the types of
the so-called 'quinarius' would seem to indicate that it was in some way
associated with the operations of the fleet upon which the survival of the
rebel regime in Britain was totally dependent.*

692   693

692 Æ *'quinarius',* Colchester (?). LAETITIA AVG. Galley r., QC in ex.
R.I.C. 124.... 50 130
692A — VIRTVS AVG. Galley l., QC in ex. *R.I.C. 128.*................................... 50 130
693 **Diocletian,** 284-305. Billon *antoninianus* of London, struck by Carausius
between 289 and 293. PAX AVGGG. Pax stg. l., S—P in field, MLXXI
in ex. *R.I.C. 9.* 70 190
694 Billon *antoninianus* of Colchester (?), same date. PROVID AVGGG.
Providentia stg. l., globe at feet, S—P in field, C in ex. *R.I.C. 22*............ 70 190

695

695 Æ *follis,* London. GENIO POPVLI ROMANI. Genius stg. l., LON in ex.
R.I.C. 1a... 200 500
*By the time the central government had recovered control of Britain in 296
the antoninianus had been replaced by the larger follis under Diocletian's
sweeping currency reform. London was retained as an official imperial
mint, but the secondary British establishment (at Colchester?) was now
abandoned. Except for its initial issue in 297 (marked 'LON') the London
mint under the tetrarchic government produced only unsigned folles
throughout its first decade of operation. Perhaps Constantius did not
wish to draw attention to his employment of a mint which had been the
creation of a rebel regime.*
696 — Similar, but without mint mark. *R.I.C. 6a.* 25 55

	F £	VF £

697　— (post-abdication coinage, after 305). PROVIDENTIA DEORVM
QVIES AVGG. Quies and Providentia stg. facing each other (no mint mark).
R.I.C. 77a. ....　40　90

697A　　　　　　　　　　　704

697A　— QVIES AVGG. Quies stg. l., holding branch and sceptre, PLN in ex.
R.I.C. 98. ....　34　80

698　**Maximian,** 286-305 and 306-308. *N aureus* of London, struck by
Carausius between 289 and 293. SALVS AVGGG. Salus stg. r., feeding
snake held in her arms, ML in ex. *R.I.C. 32.* ....　32000　72000

699　Billon *antoninianus* of London, same date. PROVIDENTIA AVGGG.
Providentia stg. l., S—P in field, MLXXI in ex. *R.I.C. 37.* ....　60　150

700　Billon *antoninianus* of Colchester (?), same date. PAX AVGGG. Pax stg.
l., S—P in field, C in ex. *R.I.C. 42.* ....　60　150

701　Æ *follis,* London. GENIO POPVLI ROMANI. Genius stg. l., LON in ex.
R.I.C. 2. ....　180　420

702　— Similar, but without mint mark. *R.I.C. 23b.* ....　26　60

703　— (post-abdication coinage, after 305). PROVIDENTIA DEORVM
QVIES AVGG. Quies and Providentia stg. facing each other (no mint mark).
R.I.C. 77b. ....　38　85

706

704　— (second reign). GENIO POP. ROM. Genius stg. l., PLN in ex. *R.I.C. 90.*　30　70

704A　— HERCVLI CONSERVATORI. Hercules stg. l., resting on club,
PLN in ex. *R.I.C. 91.* ....　42　100

705　**Constantius I,** 305-306 (Caesar 293-305). Æ *follis,* London (as Caesar).
GENIO POPVLI ROMANI. Genius stg. l., LON in ex. *R.I.C. 4a.* ....　200　500

706　— Similar, but without mint mark. *R.I.C. 30.* ....　22　50

707　— (as Augustus). Similar. *R.I.C. 52a.* ....　26　60

708　**Divus Constantius I,** deified 306. Æ *follis,* London. MEMORIA FELIX.
Altar flanked by eagles, PLN in ex. *R.I.C. 110.* ....　32　80

709　**Galerius,** 305-311 (Caesar 293-305). Æ *follis,* London (as Caesar).
GENIO POPVLI ROMANI. Genius stg. l., LON in ex. *R.I.C. 4b.* ....　180　420

		F	VF
		£	£
710	— Similar, but without mint mark. *R.I.C. 15.*	18	42
711	— (as Augustus). Similar. *R.I.C. 42.*	20	45
711A	— GENIO POP. ROM. Genius stg. l., PLN in ex. *R.I.C. 86.*	26	60
712	**Severus II,** 306-307 (Caesar 305-306). Æ *follis,* London (as Caesar). GENIO POPVLI ROMANI. Genius stg. l. (no mint mark). *R.I.C. 58a*	45	110
713	— (as Augustus). Similar. *R.I.C. 52c.*	45	110
714	**Maximinus II,** 310-313 (Caesar 305-310). Æ *follis,* London (as Caesar). GENIO POPVLI ROMANI. Genius stg. l. (no mint mark). *R.I.C. 57.*	20	50
715	—-GENIO POP. ROM. Genius stg. l., PLN in ex. *R.I.C. 89a*	22	55
716	— (as Augustus). Similar, but with star in r. field. *R.I.C. 209b*	20	50
717	**Licinius,** 308-324. Æ *follis,* London. GENIO POP. ROM. Genius stg. l., star in r. field, PLN in ex. *R.I.C. 209c.*	20	50
717A	— Similar, but with S—F in field. *R.I.C. 3.*	18	42
718	— SOLI INVICTO COMITI. Sol stg. l., holding globe, S—P in field, MSL in ex. *R.I.C. 79.*	18	45
719	**Constantine I, the Great,** 307-337 (Caesar 306-307). Æ *follis,* London (as Caesar). GENIO POPVLI ROMANI. Genius stg. l. (no mint mark). *R.I.C. 72.*	30	75
719A	— GENIO POP. ROM. Genius stg. l., PLN in ex. *R.I.C. 88b*	20	50
720	— PRINCIPI IVVENTVTIS. Prince stg. l., holding standards, PLN in ex. *R.I.C. 97.*	32	80
721	— (as Augustus). ADVENTVS AVG. Emperor on horseback l., captive on ground before, star in r. field, PLN in ex. *R.I.C. 133*	34	85
722	— COMITI AVGG. NN. Sol stg. l., holding globe and whip, same mint mark. *R.I.C. 155.*	24	60
723	— CONCORD. MILIT. Concordia stg. l., holding standards, same mint mark. *R.I.C. 195.*	22	55
724	— MARTI CONSERVATORI. Mars. stg. r., holding spear and shield, star in l. field, PLN in ex. *R.I.C. 254.*	22	55
724A	— SOLI INVICTO COMITI. Sol stg. l., holding globe, S—F in field, MLL in ex. *R.I.C. 27*	18	42
725	Æ 3, London. VICTORIAE LAETAE PRINC. PERP. Two Victories supporting shield, inscribed VOT. / P. R., over altar, PLN in ex. *R.I.C. 159.*	15	34

726

726	— VIRTVS EXERCIT. Vexillum, inscribed VOT. / XX., between two captives, PLN in ex. R.I.C. 191.	16	36
727	— BEAT. TRANQLITAS. Altar, inscribed VOT / IS / XX., surmounted by globe and three stars, PLON in ex. *R.I.C. 267*	15	34
727A	— SARMATIA DEVICTA. Victory advancing r., trampling captive, PLON and crescent in ex. *R.I.C. 289*	24	55
728	— PROVIDENTIAE AVGG. Gateway of military camp, PLON in ex. *R.I.C. 293.*	15	34

		F £	VF £
729	**Fausta,** wife of Constantine I. Æ 3, London. SALVS REIPVBLICAE. Empress stg. l., holding two children, PLON in ex. *R.I.C. 300*...............	110	300
730	**Helena,** mother of Constantine I. Æ 3, London. SECVRITAS REIPVBLICE. Empress stg. l., holding branch, PLON in ex. *R.I.C. 299*.........................	110	300
731	**Crispus,** eldest son of Constantine I, Caesar 317-326. Æ 3, London. SOLI INVICTO COMITI. Sol stg. l., holding globe, crescent in l. field, PLN in ex. *R.I.C. 144*.	18	42
731A	— VIRTVS EXERCIT. Vexillum, inscribed VOT. / XX., between two captives, PLN in ex. *R.I.C. 194*.	18	42
732	— BEATA TRANQVILLITAS. Altar, inscribed VOT / IS / XX., surmounted by globe and three stars, P—A in field, PLON in ex. *R.I.C. 211*.	16	36
733	— CAESARVM NOSTRORVM around wreath containing VOT. / X., PLON and crescent in ex. *R.I.C. 291*........................	16	36

734

		F £	VF £
734	— PROVIDENTIAE CAESS. Gateway of military camp, PLON in ex. *R.I.C. 295*....................	15	34
735	**Constantine II,** 337-340 (Caesar 317-337). Æ 3, London (as Caesar). CLARITAS REIPVBLICAE. Sol stg. l., holding globe, crescent in l. field, PLN in ex. *R.I.C. 131*.	16	36
736	— VICTORIAE LAETAE PRINC. PERP. Two Victories supporting shield, inscribed VOT. / P. R., over altar ornamented with wreath, PLN in ex. *R.I.C. 182*....................	16	36
737	— VIRTVS EXERCIT. Vexillum, inscribed VOT. / XX., between two captives, PLON in ex. *R.I.C. 190*.	16	36

737A

		F £	VF £
737A	— BEATA TRANQVILLITAS. Altar, inscribed VOT / IS / XX., surmounted by globe and three stars, PLON in ex. *R.I.C. 236*...............	15	34
738	— CAESARVM NOSTRORVM around wreath containing VOT. / X., PLON and crescent in ex. *R.I.C. 292*....................	15	34
738A	— PROVIDENTIAE CAESS. Gateway of military camp, PLON in ex. *R.I.C. 296*....................	15	34
739	**Constantius II,** 337-361 (Caesar 324-337). Æ 3, London (as Caesar). PROVIDENTIAE CAESS. Gateway of military camp, PLON in ex. *R.I.C. 298*....................	32	80

	F	VF
	£	£

740 **Magnus Maximus,** usurper in the West, 383-388. *N solidus,* London (?).
RESTITVTOR REIPVBLICAE. Emperor stg. r., holding labarum and
Victory, AVG in ex. *R.I.C. 1.* .... *Unique*

The attribution to London of this rare series has not been firmly established,
though Maximus was certainly proclaimed emperor in Britain and it is
well attested that the principal city of the British provinces bore the name
'Augusta' in the late Roman period (Ammianus Marcellinus XXVII, 8, 7;
XXVIII, 3, 7).

741

741 — VICTORIA AVGG. Two emperors enthroned facing, Victory hovering
in background between them, AVGOB in ex. *R.I.C. 2b.* 12500 40000
Maximus appears to have struck a similar type in the name of the eastern
emperor Theodosius I (cf. R.I.C. 2a), though it is presently known only
from a silver-gilt specimen preserved in the British Museum.

742 *R siliqua,* London (?). VOT. / V. / MVLT. / X. within wreath, AVG below.
R.I.C. 4.... 1200 3400
742A — VICTORIA AVGG. Victory advancing l., AVGPS in ex. *R.I.C. 3.*....... 1100 2800

4. IMITATIONS OF ROMAN COINS PRODUCED IN BRITAIN

At certain periods during the three and a half centuries of its occupation Roman Britain seems to
have been the source of much local imitation of the official imported coinage. This began soon
after the Claudian invasion in A.D. 43 when significant quantities of sestertii, dupondii and asses
(especially the last) were produced in the newly conquered territory, as evidenced by the frequency
of their occurrence in archaeological finds. The technical excellence of many of these 'copies',
together with the surprising extent of their minting, would seem to indicate that some, at least, of
these coins were produced with official sanction in order to make good an unexpected deficiency
in the currency supply. Others are much poorer and well below weight, representing the 'unofficial'
branch of this operation, some of it probably emanating from territory as yet unconquered. As
conditions in the new province settled down rapid Romanization and urbanization of British society
brought a general increase in wealth, and with it a much greater volume of currency flowing into
the country. Local imitation now virtually ceased, except for the occasional activities of criminal
counterfeiters, and this state of affairs lasted down to the great political crisis and financial collapse
of the second half of the 3rd century. At this point large scale minting of imitations of the debased
antoniniani of the late 260s and early 270s began in Britain and in the other northwestern provinces,
all of which had been serioulsy affected by the political dislocation of this turbulent era. This
class of imitations is usually referred to as 'barbarous radiates', the emperor's spiky crown being
a constant and conspicuous feature of the obverses. Most frequently copied were the antoniniani
of the Gallic rulers Tetricus Senior and Tetricus Junior (ca. 270-273) and the posthumous issues
of Claudius Gothicus (died 270). The quality of the 'barbarous radiates' is variable in the extreme,
some exhibiting what appears to be a revival of Celtic art forms, others so tiny that it is virtually

impossible to see anything of the design. Their production appears to have ended abruptly with Aurelian's reconquest of the western provinces in 273. A similar phenomenon, though on a lesser scale, occurred in the middle decades of the following century when normal life in Britain was again disrupted, not only by usurpation but additionally by foreign invasion. With supplies of currency from the Continent temporarily disrupted local imitation, particularly of the 'Æ 2' and 'Æ 3' issues of Constantius II and the usurper Magnentius, began in earnest. How long this continued is difficult to determine as life in the island province was now subject to increasingly frequent episodes of dislocation. By now urban life in Britain was in serious decline and when Roman rule ended early in the 5th century, bringing a total cessation of currency supplies, the catastrophic decline in monetary commerce in the former provinces rendered it no longer necessary for the deficiency to be made good.

		F £	VF £
743	**Agrippa,** died 12 B.C. Æ as, of irregular British mintage, imitating the Roman issue made under Agrippa's grandson Caligula, A.D. 37-41. S. C. Neptune stg. l., holding dolphin and trident. .... *The large official issue of Agrippa asses was made shortly before the Claudian invasion of Britain in A.D. 43 and would thus have comprised a significant proportion of the 'aes' in circulation at this time. In consequence, it would soon have become familiar to the new provincials providing an ideal prototype for imitation.*	55	140
744	**Claudius,** 41-54. Æ *sestertius,* of irregular British mintage. SPES AVGVSTA S. C. Spes walking l., holding flower.	130	400
745	Æ *dupondius,* of irregular British mintage. CERES AVGVSTA S. C. Ceres enthroned l., holding corn- ears and torch.	50	130

746

746	Æ *as,* of irregular British mintage. S. C. Minerva advancing r., brandishing spear and holding shield. .... *This is by far the commonest of the Claudian imitations and the prototypes must have represented the bulk of the aes coinage carried by the legions at the time of the invasion. The martial type may well have been specially selected as a suitable theme for the initial import of coinage into the newly conquered territory.*	45	120
747	**Nero Claudius Drusus,** father of Claudius, died 9 B.C. Æ *sestertius,* of irregular British mintage. TI. CLAVDIVS CAESAR AVG. P. M. TR .P. IMP. S. C. Claudius seated l. on curule chair amidst arms .... *This type was issued by Claudius half a century after his father's death and would thus have been prominently represented in the initial wave of coinage imported into the new province.*	150	450
748	**Antonia,** mother of Claudius, died A.D. 37. Æ *dupondius,* of irregular British mintage. TI. CLAVDIVS CAESAR AVG P.M. TR. P. IMP. P. P. S. C. Claudius stg. l., holding simpulum. .... *Another Claudian issue for a deceased parent, this represents one of only two dupondius types struck during this reign and would have entered Britain in significant quantities at the time of the invasion in A.D. 43.*	90	300

749A   749B   749C

		F £	VF £
749	**'Barbarous radiates',** ca. 270-273. British and Continental imitations of billon *antoniniani*, principally of Divus Claudius II (A), Tetricus Senior (B) and Tetricus Junior (C). The inscriptions are usually blundered and the types sometimes unrecognizable. British mintage can only be established by provenance.	7	15
750	**Barbarous 4th century,** mostly of the second half of the century, and principally imitated from 'Æ 2' and 'Æ 3' issues of the later Constantinian period, notably those of Constantius II ('soldier spearing fallen horseman' type), and the usurpers Magnentius and Decentius ('two Victories' type). The copies, especially those of Magnentius and Decentius, are often of excellent style and execution, though the legends frequently contain small errors. Those of Constantius II are sometimes very barbarous and poorly struck, occasionally over regular issues of the earlier Constantinian period. Again, the likelihood of British mintage can only be established by provenance.	7-12	14-18

Nigel Mills
Coins and artefacts

Wanted: all metal detecting finds

PO BOX 53126, London, E18 1YR.
Phone: 02085042569 Mobile: 07803200825
Email:nigelmillscoins@gmail.com
Website: www.nigelmills.net

Grading of Hammered Coins

As the name suggests, hammered coins were struck by hand with a hammer. This can lead to the coin being struck off centre, double struck, weak in the design, suffer cracks or flan defects. It is important to take these factors into account when assessing the grade of this series. Value is considerably reduced if the coin is holed, pierced, plugged or mounted.

Extremely Fine	**Very Fine**	**Fine**
Design and legends sharp and clear.	Design and legends still clear but with slight evidence of wear and/or minor damage.	Showing quite a lot of wear but still with design and legends distinguishable.

William I PAXS type penny

Henry VIII 1st coinage gold Angel

Edward VI silver shilling

EARLY & MIDDLE ANGLO-SAXON KINGDOMS & MINTS (c.650-973)

Approximate extent of Danelaw

Approximate extent of Hiberno-Norse Kingdom of York

NORTHUMBRIA

York

Lincoln
Chester
Newark (?)
Derby
Nottingham
Stafford
Shrewsbury
Leicester
Stamford (?)
Norwich
Tamworth
EAST ANGLIA
MERCIA
Thetford
Northampton
Huntingdon
Warwick
Hereford
Newport
Bedford
Buckingham
Hertford
Maldon
Gloucester
Oxford
Malmesbury
Wallingford
London
Bath
Rochester
Canterbury
Wilton
Winchester
KENT
Dover
Barnstaple
Langport
Lympne
Shaftesbury
Southampton
Lewes
WESSEX
Exeter
Bridport
Wareham
Chichester
Totnes

Timeline Auctions
Inc. Gregory's Est.1858

We are accepting single entries and collections
of Anglo-Saxon coins & antiquities

www.timelineauctions.com

Sold for:
£3,025

EARLY ANGLO-SAXON PERIOD, *c*. 600-*c*. 775

The withdrawal of Roman forces from Britain early in the 5th century A.D. and the gradual decline of central administration resulted in a rapid deterioration of the money supply. The arrival of Teutonic raiders and settlers, even in relatively small numbers, disrupted life and it was probably not until late in the 6th century that renewed political, cultural and commercial links with the kingdom of the Merovingian Franks led to the appearance of small quantities of Merovingian gold *tremisses* (one-third solidus) in England. A purse containing 37 such pieces (plus 3 gold blanks and 2 ingots) was found in the Sutton Hoo ship-burial. Native Anglo-Saxon gold *thrymsas* were minted from about the 630s, initially in the style of their continental prototypes or copied from obsolete Roman coinage and later in pure Anglo-Saxon style. The mixed Crondall hoard of 101 gold coins (1 Byzantine, 24 Merovingian or Frankish, 69 Anglo-Saxon, 7 others) gives structure to the arrangement of thrymsas. By the middle of the 7th century the gold coinage was being increasingly debased with silver, and gold had been superseded entirely by about 675.

These silver coins, contemporary with the *deniers or denarii* of the Merovingian Franks, are the first English pennies, though they are commonly known today as *sceats* or *sceattas* (pronounced 'skeets' or 'shatters' a term more correctly translated as 'treasure' or 'wealth'; the singular is *sceat* not *sceatta*, which is the adjective). They provide important material for the student of Anglo-Saxon art. Indeed, it could be said that, until recently, the largely anonymous, anepigraphic, nature of the sceatta coinage detracted from its numismatic character, however, Anna Gannon's work on the subtle iconography of this period has elevated its status significantly.

Though the earliest ('primary') sceats are a transition from the gold thrymsa coinage, coins of new ('secondary') style were soon developed which were also copied, and issued in substantial numbers (probably tens of millions) as a trading currency, by the Frisians of the Low Countries ('Continental'), evidencing the significant volume of North Sea trade, and their central role in the economic resurgence. Early coins are of good silver content, though the quality deteriorates early in the 8th century, with weights then averaging around 1.00gms. The secondary sceats exist in numerous varied types, though the survival rate, generally is low and for some types, extremely low. Many can be regarded as propaganda during the Conversion Period, though the iconography is often, and probably intentionally, ambiguous, to broaden their appeal to differing cultural traditions in Anglo-Saxon England. As well as the official issues there are mules and other varieties, which may be contemporary imitations; there is no clear line of demarcation. The 'eclectic' types are those which do not sit comfortably in the current, alphabetic, Serial classification. Many of the sceats were issued at the time of Aethelbald King of Mercia, (A.D. 716-757) who was overlord of the southern English, but as few bear inscriptions it is only in recent years that research has permitted their correct dating and the attribution of certain types to specific areas. The Aston Rowant (Oxon.) hoard of 324 sceats, deposited *c*. 710, separates the primary and secondary phases.

Through recent detector finds and continued research, a definitive classification is evolving but remains fluid. The arrangement given below is informed by Michael Metcalf's work on the series, developing Rigold's alphabetical classification. In this listing, the primary sceats are followed by the Continental then the secondary and, finally, the eclectic. This is not chronologically precise as there is some overlap, but has been adopted for ease of reference and identification. This list is more extensive than previously published in *Coins of England* but is not exhaustive. The catalogue numbers previously in use have been retained for the thrymsas and primary sceats but the secondary and Continental have been renumbered (the 'old' S. number given in brackets) as the issues regarded as 'eclectic' have now been given a separate section. The reference 'B.M.C.' is to the type given in *British Museum Catalogue: Anglo-Saxon Coins*. The reference *M* is to an illustration, and *M. p.* to a page, in Metcalf (below).

Major works of reference include:

Metcalf, D. M. *Thrymsas and Sceattas in the Ashmolean Museum,* Vols I-III.

Gannon, A. *Sylloge of Coins of the British Isles, vol. 63. British Museum. Anglo-Saxon Coins. Part i. Early Anglo-Saxon Coins and Continental Silver Coins of the North Sea, c.600-760.* 2013.

Gannon, A. *The Iconography of Early Anglo-Saxon Coinage* (2003)

Rigold, S. E. '*The two primary series of sceattas*', *B.N.J.*, XXX (1960).

Sutherland, C. H. V. *Anglo-Saxon Gold Coinage in the light of the Crondall Hoard* (1948).

Abramson, T. *Sceattas, An Illustrated Guide* (2006)

Op den Velde, W. & Klaassen, C. J. F. *Sceattas and Merovingian Deniers from Domburg and Westenschovwen.* (2004).

Previous years' catalogue number is shown in brackets where applicable.

ᚠ ᚢ ᚦ ᚩ ᚱ ᚳ · ᚷ ᚹ ᚻ ᚾ ᛁ ᛄ ᛇ ᛈ ᛉ ᛋ ᛏ ᛒ ᛖ ᛗ ᛚ ᛝ ᛞ ᛟ ᚪ ᚫ ᛠ ᚣ

f u th o r k z w h n i j ih p x s t b e m l ng d oe a Æ ea y

Early Anglo-Saxon Runes (Futhark)

GOLD

752

	F	VF
	£	£

A.   EARLY PIECES, OF UNCERTAIN MONETARY STATUS

751 Thrymsa. Name and portrait of Bishop Liudhard (chaplain to Queen Bertha
of Kent). R. Cross. .... *Extremely rare*

752 Solidus. Imitating solidi of Roman rulers. Blundered legends, some
with runes. .... *Extremely rare*

753   754   758

B.   CRONDALL TYPES, *c.* 620 – *c.* 645

Twelve different types, which are almost certainly English, were found in the Crondall hoard
of 1828. All are thrysmas, containing 40-70% gold.

No.	Description	F	VF
753	'Witmen' type. Bust r. with trident. R. Cross. Legend normally blundered. *M. 1-21*	1350	4000
754	London-derived type. Head r. with pseudo-legend. R. Cross. Pseudo-legend. *M. 22-32*	1450	5250
755	'Licinius' type. Elegant imitation of Roman triens. Bust l. R. VOT XX. *M. 33-41*	2250	8500
756	'LEMC' type. Head l. R. Maltese cross with letters L, E, M, C in angles, or cross on steps. *M. 42-9*	1650	6250
757	'LONDINIV' type. Facing bust, crosslets l. and r. R. Tall cross, LONDVNIV and pseudo-legend around. *M. 51-7*	2250	8000
758	Eadbald of Kent (616-40) London. Bust r. AVDVARLD REGES. R. Cross on globule, LONDENVS. Usually garbled. *M. 50*	3750	15000
758A	— Canterbury. As 758 but DOROVERNVS M. *M-*	4250	16500
759	Other crude types, usually with head or bust, R. Cross. *M. 58-72*	975	3250

C.   ULTRA-CRONDALL TYPES, *c.* 620 – *c.* 655

Thrymsas not represented in the Crondall hoard, but probably of the same date range.

760   761   762

No.	Description	F	VF
760	'Benutigo' type. Bust r., blundered legend. R. Cross on steps, runic legend (Benutigoii?)	2000	7500
761	'Wuneetton' type. Bust r., cross before. R. Cross. Blundered legend (WVNEETON or similar). *M. 77*	1450	5000
762	'York' type. Stylised face, crosslets to l. and r., squared pattern beneath. R. Cross. Blundered legend. *M. 76*	2500	9000
762A	— similar, but rev. with four 'faces' around central square. *M. p.51*	2750	10500

D.   POST-CRONDALL TYPES, *c.* 655 – *c.* 675

Pale gold types, visibly debased and sometimes almost silvery, containing 10-35% gold. The description "standard" is a reference to the Roman legionary ensign bearing the legend e.g. VOTIS X MVLTIS XX also carried in Anglo-Saxon episcopal processions. The legend is reduced to TOTII on the coinage and may be described as the "votive standard".

764	766	767	768A

		F £	VF £
764	'Crispus' type. Helmeted bust, r. CRISPVS NOB CAES. R. Cross and XX in wreath, runic legend DESAIONA. *N.7*	2000	8000
764A	'Daisy and annulet-cross' type. Flower pattern. R. annulet Latin cross in pseudo wreath.	1850	7500
765	'Concordia' type. Radiate bust r. R. Clasped hands. *N.5*	2500	9000
766	'Oath-taking' type. Bust r. or l. with hand placed against cross. R. Lyre-shaped object, or eight-rayed symbol. *N.6*	1850	7500
767	'Two emperors' type. Helmeted bust r. R. Bust of angel with wings above two facing heads. *M. 79-80*	950	3000
768	'Pada', Type Ia. Helmeted bust r. R. Runic PADA on panel. *M.p.73.*	1100	3500
768A	— Type Ib. Similar. R. Standard TTXX, PADA in runes in legend. *M. 81*	850	2750

769	771	772

769	— Type IIa. bust r. R. PADA in runes in field, blundered legend around, *M.p.73.*	750	2500
770	— Type III. bust r. R. Cross with annulets in angles, legend includes runic PADA and other lettering *M.p.73.*	700	2250
771	'Vanimundus', Type A. bust r. holding sceptre. R. Cross, with CA in lower angles. VANIMVNDVS MONE. *M.p.82*	950	3250
772	— Type B. Similar. R. Small cross in double circle of dots. *M. 84*	850	3000

SILVER

773

SCEATTA COINAGE, *c.* 675 – *c.* 760

A.   EARLY TRANSITIONAL TYPES BY THRYMSA MONEYERS, c.675 – c.685

773	'Pada', Type III. As 770, but silver. *M. 82, M. p. 73-9*	375	1350
774	'Vanimundus', Type B. As 772, but silver. *M. 85-7. M. p. 80-4*	425	1500

B.   PRIMARY PHASE, *c.* **680 –** *c.* **710**

Minted in various regions of south-eastern and eastern England.

775

	F	VF
	£	£

775   **Series A 2a**. Radiate bust r., TIC. ℞. Standard, TOTII. Several varieties.................. 80   225

776   777

776   **Series BX**. Diademed bust r., VANTAVMA or similar. ℞. Bird r. above cross
on steps, annulets and pellets in field vary. *B.M.C. 26. M. 97-9, M. p. 99*   100   275

777   **Series BI**. Diademed head r. within serpent circle. ℞. Bird r. on cross. Some with
symbols by bird. *B.M.C. 27a. M. 100-106, M. 113-16*   50   150

777A: varieties   778

777A **Series BIIIA**, Type 27a. Diademed head r. with either protruding jaw or pointed nose,
symbols before, serpent circle. ℞. Full bodied or linear bird on cross within
serpent circle, annulets either side, pellets below. *M. p. 158-65*   65   200

778   **Series BZ**. Abstract facing head. ℞. Simplified bird on cross in linear style,
blundered legend. *BMC 29a, M. 138-9. M. p. 136-7*..............................   90   240

779 C1   779 C2

779   **Series C**. Radiate bust r., similar to 775 but runic ᚠᛗᚳᚠ replaces TIC.
℞. Variety C1, standard, TOTII; variety C2, four crosses around standard,
variety C2, cross abuts standard. *B.M.C. 2b. M. 117-125, 132-2. M. P. 106-13*   45   125

780

780   Attributed to King Aethelred of Mercia (674-704). Degenerate head. ℞. 'Æthiliræd' in
runes in two lines. *M. 134-5, M. p. 120-4*   225   700

781

	F	VF
	£	£

781 **Series F**. Bust r., with pelleted helmet, blundered legend. R. Small cross on steps, arrangement of surrounding annulets and letters "T" and "I" varies, as do styles. *M. 136-7, M. p. 125-32* 65 225

782: various styles

782 **Series Z**. Broad facing portrait (Christ?) with forked or straight beard. R. Hound running r., legs straight or crossed, tail curled beneath or above, erect ears sometimes with chevrons above, various styles known. Some coarse. *BMC 66, M. 140-2, M. p. 137-8* 225 800

782A

782A **Series Z-related**. Skeletal hound r., perhaps copy of 782. R. Saltire standard or cross-crosslet design, various styles known. *M. 143-4, M. p. 138-9* 135 475

783

783 **'Vernus' group**, Types 2b, 3b and 91. Degenerate head r., VER before, execution deteriorates in later issues. R. Standard, various styles known. *M. 146-8, M. p. 140-6* 50 150

784

784 **'Saroaldo'**, Type 11. Bust r. becoming increasingly stylized R. Pseudo-legend SAROALDO(?) around standard. Some with FIT/RV inscribed (rare) or with saltire and pellets, various styles. *M. 151-3, M. p. 147-51* 80 275

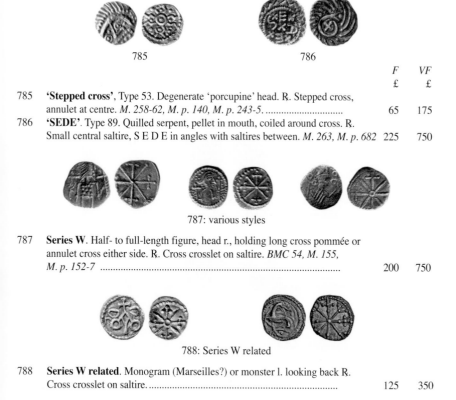

		F £	VF £
785	**'Stepped cross'**, Type 53. Degenerate 'porcupine' head. R. Stepped cross, annulet at centre. *M. 258-62, M. p. 140, M. p. 243-5.*	65	175
786	**'SEDE'**. Type 89. Quilled serpent, pellet in mouth, coiled around cross. R. Small central saltire, S E D E in angles with saltires between. *M. 263, M. p. 682*	225	750

787: various styles

787	**Series W**. Half- to full-length figure, head r., holding long cross pommée or annulet cross either side. R. Cross crosslet on saltire. *BMC 54, M. 155, M. p. 152-7*	200	750

788: Series W related

788	**Series W related**. Monogram (Marseilles?) or monster l. looking back R. Cross crosslet on saltire.	125	350

C.   CONTINENTAL ISSUES, *c.* 695 – *c.* 740

Most Continental sceattas emanate from the former Rhine mouth area, Frisia, particularly the emporia of Domburg and Dorestad. The obverse motif of Series E, commonly referred to as the "porcupine", is now recognized as a degenerate diademed bust. Series D bust takes English Series C as its prototype retaining the runic inscription ÆPA.

790

790	**Series E**. Degenerate head enclosing three bars. R Votive standard with TOTII design, various styles.	30	85

790A *VICO*

	F	VF
	£	£

790A —, **'Vico' type**. Degenerate head enclosing bars. ℞. 'Standard' with letters possibly
reading VIC (*wic*, emporium) around central annulet. *M. p. 211-16*........   35   100

790B

790B —, variety D. Degenerate head, various symbols in field. ℞. 'Standard' with four
pellets around central annulet. *Dorestad. M. 209-11.*....................................   30   80

790C

790C —, variety E. Degenerate head. ℞. 'Standard' with four lines and central annulet.
M. p. 216-19..   30   90
790D Later issues. Degenerate head. Innumerable varieties. ℞. 'Standard'.
M. 214-53, M. p. 222-42....   30   80

791

791   —, plumed bird, usually r. ℞. Standard with a variety of symmetrical geometric
symbols. *M. 190-3, M. p.206-11*   45   130

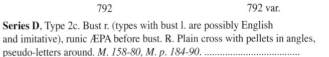

792    792 var.

792   **Series D**, Type 2c. Bust r. (types with bust l. are possibly English
and imitative), runic ÆPA before bust. ℞. Plain cross with pellets in angles,
pseudo-letters around. *M. 158-80, M. p. 184-90.*   35   100

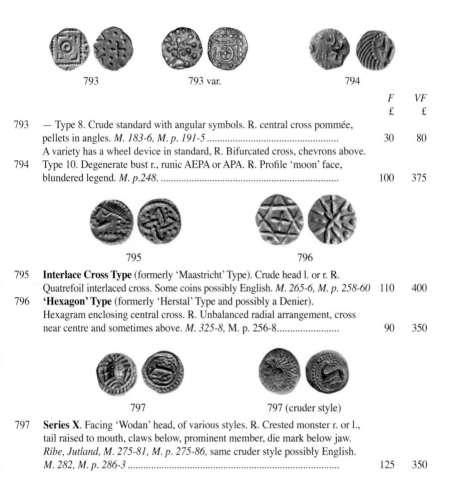

	F	VF
	£	£

793   — Type 8. Crude standard with angular symbols. R. central cross pommée,
pellets in angles. *M. 183-6, M. p. 191-5* 30   80

A variety has a wheel device in standard, R. Bifurcated cross, chevrons above.

794   Type 10. Degenerate bust r., runic AEPA or APA. R. Profile 'moon' face,
blundered legend. *M. p.248.* 100   375

795   **Interlace Cross Type** (formerly 'Maastricht' Type). Crude head l. or r. R.
Quatrefoil interlaced cross. Some coins possibly English. *M. 265-6, M. p. 258-60*   110   400

796   **'Hexagon' Type** (formerly 'Herstal' Type and possibly a Denier).
Hexagram enclosing central cross. R. Unbalanced radial arrangement, cross
near centre and sometimes above. *M. 325-8,* M. p. 256-8........................ 90   350

797   **Series X**. Facing 'Wodan' head, of various styles. R. Crested monster r. or l.,
tail raised to mouth, claws below, prominent member, die mark below jaw.
Ribe, Jutland, M. 275-81, M. p. 275-86, same cruder style possibly English.
M. 282, M. p. 286-3 125   350

SCEATTA COINAGE
D.   SECONDARY PHASE, *c.* 710 – *c.* 760

Die duplication is the exception in this coinage, with a substantial variation of execution and
fabric within each type. It is assumed that quality deteriorates over time and late issues may
be of more interest monetarily than aesthetically. This coinage was issued in all the main
regions of southern and eastern England. Some boundaries between Series remain indistinct
e.g. K and L, C and R.

800 varieties

800   **Series G**, Type 3a. Diademed bust r., heavenward gaze, cross before. R. Standard
with 3 or 4 saltires. *M. 267-70, M. p. 266-72* 65   185

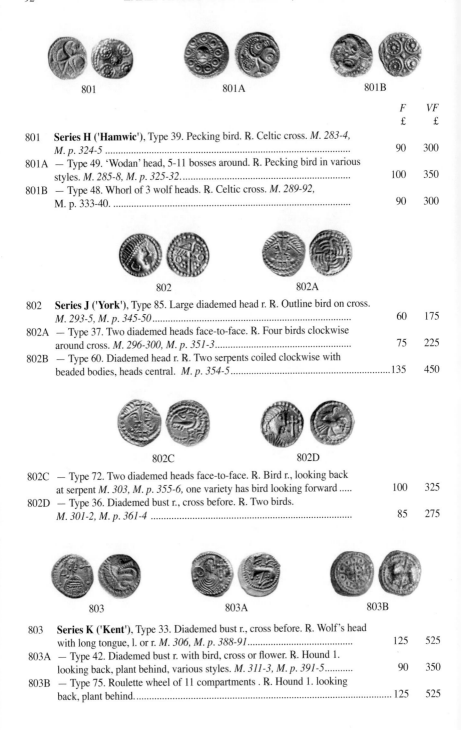

801   801A   801B

	F £	VF £
801 **Series H ('Hamwic')**, Type 39. Pecking bird. R. Celtic cross. *M. 283-4, M. p. 324-5*	90	300
801A — Type 49. 'Wodan' head, 5-11 bosses around. R. Pecking bird in various styles. *M. 285-8, M. p. 325-32*..................................	100	350
801B — Type 48. Whorl of 3 wolf heads. R. Celtic cross. *M. 289-92,* M. p. 333-40.	90	300

802   802A

	F	VF
802 **Series J ('York')**, Type 85. Large diademed head r. R. Outline bird on cross. *M. 293-5, M. p. 345-50*...................................	60	175
802A — Type 37. Two diademed heads face-to-face. R. Four birds clockwise around cross. *M. 296-300, M. p. 351-3*..............................	75	225
802B — Type 60. Diademed head r. R. Two serpents coiled clockwise with beaded bodies, heads central. *M. p. 354-5*...................................	135	450

802C   802D

	F	VF
802C — Type 72. Two diademed heads face-to-face. R. Bird r., looking back at serpent *M. 303, M. p. 355-6*, one variety has bird looking forward	100	325
802D — Type 36. Diademed bust r., cross before. R. Two birds. *M. 301-2, M. p. 361-4*	85	275

803   803A   803B

	F	VF
803 **Series K ('Kent')**, Type 33. Diademed bust r., cross before. R. Wolf's head with long tongue, l. or r. *M. 306, M. p. 388-91*..	125	525
803A — Type 42. Diademed bust r. with bird, cross or flower. R. Hound l. looking back, plant behind, various styles. *M. 311-3, M. p. 391-5*...........	90	350
803B — Type 75. Roulette wheel of 11 compartments . R. Hound l. looking back, plant behind..	125	525

803C

	F £	VF £

803C — Type 32a. Bust r. with cross before, cupped in hand. R. Wolf curled head to tail or wolf headed serpent. *M. 309, 310, M. p. 395-402* 110 450

803D

803D — — Similar. R. Wolf-headed serpent r. or l. *M. 310, M. p. 400*   85   325

803E: Series K, Type 20   obv. var.   obv. var.

803E — Type 20. Bust r. cross or chalice before. R. Standing figure in crescent boat holding cross and hawk. *M. 314-18, M. p. 402-5* 90 350

803F

803F — Type 16. Bust r. floral scroll before. R. Standing figure in crescent boat holding cross and hawk. *M. 314-18, M. p. 402-5* 90 375

804   804C   804D

804 **Series L ('London'), Type 12.** Bust r., LVNDONIA. R. Standing figure in crescent boat holding two crosses. *M. 319-22 M.p.409-11*...................... 110 475

804A — Type 13. Similar. R. Seated figure holding hawk and cross. *M.p.409.* 200 750

804B — Type 14. Similar, but bust l. R. Celtic cross. (as S822). *M. p.427.*...... 110 450

804C — Type 15. Diademed bust r. with cross, no legend. R. Standing figure holding two crosses. *M. 323-6.*.. 80 275

804D — Type 16. Bust r. with floral scroll before. R. Standing figure holding two crosses. *M. 329-30.*.. 85 300

804E — Type 17. Bust l. with floral scroll before. R. Standing figure holding two crosses.. 90 325

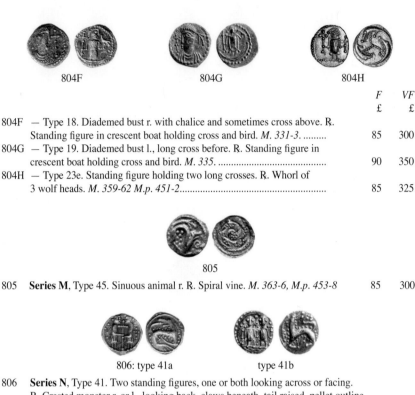

804F 804G 804H

	F £	VF £
804F — Type 18. Diademed bust r. with chalice and sometimes cross above. Ŗ. Standing figure in crescent boat holding cross and bird. *M. 331-3.*	85	300
804G — Type 19. Diademed bust l., long cross before. Ŗ. Standing figure in crescent boat holding cross and bird. *M. 335.*	90	350
804H — Type 23e. Standing figure holding two long crosses. Ŗ. Whorl of 3 wolf heads. *M. 359-62 M.p. 451-2*..	85	325

805

805 **Series M**, Type 45. Sinuous animal r. Ŗ. Spiral vine. *M. 363-6, M.p. 453-8*	85	300

806: type 41a   type 41b

806 **Series N**, Type 41. Two standing figures, one or both looking across or facing. Ŗ. Crested monster r. or l., looking back, claws beneath, tail raised, pellet outline. *M. 368-72, M.p.459-69.*	75	240

807

807 **Series O**, Type 38. Bust r. blundered legend or cable border. Ŗ. Bird r. in torc. *M. 373-5, M.p.470-2*	100	375
807A — Type 21. Similar, but peg-nosed bust l. Ŗ. Standing figure with two crosses. *M. 376, M.p.472-4.*	125	525

SPINK
founded 1666

COINS OF ENGLAND 2017
E-book available on Amazon, iBookstore,
Google, Kobo, OverDrive
and across most other platforms

For more information or enquiries please contact
Tel: +44 (0)20 7563 4000 | Email: books@spink.com
69 Southampton Row, Bloomsbury, London WC1B 4ET

WWW.SPINKBOOKS.COM

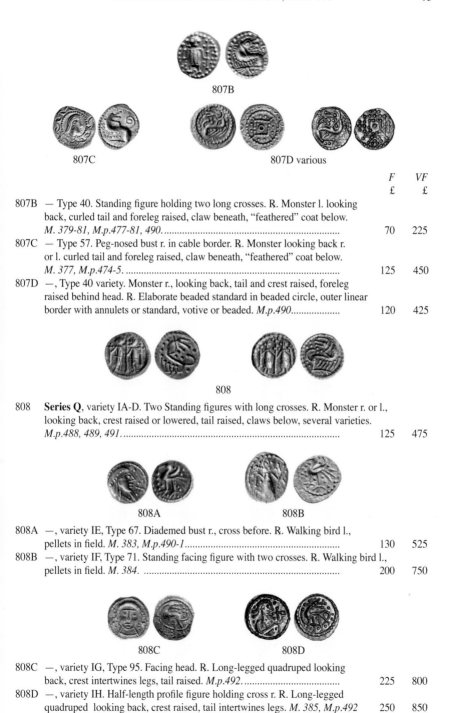

807B

807C   807D various

		F £	VF £
807B	— Type 40. Standing figure holding two long crosses. Ŗ. Monster l. looking back, curled tail and foreleg raised, claw beneath, "feathered" coat below. *M. 379-81, M.p.477-81, 490.*	70	225
807C	— Type 57. Peg-nosed bust r. in cable border. Ŗ. Monster looking back r. or l. curled tail and foreleg raised, claw beneath, "feathered" coat below. *M. 377, M.p.474-5.*	125	450
807D	—, Type 40 variety. Monster r., looking back, tail and crest raised, foreleg raised behind head. Ŗ. Elaborate beaded standard in beaded circle, outer linear border with annulets or standard, votive or beaded. *M.p.490*	120	425

808

| 808 | **Series Q**, variety IA-D. Two Standing figures with long crosses. Ŗ. Monster r. or l., looking back, crest raised or lowered, tail raised, claws below, several varieties. *M.p.488, 489, 491.* | 125 | 475 |

808A   808B

| 808A | —, variety IE, Type 67. Diademed bust r., cross before. Ŗ. Walking bird l., pellets in field. *M. 383, M.p.490-1* | 130 | 525 |
| 808B | —, variety IF, Type 71. Standing facing figure with two crosses. Ŗ. Walking bird l., pellets in field. *M. 384.* | 200 | 750 |

808C   808D

| 808C | —, variety IG, Type 95. Facing head. Ŗ. Long-legged quadruped looking back, crest intertwines legs, tail raised. *M.p.492.* | 225 | 800 |
| 808D | —, variety IH. Half-length profile figure holding cross r. Ŗ. Long-legged quadruped looking back, crest raised, tail intertwines legs. *M. 385, M.p.492* | 250 | 850 |

809

	F £	VF £

809   —, variety II. Quadruped l. or r., tail intertwines legs. R. Bird l. wings spread, cross by wing. *M.p.494*..   125   475

810

810   —, variety III. Quadruped l or r. with tail ending with triquetra. R. Bird l. or r. often with triquetra. *M.p.496*   135   500

811

811   — variety IV. Lion r. or l. R. Bird or lion r. or l. *M. p.499, 501*   140   525

812 mules of Series R and Q   812 Q/R mule

812   **Series R and Q** MULES, Type 73. Crude radiate bust r. or l. blundered runes. R. Quadruped or bird r. *M. 388, M.p.496-8 & 518,* vars. R/Q and Q/R mules   85   300

813 (R1)   813 (R3)   813 (R4)

813   **Series R**. Varieties R1-R6, bust r. on pyramidal neck. Epa in runes, sometimes retrograde. R. Standard, various angular symbols in and around. *M. 391-428, M. p. 507-14*..   45   135

813A: Series R7, Spi   813A: Series R10, Wigræd   813A: Series R11, Tilbeorht

813A   —, varieties R7-R12, Head r. or l. with no neck. Spi, Wigræd or Tilbeorht in runes r. or l. R. Standard with angular symbols. *M. 391-428, M. p. 514-23*   50   150

814

815

		F	VF
		£	£

814   **Series S**, Type 47. Female centaur 1. Palm fronds either side, tail
beaded or linear, with or without finial. R̂. Whorl of 4 wolf heads,
beaded tongues meet in centre. *M. 438-41, M. p. 537-44*   100   325

815   **Series T**, Type 9. Diademed bust r., +LEL or + TΛNVM. R̂. Degenerate
'porcupine' head l or r. *M. 442-4, M. p. 545-51*   100   375

816 varieties

816   **Series U**, Type 23. Standing figure facing or profile in crescent boat holding
two crosses. R̂. Pecking bird in vine. *M. 445-52, M. p. 552-569.*   100   375

817

817   **Series V**, Type 7. Wolf and twins. R̂. Bird in stalks of wheat. *M. 453,
M. p. 570-5.*   175   650

E.   **ECLECTIC SCEATTAS, *c*. 710 – *c*. 760**

Included here are groups of types, related often by a common reverse motif (Triquetras, Celtic cross,
interlace, saltire, annulet cross groups and Type 70) that do not easily fit into the main alphabetical
classification, even though there may be some features in common with or derived from the types
therein. There are numerous 'mules' in this coinage, typically imitative combinations of known
obverse and reverse types not official paired. Only a few of these are included.

820: C ARIP group, some varieties

820   **'Carip' group**. Bust r., CARIP, often blundered. R̂. include pecking bird,
wolf-serpent, or standing figure. *M. 336-40, M.p.416-21*   140   525

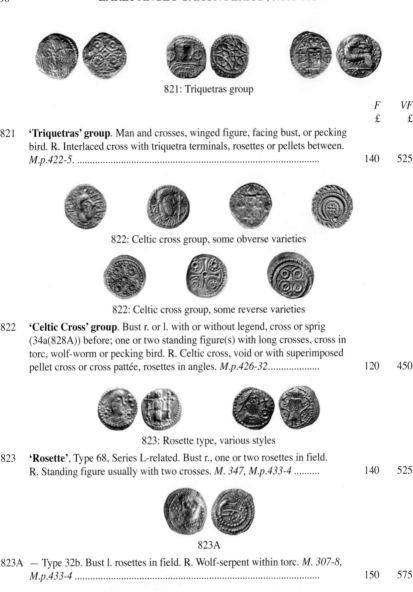

821: Triquetras group

	F £	VF £

821   **'Triquetras' group**. Man and crosses, winged figure, facing bust, or pecking
bird. R. Interlaced cross with triquetra terminals, rosettes or pellets between.
M.p.422-5.   140   525

822: Celtic cross group, some obverse varieties

822: Celtic cross group, some reverse varieties

822   **'Celtic Cross' group**. Bust r. or l. with or without legend, cross or sprig
(34a(828A)) before; one or two standing figure(s) with long crosses, cross in
torc, wolf-worm or pecking bird. R. Celtic cross, void or with superimposed
pellet cross or cross pattée, rosettes in angles. *M.p.426-32*....................   120   450

823: Rosette type, various styles

823   **'Rosette'**, Type 68, Series L-related. Bust r., one or two rosettes in field.
R. Standing figure usually with two crosses. *M. 347, M.p.433-4*   140   525

823A

823A — Type 32b. Bust l. rosettes in field. R. Wolf-serpent within torc. *M. 307-8,
M.p.433-4*   150   575

824:Monita Scorum type   824A

824   **'(Monita) Scorum' type**. Bust r., MONITA SCORVM. R. Degenerate 'porcupine'
head l., figure with two crosses, or triquetra cross. *M.p.435-6.*   325   1100
824A —. Bust r., DE LVNDONIA. R. porcupine l., SCORVM. *M.p.436.*......   350   1250

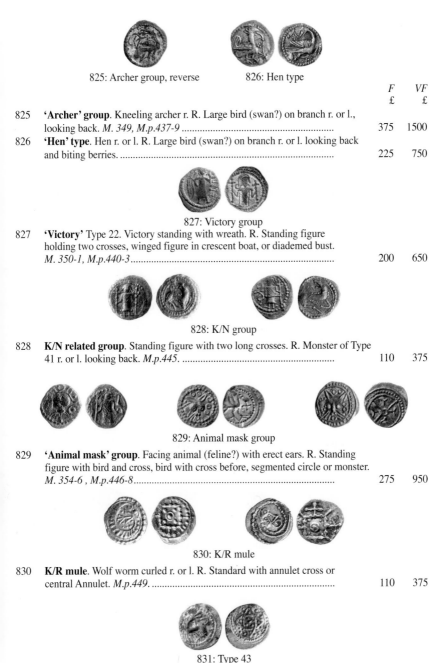

825: Archer group, reverse   826: Hen type

		F	VF
		£	£
825	**'Archer' group**. Kneeling archer r. R. Large bird (swan?) on branch r. or l., looking back. *M. 349, M.p.437-9*	375	1500
826	**'Hen' type**. Hen r. or l. R. Large bird (swan?) on branch r. or l. looking back and biting berries.	225	750

827: Victory group

| 827 | **'Victory'** Type 22. Victory standing with wreath. R. Standing figure holding two crosses, winged figure in crescent boat, or diademed bust. *M. 350-1, M.p.440-3* .... | 200 | 650 |

828: K/N group

| 828 | **K/N related group**. Standing figure with two long crosses. R. Monster of Type 41 r. or l. looking back. *M.p.445.* .... | 110 | 375 |

829: Animal mask group

| 829 | **'Animal mask' group**. Facing animal (feline?) with erect ears. R. Standing figure with bird and cross, bird with cross before, segmented circle or monster. *M. 354-6 , M.p.446-8* .... | 275 | 950 |

830: K/R mule

| 830 | **K/R mule**. Wolf worm curled r. or l. R. Standard with annulet cross or central Annulet. *M.p.449.* .... | 110 | 375 |

831: Type 43

| 831 | — Type 43. Monster of Type 40, l. looking back. R. Interlace cross. (See also S.795.) *M.p.482* .... | 250 | 750 |

832: Fledgling type

	F	VF
	£	£

832 **'Fledgling' type**. Type 33 wolf head r. R. Running fledgling with fish in mouth.
Style degenerates to linear style. .... 275 | 900

833: Saltire standard group, varieties

833 **'Saltire Standard' types**. Two standing figures or bust l. or r.. R. Saltire and
pellets in square. *M. 432-5, M.p.530-2*.. 90 | 275

833A: Saltire standard group, geometric reverses

833A 'Saltire Standard' geometric types. Double croix ancrée or annulet cross.
R. Saltire and pellets in square. *M. 432-5, M.p.530-2* .... 125 | 400

833B: Saltire standard group, Type 70

833B **Saltire-standard and geometric symbols**, Type 70. Many varieties,
typically base. R. Standard. *M. 436-7, M.p.532-4*.................................. 40 | 125

834: Annulets group: some varieties

834 **'Annulet cross' types**. Bust r. or l. with runic legend, 'Wodan' face, coiled
serpent or saltire cross. R. Annulet cross, *M.p.534-6* .... 100 | 375

835: 'Wodan' head varieties

835 **'Wodan' Head**, Type 30. Facing 'Wodan' head various styles some coarse.
R. Two standing figures, standard or Series N, type 41 monster r. *M. 429-31,
M.p.527-30.* .... 135 | 500

836: Flying monster type

836 **'Flying Monster'**. Monster in flight r. or l., looking back, tail erect. R.
     Swan-like bird r. or l., looking back, alternate with groups of pellets on
     limbs of central cross fourchée... 125   450

KINGS OF NORTHUMBRIA AND ARCHBISHOPS OF YORK

The issues associated with pre-Viking Northumbria encompass a late seventh-century emission
of gold (see 762 & 762A), followed by a series of silver sceattas and the subsequent copper alloy
Styca coinage. There are two special presentation issues, Eanred's broad Penny and Wigmund's gold
Solidus, for neither of which is there yet evidence of monetary use within the kingdom.

The stycas developed in two phases, becoming a robust currency of small-denomination coins,
which seem to have been of great practical use. Production may have ceased early in Osberht's reign,
although the old money may have continued in circulation until the Viking capture of York in 867. The
official styca coinage, however, does appear to have been overwhelmed by irregular issues, which may
reflect a period of civil war during the years *c.* 843 to *c.* 855.

James Booth's classification of the silver Sceatta coinage of the eighth century is used here, with
newly discovered types and variants added ('Sceattas in Northumbria' in Hill and Metcalf, *Sceattas in
England and on the Continent, BAR* 128 (1984), pp.71-111, and 'Coinage and Northumbrian History:
*c.*790-*c.*810, in D.M. Metcalf, *Coinage in Ninth Century Northumbria, BAR* 180 (1987), pp.57-90).

For the styca coinage of the ninth century Elizabeth Pirie provides an indispensable
illustrated corpus of the known material in her *Coins of the Kingdom of Northumbria c.700-
867*, 1996. Her classification is however over-complex for practical use, and several aspects
of it, including her division of the coins of Aethelred II between his two reigns, have not been
accepted by other scholars. The division here is that which is customarily adopted in volumes in
the SCBI series. Moneyers' names are shown as they appear on the coinage.

SILVER SCEATTA COINAGE - A: REGAL ISSUES

846: Aldfrith

846 **Aldfrith** (685-705). ALδFRIDVS in semi-uncial lettering around central boss.
     R. Lion(?) l. triple tail above 275   900

847 vars classes

847 **Eadberht** (737-758). Classes A-F. Small cross (mainly). R. Stylized stag, to
     l. or r., various ornaments 95   300

848

		F £	VF £

848 **Aethelwald Moll** (759-765) ΛD+ELΛΑΓDRE (A and R inverted) around central boss. R. His son ΛEDILRED+R (second R reversed), around central cross .... *Extremely rare*

849   850   851

849 **Alchred** (765-774). Small cross. R. Stylized stag to 1. or r., cross below.. 250 800
850 **Aethelred I** (first reign, 774-779/80). R. Stylized stag to 1. or r., triquetra
below.. 425 1350
851 **Aelfwald I** (779/80-788). R. Stylized stag to 1. or r., various ornaments.. 325 1100

SILVER SCEATTA COINAGE - B: JOINT ISSUES BY KINGS OF NORTHUMBRIA AND ARCHBISHOPS OF YORK

852   854   855

852 **Eadberht** with **Abp. Ecgberht** (737-758). Small cross. R. Mitre'd figure
holding two crosses 175 450
853 **Aethelwald Moll** with **Abp. Ecgberht** (759-765). Cross each side...... 750 2500
854 **Alchred** with **Abp. Ecgberht** (765-766). Cross each side 325 1100
855 **Aethelred I,** with **Abp. Eanbald I** (*c.* 779-780). Various motifs. 225 675

SILVER SCEATTA COINAGE - C: REGAL ISSUES WITH NAMED MONEYERS

856

856 **Aethelred I** (second reign, 789-796). R. CEOLBALD, CVDHEARD, HNIFVLA,
TIDVVLF, central motifs vary 95 325

857   858

		F	VF
		£	£
857	– Base metal. R. 'Shrine', "CVDCLS" (the moneyer Cuthgils)	325	1000
858	**Eardwulf** (first reign, 796-806). R. Small cross, CVDHEARD	675	2250

SPECIAL ISSUES

863A

| 861A | **Eanred,** *c.* 830. Æ *penny.* Bust right. R. Cross, part moline part crosslet | 3750 | 15000 |
| 863A | **Abp. Wigmund** (837-849/50). *N solidus.* Facing bust. R. Cross in wreath .... | 35000 | 150000 |

STYCA COINAGE - A: BASE SILVER REGAL ISSUES, *c.* 810 – *c.* 830

859

| 859 | **Aelfwald II** (806-808). R. Small cross, CVDhEARD .... | 275 | 900 |

860

| 860 | **Eanred** (810-841 (total reign)). R. CVDhEARD, CYNVVLF, DAEGBERCT, EADVINI,EDILECH, HERREÐ, [HEARDVVLF, correctly VVLFHEARD], HVAETRED, TIDVINI, VILHEAH, VVLFHEARD, various central motifs | 35 | 110 |

COINS OF ENGLAND & THE UNITED KINGDOM

SPINK *founded 1666*

COINS OF ENGLAND 2017

E-book available on Amazon, iBookstore, Google, Kobo, OverDrive and across most other platforms

For more information or enquiries please contact
Tel: +44 (0)20 7563 4000 | Email: books@spink.com
69 Southampton Row, Bloomsbury, London WC1B 4ET

WWW.SPINKBOOKS.COM

STYCA COINAGE - B: BASE SILVER ARCHIEPISCOPAL ISSUES, *c.* 830 – *c.* 867

861

	F	VF
	£	£
861 **Abp. Eanbald II** (796-835 (total tenure)). R̃. EODWVLF or EDILWEARD	60	175

STYCA COINAGE - C: COPPER ALLOY REGAL ISSUES, *c.* 810 – *c.* 830

862

862 **Eanred.** R̃. ALDATES, BADIGILS, BROD(E)R, FORDRED, FVLCNOD, MONNE, ODILO, W(D)IHTRED, VVLFRED, various central motifs ... 25 75

865

865 **Aethelred II** (first reign, 841-843/4), R. ALGHERE, BRODER, COENRED, CVNEMVND, EANRED, FORDRED, HVNLAF, LEOFDEGN, MONNE, ODILO, VENDELBERHT, W(D)IHTRED, VVLFRED, VVLFSIG , various central motifs 20 70

866: varieties

866 – Leofdegn's 'Special' motifs, R̃. Hound 1., various elaborate cruciform central devices, LEOFDEGN 150 600

867   868   869

867 **Redwulf** (843/4). R. ALGHERE, BROTHER, COENRED, CVDBEREhT, EANRED, FORDRED, HVAETNOD, MONNE 30 100

868 **Aethelred II** (second reign 843/4-849/50), R. EANVVLF, EARDVVLF, FORDRED, MONNE, ODILO, VVLFRED 20 65

869 **Osberht** (849/50-867). R. EANVVLF, EDELHELM, MONNE, VINIBERHT, VVLFSIXT, VVLFRED 25 85

STYCA COINAGE - D: COPPER ALLOY ARCHIEPISCOPAL ISSUES, *c. 830 – c. 867*

870 871

870	**Abp. Wigmund** (837-849/50). R. COENRED, EDELHELM, EDILVEARD, HVNLAF..	20	70
871	**Abp. Wulfhere** (849/50-900). R. VVLFRED	40	150

STYCA COINAGE - E: IRREGULAR ISSUES IN COPPER ALLOY, *c. 843/4 – c. 855*

872	**Irregular Issues** (*c*.843/4-*c*.855). Various types; legends blundered.....	20	50

Further reading: *Pirie E.J.E. Coins of the Kingdom of Northumbria c.700-867. 1996*

Nigel Mills
Coins and artefacts

Wanted: all metal detecting finds

PO BOX 53126, London, E18 1YR.
Phone: 02085042569 Mobile: 07803200825
Email:nigelmillscoins@gmail.com
Website: www.nigelmills.net

In the kingdom of the Franks a reformed coinage of good quality *deniers* struck on broad flans had been introduced by Pepin in 755 and continued by his son Charlemagne and his descendants. A new coinage of *pennies* of similar size and weighing about 20 grains (1.3 gms) was introduced into England, probably by Offa (757-96), the powerful king of Mercia, ca.780, though early pennies also exist of two little known kings of Kent, Heaberht and Ecgberht, of about the same period.

The silver penny (*Lat.* 'denarius', hence the *d.* of our £ *s. d.*) remained virtually the sole denomination of English coinage for almost five centuries, with the rare exception of occasional gold coins and somewhat less rare silver halfpence. The penny reached a weight of 24 grains (c.1.55g), i.e., a 'pennyweight' during the reign of Alfred the Great. Silver pennies of this period normally bear the ruler's name, though not always his portrait, and the name of the moneyer responsible for their manufacture.

Pennies were issued by various rulers of the Heptarchy for the kingdoms of Kent, Mercia, East Anglia, Wessex and by the Danish settlers in the Danelaw and the Hiberno-Norse kings of York, and also by the Archbishops of Canterbury and a Bishop of London. Under Eadgar, who became the sole ruler of England, a uniform coinage was instituted throughout the country, and it was he who set the pattern for the 'reformed' coinage of the later Anglo-Saxon and Norman period.

Halfpence were issued by most rulers from Alfred to Eadgar between 871-973 for S. England, and although all are rare today, it is probable that reasonable quantities were made.

Nos. 873-1378 are all silver pennies except where stated.

NB. Many pennies of the early part of this period have chipped flans and prices should be reduced accordingly.

Further Reading: R. Naismith, *The Coinage of Southern England 796-865*, 2011; C.E. Blunt, B.H.I.H. Stewart & C.S.S. Lyon, *Coinage in Tenth-century England: From Edward the Elder to Edgar's Reform*, 1989.

KINGS OF KENT

874   875

876   877

	F	VF
	£	£
873 **Heaberht** (*c.* 765). Monogram for REX. ℞. Five annulets, each containing a pellet, joined to form a cross..	7250	27500
874 **Ecgberht** (*c.* 780). Similar. ℞. Varied..	1350	6000
875 **Eadberht Praen.** Type 1. (796-798). As illustration. ℞. Varied	1350	5750
875A — Type 2. (*c.* 798). His name around, Ⓜ in centre, ℞. Moneyer's name in angles of a tribrach	1250	5500
876 **Cuthred** (798-807). *Canterbury*. Various types without portrait.............	750	3000
877 — — Portrait. ℞. Cross and wedges or A...	850	3500

878

880   881

		F	VF
		£	£
878	**Anonymous** (*c.* 822-823). *Canterbury.* As illustration or 'Baldred' style head	900	3750
879	**Baldred** (*c.* 823-825). *Canterbury.* diademed head r. ℞. DRVR CITS within inner circle	1250	5250
880	— Cross each side	850	3500
881	*Rochester.* Bust r. ℞. Cross moline or wheel design	1000	4500

ARCHBISHOPS OF CANTERBURY

882   883

881A	**Jaenberht** (765-792). New type (early). Under Ecgberht II of Kent (?). (before *c.* 780 ?) His name around small cross of pellets in centre. ℞. PONTIFEX in three lines	1500	6500
882	Under Offa of Mercia (*c.* 780-792) His name around central ornament or cross and wedges. ℞. OFFA REX in two lines	950	4500
883	— His name in three lines. ℞. OFFA or OFFA REX between the limbs of Celtic cross	1000	4750
884	**Aethelheard** (el. 792, cons. 793, d. 805). With Offa as overlord. First issue (792-?), with title *Pontifex*	850	3750

885   886

885	— Second issue (?-796), with title *Archiepiscopus*	825	3500
885A	— Third issue (*c.* 796-798), with title *Archiepiscopus*. His name and AR around EP in centre. ℞. Moneyer's name, EADGAR or CIOLHARD.....	900	4000
886	— With Coenwulf as overlord. (798-800 ?) Fourth Issue. As last. ℞. King's name in the angles of a tribrach	900	4000

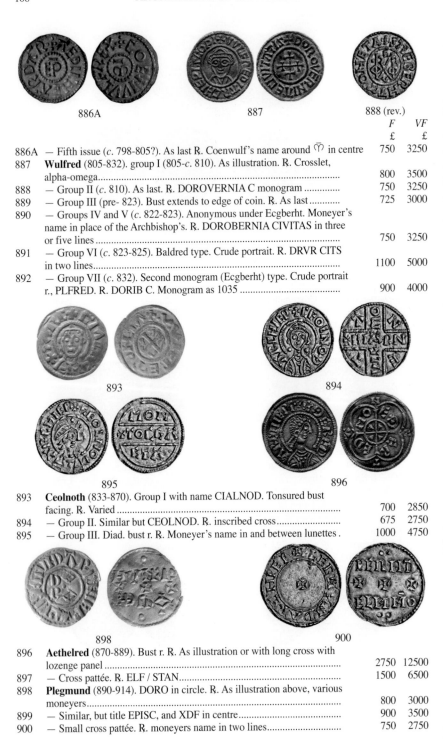

886A 887 888 (rev.)

| | F | VF |
| | £ | £ |

886A	— Fifth issue (c. 798-805?). As last R. Coenwulf's name around ᛘ in centre	750	3250
887	**Wulfred** (805-832). group I (805-c. 810). As illustration. R. Crosslet, alpha-omega..	800	3500
888	— Group II (c. 810). As last. R. DOROVERNIA C monogram	750	3250
889	— Group III (pre- 823). Bust extends to edge of coin. R. As last	725	3000
890	— Groups IV and V (c. 822-823). Anonymous under Ecgberht. Moneyer's name in place of the Archbishop's. R. DOROBERNIA CIVITAS in three or five lines	750	3250
891	— Group VI (c. 823-825). Baldred type. Crude portrait. R. DRVR CITS in two lines...	1100	5000
892	— Group VII (c. 832). Second monogram (Ecgberht) type. Crude portrait r., PLFRED. R. DORIB C. Monogram as 1035	900	4000

893 894

895 896

893	**Ceolnoth** (833-870). Group I with name CIALNOD. Tonsured bust facing. R. Varied	700	2850
894	— Group II. Similar but CEOLNOD. R. inscribed cross.........................	675	2750
895	— Group III. Diad. bust r. R. Moneyer's name in and between lunettes .	1000	4750

898 900

896	**Aethelred** (870-889). Bust r. R. As illustration or with long cross with lozenge panel	2750	12500
897	— Cross pattée. R. ELF / STAN...	1500	6500
898	**Plegmund** (890-914). DORO in circle. R. As illustration above, various moneyers..	800	3000
899	— Similar, but title EPISC, and XDF in centre.....................................	900	3500
900	— Small cross pattée. R. moneyers name in two lines...............................	750	2750

		F £	VF £
901	— Crosses moline and pommée on *obv.*	950	4000
901A	— Halfpenny. As 900	1250	5000

KINGS OF MERCIA

Until 825 Canterbury was the principal mint of the Kings of Mercia and some moneyers also struck coins for the Kings of Kent and Archbishops of Canterbury.

GOLD

902 903

902	**Offa** (757-796). Gold *dinar*. Copy of Arabic dinar of Caliph Al Mansur, dated 157 A.H. (A.D. 774), with OFFA REX added on *rev.*	135000	675000
903	Gold *penny*. Bust r., moneyer's name. R. Standing figure, moneyer's name	37500	200000

A copy of a solidus with a diademed bust appears to read CIOLHEARD and is probably Mercian of this or the following reign.
For further information see: *The Coinage of Offa and his Contemporaries* by Derek Chick, 2010.

SILVER

904 905

904	**Offa** (757-796). Light Coinage. (*c.* 780?-792) *London and Canterbury.* Various types without portraits. Small flans	575	2000
905	— (*c.* 780?-792) *London and Canterbury.* Various types with portraits. Small flans.	850	3750

906 908

906	— East Anglia. Various types with portraits. R. Some with runic letters, small flans	900	4000
907	— — Various types without portraits. R. often with runic letters, small flans	675	2400
908	Heavy Coinage (*c.* 792-796) *London, Canterbury and East Anglia.* Various types without portraits, large flans.	650	2250

909

911

		F	VF
		£	£
909	**Cynethryth** (wife of Offa). Coins as light coinage of Offa. As illustration	2250	9500
910	— *O. As rev.* of last. ℞. EOBA on leaves of quatrefoil............................	1650	7000
911	**Eadberht** (Bishop of London, died 787/789). EADBERHT EP in three lines or ADBERHT in two lines within a beaded rectangle, EP below. ℞. various with name of Offa	950	4500

912

912A

912	**Coenwulf, King of Mercia** (796-821). Gold *penny* or *Mancus* of 30 pence. London, diademed bust of Coenwulf right, finely drawn with four horizontal lines on the shoulders	45000	225000
912A	Penny Group I (796-805). *London.* Without portrait, three line inscription. ℞. Varied	650	2250
913	— *Canterbury.* Name around ⟨Ϻ⟩ as illus. below. ℞. Moneyer's name in two lines..	800	3250

914

915

914	— *Both mints.* Tribrach type..	375	1350
915	— Group II (*c.* 805-810). *Canterbury.* With portrait. Small flans. ℞. Varied but usually cross and wedges..	725	3000

916

919

916	— Groups III and IV (*c.* 810-820). *Canterbury.* Similar but larger flans. ℞. Varied	750	3000
917	— *Rochester.* Large diad. bust of coarse style. ℞. Varied. (Moneyers: Dun, Ealhstan)	800	3500
918	— *London.* With portrait generally of Roman style. ℞. Crosslet	800	3500
919	— *E. Anglia.* Crude diad. bust r. ℞. Moneyer's name LVL on leaves in arms of cross..	650	2500
920	— — *O.* as last. ℞. Various types	625	2400

921

927

	F £	VF £
921 **Ceolwulf I** (821-823). *Canterbury.* Group I. Bust r. R. Varied. (Moneyers: Oba, Sigestef)	1350	5500
922 — — Group II. *London.* Crosslet. R. Varied	950	4000
923 — — Group III. Tall cross with MERCIORV. R. Crosslet. SIGESTEF DOROBERNIA	975	4500
924 — *Rochester.* Group I. Bust r. R. Varied	1000	4750
925 — — Group IIA. As last but head r.	1000	4750
926 — — Group IIB. Ecclesiastical issue by Bp. of Rochester. With mint name, DOROBREBIA, but no moneyer	1250	5500
927 — *East Anglia.* Crude style and lettering with coarse portrait. R. Varied	950	4000

928

929

928 **Beornwulf** (823-825). Group I. *East Anglia.* Bust r. R. Moneyer's name in three lines	1200	5250
929 — Group II. *East Anglia* or *London.* R. Cross crosslet in centre	1050	4500
930 Group III. *East Anglia.* Similar to 928 but moneyer's name in two lines with crosses between	1100	5000
931 **Ludica** (825-827). Bust r. R. Moneyer's name in three lines as 928	4500	18500

932

933

932 — Similar. R. Moneyer's name around cross crosslet in centre, as 929	4750	20000
933 **Wiglaf,** first reign (827-829). *London.* Crude head r. R. Crosslet	3250	12500

COINS OF BRITAIN

PO BOX 2, MONMOUTH, NP25 3YR, UK

BNTA

E-mail: lloydbennett@coinsofbritain.com   +44(0)7714 284 939

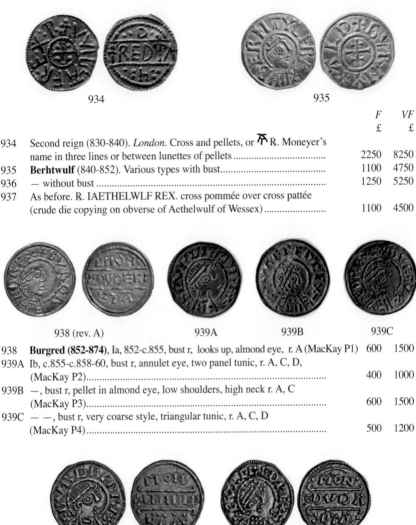

934   935

	F £	VF £
934 Second reign (830-840). *London*. Cross and pellets, or ᛤR. Moneyer's name in three lines or between lunettes of pellets	2250	8250
935 **Berhtwulf** (840-852). Various types with bust	1100	4750
936 — without bust	1250	5250
937 As before. R. IAETHELWLF REX. cross pommée over cross pattée (crude die copying on obverse of Aethelwulf of Wessex)	1100	4500

938 (rev. A)   939A   939B   939C

938 **Burgred (852-874)**, Ia, 852-c.855, bust r, looks up, almond eye, r. A (MacKay P1)	600	1500
939A Ib, c.855-c.858-60, bust r, annulet eye, two panel tunic, r. A, C, D, (MacKay P2)	400	1000
939B —, bust r, pellet in almond eye, low shoulders, high neck r. A, C (MacKay P3)	600	1500
939C — —, bust r, very coarse style, triangular tunic, r. A, C, D (MacKay P4)	500	1200

940A (rev. D)   940B (rev. C)

940A IIa, c.858/60-c.866, bust r, almond eye, neat bust, lips sometimes omitted, r. A, C, D (MacKay H1, H2)	350	900
940B — —, bust r, as Aethelberht of Wessex Floreate type (S.1054), often six pellets below neck, r. C (MacKay H3, H4)	700	1600

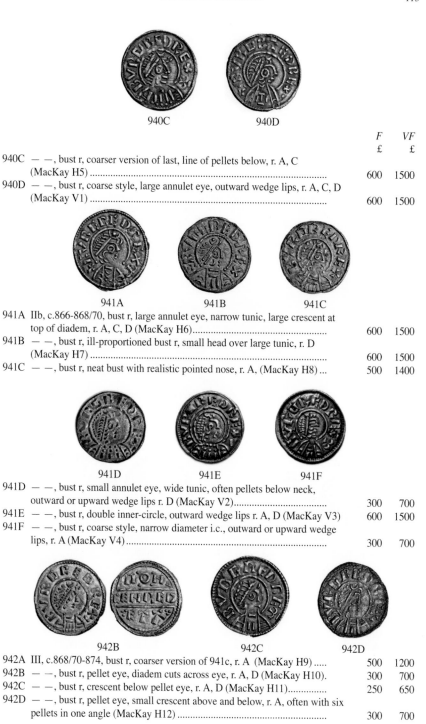

940C 940D

	F £	VF £
940C — —, bust r, coarser version of last, line of pellets below, r. A, C (MacKay H5)	600	1500
940D — —, bust r, coarse style, large annulet eye, outward wedge lips, r. A, C, D (MacKay V1)	600	1500

941A 941B 941C

941A IIb, c.866-868/70, bust r, large annulet eye, narrow tunic, large crescent at top of diadem, r. A, C, D (MacKay H6)	600	1500
941B — —, bust r, ill-proportioned bust r, small head over large tunic, r. D (MacKay H7)	600	1500
941C — —, bust r, neat bust with realistic pointed nose, r. A, (MacKay H8) ...	500	1400

941D 941E 941F

941D — —, bust r, small annulet eye, wide tunic, often pellets below neck, outward or upward wedge lips r. D (MacKay V2)	300	700
941E — —, bust r, double inner-circle, outward wedge lips r. A, D (MacKay V3)	600	1500
941F — —, bust r, coarse style, narrow diameter i.c., outward or upward wedge lips, r. A (MacKay V4)	300	700

942B 942C 942D

942A III, c.868/70-874, bust r, coarser version of 941c, r. A (MacKay H9)	500	1200
942B — —, bust r, pellet eye, diadem cuts across eye, r. A, D (MacKay H10).	300	700
942C — —, bust r, crescent below pellet eye, r. A, D (MacKay H11)	250	650
942D — —, bust r, pellet eye, small crescent above and below, r. A, often with six pellets in one angle (MacKay H12)	300	700

942E (rev. B)

	F	VF
	£	£

942E — —, bust r, rather crude, steeply pitched diadem, outward or upward wedge lips, r. A (MacKay V5)   220   500

Reverse types most commonly found are listed above; type A, closed lunettes (formerly S.938, commonly found); B, open at base and top (formerly S.939, very rare); C, open at sides (formerly S.940, rare); D, 'crooks' without lunettes semi-circles (formerly S.941 scarce); E, as D with large M symbol added above and below dividing legend (formerly S.942, very rare).
For further reading see; MacKay, The Coinage of Burgred 852-874, *BNJ 2015*

943   **Ceolwulf II** (874-*c.* 880). Bust r. ℞. Two emperors seated. Victory above   7500   35000

944

944   — ℞. Moneyer's name in angles of long cross with lozenge centre   1750   7500

KINGS OF EAST ANGLIA

945   947

945   **Beonna,** King of East Anglia, *c.* 758. Æ sceat. Pellet in centre, Runic inscription. ℞. EFE in Roman characters around saltire cross   800   3000

945A   — Similar. ℞. WILRED in runic around pellet or cross   900   3500

945B   — Similar. ℞. Interlace pattern (large flans)   1750   7500

945C   **Alberht** (749-?). Pellet in centre, AETHELBERT (runic) around ℞. Rosette in circle, TIAELRED (runic) around.   3500   15000

946   **Aethelberht** (d. 794). bust r. ℞. wolf and twins   8500   35000

946A   — King's name EDILBERHT around cross and pellets. ℞. Lozenge intersecting large cross fourchée, LVL in angles   4500   17500

947   **Eadwald** (*c.* 798). King's name in three lines. ℞. Moneyer's name in quatrefoil or around cross   950   4500

947A   — King's name around cross or Ⓜ in centre. ℞. Moneyer's name in quartrefoil   1100   5000

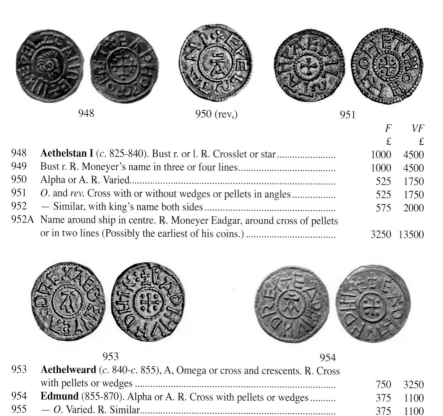

948   950 (rev,)   951

		F	VF
		£	£
948	**Aethelstan I** (*c.* 825-840). Bust r. or l. R. Crosslet or star	1000	4500
949	Bust r. R. Moneyer's name in three or four lines	1000	4500
950	Alpha or A. R. Varied	525	1750
951	*O.* and *rev.* Cross with or without wedges or pellets in angles	525	1750
952	— Similar, with king's name both sides	575	2000
952A	Name around ship in centre. R. Moneyer Eadgar, around cross of pellets or in two lines (Possibly the earliest of his coins.)	3250	13500

953   954

953	**Aethelweard** (*c.* 840-*c.* 855), A, Omega or cross and crescents. R. Cross with pellets or wedges	750	3250
954	**Edmund** (855-870). Alpha or A. R. Cross with pellets or wedges	375	1100
955	— *O.* Varied. R. Similar	375	1100

For the St. Edmund coins and the Danish issues struck in East Anglia bearing the name of Aethelred I, see Danish East Anglia.

Following the treaty of Wedmore in 880 the Viking invaders were ceded control of Eastern Mercia including all territory east of Watling street. Coinage issued in this area after 880 initially imitated Wessex types of Alfred. Independent coinages were struck from early 880s in East Anglia, the east midlands and Northumbria.

DANISH EAST ANGLIA, *c.* 885-915

956	**Aethelstan II** Guthrum (878-890), Cross pattée. R. Moneyer's name in two lines	1750	7500
957	**Oswald** (unknown except from his coins). Alpha or A. R. Cross pattée..	2250	9500
958	— Copy of Carolingian 'temple' type. R Cross and pellets	2500	10000
959	**Aethelred** (*c.*870). As last, with name Aethelred. R. As last, or cross-crosslet	1750	7500
959A	— As 954	1500	6500

Oswald and Aethelred, both unattested historically, are thought to be Anglian kings in the period after the death of Eadmund in 870 but before Guthrum took control of the East Anglia c.880.

960

962

		F	VF
		£	£
960	**St. Edmund,** memorial coinage, Æ *penny,* type as illus. above, various legends of good style	175	400
961	— Similar, but barbarous or semi-barbarous legends	165	375
962	*Halfpenny.* Similar	575	1850
963	**St. Martin of Lincoln.** Sword dividing legend. R. Cross in voided cross. LINCOI A CIVIT.	3000	13500

SOUTHERN DANELAW *c.* 880-910

964   965   970

964	**Alfred.** Imitation of London Monogram types- see 1061, 1062, some very barbarous, bust usually right, R. *Londonia* monogram (wt. c.1.2-1.4g) ..	2000	7500
964A	— Similar, crude bust, blundered legends, R. *Lincolla, ?Roiseng* monogram	4000	16000
965	— Similar to 1062, with moneyer's name (Aelfstan, Heawulf, Herewulf, Vinidat)	2750	10500
966	— Imitation of two line types (1066, 1069), small cross, R. some read REX DORO	450	1250
967	— Similar. R. 'St. Edmund type' A in centre	750	3500
968	— Imitation of Two Emperors type, as 943 and 964	3750	15000
969	*Halfpenny.* Imitation as 1063	800	2750
970	— As illustration	575	1750

Timeline Auctions
Inc. Gregory's Est.1858
We are accepting single entries and
collections of Viking coins & antiquities
www.timelineauctions.com

Sold for:
£70,180

971   975

		F	VF
		£	£
971	— Imitation of Oxford type, as 1071A, ELFRED between ORSNA and FORDA, R. Moneyer's name in two lines (sometimes divided by horizontal long cross)	750	2500
972	— *Halfpenny.* Similar, of very crude appearance	675	2000
973	**Alfred/Archbishop Plegmund.** *Obv.* ELFRED REX PLEGN	1350	5500
974	**Archbishop Plegmund.** Imitative of two line type, as 900	700	2250
975	**Earl Sihtric.** Type as 971. SCELDFOR between GVNDI BERTVS. R SITRIC COMES in two lines	4500	17500

COINAGES OF THE VIKING KINGDOM OF YORK, *c.* 895-920

References are to 'The Classification of Northumbrian Viking Coins in the Cuerdale hoard', by C. S. S. Lyon and B. H. I. H. Stewart, in Numismatic Chronicle, 1964, p. 281 ff.

975A	**Guthfrith.** GV DE F. RE Small cross. R. Moneyer's name in two lines.	3500	13500
976	**Siefred.** C. SIEFRE DIIS REX in two lines. R. EBRAICE CIVITAS (or contractions), small cross. *L. & S. Ia, Ie, Ii*	475	2000
977	— Cross on steps between. R. As last. *L. & S. If, Ij*	575	2500
978	— Long cross. R. As last. *L. & S. Ik*	475	2000

979

980   984

979	SIEFREDVS REX, cross crosslet within legend. R. As last. *L. & S. Ih...*	400	1600
980	SIEVERT REX, cross crosslet to edge of coin. R. As last. *L. & S. Ic, Ig, Im*	425	1750
981	— Cross on steps between. R. As last. *L. & S. Il*	575	2500
982	— Patriarchal cross. R. DNS DS REX, small cross. *L. & S. Va*	450	1850
983	— — R. MIRABILIA FECIT, small cross. *L. & S. VIb*	550	2250
984	REX, at ends of cross crosslet. R. SIEFREDVS, small cross. *L. & S. IIIa, b*	450	1850
985	— Long cross. R. As last. *L. & S. IIIc*	425	1650
986	*Halfpenny.* Types as 977, *L. & S. Ib;* 980, *Ic;* and 983, *VIb*	825	2500

	F £	VF £
987 **Cnut.** CNVT REX, cross crosslet to edge of coin. R. EBRAICE CIVITAS, small cross. *L. & S. Io, Iq*	400	1500
988 — — R. CVNNETTI, small cross. *L. & S. IIc*	375	1350

989   993

989 — Long cross. R. EBRAICE CIVITAS, small cross. *L. & S. Id, In, Ir*....	225	750
990 — — R. CVNNETTI, small cross. *L. & S. IIa, IId*	185	475
991 — Patriarchal cross. R. EBRAICE CIVITAS, small cross. *L. & S. Ip, Is*	185	425
992 — — R.— *Karolus* monogram in centre. *L. & S . It*	750	3000

995   998

993 — — R. CVNNETTI, small cross. *L. & S. IIb, IIe*	175	400
994 *Halfpenny.* Types as 987, *L. & S. Iq; 989, Id; 991, Is; 992, Iu; 993, IIb and e*	625	1850
995 As 992, but CVNNETTI around *Karolus* monogram. *L. & S. IIf*	650	2000
996 **Cnut and/or Siefred.** CNVT REX, patriarchal cross. R. SIEFREDVS, small cross. *L. & S. IIId*	475	1850
997 — — R. DNS DS REX, small cross. *L. & S. Vc.*	450	1750

1000   1002

998 — — R. MIRABILIA FECIT. *L. & S. VId*	300	850
999 EBRAICE C, patriarchal cross. R. DNS DS REX, small cross. *L. & S. Vb*	450	1500
1000 — — R. MIRABILIA FECIT. *L. & S. VIc*	325	900
1001 DNS DS REX in two lines. R. ALVALDVS, small cross. *L. & S. IVa*.....	1350	5250
1002 DNS DS O REX, similar. R. MIRABILIA FECIT. *L. & S. VIa*	525	1750
1003 *Halfpenny.* As last. *L. & S. VIa*	750	2250

1004

		F £	VF £
1004	**'Cnut'.** Name blundered around cross pattée with extended limbs. ℞. QVENTOVICI around small cross. *L. & S. VII*	800	2500
1005	*Halfpenny. Similar. L. & S. VII*	825	2750

1006   1009

1006	**St. Peter coinage,** *c.* 905-915. Swordless type. Early issues. SCI PETRI MO in two lines. ℞. Cross pattée	350	1100
1007	— similar. ℞. 'Karolus' monogram	900	3750
1008	*Halfpenny. Similar. ℞. Cross pattée*	750	2250
1009	**Regnald** (blundered types). RAIENALT, head to l. or r. ℞. EARICE CT, 'Karolus' monogram	3250	15000

1010

1010	— Open hand. ℞. Similar	1850	7500
1011	— Hammer. ℞. Bow and arrow	2500	9500
1012	Anonymous ℞. Sword	1350	6500

TimeLine Auctions
Inc. Gregory's **Est.1858**

We are accepting single entries
and collections of
Anglo-Saxon pennies & antiquities

www.timelineauctions.com

Sold for:
£14,880

Follow us on:

f /TimeLineAuctions

t @TimeLineAuction

ENGLISH COINS OF THE HIBERNO-NORSE VIKINGS OF YORK

	1015		1016		

		F £	VF £

EARLY PERIOD, *c.* 919-925

1013	**Sihtric** (921-927). SITRIC REX, sword. R. Cross, hammer or T............	2750	10500
1014	**St. Peter coinage.** Sword type. Late issues SCI PETRI MO, sword and hammer. R. EBORACEI, cross and pellets	1000	3750
1015	— Similar. R. Voided hammer..	1050	4000
1016	— Similar. R. Solid hammer..	1250	4500

St. Peter coins with blundered legends are rather cheaper.

LATER PERIOD, 939-954 (after the battle of Brunanburh, 937). Mostly struck at York.

1017	**Anlaf Guthfrithsson,** 939-941. Flower type. Small cross, ANLAF REX TO D. R. Flower above moneyer's name	4500	17500
1018	— Circumscription type, with small cross each side, ANLAF CVNVNC, M in field on reverse *(Derby)*	2250	10500
1018A	— Two line type. ONLAF REX. Large letter both sides *(Lincoln?)*........	2000	9500

	1019			1020	

	1021			1022	

1019	— Raven type. As illustration, ANLAF CVNVNC..................................	1500	6250
1020	**Anlaf Sihtricsson,** first reign, 941-944. Triquetra type, ANLAF CVNVNC. R. Danish standard..	1600	7000
1021	— Circumscription type (a). Small cross each side, ANLAF CVNVNC, R. MONETR..	1750	7500
1022	— Cross moline type, ANLAF CVNVN C. R. Small cross....................	1850	8500

		F £	VF £
1023	— Two line type. Small cross. R. ONLAF REX. R. Name in two lines..	1750	7500
1024	**Regnald Guthfrithsson,** 943-944. Triquetra type. As 1020. REGNALD CVNVNC	2500	12500
1025	— Cross moline type. As 1022, but REGNALD CVNVNC...................	2500	12500
1026	**Sihtric Sihtricsson,** *c.* 942. Triquetra type. As 1020, SITRIC CVNVNC	2000	9500
1027	— Circumscription type. Small cross each side	2000	9500
1027A	**Anonymous?** Two line type. Small cross ELTANGERHT. R. RERNART in two lines	1350	4500
1028	**Eric Blood-Axe,** first reign, 948. Two line type. Small cross, ERICVC REX A; ERIC REX AL; or ERIC REX EFOR. R. Name in two lines	4750	17500
1029	**Anlaf Sihtricsson,** second reign, 948-952. Circumscription type (b). Small cross each side, ONLAF REX, R. MONE..	1600	7000
1029A	— Flower type. small cross ANLAF REX R. Flower above moneyer's name................	2250	10500
1029B	— Two line type. Small cross, ONLAF REX. R. Moneyer's name in two lines................	1750	7500
1030	**Eric Blood-Axe,** second reign, 952-954. Sword type. ERIC REX in two lines, sword between. R. Small cross	5250	20000

KINGS OF WESSEX, 786-924

BEORHTRIC, 786-802

Beorhtric was dependent on Offa of Mercia and married a daughter of Offa.

1031

1031	As illustration...	6500	27500
1032	Alpha and omega in centre. R. Omega in centre	6000	25000

ECGBERHT, 802-839

King of Wessex only, 802-825; then also of Kent, Sussex, Surrey, Essex and East Anglia, 825-839, and of Mercia also, 829-830.

1035

1033	*Canterbury.* Group I. Diad. hd. r. within inner circle. R. Various.............	1250	5000
1034	— II. Non-portrait types. R. Various	900	3750
1035	— III. Bust r. breaking inner circle. R. DORIB C...................................	1050	4000

1036	*London*. Cross potent. R. LVN / DONIA / CIVIT....................................	1350	5750
1037	— — R. REDMVND MONE around TA..	1100	4500
1038	*Rochester*, royal mint. Non-portrait types with king's name ECGBEO RHT	900	3750
1039	— — Portrait types, ECGBEORHT...	1050	4250
1040	*Rochester*, bishop's mint. Bust r. R. SCS ANDREAS (APOSTOLVS)....	1350	5250

1041

1041	*Winchester*. SAXON monogram or SAXONIORVM in three lines. R. Cross	950	4000

AETHELWULF, 839-858

Son of Ecgberht; sub-King of Essex, Kent, Surrey and Sussex, 825-839; King of all southern England, 839-855; King of Essex, Kent and Sussex only, 855-858. No coins are known of his son Aethelbald who ruled over Wessex proper, 855-860.

1043   1045

1047

		F	VF
		£	£
1042	*Canterbury*. Phase I (839-c. 843). Head within inner circle. R. Various. *Br. 3*	750	3000
1043	— — Larger bust breaking inner circle. R. A. *Br. 1 and 2*	800	3250
1044	— — Cross and wedges. R. SAXONIORVM in three lines in centre. *Br. 10*	575	2000
1045	— — Similar, but OCCIDENTALIVM in place of moneyer. *Br. 11*	625	2500
1046	— Phase II (*c.* 843-848?). Cross and wedges. R. Various, but chiefly a form of cross or a large A. *Br. 4*	550	2000
1047	— — New portrait, somewhat as 1043. R. As last. *Br. 7*	750	3250
1048	— — Smaller portrait. R. As last, with *Chi/Rho* monogram. *Br. 7*	800	3250

1049

1051

1049	— Phase III (*c.* 848/851-*c.* 855). DORIB in centre. R. CANT mon. *Br. 5*	525	1850
1050	— — CANT mon. R. CAN M in angles of cross. *Br. 6*	700	2750
1051	— Phase IV (*c.* 855-859). Mostly Canterbury rarely Rochester. New neat style bust R. Large voided long cross. *Br. 8*	700	2750
1052	*Winchester.* SAXON mon. R. Cross and wedges. *Br. 9*	750	3000

AETHELBERHT, 858-865

Son of Aethelwulf; sub-King of Kent, Essex and Sussex, 858-860; King of all southern England, 860-865/6.

1053

1053A (rev.)

		F	VF
		£	£
1053	Bust r., R large voided long cross. Mostly Canterbury, also known for Rochester	700	2750
1053A	*O.* As 1053, R large cross pattée	1500	5250

1054

1054	*O.* Diad. bust r., R. Cross fleury over floreate cross	950	3750

COINS OF ENGLAND
& THE UNITED KINGDOM
PRE-DEC MAG ISSUES

SPINK
founded 1666

COINS OF ENGLAND 2017
E-book available on Amazon, iBookstore, Google, Kobo, OverDrive and across most other platforms

For more information or enquiries please contact
Tel: +44 (0)20 7563 4000 | Email: books@spink.com
69 Southampton Row, Bloomsbury, London WC1B 4ET

WWW.SPINKBOOKS.COM

Son of Aethelwulf; succeeded his brother Aethelberht.

1055

1055 As illustration, Wessex Lunettes, Canterbury, usually with bonnet ...	750	3000
1055A— —, London obv. dies in style as Burgred	800	3250
1056 Similar, but moneyer's name in four lines, Canterbury or Winchester	1050	4500

For another coin with the name Aethelred see 959 under Viking coinages.
For further reading see: *Lyons & MacKay,* BNJ 2007

ALFRED THE GREAT, 871-899

Brother and successor to Aethelred, Alfred had to contend with invading Danish armies for much of his reign. In 878 he and Guthrum the Dane divided the country, with Alfred holding all England south and west of Watling Street. Alfred occupied London in 886.

Types with portraits

1057   1058

	F £	VF £
1057 As illustration, Wessex Lunettes, Canterbury, bust with bonnet. r. R. As		
Aethelred I. *Br. 1 (name often* AELBRED)...	925	3500
1057A — —, London obv. dies in style as Burgred	950	3500
1058 — R. Long cross with lozenge centre, as 944, *Br. 5*.................................	2250	9500
1059 — R. Two seated figures, as 943. *Br. 2*...	8500	35000
1060 — R. As Archbp. Aethered; cross within large quatrefoil. *Br. 3*..............	3250	13500

1061   1062

1061 *London.* Various busts. R. LONDONIA monogram, moneyer not named	2250	8500
For contemporary Viking copies see 964.		
1062 — R. Similar, but with moneyer's name (Tilewine) added	2500	10000
1063 — *Halfpenny.* Bust r. or rarely l. R. LONDONIA monogram as 1061	950	3250
1064 *Gloucester.* R. Æ GLEAPA in angles of three limbed cross....................	5250	22500

	F £	VF £

Types without portraits

1065 King's name on limbs of cross, trefoils in angles. ℞. Moneyer's name in quatrefoil. *Br. 4.* 3500 13500

1066   1067

1066 Various styles, Cross pattée, legend in four parts. ℞. Moneyer's name in two lines. *Br. 6* 475 1600
1067 — As last, legend in three parts. ℞ as Edward the Elder, 1087 .... 500 1650
1068 — *Halfpenny.* As 1066.. 650 1850

1069

1069 *Canterbury.* As last but DORO added on *obv. Br. 6a* 550 1750
1070 *Exeter?* King name in four lines. ℞. EXA vertical 4250 16500
1071 *Winchester?* Similar to last, but PIN.. 4250 16500
1071A *Oxford.* Elfred between OHSNA and FORDA. ℞. Moneyer's name in two lines (much commoner as a Viking Imitation - see 971) 925 3750
1072 'Offering penny'. Very large and heavy. AELFRED REX SAXORVM in four lines. ℞. ELIMO in two lines i.e. (*Elimosina*, alms)........................ 13500 45000

For other pieces bearing the name of Alfred see under the Viking coinages.
For further reading see: *Lyons & MacKay, The Lunettes Coinage of Alfred the Great* BNJ 2008.

EDWARD THE ELDER, 899-924

Edward, the son of Alfred, aided by his sister Aethelflaed 'Lady of the Mericians', annexed all England south of the Humber and built many new fortified boroughs to protect the kingdom.
Rare types

1074

1073 *Br. 1. Bath?* ℞. BA.. 2250 9000
1074 — *2. Canterbury.* Cross moline on cross pommée. ℞. Moneyer's name . 1350 6000

		F	*VF*
		£	£
1075	— *3. Chester?* Small cross. ℞. Minster	2750	13500
1076	— *4.* — Small cross. ℞. Moneyer's name in single line...........................	1350	4500
1077	— *5.* — ℞. Two stars	1850	9000

1078   1079

| 1078 | — *6.* — ℞. Flower above central line, name below .... | 2000 | 9500 |

1081   1083

1079	— *7.* — ℞. Floral design with name across field......................................	2000	9500
1080	— *8.* — ℞. Bird holding twig	3250	15000
1081	— *9.* — ℞. Hand of Providence, several varieties.....................................	2750	13500
1082	— *10.* — ℞. City gate of Roman style...	1850	9000
1083	— *11.* — ℞. Anglo-Saxon burg..	1650	7000

Ordinary types

1084   1087

1084	*Br. 12.* Bust l, var. styles ℞. Moneyer's name in two lines	800	3000
1086	— *12a.* Similar, but bust r. of crude style	1250	5000
1087	— *13.* Small cross. ℞. Moneyers name in two lines...............................	225	600
1087A	— — As last, but in *gold*	27500	110000
1088	**Halfpenny**. Similar to 1087	900	3000
1088A	— — ℞. Hand of Providence..	1350	5250

Imitations of the types of Edward the Elder were also struck in the Danelaw territories. They are usually of lighter weight and coarser execution than the official Wessex issues of Edward the Elder.

AETHELSTAN, 924-939

Aethelstan, the eldest son of Edward, completed the re-conquest of territories controlled by the Danes with the capture of York in 927. He decreed that money should be coined only in a borough, that every borough should have one moneyer and that some of the more important boroughs should have more than one moneyer.

1089   1093

		F	VF
		£	£
1089	**Main issues.** Small cross. ℞. Moneyer's name in two lines.....................	275	700
1090	Diad. bust r. ℞. As last	1000	4500
1091	— ℞. Small cross	950	4000
1092	Small cross both sides..	375	1200

1095   1100

1093	— Similar, but mint name added	425	1250
1094	Crowned bust r. As illustration. ℞. Small cross	800	2750
1095	— Similar, but mint name added	850	3000
1096	**Local Issues.** *N. Mercian mints.* Star between two pellets. ℞. As 1089...	900	3750
1097	— Small cross. ℞. Floral ornaments above and below moneyer's name .	1000	4250
1098	— Rosette of pellets each side...	425	1350
1099	— Small cross one side, rosette on the other side	450	1500
1100	*N.E. mints.* Small cross. ℞. Tower over moneyer's name........................	1500	6000

1102

1101	Similar, but mint name added	1650	6250
1102	— Bust in high relief r. or l. ℞. Small cross..	1350	5500
1103	— Bust r. in high relief. ℞. Cross-crosslet...	1350	5500
1104	'Helmeted' bust or head r. ℞. As last or small cross	1100	4500
1104A	**Halfpenny.** Small cross or floral lozenge. ℞. Moneyer's name in two lines.	900	3000

Eadmund was a half brother of Aethelstan. At the start of his reign he lost the kingdom of York and faced renewed Viking incursions into North East England, however, by the end of his reign he had regained control of those territories.

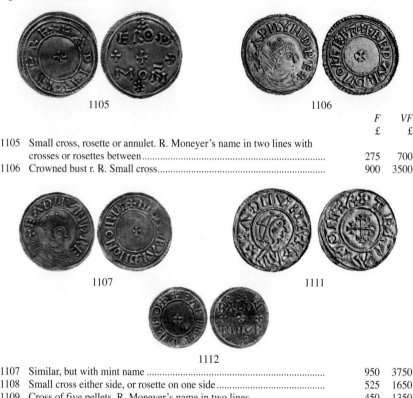

1105   1106

		F £	*VF* £
1105	Small cross, rosette or annulet. ꝶ. Moneyer's name in two lines with crosses or rosettes between	275	700
1106	Crowned bust r. ꝶ. Small cross	900	3500

1107   1111

1112

1107	Similar, but with mint name	950	3750
1108	Small cross either side, or rosette on one side	525	1650
1109	Cross of five pellets. ꝶ. Moneyer's name in two lines	450	1350
1110	Small cross. ꝶ. Flower above name	1500	6000
1111	'Helmeted' bust r. ꝶ. Cross-crosslet	1250	5000
1112	**Halfpenny.** small cross, ꝶ. Moneyer's name in two lines or one line between rosettes	925	2750
1112A	— Flower. ꝶ. As 1105	1100	3500

COINS OF ENGLAND & THE UNITED KINGDOM PRE-DECIMAL ISSUES

SPINK
founded 1666

COINS OF ENGLAND 2017
E-book available on Amazon, iBookstore, Google, Kobo, OverDrive and across most other platforms

For more information or enquiries please contact
Tel: +44 (0)20 7563 4000 | Email: books@spink.com
69 Southampton Row, Bloomsbury, London WC1B 4ET

WWW.SPINKBOOKS.COM

Eadred was another of the sons of Edward. He faced renewed Viking attempts to recover York whose last king, Eric Bloodaxe, he drove out in 954 to finally secure Northumbria for the English.

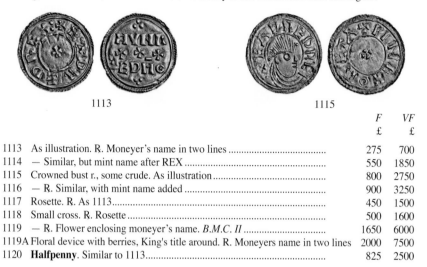

1113   1115

	F £	VF £
1113 As illustration. R. Moneyer's name in two lines	275	700
1114 — Similar, but mint name after REX	550	1850
1115 Crowned bust r., some crude. As illustration	800	2750
1116 — R. Similar, with mint name added	900	3250
1117 Rosette. R. As 1113	450	1500
1118 Small cross. R. Rosette	500	1600
1119 — R. Flower enclosing moneyer's name. *B.M.C. II*	1650	6000
1119A Floral device with berries, King's title around. R. Moneyers name in two lines	2000	7500
1120 **Halfpenny**. Similar to 1113	825	2500

HOWEL DDA, d. 949/950

Grandson of Rhodri Mawr, Howel succeeded to the kingdom of Dyfed *c.* 904, to Seisyllog *c.* 920 and became King of Gwynedd and all Wales, 942.

1121

1121 HOÞÆL REX, small cross or rosette. R. Moneyer's name in two lines . .	13500	52500

EADWIG, 955-959

Elder son of Eadmund, Eadwig lost Mercia and Northumbria to his brother Eadgar in 957.

1122   1123

1122 *Br. 1*. Type as illustration	650	1850
1123 — — Similar, but mint name in place of crosses	850	2750

		F	*VF*
		£	£
1124	— *2.* As 1122, but moneyer's name in one line	1350	4500
1125	— *3.* Similar. R̟. Floral design	1750	6500
1126	— *4.* Similar. R̟. Rosette or small cross	825	2500
1127	— *5.* Bust r. R̟. Small cross	6500	25000

1128

1128	**Halfpenny**. Small cross. R̟. Flower above moneyer's name	1200	4250
1128A	— Similar. R̟. PIN (Winchester) across field	1300	4750
1128B	— Star. R̟. Moneyer's name in two lines	950	3250

EADGAR, 959-975

King in Mercia and Northumbria from 957; King of all England 959-975. He was crowned King of England at Bath in 973 in the first coronation of an English King. His reign was largely free from Viking invasions, leading him to be given the sobriquet of 'The Peaceful'.

PRE-REFORM COINAGE BEFORE 973
It is now possible on the basis of the lettering to divide up the majority of Eadgar's coins into issues from the following regions: N.E. England, N.W. England, York, East Anglia, Midlands, S.E. England, Southern England, and S.W. England. (See 'Anglo-Saxon Coins', ed. R. H. M. Dolley.)

1129   1135

1129	*Br I.* Small cross. R̟. Moneyer's name in two lines, crosses between, trefoils top and bottom	225	525
1130	— — R̟. Similar, but rosettes top and bottom (a N.W. variety)	275	700
1131	— — R̟. Similar, but annulets between	275	700
1132	— — R̟. Similar, but mint name between (a late N.W. type)	475	1500
1133	— *2.* — R̟. Floral design	1350	5000
1133A	Voided cross, lys in angles, R̟. cross pattée dividing alpha and omega	1500	5000
1134	— *4.* Small cross either side	240	575
1135	— — Similar, with mint name	425	1350

1136

		F	VF
		£	£
1136	— — Rosette either side	275	800
1137	— — Similar, with mint name	450	1500
1138	— 5. Large bust to r. R. Small cross	950	4000
1139	— — Similar, with mint name	1350	5250
1140	**Halfpenny**. (8.5 grains / c.0.6 g)) *Br. 3*. Small cross. R. Flower above name	900	3000

1140A

1140A — — R. Mint name around cross (Chichester, Wilton)	1350	4500
1140B — Bust r. R. 'Londonia' monogram	950	3500

For Eadgar 'reform' issues see next page.

Timeline
Auctions

Inc. Gregory's **Est.1858**

We are accepting single entries and collections of
Anglo-Saxon coins & antiquities

www.timelineauctions.com

Sold for:
£14,520

Contact:
+44 [0]1277 815121
enquiries@timelineauctions.com

Follow us on:
f /TimeLineAuctions
t @TimeLineAuction

ASSOCIATION OF INTERNATIONAL ANTIQUITIES DEALERS
AIAD

BRITISH NUMISMATIC TRADE ASSOCIATION
BNTA

KINGS OF ENGLAND, 973-1066

In 973 Eadgar introduced a new coinage. A royal portrait now became a regular feature and the reverses normally have a cruciform pattern with the name of the mint in addition to that of the moneyer. Most fortified towns of burghal status were allowed a mint, the number of moneyers varying according to their size and importance: some royal manors also had a mint and some moneyers were allowed to certain ecclesiastical authorities. In all some seventy mints were active about the middle of the 11th century (see list of mints pp. 144-146).

The control of the currency was retained firmly in the hands of the central government, unlike the situation in France and the Empire where feudal barons and bishops controlled their own coinage. Coinage types were changed at intervals to enable the Exchequer to raise revenue from new dies and periodic demonetization of old coin types helped to maintain the currency in a good state. No halfpence were minted during this period. During the latter part of this era, full pennies were sheared into 'halfpennies' and 'farthings'. They are far rarer than later 'cut' coins.

Further Reading: On the initial reform of the coinage under Eadgar see K. Jonsson, *The NewEra: The Reformation of the Late Anglo-Saxon Coinage* (London: 1987). The nature and purpose of frequent periodic recoinages is explored by I. Stewart, 'Coinage and recoinage after Edgar's reform', in *Studies in Late Anglo-Saxon Coinage*, ed. K. Jonsson (Stockholm: 1990), 455-85. References to individual types for mints and moneyers for much of the first half of the period may be found in K. Jonsson, *Viking Age Hoards and Late Anglo-Saxon Coins* (Stockholm: 1986).

EADGAR, 959-975 *(continued)*

REFORM COINAGE, 973-975

1141

	F	VF
	£	£
1141 **Penny**. Reform Small Cross type. Small diademed bust left. King's name 'Eadgar'. R. Small cross, name of moneyer and mint............................	1250	3750

EDWARD THE MARTYR, 975-978

The son of Eadgar by his first wife, Æthelflaed, Edward was murdered at Corfe in Dorset.

1142

1142 Sole type. As 1141, but reading 'Eadward'.	1500	5000

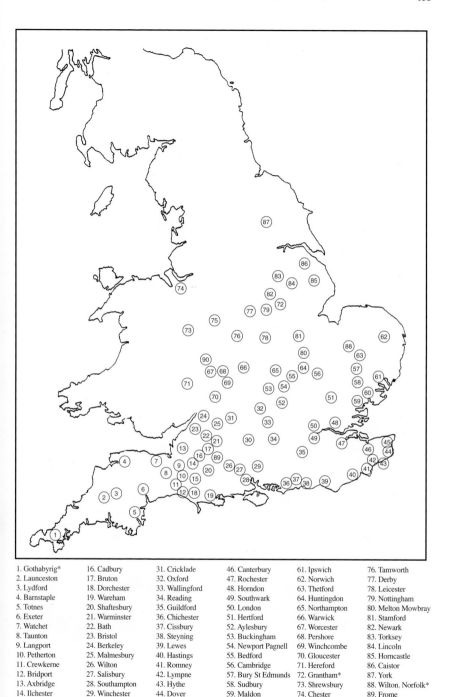

1. Gothabyrig*	16. Cadbury	31. Cricklade	46. Canterbury	61. Ipswich	76. Tamworth
2. Launceston	17. Bruton	32. Oxford	47. Rochester	62. Norwich	77. Derby
3. Lydford	18. Dorchester	33. Wallingford	48. Horndon	63. Thetford	78. Leicester
4. Barnstaple	19. Wareham	34. Reading	49. Southwark	64. Huntingdon	79. Nottingham
5. Totnes	20. Shaftesbury	35. Guildford	50. London	65. Northampton	80. Melton Mowbray
6. Exeter	21. Warminster	36. Chichester	51. Hertford	66. Warwick	81. Stamford
7. Watchet	22. Bath	37. Cissbury	52. Aylesbury	67. Worcester	82. Newark
8. Taunton	23. Bristol	38. Steyning	53. Buckingham	68. Pershore	83. Torksey
9. Langport	24. Berkeley	39. Lewes	54. Newport Pagnell	69. Winchcombe	84. Lincoln
10. Petherton	25. Malmesbury	40. Hastings	55. Bedford	70. Gloucester	85. Horncastle
11. Crewkerne	26. Wilton	41. Romney	56. Cambridge	71. Hereford	86. Caistor
12. Bridport	27. Salisbury	42. Lympne	57. Bury St Edmunds	72. Grantham*	87. York
13. Axbridge	28. Southampton	43. Hythe	58. Sudbury	73. Shrewsbury	88. Wilton. Norfolk*
14. Ilchester	29. Winchester	44. Dover	59. Maldon	74. Chester	89. Frome
15. Miborne Port	30. Bedwyn	45. Sandwich	60. Colchester	75. Stafford	90. Droitwich

*Possible location of uncertain mint

Son of Eadgar by his second wife Ælfthryth, Æthelred ascended the throne on the murder of his half-brother. He is known to posterity as 'The Unready' from 'Unrede', meaning 'without counsel', an epithet gained from the weakness of his royal government.During this reign England was subjected to Viking raids of increasing frequency and strength, and a large amount of tribute was paid in order to secure peace. Large hoards have been found in Scandinavia and the Baltic region and coins are often found peck-marked. There is a high degree of regional variation in the style of dies, particularly in Last Small Cross type, for which readers are advised to consult the following paper: C.S.S. Lyon, '*Die cutting styles in the Last Small Cross issue of c.1009-1017...*', *BNJ* 68 (1998), 21-41.

1143   1144

		F £	VF £
1143	First Small Cross type. Diademed bust left, usually with three pellets before in field. No line to indicate shoulder. *B.M.C I*	850	3000
1144	First Hand type. Diademed bust right, without sceptre. R. Hand of providence between alpha and omega, issuing from cloud composed of parallel curved or angular lines. *B.M.C IIa*	185	500
1145	— —, similar but bust left. *B.M.C IIb*	600	2000

1146   1147

1146	Second Hand type. Diademed bust right, with sceptre. R. Hand of providence between alpha and omega, issuing from clouds with edges that billow outward. *B.M.C IId*	175	475
1147	Benediction Hand type. *O.* as last. R. Hand gives Latin benediction, fields without alpha and omega. *B.M.C IIf*	1250	4000

1148   1150

1148	Crux type. Bare-headed bust left, with sceptre. R. Voided short cross with letters C, R, V, X, in angles. *B.M.C IIIa*	120	300
1149	Small Crux type. Reduced weight, small flans, sceptre inclined to bust such that the base penetrates drapery.	125	325
1150	Intermediate Small Cross type. RX at end of legend separate letters. *B.M.C I*	1250	4250

1151   1152

		F	*VF*
		£	£
1151	Long Cross type. Bare-headed bust left. R. Voided long cross. *B.M.C IVa*	120	300
1152	Helmet type. Armoured bust left in radiate helmet. *B.M.C VIII*...............	135	350
1153	As last but struck in gold.	37500	150000

1154

1154	Last Small Cross type. Diademed bust left, RX at end of legend ligated together as one letter-form. *B.M.C I*........................	100	275
1154A	— —, similar but bust right...	250	700
1155	— —, similar but bust to edge of coin....................................	650	2250

1156

| 1156 | Agnus Dei type. As illustration. *B.M.C X*... | 8000 | 27500 |

ARTHUR BRYANT COINS

Dealers in British coins and medals

www.bryantcoins.com
abcoins@live.co.uk
07768 645 686

BNTA

Son of King Swein Forkbeard of Denmark, Cnut was acclaimed king by the Danish fleet in England in 1014 but was forced to leave; Cnut returned and harried Wessex in 1015. Æthelred II died in 1016 and resistance to the Danes was continued by his son Eadmund Ironside, for whom no coins are known, but upon the latter's death in 1016 Cnut became undisputed king. The following year Cnut consolidated his position by marrying Emma of Normandy, the widow of Æthelred II.

There is a high degree of regional variation in the style of dies, particularly in Quatrefoil type, for which readers are advised to consult the following paper: M.A.S. Blackburn and C.S.S. Lyon, 'Regional die production in Cnut's Quatrefoil issue' in *Anglo-Saxon Monetary History*, ed. M.A.S. Blackburn (Leicester: 1986), 223-72. Some quatrefoil coins have pellets or a cross added in the obverse or reverse fields. There is considerable weight fluctuation within and between the types.

Substantive types

1157   1158

1159

	F	VF
	£	£
1157 Quatrefoil type (c.1017-23). Crowned bust left. *B.M.C. VIII*	120	300
1158 Pointed Helmet type (1024-1030). *B.M.C. XIV*	110	250
1159 Short Cross type (c.1029-1035/6). *B.M.C. XVI*	100	225
1159A — —, similar but sceptre replaced with a banner	750	3250

1160

Posthumous type
1160 Jewel Cross type. *B.M.C. XX*, style as 1163 in the name of Cnut.	700	2750

Type considered to have been struck under the auspices of his widow, Queen Emma of Normandy.

Harold was the illegitimate son of Cnut by Ælfgifu of Northampton and was appointed regent on behalf of his half-brother Harthacnut. Queen Emma of Normandy initially held Wessex for her son, Harthacnut, but by 1037 she had been driven from the country and Harold had been recognised as king throughout England. The principal issue was the Jewel Cross type which is also found in the name of Cnut and Harthacnut, cf. nos. 1160 and 1166.

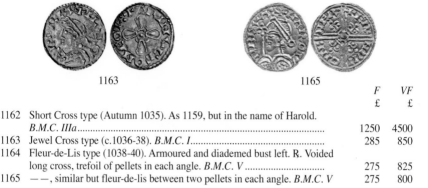

1163   1165

	F £	VF £
1162 Short Cross type (Autumn 1035). As 1159, but in the name of Harold. B.M.C. IIIa	1250	4500
1163 Jewel Cross type (c.1036-38). B.M.C. I	285	850
1164 Fleur-de-Lis type (1038-40). Armoured and diademed bust left. R. Voided long cross, trefoil of pellets in each angle. B.M.C. V	275	825
1165 — —, similar but fleur-de-lis between two pellets in each angle. B.M.C. V	275	800

HARTHACNUT, 1035-1042

Although Harthacnut was the only legitimate son of Cnut and his legitimate heir, the political situation in Denmark prevented him from leaving for England until 1040, by which time Harold had secured the kingdom. Harold's death allowed Harthacnut to reclaim England without bloodshed, but he himself died after two years of sole rule. The main variety of Harthacnut is Arm and Sceptre type from his sole reign. The Jewel Cross type from the early period is also found in the name of Cnut and Harold I, cf. nos. 1160 and 1163.

EARLY PERIOD (DURING REGENCY) 1035–7

1166 Jewel Cross type. As 1163, but in the name of Harthacnut. Diademed bust left. B.M.C. I	1350	5000

1167

1167 — —, similar but bust right. B.M.C I	1200	4500

1168

SOLE REIGN 1040–42

1168 Arm and Sceptre type. King's name given as 'Harthacnut'. Diademed bust left with sceptre in left hand, forearm visible across bust B.M.C. II	1100	4250

1169

	F £	VF £
1169 — —, Similar but king's name given as 'Cnut'.	600	1750

1170

1170 **Danish types.** Types exist in the name of Harthacnut other than those listed above and are Scandinavian in origin.	300	750

EDWARD THE CONFESSOR, 1042-1066

Son of Æthelred II and Emma of Normandy, Edward spent twenty-five years in Normandy before he was adopted into the household of his half-brother Harthacnut in 1040. On the death of Harthacnut, Edward was acclaimed king. He is known by the title 'The Confessor' owing to his piety and he was canonised after his death. There is considerable weight fluctuation within and between the types, which is often unaffected by the smallness of the flan, rather the coin might be thicker to compensate.

Further reading: P. Seaby, 'The sequence of Anglo-Saxon types 1030–1050', *BNJ* 28 (1955-7), 111–46; T. Talvio, 'The design of Edward the Confessor's coins', in *Studies in Late Anglo-Saxon Coinage*, ed. K. Jonsson (Stockholm: 1990), 489–99. A. Freeman. *The Moneyer and the Mint in the Reign of Edward the Confessor: Parts 1 and 2*, (BAR) 1985

1171   1172 (rev.)

1170A Arm and Sceptre type (1042). *B.M.C. IIIa*	1250	4500
1171 Pacx type (1042–4). Diademed bust left. ℞. Voided long cross. *B.M.C. IV*	200	600
1172 — —, Similar but ℞. voided short cross. *B.M.C. V*	210	650

1173

	F	VF
	£	£

1173   Radiate/Small Cross type (1044–6). *B.M.C. I* 120 325

1174

1175

1174   Trefoil Quadrilateral type (1046–8). *B.M.C. III* 120 350
1175   Small flan type (1048–50). *B.M.C. II* 110 275
1176   Expanding Cross type (1050–53). Light issue, small flans; weight approx.
       1.10-1.30g. *B.M.C. V* 135 400

AMR Coins
Dealers in Quality British Coins
BNTA

British Coins
Bought and Sold

Wanted: Full collections or quality single items

- Coins purchased outright
- Coins sold for clients on a commission basis
- Fine selection of quality coins always in stock
- Auction viewing and bidding service
- Valuations
- Wants lists managed

View our regularly updated stock at

www.amrcoins.com

 e-mail: info@amrcoins.com   tel: +44(0)7527 569308
P.O. Box 352, Leeds, LS19 9GG

1177   1179

	F £	VF £
1177 — —. Heavy issue, large flans; weight approx. 1.40-1.70g. *B.M.C. V*.....	135	400
1178 — —, Similar but struck in gold	42500	175000
1179 Pointed Helmet type (1053–6). Bearded bust right in pointed helmet. *B.M.C. VII*...	150	450
1180 — —, Similar but bust left.	1000	3500

TimeLine Auctions
Inc. Gregory's Est.1858

We are accepting single entries of
Anglo-Saxon and Hiberno-Norse coins & antiquities

www.timelineauctions.com

+44 [0]1277 815121
enquiries@timelineauctions.com

AIAΔ   BNTA

THE ART LOSS ■ REGISTER

Follow us on:
f /TimeLineAuctions
t @TimeLineAuction

1181

		F	VF
		£	£

1181 Sovereign/Eagles type (1056–9). King enthroned, holding orb. R. Cross, eagles in angles *B.M.C. IX* 150 450

1182

1182 Hammer Cross type (1059–62). *B.M.C. XI* 125 375

1183

1183 Facing Bust/Small Cross type (1062–5). *B.M.C. XIII* 120 325

1184

1184 Pyramids type (1065–6). *B.M.C. XV* 125 375

1185

1185 Transitional Pyramids type (c.1065). *B.M.C. XIV* 1750 6500

Most York coins of this reign have an annulet in one quarter of the reverse.

Harold was the son of Earl Godwine of Wessex, who had dominated the royal court, and was brother-in-law to Edward the Confessor. Harold successfully repulsed an invasion of Harald Hardrada of Norway, but was himself killed in the Battle of Hastings after a reign of ten months.

Further reading: H. Pagan, 'The coinage of Harold II', in *Studies in Late Anglo-Saxon Coinage*, ed. K. Jonsson (Stockholm: 1990), 177–205.

1186

	F	VF
	£	£
1186 Pax type. Crowned head left with sceptre. R. PAX across field. *B.M.C. I*	1250	3500

1187

	F	VF
1187 — —, Similar but without sceptre. *B.M.C. Ia*	1500	4250
1188 — —, Similar but head right. *B.M.C. Ib*	2750	9500

Cnut, Short Cross type (S.1159) - WULNOTH ON WINC:
moneyer Wulnoth   *mint* Winchester

William, Paxs type (S.1257) - LIFINC ON WINCE
moneyer Lifinc   *mint* Winchester

Old English special letters found on Anglo-Saxon and Norman coins:

Letter	Name	Modern Equivalent
Æ	Ash	E
Ð	Eth	Th
Ᵽ (P)	Wynn	W

In late Anglo-Saxon and Norman times coins were struck in the King's name at a large number of mints distributed in centres of population, and in times of emergency in places of refuge, across England and Wales. During the 10th century the use of a mint signature was sporadic but from the Reform type of Edgar the mint name is almost invariably given, usually in conjunction with that of the moneyer responsible, e.g. EDGAR ON BERCLE. At the peak, 71 mints struck the quatrefoil type of Cnut and 65 the PAXS type of William I and they provide a valuable insight into the economic and social structures of the period.

The output of the mints varied enormously and a dozen are exceptionally rare. Approximately 100,000 pennies survive, half of which emanate from the great centres of London, Canterbury, Lincoln, Winchester and York. At the other end of the scale a mint such as Rochester is known from about 500 coins, Derby from around 250, Guildford 100, Bedwyn 25, Horncastle 4 and Pershore 1. Many of these coins, particularly those from the great Scandinavian hoards, are in museum collections and are published in the Sylloge of Coins of the British Isles (SCBI) series.

There are too many type for mint combinations, over 1500 Saxon and 1000 Norman, to price each individually and our aim is to give an indication of value for the commonest Saxon and Norman type, in VF condition, for each of the 102 attested mints (excluding Baronial of Stephen's reign), and for a further 10 mints whose location or attribution is uncertain. The threshold VF price for a Norman coin (H1 B.M.C.15 £500) exceeds that for a Saxon coin (Cnut short cross £250) accounting for the difference in starting level. Prices for coins in lower grade would be less and there is a premium for the rarer types for each mint, but for many types, e.g. in the reigns of Harthacnut or Henry I, the value of the type itself far exceeds that of many of the constituent mints and a scarce mint is only worth a modest premium over a common one.

We also give the most characteristic mint signatures (often found abbreviated) and the reigns for which the mint is known. There are many pitfalls in identifying mints, not least that Saxon and Norman spelling is no more reliable than that of other ages and that late Saxon coins were widely imitated in Scandinavia. There is extensive literature and the specialist in this fascinating series can, for further details, consult J J North, English Hammered Coinage Vol.1.

Alf	—	Alfred the Great	Hd1	—	Harold I
EdE	—	Edward the Elder	HCn	—	Harthacnut
A'stn	—	Aethelstan	EdC	—	Edward the Confessor
Edm	—	Edmund	Hd2	—	Harold II
Edw	—	Edwig	W1	—	William I
Edg	—	Edgar	W2	—	William II
EdM	—	Edward the Martyr	H1	—	Henry I
Ae2	—	Aethelred	St	—	Stephen
Cn	—	Cnut			

Berkeley　　　　　　　　　　　Hastings

	SAXON	NORMAN
	VF	VF
	£	£
Axbridge (AXAN, ACXEPO) Edg, Ae2, Cn, HCn	4000	—
Aylesbury (AEGEL, AEEL), Ae2, Cn, EdC	3000	—
Barnstable (BARD, BEARDA) Edw, Edg, Ae2-Hd1, EdC, W1, H1	1350	1750
Bath (BADAN) EdE-A'stn, Edw-EdC, W1-St	400	900
Bedford (BEDAN, BEDEFOR) Edw-St	450	900
Bedwyn (BEDEPIN) EdC, W1	2250	4000
Berkeley (BEORC, BERCLE) EdC	8500	—
Bramber (BRAN) St	—	3000
Bridport (BRYDI, BRIPVT) A'stn, Ae2, Cn, HCn, EdC-W1	1250	1500
Bristol (BRICSTO, BRVCSTO) Ae2-St	500	700
Bruton (BRIVT) Ae2, Cn, HCn, EdC	2500	—
Buckingham (BVCIN) Edg, EdM-Hd1, HCn, EdC	3000	—
Bury St.Edmunds (EDMVN, S.EDM) EdC, W1, H1, St	1350	850
Cadbury (CADANBY) Ae2, Cn	6500	—
Caistor (CASTR, CESTR) EdM, Ae2, Cn	5000	—
Cambridge (GRANTE) Edg-St	300	900
Canterbury (DORO, CAENTPA, CNTL) Alf, A'stn, Edr, Edg-St	225	500
Cardiff (CIVRDI, CAIERDI) W1, H1, St, Mat	—	1250
Carlisle (CARD, EDEN) H1, St	—	1250
Castle Rising (RISINGE) St (type II-VII)	—	1500
Chester (LEIGE, LEGECE, CESTRE) A'stn, Edm, Edg-St	400	800
Chichester (CISSAN, CICEST) A'stn, Edg, Ae2-St	400	650
Christchurch (orig. Twynham) (TVEHAM, TPIN) W1, H1	—	3500
Cissbury (SIDESTEB, SIDMES) Ae2, Cn	3000	—
Colchester (COLN, COLECES) Ae2-St	350	650
Crewkerne (CRVCERN) Ae2, Cn, Hd1	3500	—
Cricklade (CROCGL, CRECCELAD, CRIC) Ae2-W2	1750	1750
Derby (DEORBY, DERBI) A'stn, Edm, Edg-St	1750	1750
Dorchester (DORCE, DORECES) Ae2-H1	1000	1250
Dover (DOFERA, DOFRN) A'stn, Edg, Ae2-St	300	600
Droitwich (PICC, PICNEH) EdC, Hd2	4000	—
Dunwich (DVNE) St	—	2000
Durham (DVNE, DVRHAM, DVNHO) W1-St	—	2250
Exeter (EAXA, EAXCESTRE, IEXECE) Alf, A'stn, Edw-St	300	650
Frome (FRO) Cn, HCn, EdC	3500	—
Gloucester (GLEAP, GLEPECE, GLOPEC) Alf, A'stn, Edg-St	450	750
Grantham (GRANTHA, GRE) Ae2	6500	—
Guildford (GYLD, GILDEFRI) EdM-W2	1750	3000
Hastings (HAESTINGPOR, AESTI) Ae2-St	400	800
Hedon (HEDVN) St	—	4000
Hereford (HEREFOR, HRFRD) A'stn, Edg, Ae2-St	600	850
Hertford (HEORTF, HRTFI, RET) A'stn, Edw-EdC, W1-H1	350	1500
Horncastle (HORN) EdM, Ae2	8000	—
Horndon (HORNIDVNE) EdC	8000	—
Huntingdon (HVNTEN, HVTD) Edg, Ae2-St	400	1250
Hythe (HIÐEN, HIDI) EdC, W1, W2	3000	1500
Ilchester (GIFELCST, GIVELC, IVELCS) Edg, Ae2-St	750	1500
Ipswich (GIPESWIC, GYPES) Edg-St	400	750
Langport (LANCPORT, LAGEPOR) A'stn, Cn-EdC	2500	—
Launceston (LANSTF, LANSA, SANCTI STEFANI) Ae2, W1-H1	4000	3000
Leicester (LIHER, LEHRE, LEREC) A'stn, Edg, Ae2-St	500	900
Lewes (LAEPES, LEPEEI, LAPA) A'stn, Edg-St	400	800
Lincoln (LINCOLN, NICOLE) Edr, Edg-St	225	500
London (LVNDO, LVNDENE) Alf, A'stn, Edw-St	225	500
Lydford (LYDANFOR) Edg-EdC	450	—
Lympne (LIMENE, LIMNA) A'stn, Edg-Cn	900	—
Maldon (MAELDVN, MIEL) A'stn, Edg, Ae2-Hd1, EdC-W2	500	1500
Malmesbury (MALD, MEALDMES, MELME) Edg, Ae2-W2, H1	2000	2500
Marlborough (MAERLEBI) W1, W2	—	5000
Melton Mowbray (MEDELTV) Ae2, Cn	7000	—
Milborne Port (MYLE) Ae2, Cn, EdC	6500	—

	SAXON VF £	NORMAN VF £
Newark (NEWIR, NIWOR) Edg-Cn	6500	—
Newcastle (CAST) St	—	2000
Newport (NIPANPO, NIPEPORT) Edw, Edg, EdC	5000	—
Northampton (HAMTVN, HMTI, NORHAM) Edw, Edg-St	450	700
Norwich (NORDPIC) A'stn-Edr, Edg-St	250	500
Nottingham (SNOTING) A'stn, Ae2-St	1500	1500
Oxford (OXNA, OCXEN, OXENFO) Alf, A'stn, Edr-St	400	700
Pembroke (PEI, PAN, PAIN) H1, St	—	4000
Pershore (PERESC) EdC	8500	—
Petherton (PEDR, PEDI) Cn, EdC	7000	—
Pevensey (PEFNESE, PEVEN) W1-St	—	2500
Reading (READIN, REDN) EdC	6000	—
Rhuddlan (RVDILI) W1	—	3500
Rochester (ROFEC, ROFSC) A'stn, Edg-H1	500	1250
Romney (RVMED, RVMNE) Ae2-H1	500	900
Rye (RIE) St	—	3000
Salisbury (SEREB, SEARB, SALEB) Ae2-EdC, W1-St	500	650
Sandwich (SANDPI) EdC, W1-St	600	1000
Shaftesbury (SCEFTESB, CEFT, SAFTE) A'stn, Edg-St	500	800
Shrewsbury (SCROB, SCRVBS, SALOP) A'stn, Edg, Ae2-St	650	1000
Southampton (HAMPIC, HAMTVN) A'stn, Edw-Cn	650	1250
Southwark (SVDBY, SVDGE, SVDPERC) Ae2-St	250	500
Stafford (STAFFO, STAEF) A'stn, Edg, Ae2-Hd1, EdC, W1-St	800	1250
Stamford (STANFORD) Edg-St	225	650
Steyning (STAENIG, STENIC) Cn-W2, St	350	700
Sudbury (SVDBI, SVBR) Ae2, Cn, EdC, W1-St	600	900
Swansea (SVENSEI) St	—	2500
Tamworth (TOMPEARÐ, TAMPRÐ) A'stn, Edg-Hd1, EdC, W1-St	2000	1750
Taunton (TANTVNE) Ae2-St	1000	900
Thetford (ÐEOTFOR, DTF, TETFOR) Edg-St	225	500
Torksey (TVRC, TORC) EdM-Cn	4000	—
Totnes (DARENT, TOTANES, TOTNES) A'stn, Edw-HCn, W2, H1	650	1750
Wallingford (PELINGA, PALLIG) A'stn, Edm, Edg, Ae2-H1	450	700
Wareham (PERHAM, PERI) A'stn, Edg-St	650	1200
Warminster (PORIME) Ae2-Hd1, EdC	3000	—
Warwick (PAERINC, PERPIC, PAR) A'stn (?), Edg-St	850	1250
Watchet (PECED, PICEDI, WACET) Ae2-EdC, W1-St	1750	1750
Wilton (PILTVNE) Edg-St	350	650
Winchcombe (WENCLES, PINCEL, PINCL) Edg, Ae2, Cn, HCn-W1	2000	2000
Winchester (PINTONIA, PINCEST) Alf, A'stn, Edw-St	225	500
Worcester (PIGER, PIHREC, PIREC) EdM, Ae2-St	650	900
York (EBORACI, EFORPIC, EVERWIC) A'stn, Edm, Edg-St	225	700

Mints of uncertain identification or location

	SAXON VF £	NORMAN VF £
"Brygin" (BRYGIN) Ae2	3500	—
"Dyr/Dernt" (DYR, DERNE, DERNT) EdC (East Anglia)	1500	—
"Weardburh" (PEARDBV) A'stn, Edg	4500	—
Abergavenny (?) (FVNI) W1	—	3000
Gothabyrig (GEODA, GODABYRI, IODA) Ae2-HCn	3000	—
Eye (?) (EI, EIE) St	—	3000
Peterborough (?) (BVRI) W1, St	—	3500
Richmond, Yorks (?) (R1), St (type 1)	—	1500
St Davids (?) (DEVITVN) W1	—	3500
Wilton, Norfolk (?) (PILTV) Ae2 (LSC)	2500	—
Bamborough (BCI, CIB, OBCI) Henry of Northumberland	—	6000
Corbridge (COREB) Henry of Northumberland	—	6000

Aylesbury	Barnstaple	Cricklade	Dunwich
Exeter	Frome	Guildford	Horncastle
Ilchester	London	Milborne Port	Newark
Oxford	Pevensey	Rochester	Stafford

Torksey	Winchcombe	York

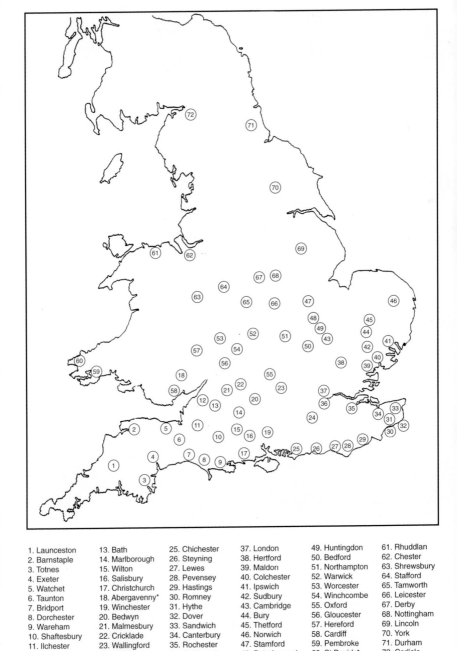

1. Launceston	13. Bath	25. Chichester	37. London	49. Huntingdon	61. Rhuddlan
2. Barnstaple	14. Marlborough	26. Steyning	38. Hertford	50. Bedford	62. Chester
3. Totnes	15. Wilton	27. Lewes	39. Maldon	51. Northampton	63. Shrewsbury
4. Exeter	16. Salisbury	28. Pevensey	40. Colchester	52. Warwick	64. Stafford
5. Watchet	17. Christchurch	29. Hastings	41. Ipswich	53. Worcester	65. Tamworth
6. Taunton	18. Abergavenny*	30. Romney	42. Sudbury	54. Winchcombe	66. Leicester
7. Bridport	19. Winchester	31. Hythe	43. Cambridge	55. Oxford	67. Derby
8. Dorchester	20. Bedwyn	32. Dover	44. Bury	56. Gloucester	68. Nottingham
9. Wareham	21. Malmesbury	33. Sandwich	45. Thetford	57. Hereford	69. Lincoln
10. Shaftesbury	22. Cricklade	34. Canterbury	46. Norwich	58. Cardiff	70. York
11. Ilchester	23. Wallingford	35. Rochester	47. Stamford	59. Pembroke	71. Durham
12. Bristol	24. Guildford	36. Southwark	48. Peterborough	60. St Davids*	72. Carlisle

Possible location of uncertain mint

William I maintained the Anglo-Saxon mint system and the practice of conducting frequent periodic recoinages by change of coin type. However, the twelfth-century witnessed a gradual transition from regional to centralised minting. Nearly seventy towns had moneyers operating under William I, but only thirty mint towns took part in the recoinage initiated by the Cross-and-Crosslets ('Tealby') coinage in 1158. Cut halfpennies and cut farthings were made during this period, but are scarce for all types up to BMC 13 of Henry I; cut coins are more frequently encountered for subsequent types.

Further reading: G.C. Brooke, *Catalogue of English Coins in the British Museum. The Norman Kings,* 2 volumes (London, 1916). (Abbr. BMC Norman Kings). I. Stewart, 'The English and Norman mints, c.600–1158', in *A New History of the Royal Mint,* ed. C.E. Challis (Cambridge, 1992), pp. 1–82.

WILLIAM I, 1066-1087

Duke William of Normandy claimed the throne of England on the death of his cousin Edward the Confessor. An important monetary reform occurred towards the close of the reign with the introduction of the *geld de moneta* assessed on boroughs. This may be seen as part of the raft of administrative reforms initiated by William I, which included the compilation of Domesday Book in 1086.

The date of the Paxs type is central to the absolute chronology of this and the subsequent reign. Currently evidence is equivocal on the matter. In BMC Norman Kings (London, 1916) it was designated the last type of the reign, an attribution maintained here, but some students regard it as having continued into the reign of William II or begun by him.

Further reading: D.M. Metcalf, 'Notes on the "PAXS" type of William I', *Yorkshire Numismatist* 1 (1988), 13–26. P.Grierson, 'Domesday Book, the geld de moneta and monetagium: a forgotten minting reform' *British Numismatic Journal* 55 (1985), 84–94.

1250   1251

		F	VF
		£	£
1250	**Penny**. *B.M.C.* 1: Profile left type.	475	1500

1252   1253

| 1251 | *B.M.C.* 2: Bonnet type. | 250 | 800 |
| 1252 | *B.M.C.* 3: Canopy type | 425 | 1350 |

1254   1255

1253	*B.M.C.* 4: Two sceptres type.	300	950
1254	*B.M.C.* 5: Two stars type.	250	800
1255	*B.M.C.* 6: Sword type.	425	1350

1256   1257

	F £	VF £
1256 *B.M.C.* 7: Profile right type (lead die struck examples exist from the Thames)	525	1650
1257 *B.M.C.* 8: Paxs type	225	550

WILLIAM II, 1087-1100

Second son of William I was killed while hunting in the New Forest. Five of the thirteen coin types in the name of 'William' have been assigned to the reign of William II, although it remains uncertain whether the Paxs type of his father continued into his reign.

1258   1259

1258 **Penny**. *B.M.C.* 1: Profile type.	900	2750
1259 *B.M.C.* 2: Cross in quatrefoil type.	750	2250

1260   1261

1260 *B.M.C.* 3: Voided cross type	700	2000
1261 *B.M.C.* 4: Cross pattée and fleury type...	750	2250

1262

1262 *B.M.C.* 5: Cross fleury and piles type...	800	2500

Henry was the third son of William I. Administrative reforms and military action to secure Normandy dominated the king's work. After the death of his son in 1120 Henry sought to guarantee the throne for his daughter Matilda, widow of German Emperor Henry V.

The coin types continue to be numbered according to BMC Norman Kings (London, 1916), but the order 1, 2, 3, 4, 5, 6, 9, 7, 8, 11, 10, 12, 13, 14, 15 is now accepted as a working hypothesis for the reign. Greater uncertainty pertains to the chronology of the coin types. The reign coincided with a period of monetary crisis. Scepticism concerning the quality of coinage led to the testing of coins by the public, hindering their acceptance in circulation. In response the government ordered all coins mutilated at issue to force the acceptance of damaged coins. Thus, a few coins of type 6 and all of those of types 7–14 have an official edge incision or 'snick'. Round halfpennies were produced and as some are found snicked they can be dated to the period when official mutilation of the coinage was ordered. In 1124 there was a general purge of moneyers in England as the royal government attempted to restore confidence in the coinage.

Further reading: M.A.S. Blackburn, 'Coinage and currency under Henry I; A review', *Anglo-Norman Studies* 13 (1991), 49–81. M.M. Archibald and W.J. Conte, 'Five round halfpennies of Henry I. A further case for reappraisal of the chronology of types', *Spink's Numismatic Circular* 98 (1990), 232–6, M. Allen 'Henry I Type 14', *BNJ* 79 (2009), 72-171.

1263   1263A   1264

	F	VF
	£	£
1263 **Penny**. *B.M.C.* 1: Annulets type	450	1500
1263A *B.M.C.* 2: Profile/cross fleury type	300	850

1265   1266

1264 *B.M.C.* 3: Paxs type	275	800
1265 *B.M.C.* 4: Annulets and piles type	350	1000

1267   1268

1266 *B.M.C.* 5: Voided cross and fleurs type	750	2500
1267 *B.M.C.* 6: Pointing bust and stars type	1250	4500
1268 *B.M.C.* 7: Facing bust/quatrefoil with piles type	325	950

1269

1270

	F	VF
	£	£

		F	VF
1269	*B.M.C.* 8: Large profile/cross and annulets type.....................................	1100	4000
1270	*B.M.C.* 9: Facing bust/cross in quatrefoil type	650	2000

1271

1272

1271	*B.M.C.* 10: Facing bust/cross fleury type	250	750
1272	*B.M.C.* 11: Double inscription type	525	1750

1273

1274

1273	*B.M.C.* 12: Small profile/cross and annulets type	375	1100
1274	*B.M.C.* 13: Star in lozenge fleury type	400	1250

1275

1276

1275	*B.M.C.* 14: Pellets in quatrefoil type...	225	700
1276	*B.M.C.* 15: Quadrilateral on cross fleury type	150	500

1277

1277A

1277	*Round halfpenny*. Facing head. R. Cross potent with pellets in angles....	2000	6500
1277A	— —, As last but reverse from penny die of type 9.	2750	9500

Stephen of Blois seized the English throne on the death of his uncle, Henry I, despite his oath to support Matilda, with whom he contended for power during his reign.

Substantive types BMC 1 and BMC 7 were the only nation-wide issues, the latter introduced after the conclusion of the final political settlement in 1153. The other substantive types, BMC 2 and BMC 6, were confined to areas in the east of England under royal control. In western England coinage was issued by or on behalf of the Angevin party (q.v. below). In areas without access to new dies from London, coinage was produced from locally made dies and initially based on the designs of regular coins of BMC 1. Particular local types were produced in the midlands and the north, associated with prominent magnates, in the king's name or occasionally in the name of barons. Entries contain references to the article by Mack (M).

Further reading: R.P. Mack, 'Stephen and the Anarchy 1135-54', *British Numismatic Journal* 35 (1966), 38–112. M.A.S. Blackburn, 'Coinage and currency', in *The Anarchy of King Stephen's Reign*, ed. E. King (Oxford, 1994), 145–205.

SUBSTANTIVE ROYAL ISSUES

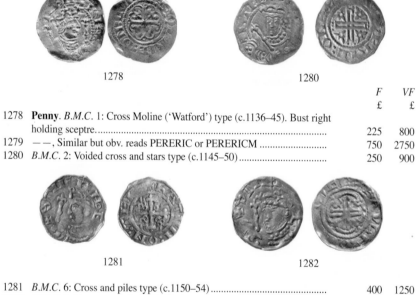

1278   1280

	F	VF
	£	£
1278 **Penny.** *B.M.C.* 1: Cross Moline ('Watford') type (c.1136–45). Bust right holding sceptre...	225	800
1279 — —, Similar but obv. reads PERERIC or PERERICM	750	2750
1280 *B.M.C.* 2: Voided cross and stars type (c.1145–50).................................	250	900

1281   1282

1281 *B.M.C.* 6: Cross and piles type (c.1150–54)..	400	1250
1282 *B.M.C.* 7: Cross pommée (Awbridge) type (c.1154–58, largely posthumous)	250	850
This type continued to be struck until 1158 in the reign of Henry II		

The types designated BMC 3, 4 and 5 are non-substantive, listed as 1300–1302.

COINS OF BRITAIN

PO BOX 2, MONMOUTH, NP25 3YR, UK

BNTA

E-mail: lloydbennett@coinsofbritain.com   +44(0)7714 284 939

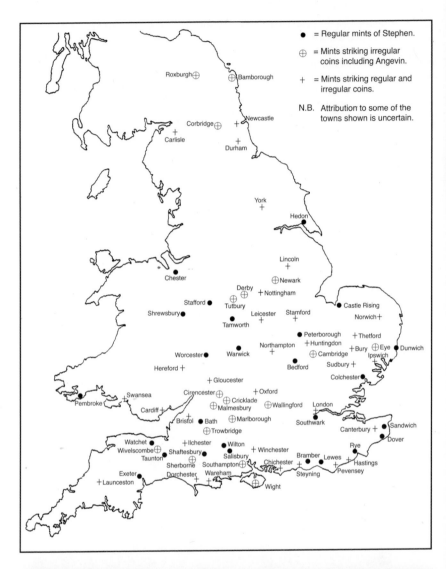

● = Regular mints of Stephen.

⊕ = Mints striking irregular coins including Angevin.

+ = Mints striking regular and irregular coins.

N.B. Attribution to some of the towns shown is uncertain.

Roxburgh ⊕

⊕ Bamborough

Corbridge ⊕

+ Newcastle

+ Carlisle

+ Durham

York +

Hedon ●

Lincoln +

Chester ●

Derby ⊕ ⊕ Newark

Stafford ● Tutbury + Nottingham

Shrewsbury ● Leicester Stamford

Tamworth Castle Rising ●

Norwich +

Worcester ● Warwick ● Peterborough ● + Thetford

Northampton + Huntingdon + Bury ⊕ Eye ● Dunwich

Hereford + ⊕ Cambridge Ipswich

Bedford ● Sudbury +

+ Gloucester Colchester ●

Swansea ● Cirencester ⊕ + Oxford

Pembroke ● Cardiff + ⊕ Cricklade ⊕ Wallingford London

Bristol ● Bath Malmesbury Southwark

⊕ Marlborough Canterbury + Sandwich ●

⊕ Trowbridge Dover ●

Watchet ● + Ilchester Wilton ● Rye ●

Wivelscombe ⊕ Shaftesbury + Winchester Bramber Lewes ●

Taunton ● Salisbury Chichester Hastings

Sherborne Southampton ⊕ Steyning Pevensey

Exeter ● Dorchester Wareham

+ Launceston Wight ⊕

Timeline **Auctions**
Inc. Gregory's **Est.1858**

We are accepting single entries and collections of Norman coins & antiquities

www.timelineauctions.com

Sold for:
£10,530

LOCAL AND IRREGULAR ISSUES OF THE CIVIL WAR

COINS STRUCK FROM ERASED DIES LATE 1130's – *c.*1145

The association of these coins with the Interdict of 1148 is erroneous. Some of the marks that disfigured the dies were probably cancellation marks, but the exigencies of the civil war required the re-employed of the dies. Other defacements may well be an overtly political statement.

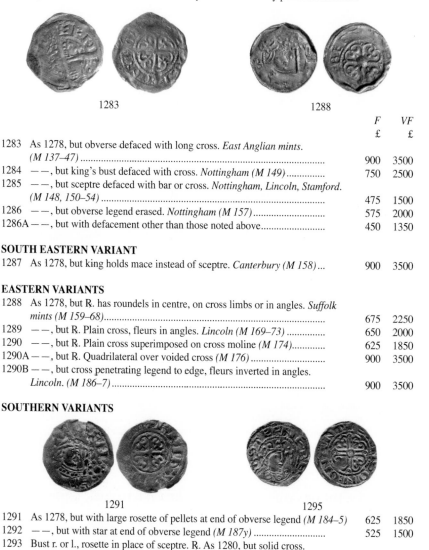

1283   1288

		F £	VF £
1283	As 1278, but obverse defaced with long cross. *East Anglian mints.* (*M 137–47*)	900	3500
1284	— —, but king's bust defaced with cross. *Nottingham (M 149)*	750	2500
1285	— —, but sceptre defaced with bar or cross. *Nottingham, Lincoln, Stamford.* (*M 148, 150–54*)	475	1500
1286	— —, but obverse legend erased. *Nottingham (M 157)*	575	2000
1286A	— —, but with defacement other than those noted above	450	1350

SOUTH EASTERN VARIANT

1287	As 1278, but king holds mace instead of sceptre. *Canterbury (M 158)*	900	3500

EASTERN VARIANTS

1288	As 1278, but R. has roundels in centre, on cross limbs or in angles. *Suffolk mints (M 159–68)*	675	2250
1289	— —, but R. Plain cross, fleurs in angles. *Lincoln (M 169–73)*	650	2000
1290	— —, but R. Plain cross superimposed on cross moline (*M 174*)	625	1850
1290A	— —, but R. Quadrilateral over voided cross (*M 176*)	900	3500
1290B	— —, but cross penetrating legend to edge, fleurs inverted in angles. *Lincoln. (M 186–7)*	900	3500

SOUTHERN VARIANTS

1291   1295

1291	As 1278, but with large rosette of pellets at end of obverse legend (*M 184–5*)	625	1850
1292	— —, but with star at end of obverse legend (*M 187y*)	525	1500
1293	Bust r. or l., rosette in place of sceptre. R. As 1280, but solid cross. (*M 181–3*)	750	2500
1295	As 1278, but king wears collar of annulets. R. voided cross moline, annulet at centre. *Southampton. (M 207–212)*	350	1250

	F £	VF £
1296	As 1278, but reverse cross penetrates legend with fleur-de-lis tips.		
	Leicester (M 177–8)..	800	2750
1297	— —, but crude work. R. Voided cross, lis outward in angles. *Tutbury*		
	(M 179)	800	2750

1298	— —, but crude work. R. Voided cross with martlets in angles. *Derby Tutbury*		
	(M 175)	2250	7500
1299	— —, but R. plain cross with T-cross in each angle *(M 180)*...................	850	3000
1300	*B.M.C.* 3: Facing bust. R. Cross pattée, fleurs inwards. *Northampton and*		
	Huntingdon (?) (M 67–71)..	1250	4000

1301	*B.M.C.* 4: Lozenge fleury type. *Lincoln or Nottingham (M 72–5)*...........	475	1650
1302	*B.M.C.* 5: Bust half-right. R. Lozenge in Cross Moline with fleurs. *Leicester*		
	(M 76)	1350	4500
1303	As 1280, but obverse legend ROBERTVS. *(M 269)*................................	2750	9500

NORTH-EASTERN AND SCOTTISH BORDER VARIANTS

1304	As 1278, but star before sceptre. R. Annulets at tips of fleurs *(M 188)* ...	850	3000
1305	— —, but voided cross penetrating legend to edge *(M 189–92)*...............	900	3250
1306	— —, but crude style *(M 276–9, 281–2)*.......................................	575	2000
1307	— —, but R. Cross with cross pattée and crescent in angles *(M 288)*	1850	6000
	King David I of Scotland		
1308	As 1305, but obverse legend DAVID REX *(M 280)*	1750	5250
	Earl Henry of Northumberland (son of King David I of Scotland)		
1309	As 1278, but legend hENRIC ERL *(M 283–5)*....................................	2000	6000
1310	— —, Similar but reverse cross fleury *(M 286–7)*	1850	5750
1311	As 1307, but obverse legend NENCI:COM *(M 289)*	2000	6000

YORK ISSUES: THE ORNAMENTED GROUP ATTRIBUTED TO YORK (*c.*1150)
King Stephen

1312	As 1278, but obverse inscription NSEPEFETI, NSEPINEI or STIEFNER.		
	R. ornamental letters WISÐGNOTA *(M 215–6)*	1350	4000

1313   1315

	F £	VF £
1313 Flag type. As 1278, but lance with pennant before face, star right. R. As 1278, letters and four ornaments in legend *(M 217)*	750	3000
1313A — —, Similar but with eight ornaments in reverse legend. *(M 217)*	800	3250
1314 As 1278, but legend STEIN and pellet lozenge for sceptre-head *(M 218)*	900	3500
1314A King standing facing, holding sceptre and standard with triple pennon. R. Cross pattée, crescents and quatrefoils in angles, ornaments in legend. ..	2750	10500

King Stephen and Queen Matilda

1315 Two full-length standing figures holding sceptre. R. Legend of ornaments. *(M 220)*	3500	13500

1317   1320

Eustace Fitzjohn

1316 EVSTACIVS, knight standing with sword. R. Cross in quatrefoil, EBORACI EDTS or EBORACI TDEFL *(M 221-222)*	1750	6000
1317 — —, Similar but reverse legend ThOMHS FILIUS VLF *(M 223)*	1850	6500
1318 — —, Similar but reverse legend of ornaments and letters. *(M 224)*	1600	5500
1319 [EVSTA]CII. FII. IOANIS, lion passant right. R. Cross moline, ornaments in legend *(M 225)*	2750	9500
1320 EISTAOhIVS, lion rampant right. R. Cross fleury, ornaments in legend *(M 226)*	2500	8500

William of Aumale, Earl of York

1320A WILLELMVS, Knight stg. r. holding sword. R. Cross in quatrefoil. As 1316	3000	10500

1322

Rodbert III de Stuteville

1321 ROBERTVS IESTV, knight holding sword on horse right. R. as 1314. *(M 228)*	4250	15000
1321A Type as 1312, but obverse legend RODBDS[T DE?] *(M 227)*	2750	9500

Henry Murdac, Archbishop of York

1322 HENRICVS EPC, crowned bust, crosier and star before. R. similar to 1314 but legend STEPHANVS REX *(M 229)*	2750	9500

UNCERTAIN ISSUES

		F	VF
		£	£
1323	Obv. as 1278. ℞. Cross pattée with annulets in angles *(M 272)*	675	2000
1324	Obv. as 1275 (Henry I, *B.M.C.* 14), but reverse as last *(M 274 extr)*	900	3000
1325	Other miscellaneous types/varieties	650	1500

THE ANGEVIN PARTY

Matilda was the daughter of Henry I and widow of German Emperor Henry V (d.1125) and had been designated heir to the English throne by her father. Matilda was Countess of Anjou by right of her second husband Geoffrey of Anjou. Matilda arrived in England in pursuit of her inheritance in 1139 and established an Angevin court at Bristol and controlled most of south-western England. Matilda's cause was championed by her half-brother, Henry I's illegitimate son, Robert, Earl of Gloucester.

The initial phase of coinage in Matilda's name copied the designs of Stephen's BMC 1 and are dated to the early 1140s. The second type was only discovered in the Coed-y-Wenallt hoard (1980). A group of coins invokes the names of past Norman kings 'William' and 'Henry' and the designs of Stephen BMC 1 and Henry I BMC 15. These coins were formally and erroneously attributed to Earl William of Gloucester and Duke Henry of Normandy. Coins of Earl William, and his father Earl Robert, of the Lion type are now known thanks to the discovery of the Box, Wiltshire hoard (1994). In addition to these great magnates a few minor barons placed their names on the coinage.

Further Reading: G. Boon, *Welsh Hoards 1979–81* (Cardiff, 1986). M.M. Archibald, 'The lion coinage of Robert Earl of Gloucester and William Earl of Gloucester', *British Numismatic Journal* 71 (2001), 71–86.

1326

Matilda (in England 1139–48)

1326	As 1278, but cruder style, legend MATILDI IMP or variant (M 230–40) *Bristol, Cardiff, Oxford and Wareham.*	1650	5000
1326A	— —, legend MATILDI IMP or IM.HE.MA. ℞. Cross pattée over fleury (Coed-y-Wenallt hoard) *Bristol and Cardiff.*..	1750	5250
1326B	— —, as last but triple pellets at cross ends (Coed-y-Wenallt hoard). *Bristol and Cardiff.*	1750	5250

Henry de Neubourg

| 1326C | Similar type to 1326A but legend hENRICI dE NOVOB (Coed-y-Wenallt hoard) *Swansea*.. | 1850 | 6500 |

Anonymous issues in the name 'King Henry' and 'King William'

1327	As 1278, but obverse legend hENRICVS or HENRICVS REX *(M 241–5)*	1250	3750
1327A	As 1295, but legend hENRIC *(M 246)*...	1250	4000
1327B	As 1326A, but hENNENNVS	1500	4500
1328	Obv. as 1278. ℞. Cross crosslet in quatrefoil *(M 254)*............................	1350	4250
1329	— —, ℞. Quadrilateral on cross fleury *(M 248–53)*................................	1100	3500

1330   1331

		F	VF
		£	£
1330	Facing bust and stars. R. Quadrilateral on cross botonnée *(M 255–8)*.....	1500	5000
1331	— —, Quadrilateral on voided cross botonnée *(M 259–61)*	1500	5000
1332	As 1329, but legend WILLEMVS or variant *(M 262)*............................	1400	4500
1333	As 1330, but legend WILLEMVS or variant *(M 263)*............................	1650	5500
1334	As 1331, but legend WILLEMVS or variant *(M 264–8)*........................	1650	5500

Earl Robert of Gloucester (1121/22–1147)

| 1334A | +ROB' COM' GLOC' (or variant), lion passant right. R. Cross fleury (Box hoard) .... | 1600 | 5250 |

Earl William of Gloucester (1147-1183)

| 1334B | +WILLEMVS, lion passant right. R. Cross fleury (Box hoard)............... | 1600 | 5250 |

Brian Fitzcount, Lord of Wallingford (?)

| 1335 | As 1330, but legend B.R:C.I.T.B.R *(M 270)* .... | 3500 | 12500 |

1336

Earl Patrick of Salisbury (?)

| 1336 | Helmeted bust r. with sword, star behind. R. As 1329. *(M 271)*............... | 3250 | 10500 |

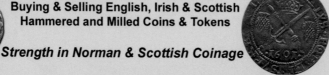

HISTORY IN COINS

Est. Feb 2001. BNTA registered
Buying & Selling English, Irish & Scottish
Hammered and Milled Coins & Tokens

Strength in Norman & Scottish Coinage

Contact details: 07944 374600 or AndrewHowitt@hotmail.com

www.HistoryInCoins.com

ENTER

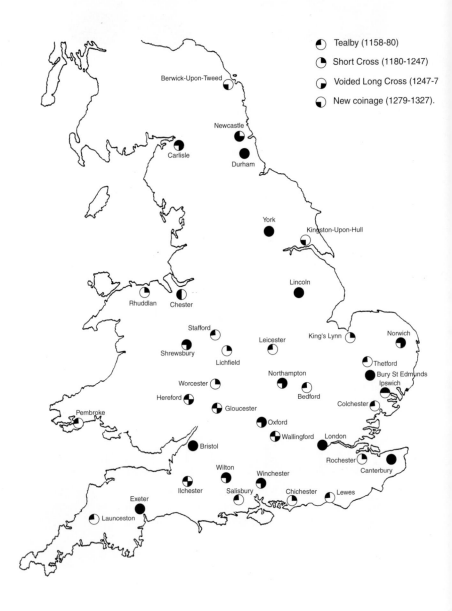

Mints and Moneyers for the Cross and Crosslets (Tealby) Coinage

	From F £
London: Accard (CD), Alwin (ABCDF), Edmund (ACDE), Geffrei (ACE), Godefrei (ACDEF), Godwin (BDE), Hunfrei (AC), Iohan (ACDEF), Lefwine (BCEF), Martin (ABC), Pieres (ACEF), Pieres Mer. (ABD), Pieres Sal. (AEF), Ricard (ABCD), Rodbert (AC), Swetman (ABC), Wid (A),	*110*
Canterbury: Alferg (A), Goldhavoc (ABCDEF), Goldeep (C), Lambrin (F), Raul (CDEF), Ricard (ABCDEF), Ricard Mr. (ABCDE), Rogier (ABCDEF), Rogier F. (A), Willem (C), Wiulf (ABCDEF),	*110*
Bedford: Arfin (A),	*Extremely Rare*
Bristol: Elaf (ACF), Rogier (ADEF), Tancard (ABD),	*250*
Bury St Edmunds: Henri (BDE), Raul (F), Willem (A),	*140*
Carlisle: Willem (ACDEF),	*140*
Chester: Andreu (A), Willem (AD),	*220*
Colchester: Alwin (AC), Pieres (CE),	*250*
Durham: Cristien (C), Iohan (B), Walter (A),	*180*
Exeter: Edwid (AC), Guncelin (AC), Rainir (BC), Ricard (A), Rogier (AD),	*220*
Gloucester: Godwin (A), Nicol (A), Rodbert (A), Sawulf (A),	*275*
Hereford: Driu (AC), Osburn (A), Stefne (A), [—]ward (A),	*250*
Ilchester: Adam (CDF), Reinard (A), Ricard (A), Rocelin (A),	*220*
Ipswich: Nicole (BCDEF), Robert (CEF), Turstain (CF),	*110*
Launceston: Willem (A),	*Extremely Rare*
Leicester: Ricard (A), Robert (A),	*250*
Lewes: uncertain (F),	*Extremely Rare*
Lincoln: Andreu (ABCDE), Godric (ABCD), Lanfram (ABCDF), Raulf (ABCDEF), Raven (ACF), Swein (ACD),	*140*
Newcastle: Willem (ACDEF),	*150*
Northampton: Ingeram (AC), Iosep (A), Pieres (A), Reimund (AC), Stefne (A), Waltier (AC), Warnier (AC),	*180*
Norwich: Gilebert (ABF), Herbert (ACD), Herbert R (A)., Hugo (ACF), Nicol (AC), Picot (ABC), Reiner (AD), Ricard (A),	*180*
Oxford: Adam (ADE), Aschetil (A), Rogier (A),	*220*
Pembroke: Walter (A),	*Extremely Rare*
Salisbury: Daniel (A), Levric (A),	*220*
Shrewsbury: Warin (A),	*Extremely Rare*
Stafford: Colbrand (AC), Willem (C),	*275*
Thetford: Siwate (ACD), Turstain (ACD), Willem (ACDF), Willem Ma (A), Willem De (A),	*140*
Wallingford: Fulke (A),	*Extremely Rare*
Wilton: Anschetil (A), Lantier (A), Willem (A),	*220*
Winchester: Herbert (AC), Hosbert (ACD), Ricard (AE), Willem (AC),	*140*
York: Cudbert (A), Gerrard (A), Godwin (AD), Griffin (AD), Herbert (ACD), Hervi (A), Iordan (A), Norman (A), Willem (A), Wulfsi (A),	*140*

Letters in brackets after moneyer's name indicate Class known to exist for the mint and moneyer combination

HENRY II, 1154-1189

CROSS-AND-CROSSLETS ('TEALBY') COINAGE, 1158-1180

Coins of Stephen's last type continued to be minted until 1158. Then a new coinage bearing Henry's name replaced the currency of the previous reign which contained a high proportion of irregular and sub-standard pennies. The new Cross and Crosslets issue is more commonly referred to as the 'Tealby' coinage, as over 6000 of these pennies were discovered at Tealby, Lincolnshire, in 1807. Twenty nine mints were employed in this re-coinage, but once the re-minting had been completed not more than a dozen mints were kept open. The issue remained virtually unchanged for twenty-two years apart from minor variations in the king's portrait. The coins tend to be poorly struck on irregular flans.

Cut coins occur with varying degrees of frequency during this issue, according to the type and local area.

Further reading: *A Catalogue of English Coins in the British Museum. The Cross-and-Crosslet ("Tealby") Type of Henry II.* (London: 1951) by D.F. Allen.

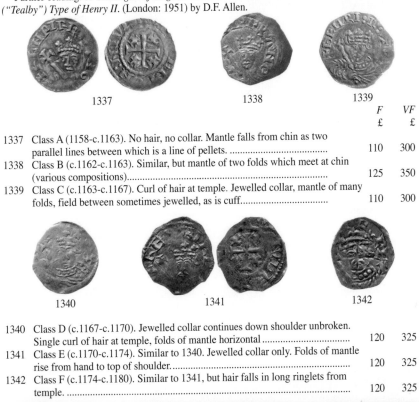

1337   1338   1339

		F	VF
		£	£
1337	Class A (1158-c.1163). No hair, no collar. Mantle falls from chin as two parallel lines between which is a line of pellets.	110	300
1338	Class B (c.1162-c.1163). Similar, but mantle of two folds which meet at chin (various compositions)	125	350
1339	Class C (c.1163-c.1167). Curl of hair at temple. Jewelled collar, mantle of many folds, field between sometimes jewelled, as is cuff	110	300

1340   1341   1342

1340	Class D (c.1167-c.1170). Jewelled collar continues down shoulder unbroken. Single curl of hair at temple, folds of mantle horizontal	120	325
1341	Class E (c.1170-c.1174). Similar to 1340. Jewelled collar only. Folds of mantle rise from hand to top of shoulder.	120	325
1342	Class F (c.1174-c.1180). Similar to 1341, but hair falls in long ringlets from temple.	120	325

Inc. Gregory's **Est.1858**

We are accepting single entries
and collections of English hammered coins

Sold for:
£411

www.timelineauctions.com

The publishers acknowledge the work of the late Prof. Jeffrey Mass for re-organising and updating the short cross series.

Further reading: *Sylloge of Coins of the British Isles Vol 56. The J.P. Mass Collection of English Short Cross Coins 1180 to 1247.* London 2002.

'SHORT CROSS' COINAGE OF HENRY II (1180-1189)

In 1180 a coinage of new type, known as the Short Cross coinage, replaced the Tealby issue. The new coinage is remarkable in that it covers not only the latter part of the reign of Henry II, but also the reigns of his sons Richard and John and on into the reign of his grandson Henry III, and the entire issue bears the name 'hENRICVS'. There are no English coins with the names of Richard or John. The Short Cross coins can be divided chronologically into various classes: ten mints were operating under Henry II and tables of mints, moneyers and classes are given for each reign.

1343   1344

1345

		F £	VF £
1343	Class 1a¹ - 1a³. Small face, square E, and/or C, and/or round M, irregular number of curls..	135	525
1343A	Class 1a⁴ and 1a⁵. Small face, seriffed X, round E and C, square M, irregular number of curls..	85	275
1344	1b. Fine portrait, curls 2 left and 5 right, stop before REX on most coins	65	200
1345	1c. Portrait less finely shaped, irregular number of curls, normally no stop before REX	50	160

RICHARD I, 1189-1199

Pennies of Short Cross type continued to be issued throughout the reign, all bearing the name hENRICVS. The coins of class 4, which have very crude portraits, continued to be issued in the early years of the next reign. The only coins bearing Richard's name are from his territories of Aquitaine and Poitou in western France.

1346   1347   1348A   1348C

1346	2. Chin whiskers made of small curls, no side whiskers, almost always 5 pearls to crown, frequently no collar, sometimes RE/X........................	110	375
1347	3. Large or small face, normally 7 pearls to crown, chin and side whiskers made up of small curls..	85	275

	F	VF
	£	£
1348A 4a. Normally 7 pearls to crown, chin and side whiskers made up of small pellets, hair consisting of 2 or more non-parallel crescents left and right	75	250
1348B 4a* Same as last, but with reverse colon stops (instead of single pellets)	90	350
1348C 4b Normally 7 pearls to crown, chin and side whiskers made up of small pellets, single (or parallel) crescents as hair left and right, frequent malformed letters	70	225

JOHN, 1199-1216

'SHORT CROSS' COINAGE *continued*. All with name hЄNRICVS

The Short Cross coins of class 4 continued during the early years of John's reign, but in 1205 a re-coinage was initiated and new Short Cross coins of better style replaced the older issues. Coins of classes 5a and 5b were issued in the re-coinage in which sixteen mints were employed. Only two of these mints (London and Durham) were still working by the end of class 5. The only coins to bear John's name are the pennies, halfpence and farthings issues for Ireland.

1349　　　　　　1350A　　　　　　　　1350B

1351　　　　　　1352　　　　　　　1354

		F	VF
1349	4c. Reversed S, square face at bottom, 5 pearls to crown, normally single crescents as hair left and right	90	325
1350A	5a1 Reversed or regular S, irregular curved lines as hair (or circular curls containing no pellets), cross pattée as initial mark on reverse, *London and Canterbury* only..	225	750
1350B	5a2 Reversed S, circular curls left and right (2 or 3 each side) containing single pellets, cross pommée as initial mark on reverse...........................	85	275
1350C	5a/5b or 5b/5a	65	200
1351	5b. Regular S, circular pelleted curls, cross pattée as initial mark on reverse	60	175
1352	5c. Slightly rounder portrait, letter X in the form of a St. Andrew's cross	55	160
1353	6a. Smaller portrait, with smaller letter X composed of thin strokes or, later, short wedges	50	150
1354	6b. Very tall lettering and long rectangular face.......................................	45	125

For further reading and an extensive listing of the English Short Cross Coinage see:
Sylloge of Coins of the British Isles. *The J. P. Mass Collection of English Short Cross Coins 1180-1247*

'SHORT CROSS' COINAGE *continued* (1216-47)

The Short Cross coinage continued for a further thirty years during which time the style of portraiture and workmanship deteriorated. By the 1220s minting had been concentrated at London and Canterbury, one exception being the mint of the Abbot of Bury St. Edmunds.

Halfpenny and farthing dies are recorded early in this issue; a few halfpennies and now farthings have been discovered. See nos 1357 D-E.

| 1355 | 1355A | 1355B |

	F £	VF £
1355 6c. Lettering now shorter, face narrow and triangular (also issued in the reign of John)	65	200
1355A 6c. orn. Various letters now ornamental in design, curls 3/3 left and right	100	350
1355B 6x. Canterbury mint only, RE/X, curls 2/2, nostril pellets outside nose...	450	1350
1355C 6d. Face less distinct in shape, N's containing a pellet along the crossbar	90	275

| 1356A | 1356B | 1356C |

1356A 7a. Small compact face, letter A (rev. only) with top coming to a point under crossbar	35	120
1356B 7b. Letter A with square top, M appears as H (rev. only)	35	120
1356C 7c. Degraded portrait, letter A and M as in 7b, large lettering (rev. only)	30	110

| 1357A | 1357C |

1357A 8a. New portrait; letter X in shape of curule; cross pattée as initial mark on reverse (early style), or cross pommée (late style)	110	325
1357B 8b. Degraded portrait, wedge-shaped X, cross pommée as initial mark ..	45	150
1357C 8c. Degraded portrait, cross pommée X, cross pommée as initial mark ..	45	150
1357D Round halfpenny in style of class 7, initial mark in shape of up-turned crescent, London mint only (dated to 1222)	2500	7000
1357E Round farthing in style of class 7, initial mark in shape of up-turned crescent, London mint only (dated to 1222)	2250	6500

Mints and Moneyers for the Short Cross Coinage

Fine

Henry II:

London: Aimer (1a-b), Alain (1a-b), Alain V (1a-b), Alward (1b), Davi (1b-c),
Fil Aimer (1a-b), Gefrei (1c), Gilebert (1c), Godard (1b), Henri (1a-b),
Henri Pi (1a), Iefrei (1a-b), Iohan (1a-b), Osber (1b), Pieres (1a-c),
Pieres M (1a-b), Randvl (1a-b), Ravl (1b-c), Reinald (1a-b), Willelm (1a-b)   50
Carlisle: Alain (1b-c)   85
Exeter: Asketil (1a-b), Iordan (1a-b), Osber (1a-b), Ravl (1b), Ricard (1b-c),
Roger (1a-c)   75
Lincoln: Edmvnd (1b-c), Girard (1b), Hvgo (1b), Lefwine (1b-c), Rodbert (1b),
Walter (1b), Will. D.F. (1b), Willelm (1b-c)   65
Northampton: Filip (1a-b), Hvgo (1a-b), Ravl (1a-c), Reinald (1a-c), Simvn (1b),
Walter (1a-c), Willelm (1a-b)   60
Oxford: Asketil (1b), Iefrei (1b), Owein (1b-c), Ricard (1b-c), Rodbert (1b),
Rodbt. F. B. (1b), Sagar (1b)   70
Wilton: Osber (1a-b), Rodbert (1a-b), Iohan (1a)   75
Winchester: Adam (1a-c), Clement (1a-b), Gocelm (1a-c), Henri (1a),
Osber (1a-b), Reinier (1b), Rodbert (1a-b)   60
Worcester: Edrich (1b), Godwine (1b-c), Osber (1b-c), Oslac (1b)   75
York: Alain (1a-b), Efrard (1a-c), Gerard (1a-b), Hvgo (1a-c), Hunfrei (1a-b),
Isac (1a-b), Tvrkil (1a-c), Willelm (1a-b)   60

Richard I

London: Aimer (2-4a), Fvlke (4a-b), Henri (4a-b), Ravl (2), Ricard (2-4b),
Stivene (2-4b), Willelm (2-4b)   70
Canterbury: Goldwine (3-4b), Hernavd (4b), Hve (4b), Ioan (4b), Meinir (2-4b),
Reinald/Reinavd (2-4b), Roberd (2-4b), Samvel (4b), Simon (4b), Vlard (2-4b)   80
Carlisle: Alein (3-4b)   125
Durham: Adam (4a), Alein (4a-b), Pires (4b)   150
Exeter: Ricard (3)   135
Lichfield: Ioan (2)   2500
Lincoln: Edmvnd (2), Lefwine (2), Willelm (2)   100
Northampton: Giferei (4a), Roberd (3), Waltir (3)   110
Northampton or Norwich: Randvl (4a-b), Willelm (4a-b)   100
Shrewsbury: Ive (4a-b), Reinald/Reinavd (4a-b), Willem (4a)   175
Winchester: Adam (3), Gocelm (3), Osbern (3-4a), Pires (4a), Willelm (3-4a)   80
Worcester: Osbern (2)   250
York: Davi (4a-b), Efrard/Everard (2-4b), Hvgo/Hve (2-4a), Nicole (4a-b),
Tvrkil (2-4a)   80

John

London: Abel (5c-6b), Adam (5b-c), Beneit (5b-c), Fvlke (4c-5b), Henri (4c-5b/5a),
Ilger (5b-6b), Ravf (5c-6b), Rener (5a/b-5c), Ricard (4c-5b), Ricard B (5b-c),
Ricard T (5a/b-5b), Walter (5c-6b), Willelm (4c-5b), Willelm B (5a/b-5c),
Willelm L (5b-c), Willelm T (5b-c)   45
Canterbury: Goldwine (4c-5c), Hernavd/Arnavd (4c-5c), Hve (4c-5c), Iohan (4c-5c),
Iohan B (5b-c), Iohan M (5b-c), Roberd (4c-5c), Samvel (4c-5c), Simon (4c-5c)   50
Bury St Edmunds: Fvlke (5b-c)   90
Carlisle: Tomas (5b)   110
Chichester: Pieres (5b/a-5b), Ravf (5b/a-5b), Simon (5b/a-5b), Willelm (5b)   80
Durham: Pieres (5a-6a)   90
Exeter: Gileberd (5a-b), Iohan (5a-b), Ricard (5a-b)   75

Ipswich: Alisandre (5b-c), Iohan (5b-c) — 60
Kings Lynn: Iohan (5b), Nicole (5b), Willelm (5b) — 125
Lincoln: Alain (5a), Andrev (5a-5c), Hve (5a/b-5c), Iohan (5a), Ravf (5a/b-5b), Ricard (5a-5b/a), Tomas (5a/b-5b) — 50
Northampton: Adam (5b-c), Roberd (5b), Roberd T (5b) — 60
Northampton or Norwich: Randvl (4c) — 80
Norwich: Gifrei (5a/b-5c), Iohan (5a-c), Renald/Renavd (5a-c) — 60
Oxford: Ailwine (5b), Henri (5b), Miles (5b) — 70
Rochester: Alisandre (5b), Hvnfrei (5b) — 90
Winchester: Adam (5a-c), Andrev (5b-c), Bartelme (5b-c), Henri (5a), Iohan (5a-c), Lvkas (5b-c), Miles (5a-c), Ravf (5b-c), Ricard (5a-b) — 50
York: Davi (4c-5b), Nicole (4c-5c), Renavd (5b), Tomas (5a/b-5b) — 50

Henry III

London: Abel (6c-7a), Adam (7b-c), Elis (7a-b), Giffrei (7b-c), Ilger (6c-7b), Ledvlf (7b-c), Nichole (7c-8c), Ravf (6c-7b), Ricard (7b), Terri (7a-b), Walter (6b-c) — 30
Canterbury: Arnold (6c/6x, 6x), Henri (6c-6c/d, 7a-c), Hivn/Ivn (6c-7b), Iohan (6c-7c, 8b-c), Ioan Chic (7b-c), Ioan F. R. (7b-c), Nichole (7c, 8b-c), Osmvnd (7b-c), Robert (6c, 7b-c), Robert Vi (7c), Roger (6c-7b), Roger of R (7a-b), Salemvn (6x, 7a-b), Samvel (6c-d, 7a), Simon (6c-d, 7a-b), Tomas (6d, 7a-b), Walter (6c-7a), Willem (7b-c, 8b-c), Willem Ta (7b-c) — 30
Bury St Edmunds: Iohan (7c-8c), Norman (7a-b), Ravf (6c-d, 7a), Simvnd (7b-c), Willelm (7a) — 35
Durham: Pieres (7a) — 80
Winchester: Henri (6c) — 125
York: Iohan (6c), Peres (6c), Tomas (6c), Wilam (6c) — 125

Irregular Local Issue
Rhuddlan (in chronological order) — 95
Group I (c. 1180 – pre 1205) Halli, Tomas, Simond
Group II (c.1205 – 1215) Simond, Henricus

Timeline Auctions
Inc. Gregory's Est.1858

Rhuddlan
Sold for: £713

We are accepting single entries and collections
of English coins & antiquities

www.timelineauctions.com

+44 [0]1277 815121; enquiries@timelineauctions.com

'LONG CROSS' COINAGE (1247-72)

By the middle of Henry's reign the Short Cross coinage in circulation was in a poor state and, in 1247, a new coinage was ordered with the cross on the reverse being extended to the edge of the coin in an attempt to prevent clipping. The earliest coins (1a) showed the names of the neither the mint nor the moneyer. Class 1b includes the name of the mint. From class 2 onwards all coins show the name of both the mint and the moneyer.

Following publication of the 1908 Brussels Hoard by Churchill and Thomas (2012) the classification of the Long Cross coinage was revised. This divided the Long Cross coinage into four phases: Phase I, 1247, Pre-provincial; Phase II, 1248-1250, Provincial when sixteen provincial mints, in addition to the main mints of London and Canterbury plus Bury St Edmunds were opened to facilitate the production and distribution of the new coins; Phase III, 1250-1272, The Post-provincial in which the mint of Durham re-opened operating intermittently; Phase IV, 1272-1280, Posthumous (see under Edward I on page 167) when the Long Cross coinage was continued in the name of Henry III through the first seven years of the reign of Edward I.

In Phases I and II the obverse features the King's head without a sceptre but during the Post-provincial phase, from class 4 onwards, the sceptre was re-introduced. No round Half-pennies or farthings were struck during the Long Cross coinage but cut halves and quarters were used in considerable numbers.

Mint marks feature on all coins from classes 1 to 4 inclusive and are an important aid to both chronology and identification. Five main varieties of mint mark exist.

1   2   3   4   5

Further reading: Ron Churchill and Bob Thomas, *The Brussels Hoard of 1908. The Long Cross Coinage of Henry III.* 2012.

THE LONG CROSS COINAGE, 1247-79

PHASE I, 1247 PRE-PROVINCIAL PHASE

1358   1359

		F	VF
		£	£
1358	Class 1a. Obv. hENRICVS REX. Rev. ANG LIE TER CI'. *mm* 1	375	1350
1359	Class 1b. Obv. hENRICVS REX ANG. Rev. LIE TER CI' LON (London), CAN (Canterbury - scarce) or AED (Bury St Edmunds - very rare). *mm* 1.	60	200
1359A	Class 1a/1b and 1b/1a mules	250	950
1360	Class 1b/2a mule. (London and Canterbury only)...................................	55	185

1361

1361	Class 2a. Obv. hENRICVS REX TERCI'. *mm* 2. Rev. Moneyer & mint.	35	110

PHASE II, 1248-50 PROVINCIAL PHASE

1361A

	F £	VF £
1361A Class 2b. Long, narrow bust, curly X or straight limbed X. Rev. Moneyer & mint. *mm* 3.	30	90

1362   1362A   1362B

	F £	VF £
1362 Class 3a1. Obv. hENRICVS REX III. Class 2 bust. *mm* 3.	25	85
1362A Class 3a2. Bust altered, eyes are round comprising pellets in crescents; often with a colon after REX. *mm* 3.	25	85
1362B Class 3ab. Neat 3a-3b transitional bust. *mm* 3.	25	75

1363   1363A   1364

	F £	VF £
1363 Class 3b. Neat round bust; beard is three pellets either side of a large central pellet. *mm* 3.	25	70
1363A Class 3bc. Smaller bust with necklines (sometimes vestigal). ENR usually ligated. *mm* 4.	30	80
1364 Class 3c. Similar but coarser bust usually with necklines and a colon after REX. Eyes are round comprising pellets in annulets. *mm* 4.	25	70

PHASE III, 1250-72 POST-PROVINCIAL PHASE

1364A   1364B

	F £	VF £
1364A Class 3d1. Small neat bust generally with a pointed chin and neck lines. Most have a colon after REX. *mm* 4.	30	80
1364B Class 3d2. Larger more rounded bust resembling class 4 coins. Ball tailed letter R (R2). *mm* 4, with a few coins featuring *mm* 5.	30	80

1365    1365a    1366    1366 detail

	F	VF
	£	£

1365   Class 4a. Bust similar to 3d2. King holds sceptre, crown has pellet ornaments.
       Legend starts at 1 o'clock. *mm* 5. 110   375
1365A Class 4ab. As above but crown has end pellets and true central fleur. *mm* 5. 110   375
1366   Class 4b. As above but crown has true half fleurs and central fleur. *mm* 5.   125   425

1367    1367A    1367B    1367B detail

1367   Class 5a1. Legend starts at 10 o'clock. Large round bust, round eyes and
       half fleur at crown ends. No *mm*.. 135   475
1367A Class 5a2. As above but crown has end pellets. Some with the letter X
       with one curved limb (Churchill/Thomas Class 5a3). 25   70
1367B Class 5a4. As above but with a jewelled crown.. 225   750

1368    1368A    1368A detail

1368   Class 5b1. Large oval bust, sometimes narrower with more pointed chin. Half
       fleur crown ends. 150   525
1368A Class 5b2. As above but crown with end pellets. 25   65

1369

1369   Class 5c. Similar but with almond eyes or wedge tailed R., variety with
       disjointed central fleur and/or no stalks.. 25   65

| 1370 | 1370A | 1370B | 1370B detail |

	F	VF
	£	£

1370   Class 5d1. Completely new and very coarse bust with crude central fleur and half fleur ends often with unusual mint spellings. 100   325

1370A Class 5d2. As above but bust is more realistic and less crude................. 60   175

1370B Class 5d3. The "Beri" type; much neater and more pleasing. Central fleur has distinctly pointed ends. 60   175

| 1371 | 1372 | 1373 | 1374 |

| 1372 detail | 1373 detail |

1371   Class 5e. Bust similar to 5d3 (but Canterbury busts usually coarser) but with jewelled crown.. 150   525

1372   Class 5f. New large and round bust similar to those from 5a to 5c with a double banded crown and a low central fleur. 25   65

1373   Class 5g. Similar bust but crown has thick single band with low central fleur. 25   60

1374   Class 5h. Similar but coarser with 'heavier' features and a more pointed chin. Crown fleur comprises three pellets often with one or more individual stalks, possibly posthumous.. 45   165

1375

1375   Gold Penny of 20 pence. As illustration. 65000   275000

Mints, Moneyers and Classes for the Long Cross Coinage

Question marks appear against certain sub classes eg Lincoln 3bc for Walter. In such cases, whilst the Brussels Hoard contained no specimens and whilst no specimen is known to Churchill and Thomas, it is thought feasible that coins of this sub-class were struck and examples may exist.

Fine
From £

London; Anonymous 1a, 1b, 1a/b, 1b/a.
    Nicole (1b/2-5c2), Henri (3a1-5g), Davi (3d1-5f), Ricard (3d1/2-5g),
    Note. Of the above four moneyers, only Nicole is known for class 4ab
    Walter (5c2-5g), Willem (5c2-5g), Ion (5c3-5g), Thomas (5g), Robert (5g),
    Renaud (5g-7), Phelip (7). 25
    Note: Coins of 5a4 and 5d1 are not known for London and coins of 5d2 are excessively
    rare.
Canterbury: Anonymous 1b. Nicole (1b/2-5g), Gilbert (1b/2-3ab, 3b-5c, 5d3-5g),
    Willem (1b/2, 2b-5g), Ion (4ab-5c, 5d2-5g), Robert/Roberd (5c-5d1, 5d3-5h)
    Walter (5c-5g), Ambroci (5g), Alein (5g-5h), Ricard (5h), Roger (5h). 25
    Note: No coin of class 2a is known for Willem but one may exist; coins of classes 4a,
    4b, 5a1 and 5b1 are not known for any Canterbury moneyer and class 5a4 is known
    only for Nicole and Ion.
Bury St Edmunds: Ion (2a-3d2, 4ab, 5a2 and 5a3), Randulf (5b2-5c, 5d3, 5f), Renaud (5g),
    Stephane (5g), Ion/Iohs (5g-7), Ioce (7). 25
Durham: Ricard (5a3, 5b2 & 5c), Roger (5g), Wilelm (5g), Roberd/Robert (6, 7)................. 50
Bristol: Elis (3ab, b, bc, c), Henri (3ab, b), Iacob (3ab, b, bc, c), Roger (3b, bc),
    Walter (3ab, b, bc)... 60
Carlisle: Adam (3ab, b, bc), Ion (3ab, b, bc, c), Robert (3ab, b, bc), Willem (3ab, b). 80
Exeter: Ion (2b, 3a, a2, ab, b), Philip (2b, 3a, a2, ab, b), Robert (2b, 3a1, a2, ab, b),
    Walter (2b2, 3a1, a2, ab, b)... 50
Gloucester: Ion (2b, 3a1, a2, ab, b, c), Lucas (2b2, 3a1, a2, ab, b, c),
    Ricard (2b, 3a1, a2, ab, b, c), Roger (2b, 3a1, a2, ab, b, c).. 50
Hereford: Henri (3ab, b, c), Ricard (3ab, b, c), Roger (3ab, b, c), Walter (3ab, b, c). 70
Ilchester: Huge (3a2, ab, b, bc, c), Ierveis (3a2, ab, b, bc, c), Randvlf (3a2, ab, b, bc, c),
    Stephe (3a2, ab, b, bc, c). 70
Lincoln: Ion (2b, 3a1, a2, ab, b, bc, c), Ricard (2b, 3a1, a2, ab, b, bc, c),
    Walter (2b, 3a1, a2, ab, b, bc, c), Willem (2b, 3a1, a2, ab, b, bc, c). 30
Newcastle: Adam (3ab, b, c), Henri (3ab, b, c), Ion (3ab, b, c), Roger (3ab, b, c). 40
Northampton: Lucas (2b, 3a1, a2, ab, b, bc, c), Philip (2b, 3a1, a2, ab, b, bc, c),
    Tomas (2b, 3a1, a2, ab, b, bc, c), Willem (2b, 3a1, a2, ab, b, bc, c). 40
Norwich: Huge (2b, 3a1, a2, ab, b, bc, c), Iacob (2b, 3a1, a2, ab, b, bc, c),
    Ion (2b, 3a, a2, ab, b, bc, c),Willem (2b, 3a1, a2, ab, b, bc, c). 40
Oxford: Adam (2b, 3a1, a2, ab, b, bc, c), Gefrei (2b, 3a1, a2, ab, b, bc, c),
    Henri (2b, 3a1, a2, ab, b, bc, c), Willem (2b, 3a1, a2, ab, b, bc, c).............................. 40
Shrewsbury: Lorens (3ab, b, bc, c), Nicole (3ab, b, bc, c), Peris (3ab, b, bc, c),
    Ricard (3ab, b, bc, c).. 70
Wallingford: Alisandre (3ab, b), Clement (3ab, b), Ricard (3ab, b), Robert (3ab, b). 70
Wilton: Huge (3ab, b, bc, c), Ion (3ab, b, bc, c), Willem (3ab, b, bc, c). 70
Winchester: Huge (2b, 3a1, a2, ab, b, bc, c), Iordan (2b, 3a1, a2, ab, b, bc, c),
    Nicole (2b, 3a1, a2, ab, b, bc, c), Willem (2b, 3a1, a2, ab, b, bc, c). 40
York: Alain (2b, 3a1, a2, ab, b, bc), Ieremie (2b, 3a1, a2, ab, b, bc), Ion (2b, 3a1,
    a2, ab, b, bc), Rener (2b, 3a1, a2, ab, b, bc), Tomas (3a2, ab, b, bc, c). 30

COINAGE IN THE NAME OF HENRY III 1272-1279

LONG CROSS COINAGE, 1247-79 *(continued)*

PHASE IV, POSTHUMOUS PHASE

These coins were struck between 1272 and 1279 during the reign of Edward I but they bear the name of Henry III. It is most likely that class 5h were also struck during these years but there are no means of separating the coins struck under Edward I from those struck before the death of Henry III; we have, therefore, included all coins of class 5h as being part of the Henry III Phase III.

The earliest coinage of Edward I, in the name of Henry III (Class 5i and 6), is of coarse style and was struck at London, Bury St. Edmunds and Durham only. Class 7, also only from these mints, is of neater style. In 1279 the Long Cross coinage was abandonned and a new coinage introduced.

Cut Halfpennies and Farthings also occur for this issue.

| 1376 | 1377 | 1378 |

	F	VF
	£	£
1376 Class 5i. Even more degraded than 5h. Most coins have ENR ligated and the line of pellets below the crown band is either missing or in a format other than a simple line of three, possibly posthumous	225	750
1377 Class 6. Crude bust with almond shaped eyes and realistic hair reaching the level of the King's mouth. Lombardic N's feature in the reverses of the coins of Bury St Edmunds	25	85
1378 Class 7. More realistic busts (several varieties) with shorter hair reaching the King's nose. Sometimes with Lombardic N's and V's	65	225

Mints, Moneyers, and Classes for Edward I 'Long Cross' Coinage

London: Phelip (VII), Renaud (VII)	*from*	65
Bury St. Edmunds: Ioce (VII), Ion or Ioh (VI, VII)	*from*	25
Durham: Roberd (VI), Robert (VII)	*from*	250

SPINK
founded 1666

COINS OF ENGLAND 2017
E-book available on Amazon, iBookstore,
Google, Kobo, OverDrive
and across most other platforms

For more information or enquiries please contact
Tel: +44 (0)20 7563 4000 | Email: books@spink.com
69 Southampton Row, Bloomsbury, London WC1B 4ET

WWW.SPINKBOOKS.COM

NEW COINAGE (from 1279).

A major re-coinage was embarked upon in 1279 which introduced new denominations. In addition to the penny, halfpence and farthings were also minted and, for the first time, a fourpenny piece called a 'Groat', wt. 89 grs., (from the French *Gros*).

The groats, though ultimately unsuccessful, were struck from more than thirty obverse dies and form an extensive series with affinities to the pence of classes 1c to 3g. The chronology of this series has now been definitively established (see Allen, M. The Durham Mint, pp. 172-179).

As mint administration was now very much centralized, the practice of including the moneyer's name in the coinage was abandoned (except for a few years at Bury St. Edmunds). Several provincial mints assisted with the re-coinage during 1279-81, then minting was again restricted to London, Canterbury, Durham and Bury.

The provincial mints were again employed for a subsidiary re-coinage in 1300 in order to remint lightweight coins and the many illegal *esterlings* (foreign copies of the English pennies, mainly from the Low Countries), which were usually of poorer quality than the English coins.

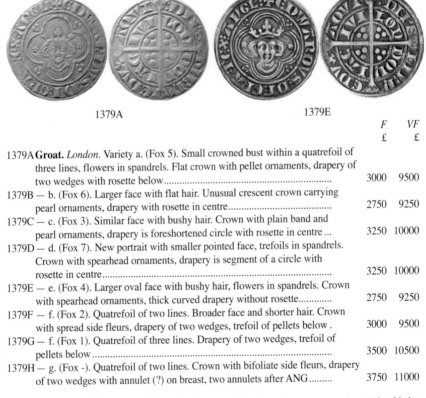

1379A   1379E

	F	VF
	£	£
1379A **Groat**. *London*. Variety a. (Fox 5). Small crowned bust within a quatrefoil of three lines, flowers in spandrels. Flat crown with pellet ornaments, drapery of two wedges with rosette below	3000	9500
1379B — b. (Fox 6). Larger face with flat hair. Unusual crescent crown carrying pearl ornaments, drapery with rosette in centre	2750	9250
1379C — c. (Fox 3). Similar face with bushy hair. Crown with plain band and pearl ornaments, drapery is foreshortened circle with rosette in centre ...	3250	10000
1379D — d. (Fox 7). New portrait with smaller pointed face, trefoils in spandrels. Crown with spearhead ornaments, drapery is segment of a circle with rosette in centre	3250	10000
1379E — e. (Fox 4). Larger oval face with bushy hair, flowers in spandrels. Crown with spearhead ornaments, thick curved drapery without rosette	2750	9250
1379F — f. (Fox 2). Quatrefoil of two lines. Broader face and shorter hair. Crown with spread side fleurs, drapery of two wedges, trefoil of pellets below .	3000	9500
1379G — f. (Fox 1). Quatrefoil of three lines. Drapery of two wedges, trefoil of pellets below	3500	10500
1379H — g. (Fox -). Quatrefoil of two lines. Crown with bifoliate side fleurs, drapery of two wedges with annulet (?) on breast, two annulets after ANG	3750	11000

Edward I groats were often mounted as brooches and gilt. Such specimens are worth considerably less

1382   1383

	F £	VF £

1380 **Penny.** *London.* Class 1a. Crown with plain band, ЄDW RЄX; Lombardic
Π on *obv;* pellet 'barred' S on rev. A with sloping top .... | 275 | 950 |
1381 — 1b. — ЄD RЄX; no drapery on bust, Roman N .... | 1350 | 5750 |
1382 — 1c. — ЄDW RЄX; Roman N, normal or reversed; small lettering ..... | 25 | 120 |
1383 — 1d. — ЄDW R;—; large lettering and face .... | 25 | 110 |

1384   1385   1386

1384 — — — Annulet below bust .... | 90 | 350 |
1385 — 2a. Crown with band shaped to ornaments; usually broken left petal
to central fleur portrait as ld. N usually reversed .... | 20 | 75 |
1386 — 2b. — tall bust; long neck; N reversed .... | 20 | 70 |

1388

1387 — 3a. Crescent-shaped contraction marks; pearls in crown, drapery is
foreshortened circle with hook ends.. | 25 | 90 |
1388 — 3b. — — drapery is segment of a circle, pearls in crown .... | 25 | 90 |
1389 — 3c. — normal crown; drapery in one piece, hollowed in centre.......... | 20 | 70 |

1391   1392   1394

1390 — 3d. — — drapery in two pieces, broad face .... | 20 | 70 |
1391 — 3e. — long narrow face (Northern mints) .... | 20 | 70 |
1392 — 3f. — broad face, large nose, rougher work, late S first used............. | 25 | 95 |
1393 — 3g. — Spread crown small neat bust, narrow face .... | 20 | 65 |
1394 — 4a. Comma-shaped contraction mark, late S always used, C and Є open | 20 | 70 |

1395   1396   1397   1398

	F	VF
	£	£
1395 — 4b. Similar, but face and hair shorter	20	65
1396 — 4c. Larger face with more copious hair; nick to band of crown	25	85
1397 — 4d. Pellet at beginning of *obv.* and *rev.* legend	20	65
1398 — 4e. Three pellets on breast, ropy hair, pellet in *rev.* legend (no pellets on Bury or Durham)	25	75

1399   1400

1399 — 5a. Well spread coins, pellet on breast, face as 1398, A normally unbarred	30	100
1400 — 5b. Coins more spread, tall lettering, long narrow face, pellet on breast	25	90

1401   1402   1403

1401 — 6a. Smaller coins, smaller lettering with closed E (from now on) initial cross almost plain, crown with wide fleurs, crude appearance	90	350
1402 — 6b. Initial cross pattée	50	175
1403 — 7a. Rose on breast (except Bury), short hair; almond-shaped eyes, double barred N	35	110

1404   1406   1406A

1404 — 7b. Rose on breast (London only) longer hair, new crown	40	135
1405 — 8a. Crown resembling 7b with central fleur usually broken	25	80
1406 — 8b. Similar to 1405 with wider drapery, top-tilted S	25	80
1406A — 8c — — Crown with very arched band	25	95

1407

		F £	VF £

1407 — 9a. Drapery of two wedges, pellet eyes, crown of 8a-b or new flatter one; often star on breast... 20 60

1408 — 9b. Small coins; Roman N, normal, un-barred, or usually of pot-hook form; often star or (very rarely) pellet on breast. Some Durham coins are from locally made dies................................ 20 60

1408A – 9c. Larger crude lettering with barred A and abbreviation marks. (only found in combination with dies of 9b or 10ab, except Bury).......... 35 125

1409 - 10ab   1409B - 10ab

1409 — 10ab. ЄDWARD. Bifoliate crown (converted 9b or new taller one). Narrow incurved lettering.. 20 50

1409A — 10ab. Similar with annulet on breast or a pellet each side of head and on breast.. 100 350

1409B — 10ab. ЄDWAR (rarely ЄDWR). Similar to 1409. A few early coins have the trifoliate crown of 9b.................................... 20 50

1410   1411

Crown 1   Crown 2   Crown 3   Crown 4   Crown 5

1410 — 10cf1. Crown 1 (Axe-shaped central fleur, wedge-shaped petals). ЄDWA from now on. Stub-tailed. R.......................... 20 50

1411 — 10cf2. Crown 2 (Well-shaped central lis, no spearheads). Spreading hair. 20 50

1413   1414

	F	VF
	£	£

1412 — 10cf3. Crown 3 (Left-hand arrowhead inclines to right). Early coins
      have the broken lettering of 10cf2; later have new lettering with round-
      backed Є. .... 20 | 50

1413 — 10cf4. Crown 4 (Neat with hooked petal to right-hand side fleur)...... 25 | 80

1414 — 10cf5. Crown 5 (taller and more spread, right-hand ornament inclines
      to left). Later coins are on smaller flans. .... 20 | 55

Some of the coins of class 10cf3 (c.1307-9), and all of the coins of classes 10cf4 and 10cf5 (c.1309-10), were struck in the reign of Edward II.

For a more detailed classification of Class 10, see 'Sylloge of British Coins, 39, The J. J. North Collection, Edwardian English Silver Coins 1279-1351', The Classification of Class 10, c. 1301-10, by C. Wood.

Prices are for full flan, well struck coins.

The prices for the above types are for London. For coins of the other mints see following pages; types are in brackets, prices are for the commonest type of each mint.

| Berwick Type 1 | Type II | Type III | Type IV |

No.	Description	F	VF
1415	*Berwick-on-Tweed.* (Blunt types I-IV) Local dies	25	75
1416	*Bristol.* (2; 3b; c, d; 3f, g; 9b)	20	65
1417	*Bury St. Edmunds.* Robert de Hadelie (3c, d, g; 4a, b, c)	45	125
1418	— Villa Sci Edmundi (4e; 5b; 6b; 7a; 8ab, 9a – 10 cf 5)..........................	20	50
1419	*Canterbury.* (2; 3b-g; 4; 5; 7a; 7b; 9;10)...................................	20	50
1420	*Chester.* (3g; 9b)..	30	90
1421	*Durham.* Plain cross *mm* (9b; 10ab; 10cf 2-3; 10cf 5)......................	20	50
1422	— Bishop de Insula (2; 3b, c, e, g; 4a)	20	50
1423	— Bishop Bec (4b-e; 5b; 6b; 7b; 9a, 9b, 10) with *mm.* cross moline.......	20	50
1424	— — (4b) cross moline in one angle of *rev*..................................	150	425
1425	*Exeter.* (9b)...	25	80
1426	*Kingston-upon-Hull.* (9b)	30	90
1427	*Lincoln.* (3c, d, f, g)	20	50
1428	*Newcastle-upon-Tyne.* (3e; 9b; 10ab).......................................	20	50
1429	*York.* Royal mint (2; 3b, c, d, e, f; 9b)	20	50
1430	— Archbishop's mint (3e, f; 9b). R. Quatrefoil in centre	20	50
1431	**Halfpenny,** *London.* Class 3b. ЄDWR ANGL DNS hYB, drapery composed of curved line with wedges above	40	135
1432	— 3c Drapery composed of two wedges.......................................	25	80

1434A

	F	VF
	£	£
1433　— 3g. New wide crown, thick-waisted S, drapery as 3b..........................	25	80
1433A — — 4c. Narrower crown, drapery of two unequal wedges....................	30	110
1433B — — Similar, pellet before LON	40	140
1434　— 4e. Single-piece collar with (usually) three pellets on breast.............	45	160
1434A — 6. Small face with short hair, large coarse crown, closed Є................	50	175
1435　— 7. Larger face with square jaw, open Є, usually double-barred N.......	40	135
1436　— 8. Similar, new crown with straight sides...	45	160
1437　— 10. ЄDWAR R ANGL DNS hYB, bifoliate or trifoliate crown, new waisted letters	30	100

The above prices are for London; halfpence of the mints given below were also struck.

	F	VF
1438　*Berwick-on-Tweed.* (Blunt types I, II and III)...	50	150
1439　*Bristol.* Class 3c, 3g, 4c	35	110
1440　*Lincoln.* Class 3c..	40	135
1441　*Newcastle.* Class 3e, single pellet in each angle of *rev.*.........................	50	150
1442　*York.* Class 3c-e...	35	110

1443A　　　　　　　　　1445

	F	VF
1443　**Farthing,** *London.* Class 1a. Base silver issue (6.65 grains), ЄDWARDVS RЄX. bifoliate crown with no intermediate jewels, inner circle. R. LONDONIЄNSIS, (rarely LONDRIЄNSIS), ...	50	175
1443A — 1c. Similar trifoliate crown..	40	135
1444　— 2. Smaller face, trifoliate crown with intermediate jewels................	25	90
1445　— 3c. New tapering face, wide at top, crown with curved band.............	25	100
1445A — 3de. Sterling silver issue (5.51 grains.) Є R ANGLIЄ bust (usually) to bottom of coin, no inner circle. R. LONDONIЄNSIS	25	110
1446　— 3g. Similar, new wide crown with curving side fleurs.	25	90
1446A — 4de. Similar to 3de. R̩. CIVITAS LONDON	30	135
1446B — 5. Similar, crude wide crown.	30	135
1447　— 6-7. New large face with wide cheeks, pellet or almond eyes.............	25	90
1448　— 8. Similar, small rounded face, tall crude crown	30	135
1449　— 9a. Є R̩ ANGL DN, small tapering face, (a variety has the face of class 6-7)...	35	150
1449A — 9b. Small ugly face, usually wide crown with outwards-sloping sides..	40	175
1450　— 10 ЄDWARDVS REX (-, A, AN or ANG,) large bust within inner circle.	25	90
Type 1450 often appears on oval flans.		

It is now thought that the order of London Farthings is class 4de, 6-7, 5, 9a, 8, 9b

1446   1452

	F	VF
	£	£
1451 *Berwick-on-Tweed.* (Blunt type I, IIIb)...	125	450
1452 *Bristol.* Class 2, 3c, 3de	35	125
1453 *Lincoln.* Class 3de...	35	125
1453A *Newcastle.* Class 3de, R NOVI CASTRI........................	200	750
1454 *York.* Class 2, 3c, 3de...	40	150

For further information see*: Farthings and Halfpennies, Edward I and II,* P. and B R Withers, 2001

EDWARD II, 1307-27

The coinage of this reign differs only in minor details from that of Edward I. No groats were issued
in the years *c.* 1282-1351.

1458 (12a)   1459 (13)   1460 (14)

1461 (15a)   1462 (15b)   1463 (15c)

1455	**Penny,** *London.* Class 11a. Broken spear-head or pearl on l. side of crown; long narrow face, straight-sided N; round back to C and Є	20	75
1456	— 11b. — Є with angular back (till 15b), N with well-marked serifs (late)	25	80
1457	— 11c. — — A of special form	45	150
1458	— 12a. Central fleur of crown formed of three wedges; thick cross *mm.*	25	90
1458A	— 12b — Crown with diamond-shaped petals and cruciform central fleur; cross of four wedges *mm*	50	175
1458B	— 12c — Crown with heart-shaped petals; cross pattée *mm*..................	60	225
1459	— 13. Central fleur of crown as Greek double axe	25	75
1460	— 14. Crown with tall central fleur; large smiling face with leering eyes	20	75
1461	— 15a. Small flat crown with both spear-heads usually bent to l.; face of 14	25	85
1462	— 15b. — very similar, but smaller face...	25	80
1463	— 15c. — large face, large Є	25	85

Berwick Type V	Type VI	Type VII

		F	*VF*
		£	£
1464	*Berwick-on-Tweed*. (Blunt types V, VI and VII) Local dies except V......	25	85
1465	*Bury St. Edmunds*. (11; 12; 13; 14; 15)...	20	75
1466	*Canterbury*. (11; 12a; 13; 14; 15)	20	75
1467	*Durham*. King's Receiver (11a), *mm*. plain cross......................................	20	75
1468	— Bishop Bec. (11a), *mm*. cross moline	20	75
1469	— Bishop Kellawe (11; 12a; 13), crozier on *rev*.	25	80
1470	— Bishop Beaumont (13; 14; 15), *mm*. lion with lis...............................	25	90
1471	*mm*. plain cross (11a, 14, 15c)	45	150

1472

1472	**Halfpenny,** *London*. Class 10-11, ЄDWARDVS REX (-, A, AN, ANG, ANGL or ANGLI,) bifoliate or trifoliate crown	45	175
1473	— *Berwick-on-Tweed*. (Blunt type V)	110	325

1474

1474	**Farthing,** *London*. Class 11, 13, ЄDWARDVS REX (-, A, AN, or AG), face with pellet eyes...	30	100
1475	— *Berwick-on-Tweed*. (Blunt type V)	175	525

SPINK
founded 1666

COINS OF ENGLAND 2017
E-book available on Amazon, iBookstore,
Google, Kobo, OverDrive
and across most other platforms

For more information or enquiries please contact
Tel: +44 (0)20 7563 4000 | Email: books@spink.com
69 Southampton Row, Bloomsbury, London WC1B 4ET

WWW.SPINKBOOKS.COM

During Edward's early years small quantities of silver coins were minted following the standard of the previous two reigns, but in 1335 halfpence and farthings were produced which were well below the .925 Sterling silver standard. In 1344 an impressive gold coinage was introduced comprising the Double Florin or Double Leopard valued at six shillings, and its half and quarter, the Leopard and the Helm. The design of the Florin was based on the contemporary gold of Philip de Valois of France.

The first gold coinage was not successful and it was replaced later the same year by a heavier coinage, the Noble, valued at 6s. 8d, i.e., 80 pence, half a mark or one third of a pound, together with its fractions. The Noble was lowered in weight in two stages over the next few years, being stabilized at 120 grains in 1351. With the signing of the Treaty of Bretigni in 1360 Edward's title to the Kingdom of France was omitted from the coinage, but it was resumed again in 1369.

In 1344 the silver coinage had been re-established at the old sterling standard, but the penny was reduced in weight to just over 20 grains and in 1351 to 18 grains. Groats were minted again in 1351 and were issued regularly henceforth until the reign of Elizabeth.

Subsequent to the treaty with France which gave England a cross-channel trading base at Calais, a mint was opened there in 1363 for minting gold and silver coins of English type. In addition to coins of the regular English mints, the Abbot of Reading also minted silver pence, halfpence and farthings with a scallop shell in one quarter of the reverse while coins from Berwick display one or two boar's or bear's heads.

There is evidence of re-use of dies at later periods, e.g. 3rd coinage halfpennies.

For further study of the English Hammered Gold Coinage see: Sylloge of Coins of the British Isles, 47, the Herbert Schneider Collection Volume One, by Peter Woodhead. 1996.

Mintmarks

✠	✠	⳨	✚	♔	✠	✠	✚
6	1	2	3	74	4	5	7a

1334-51	Cross pattée (6)		1356	Crown (74)
1351-2	Cross 1 (1)		1356-61	Cross 3 (4)
1351-7	Crozier on cross end (76a, *Durham*)		1361-9	Cross potent (5)
1352-3	Cross 1 broken (2)		1369-77	Cross pattée (6)
1354-5	Cross 2 (3)			Plain cross (7a)

The figures in brackets refer to the plate of mintmarks in Appendix III.

TimeLine Auctions
Inc. Gregory's **Est.1858**

We are accepting single entries and collections
of English hammered coins

Follow us on: +44 [0]1277 815121; enquiries@timelineauctions.com
f /TimeLineAuctions
t @TimeLineAuction   **www.timelineauctions.com**

GOLD
(No gold coinage issued before 1344)

THIRD COINAGE, 1344-51, First period, 1344

1476   1477   1478

	F	VF
	£	£

1476 **Double-florin (Double Leopard).** (=6s.; wt. 108 grs., 6.99g.). King enthroned beneath canopy; crowned leopard's head each side. R. Cross in quatrefoil   75000   350000
1477 **Florin.** Leopard sejant with banner l. R. Somewhat as last   27500   125000
1478 **Half-florin.** Helmet on fleured field. R. Floriate cross   15000   75000

Second period, 1344-46
1479 **Noble** (=6s. 8d., wt. 138.46 grs., 8.97g.). King stg. facing in ship with sword and shield. R. L in centre of royal cross in tressure...................................   17500   90000
1479A **Half-noble.** Similar   5750   22500
1480 **Quarter-noble.** Shield in tressure. R. As last..   2250   8500

1481

1482

Third period, 1346-51
1481 **Noble** (wt. 128.59 grs., 8.33g.). As 1479, but Є in centre; large letters ...   2500   9500
1482 **Half-noble.** Similar   2250   8000
1483 **Quarter-noble.** As 1480, but Є in centre...   300   950

FOURTH COINAGE, 1351-77

Reference: L. A. Lawrence, *The Coinage of Edward III from 1351*.

Pre-treaty period, 1351-61. With French title.

		F £	VF £
1484	**Noble** (wt. 120 grs., 7.77g.), series B (1351). Open Є and C, Roman M; *mm.* cross 1 (1)	1200	4250
1485	— — *rev.* of series A (1351). Round lettering, Lombardic M and N; closed inverted Є in centre	1250	4500
1486	C (1351-1352). Closed Є and C, Lombardic M; *mm.* cross 1 (1)	850	3250
1487	D (1352-1353). *O.* of series C. R. *mm.* cross 1 broken (2)	1750	6500

1490   1498

1488	E (1354-1355). Broken letters, V often has a nick in r. limb; *mm.* cross 2 (3)	800	3000
1489	F (1356). *mm.* crown (74)	1100	4000
1490	G (1356-1361). *mm.* cross 3 (4). Many varieties	800	3000
1491	**Half-noble,** B. As noble with *rev.* of series A, but closed Є in centre not inverted	750	2750
1492	C. *O.* as noble. *Rev.* as last	850	3000
1493	E. As noble	1000	3500
1494	G. As noble. Many varieties	675	2250
1495	**Quarter-noble,** B. Pellet below shield. R. Closed Є in centre	350	900
1496	C. *O.* of series B. *Rev.* details as noble	400	1100
1497	E. *O.* as last. *Rev.* details as noble, pellet in centre	375	950
1498	G. *mm.* cross 3 (4). Many varieties	325	800

Transitional treaty period, 1361. French title omitted, replaced by that of Aquitaine on the noble and (rarely) on the half-noble, but not on the quarter-noble; irregular sized letters; *mm.* cross potent (5).

1499

1499	**Noble.** R. Pellets or annulets at corners of central panel	1100	4000

1504

		F £	*VF* £
1500	**Half-noble.** Similar	525	1600
1501	**Quarter-noble.** Similar. Many varieties. Pellet and rarely Є in centre....	275	700

Treaty period, 1361-69. Omits FRANC, new letters, usually curule-shaped X; *mm.* cross potent(5).

1502	**Noble.** *London.* Saltire or nothing before ЄDWARD..............................	850	3000
1503	— Annulet before ЄDWARD (with, rarely, crescent on forecastle).........	800	2750
1504	*Calais.* C in centre of *rev.,* flag at stern of ship	900	3250
1505	— — without flag..	925	3250

1506   1508

1506	**Half-noble.** *London.* Saltire before ЄDWARD......................................	550	1750
1507	— Annulet before ЄDWARD	575	1850
1508	*Calais.* C in centre of *rev.,* flag at stern of ship	800	2750
1509	— — without flag...	900	3250
1510	**Quarter-noble.** *London.* As 1498. R. Lis in centre................................	275	675
1511	— — annulet before ЄDWARD	275	675
1512	*Calais.* R. Annulet in centre..	325	825
1513	— — cross in circle over shield	300	800
1514	— R. Quatrefoil in centre; cross over shield	400	1100
1515	— — crescent over shield..	425	1250

Post-treaty period, 1369-1377. French title resumed.

1516	**Noble.** *London.* Annulet before ЄD. R. Treaty period die......................	1500	5250
1517	— — — crescent on forecastle..	1100	3750
1518	— — post-treaty letters. R. Є and pellet in centre..................................	900	3250
1519	— — — R. Є and saltire in centre..	1100	3750
1520	*Calais.* Flag at stern. R. Є in centre...	950	3500

1521

		F	VF
		£	£
1521	— — *Rev.* as 1518, with Є and pellet in centre	900	3250
1522	— As 1520, but without flag. R. Є in centre	1100	3750
1523	**Half-noble.** *London.* *O.* Treaty die. *Rev.* as 1518	1850	6500
1524	*Calais.* Without AQT, flag at stern. R. Є in centre	1650	6000
1525	— — R. Treaty die with C in centre	1750	6250

SILVER

FIRST COINAGE, 1327-35 (0.925 fineness)

1526   1530

1526	**Penny.** *London.* As Edw. II; Fox class XVd with Lombardic n's	325	1000
1527	*Bury St. Edmunds.* Similar	425	1350
1528	*Canterbury; mm.* cross pattée with pellet centre	225	700
1529	— — three extra pellets in one quarter	200	650
1530	*Durham.* R. Small crown in centre	575	1750
1530A	*Reading.* R. Escallop in 2nd quarter	600	1750
1531	*York.* As 1526, but quatrefoil in centre of *rev;* three extra pellets in TAS quarter	175	575
1532	— — — pellet in each quarter of *mm*	175	575

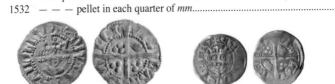

1535   1537   1539

1534	— — — Roman N's on *obv.*	175	575
1535	*Berwick* (1333-1342, Blunt type VIII). Bear's head in one quarter of *rev.*	525	1500
1536	**Halfpenny.** *London.* Indistinguishable from EDWARD II (cf. 1472)	45	175
1537	*Berwick* (Bl. VIII). Bear's head in one or two quarters	85	275
1538	**Farthing.** *London.* Indistinguishable from those of EDWARD II (cf. 1474)	30	100
1539	*Berwick* (Bl. VIII). As 1537	90	300

1540

1542

	F	VF
	£	£

SECOND COINAGE, 1335-43 (0.833 fineness)

1540 **Halfpenny.** *London.* ЄDWARDVS RЄX AN(G). Six-pointed star after
    AN and before LON. Bifoliate or trifoliate crown. 25   85

1540A — — New tall crown. Star of eight or six points after ANG and DON
    and before CIVI or none on rev. 25   90

1541 *Reading.* Escallop in one quarter, star before or after mint 175   575

1542 **Farthing.** *London.* A (N), six-pointed star after A (rarely omitted) and
    before LON, flat crown. 25   80

1542A — ANG, star after ANG and before LON or after DON, tall crown. 25   85

THIRD OR FLORIN COINAGE, 1344-51. Bust with bushy hair. (0.925 fine, 20 grs., 1.30g.)

1543

1544

Reverses: I. Lombàrdic Π II. Roman N. III. Reversed N. IV. Reversed Double-barred N.

1543 **Penny.** Fox proposed 'Class XVI'. *London.* Class 1. ЄDW, Lombardic N. Rev. I.   20   95

1544 — — Class 2, ЄDWA, Lombardic N. Rev. I, II. 20   90

1545 — — Class 3. ЄDW. Roman N. Rev. I, II, III. 20   90

1546 — — Class 4. ЄDW. Reversed N. Rev. I, II, III, IV (doubtful) 20   90

1546A — Unusual types designated A to E. 35   125

1547 — Canterbury. Class 2. as 1544. Rev. I. 60   175

1548 — — Class 4. as 1546 Rev. I. 45   150

1549 *Durham,* Sede Vacante (possibly 1345 issues of Bishop Richard de Bury
    or Bishop Hatfield). A, ЄDWR rev. No marks 30   110

1550 — — B, similar, ЄDWAR R. 45   150

1551 — Bp. Hatfield. C, similar, but pellet in centre of *rev.* 50   160

1552 — — — Crozier on *rev.* 50   160

1553 — — — — with pellet in centre of *rev.* 60   175

1554 — — D, ЄDWARDVS RЄX AIΠ, crozier on *rev.* 75   225

1555

1555 *Reading. obv.* as 1546. R. Escallop in one quarter. 200   750

1555A — — ЄDWARDVS RЄX AΠG. Rev. as 1555. 225   800

1556 *York. obv.* as 1546. R. Quatrefoil in centre 30   100

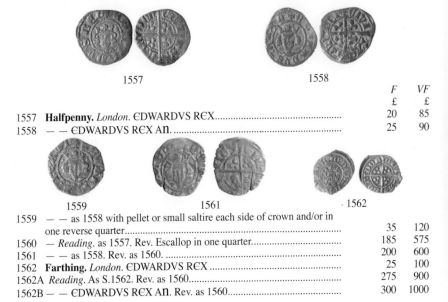

1557   1558

	F	VF
	£	£
1557 **Halfpenny.** *London.* ЄDWARDVS RЄX............	20	85
1558 — — ЄDWARDVS RЄX An.	25	90

1559   1561   1562

1559 — — as 1558 with pellet or small saltire each side of crown and/or in one reverse quarter................................	35	120
1560 — *Reading.* as 1557. Rev. Escallop in one quarter..................	185	575
1561 — — as 1558. Rev. as 1560.	200	600
1562 **Farthing.** *London.* ЄDWARDVS RЄX	25	100
1562A *Reading.* As S.1562. Rev. as 1560.............	275	900
1562B — — ЄDWARDVS RЄX An. Rev. as 1560........	300	1000

FOURTH COINAGE, 1351-77

Reference: L. A. Lawrence, *The Coinage of Edward III from 1351.*
A large variety of mules exist between styles and issue.

Pre-treaty period, 1351-61. With French title.

1563   1565

1567

1563 **Groat** (=4d., 72 grs., 4.66g.). *London,* series B (1351). Roman M, open C and Є; *mm.* cross 1	125	475
1564 — — — crown in each quarter....................	3250	9500
1565 — C (1351-2). Lombardic Ṃ, closed Ç and Є, R with wedge-shaped tail; *mm.* cross 1	45	210
1566 — D (1352-3). R with normal tail; *mm.* cross 1 or cross 1 broken (2).....	50	225
1567 — E (1354-5). Broken letters, V often with nick in r. limb; *mm.* cross 2 (3)	40	165

		F	VF
		£	£
1568	— — — lis on breast..	45	210
1569	— F (1356). *mm.* crown (74)..	50	225

1570

1572

1570	— G (1356-61). Usually with annulet in one quarter and sometimes under bust, *mm.* cross 3 (4). Many varieties..	40	185
1571	*York,* series D. As London	175	675
1572	— E. As London	60	250

1573

1581

1573	**Halfgroat.** *London,* series B. As groat	80	275
1574	— C. As groat	30	110
1575	— D. As groat	35	125
1576	— E. As groat	35	120
1577	— F. As groat	40	135
1578	— G. As groat	35	125
1579	— — — annulet below bust	40	140
1580	*York,* series D. As groat..	70	250
1581	— E. As groat	45	150
1582	— — — lis on breast...	65	225
1583	**Penny.** *London.* Series A (1351). Round letters, Lombardic m and n, annulet in each quarter; *mm.* cross pattée	80	275

1584

1585

1591

1584	— C. Details as groat, but annulet in each quarter	20	95
1585	— D. Details as groat, but annulet in each quarter	25	100
1586	— E. Sometimes annulet in each quarter.....................................	20	95
1587	— F. Details as groat...	20	95
1588	— G. Details as groat..	20	90

		F	*VF*
		£	£
1589	— — — annulet below bust...	25	100
1590	— — — saltire in one quarter	30	135
1591	*Durham*, Bp. Hatfield. Series A. As 1583, but extra pellet in each quarter, VIL LA crozier DVRRЄM and VIL crozier LA DVRRЄM	60	225
1592	— C. Details as groat. R. Crozier, CIVITAS DVNЄLMIЄ	25	110
1593	— D — — —..	30	125
1594	— E — — —...	35	135
1595	— F — R. Crozier, CIVITAS DVRЄMЄ...	30	125
1596	— G — — —...	30	125
1597	— — — — — annulet below bust	35	135
1598	— — — — — saltire in one quarter	45	175
1599	— — — — — annulet on each shoulder	35	150
1600	— — — — — trefoil of pellets on breast	35	150
1601	— — — R. Crozier, CIVITAS DVRЄLMIЄ	45	175
1602	*York*, Royal Mint. Series D	30	110
1603	— — E...	25	100
1604	— Archb. Thoresby. Series D. R. Quatrefoil in centre	30	120
1605	— — G —	25	100
1606	— — — annulet or saltire on breast...	30	125

		F	*VF*
1607	**Halfpenny.** *London.* Series E. ЄDWARDVS RЄX An..........................	60	225
1608	— G, but with *obv.* of F (*mm.* crown). Annulet in one quarter.................	110	400
1609	**Farthing.** *London.* Series E. ЄDWARDVS RЄX	90	350
1609A	— — Series G. Annulet in one quarter..	110	425

Transitional treaty period, 1361. French title omitted, irregular sized letters; *mm.* cross potent (5).

| 1610 | **Groat.** *London.* Annulet each side of crown ....| 375 | 1500 |

1611	**Halfgroat.** Similar, but only seven arches to tressure	100	350
1612	**Penny,** *London.* Omits RЄX, annulet in two upper qtrs. of *mm.*..............	80	300
1613	*York,* Archb. Thoresby. Similar, but quatrefoil enclosing pellet in centre of *rev.* ...	50	175
1614	*Durham.* Bp. Hatfield. Similar. R. Crozier, CIVITAS DORЄLMЄ.........	55	200
1615	**Halfpenny.** Two pellets over *mm.*, ЄDWARDVS RЄX An...................	110	450

Treaty period, 1361-69. French title omitted, new letters, usually 'Treaty' X, rarely curule chair X *mm.* cross potent (5).

		F	VF
		£	£
1616	**Groat,** *London.* Many varieties	70	250
1617	— Annulet before ЄDWARD	75	260
1618	— Annulet on breast	110	400

1617   1618

1619	*Calais.* As last	125	425

1620

1620	**Halfgroat,** *London.* As groat	50	175
1621	— — Annulet before ЄDWARDVS	50	175
1622	— — Annulet on breast	60	200
1623	*Calais.* As last	110	350
1624	**Penny,** *London.* ЄDWARD AПGL R, etc	35	125
1625	— — — pellet before ЄDWARD	40	135
1626	*Calais.* R. VILLA CALЄSIE	130	475
1627	*Durham.* R. CIVITAS DVПЄLMIS	50	175
1628	— R. Crozier, CIVITAS DVRЄMЄ	40	135
1629	*York,* Archb. Thoresby. Quatrefoil in centre of *rev.,* ЄDWARDVS DЄI G RЄX AП	40	135
1630	— — — ЄDWARDVS RЄX AПGLI	30	110
1631	— — — — quatrefoil before ЄD and on breast	35	120
1632	— — — — annulet before ЄD	35	120
1633	— — — ЄDWARD AПGL R DПS HYB	40	135
1634	**Halfpenny.** ЄDWARDVS RЄX AП, pellet stops	30	110

1635   1636

1635	— Pellet before ЄD, annulet stops	30	110
1636	**Farthing.** ЄDWARDVS RЄX, pellet or no stops	150	525

Post-treaty period, 1369-77. French title resumed, X like St. Andrew's cross; *mm.* 5, 6, 7a.

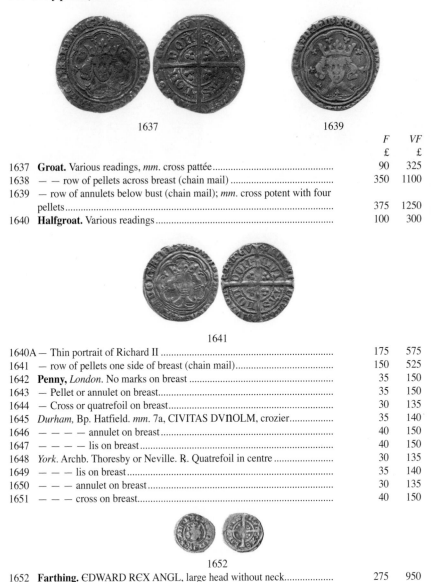

1637   1639

		F £	VF £
1637	**Groat.** Various readings, *mm.* cross pattée	90	325
1638	— — row of pellets across breast (chain mail)	350	1100
1639	— row of annulets below bust (chain mail); *mm.* cross potent with four pellets	375	1250
1640	**Halfgroat.** Various readings	100	300

1641

1640A	— Thin portrait of Richard II	175	575
1641	— row of pellets one side of breast (chain mail)	150	525
1642	**Penny,** *London.* No marks on breast	35	150
1643	— Pellet or annulet on breast	35	150
1644	— Cross or quatrefoil on breast	30	135
1645	*Durham,* Bp. Hatfield. *mm.* 7a, CIVITAS DVnOLM, crozier	35	140
1646	— — — — annulet on breast	40	150
1647	— — — — lis on breast	40	150
1648	*York.* Archb. Thoresby or Neville. R. Quatrefoil in centre	30	135
1649	— — — lis on breast	35	140
1650	— — — annulet on breast	30	135
1651	— — — cross on breast	40	150

1652

1652	**Farthing.** EDWARD REX ANGL, large head without neck	275	950

For further reading see:
Halfpennies and Farthings of Edward III and Richard II. *Paul and Bente R. Withers, 2002.*

There was no change in the weight standard of the coinage during this reign and the coins evolve from early issues resembling those of Edward III to late issues similar to those of Henry IV.

There is no overall, systematic classification of the coins of Richard II but a coherent scheme for the gold coinage has been worked out and is published in the Schneider Sylloge (SCBI 47). This classification has been adopted here.

Reference: *Silver coinages of Richard II, Henry IV and V.* (B.N.J. 1959-60 and 1963).

Mintmark: cross pattée (6)

GOLD

	F £	VF £
1653 **Noble,** *London.* Style of Edw. III. IA. Lis over sail	1500	5250

1654

1658

1654	— IB. Annulet over sail..	1100	3750
1655	French title omitted. IIA. Crude style, saltire over sail. IIB. Fine style, trefoil over sail. IIC. Porcine style, no mark over sail	1100	3750
1656	French title resumed. IIIA. Fine style, no marks....................................	1200	4000
1657	— IIIB. Lis on rudder. IIIC. Trefoil by shield	1200	4000
1658	Henry IV style. IVA. Escallop on rudder. IVB. Crescent on rudder.........	1650	5750
1659	*Calais.* With altered obverse of Edw. III, Edw. III lettering....................	2250	7500
1660	Style of Edw. III. IB. New lettering. Voided quatrefoil over sail	1350	4500

1661

1661	French title omitted. IIA. Crude style, no marks. IIB. Fine style, trefoil over sail. IIC. Porcine style, no marks..	1200	4000
1662	French title resumed. IIIA. Fine style, no marks	1250	4250
1663	— IIIB. Lion on rudder. IIIC. Two pellets by shield	1650	5750

	F £	VF £

1664 **Half-noble,** *London.* With altered *obv.* of Edw. III. Usually muled with
   rev. or altered *rev.* of Edw. III 1650   5250

1665   1673

		F £	VF £
1665	Style of Edw. III. IB. No marks or saltire over sail............................	1250	4500
1666	French title omitted. IIA. New style, no marks...................................	1350	4750
1667	French title resumed. IIIA. No marks. IIIB. Lion on rudder..............	1250	4500
1668	Henry IV style. IVB. Crescent on rudder	1500	5500
1669	*Calais.* Mule with *obv.* or *rev.* of Edw. III..	1850	6500
1670	Style of Edw. III. IB. Quatrefoil over sail	1650	6000
1671	Late style. French title. IIIA. No marks. IIIB. Saltire by rudder	1500	5500
1672	**Quarter-noble,** *London.* IA. R in centre of *rev.*	450	1250
1673	IB Lis in centre of *rev.*	400	1100
1674	— lis or cross over shield	450	1250

1675   1677

		F £	VF £
1675	IIIA. Pellet in centre of *rev.*..	400	1100
1676	IIIB. Trefoil of annulets over shield or trefoils in spandrels..............	475	1500
1677	IVA. Escallop over shield	450	1350

COINS OF ENGLAND & THE UNITED KINGDOM PRE-DECIMAL ISSUES

STANDARD CATALOGUE OF BRITISH COINS SPINK 2017

SPINK
founded 1666

COINS OF ENGLAND 2017
E-book available on Amazon, iBookstore,
Google, Kobo, OverDrive and across
most other platforms

For more information or enquiries please contact
Tel: +44 (0)20 7563 4000 | Email: books@spink.com
69 Southampton Row, Bloomsbury, London WC1B 4ET

WWW.SPINKBOOKS.COM

SILVER

1680

		F	VF
		£	£
1678	**Groat.** I. Style of Edw. III, F *(i.e. et)* before FRANC, etc.	525	2250
1679	II. New lettering, retrograde Z before FRANC, etc.	450	1850
1680	III. Bust with bushy hair, 'fishtail' serifs to letters	475	2000
1681	IV. New style bust and crown, crescent on breast	1500	6500

1682

1682	**Halfgroat.** II. New lettering; with or without French title	225	850
1683	III. As 1680	250	900
1684	— — with *obv.* die of Edw. III (1640A)	275	950
1685	IV. As 1681, with or without crescent on breast	375	1350
1686	**Penny,** *London*. I Lettering as 1678, RICARDVS RЄX AnGLIЄ	165	625
1688	— II. As 1679, Z FRAnC lis on breast	175	675

1688

1689	— III. As 1680, RICARD RЄX AnGLIЄ, fish-tail letters	185	700
1690	*York*. I. Early style, usually with cross or lis on breast, quatrefoil in centre of *rev.*	65	300
1691	— II. New bust and letters, no marks on breast	65	300

1692

1692	— Local dies. Pellet above each shoulder, cross on breast, REX ANGLIE or ANGILIE..	75	325
1693	— — — REX DNS ЄB	85	350
1694	— — — REX ANG FRANC...	80	375
1695	— III. As 1680, REX ANGL Z FRANC (scallop after TAS).............	75	325
1696	— IV. Very bushy hair, new letters, R. R in centre of quatrefoil........	135	550
1697	*Durham.* Cross or lis on breast, DVNOLM	125	475

1698   1699

1698	**Halfpenny.** Early style. LONDON, saltire or annulet (rare) on breast	45	150
1699	Intermediate style. LONDON, no marks on breast	35	120
1700	Type III. Late style. Similar, but fishtail letters	35	125
1700A	Type IV. Short, stubby lettering...	40	135

1701   1704A

1701	**Farthing.** Small bust and letters..	110	450
1703	Similar but no neck	110	450
1704	Rose in each angle of *rev.* instead of pellets	135	525
1704A	Large head with broad face as Henry IV	150	575

For further reading see:
Halfpennies and Farthings of Edward III and Richard II. P. and B. R. Withers, 2002.

AMR Coins
Dealers in Quality British Coins
BNTA

British Coins Bought and Sold
www.amrcoins.com
email: info@amrcoins.com
tel: +44 (0)7527 569308

HENRY IV, 1399-1413

In 1412 the standard weights of the coinage were reduced, the noble by 12 grains and the penny by 3 grains, partly because there was a scarcity of bullion and partly to provide revenue for the king, as Parliament had not renewed the royal subsidies. As in France, the royal arms were altered, three fleur-de-lis taking the place of the four or more lis previously displayed.

Mintmark: cross pattée (6)　

GOLD

HEAVY COINAGE, 1399-1412

1706 　　　　　　　　　　1707

		F	*VF*
		£	£
1705	**Noble** (120 grs., 7.77g.), *London*. Old arms with four lis in French quarters; crescent or annulet on rudder	6500	22500
1706	— New arms with three lis; crescent, pellet or no marks on rudder	6250	20000
1707	*Calais*. Flag at stern, old arms; crown on or to l. of rudder	8000	27500

1709

1708	— — new arms; crown or saltire on rudder	7500	25000
1709	**Half-noble**, *London*. Old arms	5250	17500
1710	— new arms	5000	16500
1711	*Calais*. New arms	6250	22500
1712	**Quarter-noble**, *London*. Crescent over old arms	1350	4500
1713	— — — new arms	1250	4250
1714	*Calais*. New arms. R. *Mm.* crown	1500	5250

1715

	F £	*VF* £

LIGHT COINAGE, 1412-13

| 1715 | **Noble** (108 grs., 6.99g.). Trefoil, or trefoil and annulet, on side of ship. R. Trefoil in one quarter | 1750 | 6000 |
| 1716 | **Half-noble.** Similar, but always with annulet | 2000 | 7500 |

1717

| 1717 | **Quarter-noble.** Trefoils, or trefoils and annulets beside shield, lis above. R. Lis in centre | 650 | 2000 |

SILVER

HEAVY COINAGE, 1399-1412

1718	**Halfgroat** (36 grs., 2.33g.). Star on breast	1500	5250
1718A	— Muled with Edw. III (1640A) *obv.*	750	2500
1719	**Penny,** *London.* Similar, early bust with long neck	850	3000
1720	— later bust with shorter neck, no star on breast	850	3000

1722   1723   1725

1722	*York* Bust with broad face, round chin	475	1500
1723	**Halfpenny.** Early small bust	225	750
1724	— later large bust, with rounded shoulders,	250	800
1725	**Farthing.** Face without neck	850	2500

LIGHT COINAGE, 1412-13

1726

1732

	F £	VF £
1726 **Groat** (60 grs., 3.88g.). I. Pellet to l., annulet to r. of crown; altered die of Richard II	2500	9000
1727 New dies; II. Annulet to l., pellet to r. of crown, 8 or 10 arches to tressure	2250	8000
1728 — III. Similar but 9 arches to tressure	2000	7000
1729 **Halfgroat.** Pellet to l., annulet to r. of crown	1250	3500
1730 Annulet to l., pellet to r. of crown	950	2750
1731 **Penny,** *London.* Annulet and pellet by crown; trefoil on breast and before CIVI	900	2750
1732 — — annulet or slipped trefoil before LON	950	3000
1733 — Pellet and annulet by crown	950	3000
1734 *York.* Annulet on breast. R. Quatrefoil in centre	450	1250
1735 *Durham.* Trefoil on breast, DVNOLM	425	1100

1737

1738

	F £	VF £
1737 **Halfpenny.** New dies; annulets by crown or neck, or no marks	275	800
1738 **Farthing.** Face, no bust; trefoil after REX	750	2250

For further information see:
Halfpennies and Farthings of Henry IV, V and VI. P. and B. R. Withers, 2003.

TimeLine Auctions
Inc. Gregory's Est.1858

Sold for:
£3,627

Follow us on:

f /TimeLineAuctions
t @TimeLineAuction

We are accepting
single entries and collections
of English hammered coins

www.timelineauctions.com

There was no change of importance in the coinage of this reign. There was, however, a considerable development in the use of privy marks which distinguished various issues, except for the last issue of the reign when most marks were removed. The Calais mint, which had closed in 1411, did not re-open until just before the end of the reign. There is now some uncertainty as to whether types A and B of Henry V should be given to Henry IV.

Mintmarks

Cross pattée (4)   Pierced cross with   Pierced cross (18).
                     pellet centre (20)

GOLD

		F £	VF £
1739	**Noble.** A. Quatrefoil over sail and in second quarter of *rev.* Short broad letters, no other marks	2000	7500
1740	— B. Ordinary letters; similar, or with annulet on rudder	1350	4500
1741	— C. Mullet by sword arm, annulet on rudder	1200	4000

1742   1744

		F £	VF £
1742	— — — broken annulet on side of ship	1100	3750
1743	—D. Mullet and annulet by sword arm, trefoil by shield, broken annulet on ship	1250	4250
1744	— E. Mullet, or mullet and annulet by sword arm, trefoil by shield, pellet by sword point and in one quarter, annulet on side of ship	1200	4000
1745	— — Similar, but trefoil on ship instead of by shield	1250	4250
1746	— F. Similar, but no pellet at sword point, trefoil in one quarter	1350	4500
1747	— G. No marks; annulet stops, except for mullet after first word	1750	6000
1748	**Half Noble.** B. As noble; Hen. IV *rev.* die	2250	7500
1749	— C. Broken annulet on ship, quatrefoil below sail	950	3250
1750	— — Mullet over shield, broken annulet on *rev.*	900	3000
1751	— F. Similar, but no annulet on ship, usually trefoil by shield	1000	3500
1752	— F/E. As last, but pellet in 1st and annulet in 2nd quarter	1100	4000

1753

1756

	F	VF
	£	£
1753 — G. As noble, but quatrefoil over sail, mullet sometimes omitted after first word of *rev.*	1000	3500
1754 **Quarter Noble.** A. Lis over shield and in centre of *rev.* Short broad letters; quatrefoil and annulet beside shield, stars at corners of centre on *rev.*	700	1850
1755 — C. Ordinary letters; quatrefoil to l., quat. and mullet to r. of shield	425	1050
1756 — — — annulet to l., mullet to r. of shield	325	750
1757 — F. Ordinary letters; trefoil to l., mullet to r. of shield	375	900
1758 — G. — no marks, except mullet after first word	425	1050

SILVER

1759

1759 **Groat.** A. Short broad letters; 'emaciated' bust	1100	3750
1760 — — muled with Hen. IV *obv*	1750	5750
1761 — — muled with Hen. IV *rev*	1350	4250

1762B

1767

1762 B. Ordinary letters; 'scowling' bust	425	1350
1762A — — mullet in centre of breast	450	1500
1762B — — mullet to r. of breast	575	2000
1763 — — muled with Hen. IV	1050	3250
1764 C. Normal 'frowning' bust	325	1100
1765 — — mullet on r. shoulder	150	575
1766 — — R muled with Hen. IV	625	2250
1767 G. Normal 'frowning' bust; no marks	375	1350
1768 **Halfgroat.** A. As groat, but usually with annulet and pellet by crown	750	3000

	F	VF
	£	£
1769 B. Ordinary letters; no marks..	325	1250
1770 — — muled with Hen. IV *obv.*..	1000	3500
1771 C. Tall neck, broken annulet to l. of crown...	125	450
1772 — — — mullet on r. shoulder	150	525

1774   1775   1788

	F	VF
1773 — — — mullet in centre of breast	120	375
1774 F. Annulet and trefoil by crown, mullet on breast	125	450
1775 G. New neat bust: no marks...	120	375
1776 **Penny.** *London.* Altered Hen. IV *obv.* with mullet added to l. of crown..	750	2500
1777 — A. Letters, bust and marks as 1768	275	950
1778 — C. Tall neck, mullet and broken annulet by crown	45	200
1779 — D. Similar, but whole annulet	50	225
1780 — F. Mullet and trefoil by crown	50	225
1781 — G. New neat bust, no marks, DI GRA	60	240
1782 *Durham.* C. As 1778 but quatrefoil at end of legend...........................	45	185
1783 — D. As 1779	45	185
1784 — G. Similar, but new bust. R. Annulet in one qtr.	45	200
1785 *York.* C. As 1778, but quatrefoil in centre of *rev.*...............................	40	165
1786 — D. Similar, but whole annulet by crown	40	165
1787 — E. As last, but pellet above mullet	60	240
1788 — F. Mullet and trefoil by crown	40	165
1789 — — Trefoil over mullet to l., annulet to r. of crown............................	50	225
1790 — G. Mullet and trefoil by crown (London dies).................................	45	185

1791   1796   1798

	F	VF
1791 — — Mullet and lis by crown, annulet in one qtr. (usually local dies)....	40	175
1792 **Halfpenny.** A. Emaciated bust, annulets by crown	175	650
1793 — altered dies of Hen. IV..	225	800
1794 C. Ordinary bust, broken annulets by crown	30	110
1795 D. Annulets, sometimes broken, by hair...	35	125
1796 F. Annulet and trefoil by crown	35	125
1797 G. New bust; no marks, (usually muled with Henry VI annulet *rev.*)	45	150
1797A **Farthing.** *London.* B. Very large head	450	1500
1798 — G. Small face with neck...	300	800
1798A *Calais.* G. as 1798, VILLA CALIS	450	1500

For further information see:
Halfpennies and Farthings of Henry IV, V and VI. P and B. R. Withers, 2003.

The supply of gold began to dwindle early in the reign, which accounts for the rarity of gold after 1426. The Calais mint had reopened just before the death of Henry V and for some years a large amount of coin was struck there. It soon stopped minting gold; the mint was finally closed in 1440. A royal mint at York was opened for a short time in 1423/4.

Marks used to denote various issues become more prominent in this reign and can be used to date coins to within a year or so.

Reference: C. A. Whitton Heavy Coinage of Henry VI. (B.N.J. 1938-41).

Mintmarks

136 7a 105 18 133 8 9 15

1422-7	Incurved pierced cross (136)	1422-34	Cross pommée (133)
1422-3	Lis (105, York)	1427-34	Cross patonce (8)
1422-60	Plain cross (7a, intermittently		Cross fleury (9)
	Lis (105, on gold)	1434-35	Voided cross (15)
1422-27	Pierced cross (18)	1435-60	Cross fleury (9)
1460	Lis (105, on rev. of some groats)		

For Restoration mintmarks see page 198.

GOLD

1799

		F £	VF £
Annulet issue, 1422-c.1430			
1799	**Noble.** *London.* Annulet by sword arm, and in one spandrel on *rev.;* trefoil stops on *obv.* with lis after hЄnRIC, annulets on *rev.,* with mullet after IhC	950	3000
1800	— Similar, but *obv.* from Henry V die	2000	7000
1801	— As 1799, but Flemish imitative coinage	850	2500

1802

1802	*Calais.* As 1799, but flag at stern and C in centre of *rev*	1350	4500

		F	VF
		£	£
1803	— — with h in centre of *rev.*	1200	4000
1804	*York.* As London, but with lis over stern..	1500	5000

1805

1805	**Half-noble.** *London.* As 1799..	725	2250
1806	— Similar, but *obv.* from Henry V die..	1200	4000
1807	*Calais.* As noble, with C in centre of *rev.*	1500	5000
1808	— — with h in centre of *rev.*	1350	4500
1809	*York.* As noble..	1500	5000
1810	**Quarter-noble.** *London.* Lis over shield; *mm.* large lis	300	700
1811	— — — trefoil below shield..	325	750
1812	— — — pellet below shield	325	800
1813	*Calais.* Three lis over shield; *mm.* large lis..	425	1250

1814

1819

1814	— Similar but three lis around shield...	350	950
1815	— As 1810, but much smaller *mm.*..	325	850
1816	*York.* Two lis over shield..	350	950

Rosette-mascle issue, c.1430-31

1817	**Noble.** *London.* Lis by sword arm and in *rev.* field; stops, rosettes, or		
	rosettes and mascles..	1850	6500
1818	*Calais.* Similar, with flag at stern	2250	8500
1819	**Half-noble.** *London.* Lis in *rev.* field; stops, rosettes and mascles...........	2500	9500
1820	*Calais.* Similar, flag at stern; stops, rosettes...	3250	12000
1821	**Quarter-noble.** *London.* As 1810; stops, as noble....................................	1000	3500
1822	— without lis over shield..	1100	3750
1823	*Calais.* Lis over shield, rosettes r. and l., and rosette stops	1100	3750

Pinecone-mascle issue, c.1431-2/3

1824

		F	VF
		£	£
1824	**Noble.** Stops, pinecones and mascles	1850	6500
1825	**Half-noble.** *O.* Rosette-mascle die. R. As last	3000	11000
1826	**Quarter-noble.** As 1810, but pinecone and mascle stops	1200	4000

1828

Leaf-mascle issue, c.1432/3-6

1827	**Noble.** Leaf in waves; stops, saltires with two mascles and one leaf	4250	15000
1828	**Half-noble.** (Fishpool hoard and Reigate hoard)	3250	12500
1829	**Quarter-noble.** As 1810; stops, saltire and mascle; leaf on inner circle of *rev.*	1250	4500

Leaf-trefoil issue, c.1436-8

1830	**Noble.** Stops, leaves and trefoils	3000	11000
1830A	**Half-noble.**	3250	12500
1831	**Quarter-noble.** Similar	1250	4500

Trefoil issue, 1438-43

1832	**Noble.** Trefoil to left of shield and in *rev.* legend	3000	11000

Leaf-pellet issue, 1445-54

1833	**Noble.** Annulet, lis and leaf below shield	3500	13500

Cross-pellet issue, 1454-61

1834	**Noble.** Mascle at end of *obv.* legend	4250	15000

ARTHUR BRYANT COINS

Dealers in British coins and medals

www.bryantcoins.com
abcoins@live.co.uk
07768 645 686

Muling exists in Henry VI coins spanning two or three issues. Full flan coins in the smaller denominations are difficult to find.

SILVER

Annulet issue, 1422-30

1835    1836

	F	VF
	£	£
1835 **Groat.** *London.* Annulet in two quarters of *rev.*	40	145
1836 *Calais.* Annulets at neck. R. Similar.	40	140
1837 — — no annulets on *rev.*	65	250

1838

1838 *York.* Lis either side of neck. R. As 1835	1250	3500
1839 **Halfgroat.** *London.* As groat	40	150

1840    1843

1840 *Calais.* As 1836.	30	120
1841 — — no annulets on *rev.*	40	140
1843 *York.* As groat.	900	2750

1845

1844 **Penny.** *London.* Annulets in two qtrs.	30	110
1845 *Calais.* Annulets at neck. R. As above.	30	100

	F	VF
	£	£
1847 *York*. As London, but lis at neck	900	2750
1848 **Halfpenny.** *London*. As penny	20	80
1849 *Calais*. Similar, but annulets at neck	20	80

1850

1852

1850 *York*. Similar, but lis at neck	475	1500
1851 **Farthing.** *London*. As penny, but *mm.* cross pommée	100	350
1852 *Calais*. Similar, but annulets at neck	135	475
1852A *York*. Similar, but lis at neck	575	1500

Annulet-trefoil sub-issue

1854

1855

1854 **Groat.** *Calais,* as 1836 but trefoil to l. of crown, R trefoil after POSVI and only one annulet	70	225
1855 **Halfgroat.** *Calais,* similar, usually a mule with annulet issue.	55	175
1856 **Penny.** *Calais*. Similar, only one annulet on *rev*	80	275

Rosette-mascle issue, 1430-31. All with rosettes (early) or rosettes and mascles somewhere in the legends.
| 1858 **Groat.** *London*. .... | 65 | 225 |

1859

1861

1859 *Calais*	45	150
1860 — mascle in two spandrels	60	175
1861 **Halfgroat.** *London*.	100	325

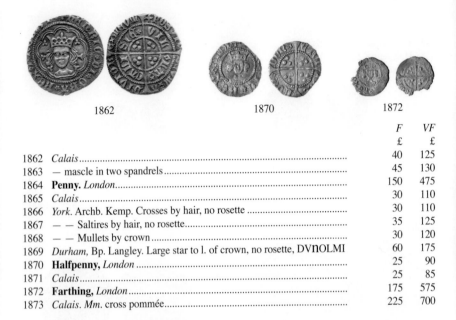

1862   1870   1872

		F £	VF £
1862	*Calais*..	40	125
1863	— mascle in two spandrels..	45	130
1864	**Penny.** *London*..	150	475
1865	*Calais*..	30	110
1866	*York.* Archb. Kemp. Crosses by hair, no rosette	30	110
1867	— — Saltires by hair, no rosette...	35	125
1868	— — Mullets by crown...	30	120
1869	*Durham,* Bp. Langley. Large star to l. of crown, no rosette, DVnOLMI	60	175
1870	**Halfpenny,** *London*	25	90
1871	*Calais*..	25	85
1872	**Farthing,** *London*..	175	575
1873	*Calais. Mm.* cross pommée..	225	700

Pinecone-mascle issue, 1431-32/3. All with pinecones and mascles in legends.

1874   1876

		F	VF
1874	**Groat,** London...	50	160
1875	*Calais*...	45	150
1876	**Halfgroat,** *London*	60	175
1877	*Calais*...	45	130
1878	**Penny,** *London*...	50	175
1879	*Calais*...	40	125
1880	*York,* Archb. Kemp. Mullet by crown, quatrefoil in centre of *rev.*	40	135
1881	— — rosette on breast, no quatrefoil...	40	135
1882	— — mullet on breast, no quatrefoil	45	150
1883	*Durham,* Bp. Langley. DVnOLMI...	50	165

1884

1886

		F	VF
		£	£
1884	**Halfpenny,** *London*	20	80
1885	*Calais*	25	90
1886	**Farthing,** *London*	135	500
1887	*Calais. Mm.* cross pommée	175	650

Leaf-mascle issue, 1432/3-6. Usually with a mascle in the legend and a leaf somewhere in the design.

1888	**Groat.** *London.* Leaf below bust, all appear to read DOnDOn	450	1350
1889	— — *rev.* of last or next coinage	150	525

1890

1892

1890	*Calais.* Leaf below bust, and usually below MEVM	135	450
1891	**Halfgroat.** *London.* Leaf under bust, pellet under TAS and DON.	165	575
1892	*Calais.* Leaf below bust, and sometimes on *rev.*	135	450
1893	**Penny.** *London.* Leaf on breast, no stops on *rev.*	65	200
1894	*Calais.* Leaf on breast and below SIE	75	225
1895	**Halfpenny.** *London.* Leaf on breast and on *rev.*	35	100
1896	*Calais.* Leaf on breast and below SIE	75	225

1897

1902

Leaf-trefoil issue, 1436-8. Mostly with leaves and trefoil of pellets in the legends.

1897	**Groat.** *London.* Leaf on breast	85	250
1898	— without leaf on breast	85	250
1899	*Calais.* Leaf on breast	400	1250
1900	**Halfgroat.** *London.* Leaf on breast; *mm.* plain cross	70	225
1901	— *O. mm.* cross fleury; leaf on breast	65	200
1902	— — without leaf on breast	70	225
1902A	*Calais.* leaf on breast, mule with leaf mascle *rev.*	175	600

		F	VF
		£	£
1903	**Penny.** *London.* Leaf on breast...	80	250
1903A	*Calais.* Similar...	275	750
1904	*Durham,* Bp. Neville. Leaf on breast. R. Rings in centre, no stops, DVnOLM	110	350

	1905	1907	
1905	**Halfpenny.** *London.* Leaf on breast	25	90
1906	— without leaf on breast..	25	95
1906A	*Calais.* leaf on breast, mule with leaf mascle rev.	100	325
1907	**Farthing.** *London.* Leaf on breast; stops, trefoil and saltire on *obv.*........	135	450

Trefoil issue, 1438-43. Trefoil of pellets either side of neck and in legend, leaf on breast.

1910

1908	**Groat.** *London.* Sometimes a leaf before LON.	80	250
1909	— Fleurs in spandrels, sometimes extra pellet in two qtrs.	85	275
1910	— Trefoils in place of fleurs at shoulders, none by neck, sometimes extra pellets...	90	300
1911	*Calais*..	225	800

	1911A	1912A	
1911A	**Halfgroat,** *London* Similar, but trefoil after DEUM and sometimes after POSVI Mule only with leaf trefoil *obv.*....................	150	475
1911B	— *Calais Obv.* Similar to 1911, mule with leaf mascle *rev.*.....................	250	850
1912	**Halfpenny,** *London*	25	100
1912A	**Farthing,** *London*	200	675

HAMMERED BRITISH COINS

Hammered coins bought and sold

www.hammeredbritishcoins.com
mail@hammeredbritishcoins.com
07825226435

Trefoil pellet issue, 1443-5

1913

		F	*VF*
		£	£
1913	**Groat.** Trefoils by neck, pellets by crown, small leaf on breast; sometimes extra pellet in two quarters	100	325

1915   1917

Leaf-pellet issue, 1445-54. Leaf on breast, pellet each side of crown, except where stated.

1914	**Groat.** ANGL; extra pellet in two quarters	60	225
1915	*Similar,* but ANGLI	60	210
1916	— — trefoil in *obv.* legend	75	275
1917	Leaf on neck, fleur on breast, R often extra pellet in two quarters	60	225
1918	As last, but two extra pellets by hair	275	900
1919	**Halfgroat.** As 1914 *mm.* Cross patonce	85	300
1920	Similar, but *mm.* plain cross, some times no leaf on breast, no stops	75	250
1921	**Penny.** *London.* Usually extra pellets in two quarters	55	160
1922	— — pellets by crown omitted	55	175
1923	— — trefoil in legend	60	185
1924	*York,* Archb. Booth. R. Quatrefoil and pellet in centre	40	135
1925	— — two extra pellets by hair (local dies)	40	135
1926	*Durham,* Bp. Neville. Trefoil in *obv.* legend. R. Two rings in centre of cross	60	175

1928   1930

1927	— — Similar, but without trefoil	60	175
1928	**Halfpenny.** Usually extra pellet in two quarters	20	80
1929	— *mm.* plain cross	20	80
1930	**Farthing.** As last	135	475

Unmarked issue, 1453-4

1931   1935

		F £	VF £
1931	**Groat.** No marks on *obv.*; two extra pellets on *rev.*	525	1750
1932	— four extra pellets on *rev.*	650	2250
1933	**Halfgroat.** As 1931	375	1250

Cross-pellet issue, 1454-61

1934	**Groat.** Saltire either side of neck, pellets by crown, leaf and fleur on breast, extra pellets on *rev.*	650	2000
1935	Saltire on neck, no leaf, pellets by crown, usually mullets in legend; extra pellets on *rev.*	100	325
1936	— Similar, but mascles in place of mullets on *obv.*	125	375
1937	— — pellets by hair instead of by crown	175	575
1938	**Halfgroat.** Saltire on neck, pellets by crown and on *rev.*, mullets in legend	275	950

1940   1943   1944

1939	**Penny.** *London.* Saltire on neck, pellets by crown and on *rev.*, mascle(s), or mullet and mascle in legend	150	475
1940	*York,* Archb. Wm. Booth. Saltires by neck, usually leaf on breast, pellets by crown. ℞. Cross in quatrefoil in centre.	55	175
1941	*Durham,* Bp. Laurence Booth. Saltire and B or B only at neck, pellets by crown. ℞. Rings in centre	65	225
1942	**Halfpenny.** Saltires by neck, usually two extra pellets on *rev.*	35	125
1943	Similar, but saltire on neck, sometimes mullet after hЄnRIC	25	90
1944	**Farthing.** Saltire on neck, usually pellets by crown and on *rev.*, but known without either.	225	700

For further information see:
Halfpennies and Farthings of Henry IV, V and VI. P. and B. R. Withers, 2003.

Lis-pellet issue, 1456-61

1945

1945	**Groat.** Lis on neck; pellets by crown. ℞. Extra pellets	250	800

EDWARD IV, First Reign, 1461-70

In order to increase the supply of bullion to the mint the weight of the penny was reduced to 12 grains in 1464, and the current value of the noble was raised to 8s. 4d. Later, in 1465, a new gold coin was issued, the Ryal or 'Rose Noble', weighing 120 grains and having a value of 10s. However, as 6s. 8d. had become the standard professional fee the old noble was missed, and a new coin was issued to take its place, the Angel of 80 grains.

Royal mints were set up in Bristol, Coventry, Norwich and York to help with the recoinage. The Coventry and Norwich mints were not open for long, but the York and Bristol mints remained open until 1471 and 1472 respectively.

Reference: C. E. Blunt and C. A Whitton, *The Coinage of Edward IV and Henry VI (Restored)*, B.N.J. 1945-7.

Mintmarks

105	9	7a	33	99	28	74	11

1461-4	Lis (105)		1467-70	Lis (105, *York*)	
	Cross fleury (9)		1467-8	Crown (74)	(often
	Plain cross (7a)			Sun (28)	combined)
1464-5	Rose (33 and 34)		1468-9	Crown (74)	(sometimes
1464-7	Pall (99, *Canterbury*)			Rose (33)	combined)
1465-6	Sun (28)		1469-70	Long cross	
1466-7	Crown (74)			fitchee (l.c.f) (11)	(often
				Sun (28)	combined)

GOLD

HEAVY COINAGE, 1461-4

1946

	F	VF
	£	£

1946	**Noble** (=6s. 8d., wt. 108 grs., 6.99g.). Normal type, but *obv.* legend commences at top left, lis below shield; *mm.*-/lis (Spink's sale May 1993)	4750	17500
1947	— Quatrefoil below sword arm; *mm.* rose/lis	5250	20000
1948	— R. Roses in two spandrels; *mm.* rose	5750	22500
1949	**Quarter-noble**	1750	6000

AMR Coins

Dealers in Quality British Coins

BNTA

British Coins Bought and Sold

www.amrcoins.com

email: info@amrcoins.com

tel: +44 (0)7527 569308

1950

		F	*VF*
		£	£

LIGHT COINAGE, 1464-70

1950	**Ryal** or rose-noble (=10s., wt. 120 grs., 7.77g), *London*. As illustration. Large fleurs in spandrels; *mm*. 33-74...	850	3000
1951	— — Small trefoils in spandrels; *mm*. 74-11	850	3000

1952

1952	— Flemish imitative coinage (mostly 16th cent. on a large flan).............	750	2500
1953	*Bristol*. B in waves, large fleurs; *mm*. sun, crown	1200	4000
1954	— — small fleurs in spandrels; *mm*. sun, crown......................................	1200	4000
1955	*Coventry*. C in waves; *mm*. sun...	1850	6250
1956	*Norwich*. n in waves; *mm*. sun, rose	2000	6500
1957	*York*. Є in waves, large fleurs in spandrels, *mm*. sun, lis.........................	1000	3500
1958	— — small fleurs, *mm*. sun. lis	1100	3750
1959	**Half-ryal.** *London*. As 1950	750	2250
1960	*Bristol*. B in waves; *mm*. sun, sun/crown..	1350	4750
1961	*Coventry*. C in waves; *mm*. sun...	5000	17500
1962	*Norwich*. n in waves; *mm*. rose...	4000	13500

1963   1965

		F	VF
		£	£
1963	*York.* Є in waves; *mm.* 28, 105, 33/105	850	2750
1963A	Similar but lis instead of Є in waves (probably York)...........	1000	3500
1964	**Quarter-ryal.** Shield in tressure of eight arcs, rose above. R. Somewhat		
	as half ryal; *mm.* sun/rose	1250	4500
1965	Shield in quatrefoil. Є above, rose on l., sun on r.; *mm.* 33/28-74/33	400	1100
1966	— — sun on l., rose on r.; *mm.* 74-11..........................	425	1250

1967

1967	**Angel** (=6s. 8d., wt. 80 grs., 5.18g). St. Michael spearing dragon. R. Ship, rays of		
	sun at masthead, large rose and sun beside mast; *mm.*-/33.....................	9500	35000
1968	— — small rose and sun at mast; *mm.*-/74..........................	10000	37500

SILVER

1969   1972

HEAVY COINAGE, 1461-4

1969	**Groat** (60 grs., 3.88g). Group I, lis on neck, pellets by crown; *mm.* 9, 7a,		
	105, 9/105	150	475
1970	— Lis on breast, no pellets; *mm.* plain cross, 7a/105	165	525
1971	— — with pellets at crown; *mm.* plain cross..........................	175	575
1972	II, quatrefoils by neck, crescent on breast; *mm.* rose..............	145	450
1973	III, similar but trefoil on breast; *mm.* rose	140	425

1974

1979

		F	VF
		£	£
1974	— — — eye in *rev.* inner legend, *mm.* rose	110	325
1975	— Similar, but no quatrefoils by bust	225	750
1976	— — Similar, but no trefoil on breast	175	575
1977	IV, annulets by neck, eye after TAS; *mm.* rose	300	1000
1978	**Halfgroat.** I, lis on breast, pellets by crown and extra pellets in two qtrs.; *mm.* 9, 7a	375	1500
1979	II, quatrefoils at neck, crescent on breast; *mm.* rose	275	950
1980	III, similar, but trefoil on breast, eye on rev.; *mm.* rose	225	650
1981	— Similar, but no mark on breast	225	650
1982	IV, annulets by neck, sometimes eye on *rev.; mm.* rose	250	800
1983	**Penny** (15 grs.), *London.* I, marks as 1978, but mascle after RЄX; *mm.* plain cross	350	1250
1984	II, quatrefoils by neck; *mm.* rose	225	750

1985   1991   1994

1985	III, similar, but eye after TAS; *mm.* rose	200	675
1986	IV, annulets by neck; *mm.* rose	200	675
1987	*York,* Archb. Booth. Quatrefoils by bust, voided quatrefoil in centre of *rev.; mm.* rose	125	350
1988	*Durham. O.* of Hen. VI. R. DVΠOLIП	120	325
1988A	(ca.1461-c.1462). Local dies, mostly with rose in centre of rev.; *mm.* 7a, 33	35	130
1989	**Halfpenny.** I, as 1983, but no mascle	65	225
1990	II, quatrefoils by bust; *mm.* rose	35	140
1991	— saltires by bust; *mm.* rose	35	135
1992	III, no marks by bust; *mm.* rose	35	140
1992A	—saltires by bust, eye after TAS, *mm.* rose	100	350
1993	IV, annulets by bust; *mm.* rose	35	140
1994	**Farthing.** I, pellets by crown, extra pellets on rev., with or without lis on breast	250	900
1994A	II. saltires by bust; *mm.* rose	250	900
1994B	III, no marks by bust; *mm.* rose	225	850

LIGHT COINAGE, 1464-70. There is a great variety of groats and we give only a selection. Some have pellets in one quarter of the reverse, or trefoils over the crown; early coins have fleurs on the cusps of the tressure, then trefoils or no marks on the cusps, while the late coins have only trefoils.

		F	VF
		£	£
1995	**Groat** (48 grs., 3.11g), *London.* Annulets at neck, eye after TAS; *mm.* 33 (struck from heavy dies, IV)	125	475
1996	— — — Similar, but new dies, eye after TAS or DON	110	425
1997	— Quatrefoils at neck, eye; rose (heavy dies, III)	100	350
1998	— — — Similar, but new dies, eye in *rev.* legend	110	375
1999	— No marks at neck, eye; *mm* rose	150	525
2000	— Quatrefoils at neck, no eye; *mm.* 33, 74, 28, 74/28, 74/33, 11/28	40	140

	2001	2002		
2001	— — — rose or quatrefoil on breast; *mm.* 33, 74/28		45	150
2002	— No marks at neck; *mm.* 28, 74, 11/28, 11		50	165
2003	— Trefoils or crosses at neck; *mm.* 11/33, 11/28, 11		45	150
2004	*Bristol.* B on breast, quatrefoils at neck; *mm.* 28/33, 28, 28/74, 74, 74/28		60	185
2005	— — trefoils at neck; *mm.* sun		80	275
2006	— — no marks at neck; *mm.* sun		150	525
2007	— Without B, quatrefoils at neck; *mm.* sun		135	475
Bristol is variously rendered as BRESTOLL, BRISTOLL, BRESTOW, BRISTOW.				
2008	*Coventry.* C on breast, quatrefoils at neck, COVETRE; *mm.* 28/33, 28...		140	475
2009	— — Local dies, similar; *mm.* rose		175	575
2010	— — — as last, but no C or quatrefoils		175	575
2011	Norwich. N on breast, quatrefoils at neck, NORWIC or NORVIC, *mm.* 28/33, 28		125	375
2012	*York.* E on breast, quatrefoils at neck, EBORACI; *mm.* 28, 105/74, 105, 105/28		60	185
2013	— Similar, but without E on breast, *mm.* lis		135	425
2014	— E on breast, trefoils at neck; *mm.* 105/28, 105		65	200
2015	**Halfgroat.** *London.* Annulets by neck (heavy dies); *mm.* 33		275	850

2016

2016	— Quatrefoils by neck; *mm.* 33/-, 28/-, 74, 74/28	60	175
2017	— Saltires by neck; *mm.* 74, 74/28	65	180
2018	— Trefoils by neck; *mm.* 74, 74/28, 11/28	65	180
2019	— No marks by neck; *mm.* 11/28	90	275

		F £	VF £
2020	*Bristol.* Saltires or crosses by neck; *mm.* 33/28, 28, 74, 74/-......	135	450
2021	— Quatrefoils by neck; *mm.* 28/-, 74, 74/-..............................	125	425
2022	— Trefoils by neck; *mm.* crown	135	475
2023	— No marks by neck; *mm.* 74/28	150	500
2024	*Canterbury,* Archb. Bourchier (1464-7). Knot below bust; quatrefoils by neck; *mm.* 99/-, 99, 99/33, 99/28	40	150
2025	— — — quatrefoils omitted *mm.* 99	40	150
2026	— — — saltires by neck; *mm.* 99/-, 99/28.............................	50	170
2026A	— — — trefoils by neck; *mm.* 99..	55	185
2027	— — — wedges by hair and/or neck; *mm.* 99, 99/–, 99/33, 99/28	45	160
2028	— — As 2024 or 2025, but no knot..	50	170
2029	— (1467-9). Quatrefoils by neck; *mm.* 74, 74/-	50	165
2030	— — Saltires by neck; *mm.* 74/-, 74	50	165
2031	— — Trefoils by neck; *mm.* 74, 74/-, 74/28, 33.......................	45	150
2032	— No marks by neck; *mm.* sun...	75	250
2033	*Coventry.* Crosses by neck; *mm.* sun	750	2250
2034	*Norwich.* Quatrefoils or saltires by neck; *mm.* sun..................	575	1750

2035   2063

		F £	VF £
2035	*York.* Quatrefoils by neck; *mm.* sun, lis, lis/-	85	300
2036	— Saltires by neck; *mm.* lis	75	275
2037	— Trefoils by neck; *mm.* lis, lis/-	85	325
2038	— Є on breast, quatrefoils by neck; *mm.* lis/-	75	275
2039	**Penny** (12 grs., 0.77g.), *London.* Annulets by neck (heavy dies); *mm.* rose	200	650
2040	— Quatrefoils by neck; *mm.* 74, sun. crown	65	225
2041	— Trefoil and quatrefoil by neck; *mm.* crown........................	65	225
2042	— Saltires by neck; *mm.* crown	65	225
2043	— Trefoils by neck; *mm.* crown, long cross fitchée	70	250
2044	— No marks by neck; *mm.* long cross fitchée	100	350
2045	*Bristol.* Crosses, quatrefoils or saltires by neck, BRISTOW; *mm.* crown	125	475
2046	— Quatrefoils by neck; BRI(trefoil)STOLL	135	525
2047	— Trefoil to r. of neck BRISTOLL	135	525
2048	*Canterbury,* Archb. Bourchier. Quatrefoils or saltires by neck, knot on breast; *mm.* pall..	70	240
2049	— — Similar, but no marks by neck	70	240
2050	— — As 2048, but no knot..	75	275
2051	— — Crosses by neck, no knot	70	240
2052	— Quatrefoils by neck; *mm.* crown.......................................	135	525
2053	— King's Receiver (1462-4). Local dies, mostly with rose in centre of rev.; *mm.* 7a, 33..	35	130
2054	— *Durham,* Bp. Lawrence Booth (1465-70). B and D by neck, B on *rev.; mm.* 33	30	140
2055	— — Quatrefoil and B by neck; *mm.* sun	35	130
2056	— — B and quatrefoil by neck; *mm.* crown............................	40	140
2057	— — D and quatrefoil by neck; *mm.* crown............................	40	140
2058	— — Quatrefoils by neck; *mm.* crown...................................	35	130
2059	— — Trefoils by neck; *mm.* crown	40	140
2060	— Lis by neck; *mm.* crown..	35	130

	F	VF
	£	£

2061 *York,* Sede Vacante (1464-5). Quatrefoils at neck, no quatrefoil in centre
of *rev.; mm.* sun, rose 40 150

2062 — Archb. Neville (1465-70). Local dies, G and key by neck, quatrefoil
on *rev.; mm.* sun, plain cross 30 120

2063 — — London-made dies, similar; *mm.* 28, 105, 11 .... 35 140

2064 — — Similar, but no marks by neck; *mm.* large lis 40 150

2065 — — — Quatrefoils by neck; *mm.* large lis 40 150

2066 — — — Trefoils by neck; *mm.* large lis 35 140

2068   2077

2067 **Halfpenny,** *London.* Saltires by neck; *mm.* 34, 28, 74 .... 25 120

2068 — Trefoils by neck; *mm.* 28, 74, 11 .... 25 120

2069 — No marks by neck; *mm.* 11 .... 35 135

2070 *Bristol.* Crosses by neck; *mm.* crown.. 100 350

2071 — Trefoils by neck; *mm.* crown 90 325

2072 *Canterbury.* Archb. Bourchier. No marks; *mm.* pall............................... 65 225

2072A — — Trefoils by neck, *mm.* pall.. 65 225

2073 — Saltires by neck; *mm.* crown... 60 185

2074 — — Trefoils by neck; *mm.* crown 60 185

2074A *Norwich.* Quatrefoils by neck., *mm.* Sun 350 900

2074B — — Trefoils by neck; *mm.* crown 400 1000

2075 *York.* Royal mint. Saltires by neck; *mm.* lis/-, sun/-................................... 45 150

2076 — — Trefoils by neck; *mm.* lis/- 40 140

2077 **Farthing,** *London.* ЄDWARD DI GRA RЄX, trefoils by neck, *mm.* crown 375 1100

Full flan coins are difficult to find in the smaller denominations.

For further information see:
Halfpennies and Farthings of Edward IV to Henry VII. P. and B. R. Withers, 2004.

Timeline
Auctions
Inc. Gregory's **Est.1858**

We are accepting single entries
and collections
of coins & antiquities

www.timelineauctions.com

Sold for:
£14,880

Follow us on:
f /TimeLineAuctions
t @TimeLineAuction

The coinage of this short restoration follows closely that of the previous reign. Only angel gold was issued, the ryal being discontinued. Many of the coins have the king's name reading hꞓnRICV — another distinguishing feature is an R that looks like a B.

Mintmarks

Cross pattée (6)   Rose (33, Bristol)
Restoration cross (13)   Lis (105)
Trefoil (44 and 45)   Short cross fitchée (12)

GOLD

2078

		F £	VF £
2078	**Angel,** *London.* As illus. but no B; *mm.* -/6, 13, -/105, none	1750	5500
2079	*Bristol.* B in waves; *mm.* -/13, none..	2500	9000
2080	**Half-angel,** *London.* As 2078; *mm.* -/6, -/13, -/105..........................	4500	13500
2081	*Bristol.* B in waves; *mm.* -/13	6000	17500

SILVER

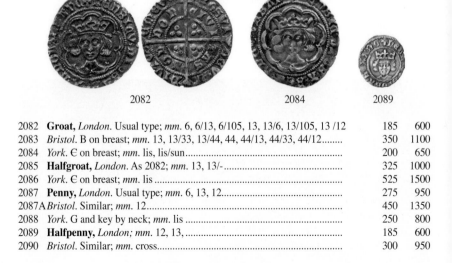

2082   2084   2089

2082	**Groat,** *London.* Usual type; *mm.* 6, 6/13, 6/105, 13, 13/6, 13/105, 13 /12	185	600
2083	*Bristol.* B on breast; *mm.* 13, 13/33, 13/44, 44, 44/13, 44/33, 44/12........	350	1100
2084	*York.* Ꞓ on breast; *mm.* lis, lis/sun...	200	650
2085	**Halfgroat,** *London.* As 2082; *mm.* 13, 13/-...............................	325	1000
2086	*York.* Ꞓ on breast; *mm.* lis	525	1500
2087	**Penny,** *London.* Usual type; *mm.* 6, 13, 12.................................	275	950
2087A	*Bristol.* Similar; *mm.* 12..	450	1350
2088	*York.* G and key by neck; *mm.* lis	250	800
2089	**Halfpenny,** *London; mm.* 12, 13, ...	185	600
2090	*Bristol.* Similar; *mm.* cross...	300	950

The Angel and its half were the only gold denominations issued during this reign. The main types and weight standards remained the same as those of the light coinage of Edward's first reign. The use of the 'initial mark' as a mintmark to denote the date of issue was now firmly established.

Mintmarks

33	105	12	55	44	55	28	56	17

30	37	6	18	19	20	31	11	38

1471-83	Rose (33, *York & Durham*)	1473-7	Cross pattée (6)
	Lis (105, *York*)		Pierced cross 1 (18)
1471	Short cross fitchee (12)	1477-80	Pierced cross and
1471-2	Annulet (large, 55)		pellet (19)
	Trefoil (44)		Pierced cross 2 (18)
	Rose (33, *Bristol*)		Pierced cross, central
1471-3	Pansy (30, *Durham*)		pellet (20)
1472-3	Annulet (small, 55)		Rose (33, *Canterbury*)
	Sun (28, *Bristol*)	1480-3	Heraldic cinquefoil (31)
1473-7	Pellet in annulet (56)		Long cross fitchee
	Cross and four pellets (17)		(11, *Canterbury*)
	Cross in circle (37)	1483	Halved sun and rose (38)
			(Listed under Ed. IV/V.)

GOLD

2091   2093

		F	VF
		£	£
2091	**Angel.** *London.* Type as illus.; *mm.* 12, 55, 56, 17, 18, 19, 31	800	2500
2092	*Bristol.* B in waves; *mm.* small annulet	3500	12500
2093	**Half-angel.** As illus.; *mm.* 55, cross in circle, 19, 20/19, 31	700	2250
2094	King's name and title on rev.; *mm.* 12/-	900	3000
2095	King's name and the title both sides; *mm.* 55/-	950	3250

SILVER

2097

	F £	VF £
2096 **Groat,** *London*. Trefoils on cusps, no marks by bust; *mm.* 12-37	60	200
2097 — — roses by bust; *mm.* pellet in annulet	125	400
2098 — Fleurs on cusps; no marks by bust; *mm.* 18-20	65	210
2099 — — pellets by bust; *mm.* pierced cross	80	275
2100 — — rose on breast; *mm.* 31	75	240

2101   2107

2101 *Bristol*. B on breast no marks by bust; *mm.* 33, 33/55, 28/55, 55, 55/-, 28	200	650
2102 *York*. Є on breast no marks by bust; *mm.* lis	210	675
2103 **Halfgroat,** *London*. As 2096; *mm.* 12-31	65	250
2104 *Bristol*. B on breast; *mm.* 33/12	275	950
2105 *Canterbury*. Archb. Bourchier. As 2103; *mm.* 33, 11, 11/31, 31	45	175
2106 — C on breast; *mm.* rose	40	160
2107 — — Ɍ. C in centre; *mm.* rose	40	160
2108 — — Ɍ. Rose in centre; *mm.* rose	40	160
2109 *York*. No. Є on breast; *mm.* lis	175	575
2110 **Penny,** *London*. No marks by bust; *mm.* 12-31	55	200
2111 *Bristol*. Similar; *mm.* rose	185	625
2112 *Canterbury*. Archb. Bourchier. Similar; *mm.* 33, 11	65	225
2113 — C on breast; *mm.* rose	75	275
2114 *Durham,* Bp. Booth (1471-6). No marks by neck; *mm.* 12, 44	30	100

2115   2116

2115 — — D in centre of *rev.;* B and trefoil by neck; *mm.* 44, 33, 56	30	100
2116 — — — two lis at neck; *mm.* rose	30	110
2117 — — — crosses over crown, and on breast; *mm.* rose	30	110
2118 — — — crosses over crown, V under CIVI; *mm.* rose, pansy	35	110
2119 — — — B to l. of crown, V on breast and under CIVI	30	100

		F	VF
		£	£
2120	— — — As last but crosses at shoulders	30	100
2121	— — R. D in centre; *mm.* rose	30	110
2122	— Bp. Dudley (1476-83). V to r. of neck; as last	35	110

2123   2125   2131

2123	— — D and V by neck; as last, but *mm.* 31	30	100

Nos. 2117-2123 are from locally-made dies.

2124	*York*, Archb. Neville (1471-2). Quatrefoils by neck. R. Quatrefoil; *mm.* 12 (over lis)	45	165
2125	— — Similar, but G and key by neck; *mm.* 12 (over lis)	30	110
2126	— Neville suspended (1472-5). As last, but no quatrefoil in centre of *rev.*	35	135
2126A	— — no marks by bust, similar; *mm.* annulet	40	145
2127	— — No marks by neck, quatrefoil on *rev.; mm.* 55, cross in circle, 33..	30	110
2128	— — Similar but Є and rose by neck; *mm.* rose	25	100
2129	— Archb. Neville restored (1475-6). As last, but G and rose	30	110
2130	— — Similar, but G and key by bust	25	100
2131	— Sede Vacante (1476). As 2127, but rose on breast; *mm.* rose	35	135
2132	— Archb. Lawrence Booth (1476-80). B and key by bust, quatrefoil on *rev.; mm.* 33, 31	25	100
2133	— Sede Vacante (1480). Similar, but no quatrefoil on rev.; *mm.* rose	35	120

2134   2140

2134	— Archb. Rotherham (1480-3). T and slanting key by neck, quatrefoil on *rev.; mm.* 33	30	110
2135	— — — Similar, but star on breast	40	135
2136	— — — Star on breast and to r. of crown	45	150
2137	**Halfpenny**, *London.* No marks by neck; *mm.* 12-31	20	90
2138	— Pellets at neck; *mm.* pierced cross	30	100
2139	*Canterbury* (Archbishop Bourchier). C on breast and in centre of *rev.; mm.* rose	80	250
2140	— C on breast only; *mm.* rose	75	225
2141	— Without C either side; *mm.* 11	75	225
2142	*Durham*, Bp. Booth. No marks by neck. R. DЄRA̅ M, D in centre; *mm.* rose	150	450
2142A	— — Lis either side of neck. R. with or without D in centre	175	500
2142B	— — B to l. of crown, crosses at shoulders. R. with or without D. in centre; *mm.* rose	175	500
2143	— — — Bp. Dudley V to l. of neck; as last	160	475

Full flan coins are very difficult to find in the small denominations.

On 12th February 1483, the prolific cinquefoil coinage of Edward IV came to an end and an indenture between the king and the new master of the mint, Bartholomew Reed, saw the introduction of the sun and rose mintmark.

Edward IV died on 9th April 1483, but the sun and rose coinage continued, essentially unaltered, through the short reign of Edward V and into the reign of Richard III, ending with the indenture of 20th July 1483, with Robert Brackenbury, who had been Richard's ducal treasurer, and the introduction of the boar's head mintmark.

New dies prepared after the accession of Richard III on 26th June 1483, bear his name but coins of the sun and rose coinage struck under Edward IV and Edward V can only be distinguished by arranging the dies in sequence. This is possible for the angels (Schneider Sylloge, SCBI 47, p.41) but has not yet been achieved for the silver coinage.

Mintmark: Halved sun and rose.　

GOLD

2144A

		F	VF
		£	£
2144	**Angel.** Type As 2091, reading EDWARD DEI GRA (Edward IV)..........	5000	15000
2144A	— Similar but reading EDWARD DI GRA (Edward V)..........................	12500	35000
2145	**Half-angel.** As 2093 (probably Edward IV)..	4500	15000

SILVER

2146

2146	**Groat.** *London,* pellet below bust, reading EDWARD or EDVARD.......	1100	4000
2146A	— — No pellet below, reading EDWARD or EDWRD...........................	1000	3750
2147	**Penny.** *London* As 2110	1250	4500
2148	**Halfpenny.** *London* As 2137...	325	950

Richard's coinage follows the pattern of previous reigns. The portrait on the silver denominations remains stylised, though increasingly distinctive. It can be divided into three types according to mintmark. Type 1, the first sun and rose coinage, lasted 24 days to 20th July 1483. Type 2, the boar's head coinage, was issued until about June 1484. Type 3, the second sun and rose coinage, was struck until the end of the reign (Schneider Sylloge, SCBI 47, pp. 41-2).

It is evident that coin dies were stored in a 'loose-box' system which led to extensive muling between types. As an interim measure, after the indenture of 20th July 1483, at least eleven existing sun and rose obverse dies, both gold and silver, were overpunched with the boar's head mark. The seven overpunched groat dies included four Edward IV/V dies, then still in use, and three dies of Richard III type 1.

Mintmarks

| SR1 | BH1 | BH2 | SR2 | SR3 | 105 | 33 |

Halved sun and rose, 1, 2 and 3.
Boar's head, 1 (62) 2 (63).
Lis (105, *Durham*)
Rose only (33).

GOLD

2150   2152

		F	VF
		£	£
2149	**Angel.** 1. Reading RICARD. R. R and rose by mast; *mm.* sun and rose 1	5500	18500
2150	— 2a. Reading EDWARD. R. E and rose or R and rose by mast; *mm.* boar's head 1 over sun and rose 1/sun and rose 1	7500	27500
2151	— 2b. Reading RICARD. R. R and rose by mast; mm. boar's head 1 over sun and rose 1/sun and rose 1, boar's head 1, boar's head 2 (often muled)	5250	17500
2152	— 3. Reading RICARD or RICAD; *mm.* sun and rose 2	5000	16500

2153

| 2153 | **Half-angel.** 2b. R. R and rose by mast; *mm.* boar's head 1 | 7000 | 25000 |

SILVER

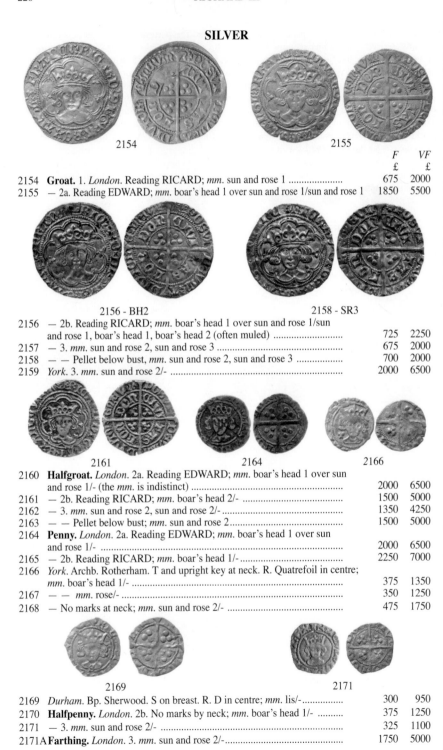

2154   2155

2156 - BH2   2158 - SR3

2161   2164   2166

2169   2171

		F £	VF £
2154	**Groat.** 1. *London.* Reading RICARD; *mm.* sun and rose 1	675	2000
2155	— 2a. Reading EDWARD; *mm.* boar's head 1 over sun and rose 1/sun and rose 1	1850	5500
2156	— 2b. Reading RICARD; *mm.* boar's head 1 over sun and rose 1/sun and rose 1, boar's head 1, boar's head 2 (often muled)	725	2250
2157	— 3. *mm.* sun and rose 2, sun and rose 3	675	2000
2158	— — Pellet below bust, *mm.* sun and rose 2, sun and rose 3	700	2000
2159	*York.* 3. *mm.* sun and rose 2/-	2000	6500
2160	**Halfgroat.** *London.* 2a. Reading EDWARD; *mm.* boar's head 1 over sun and rose 1/- (the *mm.* is indistinct)	2000	6500
2161	— 2b. Reading RICARD; *mm.* boar's head 2/-	1500	5000
2162	— 3. *mm.* sun and rose 2, sun and rose 2/-	1350	4250
2163	— — Pellet below bust; *mm.* sun and rose 2	1500	5000
2164	**Penny.** *London.* 2a. Reading EDWARD; *mm.* boar's head 1 over sun and rose 1/-	2000	6500
2165	— 2b. Reading RICARD; *mm.* boar's head 1/-	2250	7000
2166	*York.* Archb. Rotherham. T and upright key at neck. R. Quatrefoil in centre; *mm.* boar's head 1/-	375	1350
2167	— — *mm.* rose/-	350	1250
2168	— No marks at neck; *mm.* sun and rose 2/-	475	1750
2169	*Durham.* Bp. Sherwood. S on breast. R. D in centre; *mm.* lis/-	300	950
2170	**Halfpenny.** *London.* 2b. No marks by neck; *mm.* boar's head 1/-	375	1250
2171	— 3. *mm.* sun and rose 2/-	325	1100
2171A	**Farthing.** *London.* 3. *mm.* sun and rose 2/-	1750	5000

HENRY VII, 1485-1509

For the first four years of his reign Henry's coins differ only in name and mintmark from those of his predecessors, but from 1489 radical changes were made in the coinage. On the Groat and subsequently on the lesser denominations the tradional open crown was replaced with an arched imperial crown. Though the pound sterling had been a denomination of account for centuries, a pound coin had never been minted. Now a magnificent gold pound was issued, and, from the design of the king enthroned in majesty, was called a 'Sovereign'. A small simplified version of the Sovereign portrait was at the same time introduced on the silver pence. The reverse of the gold 'Sovereign' had the royal arms set in the centre of a Tudor rose. A few years later the angel was restyled and St. Michael, who is depicted about to thrust Satan into the Pit with a cross-topped lance, is no longer a feathered figure but is clad in armour of Renaissance style. A gold ryal of ten shillings was also minted again for a brief period.

The other major innovation was the introduction of the shilling (testoon) in the opening years of the 16th century. It is remarkable for the very fine profile portrait of the king which replaces the representational image of a monarch that had served on the coinage for the past couple of centuries. This new portrait was also used on groats and halfgroats but not on the smaller denominations.

Mintmarks

| 39 | 41 | 40 | 42 | 33 | 11 | 7a | 123 |

| 105 | 76b | 31 | 78 | 30 | 91 | 43 | 57 |

| 85 | 94 | 118 | 21 | 33 | 53 |

1485-7	Halved sun and rose (39)		1495-8	Pansy (30)
	Lis upon sun and rose (41)			Tun (123, *Canterbury*)
	Lis upon half rose (40)			Lis (105, York)
	Lis-rose dimidiated (42)		1498-9	Crowned leopard's head (91)
	Rose (33, *York*)			Lis issuant from rose (43)
1487	Lis (105)			Tun (123, *Canterbury*)
	Cross fitchée (11)		1499-1502	Anchor (57)
1487-8	Rose (33)		1502-4	Greyhound's head (85)
	Plain cross (7a, *Durham*)			Lis (105, profile issue only)
1488-9	No marks			Martlet (94, *York*)
1489-93	Cinquefoil (31)		1504-5	Cross-crosslet (21)
	Crozier (76b, *Durham*)		1504-9	Martlet (94, (*York, Canterbury*)
1492	Cross fitchée (11, gold only)			Rose (33, *York* and
1493-5	Escallop (78)			*Canterbury*)
	Dragon (118, gold only)		1505-9	Pheon (53)
	Lis (105, *Canterbury and York*			
	Tun (123, *Canterbury*)			

GOLD

		F	VF
		£	£
2172	**Sovereign** (20s; wt. 240 grs., 15.55g). Group I. Large figure of king sitting on backless throne. ℞. Large shield crowned on large Tudor rose. *mm.* 31 ..	100000	525000
2173	— Group II. Somewhat similar but throne has narrow back, lis in background. ℞. Large Tudor rose bearing small shield. *mm.* -/11	75000	325000

2174

2174	— III. King on high-backed very ornamental throne, with greyhound and dragon on side pillars. ℞. Shield on Tudor rose; *mm.* dragon............	35000	150000
2175	— IV. Similar but throne with high canopy breaking legend and broad seat, *mm.* 105/118, (also with no *obv.* i.c. *mm.* 105/118, very rare)..................	27500	125000
2176	— Narrow throne with a portcullis below the king's feet (like Henry VIII); *mm.* 105/21, 105/53	22500	95000
2177	**Double-sovereign** and **Treble-sovereign** from same dies as 2176. These piedforts were probably intended as presentation pieces *mm.* 105/21, 105/53	100000	525000

2178

2178	**Ryal** (10s.). As illustration: *mm.* -/11	30000	135000
2179	**Angel** (6s. 8d). I. Angel of old type with one foot on dragon. ℞. PER CRVCEM. etc., *mm.* 39, 40, (also muled both ways)...............................	1500	5250
2179A	— With Irish title, and legend over angel head. mm. 33/-........................	1600	5500
2180	— — Name altered from RICARD? and h on *rev.* from ℞. mm. 41/39, 41/40, 41/-, 39/?..	1750	5750

2181   2183

2187

		F	VF
		£	£
2181	II. As 2179, but *mm.* none. 31/-.	1350	4500
2181A	II/III mule. *mm.* 31/78, ℞. PER CRUC or AVTEM TRANS	1400	4750
2182	As 2181. ℞. IhC AVTEM TRANSIENS etc.; *mm.* none, 31/-	1500	5000
2183	III. New dies, angel with both feet on dragons; (large straight lettering) *mm.* 78-85 except 91 (many mules exist)	650	2000
2183A	— Angel with very small wings. *mm.* escallop	725	2250
2184	— — R. IhC AVTEM TRANSIENS, etc.; *mm.* escallop	1100	4000
2185	IV. Small square lettering; *mm.* 85 (also muled with 2183)	725	2250
2186	— Tall thin lettering; *mm.* 21 (also muled with 2185 obv.)	725	2250
2187	V. Large crook-shaped abbreviation after hEnRIC; *mm.* 21 and 53 (combinations and mules exist)	675	2100
2188	**Half-angel or angelet.** I. Mm. 39, 41, (old dies RIII altered)	1750	5750
2189	III. Angel with both feet on dragon: *mm.* 30, 57/30, 30/85	800	2500
2190	IV. Small square lettering; *mm.* rose *mm.* -/85	725	2250
2191	— *Obv.* as last. R. Tall thin lettering; *mm.* 33/21	800	2500
2192	V. As angel; *mm.* pheon, cross-crosslet	675	2100

SILVER

Facing bust issues. Including 'Sovereign' type pennies.

2193	**Groat.** I. Open crown; *mm.* 40 (rose on bust), 39-42 and none (combinations)	95	350

2194   2195

2194	— — crosses or saltires by neck, 41, 40, 105-33 and none (combinations)	110	400
2195	IIa. Large bust with out-turned hair, crown with two plain arches; *mm.* none, 31, 31/-, 31/78	75	225

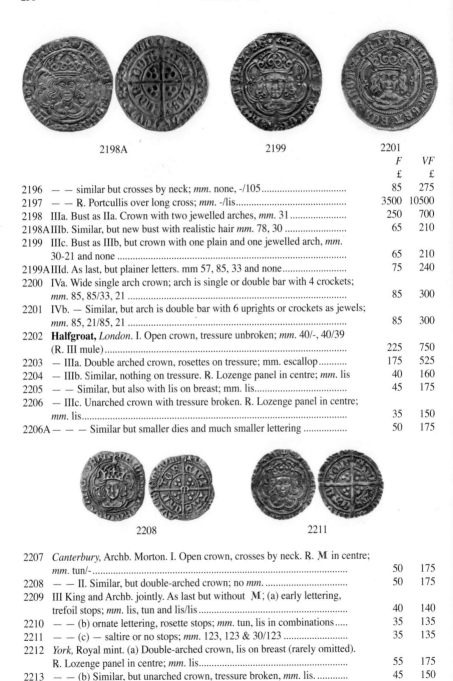

2198A　　　　　　　　　　2199　　　　　　　2201

	F	VF
	£	£
2196 — — similar but crosses by neck; *mm.* none, -/105.................................	85	275
2197 — — ℞. Portcullis over long cross; *mm.* -/lis..	3500	10500
2198 IIIa. Bust as IIa. Crown with two jewelled arches, *mm.* 31	250	700
2198A IIIb. Similar, but new bust with realistic hair *mm.* 78, 30	65	210
2199 IIIc. Bust as IIIb, but crown with one plain and one jewelled arch, *mm.*		
30-21 and none	65	210
2199A IIId. As last, but plainer letters. mm 57, 85, 33 and none........................	75	240
2200 IVa. Wide single arch crown; arch is single or double bar with 4 crockets;		
mm. 85, 85/33, 21	85	300
2201 IVb. — Similar, but arch is double bar with 6 uprights or crockets as jewels;		
mm. 85, 21/85, 21	85	300
2202 **Halfgroat,** *London.* I. Open crown, tressure unbroken; *mm.* 40/-, 40/39		
(℞. III mule)...	225	750
2203 — IIIa. Double arched crown, rosettes on tressure; mm. escallop..........	175	525
2204 — IIIb. Similar, nothing on tressure. ℞. Lozenge panel in centre; *mm.* lis	40	160
2205 — — Similar, but also with lis on breast; mm. lis....................................	45	175
2206 — IIIc. Unarched crown with tressure broken. ℞. Lozenge panel in centre;		
mm. lis..	35	150
2206A — — — Similar but smaller dies and much smaller lettering	50	175

2208　　　　　　　　　　2211

2207 *Canterbury,* Archb. Morton. I. Open crown, crosses by neck. ℞. Ⰼ in centre;		
mm. tun/-	50	175
2208 — — II. Similar, but double-arched crown; no *mm.*	50	175
2209 III King and Archb. jointly. As last but without Ⰼ; (a) early lettering,		
trefoil stops; *mm.* lis, tun and lis/lis..	40	140
2210 — — (b) ornate lettering, rosette stops; *mm.* tun, lis in combinations.....	35	135
2211 — — (c) — saltire or no stops; *mm.* 123, 123 & 30/123	35	135
2212 *York,* Royal mint. (a) Double-arched crown, lis on breast (rarely omitted).		
℞. Lozenge panel in centre; *mm.* lis..	55	175
2213 — — (b) Similar, but unarched crown, tressure broken, *mm.* lis.	45	150

	F	*VF*
	£	£

2214	— Archb. Savage. (a) Double-arched crown, keys at neck, no tressure; ornate lettering; *mm.* martlet...	40	140
2215	— — (b) Similar, but fleured tressure, small square lettering; *mm.* martlet	45	150
2216	— — (c) As last, but tall thin lettering; *mm.* martlet	45	150
2217	— As last but no keys; *mm.* martlet...	50	165

2221   2226

2218	**Penny.** Old type. London; *mm.* 40/-	175	600
2219	— — — crosses by bust, mm. small cross (obv.)....................................	225	675
2220	— *Canterbury,* Archb. Morton. Open crown, *mm.* tun/- R̈. M in centre .	200	600
2221	— — King and Archb. jointly, arched crown; *mm.* tun, tun/-	65	225
2222	— *Durham,* Bp. Sherwood. S on breast. R. D in centre; *mm.* 7a/-...........	55	200
2223	— *York,* Archb. Rotherham. With or without cross on breast, *mm.* 33/-, T and cross or key at neck. R. h in centre......................................	45	175
2224	— — — T and trefoil at neck. R. Quatrefoil in centre and two extra pellets; *mm.* 39/-	40	150
2225	'Sovereign' type. *London.* Early lettering, no stops, no pillars to throne; no *mm.*..	100	350
2226	— — — single pillar on king's right side, trefoil stops; no *mm.* or 31/-..	40	140
2227	— — Ornate letters, rosette stops, single pillar; *mm.* lis (can be muled with above)	55	200
2228	— — saltire stops or none, two pillars; *mm.* none, -/30	40	140
2229	— — Similar, but small square lettering; no *mm.*	45	150
2230	— — Similar, but lettering as profile groats two double pillars; *mm.* 21, 53, none (sometimes on one side only)	40	140

2231   2233   2235

2231	— *Durham,* Bp. Sherwood. Crozier to r. of king, throne with one pillar. R. D and S beside shield..	40	140
2232	— — Throne with two pillars, no crozier. R. As last	45	150
2233	— — Bp. Fox. Throne with one pillar. R. Mitre above shield, RD or DR at sides, no *mm.*...	30	120
2234	— — Similar, but two pillars..	35	125
2235	*York,* Archb. Rotherham. Keys below shield; early lettering, trefoil stops, no pillars to throne, no *mm.*	35	125
2236	— — — single pillar	30	120
2237	— — — ornate lettering, rosette or no stops,......................................	35	125
2238	— — — two pillars sometimes with crosses between legs of throne	35	120

2239   2244A   2245

2249   2250

		F	*VF*
		£	£
2239	**Halfpenny,** *London.* I. Open crown; *mm.* 40, 42	35	125
2240	— — — trefoils at neck; no *mm.,* rose	40	135
2241	— — — crosses at neck; *mm.* rose, cross fitchée....................................	35	125
2242	— II. Double arched crown; *mm.* cinquefoil, none	30	85
2243	— — — saltires at neck; no *mm.*...	30	85
2244	— IIIa. Crown with single arch, ornate lettering; no *mm.,* pansy............	25	80
2244A	— IIIb. Similar but with rosette stops; *mm.* none, rose, lis	35	110
2245	— IIIc. Much smaller portrait; *mm.* pheon, lis, none	25	85
2246	*Canterbury,* Archb. Morton. I. Open crown, crosses by neck; ℞. M in centre	75	250
2247	— — II. Similar, but arched crown, saltires by bust; *mm.* profile eye (82)	75	250
2247A	— — — no marks at neck..	70	225
2248	— III. King and Archb. Arched crown; *mm.* lis, none.............................	40	125
2249	*York,* Archb. Savage. Arched crown, key below bust to l or r. *mm.* martlet	50	150
2250	**Farthing,** *London.* hЄNRIC DI GRA RЄX (A), arched crown	450	1500

*No.s 2239-49 have *mm.* on *obv.* only.

Profile issue

2251	**Testoon** (ls.). Type as groat. hЄNRIC (VS); *mm.* lis...............................	15000	35000
2252	— hЄNRIC VII; *mm.* lis	16000	40000

2253   2254

2253	— hЄNRIC SЄPTIM; *mm.* lis	17500	45000
2254	**Groat,** *Tentative issue* (contemporary with full-face groats). Double band to crown, hЄNRIC VII; *mm.* none, 105/-, -/105: 105/85, 105, 85, 21	275	1000
2255	— — — tressure on *obv.;* *mm.* cross-crosslet...	2500	9500
2256	— — hЄNRIC (VS); *mm.* 105, -/105, 105/ 85, none	450	1500
2257	— — hЄNRIC SЄPTIM; *mm.* -/105..	2250	8500

2258

		F	VF
		£	£
2258	*Regular issue.* Triple band to crown; *mm.* 21, 53 (both *mm.*s may occur on *obv.* or *rev.* or both)	135	400
2259	**Halfgroat,** *London.* As last; *mm.* 105, 53/105, 105/53, 53	90	350
2260	— — no numeral after King's name, no *mm.*, -/lis	225	750
2261	*Canterbury,* King and Archb. As London, but *mm.* 94, 33, 94/33	70	250

2262   rev. enlarged

| 2262 | *York,* Archb. Bainbridge. As London, but two keys below shield; *mm.* 94, 33, 33/94 | 70 | 250 |

2263

| 2263 | — — XB beside shield; *mm.* rose/martlet | 200 | 600 |
| 2263A | — — Similar but two keys below shield *mm.* rose(?)/martlet | 225 | 675 |

COINS OF BRITAIN
PO BOX 2, MONMOUTH, NP25 3YR, UK
BNTA

E-mail: lloydbennett@coinsofbritain.com +44(0)7714 284 939

Henry VIII is held in ill-regard by numismatists as being the author of the debasement of England's gold and silver coinage; but there were also other important numismatic innovations during his reign. For the first sixteen years the coinage closely followed the pattern of the previous issues, even to the extent of retaining the portrait of Henry VII on the larger silver coins.

In 1526, in an effort to prevent the drain of gold to continental Europe, the value of English gold was increased by 10%, the sovereign to 22s. 0d. and the angel to 7s. 4d., and a new coin valued at 4s. 6d. — the Crown of the Rose — was introduced as a competitor to the French *écu au soleil*. The new crown was not a success and within a few months it was replaced by the Crown of the Double Rose valued at 5s but made of gold of only 22 carat fineness, the first time gold had been minted below the standard 23c. At the same time the sovereign was again revalued to 22s. 6d. and the angel to 7s. 6d., with a new coin, the George Noble, valued at 6s. 8d. (one-third pound).

The royal cyphers on some of the gold crowns and half-crowns combine the initial of Henry with those of his queens: Katherine of Aragon, Anne Boleyn and Jane Seymour. The architect of this coinage reform was the chancellor, Cardinal Thomas Wolsey, who besides his other changes had minted at York a groat bearing his initials and cardinal's hat in addition to the other denominations normally authorized for the ecclesiastical mints.

When open debasement of the coinage began in 1544 to help finance Henry's wars, the right to coin of the archbishops of Canterbury and York and of the bishop of Durham was not confirmed. Instead, a second royal mint was opened in the Tower as in subsequent years were six others, at Southwark, York, Canterbury, Bristol, Dublin and Durham House in the Strand. Gold, which fell to 23c. in 1544, 22c. in 1545, and 20c. in 1546 was much less debased than silver which declined to 9oz 2dwt. in 1544, 6oz 2dwt. in 1545 and 4oz 2dwt. in 1546. At this last standard the blanched silver surface of the coins soon wore away to reveal the copper alloy beneath which earned for Henry the nickname 'Old Coppernose'.

Mintmarks

53	69	70	108	33	94	73	11
105	22	23	30	78	15	24	110
52	72a	44	8	65a	114	121	90
36	106	56	S	E	116	135	

1509-26		1509-14	Martlet (94, *York*)
	Pheon (53)	1509-23	Radiant star (22, *Durham & York*)
	Castle (69)	1513-18	Crowned T (135, Tournai)
	Castle with H (70, gold)	1514-26	Star (23, *York & Durham*)
	Portcullis crowned (108)		Pansy (30, *York*)
	Rose (33, *Canterbury*)		Escallop (78, *York*)
	Martlet (94, *Canterbury*)		Voided cross (15, *York*)
	Pomegranate (73, but broader, *Cant.*)	1523-26	Spur rowel (24, *Durham*)
	Cross fitchée (11, *Cant.*)		
	Lis (105, *Canterbury, Durham*)		

1526-44	Rose (33)
	Lis (105)
	Sunburst 110)
	Arrow (52)
	Pheon (53)
	Lis (106)
	Star (23, *Durham*)
1526-9	Crescent (72a, *Durham*)
	Trefoil (44 variety, *Durham*)
	Flower of eight petals and circle centre (*Durham*)
1526-30	Cross (7a, sometimes slightly voided, *York*)
	Acorn (65a, *York*)

1526-32	Cross patonce (8, *Cant.*)
	T (114, *Canterbury*)
	Uncertain mark (121, *Canterbury*)
1529-44	Radiant star (22, *Durham*)
1530-44	Key (90, *York*)
1533-44	Catherine wheel (36, *Canterbury*)
1544-7	Lis (105 and 106)
	Pellet in annulet (56)
	S (Southwark)
	Є or E (Southwark)
1546-7	WS monogram (116, *Bristol*)

GOLD

FIRST COINAGE, 1509-26

2265

		F	VF
		£	£
2264	**Sovereign** (20s; wt. 240grs., 15.55g.). Similar to last sov. of Hen. VII; *mm.* 108	11000	37500
2264A	**Ryal** (10s.) King in ship holding sword and shield. ℞. Similar to 1950, *mm.*-/108	*Extremely rare*	
2265	**Angel** (6s. 8d.). As Hen. VII, but hЄnRIC? VIII DI GRA RЄX, etc.; *mm.* 53, 69, 70, 70/69, 108, ℞. May omit h and rose, or rose only; *mm.* 69, 108	750	2250
2266	**Half-angel.** Similar (sometimes without VIII), *mm.* 69, 70, 108/33, 108	675	1850

SECOND COINAGE, 1526-44

2267

| 2267 | **Sovereign** (22s. 6d; wt. 240grs., 15.55g.). As 2264, ℞. single or double tressure *mm.* 110, 105, 105/52 .... | 10000 | 35000 |
| 2268 | **Angel** (7s. 6d.). As 2265, hЄnRIC VIII D(I) G(RA) R(ЄX) etc,; *mm.* 110, 105 .... | 1200 | 4000 |

		F £	VF £
2269	**Half-angel.** Similar; *mm.* lis..	1250	4500

2270   2272

2270	**George-noble** (6s. 8d.). As illustration; *mm.* rose	8500	35000
2270A	— Similar, but more modern ship with three masts, without initials hR. R.		
	St. George brandishing sword behind head..	9500	42500
2271	**Half-George-noble.** Similar to 2270 *mm* rose, lis................................	8000	35000
2272	**Crown of the rose** (4s. 6d., 23 c. 3 $^1/_2$ gr.). As illustration; *mm.* rose,		
	two legend varieties	7000	25000
2273	**Crown of the double-rose** (5s., 22 c). Double-rose crowned, hK (Henry and		
	Katherine of Aragon) both crowned in field. R. Shield crowned; *mm.* rose	725	2500

2274   2285

2274	— hK both sides; *mm.* rose/lis, lis, arrow	725	2500
2275*	— hK/hA or hA/hK; *mm.* arrow	2250	7500
2276*	— hR/hK or hI/hR; *mm.* arrow	1000	3250
2277	— hA (Anne Boleyn); *mm.* arrow	2500	9000
2278	— hA/hR; *mm.* arrow	2250	7500
2279	— hI (Jane Seymour); *mm.* arrow	750	2500
2280*	— hK/hI; *mm.* arrow	1100	3500
2281	— hR/hI; *mm.* arrow...	1000	3250
2282	— hR (Rex); *mm.* arrow...	750	2500
2283	— — *mm.* pheon...	1100	3500
2284	**Halfcrown.** Similar but king's name henric 8 on *rev.,* no initials; *mm.* rose	1350	4500
2285	— hK uncrowned on *obv.; mm.* rose...	725	2000
2286	— hK uncrowned both sides; *mm.* rose/lis, lis, arrow..............................	725	2000
2287	— hI uncrowned both sides; *mm.* arrow	800	2500
2288	— hR uncrowned both sides; hIB REX; *mm.* pheon	900	3000

*The hK initials may on later coins refer to Katherine Howard (Henry's fifth wife).

THIRD COINAGE, 1544-7

2291

	F	VF
	£	£

2289 **Sovereign,** I (20s., Wt. 200 grs., 12.96g., 23 ct.). Large module, similar to 2291 but king with large head; *mm.* lis 35000 150000

2290 II (20s., wt. 200 or 192 grs., 23, 22 or 20 ct.). *Tower.* As illustration; *mm.* lis, pellet in annulet/lis 6500 22500

2291 — *Southwark.* Similar; *mm.* S, Є/S 6500 22500

2292 — — Similar but Є below shield; *mm.* S/Є 7500 25000

2293 — *Bristol.* As London but *mm.* WS/- 12500 40000

2294   2303

2294 **Half-sovereign** (wt. 100 or 96 grs., 6.22g.), *Tower.* As illus.; *mm.* lis, pellet in annulet 800 2750

2295 — Similar, but with annulet on inner circle (either or both sides) 850 3000

2296 *Southwark. mm.* S 850 3000

2297 — Є below shield; *mm.* S, Є, S/Є, Є/S, (known without sceptre; *mm.* S) 800 2750

2298 *Bristol.* Lombardic lettering; *mm.* WS, WS/- 1750 6500

2299 **Angel** (8s., 23 c). Annulet by angel's head and on ship, hЄnRIC' 8; *mm.* lis 750 2250

2300 — Similar, but annulet one side only or none 800 2400

2300A— Similar, but three annulets on ship, *mm.* lis 1350 4500

2301 **Half-angel.** Annulet on ship; *mm.* lis 675 2000

2302 — No annulet on ship; *mm.* lis 725 2250

2303 — Three annulets on ship; *mm.* lis 900 2750

2304

		F	VF
		£	£
2304	**Quarter-angel** Angel wears armour; *mm.* lis	800	2400
2304A—	Angel wears tunic; *mm.* lis...	825	2500
2305	**Crown,** *London.* Similar to 2283, but hЄNRIC' 8 ; Lombardic lettering; *mm.* 56	675	2000
2306	— without RVTILAПS; *mm.* 56...	725	2250
2307	— — — with annulet on inner circle	725	2250
2307A—	King's name omitted. DEI GRA both sides, *mm.* 56...........................	900	3000
2308	— *Southwark.* As 2306; *mm.* S, Є, E/S, Є/-, E/Є	800	2500
2309	*Bristol.* hЄNRIC VIII. ROSA etc. Ʀ. D G, etc.; *mm.*-/WS	750	2250
2309A—	— with initials H R transposed on rev...	850	2500
2310	— Similar but hЄNRIC(VS) 8 Ʀ. DЄI) G(RA); *mm.* -/WS, WS	750	2250
2311	**Halfcrown,** *London.* Similar to 2288; *mm.* 56, 56/-.............................	475	1500
2312	— — with annulet on inner circle *mm.* 56...	525	1600
2313	*Southwark.* As 2311; *mm.* S	575	1750
2314	— *O.* hЄNRIC 8 ROSA SINЄ SPIП. Ʀ. DЄI GRA, etc.; *mm.* Є	575	1750
2315	*Bristol. O.* RVTILAПS, etc. Ʀ. hЄNRIC 8; *mm.* WS/-..........................	725	2250

For other gold coins in Henry's name see page 221-2.

SILVER

FIRST COINAGE, 1509-26

2316   2322

2316	**Groat.** Portrait of Hen. VII. *London mm.* 53, 69, 108, 108 over 135.......	110	400
2317	— *Tournai; mm.* crowned T. Ʀ. CIVITAS TORПACЄП*, dated 1513 ...	850	3000
2318	**Halfgroat.** Portrait of Hen. VII. London; *mm.* 108, 108/-	110	450
2319	— *Canterbury,* Archb. Warham. POSVI *rev.; mm.* rose..........................	135	525
2320	— — — WA above shield; *mm.* martlet...	100	350
2321	— — — WA beside shield; *mm.* cross fitchee..	100	350
2322	— — CIVITAS CAПTOR *rev.,* similar; *mm.* 73, 105, 11/105.................	75	225
2323	— *York,* POSVI *rev.,* Archb. Bainbridge (1508-14). Keys below shield; *mm.* martlet..	90	300
2324	— — — XB beside shield no keys; *mm.* martlet	100	350
2325	— — — Archb. Wolsey (1514-30). Keys and cardinal's hat below shield; *mm.* 94, 22..	175	625
2326	— — CIVITAS ЄBORACI *rev.* Similar; *mm.* 22, 23, 30, 78, 15, 15/78..	75	250
2327	— — As last with TW beside shield; *mm.* voided cross...........................	125	425
2327A—	*Tournai.* As 2317...	900	2750

*Non-portrait groats and half-groats exist of this mint, captured during an invasion of France in 1513. (Restored to France in 1518.)

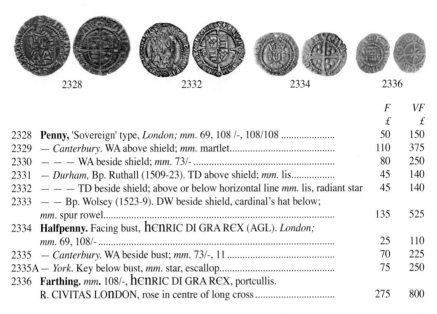

	2328	2332	2334	2336

		F £	VF £
2328	**Penny,** 'Sovereign' type, *London; mm.* 69, 108 /-, 108/108	50	150
2329	— *Canterbury.* WA above shield; *mm.* martlet..	110	375
2330	— — — WA beside shield; *mm.* 73/-	80	250
2331	— *Durham,* Bp. Ruthall (1509-23). TD above shield; *mm.* lis.................	45	140
2332	— — — TD beside shield; above or below horizontal line *mm.* lis, radiant star	45	140
2333	— — Bp. Wolsey (1523-9). DW beside shield, cardinal's hat below; *mm.* spur rowel..	135	525
2334	**Halfpenny.** Facing bust, hεnRIC DI GRA RεX (AGL). *London; mm.* 69, 108/-	25	110
2335	— *Canterbury.* WA beside bust; *mm.* 73/-, 11	70	225
2335A	— *York.* Key below bust, *mm.* star, escallop..	75	250
2336	**Farthing.** *mm.* 108/-, hεnRIC DI GRA RεX, portcullis. R̊. CIVITAS LOnDOn, rose in centre of long cross	275	800

SECOND COINAGE, 1526-44

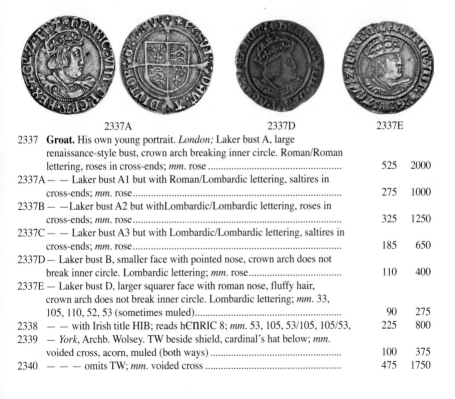

	2337A	2337D	2337E

		F	VF
2337	**Groat.** His own young portrait. *London;* Laker bust A, large renaissance-style bust, crown arch breaking inner circle. Roman/Roman lettering, roses in cross-ends; *mm.* rose	525	2000
2337A	— — Laker bust A1 but with Roman/Lombardic lettering, saltires in cross-ends; *mm.* rose..	275	1000
2337B	— —Laker bust A2 but withLombardic/Lombardic lettering, roses in cross-ends; *mm.* rose..	325	1250
2337C	— — Laker bust A3 but with Lombardic/Lombardic lettering, saltires in cross-ends; *mm.* rose..	185	650
2337D	— Laker bust B, smaller face with pointed nose, crown arch does not break inner circle. Lombardic lettering; *mm.* rose...................................	110	400
2337E	— Laker bust D, larger squarer face with roman nose, fluffy hair, crown arch does not break inner circle. Lombardic lettering; *mm.* 33, 105, 110, 52, 53 (sometimes muled)...	90	275
2338	— — with Irish title HIB; reads hεnRIC 8; *mm.* 53, 105, 53/105, 105/53, rose.........	225	800
2339	— *York*, Archb. Wolsey. TW beside shield, cardinal's hat below; *mm.* voided cross, acorn, muled (both ways)	100	375
2340	— — — omits TW; *mm.* voided cross	475	1750

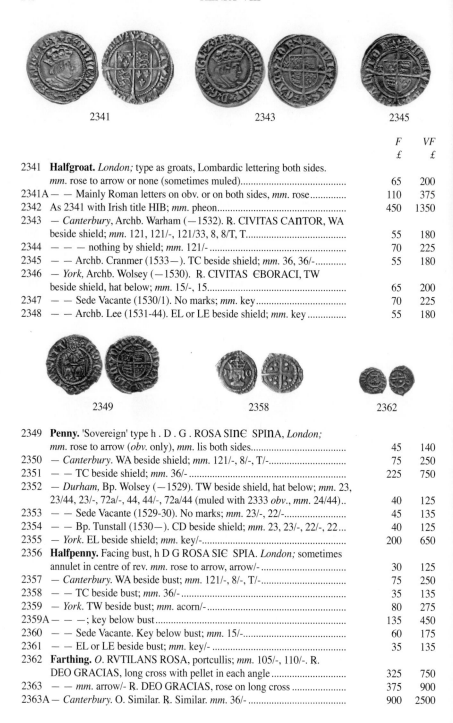

2341   2343   2345

	F £	VF £
2341 **Halfgroat.** *London;* type as groats, Lombardic lettering both sides. *mm.* rose to arrow or none (sometimes muled)	65	200
2341A — — Mainly Roman letters on obv. or on both sides, *mm.* rose	110	375
2342 As 2341 with Irish title HIB; *mm.* pheon	450	1350
2343 — *Canterbury,* Archb. Warham (−1532). R. CIVITAS CAПTOR, WA beside shield; *mm.* 121, 121/-, 121/33, 8, 8/T, T	55	180
2344 — — — nothing by shield; *mm.* 121/-	70	225
2345 — — Archb. Cranmer (1533−). TC beside shield; *mm.* 36, 36/-	55	180
2346 — *York,* Archb. Wolsey (−1530). R. CIVITAS ЄBORACI, TW beside shield, hat below; *mm.* 15/-, 15	65	200
2347 — — Sede Vacante (1530/1). No marks; *mm.* key	70	225
2348 — — Archb. Lee (1531-44). EL or LE beside shield; *mm.* key	55	180

2349   2358   2362

2349 **Penny.** 'Sovereign' type h . D . G . ROSA SIПЄ SPIПA, *London;* *mm.* rose to arrow (*obv.* only), *mm.* lis both sides	45	140
2350 — *Canterbury.* WA beside shield; *mm.* 121/-, 8/-, T/-	75	250
2351 — — TC beside shield; *mm.* 36/-	225	750
2352 — *Durham,* Bp. Wolsey (−1529). TW beside shield, hat below; *mm.* 23, 23/44, 23/-, 72a/-, 44, 44/-, 72a/44 (muled with 2333 *obv.*, *mm.* 24/44)..	40	125
2353 — — Sede Vacante (1529-30). No marks; *mm.* 23/-, 22/-	45	135
2354 — — Bp. Tunstall (1530−). CD beside shield; *mm.* 23, 23/-, 22/-, 22	40	125
2355 — *York.* EL beside shield; *mm.* key/-	200	650
2356 **Halfpenny.** Facing bust, h D G ROSA SIЄ SPIA. *London;* sometimes annulet in centre of rev. *mm.* rose to arrow, arrow/-	30	125
2357 — *Canterbury.* WA beside bust; *mm.* 121/-, 8/-, T/-	75	250
2358 — — TC beside bust; *mm.* 36/-	35	135
2359 — *York.* TW beside bust; *mm.* acorn/-	80	275
2359A — — —; key below bust	135	450
2360 — — Sede Vacante. Key below bust; *mm.* 15/-	60	175
2361 — — EL or LE beside bust; *mm.* key/-	35	135
2362 **Farthing.** *O.* RVTILANS ROSA, portcullis; *mm.* 105/-, 110/-. R. DEO GRACIAS, long cross with pellet in each angle	325	750
2363 — — *mm.* arrow/- R. DEO GRACIAS, rose on long cross	375	900
2363A — *Canterbury.* O. Similar. R. Similar. *mm.* 36/-	900	2500

2364

	F	VF
	£	£

THIRD COINAGE, 1544-7 (Silver progressively debased. 9oz (2dwt), 6oz (2dwt) 4oz (2dwt)).

2364 **Testoon.** *Tower.* hεnRIC'. VIII, etc. R. Crowned rose between crowned h
and R.POSVI, etc.; *mm.* lis, lis and 56, lis/two lis 1250 6500

2365 — hεnRIC 8, *mm.* 105 and 56, 105/56, 105 and 56/56, 56 .... 750 4250

2366 — — annulet on inner circle of rev. or both sides; *mm.* pellet in annulet 800 4500

2367

2367 — *Southwark.* As 2365. R. CIVITAS LOnDOn; *mm.* S, Є, S/Є, Є/S 750 4250

2368 — *Bristol. mm.*-/WS monogram. (Tower or local dies.) 1100 6000

2369 Bust 1   2374 Bust 2

2369 **Groat.** *Tower.* As ill. above, busts 1, 2, 3; *mm.* lis/-, lis 100 550

2369A Bust 1, R. As second coinage; i.e. saltires in forks; *mm.* lis 125 650

2370 Bust 2 or 3 annulet on inner circle, both sides or rev. only 110 600

2371 *Southwark.* As 2367, busts 1, 2, 3, 4; no *mm.* or lis/-; S or S and Є or
Є in forks 100 550

2372 *Bristol. Mm.*-/WS monogram, Bristol bust and Tower bust 2 or 3 .... 100 550

2373 *Canterbury.* Busts 1, 2, (2 var); no *mm*, or lis/– 100 550

2374 *York.* Busts 1 var., 2, 3, no *mm* 100 550

2377   2384   2385   2388A

		F	VF
		£	£
2375	**Halfgroat.** *Tower.* As 2365, bust 1; *mm.* lis, none	75	325
2376	*Southwark.* As 2367, bust 1; no *mm.*; S or Є and S in forks	110	375
2377	*Bristol. Mm.*-/WS monogram	75	300
2378	*Canterbury.* Bust 1; no *mm.*	60	225
2379	*York.* Bust 1; no *mm.*	70	275
2380	**Penny.** *Tower.* Facing bust; no *mm.* or lis/-	50	175
2381	*Southwark.* Facing bust; *mm.* S/-, Є/-, -/Є	85	300
2382	*Bristol.* Facing bust; no *mm.* (Tower dies or local but truncated at neck)	60	200
2383	*Canterbury.* Facing bust; no *mm.*	50	175
2384	*York.* Facing bust; no *mm.*	50	175
2385	**Halfpenny.** *Tower.* Facing bust; pellet in annulet in *rev.* centre, no *mm.* or lis/-	60	175
2386	*Bristol.* Facing bust; no *mm.*	75	250
2387	*Canterbury.* Facing bust; no *mm.*, (some read H 8)	55	150
2388	*York.* Facing bust; no *mm.*	45	135
2388A	**Farthing** *obv.* Rose. R. Cross and pellets	850	2500

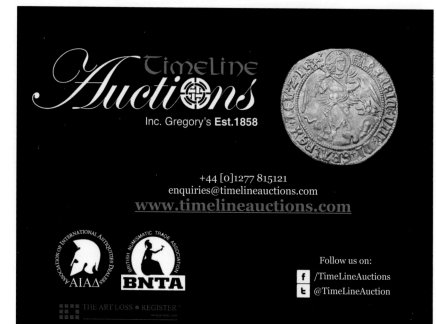

Timeline Auctions
Inc. Gregory's Est.1858

+44 [0]1277 815121
enquiries@timelineauctions.com
www.timelineauctions.com

AIAΔ
BNTA

THE ART LOSS ● REGISTER

Follow us on:
f /TimeLineAuctions
t @TimeLineAuction

These coins were struck during the reign of Edward VI but bear the name and portrait of Henry VIII, except in the case of the half-sovereigns which bear the youthful head of Edward.

Mintmarks

56	105	52	K	E	116

66	115	33	122	t	94

GOLD

	F	VF
	£	£
2389 **Sovereign** (20 ct.), *London*. As no. 2290, but Roman lettering; *mm*. lis..	8500	27500
2390 — *Bristol*. Similar but *mm*. WS...	12500	40000

2391

2393

2391 **Half-sovereign.** As 2294, but with youthful portrait with sceptre. *Tower*; *mm*. 52, 105, 94 (various combinations)..	725	2200
2391A — Similar but no sceptre; *mm*. 52, 52/56	750	2250
2392 — — — K below shield; *mm*.-/K, none,. E/-	750	2250
2393 — — — grapple below shield; *mm*. 122, none, 122/-, -/122.	800	2400
2394 — *Southwark*. *Mm*. E, E/-, -/E, Є /E. Usually Є or E (sometimes retro-grade) below shield (sceptre omitted; *mm*. -/E)..	725	2200
2394A — — — R. As 2296; *mm*.-/S..	900	2750

2395

	F	VF
	£	£
2395 **Crown.** Similar to 2305. *London; mm.* 52, 52/-, -/K, 122, 94, ...	650	2000
2396 — Similar but transposed legends without numeral; *mm.* -/arrow	700	2250
2396A — As 2395, but omitting RVTILANS; *mm.* arrow	700	2250
2396B Similar, but RVTILANS both sides; *mm.* arrow	850	2750
2397 — *Southwark.* Similar to 2396; *mm.* E	750	2500
2398 — — King's name on *obv.; mm.* E/-, -/E	700	2250
2399 **Halfcrown.** Similar to 2311. *London; mm.* 52, K/-, 122/-, 94, -/52	650	1750
2399A As last but E over h on *rev., mm.* 56/52	1000	3000
2399B As 2399 but RVTILANS etc. on both sides, *mm.* arrow	700	2250
2400 — *Southwark. mm.* E, E/-, -/E	675	2000

SILVER

AR (4oz .333)

2401 **Testoon.** *Tower.* As 2365 with lozenge stops one side; -/56, 56..........	1750	9500

2403   2403 Bust 4   2403 Bust 6

Some of the Bristol testoons, groats and halfgroats with WS monogram were struck after the death of Henry VIII but cannot easily be distinguished from those struck during his reign.

	F	VF
2403 **Groat.** *Tower.* Busts 4, 5, 6 (and, rarely, 2). R. POSVI, etc.; *mm.* 105-94 and none (frequently muled)..	85	500
2404 — *Southwark.* Busts 4, 5, 6. R. CIVITAS LONDON; no *mm.* -/E; lis/-, -/lis, K/E; roses or crescents or S and Є in forks, or rarely annulets	80	475
2405 — *Durham House.* Bust 6. R. REDDE CVIQVE QVOD SVVM EST; *mm.* bow..	225	950
2406 — *Bristol. mm.* WS on *rev.* Bristol bust B, Tower bust 2 and 3	100	525
2407 — — *mm.* TC on *rev.* Similar, Bristol bust B	120	600
2408 — *Canterbury.* Busts 5, 6; no *mm.* or rose/-	75	425
2409 — *York.* Busts 4, 5, 6; no *mm.* or lis/-, -/lis...	75	425

2411   2416

		F	VF
		£	£
2410	**Halfgroat.** Bust 1. *Tower*. POSVI, etc.; *mm.* 52, 52/-, 52/K , -/K, 52/122, 122, -/122	90	350
2411	— *Southwark*. CIVITAS LONDON; *mm.* E, -/E, none, 52/E, K/E	60	200
2412	— *Durham House*. R. REDD, etc.; *mm.* bow, -/bow	375	1350
2413	— *Bristol*. *Mm.* WS on *rev.*	75	300
2414	— — *mm.* TC on *rev.*	90	350
2415	— *Canterbury*. No *mm.* or t/-, -/t,	45	185
2416	— *York*. No *mm.*, bust 1 and three-quarter facing	65	250

2417   2418

2417	**Penny.** *Tower*. CIVITAS LONDON. Facing bust; *mm.* 52/-, -/52, -/K, 122/-, -/122, none	50	175
2418	— — three-quarter bust; no *mm.*	50	180
2419	— *Southwark*. As 2417; *mm.* E, -/E	55	185
2420	— *Durham House*. As groat but shorter legend; *mm.* -/bow	450	1500

2421   2426   2428

2421	— *Bristol*. Facing busts, as 2382 but showing more body, no *mm.*	75	275
2422	— *Canterbury*. Similar to 2417	50	175
2423	— — three-quarter facing bust; no *mm.*	55	180
2424	— *York*. Facing bust; no *mm.*	50	175
2425	— — three-quarter facing bust; no *mm.*	60	200
2426	**Halfpenny.** *Tower*. *mm* 52?, none	45	140
2427	— *Canterbury*. No *mm.*, sometimes reads H8	50	150
2428	— *York*. No *mm.*	45	140

COINS OF BRITAIN
PO BOX 2, MONMOUTH, NP25 3YR, UK

BNTA

E-mail: lloydbennett@coinsofbritain.com   +44(0)7714 284 939

The 4 oz. 2.5dwt coins of Henry VIII and those issued under Edward in 1547 and 1548 caused much disquiet, yet at the same time government was prevented by continuing financial necessity from abandoning debasement. A stratagem was devised which entailed increasing the fineness of silver coins, thereby making them appear sound, while at the same time reducing their weight in proportion so that in practice they contained no more silver than hitherto. The first issue, ordered on 24 January 1549, at 8 oz.2 dwt. fine produced a shilling which, at 60 gr., was so light that it was rapidly discredited and had to be replaced in April by another at 6 oz. 2 dwt. Weighing 80 gr., these later shillings proved acceptable.

Between April and August 1551 the issue of silver coins was the worst ever – 3 oz. 2dwt. fine at 72s per lb. before retrenchment came in August, first by a 50% devaluation of base silver coin and then by the issue of a fine standard at 11oz. 1dwt. 'out of the fire'. This was the equivalent of 11oz.3dwt. commixture, and means that since sterling was only 11oz. 2dwt., this issue, which contained four new denominations – the crown, halfcrown, sixpence and threepence – was in effect the finest ever issued under the Tudors.

Some base 'pence' were struck in parallel with the fine silver, but at the devalued rate, they and the corresponding 'halfpence' were used as halfpence and farthings respectively.

The first dates on English coinage appear in this reign, first as Roman numerals and then on the fine issue crowns and halfcrowns of 1551-3, in Arabic numerals.

Mintmarks

66	52	35	115	E	53	122

t	T	111	Y	126	94	91A

92	105	y	97	123	78	26

1547-8	Arrow (52)		
	E (Southwark)		
1548-50	Bow (66, *Durham House*)	1550	Martlet (94)
1549	Arrow (52)	1550	Leopard's head (91A)
	Grapple (122)	1550-1	Lion (92)
	Rose (35, *Canterbury*)		Lis (105, *Southwark*)
	TC monogram (115, *Bristol*)		Rose (33)
	Pheon (53)	1551	Y or y (117, *Southwark*)
	t or T (*Canterbury*)		Ostrich's head (97, gold only)
1549-50	Swan (111)	1551-3	Tun (123)
	Roman Y (*Southwark*)		Escallop (78)
1549-50	6 (126 gold only)	1552-3	Pierced mullet (26, *York*)

GOLD

First period, Apr. 1547-Jan. 1549

2430

	F	VF
	£	£

2429 **Half-sovereign** (20 c). As 2391, but reading EDWARD 6. Tower; *mm.*
arrow 2250 9000

2430 — *Southwark* (Sometimes with E or Є below shield); *mm.* E................ 1750 6500

2431 **Crown.** RVTILANS, etc., crowned rose between ER both crowned. R.
EDWARD 6, etc., crowned shield between ER both crowned; *mm.* arrow,
E over arrow/- 2250 9000

2431A — *Obv.* as last. R. As 2305, *mm.* 52/56 .... 2000 7500

2432 **Halfcrown.** Similar to 2431, but initials not crowned; *mm.* arrow 1500 5000

Second period, Jan. 1549-Apr. 1550

2433

2433 **Sovereign** (22 ct). As illustration; *mm.* arrow, –/arrow, Y,...................... 6250 18500

2434 **Half-sovereign.** Uncrowned bust. *Tower.* TIMOR etc., MDXLIX on
obv. mm. arrow 3750 12500

2435

2435 — — SCVTVM, etc., as illustration; *mm.* arrow, **6**, Y............................ 1850 6750

	F	VF
	£	£
2436 — *Durham House.* Uncrowned, 1/2 length bust with MDXLVIII at end of		
obv. legend; *mm.* bow; SCVTVM etc.	7500	27500
2437 — Normal, uncrowned bust. LVCERNA, etc., on *obv.; mm.* bow	6500	22500
2437A — Normal, uncrowned bust. SCVTVM, etc. but with *rev.* as 2440, *mm.* bow	5250	17500

2438   2441

2438 — *London, Southwark.* Crowned bust. EDWARD VI, etc. R. SCVTVM, etc.;		
mm. 52, 122, 111/52, 111, Y, 94...	1750	6250
2439 — *Durham House.* Crowned, half-length bust; *mm.* bow	7500	27500
2440 — — King's name on *obv.* and *rev.; mm.* bow (mule of 2439/37)...........	8000	30000
2441 **Crown.** Uncrowned bust, as 2435; *mm.* 6, Y, 52/-, Y/-	2250	8500
2442 — Crowned bust, as 2438; *mm.* 52, 122, 111, Y (usually *obv.* only)........	2000	7000
2443 **Halfcrown.** Uncrowned bust; R. As 2441, *mm.* arrow, Y, Y/-, 52/-	2250	8000
2444 — Crowned bust, as illus. above; *mm.* 52, 52/111, 111, 122, Y, Y/-	1650	5750
2445 — Similar, but king's name on *rev., mm.* 52, 122.....................................	1750	6000

Third period, 1550-3, Fine Gold (23 ct.)

| 2446 **Sovereign** (30s., 240grs., 15.55g.). King on throne; *mm.* 97, 123 .... | 32500 | 125000 |

2444   2448

2447 **Double sovereign.** From the same dies, *mm.* 97	100000	450000
2448 **Angel** (10s.). As illustration; *mm.* 97, 123..	12500	40000
2449 **Half-angel.** Similar, *mm.* 97	11000	35000

2450

| | F | VF |
| | £ | £ |

Crown Gold (22 ct.)

2450 **Sovereign**. (=20s., 174.6 grs., 11.31g.). Half-length
figure of king r., crowned and holding sword and orb. R. Crowned shield
with supporters; *mm.* y, tun... 5750 17500

2451

2451 **Half-sovereign**. As illustration above; *mm.* y, tun 1850 6500
2452 **Crown**. Similar, but *rev.* SCVTVM etc., *mm.* y, tun 2250 7500
2453 **Halfcrown**. Similar, *mm.* tun, y... 2500 8500

*Small denominations often occur creased or straightened.

SILVER

First period, Apr. 1547-Jan. 1549

2454   2455

2454 **Groat**. Crowned bust r. *Tower*. R. Shield over cross, POSVI, etc.; *mm.* arrow   750 4250
2455 — As last, but EDOARD 6, *mm.* arrow.. 800 4500
2456 *Southwark*. *Obv.* as 2454. R. CIVITAS LONDON; *mm.*-/E or none,
sometimes S in forks... 750 4250
2457 **Halfgroat**. *Tower*. *Obv.* as 2454; *mm.* arrow... 650 2500
2458 *Southwark*. As 2456; *mm.* arrow, E on reverse only................................. 575 2000

2459 2462

	F	VF
	£	£
2459 *Canterbury*. Similar. No *mm.*, reads EDOARD or EDWARD (rare)	350	1350
2460 **Penny**. *Tower*. As halfgroat, but E.D.G. etc. R. CIVITAS LONDON; *mm.* arrow	450	1500
2461 *Southwark*. As last, but *mm.* -/E...	500	1650
2462 *Bristol*. Similar, but reads ED6DG or E6DG no *mm.*............................	450	1500
2463 **Halfpenny**. *Tower. O.* As 2460, *mm.* E (?). R. Cross and pellets	450	1500
2464 *Bristol*. Similar, no *mm.* but reads E6DG or EDG....................................	525	1750

Second period, Jan. 1549-Apr. 1550

At all mints except Bristol, the earliest shillings of 1549 were issued at only 60 grains but of 8 oz. 2 dwt standard. This weight and size were soon increased to 80 grains, (S.2466 onwards), but the fineness was reduced to 6 oz. 2 dwt so the silver content remained the same. Dies, mm G were prepared for a coinage of 80gr shillings at York, but were not used. Coins from the *mm* are found suitably overmarked, from other mints, S.2466-8. The shilling bust types are set out in *J. Bispham 'The Base Silver Shillings of Edward VI; BNJ 1985.*

Bust 1   2465A   Bust 2

First Issue, 60 grs., 3.88g., 8oz. 2 dwt.

2465 **Shilling**. *Tower*. Broad bust with large crown. *Obv.* TIMOR etc. MDXLIX. R. Small, oval garnished shield dividing ER. EDWARD VI etc., *mm.* 52, no *mm*, Bust 1; *mm*, –/52, Bust 2 (very rare)	250	1350
2465A*Southwark*. As last, Bust 1, *mm.* Y, EY/Y...	225	1250
2465B*Canterbury*. As last, Bust 1, *mm.* -/rose..	300	1650

2465C

2465C *Durham House*. Bust with elaborate tunic and collar TIMOR etc. MDXLIX. R. Oval shield, very heavily garnished in different style. EDWARD VI etc., *mm.* bow (2469) 275   1500

Second Issue, debased, 80 grs., 5.18g., 6oz. 2 dwt.

Bust 3   Bust 4

Bust 5   2466C   2468

2472

		F	*VF*
		£	£
2466	*Tower.* Tall, narrow bust with small crown. *Obv.* EDWARD VI etc. MDXLIX or MDL. R. As 2465 but TIMOR etc., Busts 3, 4 and 5, *mm.* 52-91a (frequently muled)	150	900
2466A	— *Obv.* as last, MDXLIX. R. Heavily garnished shield, Durham House style, Bust 3 *mm.* grapple	375	1750
2466B	*Southwark.* As 2466, Busts 3, 4 and 5 *mm.* Y, Y/swan	150	850
2466C	— — — Bust 4; R. as 2466A. *mm.* Y	375	1750
2467	*Bristol. Obv.* similar to 2466, Bust 3 or local die R. Shield with heavy curved garniture or as 2466, *mm.* TC, or TC over G	950	4500
2468	*Canterbury.* As 2466, Bust 3 and 4 *mm.* T, T/t, t/T, t or t over G	240	1250
2470	*Durham House.* Bust as 2465C. INIMICOS etc., no date. R. EDWARD etc.	225	1200
2472	— Bust similar to 2466. EDWARD VI etc. R. INIMICOS etc.	200	1050
2472A	— As last but legends transposed	325	1650
2472B	*Tower.* Elegant bust with extremely thin neck. Bust 6, R. As 2466, *mm.* martlet	450	2250
2472C	*Southwark.* As last, Bust 6, *mm.* Y	225	1350

For coins of Edward VI countermarked, see p. 236

Third period, 1550-3

Very base issue (1551) ca. 70grs., ca. 4.88g., 3oz. 2 dwt.

2473 Bust 6   2474   2476

		F £	VF £
2473	**Shilling**, *Tower*. As 2472B. MDL or MDLI, *mm.* lion, rose, lion/rose	175	950
2473A	*Southwark*. As last, *mm.* lis/Y, Y/lis, lis	175	950
2474	**Base Penny**. *London. O*. Rose. ℞. Shield; *mm.* escallop (*obv.*)	55	250
2475	— — *York. Mm.* mullet (*obv.*) as illustration	50	225
2476	**Base Halfpenny**. As penny, but single rose	175	850

* The base penny and halfpenny were used as halfpenny and farthing respectively.
Note: Irish very base shillings exist which are all dated MDLII, a date that does not occur for
English issued shillings.

Fine silver issue, (1551-3) 460grs., 30g., 11oz. 3 dwt.

2478

| 2478 | **Crown**. King on horseback with date below horse. ℞. Shield on cross; *mm.* y. 1551; tun, 1551-3 (1553, wire line inner circle may be missing) . | 900 | 3000 |

2479

| 2479 | **Halfcrown**. Walking horse with plume; *mm.* y, 1551 | 600 | 2000 |
| 2480 | Galloping horse without plume; *mm.* tun, 1551-3 | 625 | 2250 |

2482

2483   2484

		F	VF
		£	£
2481	Large walking horse without plume; *mm.* tun, 1553	950	3500
2482	**Shilling**. Facing bust, rose l., value XII r. *mm.* y, tun (several bust varieties)	100	400
2483	**Sixpence**. *London*. Similar value VI, as illustration; *mm.* y/-, -/y, y, tun (bust varieties)	120	500
2484	*York*. As last, but rev. reads CIVITAS ЄBORACI; *mm.* mullet	200	1250

2485   2486

2485	**Threepence**. *London*. As sixpence, but value III; *mm.* tun	185	1000
2486	*York*. As 2484, but III by bust	425	2000

2487   2487A

2487	**Penny**. 'Sovereign' type; *mm.* tun	1250	4500
2487A	**Farthing**. *O*. Portcullis, *R* Cross and Pellets	1350	4500

SPINK

LONDON
1666

ALSO AVAILABLE FROM SPINK

ENGLISH COINS 1180-1551
by Lord Stewartby

This book is an indispensable point of reference for students, curators, dealers and collectors. It is also a ready source of information for historians and others with a more general interest in English medieval coins.

Price: £45 + postage

To order your copy, please contact the Spink Books Department:
Tel: +44 (0)20 7563 4046 | Email: books@spink.com
SPINK LONDON | 69 Southampton Row | Bloomsbury | London | WC1B4ET
LONDON | NEW YORK | HONG KONG | SINGAPORE | LUGANO

#SPINK_AUCTIONS   WWW.SPINK.COM   WWW.SPINKBOOKS.COM

Mary brought English coins back to the sterling standard and struck all her gold coins at the traditional fineness of 0.995. The mintmarks usually appear at the end of the first or second word of the legends.

Pomegranate   Halved rose and castle

GOLD

2488

	F	VF
	£	£

2488 **'Fine' Sovereign** (30s.). Queen enthroned. R̩. Shield on rose, MDLIII, MDLIIII and undated, *mm.* pomegranate, half-rose (or mule) 8500 27500

2489

2490

2489 **Ryal** (15s.). As illus, MDLIII. R̩. As 1950 but A DNO etc. *mm.* pomegranate/- 32500 110000

2490 **Angel** (10s.). Class I, annulet stops; *mm.* pomegranate............................ 2000 6000

2490A — Class II, pellet stops, *mm.* pomegranate (often muled with class I reverse) 2100 6250

2490B — Class III, pellet stops, large Roman letters, *mm.* half-rose and castle . 2250 7500

2491 **Half-angel**. Similar; *mm.* pomegranate, pomegranate/- 5250 15000

SILVER

2492

		F £	VF £
2492	**Groat**. Crowned bust l. R̃. VERITAS, etc.; *mm.* pomegranate, pomegranate/-	125	525
2493	**Halfgroat**. Similar	650	2250
2494	**Penny**. Similar, but M. D. G. ROSA, etc.	575	2000

2495

2495	— As last. R̃. CIVITAS LONDON; no *mm.*	575	2000

Timeline Auctions

Inc. Gregory's **Est.1858**

Sold for:
£34,720

We are accepting
single entries and collections
of coins & antiquities

+44 [0]1277 815121; enquiries@timelineauctions.com

www.timelineauctions.com

Follow us on:

f /TimeLineAuctions
t @TimeLineAuction

ASSOCIATION OF INTERNATIONAL ANTIQUITIES DEALERS
AIAΔ

BRITISH NUMISMATIC TRADE ASSOCIATION
BNTA

The groats and smaller silver coins of this period have Mary's portrait only, but the shillings and sixpences show the bust of the queen's husband, Philip of Spain.

Mintmarks

Lis (105   Half-rose and castle

GOLD

2496A

		F	VF
		£	£
2496	**Angel**. As illustration; wire line inner circles, calm sea, *mm.* lis	5750	22000
2496A	— — New-style, large wings, wire line i.c.	6000	22500
2496B	— — As above but beaded i.c.	6250	23000
2497	**Half-angel**. Similar to 2496	12500	35000

SILVER

2497A

		F	VF
2497A	**Halfcrown (Pattern)**. As illustration. Bust of Philip r., crown above, date 1554 below. R. Bust of Mary l. crown and date 1554 above, without mark of value, no *mm*...	13500	45000
2498	**Shilling**. Busts face-to-face, full titles, undated, no *mm*.	400	1800
2499	— — — also without mark of value	450	2000

AMR Coins
Dealers in Quality British Coins

BNTA

British Coins Bought and Sold
www.amrcoins.com
email: info@amrcoins.com
tel: +44 (0)7527 569308

2500

		F £	VF £
2500	— — 1554	400	1800
2501	— English titles only 1554, 1555	425	1850
2501A	— — undated	525	2250
2502	— — without mark of value, 1554, 1555 (rare)	450	2000
2503	— — date below bust, 1554, 1555	3500	12500
2504	— — As last, but without ANG., 1555	4000	13500

2505   2506

		F £	VF £
2505	**Sixpence**. Similar. Full titles, 1554 (and undated?)	425	1750
2506	— English titles only, 1555 (no *mm.*, rare), 1557 (*mm.* lis, rounder garnishing)	400	1650
2506A	— As last but heavy beaded i.c. on obv. 1555. (Irish 4d. obv. mule)	450	1850
2507	— — date below bust, 1554, 1557 (very rare)	1250	5250

2508   2510A

		F £	VF £
2508	**Groat**. Crowned bust of Mary l. ℞. POSVIMVS etc. (several legend vars.); *mm.* lis	110	475
2509	**Halfgroat**. Similar, but POSVIM, *mm.* lis	425	1750
2510	**Penny**. Similar to 2495, but P. Z. M. etc.; *mm.* lis	400	1600
2510A	**Base penny**, but P. Z. M . etc.; *mm.* halved rose and castle or castle/–, (used as a halfpenny)	65	225

Elizabeth's coinage is particularly interesting on account of the large number of different denominations issued. 'Crown' gold coins were again issued as well as the 'fine' gold denominations. In 1560 the base shillings of Edward VI's second and third coinages were called in and countermarked for recirculation at reduced values. Smaller debased coins were also devalued but not countermarked. The old debased groat became a three halfpence and other coins in proportion. The normal silver coinage was initially struck at 0.916 fineness as in the previous reign but between 1560 and 1577 and after 1582 the old sterling standard of 0.925 was restored. Between 1578 and 1582 the standard was slightly reduced and the weights were reduced by 1/32nd in 1601. Gold was similarly reduced slightly in quality 1578-82, and there was a slight weight reduction in 1601.

To help alleviate the shortage of small change, and to avoid the expense of minting an impossibly small silver farthing, a threefarthing piece was introduced to provide change if a penny was tendered for a farthing purchase. The sixpence, threepence, threehalfpence and threefarthings were marked with a rose behind the queen's head to distinguish them from the shilling, groat, half-groat and penny.

Coins of exceedingly fine workmanship were produced in a screw press introduced by Eloye Mestrelle, a French moneyer, in 1561. With parts of the machinery powered by a horse-drawn mill, the coins produced came to be known as 'mill money'. Despite the superior quality of the coins produced, the machinery was slow and inefficient compared to striking by hand. Mestrelle's dismissal was engineered in 1572 and six years later he was hanged for counterfeiting.

Mintmarks

1ST ISSUE	2ND ISSUE		3RD & 4TH ISSUES				
106	21	94	23	53	33	107	92
			74	71	77	65b	27

5TH ISSUE			6TH ISSUE				
7	14	113	60	54	79	72b	86

7TH ISSUE							
1	2		123	124	90	57	0

First Issue
1558-60 Lis (106)
Second Issue
1560-1 Cross crosslet (21)
Martlet (94)
Third & Fourth Issue
1560-6 Star (23, milled)
1561-5 Pheon (53)
1565 Rose (33)
1566 Portcullis (107)
1566-7 Lion (92)
1567-70 Coronet (74)

Lis (106, milled)
1569-71 Castle (71)
1572-3 Ermine (77)
1573-4 Acorn (65b)
1573-8 Eglantine (27)
Fifth Issue
1578-9 Greek cross (7)
1580-1 Latin cross (14)
1582 Sword (113)
Sixth Issue
1582-3 Bell (60)
1582-4 A (54)

1584-6 Escallop (79)
1587-9 Crescent (72b)
1590-2 Hand (86)
1592-5 Tun (123)
1594-6 Woolpack (124)
1595-8 Key (90)
1598-1600 Anchor (57)
1600 **0**
Seventh Issue
1601-2 **1**
1602 **2**

N.B. *The dates for* mms *sometimes overlap. This is a result of using up old dies, onto which the new mark was punched.*

GOLD

HAMMERED COINAGE
First to Fourth issues, 1559-78. ('Fine' gold of 0.994. 'Crown' gold of 0 .916 fineness. Sovereigns of 240 grs., 15.55g.). Mintmarks; lis to eglantine.

	F	VF
	£	£

			F	VF
2511	**'Fine' Sovereign** (30 s.) Queen enthroned, tressure broken by throne, reads Z not ET, no chains to portcullis. R. Arms on rose; *mm*. lis............		9500	35000

2512

			F	VF
2512	— — Similar but ET, chains on portcullis; *mm*. crosslet		7000	22500

2513　　　　　　　　　　　　　　　　　　2517

			F	VF
2513	**Angel**. St. Michael. R. Ship. Wire line inner circles; *mm*. lis..................		1850	6000
2513A	— Similar, but beaded i.c. on *obv*., *mm*. lis		2250	7500
2514	— — Similar, but beaded inner circles; ship to r.; *mm*. 106, 21, 74, 27,..		1200	3500
2515	— — — Similar, but ship to l.; *mm*. 77-27		1250	3650
2516	**Half Angel**. As 2513, wire line inner circles; *mm*. lis		2250	7500
2516A	— As last, but beaded i.c.s, legend ends. Z.HIB		1500	5000
2517	— As 2514, beaded inner circles; *mm*. 106, 21, 74, 77-27.......................		950	3000
2518	**Quarter Angel**. Similar; *mm*. 74, 77-27..		850	2750
2519	**Half Pound** (10 s.) Young crowned bust l. R. Arms. Wire line inner circles; *mm*. lis		5250	18500

HAMMERED BRITISH COINS

Hammered coins bought and sold

www.hammeredbritishcoins.com
mail@hammeredbritishcoins.com
07825226435

2520   2524

	F	VF
	£	£
2520 — Similar, but beaded inner circles; *mm.* 21, 33-107	1650	5000
2520A — — Smaller bust; *mm.* lion	1750	6000
2520B — — Broad bust, ear visible; *mm.* 92, 74, 71	1650	5000
2521 **Crown**. As 2519; *mm.* lis	3000	9500
2522 — Similar to 2520; *mm.* 21, 33-107	1250	3500
2522A — Similar to 2520B; *mm.* 74, 71, 92	1350	3750
2523 **Half Crown**. As 2519; *mm.* lis	2250	7500
2524 — Similar to 2520; *mm.* 21, 33-107 (2 busts)	1100	3250
2524A — Similar to 2520B; *mm.* 107-71	1250	3500

Fifth Issue, 1578-82 (`Fine' gold only of 0.992). *Mms* Greek cross,
Latin cross and sword.

2525 **Angel**. As 2514; *mm.* 7, 14, 113	1000	3000
2526 **Half Angel**. As 2517; *mm.* 7, 14, 113	950	3000
2527 — Similar, but without E and rose above ship; *mm.* latin cross	1100	3500
2528 **Quarter Angel**. As last; *mm.* 7, 14, 113	850	2750

Sixth Issue, 1583-1600 (`Fine' gold of 0.995, `crown' gold of 0.916; pound of 174.5 grs. wt.).
Mintmarks: bell to **O**.

2529

2529 **Sovereign** (30 s:). As 2512, but tressure not normally broken by back of throne; *mm.* 54-123	6000	17500

2530

	F	VF
	£	£

2530 **Ryal** (15 s.). Queen in ship. R. Similar to 1950; *mm.* 54-86 (*rev.* only) .. 22500 70000

Note: Contemporary imitations of the Elizabeth Ryal are known for the Low Countries.

2531

2531	**Angel**. As 2514; *mm.* 60-123, 90-O	950	3000
2532	**Half Angel**. As 2517; *mm.* 60-86, 90-57	1000	3250

2535

2533	**Quarter Angel**. As 2518; *mm.* 60-123, 90-57/–	850	2750
2534	**Pound** (20 s.). Old bust l., with elaborate dress and profusion of hair; *mm.*, lion and tun/tun, 123-O	2750	10000
2535	**Half Pound**. Similar; *mm.* tun	2350	7500
2535A	— Similar but smaller bust with less hair; *mm.* 123-O	2250	7000

2536

2536	**Crown**. Similar to 2534; *mm.* 123-90. O	2250	7000
2537	**Half Crown**. Similar; *mm.* -/123, 123-0, O	1500	4500

Seventh Issue, 1601-3 ('Fine' gold of 0.994, 'crown' gold of 0.916; Pound of 172 gr.). Mintmarks: **1** and **2**

		F	VF
		£	£
2538	**Angel**. As 2531; *mm*. **1, 2**..	2000	6000
2539	**Pound**. As 2534; *mm*. **1, 2**...	3250	11500
2540	**Half Pound**. As 2535A; *mm*. **1, 2**	3500	12000
2541	**Crown**. As 2536; *mm*. **1, 2**..	2750	8500
2542	**Half Crown**. As 2537; *mm*. **1, 2**...	2500	7500

MILLED COINAGE, 1561-70

2543

2543	**Half Pound**. Crowned bust l.; *mm*. star, lis...	3000	9500
2544	**Crown**. Similar; *mm*. star, lis	2500	7500
2545	**Half Crown**. Similar; *mm*. star, lis...	3500	10500

For further details on the Gold milled coinage, *see* D. G. Borden & I.D. Brown *'The milled coinage of Elizabeth I'*. BNJ 53, 1983

TimeLine Auctions
Inc. Gregory's **Est.1858**

We are accepting single entries and collections of coins & antiquities

www.timelineauctions.com

Contact either Brett Hammond or Christopher Wren on
+44 [0]1277 815121

enquiries@timelineauctions.com

Follow us on:

f /TimeLineAuctions

t @TimeLineAuction

AIAΔ   BNTA

SILVER

HAMMERED COINAGE
Countermarked Edward VI base shillings (1560)

2546   2547

	Fair	*F*
	£	£
2546 **Fourpence-halfpenny**. Edward VI 2nd period 6oz and 8oz shillings	1350	4500
cmkd on obv. with a portcullis; *mm*. 66, –/33, 52, t, 111, Y and 122		
2547 **Twopence-farthing**. Edward VI 3rd period 3 oz. shillings	1650	5750
countermarked on obverse with a seated greyhound; *mm*. 92. 105, 35 and 87		
N.B. *Occasionally the wrong countermark was used*		

First Issue, 1559-60 (.916 fine, shillings of 96 grs., 6.22g.)

2549   2551

1A   1B   1D   2A   2B

	F	*VF*
	£	£
2548 **Shilling**. Without rose or date. ELIZABET(H), wire line inner circles,		
pearls on bodice, busts 1A, and 1B; *mm*. lis.	525	2500
2549 — Similar, ELIZABETH, wire line and beaded inner circles, busts 1A, 1D,		
2A and 2B; *mm*. lis..	185	1050

1F   1E 2550 only   1G

		F	VF
		£	£
2550	**Groat**. Without rose or date, wire line or no inner circle, (busts 1F and 1E); *mm*. lis	135	675
2551	— Similar, wire line and beaded inner circles, bust 1F; *mm*. lis...........	85	450
2551A	— — Small bust 1G and shield (from halfgroat punches); *mm*. lis......	100	575

2551A   2552   2553

2552	**Halfgroat**. Without rose or date, wire line inner circles; *mm*. lis.........	150	750
2553	**Penny**. Without rose or date, wire line inner circles; *mm*. lis...............	250	1250
2554	— Similar but dated 1558 on *obv*.; *mm*. lis..	525	2250
2554A	— Similar to 2553, but wire line and beaded inner circles.; *mm*. lis	275	1350

Second Issue, 1560-1 (0.925 fineness, shilling of 96 grs., 6.22g.)

2555   2557

2558

3A   3B   3C   3J

2555	**Shilling**. Without rose or date, beaded inner circles. ET instead of Z busts 3A, 3B, 3C and 3J; *mm*. 21, 94	100	525
2555A	— large bust with pearls on bodice as 2548; *mm*. 21, bust 1A, 94, bust 1B	150	850
2556	**Groat**. Without rose or date, bust as 2551; *mm*. 21, 94	70	300
2557	**Halfgroat**. Without rose or date; *mm*. 21, 94..	35	150
2558	**Penny**. Without rose or date (three bust varieties); *mm*. 21, 94............	35	135

Third and Fourth Issues, 1561-77 (Same fineness and weight as last)

	2559	2561	2561B		

<table>
<tr><td></td><td></td><td>F
£</td><td>VF
£</td></tr>
<tr><td>2559</td><td>Sixpence. With rose and date, large flan (inner beaded circle 19mm), large bust 3D with hair swept back, 1561; mm. pheon.....................................</td><td>135</td><td>650</td></tr>
<tr><td>2560</td><td>— Similar, small bust 1F, 1561; mm. pheon...</td><td>70</td><td>325</td></tr>
</table>

3D 2559 only	1F 2560	3E 2561B only

2562	4B 2562

2561	— Smaller flan (inner beaded circle 17.5mm). Small bust 1F, 1561-6; *mm.* 53-107	60	275
2561B	— Similar, very large bust 3E, 1563-5; *mm.* pheon.................................	80	375
2562	— Intermediate bust 4B, ear shows, 1566-73; *mm.* 92-77	55	225
2562A	— Similar, without date; *mm.* lion, coronet, ermine................................	750	2250

2563	5A 2563	2565

2563	— Larger bust 5A, 1573-7; *mm.* 77-27..	50	225
2564	**Threepence**. With rose and date 1561, large flan (inner circle 15mm.); *mm.* pheon	50	225
2565	— smaller flan (inner circle 14mm.). Regular bust, 1561-7; *mm.* 53-92 .	40	185

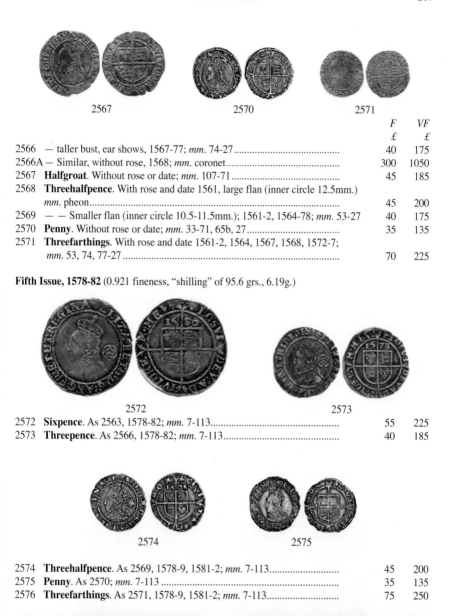

2567   2570   2571

		F	VF
		£	£
2566	— taller bust, ear shows, 1567-77; *mm.* 74-27	40	175
2566A	— Similar, without rose, 1568; *mm.* coronet....................................	300	1050
2567	**Halfgroat**. Without rose or date; *mm.* 107-71	45	185
2568	**Threehalfpence**. With rose and date 1561, large flan (inner circle 12.5mm.) *mm.* pheon..	45	200
2569	— — Smaller flan (inner circle 10.5-11.5mm.); 1561-2, 1564-78; *mm.* 53-27	40	175
2570	**Penny**. Without rose or date; *mm.* 33-71, 65b, 27	35	135
2571	**Threefarthings**. With rose and date 1561-2, 1564, 1567, 1568, 1572-7; *mm.* 53, 74, 77-27	70	225

Fifth Issue, 1578-82 (0.921 fineness, "shilling" of 95.6 grs., 6.19g.)

2572   2573

2572	**Sixpence**. As 2563, 1578-82; *mm.* 7-113...	55	225
2573	**Threepence**. As 2566, 1578-82; *mm.* 7-113..	40	185

2574   2575

2574	**Threehalfpence**. As 2569, 1578-9, 1581-2; *mm.* 7-113..........................	45	200
2575	**Penny**. As 2570; *mm.* 7-113	35	135
2576	**Threefarthings**. As 2571, 1578-9, 1581-2; *mm.* 7-113............................	75	250

HAMMERED BRITISH COINS

Hammered coins bought and sold

www.hammeredbritishcoins.com
mail@hammeredbritishcoins.com
07825226435

Sixth Issue, 1582-1600 (0.925 fineness, shilling of 96 grs., 6.22g.)

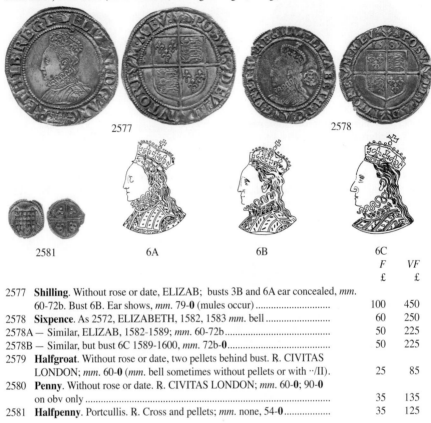

2577   2578

2581   6A   6B   6C

		F £	VF £
2577	**Shilling**. Without rose or date, ELIZAB; busts 3B and 6A ear concealed, *mm.* 60-72b. Bust 6B. Ear shows, *mm.* 79-**0** (mules occur)	100	450
2578	**Sixpence**. As 2572, ELIZABETH, 1582, 1583 *mm.* bell	60	250
2578A	— Similar, ELIZAB, 1582-1589; *mm.* 60-72b	50	225
2578B	— Similar, but bust 6C 1589-1600, *mm.* 72b-**0**	50	225
2579	**Halfgroat**. Without rose or date, two pellets behind bust. Ŗ. CIVITAS LONDON; *mm.* 60-**0** (*mm.* bell sometimes without pellets or with ··/II).	25	85
2580	**Penny**. Without rose or date. Ŗ. CIVITAS LONDON; *mm.* 60-**0**; 90-**0** on obv only	35	135
2581	**Halfpenny**. Portcullis. Ŗ. Cross and pellets; *mm.* none, 54-**0**	35	125

Seventh Issue, 1601-2 (0.925 fineness, shilling of 92.9 grs., 6.02)

2582

2582	**Crown**. As illustration, *mm.* **1**	1500	4750
2582A	– Similar, *mm.* **2**	3250	11000

2583

2588

		F £	VF £
2583	**Halfcrown**. As illustration, *mm*. **1**	1000	3000
2583A	– Similar, *mm*. **2**	3750	12500
2584	**Shilling**. As 2577; bust 6B *mm*. **1, 2**	110	500
2585	**Sixpence**. As 2578B, 1601-2; *mm*. **1, 2**	60	250
2586	**Halfgroat**. As 2579, *mm*. **1, 2**	25	85
2587	**Penny**. As 2580, *mm*. **1, 2**	35	135
2588	**Halfpenny**. As 2581, *mm*. **1, 2**	35	135

MILLED COINAGE 1561-71

2589	**Shilling**. Without rose or date; *mm*. star. Plain dress, large size (over 31 *mm*.)	750	3000
2590	— decorated dress, large size	350	1500
2591	— — intermediate size (30-31 *mm*.)	275	1100
2592	— — small size (under 30 *mm*.)	250	950

2593

2594

2593	**Sixpence**. Small bust, large rose. R. Cross fourchee, 1561 *mm*. star	125	450
2594	Tall narrow bust with plain dress, large rose, 1561-2; *mm*. star	110	425

2595

2596

2595	— similar, but decorated dress, 1562	110	425
2596	Large broad bust, elaborately decorated dress, small rose, 1562; *mm*. star	110	425
2597	— — cross pattée on *rev*., 1562, 64 *mm*. star	125	450

2599

		F	VF
		£	£
2598	— similar, pellet border, 1562-4	125	450
2598A	Bust with low ruff, raised rim, 1564, 1566 (both overdates)	135	500
2599	Small bust, 1567-8, R. As 2593; *mm.* lis	110	425

2600   2601

2600	Large crude bust breaking legend; 1570, *mm.* lis; 1571/0, *mm.* castle (over lis)	325	1350
2601	**Groat**. As illustration	150	675
2602	**Threepence**. With rose, small bust with plain dress, 1561	165	700
2603	Tall narrow decorated bust with medium rose, 1562	135	575
2604	Broad bust with very small rose, 1562	140	600
2605	Cross pattée on *rev.*, 1563, 1564/3	200	750

2606

| 2606 | **Halfgroat**. As groat | 165 | 700 |
| 2607 | **Threefarthings**. E . D . G . ROSA, etc., with rose. R. CIVITAS LONDON, shield with 1563 above | 3000 | 7500 |

Further reading:
The Hammered Silver Coins produced at the Tower Mint during the reign of Elizabeth I.
I. D. Brown, C. H. Comber and W. Wilkinson. 2006.
The Milled Coinage of Elizabeth I. D. G. Borden and I. D. Brown. *BNJ* 53, 1983

EAST INDIA COMPANY TRADE COINAGE - 'Portcullis money'

Trade coins of 8, 4, 2, and 1 Testerns were coined at the Tower Mint in 1600/1 for the first voyage of the incorporated 'Company of Merchants of London Trading into the East Indies'. The coins bear the royal arms on the obverse and a portcullis on the reverse and have the *mm*. **O**. They were struck to the weights of the equivalent Spanish silver 8, 4, 2 and 1 reales.

2607A

	F	VF
	£	£
2607A Eight testerns	6250	18500

2607B

2607B Four testerns	3000	9500

2607C

2607D

2607C Two testerns	2500	7250
2607D One testern	1750	5250

THE HOUSE OF STUART 1603-49

JAMES I, 1603-25

With the accession of James VI of Scotland to the English throne, the royal titles and coat of arms are altered on the coinage; on the latter the Scottish rampant lion and the Irish harp now appear in the second and third quarters. In 1604 the weight of the gold pound was reduced and the new coin became known as the 'Unite'. Fine gold of 0·979 and crown gold of 0·916 fineness were both issued, and a gold four-shilling piece was struck 1604-19. In 1612 all the gold coins had their values raised by 10%; but in 1619 the Unite was replaced by a new, lighter 20s. piece, the 'Laurel', and a lighter rose-ryal, spur-ryal and angel were minted.

In 1613 the king granted Lord Harington a licence to coin farthings of copper as a result of repeated public demands for a low value coinage; this was later taken over by the Duke of Lennox. Towards the end of the reign coins made from silver sent to the mint from the Welsh mines had the Prince of Wales's plumes inserted over the royal arms.

Mintmarks

125	105	33	79	84	74	90
60	25	71	45	32	123	132
72b	7a	16	24	125	105	46

First coinage
1603-4   Thistle (125)
1604-5   Lis (105)

Second coinage
1604-5   Lis (105)
1605-6   Rose (33)
1606-7   Escallop (79)
1607   Grapes (84)
1607-9   Coronet (74)

1609-10   Key (90)
1610-11   Bell (60)
1611-12   Mullet (25)
1612-13   Tower (71)
1613   Trefoil (45)
1613-15   Cinquefoil (32)
1615-16   Tun (123)
1616-17   Book on lectern (132)

1617-18   Crescent (72b, gold)

1618-19   Plain cross (7a)
1619   Saltire cross (16, gold)

Third coinage
1619-20   Spur rowel (24)
1620-1   Rose (33)
1621-3   Thistle (125)
1623-4   Lis (105)
1624   Trefoil (46)

SPINK
founded 1666

COINS OF ENGLAND 2017
E-book available on Amazon, iBookstore,
Google, Kobo, OverDrive
and across most other platforms

For more information or enquiries please contact
Tel: +44 (0)20 7563 4000 | Email: books@spink.com
69 Southampton Row, Bloomsbury, London WC1B 4ET
WWW.SPINKBOOKS.COM

GOLD

FIRST COINAGE, 1603-4 (Obverse legend reads D' . G' . ANG : SCO : etc.)

	F £	VF £
2608 **Sovereign** (20s; 171.9 grs., 11.14g.). King crowned r., half-length, first bust with plain armour. R. EXVRGAT, etc.; *mm.* thistle	2750	13000
2609 — second bust with decorated armour; *mm.* thistle, lis............................	3000	13500

	2610	2611

	F £	VF £
2610 **Half-sovereign**. Crowned bust r. R. EXVRGAT, etc.; *mm.* thistle	4500	17500
2611 **Crown**. Similar. R. TVEATVR, etc.; *mm.* 125, 105/125	2250	9000
2612 **Halfcrown**. Similar; *mm.* thistle, lis...	900	2750

N.B. *The Quarter-Angel of this coinage is considered to be a pattern (possibly a later strike), although coin weights are known.*

SECOND COINAGE, 1604-19 (Obverse legend reads D' G' MAG : BRIT : etc.)

2613

	F £	VF £
2613 **Rose-ryal** (30s., 33s. from 1612; 213.3 grs., 13.83g.) (Fine gold, 23 ct.). King enthroned. R. Shield on rose; *mm.* 33-90, 25-132	3250	12000

ARTHUR BRYANT COINS

Dealers in British coins and medals

www.bryantcoins.com

abcoins@live.co.uk

07768 645 686

BNTA

2614

		F £	VF £
2614	**Spur ryal** (15s., 16s. 6d. from 1612). King in ship; *mm.* 33, 79, 74, 25-32, 132	7500	30000
2615	**Angel** (10s., 11s. from 1612). Old type but larger shield; *mm.* 33-74, 60-16..	1650	5000
2616	— — pierced for use as touch-piece	700	2250
2617	**Half-angel** (5s., 5s. 6d. from 1612; 154.8 grs., 10.03 g.) (Crown gold, 22 ct.). Similar; *mm.* 71-132, 7a, 16	3500	13500
2618	**Unite** (20s., 22s. from 1612). Half-length second bust r. R. FACIAM etc.; *mm.* lis or rose..	725	2000

2619

2619	— fourth bust; *mm.* rose to cinquefoil..	625	1650
2620	— fifth bust; *mm.* cinquefoil to saltire.......................................	625	1650
2621	**Double-crown.** Third bust r. R. HENRICVS, etc.; *mm.* lis or rose	450	1350

2623

2622	Fourth bust; *mm.* rose to bell	425	1250
2623	Fifth bust; *mm.* key, mullet to saltire	425	1250

2624   2627

	F	VF
	£	£
2624 **Britain crown**. First bust r.; *mm*. lis to coronet	300	750
2625 Third bust; *mm*. key to cinquefoil..	300	750
2626 Fifth bust; *mm*. cinquefoil to saltire..	275	700
2627 **Thistle crown** (4s.). As illus.; *mm*. lis to plain cross	275	700
2628 – IR on only one side or absent both sides; *mm*. 79, 74, 71-123...........	300	750
2629 **Halfcrown**. I' D' G' ROSA SINE SPINA. First bust; *mm*. lis to key	225	475
2630 Third bust; *mm*. key to trefoil, trefoil/tower...	225	475
2631 Fifth bust; *mm*. cinquefoil to plain cross	225	475

THIRD COINAGE, 1619-25

2632 **Rose-ryal** (30s.; 194.2 grs., 12.58 g.) (Fine gold, 23 ct.). King enthroned. R. XXX above shield; lis, lion and rose emblems around; *mm*. 24, 125, 105	4000	15000
2633 Similar but plain back to throne; *mm*. trefoil..	4250	16500

2634   2635

2634 **Spur-ryal** (15s.). As illus. R. Somewhat like 2614, but lis are also crowned. *mm*. 24-125, 46	7500	30000
2635 **Angel** (10s.) of new type; *mm*. 24-46...	2250	7000
2636 – pierced for use as touch-piece..	700	2250

AMR Coins
Dealers in Quality British Coins

BNTA

British Coins Bought and Sold

www.amrcoins.com

email: info@amrcoins.com

tel: +44 (0)7527 569308

2637   2638

		F	VF
		£	£
2637	**Laurel** (20s.; 140.5 grs., 9.10 g.) (Crown gold, 22 ct.). First (large) laur, bust l.; *mm.* 24, 24/-	1000	3500
2638	Second, medium, square headed bust, 'SS' tie ends; *mm.* 24, 33	700	2000
2638A	Third, small rounded head, ties wider apart; *mm.* 33, 105, 125.................	650	1750
2638B	Fourth head, very small ties; *mm.* 105, 46..	625	1650
2638C	Fourth head variety, tie ends form a bracket to value; *mm.* lis	650	1750

2639

2639	Fifth, small rather crude bust; *mm.* trefoil	2500	8500

2641A   2642A

2640	**Half-laurel**. First bust; *mm.* spur rowel..	500	1600
2641	— As 2638A; *mm.* rose..	525	1650
2641A	— As 2638B; *mm.* 33-46, 105/-...	450	1400
2642	**Quarter-laurel**. Bust with two loose tie ends; *mm.* 24-105....................	275	700
2642A	Bust as 2638C; *mm.* 105, 46, 105/46...	260	675
2642B	As last but beaded, i.c. on *rev.* or both sides; *mm.* 105, 46......................	275	700

Rev. mm. on $^1/_2$ *and* $^1/_4$ *laurels normally follows REGNA.*

SILVER

2644

	F	VF
	£	£

FIRST COINAGE, 1603-4

| 2643 | **Crown**. King on horseback. Ꞧ. EXVRGAT, etc., shield; *mm*. thistle, lis. | 1250 | 3750 |
| 2644 | **Halfcrown**. Similar .... | 1100 | 5250 |

2645   2646

2645	**Shilling**. First bust, square-cut beard. Ꞧ. EXVRGAT, etc.; *mm*. thistle ...	100	525
2645A	— transitional bust, nape of neck shows above broad collar, crown similar to first bust, shoulder armour as second bust, *mm*. thistle	125	650
2646	— Second bust, beard appears to merge with collar; *mm*. thistle, lis	75	300

2647   2648

| 2647 | **Sixpence**. First bust; 1603; *mm*. thistle .... | 75 | 375 |
| 2648 | Second bust; 1603-4; *mm*. thistle, lis .... | 55 | 275 |

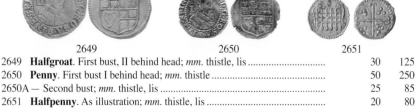

2649   2650   2651

2649	**Halfgroat**. First bust, II behind head; *mm*. thistle, lis	30	125
2650	**Penny**. First bust I behind head; *mm*. thistle	50	250
2650A	— Second bust; *mm*. thistle, lis	25	85
2651	**Halfpenny**. As illustration; *mm*. thistle, lis	20	80

SECOND COINAGE, 1604-19

2652

		F	VF
		£	£
2652	**Crown**. King on horseback. R. QVAE DEVS, etc. *rev.* stops; *mm.* 105-84	1100	3250
2653	**Halfcrown**. Similar; *mm.* 105-79	1500	5750
2654	**Shilling**. Third bust, beard cut square and stands out (*cf.* illus. 2657); *mm.* lis, rose	70	300
2655	— Fourth bust, armour plainer (*cf.* 2658); *mm.* 33-74, 90 over 74, or 60 over 74	70	300

2656

2656	— Fifth bust, similar, but hair longer; single-arched crown, *mm.* 74; higher double-arched crown, *mm.* 74 (rare), 90-7a	75	325

2657

2658

2657	**Sixpence**. Third bust; 1604-6; *mm.* lis, rose, escallop	60	240
2658	— Fourth bust; 1605-16; *mm.* rose to book, 90/60, 25/60	65	250
2658A	— Fifth bust, 1618; *mm.* plain cross	900	3000

2659

	F	VF
	£	£

2659 **Halfgroat**. As illus. but larger crown on *obv.*; *mm.* lis to coronet............ 20 70
2660 — — Similar, but smaller crown on *obv.*; *mm.* coronet to plain cross...... 20 70
2660A As before, but TVEATVR legend both sides; *mm.* plain cross over book 35 110
2661 **Penny**. As halfgroat but no crowns; *mm.* 105-32,7a and none, -/84, 32/- 20 70
2662 — As before but TVEATVR legend both sides; *mm.* mullet.................. 35 100
2663 **Halfpenny**. Rose, ℞ Thistle (with *mm.*) 105-25, 32; all *mms* on rev. only 15 65

THIRD COINAGE, 1619-25

2664 **Crown**. As 2652, with plain or grass ground line, colon stops on *obv.*, no
stops on *rev.*; *mm.* 33-46.. 750 1850

2665

2665 — — plume over shield; *mm.* 125-46 .... 950 3000

2667

2666 **Halfcrown**. As 2664 with plain or grass ground line; all have bird-
headed harp; *mm.* 33-46... 225 750
2666A — — Similar but no ground line; *mm.* rose.. 475 1750

2668   2669

		F	VF
		£	£
2667	— — Plume over shield; groundline *mm.* 125-46	350	1350
2668	**Shilling**. Sixth (large) bust, hair longer and very curly; *mm.* 24-46	80	350
2669	— — plume over shield; *mm.* 125-46	175	825

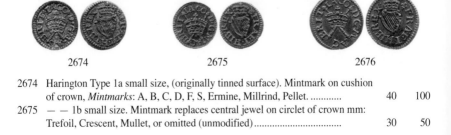

2670   2672   2673

2670	**Sixpence**. Sixth bust; 1621-4; *mm.* 33-46; 1621/0, *mm.* rose	70	275
2671	**Halfgroat**. As 2660 but no stops on *rev.*; *mm.* 24-46 and none, 105 and 46, 46/- *mm.* 24 with *rev.* stops known	20	60
2671A	Similar but no inner circles; *mm.* lis, trefoil over lis	25	70
2672	**Penny**. As illus.; *mm.* 24, 105, two pellets, none, trefoil,	20	60
2672A	— Similar but without inner circles on one or both sides; *mm.* lis, two pellets	20	60
2673	**Halfpenny**. As 2663, but no *mm.*	15	50

COPPER

For further details see Tim Everson, *The Galata Guide to the Farthing Tokens of James I and Charles I*

Farthings

2674   2675   2676

2674	Harington Type 1a small size, (originally tinned surface). Mintmark on cushion of crown, *Mintmarks*: A, B, C, D, F, S, Ermine, Millrind, Pellet.	40	100
2675	— — 1b small size. Mintmark replaces central jewel on circlet of crown mm: Trefoil, Crescent, Mullet, or omitted (unmodified)	30	50

		F	VF
		£	£

2675A — — 1c small size. Mintmark below crown, *mm*: :<............................ 40 100
2676 — — 2 normal size. Mintmark on reverse only, *mm*: Cinquefoil, Cross
 saltire, Lis, Mullet, Trefoil.. 20 40
2676A — — 3, large crown and harp, mintmark on reverse only, *mm* Martlet... 30 70
2677 Lennox Type 1, mintmark on reverse only; *mm*: Bell, Tower 35 70

| 2678 | 2679 | 2680 |

2678 — — 2, mintmark both sides, *mm*: Flower, Fusil..................................... 10 30
2679 — — 3, mintmark on obverse only, *mm*: Annulet, Coronet, Cross flory
 fitchée, Cross patée fourchée, Dagger, Eagle's head, Fusil, Key (horizontal),
 Lion passant, Quatrefoil, Rose (double), Roundel, Thistlehead, Trefoil, Tun,
 Turtle, Woolpack.. 10 30
2679A Contemporary counterfeits of Lennox Type 3, *mm*: A, Annulet, Coronet,
 Crescent, Cross (plain or patée), Dagger, Fusil, Key, Mascle, Roundel,
 Star (pierced), Stirrup, Trefoil, Triangle, Triangle with pellet below, Tun 10 25
2680 — — 4, as 3 but with larger, 9 jewel, crowns, *mm*: A, Dagger, Fusil, Lion
 rampant, Lis (three), Mascle, Stirrup, Trefoil, Triangle............................ 10 30
2680A Contemporary forgeries of Lennox Type 4, *mm* A, Annulet, Dagger, Fusil,
 Lis, Mascle, Pellets (four), Tun, ... 10 25
2681 — — 5, oval flan, legend starts at bottom left, *mm* Cross patée 60 120

Lennox Type 5, the oval farthings, were issued for use in Ireland

TimeLine Auctions

Inc. Gregory's **Est.1858**
We are accepting single entries and collections
of coins & antiquities

www.timelineauctions.com

+44 [0]1277 815121
enquiries@timelineauctions.com

Sold for:
£1,815

Follow us on:
f /TimeLineAuctions
t @TimeLineAuction

AIAΔ   BNTA

Numismatically, this reign is one of the most interesting. Some outstanding machine-made coins were produced by Nicholas Briot, a French die-sinker, but they could not be struck at sufficient speed to supplant hand-hammering methods, and the weights often had to be adjusted by blank filing. In 1637 a branch mint was set up at Aberystwyth to coin silver extracted from the Welsh mines and dies supplied from Tower Mint. After the king's final breach with Parliament the parliamentary government continued to issue coins at London with Charles's name and portrait until the king's trial and execution. The coinage of copper farthings continued to be manufactured privately under licences held first by the Duchess of Richmond and, lastly, by Lord Maltravers. Parliament took control of the Token House in 1643, and production ceased the following year.

During the Civil War coins were struck at a number of towns to supply coinage for those areas of the country under Royalist control. Many of these coins have an abbreviated form of the 'Declaration' made at Wellington, Shropshire, Sept., 1642, in which Charles promised to uphold the Protestant Religion, the Laws of England and the Liberty of Parliament. Amongst the more spectacular pieces are the gold triple unites and the silver pounds and half-pounds struck at Shrewsbury and Oxford, and the emergency coins, some made from odd-shaped pieces of silver plate during the sieges of Newark, Scarborough, Carlisle and Pontefract.

Mintmarks

105	10	96	71	57	88	101	35
87	107	60	70	123	57	119a	23
	119b	98	112	81	120	109	

Tower Mint under Charles I

1625	Lis (105)		1633-4	Portcullis (107)
1625-6	Cross Calvary (10)		1634-5	Bell (60)
1626-7	Negro's head (96)		1635-6	Crown (75)
1627-8	Castle (71)		1636-8	Tun (123)
1628-9	Anchor (57)		1638-9	Anchor (57)
1629-30	Heart (88)		1639-40	Triangle (119a)
1630-1	Plume (101)		1640-1	Star (23)
1631-2	Rose (35)		1641-3	Triangle in circle
1632-3	Harp (87)			(119b)

Tower Mint under Parliament

1643-4	P in brackets (98)
1644-5	R in brackets (112)
1645	Eye (81)
1645-6	Sun (120)
1646-8	Sceptre (109)

Mint mark no. 57 maybe upright, inverted, or horizontal to left or right.

59	B	58*var*	58

Briot's Mint

1631-2	Flower and B (59)	1638-9	Anchor (57)
1632	**B**		Anchor and B (58)
			(B upright or on side)
			Anchor and Mullet (58v)

61	104	35	92	103	6	65b	71
89	91*var*	131	84	94*var*	64	93	34
102	67	127	128	129	25	83	100
	134	71	A	B	75		

Provincial and Civil War Mints

1638-42	Book (61, *Aberystwyth*)		1643-4	Boar's head (64 *Worcs.* or *Shrews.*)
1642	Plume (104, *Shrewsbury*)			Lion rampant (93, *Worcs.* or *Shrews.*)
	Pellets or pellet (*Shrewsbury*)			Rosette (34, *Worcs.* or *Shrews.*)
1642-3	Rose (35, *Truro*)		1643-5	Plume (102, *Bristol*)
	Bugle (134, *Truro*)			Br. (67, *Bristol*)
1642-4	Lion (92, *York*)			Pellets (*Bristol*)
1642-6	Plume (103, *Oxford*)			Rose (35, *Exeter*)
	Pellet or pellets (*Oxford*)			Rosette (34, *Oxford*)
	Lis (105, *Oxford*)		1643-6	Floriated cross (127, *Oxford*)
1643	Cross pattee (6, *Bristol*)		1644	Cross pattee (6, *Oxford*)
	Acorn (65b, *Bristol*)			Lozenge (128, *Oxford*)
	Castle (71, *Worcester* or *Shrewsbury*)			Billet (129, *Oxford*)
	Helmet (89, *Worcester* and *Shrewsbury*)			Mullet (25, *Oxford*)
1643-4	Leopard's head (91 *var. Worcester*)		1644-5	Gerb (83, *Chester*)
	Two lions (131, *Worcester*)			Pear (100, *Worcester*)
	Lis (105, *Worcs.* or *Shrews.*)			Lis (105, *Hereford?*)
	Bunch of grapes (84, *Worcs.* or *Shrews.*)			Castle (71, *Exeter*)
	Bird (94 var., *Worcs.* or *Shrews.*)		1645-6	Plume (102, *Ashby, Bridgnorth*)
			1645	A (*Ashby*)
			1646	B (*Bridgnorth*)
			1648-9	Crown (75, *Aberystwyth Furnace*)

THE ART LOSS ■ REGISTER™

Timeline Auctions
Inc. Gregory's Est.1858

We are accepting single entries
and collections of Charles I coins

www.timelineauctions.com

ASSOCIATION OF INTERNATIONAL ANTIQUITIES DEALERS
AIAD
BRITISH NUMISMATIC TRADE ASSOCIATION
BNTA

GOLD COINAGE

TOWER, UNDER THE KING (1625-42), AND UNDER PARLIAMENT (1642-9)

For bust varieties on Tower Mint Gold see H. Schneider BNJ 1955-61
Numbers in brackets following each entry refer to numbers employed in previous editions of this catalogue

		F £	VF £
2682	**Angel**. St. Michael slaying dragon, no mark of value. R. Three masted ship, royal arms on mainsail; mm. lis, cross calvary..............................	4250	13500
2682A	— — — pierced for use as touch-piece (2683).......................................	1350	4500
2683	— X in field to right of St. Michael; m.m. negro's head, castle, anchor, heart, castle and negro's head/castle, anchor and castle/anchor (2684)	3000	10000
2683A	— — — pierced for use as touch-piece (2685)	900	2750
2684	— X in field to left of St. Michael; mm. negro's head, heart, rose, harp, portcullis, bell, crown, tun, anchor, triangle, star, triangle-in-circle (2686)	2750	9000

2684A   2685

		F £	VF £
2684A	— — — pierced for use as touch-piece (2687)..	800	2500
2685	**Unite**. Group A, first bust, in coronation robes, bust 1, high double-arched crown. R. Square-topped shield, plain or elaborate garnishing; mm. lis (2688, 2688A)...	750	2000
2686	— — bust 1a, flatter single-arched crown; mm. lis, cross calvary (2689, 2689A)	800	2250
2687	Group B, second bust, in ruff, armour and mantle. R. Square-topped shield; m.m. cross calvary, negro's head, castle, anchor, heart (2690)	750	2000

2688

		F £	VF £
2688	— — more elongated bust, usually dividing legend, mm. anchor, heart, plume (2690A)...	750	2000
2689	— — — anchor below bust; mm. (2691)	2250	7500
2689A	Group B/C mule. R. Oval shield with CR at sides; mm. plume (2691A)	1100	3500
2690	Group C, third bust, shorter with heavier armour. R. Oval shield with CR at sides; mm. plume, rose (2692)	750	2000
2691	Group D, fourth bust, with falling lace collar, bust 4, large bust with jewelled crown.R. Oval shield with CR at sides; mm. harp, portcullis (2693)	700	1850

	F £	VF £
2692 — — bust 5, smaller bust, unjewelled crown; mm. portcullis, bell, crown, tun, anchor, triangle, star (2693A)	700	1850
2693 — — — (under Parliament); mm. (P), (P)/- (2710)	1500	5000
2694 Group F, sixth 'Briot's' bust, with stellate lace collar. R. Oval shield with CR at sides, mm. triangle, star, triangle-in-circle (2694)	850	2250
2695 — — (under Parliament); mm. (P), (R) (2711)	1650	5250

2696

2696 Group G, (under Parliament), seventh bust, smaller collar; mm. eye, sun, sceptre (2712)	1850	6000

2697

2697 **Double-crown.** Group A, first bust, in coronation robes, bust 1, high double-arched crown, both arches jewelled. R. Square-topped shield; mm. lis (2696)	525	1650
2698 — — bust 1a, flatter crown, outer arch only jewelled; m.m. lis, cross calvary (2696A)	475	1500

2699

2699 Group B, second bust, in ruff, armour and mantle, bust 2. R. Square-topped shield; mm. cross calvary, negro's head, castle, anchor (2697)	425	1250
2700 — — busts 3-4, more elongated bust, usually dividing legend; mm. anchor, heart, plume (2697A)	450	1400
2700A Group B/C mule, elongated bust dividing legend. R. oval shield, *mm.* plume	650	2000
2701 Group C, third bust, bust 5. R. Oval shield with CR at sides; mm. plume, rose (2698)	525	1650

		F	VF
		£	£

2702 Group D, fourth bust, with falling lace collar, bust 6, large bust with jewelled
crown. ℞. Oval shield with CR at sides; mm. harp, crown (2699) .... | 500 | 1500

2703 — — bust 7, smaller head, inner or both arches of crown unjewelled; mm. harp,
portcullis, bell, crown, tun, anchor (2699A-C)..................................... | 475 | 1400

2703A— — — Group Da, (under Parliament), re-cut Group D bust punches;
m.m. eye (2713) .... | 1250 | 4000

2704 Group E, fifth bust, 'Aberystwyth' bust, bust 8, double-arched crown. ℞. Oval
shield with CR at sides; m.m. anchor (2700)... | 750 | 2500

2705 — — bust 9, smaller 'Aberystwyth' bust, single-arched crown; m.m. anchor,
triangle (2700A)... | 700 | 2250

2705A— — — Group Ea, (under Parliament), re-cut bust 9; m.m. sun, sceptre (2714) | 1050 | 3500

2706 Group F, sixth 'Briot's' bust, with stellate lace collar, bust 10. ℞. Oval shield
with CR at sides; mm. triangle, star, triangle-in-circle (2701)................. | 500 | 1500

2707 — — (under Parliament); mm. (P), (R) (2715) .... | 700 | 2250

2708 Group H, (under Parliament), bust 11, dumpy crude bust, single flat-arched
crown; mm. sun (2716).. | 1350 | 4500

2710   2715

2709 **Crown**. Group A, first bust, in coronation robes, bust 1 var, tall narrow bust,
double-arched crown. ℞. Square-topped shield; mm. lis (2703)............. | 300 | 825

2710 — bust 1, broader, less angular bust; m.m. lis, cross calvary (2703A).... | 325 | 850

2711 Group B, second bust, in ruff, armour and mantle, bust 2. ℞. Square-topped
shield; mm. cross calvary, negro's head, castle (2704)........................... | 275 | 750

2712 — — bust 3, narrower; more elongated bust; m.m. anchor, heart, plume
(2704A).. | 275 | 725

2713 — — — anchor below bust; mm. anchor (2704B)................................. | 700 | 2250

2713A Group B/C mule. ℞. Oval shield with CR at sides; mm. plume, rose (2705) | 300 | 750

2714 Group C, third bust, bust 4. ℞. Oval shield with CR at sides; mm. plume
(2706) .... | 375 | 1000

2715 Group D, fourth bust, with falling lace collar, busts 5, 7. ℞. Oval shield
with CR at sides; m.m. harp, -/harp, portcullis, portcullis/bell, bell, crown,
tun, anchor, triangle, star/triangle, star, triangle-in-circle (2707) .... | 250 | 650

2716 — — (under Parliament), bust 5, jewelled crown; m.m. (P), (R), eye, sun
(2717).. | 350 | 950

2716A— — (under Parliament), bust 6, unjewelled crown; m.m. eye, sun, sceptre
(2717A)... | 400 | 1050

2717 Group E, fifth bust, small 'Aberystwyth' bust, bust 8. ℞. Oval shield
with CR at sides; mm. anchor (2708) .... | 450 | 1250

2721C — Group F, sixth 'Briot's' bust, bust 9, only known as Briot/hammered
mule (see 2721C below)... | 1250 | 4500

	F £	*VF* £

NICHOLAS BRIOT'S COINAGES, 1631-2 and 1638-9
MILLED ISSUES, 1631-2

2718 **Angel**. Type somewhat as Tower but smaller and neater; *mm*. -/B 9500 35000

2719

2719	**Unite**. As illustration. R. FLORENT etc.; *mm*. flower and B/B...............	4000	12500
2720	**Double-crown**. Similar but X. R. CVLTORES, etc. *mm*. flower and B/B	2000	6000
2720A	Similar but King's crown unjewelled: *mm*. flower and B/B, B	2100	6250
2721	**Crown**. Similar; *mm*. B	4500	15000

BRIOT'S HAMMERED ISSUES, 1638-9

2721A	**Unite**. Briot's (sixth) bust, large lace collar. R. FLORENT etc., Briot's square-topped shield dividing crowned C R; *mm*. anchor........................	7000	25000
2721B	**Double-crown**. Briot's bust, similar. R. CVLTORES etc., square-topped shield dividing crowned C R; *mm*. anchor..	2250	7500
2721C	**Crown**. Briot's bust, similar. R. CVLTORES etc., oval shield dividing crowned C R (a Briot hammered issue/Tower mule); *mm*. anchor...........	1250	4500

GOLD COINAGES

PROVINCIAL ISSUES AND COINAGES OF THE ENGLISH CIVIL WAR, 1642-9
CHESTER, 1644

2722	**Unite**. As Tower. Somewhat like a crude Tower sixth bust. R. Crowned, oval shield, crowned CR, *mm*. plume	22500	85000

SHREWSBURY, 1642 (See also 2749)

2723	**Triple unite**, 1642. Half-length figure l holding sword and olive-branch; *mm*.: R. EXVRGAT, etc., around RELIG PROT, etc., in two wavy lines. III and three plumes above, date below	65000	275000

BucksCoins

M. 07825 44 00 85   T. 01603 92 70 20
buckscoins1@aol.co.uk
www.stores.ebay.co.uk/BucksCoins

St Mary's House
Duke Street • Norwich
Norfolk NR3 1QA

PCGS AUTHORIZED DEALER

Specialists in
Celtic, hammered,
milled and world coins.
Investment gold, tokens,
commemorative
medals and
banknotes.

BNTA   ANA MEMBER   IBNS MEMBER

2727

| | | F | VF |
| | | £ | £ |

OXFORD, 1642-6

2724	**Triple unite**. As last, but *mm*. plume, tall narrow bust, 1642..................	12000	30000
2725	Similar, 1643	20000	65000
2725A	Large bust of fine style. King holds short olive branch; *mm*. small lis	45000	175000
2726	As last, but taller bust, with scarf behind shoulder, 1643, *mm*. plume	13000	35000
2727	Similar, but without scarf, longer olive branch, 1643	12500	32500
2728	Similar, but OXON below 1643, rosette stops	22500	75000
2729	Smaller size, olive branch varies, bust size varies, 1644 OXON	13500	37500
2730	— Obv. as 2729, 1644 / OX	14000	40000
2731	**Unite**. Tall thin bust. R. 'Declaration' in two wavy lines, 1642; *no mm*...	3000	10000
2732	— R. 'Declaration' in three lines on continuous scroll, 1642-3	3250	10500
2733	Tall, well-proportioned bust. R. Similar, 1643, no *mm*...........................	3750	13500
2734	Shorter bust, king's elbow not visible. R. Similar, 1643; *mm*. plume/-....	2500	9000

2735

2735	Similar but longer olive branch curving to l. 1644 / OX; *mm*. plume	2750	9500
2735A	Similar, but dumpy bust breaking lower i.c., small flan	2750	9500
2736	Tall bust to edge of coin. R. Similar, 1643	7000	25000
2737	As 2734. R. 'Declaration' in three straight lines, 1644 / OX (as shilling rev. S2971)..	5250	17500
2738	Similar to 2734, but smaller size; small bust, low olive branch. 1645.....	4000	15000
2739	— R. Single plume above 'Declaration', 1645-6 / OX; *mm*. plume, rosette, none	3500	12500
2740	**Half-unite**. 'Declaration' in three straight lines, 1642.............................	3250	10000
2741	'Declaration' on scroll; *mm*. plume; 1642-3	3000	9500

2742

		F	VF
		£	£
2742	Bust to bottom of coin, 1643; Oxford plumes	2500	7500
2743	— 1644 / OX. Three Shrewsbury plumes (neater work)	3500	12000

BRISTOL, 1643-5

| 2744 | **Unite**. Somewhat as 2734; Two busts known. *mm.* Br. or Br/ plumelet.; 1645 | 22500 | 85000 |
| 2745 | **Half-unite**. Similar 1645 | 13500 | 40000 |

TRURO, 1642–3

| 2745A | **Half-Unite**. Crowned bust l. (similar to Tower 4th bust). Ṛ. CVLT, etc., crowned shield | 13500 | 40000 |

EXETER, 1643–5

| 2746 | **Unite**. *obv.* sim. to early Oxford bust. Ṛ. FLORENT, etc., crowned oval shield between crowned CR, *mm.* rose | 25000 | 90000 |
| 2747 | — Ṛ. CVLTORES, etc., similar but no CR | 25000 | 90000 |

WORCESTER, 1643-4

| 2748 | **Unite**. Crude bust Ṛ. FLORENT, etc., double annulet stops, crowned oval shield, lion's paws on either side of garniture, no *mm.* | 22500 | 85000 |

SALOPIA (SHREWSBURY) , 1644

| 2749 | **Unite**. *Obv.* bust in armour. Ṛ. Cr. shield, crowned CR. *mm.* lis/- | 25000 | 90000 |

COLCHESTER BESIEGED, 1648

| 2750 | **Ten Shillings** Gateway of castle between CR; below OBS COL 16 S/X 48. Uniface – now considered a later concoction | | |

PONTEFRACT BESIEGED, 1648-9. After the death of Charles I, in the name of Charles II

| 2751 | **Unite**. DVM : SPIRO : SPERO around CR crowned. CAROLVS : SECVИDVS : 16 48, castle, OBS on l., PC above. | 70000 | 250000 |
| 2752 | **Unite**. CAROL : II, etc., around HANC : DEVS, etc. Ṛ. POST : MORTEM, etc.,around castle. *Octagonal* | 65000 | 225000 |

SILVER COINAGES

TOWER, UNDER THE KING (1625-42), AND UNDER PARLIAMENT (1642-9)

2753	**Crown**. Group I, first horseman, type 1a, king on horseback left, horse caparisoned with plume on head and crupper. R. Square-topped shield over long cross fourchee; mm. lis, cross calvary	700	2250
2754	— — 1b. R. Plume above shield, no cross fourchee; mm. lis, cross calvary, castle	1350	4750
2755	Group II, second horseman, type 2a, smaller horse, plume on head only, cross on housing. R. Oval shield over cross fourchee, CR above; mm. harp	650	2000
2756	— — 2b1. R. Plume between CR above shield, no cross fourchee; mm. plume, rose	750	2750
2757	— — 2b2. R. Plume between CR, cross fourchee; mm. harp	900	3250

2758

	F £	VF £
2758 Group III, third horseman, type 3a, horse without caparisons, sword upright. R. Oval shield without CR; mm. bell, crown, tun, anchor, triangle, star..	650	2000
2759 — — 3b. R. Plume above shield; mm. portcullis, crown, tun.................	750	2750
2760 'Briot's' horseman with groundline, lozenge stops on obverse; mm. triangle in circle	5250	18500
2761 Group IV, (under Parliament), fourth horseman, type 4, foreshortened horse R. Oval shield; mm. (P), (R), eye, sun (2838)	700	2250
2762 Group V, (under Parliament), fifth horseman, type 5, tall spirited horse; mm. sun (2839)..	900	3250

2763

2763 **Halfcrown**. Group I, first horseman, type 1a1, horse caparisoned with plume on head and crupper, rose on housings, ground-line. R. Square-topped shield over long cross fourchee; mm. lis (2761)	425	1750
2764 — — 1a2. No rose on housings, no ground-line; mm. lis, cross calvary (2762)	225	900
2765 — — — ground-line; mm. lis (2762A)...	425	1750
2766 — — 1a3. No rose on housings, no ground-line. R. No long cross, heavy or light garnishing to shield; mm. cross calvary*, negro's head, castle (2763-2763B)	225	900
2767 — — — 1b. R. Plume above shield, heavy or light garnishing; mm. lis, cross calvary*, negro's head, castle, anchor (2765, 2765A).............................	575	2250
2768 Group II, second horseman, type 2/1b, plume on horse's head only, rose on housings. R. Plume over shield; mm. heart, plume (2766).......................	1050	3500
2769 — — 2a. Smaller horse, cross on housings. R. Oval shield with CR above (CR divided by rose (very rare), lis over rose (rare), or lis); mm. plume, rose, plume/rose (2767)	90	375
2770 — — — 2b. R. Plume between CR above shield; mm. plume, rose (2768)	250	950

2771

	F	VF
	£	£

2771 — — 2c. R. Oval draped shield with CR at sides; mm. harp, portcullis,
portcullis/harp (2769) 80 350

2772 — — — 2d. R. Plume above shield; mm. harp (2770) 1500 5250

2776   2779

2773 Group III, third horseman, type 3a1, no caparisons on horse, scarf flying
from king's waist. R. Oval garnished shield; mm. bell, bell/crown, crown,
tun, triangle (2771) 65 250

2774 — — — 3b. R. Plume above shield; mm. portcullis, bell, crown, tun (2772) 110 525

2775 — — 3a2. King wears cloak flying from shoulder. R. Oval garnished shield;
mm. tun, anchor, triangle, star, triangle-in-circle (2773) 60 240

2776 — — — — rough ground under horse; mm. triangle, star (2774) 60 240

2777 — — horseman of finer style, short busy tail, cloak like arrowhead behind
shoulder, no ground below; mm. triangle, star (2773 var.) 110 450

2778 — — 3a3, (under Parliament), no ground, cruder workmanship; mm. (P),
(R), eye, sun (2840) 50 200

2779 Group IV, fourth horseman, type 4, foreshortened horse. R. Oval
garnished shield; mm. star, triangle in circle (2775) 55 225

2779A — — (under Parliament); mm. (P) (2841) 125 575

2779B — —, transitional type 4/5, mm. sun... 110 525

2780 Group V, (under Parliament), fifth horseman, type 5, tall spirited horse.
R. Oval garnished shield; mm. sun, sceptre (2842).................................. 70 250

Light weight half crowns (204 grains) exist of No. 2766 and 2767, mm. cross calvary

HAMMERED BRITISH COINS

Hammered coins bought and sold

www.hammeredbritishcoins.com
mail@hammeredbritishcoins.com
07825226435

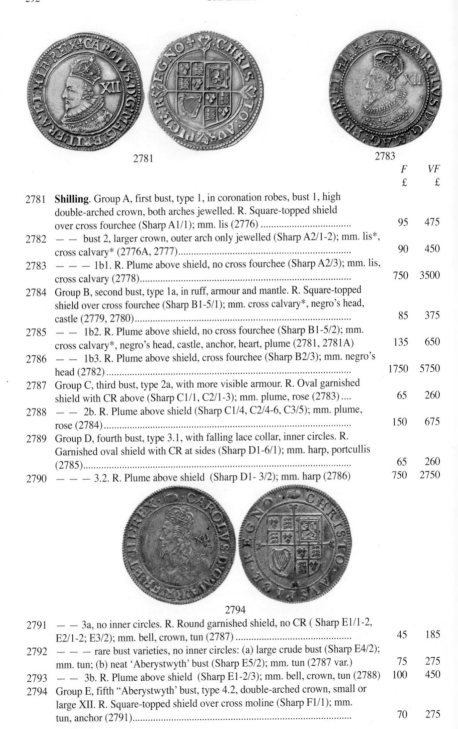

2781

2783

		F	VF
		£	£

2781 **Shilling**. Group A, first bust, type 1, in coronation robes, bust 1, high double-arched crown, both arches jewelled. R. Square-topped shield over cross fourchee (Sharp A1/1); mm. lis (2776) 95 475

2782 — — bust 2, larger crown, outer arch only jewelled (Sharp A2/1-2); mm. lis*, cross calvary* (2776A, 2777)... 90 450

2783 — — — 1b1. R. Plume above shield, no cross fourchee (Sharp A2/3); mm. lis, cross calvary (2778).. 750 3500

2784 Group B, second bust, type 1a, in ruff, armour and mantle. R. Square-topped shield over cross fourchee (Sharp B1-5/1); mm. cross calvary*, negro's head, castle (2779, 2780).. 85 375

2785 — — 1b2. R. Plume above shield, no cross fourchee (Sharp B1-5/2); mm. cross calvary*, negro's head, castle, anchor, heart, plume (2781, 2781A) 135 650

2786 — — 1b3. R. Plume above shield, cross fourchee (Sharp B2/3); mm. negro's head (2782) 1750 5750

2787 Group C, third bust, type 2a, with more visible armour. R. Oval garnished shield with CR above (Sharp C1/1, C2/1-3); mm. plume, rose (2783) 65 260

2788 — — 2b. R. Plume above shield (Sharp C1/4, C2/4-6, C3/5); mm. plume, rose (2784)... 150 675

2789 Group D, fourth bust, type 3.1, with falling lace collar, inner circles. R. Garnished oval shield with CR at sides (Sharp D1-6/1); mm. harp, portcullis (2785).. 65 260

2790 — — — 3.2. R. Plume above shield (Sharp D1- 3/2); mm. harp (2786) 750 2750

2794

2791 — — 3a, no inner circles. R. Round garnished shield, no CR (Sharp E1/1-2, E2/1-2; E3/2); mm. bell, crown, tun (2787) 45 185

2792 — — — rare bust varieties, no inner circles: (a) large crude bust (Sharp E4/2); mm. tun; (b) neat 'Aberystwyth' bust (Sharp E5/2); mm. tun (2787 var.) 75 275

2793 — — 3b. R. Plume above shield (Sharp E1-2/3); mm. bell, crown, tun (2788) 100 450

2794 Group E, fifth "Aberystwyth' bust, type 4.2, double-arched crown, small or large XII. R. Square-topped shield over cross moline (Sharp F1/1); mm. tun, anchor (2791).. 70 275

	F £	VF £

2795 — — 4.1, larger bust, single-arched crown, small or large XII (Sharp F2/1); mm. tun, anchor (2789) 70 300

2796 — — 4.3, smaller bust, single-arched crown, large XII (Sharp F3/1-2); mm. tun, anchor, triangle (2792) 50 225

2797   2800

2797 — — 4.1var., larger bust with rounded shoulder, large XII (Sharp F5/1-2); mm. anchor, triangle (2790) 50 225

2798 — — rare bust varieties : (a) small 'Aberystwyth' bust, double-arched crown (Sharp F4/1); mm. anchor (to right); (b) small 'Briot's' bust, with stellate lace collar, single-arched crown (Sharp F6/1-2); mm. triangle; (c) small 'Aberystwyth' bust, single-arched crown (Sharp F7/2); mm. triangle-in-circle (2790 var.) 100 475

2803   2804

2799 Group F, sixth large 'Briot's' bust, type 4.4, with stellate lace collar, double-arched crown. R. Square-topped shield over cross moline (Sharp G 1/1-2); mm. triangle, star, triangle-in-circle (2793) 35 145

2800 — — — (under Parliament) (Sharp G1-2/2); mm. (P), (R), eye, sun (2843) 35 145

2801 — — 4.4 var., (under Parliament), small thin bust, 'nick' below truncation (Sharp G3/2); mm. sun (2843A) 325 1250

2802 Group G, (under Parliament), seventh bust, type 4.5, tall coarse narrow bust. R. Square-topped shield over cross moline (Sharp H1/1); mm. sun, sceptre (2844) 60 250

2803 — — 4.6, shorter slim better proportioned bust (Sharp H2/2); mm. sceptre (2845) 70 275

2804 — — — short broad bust (Sharp H3/2); mm. sceptre (2845A) 85 375

Light weight shillings (81.75 grains) exist of No. 2782, mm. lis, cross calvary over lis; No. 2784, mm. cross calvary; and No. 2785 mm. cross calvary

See Sharp BNJ 1977,for shilling bust varieties including fine work coins- see Holt, Hulett and Lyle, BNJ 2014.

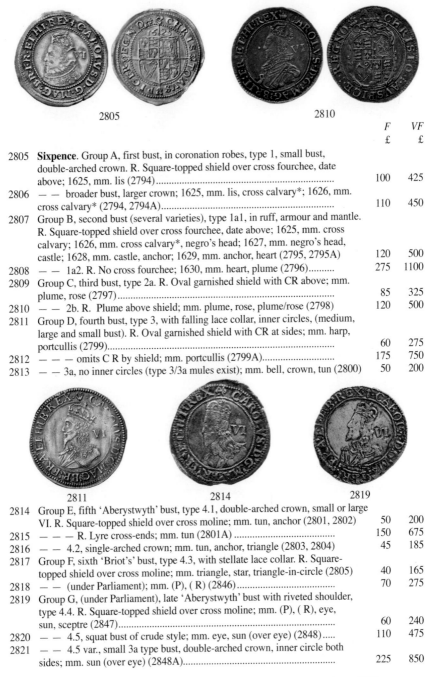

2805   2810

		F	VF
		£	£
2805	**Sixpence.** Group A, first bust, in coronation robes, type 1, small bust, double-arched crown. R. Square-topped shield over cross fourchee, date above; 1625, mm. lis (2794)...	100	425
2806	— — broader bust, larger crown; 1625, mm. lis, cross calvary*; 1626, mm. cross calvary* (2794, 2794A)...	110	450
2807	Group B, second bust (several varieties), type 1a1, in ruff, armour and mantle. R. Square-topped shield over cross fourchee, date above; 1625, mm. cross calvary; 1626, mm. cross calvary*, negro's head; 1627, mm. negro's head, castle; 1628, mm. castle, anchor; 1629, mm. anchor, heart (2795, 2795A)	120	500
2808	— — 1a2. R. No cross fourchee; 1630, mm. heart, plume (2796)..........	275	1100
2809	Group C, third bust, type 2a. R. Oval garnished shield with CR above; mm. plume, rose (2797)...	85	325
2810	— — 2b. R. Plume above shield; mm. plume, rose, plume/rose (2798)	120	500
2811	Group D, fourth bust, type 3, with falling lace collar, inner circles, (medium, large and small bust). R. Oval garnished shield with CR at sides; mm. harp, portcullis (2799)...	60	275
2812	— — — omits C R by shield; mm. portcullis (2799A)............................	175	750
2813	— — 3a, no inner circles (type 3/3a mules exist); mm. bell, crown, tun (2800)	50	200

2811   2814   2819

2814	Group E, fifth 'Aberystwyth' bust, type 4.1, double-arched crown, small or large VI. R. Square-topped shield over cross moline; mm. tun, anchor (2801, 2802)	50	200
2815	— — — R. Lyre cross-ends; mm. tun (2801A)	150	675
2816	— — 4.2, single-arched crown; mm. tun, anchor, triangle (2803, 2804)	45	185
2817	Group F, sixth 'Briot's' bust, type 4.3, with stellate lace collar. R. Square-topped shield over cross moline; mm. triangle, star, triangle-in-circle (2805)	40	165
2818	— — (under Parliament); mm. (P), (R) (2846)......................................	70	275
2819	Group G, (under Parliament), late 'Aberystwyth' bust with riveted shoulder, type 4.4. R. Square-topped shield over cross moline; mm. (P), (R), eye, sun, sceptre (2847)...	60	240
2820	— — 4.5, squat bust of crude style; mm. eye, sun (over eye) (2848).....	110	475
2821	— — 4.5 var., small 3a type bust, double-arched crown, inner circle both sides; mm. sun (over eye) (2848A)..	225	850

Light weight sixpences (40.85 grains) exist of No. 2806, 1625, mm. cross calvary, 1626, mm. cross calvary; and No. 2807, 1626, mm. cross calvary

2822   2824   2832

	F £	VF £

2822 **Halfgroat**. Group A, without bust, crowned rose each side, type 1, inner
circles on one or both sides;mm. lis, lis/-, cross calvary, castle, none (2806) | 25 | 100

2823 — — 1a, without inner circles; mm. negro's head, castle, anchor, heart,
plume (2807).. | 25 | 100

2824 Group B, second bust, type 2a, in ruff and mantle. R. Oval shield; mm.
plume, rose (2808)... | 25 | 110

2825 — — 2b. R. plume above shield; mm. plume, plume/-, rose (2809) ...... | 35 | 150

2826 Group C, third bust, more armour, crown breaks inner circle; mm. plume,
rose (2809A)... | 25 | 110

2827 — — R. Plume above shield; mm. plume (2809B)..................................... | 35 | 150

2828 Group D, fourth bust, type 3.1, no inner circles. R. Oval shield dividing
C R; mm. harp, portcullis crown (2810)... | 20 | 80

2829 — — — — 3.2-4, inner circle on one or both sides; mm. harp, portcullis,
../harp (2811-13) .... | 20 | 80

2830 — — — 3.5-6. R. Oval shield, no C R, no inner circle or obv. only; mm. harp,
portcullis (2814-15) .... | 25 | 90

2831 — — 3a1. R. Rounder shield, no inner circles; mm. bell, crown, tun, anchor,
triangle (2816) .... | 20 | 80

2832 — — 3a2-3, inner circles on obverse or both sides; mm. anchor, triangle, star,
triangle-in-circle (2817-18) .... | 25 | 85

2833 — — — (under Parliament), type 3a3, inner circles both sides; mm. (P)/triangle-
in-circle, (P), (R), eye, sun, sceptre (2849)... | 20 | 80

2834 Group E, fifth 'Aberystwyth' bust, types 3a4-5, no inner circles or on reverse
only; mm. anchor (2819-20).. | 35 | 135

2835 — — 3a6, very small bust (from penny puncheon), no inner circles; mm.
anchor (2821)... | 40 | 150

2836 Group G, (under Parliament), seventh bust, type 3a7, older bust with pointed
beard; mm. eye, sun, sceptre (2850) .... | 20 | 80

2837 **Penny**. Group A, without bust, rose each side, type 1, inner circles; mm.
lis, negro's head, one or two pellets (2822)... | 20 | 80

2838 — — 1a, no inner circles; mm. lis, anchor, one or two pellets (2823).... | 20 | 80

2839 — — 1b, inner circle on reverse; mm. negro's head/two pellets (2824). | 35 | 135

2840 Group B, second bust, type 2, in ruff and mantle. R. Oval shield, inner
circles; mm. plume, plume/rose, rose (2825) .... | 30 | 120

2841 — — 2.1, no inner circles; mm. plume, rose (2826)............................... | 30 | 110

2842 Group C, third bust, type 2a1, more armour visible, no inner circles;
mm. plume, plume/rose, rose (2827).. | 25 | 95

2843 — — 2a2-4, inner circles on obverse, both sides or reverse; mm. plume,
rose (2828-30).. | 25 | 95

2845

2851

	F £	VF £
2844 Group D, fourth bust, type 3.1, with falling lace collar. R. CR by shield, no inner circles; mm. harp, one or two pellets (2831)	20	75
2845 — — — 3.2, no C R by shield, no inner circles; mm. harp, portcullis, pellets, none (2832)	20	75
2846 — — — — 3.3-4, inner circles on obverse or reverse; mm. harp, two pellets (2833-34)	20	80
2847 — — 3a1, shield almost round with scroll garniture, no inner circles; mm. bell, triangle, one to four pellets, none (2835)	20	70
2848 — — 3a1 var., inner circle on one or both sides; mm. triangle/two pellets (2835A)	25	90
2849 Group E, fifth 'Aberystwyth' bust, type 3a3, inner circle on obverse or none; mm. triangle, anchor, one or two pellets, none (2836)	20	80
2850 Group G, (under Parliament), seventh bust, type 3a2, older bust, inner circle on obverse only; mm. one or two pellets (2851)	25	85
2851 **Halfpenny**. Rose each side, no legend or mm (2837)	15	50

NICHOLAS BRIOT'S COINAGE, 1631-9

FIRST MILLED ISSUE, 1631-2

2852 **Crown**. King on horseback. R. Crowned shield between CR crowned; *mm.* flower and B / B	1100	3000

2853

2853 **Halfcrown**. Similar	575	1650
2854 **Shilling**. Briot's early bust with falling lace collar. R. Square-topped shield over long cross fourchee; R. Legend starts at top or bottom (extr. rare) *mm.* flower and B/B, B	450	1250

2855

2855 **Sixpence**. Similar, but VI behind bust; *mm.* flower and B/B, flower and B/-	175	450

2856

2856A

		F £	VF £

2856 **Halfgroat**. Briot's bust, B below, II behind. R. IVSTITIA, etc., square-
topped shield over long cross fourchee 75 200

2856A Pattern halfgroat. Uncrowned bust in ruff r. R. crowned, interlocked Cs.
(North 2687). (Included because of its relatively regular appearance.) ... 70 175

2857 **Penny**. Similar, but I behind bust, B below bust; position of legend may vary 75 200

SECOND MILLED ISSUE, 1638-9

2859

2858 **Halfcrown**. As 2853, but *mm.* anchor and B... 450 1250

2859 **Shilling**. Briot's late bust, the falling lace collar is plain with broad lace
border, no scarf. R. As 2854 but cross only to inner circle; *mm.* anchor and
B, anchor or muled 200 575

2860 **Sixpence**. Similar, but VI; *mm.* anchor, anchor and mullet/anchor.......... 85 275

The last two often exhibit flan reduction marks.

HAMMERED ISSUE, 1638-9

2861 **Halfcrown**. King on Briot's style horse with ground line. R. Square-topped
shield; *mm.* anchor, triangle over anchor. Also muled with Tower *rev*..... 400 1250

2862 **Shilling**. Briot's first hammered issue, Sim. to 2859; R. Square-topped
shield over short cross fleury, contraction stops on *obv.*, pellet stops
rev. mm. anchor 750 3000

2862A — Briot's second hammered issue. As 2862 but lozenge stops both sides.
mm. anchor, triangle over anchor or triangle... 275 900

2862B Tower, Group E, obv. type 4.1 var. (S.2797) above R. as Briot's 1st or 2nd
hammered issue; mm. Δ over anchor... 525 1750

2862C Tower, Group F, obv. type 4.4 (S.2799 above) R. as Briot's 2nd hammered
issue; mm Δ/Δ over anchor. 275 900

COINS OF BRITAIN
PO BOX 2, MONMOUTH, NP25 3YR, UK

BNTA

E-mail: lloydbennett@coinsofbritain.com   +44(0)7714 284 939

YORK, 1643-4. *Mm. Lion*

2867

		F	VF
		£	£
2863	**Halfcrown**. 1. Ground-line below horse. R. Square-topped shield between CR..	575	2250
2864	— 2. — R. Oval shield as Tower 3a, groundline grass or dotted.............	525	2000
2865	— 3. No ground-line. R. Similar...	500	2000
2866	— 4. As last, but EBOR below horse with head held low. Base metal, often very base (*These pieces are contemporary forgeries*)......................	100	300
2867	— 5. Tall horse, mane in front of chest, EBOR below. R. Crowned square-topped shield between CR, floral spray in legend	350	1100

2868

		F	VF
		£	£
2868	— 6. As last, but shield is oval, garnished (*rev.* detail variations)............	325	1000
2869	— 7. Similar, but horse's tail shows between legs. R. Shield as last, but with lion's skin garniture, no CR or floral spray	300	950

2870   2872

2870	**Shilling**. 1. Bust in scalloped lace collar similar to 3¹. R. EBOR above square-topped shield over cross fleury..	225	750
2871	— 2. Similar, but bust in plain armour, mantle; coarse work..................	250	800
2872	— 3. Similar R. EBOR below oval shield..	250	800
2873	— 4. — Similar, but crowned oval shield (*obv.* finer style).....................	200	650
2874	— 5. — As last, but lion's skin garniture	200	650
2875	**Sixpence**. *Obv.* Sim. to 2870. Crowned oval shield	300	950

2876   2877

2876	— — Crowned CR at sides	250	800
2877	**Threepence**. As type 1 shilling, but III behind bust. R. As 2870............	75	250

ABERYSTWYTH, 1638/9-42. *Mm.* book.
Plume 1=with coronet and band. Plume 2=with coronet only

2878

		F £	VF £
2878	**Halfcrown**. Horseman similar to 2773, but plume 2 behind. R. Oval garnished shield with large plume above. *Obv.* plume 2, *rev.* plume 1.....	1000	4750
2879	— Similar to 2774, plume 1 behind King, ground below horse. *Obv.* squat plume 1, *rev.* plume 1	1100	5000
2880	As 2773 but more spirited horse, no ground. FRAN ET HIB, plume 2/1	950	4500

2881

2881	**Shilling**. Bust with large square lace collar, plume 2 before, small XII. R. As Tower 3b...	450	1750
2882	— inner circle on *rev.*	375	1500
2883	As 2881, but large plume 1 or 2, large XII, inner circles, large or small shield	375	1500

2884   2886

2884	As last, but small narrow head, square lace collar, large or square plume	400	1600
2885	Small Briot style face, small crown, plume 2, large shield	475	1850
2885A	**Sixpence**. *Obv.* as Tower bust 3a, plume before. R. as 2889; inner circles both sides, *mm.* book (*obv.* only)..	400	1350
2886	Somewhat as 2881, but double-arched crown, small VI; no inner circles	250	850
2887	Similar to 2886, but single arched crown, plume 2, inner circle *obv.* Large VI	275	900
2888	Similar, but with inner circles both sides...	300	950
2889	— — *Rev.* with small squat-shaped plume above, sometimes no *rev. mm.*	275	900

		F £	VF £
2890	Bust as the first Oxford sixpence; with crown cutting inner circle	325	1100

2891   2894

2891	**Groat.** Large bust, lace collar, no armour on shoulder. Crown breaks or touches inner circle. R. Shield, plume 1 or 2..	70	185
2892	— Similar, armour on shoulder, shorter collar. R. Similar......................	75	225
2893	— Smaller, neater bust well within circle. R. Similar	70	200
2894	**Threepence.** Small bust, plume 2 before. R. Shield, plume 1 or 2 above, *obv.* legend variations...	55	160
2895	— Similar, but crown cuts i.c. squat pl. on *obv.*, R. Pl. 2, *obv.* legend variations..	60	175
2900	**Halfgroat.** Bust as Tower type 3. R. Large plume. No inner circles, *mm.* pellet/book,book	60	200
2900A	Bust as 2886. R. As last, no inner circle	55	175

2901   2903   2907

2901	Bust with round lace collar; single arch crown, inner circles, colon stops	50	150
2902	After Briot's bust, square lace collar: inner circles..................................	50	150
2903	**Penny.** As 2901; CARO; no inner circles	75	275
2904	As 2901; CARO; inner circles...	70	250
2905	As last but reads CAROLVS; inner circles..	80	300

Simon Willis Coins

Welcome. Please visit our coin website! You can find a summary of the current coins for sale which we aim to update on a regular basis.

We deal with quality hammered and early milled British coins, having good eye appeal and provenance .

Feel free to call: **+44 (0) 7908 240978**

Or email us anytime at

		F	*VF*
		£	£
2906	*Obv.* similar to 2890, tall narrow bust, crown touches inner circle	85	325
2907	**Halfpenny**. No legend. *O*. Rose. R. Plume	250	950

ABERYSTWYTH-FURNACE, 1648/9. *Mm.* crown

		F	*VF*
2908	**Halfcrown**. King on horseback. R. Sim. to 2878...............	1750	7500
2909	**Shilling**. Aberystwyth type, but *mm.* crown	3250	12500
2910	**Sixpence**. Similar	1500	4500

2911   2913

2911	**Groat**. Similar	225	750
2912	**Threepence**. Similar..........................	250	850
2913	**Halfgroat**. Similar. R. Large plume	275	950
2914	**Penny**. Similar..............................	750	2500

UNCERTAIN MINTS

2915

2915	**Halfcrown**. As illustration, (Hereford?) dated 1645 or undated	3500	12500
2915A	**Halfcrown**. (Compton House) Scarf with long sash ends. CH (Chirk castle?)		
	below horse. R. Oval shield 1644..	4000	15000
2915B	— — R. Crowned oval shield, lion paws	3750	13500

SHREWSBURY, 1642. Plume without band used as *mm.* or in field.

2917	**Pound**. King on horseback, plume behind, from the puncheon of Tower grp. 3 crowns.		
	R. Declaration between two straight lines, XX and three Shrewsbury		
	plumes above, 1642 below; *mm.* pellets, pellets/-	4500	15000
2918	Similar, but Shrewsbury horse walking over pile of arms; no *mm.*, pellets	3750	12500
2919	As last, but cannon amongst arms and only single plume and XX above		
	Declaration, no *mm.*..	7250	25000
2920	**Half-pound**. As 2917, but X; *mm.* pellets	2000	6500
2921	Similar, but only two plumes on *rev.*; *mm.*, pellets................................	3750	12500
2922	Shrewsbury horseman with ground-line, three plumes on *rev.*; *mm.*, none,		
	pellets/-	1800	5750
2923	— with cannon and arms or arms below horse; *mm.* pellets/-..................	1850	6000

			F	VF
			£	£
2924		— no cannon in arms, no plume in *obv.* field; *mm.* plume/pellets, plume/-	1250	3750
2925	**Crown.** Aberystwyth horseman from the puncheon of a Tower halfcrown			
		no ground line	22500	75000

2926

2926	Shrewsbury horseman with ground-line; *mm.* -/pellets, pellets/-, none ...	1100	3500
2927	**Halfcrown.** *O.* From Aberystwyth die; (S2880); *mm.* book. R. Single plume		
	above Declaration, 1642	3250	12500
2928	Sim. to Aberystwyth die, fat plume behind. R. Three plumes above		
	Declaration; *mm.* pellets, pellets/-	950	4000
2929	Shrewsbury horseman, no ground line. R. As 2927, single plume, no *mm.*	1100	4500
2929A	— — R. As 2933	950	4000

2930

2930	— R. 2: plume; 6, above Declaration	2000	8500
2931	— with ground-line. R. Similar...	2000	8500
2932	— — R. As 2927, single plume...	1100	4500
2933	— — R. Three plumes above Declaration; *mm.* none or pellets	900	3500
2933A	— — R. Aberystwyth die, plume over shield; *mm.* -/book......................	3250	12500
2934	As 2933 but no plume behind king; *mm.* plume/pellets	900	3500
2935	**Shilling.** *O.* From Aberystwyth die; S2885 *mm.* book. R. Declaration type	1750	6000
2936	*O.* From Shrewsbury die. R. Similar..	3000	12500

OXFORD, 1642-6. *Mm.* usually plume with band, except on the smaller denominations when it is lis or pellets. There were so many dies used at this mint that we can give only a selection of the more easily identifiable varieties.

For many years Oxford Halfcrowns and Shillings have been catalogued according to Morrieson obverse die varieties. In many cases, these are very small and difficult to identify. We have, therefore, simplified the obverse classification and used the available space to expand the listing of the more interesting reverse varieties.

2943

		F	VF
		£	£
2937	**Pound**. Large horseman over arms, no exergual line, fine workmanship. R. Three Shrewsbury plumes and XX above Declaration, 1642 below; *mm.* plume/pellets..	9500	32500
2938	— Similar, but three Oxford plumes, 1643; *mm.* as last............................	8500	27500
2939	Shrewsbury horseman trampling on arms, exergual line. R. As last, 1642	3250	10000
2940	— — cannon amongst arms, 1642-3; *mm.* similar....................................	3000	9500
2941	— as last but exergue is chequered, 1642; *mm.* similar...........................	5750	17500
2942	Briot's horseman, 1643; *mm.* similar..	7500	25000
2943	O. As 2937. R. Declaration in cartouche, single large plume above, 1644 OX below...	20000	65000
2944	**Half-pound**. Shrewsbury horseman over arms, Oxford plume behind. R. Shrewsbury die, 1642; mm. plume/-..	1400	3500
2945	— R. Three Oxford plumes above, 1642; mm. plume/-...........................	1350	3250
2945A	— — 1643; *mm.* plume/-	1350	3250
2946	**Crown.** Shrewsbury die with groundline. R. Three Oxford plumes, 1642; no mm.	1200	3500
2946A	— — 1643; no *mm.*	1200	3500
2947	Oxford horseman, grass below. R. Three Oxford plumes, 1643; *mm.* plume/-..	1350	3750

COINS OF BRITAIN
PO BOX 2, MONMOUTH, NP25 3YR, UK   BNTA

E-mail: lloydbennett@coinsofbritain.com   +44(0)7714 284 939

2948

		F	VF
		£	£
2948	Rawlins' crown. King riding over a view of the city. R. Floral scrolls above and below Declaration, date in script, 1644 OXON; *mm.* floriated cross/- *(Electrotypes and copies of this coin are common)*	32500	110000
2949	**Halfcrown.** *O.* Shrewsbury die with groundline, plume behind. R. Oxford die, declaration in two lines, three Oxford plumes above, 1642 below; no *mm.*	900	3500
2950	— no plume behind. R. as last, 1642; *mm.* plume/-	525	2000
2951	Shrewsbury horseman with groundline, Oxford plume behind. R. Shrewsbury die, 1642; *mm.* plume/-	500	1850
2952	— R. Three Oxford plumes, 1642; *mm.* plume/-	275	900
2953	— — without groundline, 1642; *mm.* plume/-	275	900

2954   2955

2954	Oxford horseman without groundline, 1643; *mm.* plume/-	260	850
2954A	— — R. Shrewsbury die, 1642; *mm.* plume/- or no *mm.*	500	1850
2955	— with groundline. R. Three Oxford plumes, 1643; *mm.* plume/-	260	850
2956	Briot horseman, grassy, rocky or uneven ground. R. Three Oxford plumes, 1643; *mm.* plume/-, plume & rosette/-	225	750
2957	— — 1643 OX; *mm.* plume/rosette, rosette	240	800

2961   2965A

	F	VF
	£	£
2958 — — 1644 OX; *mm.* plume/-	250	825
2958A — — lozenges by OX, 1644 OX; *mm.* plume/-	275	850
2959 — — 1645 OX; *mm.* plume/-, plume/rosette	275	850
2959A — — pellets by date, 1645 OX; *mm.* plume/-	300	925
2960 — — 1646 OX; *mm.* plume/-	275	850
2961 — — pellets or annulets by plumes and date, 1646 OX; *mm.* plume/- ...	300	950
2962 — R. Large central plume and two Oxford plumes, 1643; *mm.* plume/-	275	850
2963 — — 1643 OX; *mm.* plume/-, rosette/-, plume & rosette/rosette, plume & rosette/-	250	800
2964 — — rosettes by OX, 1643 OX; *mm.* rosette/-, plume & rosette/-	300	925
2965 — — plain, pellets or lozenges by plumes and/or OX, 1644 OX; *mm.* plume/- plume/rosette, rosette	225	750
2965A — — date in script, 1644 OX; *mm.* plume/-	250	800
2966 — — rosettes by plumes and date, 1644 OX; *mm.* plume & rosette/rosette	375	1250
2967 — — small plumes by date, 1644 OX; *mm.* plume & rosette/-, rosette ..	450	1500
2968 — R. Large central plume and two small Shrewsbury plumes, lozenges in field, date in script, 1644 OX; *mm.* plume/rosette	425	1350
2969 — — small plumes by date, pellets by OX, 1644 OX; *mm.* plume/-	450	1500
2970 **Shilling.** *O.* Shrewsbury die. R. Declaration in three lines, three Oxford plumes above, 1642; *mm.* plume/-	1350	4500

2971

2971 Oxford bust (small). R. Three Oxford plumes, 1642; *mm.* Oxford plume/-,	275	900
2972 Oxford bust (small or large). R. Three Oxford plumes, 1643; *mm.* Oxford plume/-, Oxford plume/rosette	275	900
2972A — — pellets by date, 1644; *mm.* plume/-	325	1050
2972B — — 1644 OX; mm. plume/rosette	325	1050
2973 — R. Oxford and two Shrewsbury plumes, lozenges by date, 1644 OX; *mm.* plume/-	375	1250
2974 — R. Three Shrewsbury plumes, 1643; *mm.* plume/-	300	1000

	F £	VF £
2975 Fine Oxford bust. R. Three Oxford plumes, lozenges in field, 1644 OX; *mm.* Shrewsbury plume/-	275	900
2975A — — large date in script, 1644 OX; *mm.* plume/-	325	1050
2976 — 1645 OX; *mm.* plume/-	2250	7500
2976A — R. Oxford and two Shrewsbury plumes, 1644 OX; *mm.* plume/-	375	1250
2977 — R. Three Shrewsbury plumes, 1644 OX; *mm.* plume/-	350	1100
2978 — — annulets or pellets at date, 1646; *mm.* plume/floriated cross, plume/-	325	1050

2979

	F £	VF £
2979 Rawlins' die. Fine bust with R. on truncation. R. Three Oxford plumes, rosettes or lozenges by plumes, lozenges by date, 1644 OX; *mm.* Shrewsbury plume/rosette, Shrewsbury plume/-	1000	3750
2979A — — pellets by date, no OX, 1644; *mm.* plume/-	1100	4000
2979B — R. Oxford and two Shrewsbury plumes, 1644 OX; *mm.* plume/-	1250	4250

2980A

	F £	VF £
2980 **Sixpence.** O. Aberystwyth die R. Three Oxford plumes, 1642; *mm.* book/-	325	1000
2980A — — 1643; *mm.* book/-	300	950
2981 — R. Three Shrewsbury plumes, 1643; *mm.* book/-	275	850
2982 — R. Shrewsbury plume and two lis, 1644 OX (groat rev. die); *mm.* book/-	575	2000
2983 **Groat.** O. Aberystwyth die. R. Shrewsbury plume and two lis, 1644 OX; *mm.* book/-	250	850
2984 — R. Three Shrewsbury plumes, 1644 OX; mm. book/-	275	900

2985

	F £	VF £
2985 Oxford bust within inner circle. R. As 2983, 1644 OX; mm. floriated cross/-	175	625

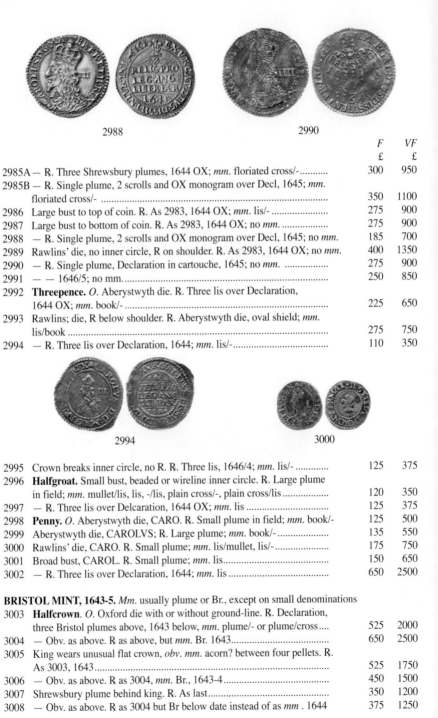

2988   2990

	F	VF
	£	£
2985A — R. Three Shrewsbury plumes, 1644 OX; *mm.* floriated cross/-...........	300	950
2985B — R. Single plume, 2 scrolls and OX monogram over Decl, 1645; *mm.* floriated cross/-	350	1100
2986 Large bust to top of coin. R. As 2983, 1644 OX; *mm.* lis/-	275	900
2987 Large bust to bottom of coin. R. As 2983, 1644 OX; no *mm.*	275	900
2988 — R. Single plume, 2 scrolls and OX monogram over Decl, 1645; no *mm.*	185	700
2989 Rawlins' die, no inner circle, R on shoulder. R. As 2983, 1644 OX; no *mm.*	400	1350
2990 — R. Single plume, Declaration in cartouche, 1645; no *mm.*	275	900
2991 — — 1646/5; no mm..	250	850
2992 **Threepence.** *O.* Aberystwyth die. R. Three lis over Declaration, 1644 OX; *mm.* book/-...	225	650
2993 Rawlins; die, R below shoulder. R. Aberystwyth die, oval shield; *mm.* lis/book	275	750
2994 — R. Three lis over Declaration, 1644; *mm.* lis/-...................................	110	350

2994   3000

2995 Crown breaks inner circle, no R. R. Three lis, 1646/4; *mm.* lis/-	125	375
2996 **Halfgroat.** Small bust, beaded or wireline inner circle. R. Large plume in field; *mm.* mullet/lis, lis, -/lis, plain cross/-, plain cross/lis	120	350
2997 — R. Three lis over Delcaration, 1644 OX; *mm.* lis	125	375
2998 **Penny.** *O.* Aberystwyth die, CARO. R. Small plume in field; *mm.* book/-	125	500
2999 Aberystwyth die, CAROLVS; R. Large plume; *mm.* book/-	135	550
3000 Rawlins' die, CARO. R. Small plume; *mm.* lis/mullet, lis/-	175	750
3001 Broad bust, CAROL. R. Small plume; *mm.* lis.......................................	150	650
3002 — R. Three lis over Declaration, 1644; *mm.* lis	650	2500

BRISTOL MINT, 1643-5. *Mm.* usually plume or Br., except on small denominations

3003 **Halfcrown.** *O.* Oxford die with or without ground-line. R. Declaration, three Bristol plumes above, 1643 below, *mm.* plume/- or plume/cross....	525	2000
3004 — Obv. as above. R as above, but *mm.* Br. 1643.....................................	650	2500
3005 King wears unusual flat crown, *obv. mm.* acorn? between four pellets. R. As 3003, 1643..	525	1750
3006 — Obv. as above. R as 3004, *mm.* Br., 1643-4..	450	1500
3007 Shrewsbury plume behind king. R. As last..	350	1200
3008 — Obv. as above. R as 3004 but Br below date instead of as *mm* . 1644	375	1250

3009

| | | F | VF |
| | | £ | £ |

3009 — Obv. as 3007 but Br below horse. R̶ as above but 1644-5................... 350 1200
3010 — Obv. as above. R̶ as 3004, *mm.* Br. and Br. below date, 1644-5.......... 400 1300
3011 **Shilling.** *O.* Oxford die. R̶. Declaration, 1643, 3 crude plumes above, no *mm.* 625 2000

3012 3014

3012 — — R̶ Similar, but *mm.* Br., 1643-4, less crude plumes........................ 400 1350
3013 —Obv. Coarse bust. R̶. As 3011, no *mm.*, 1643 .... 1050 3500
3014 — — Coarse bust, R̶. as 3012, *mm.* Br, but 1644.................................... 500 1650

3016A 3017

3015 Obv. Bust of good style, plumelet before face. R̶. As 3012 *mm.* Br. but 1644-5 375 1300
3016 — — R̶.as 3012, 1644, but Br below date instead of *mm.* 425 1400
3016A — — R̶ as 3012, 1644 but plume and plumelet either side...................... 350 1250
3017 —Obv. Taller bust with high crown, no plumelets before, *mm.* Br. on its side. R̶
As 3016 Br.below 1644-5... 500 1650
3018 —Obv. As 3017 but no *mm.* R̶ as above but *mm.* Br., no Br below 1644-5 525 1750
3018A — — R̶ as above but plume and plumelets, 1645 .... 675 2250
3019 **Sixpence.** Small bust, nothing before. R̶. Declaration surrounded by
CHRISTO etc., 1643; *mm.* ./Br.. 525 1750

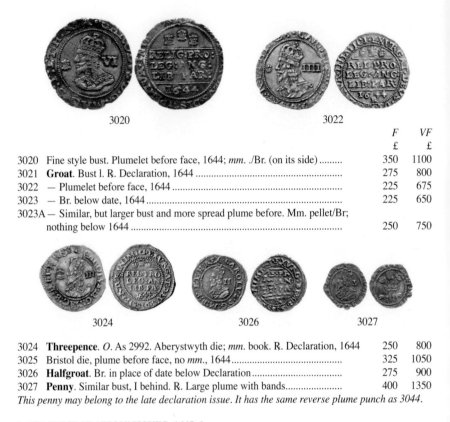

3020   3022

	F	VF
	£	£
3020 Fine style bust. Plumelet before face, 1644; *mm.* ./Br. (on its side)	350	1100
3021 **Groat**. Bust l. R. Declaration, 1644	275	800
3022 — Plumelet before face, 1644	225	675
3023 — Br. below date, 1644	225	650
3023A— Similar, but larger bust and more spread plume before. Mm. pellet/Br;		
nothing below 1644	250	750

3024   3026   3027

3024 **Threepence**. *O.* As 2992. Aberystwyth die; *mm.* book. R. Declaration, 1644	250	800
3025 Bristol die, plume before face, no *mm.*, 1644..	325	1050
3026 **Halfgroat**. Br. in place of date below Declaration..................................	275	900
3027 **Penny**. Similar bust, I behind. R. Large plume with bands......................	400	1350

This penny may belong to the late declaration issue. It has the same reverse plume punch as 3044.

LATE 'DECLARATION' ISSUES, 1645-6

After Bristol surrendered on 11 September 1645, many of the Royalist garrison returned unsearched to Oxford and the Bristol moneyers appear to have continued work, using altered Bristol dies and others of similar type bearing the marks A, B and plume. Ashby de la Zouch was reinforced from Oxford in September 1645 and, following its fall on 28 February 1646, Royalist forces marched to Bridgnorth-on-Severn, holding out until 26 April 1646. Mr Boon suggested (cf. SCBI 33, p. xli) that Ashby and Bridgnorth are plausible mint sites and the most likely candidates for the A and B marked issues, if these do indeed represent fixed mint locations.

ASHBY DE LA ZOUCH, 1645

3028 **Halfcrown**. Horseman of Bristol type, A below. R. Altered Bristol die. A		
(over Br) below date, 1645; *mm.* plume/A (over Br)	3000	10500
3029 - - R. A below date (new die), 1645; *mm.* plume/A	3000	10500
3030 - - R. Nothing below date 1645; *mm.* plume/A....................................	2750	9000
3031 **Shilling**. Crowned bust left. R. Declaration type, A below date, 1645; mm.		
plume/A	1500	4750

3032

		F	*VF*
		£	£
3032	- plumelet before face, 1645; *mm.* plume/A	1600	5000
3033	**Sixpence.** Bust of Bristol style, plumelet before face. R. Declaration type, 1645; *mm.* A (on its side)/-	1100	3250
3034	**Groat.** Similar, plumelet before face, 1645; *mm.* A (on its side)/-	950	2750
3035	**Threepence.** Similar, plumelet before face. R. Single plumelet above Declaration, 1645; no *mm.*	750	2250

BRIDGNORTH-ON-SEVERN, 1646

| 3036 | **Halfcrown.** Horseman of Bristol type, A below (same die as 3028-30). R. Scroll above Declaration, B below, 1646; *mm.* plume/A .... | 3500 | 12500 |
| 3036A | - R. Nothing below date, 1646; *mm.* plume/- .... | 2750 | 9000 |

3037

3037	- plumelet (over A) below horse (same die as 3028-30 recut). R. Nothing below date, 1646; *mm.* plume, plume/-	1500	4750
3038	- - plumelet below date, 1646; *mm.* plume	1500	4750
3039	**Shilling.** Crowned bust left, plumelet before face (same die as 3032). R. Scroll above Declaration, 1646; *mm.* plume/plumelet	575	2000
3039A	- Bristol obverse die, nothing before face. R. Scroll above Declaration, 1646; 2000 *mm.* Br/-	750	2500
3040	- - plume before face (altered die of 3039A), 1646; *mm.* plumelet (over Br)/-	575	2000

3041   3042

| | | F | VF |
| | | £ | £ |

3041 **Sixpence.** Crowned bust left, plume before face. R. Scroll above Declaration,
1646; *mm.* B/- 250   900
3042 **Groat.** Similar, plumelet before face, 1646; *mm.* plumelet, plumelet/- 185   575
3043 **Threepence.** Similar, plumelet before face. R. Single plume above
Declaration, 1646; *mm.* plumelet/- 225   675
3044 **Halfgroat.** Crowned bust left, II behind. R. Large plume with bands dividing
date, 1646; no *mm.* 425   1250

3045   3047

TRURO, 1642-3. *Mm.* rose except where stated
3045 **Crown.** King on horseback, head in profile, sash flies out in two ends.
R. CHRISTO, etc., round garnished shield 475   1250
3046 **Halfcrown.** King on walking horse, groundline below, R. Oblong shield,
CR above, *mm.* bugle/– 3000   12500
3047 Galloping horse, king holds baton. R. Oblong shield, CR at sides 3000   12500
3048 Walking horse, king holds sword. R. Similar 850   3250
3049 — R. Similar, but CR above 900   3500
3050 Galloping horse, king holds sword. R. Similar, but CR at sides 1100   4500
3051 — R. Similar, but CR above 1200   4750
3052 Trotting horse. R. Similar, but CR at sides 900   3500
3053 **Shilling.** Small bust of good style. R. Oblong shield 4250   13500

EXETER, 1643-6. Undated or dated 1644-5 *Mm.* rose except where stated
3054 **Half-pound.** King on horseback, face towards viewer, sash in large bow.
R. CHRISTO, etc., round garnished shield. Struck from crown dies of 3055
on a thick flan 6500   20000
3055 **Crown.** King on horseback, sash in large bow. R. Round garnished
shield 475   1500

		F	VF
		£	£
3056	— Shield garnished with twelve even scrolls	575	1750
3057	As 3055, R Date divided by *mm.* 16 rose 44	525	1650
3058	— R Date to l. of *mm.* 1644	450	1250
3059	— *mm*: rose/Ex, 1645	525	1650
3060	King's sash flies out in two ends; *mm.* castle/rose, 1645	600	1850
3061	— *mm.* castle/Ex, 1645	475	1500
3062	— *mm.* castle, 1645	375	1000
3063	**Halfcrown**. King on horseback, sash tied in bow. R. Oblong shield CR at sides	900	3750
3064	— R. Round shield with eight even scrolls	375	1250

3065

| 3065 | — R. Round shield with five short and two long scrolls .... | 300 | 800 |
| 3066 | — R. Oval shield with angular garnish of triple lines............................ | 750 | 2750 |

3067

3067	Briot's horseman with lumpy ground. R. As 3064	400	1350
3068	— R. As 3065	375	1250
3069	— R. As 3066	750	2750
3070	— R. As 3065, date to l. of *mm.* 1644	525	1750

3071

| 3071 | King on spirited horse galloping over arms. R. Oval garnished shield, 1642 in cartouche below .... | 6500 | 20000 |

		F	VF
		£	£
3072	— R. As 3070, date to 1. of *mm*. 1644-5	7000	22500
3073	— R. *mm*. castle, 1645	7500	25000
3074	Short portly king, leaning backwards on ill-proportioned horse,		
	1644, 16 rose 44	1500	5250
3075	Horse with twisted tail, sash flies out in two ends R. As 3064	600	1850

3076

		F	VF
3076 —	R. As 3070, date divided by *mm*. 16 rose 44, or date to 1. of *mm*. 1644-5	525	1750
3077	— R. *mm*. castle, 1645	575	1850
3078	— R. *mm*. Ex, 1645	550	1800
3079	— R. Declaration type; *mm*. Ex. 1644-5	3750	12500
3080	— R. Similar, Ex also below declaration, 1644	3500	12000
3081	**Shilling.** Large Oxford style bust. R. Round shield with eight even scrolls	1250	4500
3082	— R. Oval shield with CR at sides	1650	5750
3083	Normal bust with lank hair. R. As 3081	700	2250
3083A —	R. As 3082	1650	5750
3084	— R. Round shield with six scrolls	525	1650

3085

		F	VF
3085	— R. Similar, date 1644, 45 to left of rose *mm*. 16 rose 44 (rare),		
	1644 to right of rose (very rare)....................................	375	1100
3086	— R. Declaration type, 1645	2250	7000

3087A

		F	VF
3087	**Sixpence.** Similar to 3085, large bust and letters 1644 rose.....................	300	900
3087A —	Smaller bust and letters from punches used on 3088, small or large		
	VI, 16 rose 44	325	950

	F	VF
	£	£
3088 **Groat**. Somewhat similar but 1644 at beginning of *obv.* legend..............	135	450

	3089	3090	3092		
3089	**Threepence**. Similar. R. Square shield, 1644 above.............................			125	400
3090	**Halfgroat**. Similar, but II. R. Oval shield, 1644			225	700
3091	— R. Large rose, 1644..			250	750
3092	**Penny**. As last but I behind head..			275	800

WORCESTER, 1644-45

3093	**Halfcrown**. King on horseback l., W below; *mm.* two lions. R. Declaration type 1644 altered from 1643 Bristol die; *mm.* pellets.............................	1750	6500
3094	— R. Square-topped shield; *mm.* helmet, castle......................................	1100	4750
3095	— R. Oval shield; *mm.* helmet..	1250	5000

3096

3096	Similar but grass indicated; *mm.* castle. R. Square-topped shield; *mm.* helmet or pellets...	900	3750
3097	— R. Oval draped shield, lis or lions in legend......................................	975	4000
3098	— R. Oval shield CR at sides, roses in legend	1000	4250
3099	— R. FLORENT etc., oval garnished shield with lion's paws each side .	1000	4250
3100	Tall king, no W or *mm.* R. Oval shield, lis, roses, lions or stars in legend	900	3750
3101	— R. Square-topped shield; *mm.* helmet...	975	4000
3102	— R. FLORENT, etc., oval shield; no *mm.*...	1000	4250
3103	Briot type horse, sword slopes forward, ground-line. R. Oval shield, roses in legend; *mm.* 91v, 105, none (combinations)......................................	1000	4250
3104	— Similar, but CR at sides, 91v/-..	1100	4500
3105	Dumpy, portly king, crude horse. R. As 3100; *mm.* 91v, 105, none	975	4000

COINS OF BRITAIN
PO BOX 2, MONMOUTH, NP25 3YR, UK

BNTA

E-mail: lloydbennett@coinsofbritain.com   +44(0)7714 284 939

3106

	F	VF
	£	£

3106　Thin king and horse. R. Oval shield, stars in legend; *mm.* 91v, none...... 900 3750

WORCESTER OR SALOPIA (SHREWSBURY), 1643-4

3107　**Shilling**. Bust of king l., adequately rendered. R. Square-topped shield;
　　　mm. castle 1850 7500
3108　— R. CR above shield; *mm.* helmet and lion 1850 7500
3109　— R. Oval shield; *mm.* lion, pear 1650 6500
3110　— Bust a somewhat crude copy of last (two varieties); *mm.* bird, lis.
　　　R. Square-topped shield with lion's paws above and at sides; *mm.* boar's
　　　head, helmet.. 1750 7000

3108

3111　— — CR above 1750 7000
3112　— R. Oval shield, lis in legend; *mm.* lis 1500 5250
3113　— R. Round shield; *mm.* lis, 3 lis.. 1500 5250
3114　Bust r.; *mm.* pear/-, pear/lis. R. draped oval shield with or without CR.
　　　(Halfcrown reverse dies)... 3250 12500
3115　**Sixpence**. As 3110; *mm.* castle, castle/boar's hd 1350 4250

3116

3117

3116　**Groat**. As 3112; *mm.* lis/helmet, rose/helmet... 600 1750
3117　**Threepence**. Similar; *mm.* lis.. 275 825
3118　**Halfgroat**. Similar; *mm.* lis (*O.*) various (R.)... 325 900

	F £	VF £

SALOPIA (SHREWSBURY), 1644

3119 **Halfcrown.** King on horseback l. SA below; *mm*. lis. R. (*mm*. lis, helmet,
lion rampant, none). Cr. oval shield; CHRISTO etc. *mm*. helmet .... | 4500 | 15000

3120 — R. FLORENT, etc., crowned oval shield, no *mm*. .... | 4500 | 15000

3121 — SA erased or replaced by large pellet or cannon ball; *mm*. lis in legend,
helmet. R. As 3119... | 2250 | 7500

3122 Tall horse with mane blown forward, nothing below; *mm*. lis. R.
Large round shield with crude garniture; *mm*. helmet.............................. | 1100 | 4500

3123 — R. Uncrowned square-topped shield with lion's paw above and at sides;
mm. helmet.. | 1250 | 5000

3124 — R. Small crowned oval shield; *mm*. various .... | 975 | 4000

3125

3125 — R. As 3120 .... | 1000 | 4250

3126 Finer work with little or no mane before horse. R. Cr. round or oval shield | 1100 | 4500

3127 Grass beneath horse. R. Similar; *mm*. lis or rose .... | 1350 | 5250

3128 Ground below horse. R. As 3120.. | 2000 | 7500

HARTLEBURY CASTLE (WORCS.), 1646

3129

3129 **Halfcrown.** *O. Mm*. pear. R. HC (Hartlebury Castle) in garniture below
shield; *mm*. three pears .... | 1500 | 5000

CHESTER, 1644

3130

		F	VF
		£	£
3130	**Halfcrown**. As illus. Ɽ. Oval shield; *mm.* three gerbs and sword............	1000	4000
3131	— Similar, but without plume or CHST; Ɽ. Cr. oval shield with lion skin; *mm.* prostrate gerb; -/cinquefoil, ⁻/⋮	900	3750
3132	— Ɽ. Crowned square-topped shield with CR at sides both crowned *rev.*; *mm.* cinquefoil (these dies were later crudely recut)	1500	5750
3133	As 3130, but without plume or CHST. Ɽ. Declaration type, 1644 *rev.*; *mm.* plume	1250	5000
3133A	**Shilling**. Bust l. Ɽ. Oval garnished shield; *mm.* ∴ (obv. only)	3500	9500
3133B	— Ɽ. Square-topped shield; *mm.* as last...................................	3500	9500
3133C	— R . Shield over long cross...	3250	9000
3134	**Threepence**. Ɽ. Square-topped shield; *mm.*-/ prostrate gerb	900	3000

WELSH MARCHES? 1644

3135

| 3135 | **Halfcrown**. Crude horseman, l. Ɽ. Declaration of Bristol style divided by a dotted line, 3 plumes above, 1644 below .... | 1350 | 4500 |

HAMMERED BRITISH COINS

Hammered coins bought and sold

www.hammeredbritishcoins.com
mail@hammeredbritishcoins.com
07825226435

CARLISLE, 1644-5

3137   3139

		F	VF
		£	£
3136	**Three shillings**. Large crown above C R between rosettes III. S below. rev. OBS . CARL / . 1645, rosette below	13500	32500
3137	Similar but :- OBS :/-: CARL :./.1645, rosette above and below	12500	30000
3138	**Shilling**. Large crown above C R between trefoil of pellets, XII below. *rev.* as 3137	7500	16500
3139	R. Legend and date in two lines	8000	17500

Note. *(3136-39) Round or Octagonal pieces exist.*

NEWARK, 1645-6

3140   3142

3140	**Halfcrown**. Large crown between CR ; below, XXX. *rev.* OBS / NEWARK / 1645	950	2500
3140A	— Similar 1646	925	2400
3141	**Shilling**. Similar but crude flat shaped crown, NEWARKE, 1645	950	2500
3142	Similar but normal arched crown, 1645	750	1750
3143	— NEWARK, 1645 or 1646	725	1650

3144   3146

	F	VF
	£	£
3144 **Ninepence**. As halfcrown but IX, 1645 or 1646	700	1700
3145 — NEWARKE, 1645..	725	1800
3146 **Sixpence**. As halfcrown but VI, 1646...	850	2000

PONTEFRACT, June 1648-March 1649. Before execution of Charles I

3147 **Two shillings** (lozenge shaped). DVM : SPIRO : SPERO around CR crowned. R. Castle surrounded by OBS, PC, sword and 1648, weight: c.9-10g. ...	7500	27500

3148

3148 **Shilling** (lozenge shaped, octagonal or round). Similar...........................	2500	6500
3149 — Similar but XII on r. dividing PC	2400	6250

After the execution of Charles I (30 Jan. 1649), in the name of Charles II

3150

3150 **Shilling** (octagonal). *O*. As last. R. CAROLVS : SECV*N* DVS : 1648, castle gateway with flag dividing PC, OBS on l., cannon protrudes on r.	2500	6500
3151 CAROL : II : etc., around HANC : DE / VS : DEDIT 1648. R. POST : MORTEM : PATRIS : PRO : FILIO around gateway etc. as last	2750	7500

SCARBOROUGH, July 1644-July 1645*

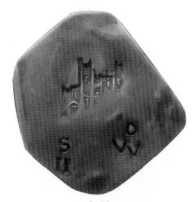

3156

3165

3169

	VF
Type I. Large Castle with gateway to left, SC and value Vs below	
3152 **Crown.** (various weights)	65000
Type II. Small Castle with gateway, no SC, value punched on flan	
3153 **Five shillings and eightpence.**...	60000
3154 **Crown.** Similar..	75000
3155 **Three shillings.** Similar	45000
3156 **Two shillings and tenpence.** Similar	45000
3157 **Two shillings and sevenpence.** Similar	45000
3158 **Halfcrown.** Similar..	50000
3159 **Two shillings and fourpence.** Similar	45000
3162 **One shilling and sixpence.** Similar to 3159...	40000
3163 **One shilling and fourpence.** Similar	40000
3164 **One shilling and threepence.** Similar..	40000
3165 **Shilling.** Similar..	50000
3166 **Sixpence.** Similar	35000
3167 **Groat.** Similar...	30000

*No research has been done on this complicated series for many years but a detailed overview was set out in the 'Slaney' catalogue, Spink auction 229, 14 May 2015.

VF

UNCERTAIN CASTLE

Type III. Castle gateway with two turrets, value punched below

		VF
3168	**Two shillings and twopence**	17500
3169	**Two shillings.** Castle punched twice.............	17500
3170	**One shilling and sixpence.** Similar to 3168.........	15000
3171	**One shilling and fourpence.** Similar.............	15000
3172	**One shilling and threepence.** Similar.............	15000
3173	**One shilling and twopence.** Similar.............	14500
3174	**One shilling and one penny.** Similar.............	14500
3175	**Shilling.** Similar.............	17500
3176	**Elevenpence.** Similar.............	13500
3177	**Tenpence.** Similar.............	13500
3178	**Ninepence.** Similar.............	13500
3178A	**Eightpence.** Similar.............	12500
3179	**Sevenpence.** Similar.............	12500
3180	**Sixpence.** Similar.............	15000

COPPER

For further details see Tim Everson, *The Galata Guide to the Farthing Tokens of James I and Charles I*

Farthings

3182　　　　　　　　　　　　3183

		F £	VF £
3181	Richmond 1a, colon stops, CARO over IACO, five jewel crowns on obverse, mm on obverse only; *mm*: Coronet, Crescent with mullet.	20	50
3182	—— 1b, colon stops, CARO over IACO, nine jewel crowns on obverse, *mm*: Dagger, Mascle.............	20	50
3183	—— 2 CARO, colon stops, *mm* on obverse only, *mm*: Lombardic A, Lombardic A with pellet below, Annulet, Annulet with pellet within, Bell, Book, Castle, Cinquefoil, Crescent (large and small), Cross (pellets in angles), Cross calvary, Cross patée, Cross patée fitchée, Cross patonce, Cross patonce in saltire, Cross saltire, Dagger, Ermine, Estoile (pierced), Eye, Fish hook, Fleece, Fusil, Fusils (two), Halberd, Harp, Heart, Horseshoe, Key (vertical), Leaf, Lion passant, Lis (large), Lis (demi), Lis (three), Martlet, Mascle with pellet within, Nautilus, Pike-head, Rose (single), Shield, Star, Tower, Trefoil, Tun, Woolpack, Woolpack over Crescent.............	10	30
3183A	—— CARA farthings (Contemporary forgeries manufactured from official punches. Usually F for E in REX), mm on obverse only; *mm*: Annulet, Coronet, Cross patée fourchée, Dagger, Fusil, Key, Mascle, Trefoil, Tun.............	150	300
3183B	—— Contemporary forgeries of Richmond Type 2, mm: Lombardic A, Annulet, Annulet with saltire within, Barbell and pellets, Cross (pellets in angles), Cross patée, Cross patonce, Cross patonce in saltire, Cross saltire, Dagger, Fusil, Heart, Horseshoe, Key (horizontal), Lis (large), Lis, Lis demi, Lis (three), Lis (two), Mascle, Mascle with pellet within, Rose, Star, Thistlehead, Tower, Triangle, Triangle (inverted), Tun.............	5	15

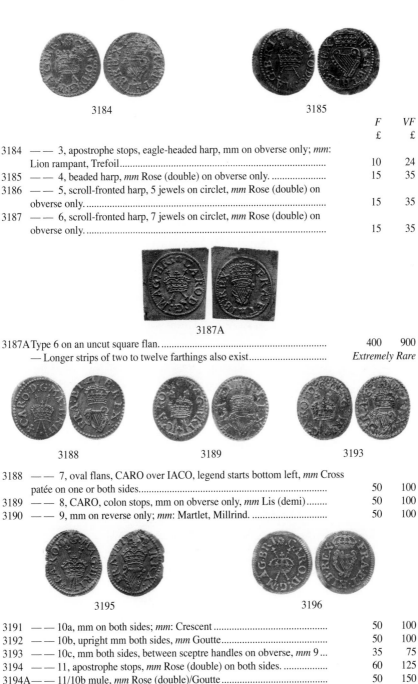

3184

3185

	F	VF
	£	£

3184 — — 3, apostrophe stops, eagle-headed harp, mm on obverse only; *mm*: Lion rampant, Trefoil.. 10 24

3185 — — 4, beaded harp, *mm* Rose (double) on obverse only. 15 35

3186 — — 5, scroll-fronted harp, 5 jewels on circlet, *mm* Rose (double) on obverse only.. 15 35

3187 — — 6, scroll-fronted harp, 7 jewels on circlet, *mm* Rose (double) on obverse only.. 15 35

3187A

3187A Type 6 on an uncut square flan.. 400 900

— Longer strips of two to twelve farthings also exist............................ *Extremely Rare*

3188   3189   3193

3188 — — 7, oval flans, CARO over IACO, legend starts bottom left, *mm* Cross patée on one or both sides.. 50 100

3189 — — 8, CARO, colon stops, mm on obverse only, *mm* Lis (demi)........ 50 100

3190 — — 9, mm on reverse only; *mm*: Martlet, Millrind. 50 100

3195   3196

3191 — — 10a, mm on both sides; *mm*: Crescent 50 100

3192 — — 10b, upright mm both sides, *mm* Goutte.. 50 100

3193 — — 10c, mm both sides, between sceptre handles on obverse, *mm* 9 ... 35 75

3194 — — 11, apostrophe stops, *mm* Rose (double) on both sides. 60 125

3194A — — 11/10b mule, *mm* Rose (double)/Goutte 50 150

3195 — — 12, *mm* Rose (double) on obverse only... 45 90

3196 Transitional Issue Farthings, double arched crowns, mm on obverse only; *mm*: Harp, Quatrefoil... 20 50

	F	*VF*
	£	£
3197 Maltravers Type 1, inner circles, mm on obverse only; *mm*: Rose (double), Woolpack............................	50	100
3197A Counterfeits of Maltravers Type 1, *mm*: Bell, Lis, Tun, Woolpack..........	15	35
3198 — — 2, mm both sides; *mm*: Bell, Lis (large), Lis (small), Martlet, Rose (double), Woolpack...................	15	35
3198A Counterfeits of Maltravers Type 2, *mm*: Bell, Cross patée, Harp, Lis (small), Mascle, Star, Woolpack	15	35

3199   3200

3199 — — 3, different mm on each side; *mm*: Woolpack/Rose (double), Martlet/ Bell, Woolpack/Portcullis, Lis/Portcullis, Harp/Bell, Harp/Billet............	15	35
3199A Counterfeits of Maltravers Type 3, *mm*: Bell/Cross patée fitchée, Bell/ Woolpack, Cross patée fitchée/Bell, Tun/Bell, Woolpack/Lis.................	15	35
3200 Maltravers Oval Type 4, no inner circles, legend starts bottom left, mm Lis (large) on both sides................	75	150

Richmond Types 7 to 12 and Maltravers Type 4, 3188 to 3195 and 3200, the oval farthings, were issued for use in Ireland.

3201   3202   3203

(There is frequent muling between types in the Rose Farthing sequence)

3201 Rose Type 1, large double-arched crowns, sceptres within inner Circle, BRIT, mm on obv. or rev. or both; *mm*: Lis, Martlet................................	45	90
3202 — — 2, similar but small crowns and sceptres just cross inner circle, BRIT, mm on obverse only or both sides, *mm* Lis	30	75
3203 — — 3, similar but crowns with pointed sides and sceptres almost to outer circle, BRIT, *mm* Lis, Cross patée, Mullet, Crescent...............................	15	35

3204   3206   3207

3204 - - Mules of Type 3 with Types 4a and 4b, *mm* Lis, Mullet, Crescent........	15	35
3205 - - 4a Single arched crowns, Long legends with CAROLVS, MAG, FRAN and HIB, *mm*: Lis, Mullet, Crescent.	10	25
3206 — — 4b Single arched crowns, Short legends with CAROLV, MA, FRA and HI, *mm*: Mullet, Crescent................	10	25
3206A Counterfeits of Rose type 4, *mm* Crescent...............................	20	45
3207 — — 5, sceptres below crown, *mm* Mullet on both sides	35	75

The Rose farthings were also authorised for use in Ireland but do not seem to have reached there.

The coins struck during the Commonwealth have inscriptions in English instead of Latin as a truer expression of Protestantism. St. George's cross and the Irish harp take the place of the royal arms. The silver halfpenny was issued for the last time. Coins with *mm.* anchor were struck during the protectorship of Richard Cromwell.

Mintmarks

1649-57 Sun   1658-60 Anchor

GOLD

3208

	F £	VF £		F £	VF £
3208 Unite. As illustration; *mm.* sun,					
1649	2750	8000	1654	2400	6000
1650	2500	6500	1655	3750	10500
1651	2250	5500	1656	2750	7500
1652	2500	6500	1657	2750	7500
1653	2250	5500			
3209 Similar, *mm.* anchor,					
1658	9500	25000	1660	8500	22500

3210

3210 **Double-crown.** Similar; but X; *mm.* sun,					
1649	2250	7000	1654	1850	6000
1650	1800	5750	1655	2750	9500
1651	1700	5000	1656	3000	10000
1652	1850	6000	1657	2750	9500
1653	1700	5000			
3211 Similar, *mm.* anchor, 1660				4500	15000

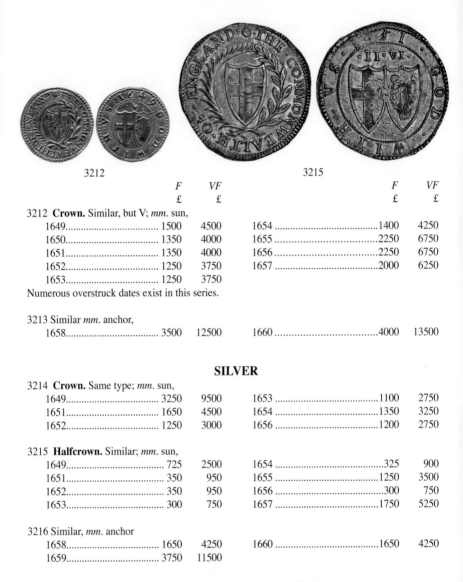

3212   3215

	F £	VF £		F £	VF £
3212 Crown. Similar, but V; *mm*. sun,					
1649	1500	4500	1654	1400	4250
1650	1350	4000	1655	2250	6750
1651	1350	4000	1656	2250	6750
1652	1250	3750	1657	2000	6250
1653	1250	3750			

Numerous overstruck dates exist in this series.

3213 Similar *mm*. anchor,					
1658	3500	12500	1660	4000	13500

SILVER

3214 Crown. Same type; *mm*. sun,					
1649	3250	9500	1653	1100	2750
1651	1650	4500	1654	1350	3250
1652	1250	3000	1656	1200	2750

3215 Halfcrown. Similar; *mm*. sun,					
1649	725	2500	1654	325	900
1651	350	950	1655	1250	3500
1652	350	950	1656	300	750
1653	300	750	1657	1750	5250

3216 Similar, *mm*. anchor					
1658	1650	4250	1660	1650	4250
1659	3750	11500			

ARTHUR BRYANT COINS

Dealers in British coins and medals

www.bryantcoins.com
abcoins@live.co.uk
07768 645 686

BNTA

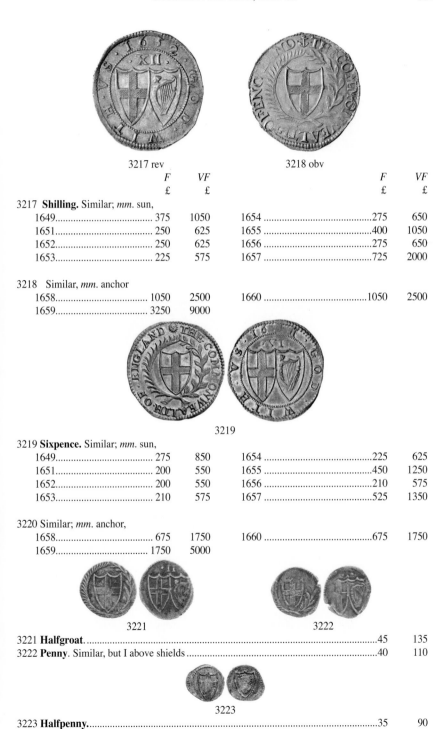

3217 rev   3218 obv

	F	VF			F	VF
	£	£			£	£

3217 Shilling. Similar; *mm.* sun,

1649	375	1050		1654	275	650
1651	250	625		1655	400	1050
1652	250	625		1656	275	650
1653	225	575		1657	725	2000

3218 Similar, *mm.* anchor

| 1658 | 1050 | 2500 | | 1660 | 1050 | 2500 |
| 1659 | 3250 | 9000 | | | | |

3219

3219 Sixpence. Similar; *mm.* sun,

1649	275	850		1654	225	625
1651	200	550		1655	450	1250
1652	200	550		1656	210	575
1653	210	575		1657	525	1350

3220 Similar; *mm.* anchor,

| 1658 | 675 | 1750 | | 1660 | 675 | 1750 |
| 1659 | 1750 | 5000 | | | | |

3221   3222

3221 Halfgroat. 45   135
3222 Penny. Similar, but I above shields 40   110

3223

3223 Halfpenny. 35   90

Oliver Cromwell, 'the Great Emancipator' was born on 25th April 1599 in Huntingdon. He married Elizabeth Bourchier in August 1620 and had nine children seven of whom survived infancy. The Protectorate was established on 16th December 1653, with work on the production of portrait coins authorised in 1655. Although often referred to as patterns, there is in fact nothing to suggest that the portrait coins of Oliver Cromwell were not *intended* for circulation. Authorised in 1656, the first full production came in 1657 and was followed by a second more plentiful one before Cromwell's death on 3rd September 1658. All coins were machine made, struck from dies by Thomas Simon (1618-1665) in the presses of the Frenchman, Pierre Blondeau. Later, some of Simon's puncheons were sold in the Low Countries and an imitation Crown was made there. Other Dutch dies were prepared and some found their way back to the Mint, where in 1738 it was decided to strike a set of Cromwell's coins. Shillings and Sixpences were struck from the Dutch dies, and Crowns from new dies prepared by John Tanner. Dutch and Tanner Halfbroads were also made. Oliver was succeeded as Lord Protector by his son Richard for whom no coins were struck.

GOLD

	F £	VF £	EF £
3224 **Fifty shillings**. Laur. head l. ℞. Crowned Shield of the Protectorate, die axis ↑↓ 1656 from the same dies as the Broad........................	25000	75000	175000

Lettered edge PROTECTOR · LITERIS · LITERÆ · NUMMIS · CORONA · ET · SALUS

3225
1656 gold Broad

3225 **Broad.** of Twenty Shillings. Laur. head l. ℞. Crowned Shield of the
Protectorate, but grained edge die axis ↑↓ 1656. .... 5250 15000 37500

SILVER

3226
1658 Crown 8 over 7 - Die flawed drapery

3226	**Crown.** Dr. bust l. ℞. Crowned shield, 1658/7. Lettered edge ↑↓	1750	3500	8000
3226A	**Crown.** Dutch copy, similar with A ⅄G legend 1658	2000	5000	17500
3226B	**Crown.** Tanner's copy (struck 1738) dated 1658	2000	5000	17500

	F	VF	EF
	£	£	£

3227 **Halfcrown.** Dr. bust l. R. Crowned shield 1656 HI type
legend, lettered edge, die axis ↑↓   2750   7500   17500

3227A
1658 Halfcrown with HIB obverse legend

3227A **Halfcrown.** Similar, 1658 HIB type legend, lettered edge, die axis ↑↓   1250   2500   6000

3228	3230
1658 Shilling	Copper Farthing

3228 **Shilling.** Dr. bust l. R. Crowned shield, grained edge, 1658 die
axis ↑↓   850   1750   4500

3229 **Sixpence.** Similar 1658 die axis ↑↓ ....   *Extremely rare*

Dutch copies (ESC 1506) are more often found

COPPER

3230 **Farthing.** Dr. bust l. R. CHARITIE AND CHANGE, shield ↑↓..   3500   8500   1750
There are also other reverse types for this coin, and an obverse with mullet on top.

Timeline Auctions
Inc. Gregory's **Est.1858**

We are accepting single entries
and collections of antiquities & milled coins

Sold for:
£5,808

www.timelineauctions.com

CHARLES II, 1660-85

Charles II was born at St James Palace on 29th May 1630. He spent a long exile in France and returned after the fall of the Protectorate in 1660. The Restoration commenced and he married Catherine of Braganza, but he bore no legitimate successor. Charles II died on 6th February 1685.

For the first two years after the Restoration the same denominations, apart from the silver crown, were struck as were issued during the Commonwealth although the threepence and fourpence were soon added. Then, early in 1663, the ancient hand hammering process was finally superceded by the machinery of Blondeau.

For the emergency issues struck in the name of Charles II in 1648/9, see the siege pieces of Pontefract listed under Charles I, nos. 3150-1.

HAMMERED COINAGE, 1660-2

Mintmark: Crown.

GOLD

3301

3302   3303

		F £	VF £
First issue. Without mark of value; *mm.* crown on *obv.* only			
3301	**Unite** (20s.). Type as illustration	2250	6750
3302	**Double-crown.** As illustration	1500	4500
3303	**Crown.** Similar	1650	5000

3304   3305

Second issue. With mark of value; *mm.* crown on *obv.* only			
3304	**Unite.** Type as illustration	1750	5250
3305	**Double-crown.** As illustration	1500	4500
3306	**Crown.** Similar	2000	6500

SILVER

3307

	F £	VF £

First issue. Without inner circles or mark of value; *mm*. crown on *obv*. only

| 3307 | **Halfcrown**. Crowned bust, as 3308... | 1500 | 5250 |

3308   3309

3308	**Shilling**. Similar. (Also known with smaller harp on reverse.).................	450	1750
3309	**Sixpence**. Similar	375	1250
3310	**Twopence**. Similar...	50	150
3311	**Penny**. Similar...	40	120
3312	As last, but without mintmark	50	135

3313   3316

Second issue. Without inner circles, but with mark of value; *mm*. crown on *obv*. only

3313	**Halfcrown**. Crowned bust...	1250	4500
3314	**Shilling**. Similar	750	2500
3315	**Sixpence**. Similar	1350	3500
3316	**Twopence**. Similar, but mm. on obv. only	90	300

		F	VF
		£	£
3317	Similar, but mm. both sides (machine made)	20	80
3318	Bust to edge of coin, legend starts at bottom l. (machine made, single arch crown)..	20	75
3319	**Penny**. As 3317	25	90
3320	As 3318 (single arch crown)...	20	80

3321   3326

Third issue. With inner circles and mark of value; *mm.* crown on both sides

3321	**Halfcrown**. Crowned bust to i.c. (and rarely to edge of coin)	225	700
3322	**Shilling**. Similar, rarely *mm.* crown on *obv.* only. (Also known with smaller harp on reverse.)	135	575
3323	**Sixpence**. Similar	110	475
3324	**Fourpence**. Similar	40	125
3325	**Threepence**. Similar...	25	90
3326	**Twopence**. Similar..	20	70
3327	**Penny**. Similar..	20	75

Timeline Auctions

Inc. Gregory's **Est.1858**

www.timelineauctions.com

Sold for:
£45,880

+44 [0]1277 815121
enquiries@timelineauctions.com

Follow us on:

f /TimeLineAuctions
t @TimeLineAuction

AIAΔ   BNTA

M&H COINS

RARE AND HIGH GRADE ENGLISH HAMMERED & MILLED COINS BOUGHT & SOLD

www.mhcoins.co.uk

Tel : + 44 (0) 7504 804019   Email : info@mhcoins.co.uk

SOURCING COINS

EXPERTS IN SOURCING OLD ENGLISH
MILLED AND HAMMERED COINS.

Milled & Hammered Gold & Silver Coins Wanted

Address: PO Box 6408, Basildon, SS14 0PR
Phone: (01268) 208283

www.sourcingcoins.co.uk

Grading of Early and Later Milled Coinage

Milled coinage refers to coins that are struck by dies worked in a mechanical coining press. The early period is defined from the time of the successful installation of Peter Blondeau's hand powered machinery at the mint, initiated to strike the first portrait coins of Oliver Cromwell in 1656. The early period continuing until the advent of Matthew Boulton's steam powered presses from 1790. The coinage of this early period is therefore cruder in its execution than the latter. When pricing coins of the early peiod, we only attribute grades as high as extremely fine, and as high as uncirculated for the latter period. Most coins that occur of the early period in superior grades than those stated, in particular copper coins retaining full original lustre, will command considerably higher prices, due to their rarity. We suggest the following definitions for grades of preservation:

Milled Coinage Conditions

Proof A very carefully struck coin from specially prepared dies, to give a superior definition to the design, with mirror-like fields. Occurs occasionally in the Early Milled Coinage, more frequently in the latter period. Some issues struck to a matt finish for Edward VII.

FDC *Fleur-de-coin.* Absolutely flawless, untouched, without wear, scratches, marks or hairlines. Generally applied to proofs.

UNC *Uncirculated.* A coin in as new condition as issued by the Mint, retaining full lustre or brilliance but, owing to modern mass-production methods of manufacture and storage, not necessarily perfect.

EF *Extremely Fine.* A coin that exhibits very little sign of circulation, with only minimal marks or faint wear, which are only evident upon very close scrutiny.

VF *Very Fine.* A coin that exhibits some wear on the raised surfaces of the design, but really has only had limited circulation.

F *Fine.* A coin that exhibits considerable wear to the raised surfaces of the design, either through circulation, or damage perhaps due to faulty striking

Fair *Fair.* A coin that exhibits wear, with the main features still distinguishable, and the legends, date and inscriptions still readable.

Poor *Poor.* A coin that exhibits considerable wear, certainly with milled coinage of no value to a collector unless it is an extremely rare date or variety.

Examples of Condition Grading

Early Milled

Gold Ν   Silver Ρ   Copper Æ

Extremely Fine

Gold ᴀᴠ   Silver ᴬᴿ   Copper Æ

Very Fine

Fine

George III   *James II*   *George II*
Guinea   *Crown*   *old head Halfpenny*

Later Milled

Gold ᴀᴠ   Silver ᴬᴿ   Copper Æ

Uncirculated

Gold Aν   Silver AR   Copper Æ

Extremely Fine

Very Fine

Fine

Victoria
Jubilee head Sovereign

George IV
laureate bust Crown

Victoria
Young head Halfpenny

MILLED COINAGE, 1662-85

Early in 1663, the ancient hand hammering process was finally superceded by the machinery of Blondeau. John and Joseph Roettier, two brothers, engraved the dies with a safeguard against clipping, the larger coins were made with the edge inscribed DECVS ET TVTAMEN and the regnal year. The medium-sized coins were given a grained edge.

The new gold coins were current for 100s., 40s., 20s. and 10s., and they came to be called 'Guineas' as the gold from which some of them were made was imported from Guinea by the Africa Company (whose badge was the Elephant and Castle). It was not until some years later that the Guinea increased in value to 21s. and more. The Africa Co. badge is also found on some silver and so is the plume symbol indicating silver from the Welsh mines. The four smallest silver denominations, though known today as 'Maundy Money', were actually issued for general circulation: at this period the silver penny was probably the only coin distributed at the Royal Maundy ceremonies. Though never part of the original agreement, smaller coins were eventually also struck by machinery.

A good regal copper coinage was issued for the first time in 1672, but later in the reign, farthings were struck in tin (with a copper plug) in order to help the Cornish tin industry.

Engravers and designers: John Roettier (1631-1700), Thomas Simon (1618-1665)

GOLD

3328
1672 First bust type Five-Guineas

	F £	VF £	EF £		F £	VF £	EF £

3328 Five Guineas. First laur. bust r., pointed trun., regnal year on edge in words, die axis ↑↓
(e.g. 1669=VICESIMO PRIMO), R. Crowned cruciform shields, sceptres in angles

	F	VF	EF		F	VF	EF
1668 VICESIMO	4000	12500	50000	1671 – TERTIO	4250	13500	55000
1668 V. PRIMO	4250	13500	55000	1672 – QVARTO	4000	13000	52500
1669 – PRIMO........	4000	12500	50000	1673 – QVINTO........	4000	13000	52500
1670 – SECVNDO..	4000	12500	50000	1674 – QVINTO..................			*Extremely rare*
1670 – Similar proof *FDC* —	—	175000		1674 – SEXTO	4500	14500	60000

3328A Five Guineas. First bust. Similar hair of different style. Shorter ties

					F	VF	EF
1674 QVINTO			*Extremely rare*	1676 – OCTAVO	4250	13500	55000
1675 V. SEPTIMO..	4250	13500	55000	1677 – NONO............	4000	12500	50000
1676 – SEPTIMO ...	4000	13000	52500	1678/7 – TRICESIMO..	4000	13000	52500

3329   Five Guineas. First bust with elephant below, similar die axis ↑↓

	F	VF	EF		F	VF	EF
1668 VICESIMO ...	3750	11000	45000	1675 V. SEPTIMO.....	4500	14000	57500
1669 – PRIMO........	4500	14000	57500	1677/5 – NONO............	4750	14500	60000

3330

1676 Five-Guineas with elephant and castle provenance mark

	F	VF	EF		F	VF	EF
	£	£	£		£	£	£

3330 Five Guineas. First bust with elephant and castle below, similar die axis ↑↓

1675 – SEPTIMO ...	4750	14500	60000	1677 – NONO............	4500	14000	57500
1676 – OCTAVO.....	4250	13500	55000	1678/7 – TRICESIMO..	4500	14000	57500

3331 Five Guineas. Second laur. bust r., rounded trun. similar die axis ↑↓

1678/7 TRICESIMO.	4000	12500	50000	1682 T. QVARTO	3750	12000	47500
1679 – PRIMO........	3750	12000	47500	1683 – QVINTO........	3750	12000	47500
1680 – SECVNDO..	4000	12500	50000	1683/2 – QVINTO.......	4000	12500	50000
1681 – TERTIO.......	4000	12500	50000	1684 – SEXTO	3750	12000	47500

3332 Five Guineas. Second laur. bust r., with elephant and castle below, similar die axis ↑↓

1680 T. SECVNDO	4500	14000	57500	1683 T. QVINTO.......	4250	13500	55000
1681 – TERTIO.......	4250	13500	55000	1684 – SEXTO	4000	12500	50000
1682 – QVARTO.....	4000	12500	50000				

3333

1664 First bust type Two Guineas

3333 Two Guineas. First laur. bust r., pointed trun. R. Crowned cruciform shields, sceptres in angles, die axis ↑↓

1664	2250	5000	17500	1671	2750	6500	25000
1665		*Extremely rare*		1673		*Extremely rare*	
1669		*Extremely rare*					

3334

1664 Two Guineas with elephant only below

3334 Two Guineas. First bust with elephant below, similar die axis ↑↓

1664..	1850	4250	13500

Knightsbridge Coins

We are always keen to purchase coins and medallions
especially British, American and Australian in choice
condition, either singly or in collections

We are happy to travel to view collections and we can
arrange valuations for insurance or probate purposes. If
you have coins and are thinking of selling, please do not
hesitate to contact:

Knightsbridge Coins
43 Duke Street, St James's, London SW1Y 6DD
Phone: +44 (0)20 7930 7597 | Fax: +44 (0)20 7930 8214
info@knightsbridgecoins.com | www.knightsbridgecoins.com

Knightsbridge Coins
Celebrating 50 years in Numismatics

St James's Auctions

Auctioneers of rare coins

George V, sovereign, 1920S
Sold for £525,000 in 2015
The only UK auctioneers to have sold
two different 1920S sovereigns

0% Commission for lots over £1000

There are no hidden costs, you get the entire hammer price!
For more information please contact:

St James's Auctions Ltd.
10 Charles II Street, London SW1Y 4AA
Phone: +44 (0)20 7930 7888
Fax: +44 (0)20 7930 8214
Email: info@stjauctions.com
www.stjauctions.com

3335
1675 Two Guineas - second bust

3339
1663 Guinea first bust, elephant below

	F	VF	EF		F	VF	EF
	£	£	£		£	£	£

3335 Two Guineas. Second laur. bust r., rounded trun, similar die axis ↑↓

1675	1850	4500	17500	1680	2000	5500	20000
1676	1850	4500	17500	1681	1750	4250	16500
1677	1750	4250	16500	1682	1750	4250	16500
1678/7	1700	4000	16500	1683	1750	4250	16500
1679	1750	4250	16500	1684	1800	4500	17500

3336 Two Guineas. Second bust with elephant and castle below, similar die axis ↑↓

1676	1850	5000	18500	1682	1850	5000	18500
1677		*Extremely rare*		1683	2000	5500	20000
1678	1850	5000	18500	1684	1850	5000	18500

3337 Two Guineas. Second bust with elephant only below, die axis ↑↓ 1678 ...   *Extremely rare*

3337A Broad of 20s. Laur. and dr. bust r. R. Crowned shield of arms (approx. 3400 issued),
die axis ↑↓ 1662 . 2000   4750   12500

3338 Guinea. First laur. bust r., R. Crowned cruciform shields, die axis
↑↓ 1663 4000   15000   55000

3339 Guinea. First bust with elephant below, similar die axis ↑↓ 1663 3000   9500   32500

3340 Guinea. Second laur. bust r.,similar die axis ↑↓

| 1663 | 3250 | 10000 | 40000 | 1664 | 2250 | 7500 | 27500 |

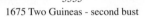

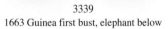

3341
1664 Guinea second bust elephant below

3342
1666 Guinea - third bust

3341 Guinea. Second bust with elephant below, similar die axis ↑↓1664..3500   10500   42500

3342 Guinea. Third laur. bust r. similar die axis ↑↓

1664	1000	3500	15000	1669	950	3000	13500
1665	950	3000	13500	1670	950	3000	13500
1666	950	3000	13500	1671	950	3000	13000
1667	950	3000	13500	1672	1000	3500	15000
1668	925	2750	13000	1673	1000	3500	15000

3343 Guinea. Third laur. bust r., with elephant below, similar die axis ↑↓

| 1664 | 1750 | 5500 | 20000 | 1668 | | *Extremely rare* | |
| 1665 | 1750 | 5500 | 20000 | | | | |

	3344				3345	
	1679 Guinea - Fourth bust				1682 - Fourth bust - elephant below	
	F	VF	EF		F	VF	EF
	£	£	£		£	£	£

3344 Guinea. Fourth laur. bust r., rounded trun. similar die axis ↑↓

	F	VF	EF		F	VF	EF
1672	750	2600	9750	1679	700	2250	9250
1673	725	2500	9500	1679 ' O' over' o' on it's side and			
1674	750	2600	9750	R of FRA over A	775	2600	9750
1675	750	2500	9500	1680	700	2250	9250
1675 CRAOLVS error	3500	—	—	1680 8 over 7 and O over			
1676	700	2250	9250	inv. 9 or 6 in date	775	2750	10000
1676/4	725	2500	9500	1681	725	2500	9500
1677	700	2250	9250	1682	725	2500	9500
1677 GRATIR error	2750	—	—	1682 rev.@90° axis	775	2600	9750
1677 CAROLVS error	750	2750	10000	1683	700	2250	9250
1678	700	2250	9250	1684	725	2500	9500

3345 Guinea. Fourth laur. bust r., with elephant and castle below, similar die axis ↑↓

	F	VF	EF		F	VF	EF
1674		*Extremely rare*		1679	900	3750	13500
1675	900	3750	13500	1680	900	3750	13500
1676	850	3500	13000	1681	900	3750	13500
1677	850	3500	13000	1682	900	3750	13500
1677 GRATIR error	3250	—	—	1683	850	3500	13000
1678	850	3500	13000	1684	900	3750	13500

3346 Guinea. — — with elephant below bust, similar die axis ↑↓

1677/5		*Extremely rare*		1678	3250	11000	—

3347
1669 Half-Guinea, first bust

3347 Half-Guinea. First laur. bust r., pointed trun.℟. Crowned cruciform shields, sceptres in angles die axis ↑↓

	F	VF	EF		F	VF	EF
1669	525	1750	6000	1671	600	1850	6500
1670	500	1600	5750	1672	525	1750	6000

3348 - 1684 Half-Guinea, second bust

	F	VF	EF		F	VF	EF
	£	£	£		£	£	£

3348 Half-Guinea. Second laur. bust r., rounded trun. similar die axis ↑↓

1672	475	1500	4500	1678/7	500	1600	4750
1673	500	1600	4750	1679	475	1500	4500
1674	525	1650	5250	1680	475	1500	4500
1675	500	1600	4750	1681	500	1600	4750
1676	475	1500	4500	1682	475	1500	4500
1676/4	500	1600	4750	1683	475	1500	4500
1677	500	1600	4750	1684	475	1500	4500
1678	500	1600	4750				

3349 Half-Guinea. Second bust with elephant and castle below, similar die axis ↑↓

1676	700	2250	8250	1681	700	2250	8250
1677	675	2000	8000	1682	675	2000	8000
1678/7	675	2000	8000	1683		*Extremely rare*	
1680	700	2250	8250	1684	675	2000	8000

SILVER

3350 - 1662 Crown, first type, rose below bust

3350 Crown. First dr. bust r., rose below, numerous varieties in length and style of hair ties. R.
Crowned cruciform shields, interlinked C's in angles edge undated,
die axis ↑↓ 1662 .... 200 | 1250 | 10000

3350A Crown. — — Similar, die axis ↑↑ 1662 .... 275 | 1350 | —

3350B Crown. — striped cloak to drapery, 1662 similar die axis ↑↓ .... 300 | 1500 | —

3350C Crown. — — II of legend at 12 o'clock, similar die axis ↑↓ 1662 .. 2000 | — | —

3351 Crown. — — edge dated, similar die axis ↑↓ or ↑↑ 1662 .... 200 | 1250 | 10000

3352 Crown. — legend re-arranged no rose, edge dated, similar die
axis ↑↓ 1662 .... 250 | 1350 | 10500

3353 Crown. — — edge not dated, similar die axis ↑↓ 1662 .... 200 | 1100 | 9000

3354 Crown. — — shields altered, 1663, similar regnal year on edge in
Roman figures ANNO REGNI XV die axis ↑↓ .... 180 | 900 | 7500

1663 no stops on reverse .... 185 | 950 | 8000

1663 edge not dated, as 3350 .... *Extremely rare*

3354A

	F	VF	EF		F	VF	EF
	£	£	£		£	£	£

3354A Pattern 'Petition' Crown, 1663 by Thomas Simon. Laur. Bust r. of fine style in high relief, *Simon* below, edge inscription of Simon's 'petition': THOMAS SIMON. MOST. HVMBLY. PRAYS. YOVR MAJESTY etc., etc. 40000 135000 425000

3354B Pattern 'Reddite' Crown, 1663, by Thomas Simon, struck from the same dies, edge inscription: REDDITE. QVAE. CESARIS etc., etc. 30000 110000 375000

3355 Crown. Second dr. bust r. smaller than first bust and with curving tie to wreath. Regnal year on edge in Roman figures (e.g. 1664 = XVI), die axis ↑↓

1664 edge XVI........	180	950	6500	1665 XVII....................	1250	3750	—
1664 Proof *FDC*.........	—	—	52500	1666 XVIII....................	300	1250	7250
1665 XVI................	1500	—	—	1666 XVIII RE·X	325	1300	7500
1665/4 XVII	1350	4000	—	1667 XVIII..................	3750	—	—

3356 Crown. Second bust elephant below, similar, die axis ↑↓

1666 XVIII................	850	3000	18500	1666 XVIII RE·X	875	3000	—

3357
1668 Crown - second bust

3357 Crown. Second bust, similar, Regnal year on edge in words (e.g. 1667= DECIMO NONO) die axis ↑↓

1667 D. NONO	220	800	7000	1669 V· PRIMO.............	325	1350	—
1667 — AN.· REG.·..	220	800	7000	1669/8 V· PRIMO..........	375	1500	—
1668 VICESIMO	200	700	6500	1670 V. SECVNDO	200	700	6500
1668 — error edge				1670/69 V. SECVND......	250	800	7000
inverted......................	350	—	—	1671 V· TERTIO	200	700	6500
1668/7 VICESIMO	225	800	6750	1671 — T/R in ET	325	1000	—
1668/5 VICESIMO		*Extremely rare*		1671 — ET over FR	350	1200	—

3358
Third bust Crown

	F £	VF £	EF £		F £	VF £	EF £

3358 Crown. Third dr. bust r. much larger and broader than second bust, tie nearly straight. From end of tie to top of nose is 20mm. R.Similar die axis ↑↓

	F	VF	EF		F	VF	EF
1671 V. TERTIO.......	175	700	6000	1675 —	750	2750	—
1671 V. QVARTO.......	450	1500	—	1676 V. OCTAVO	175	700	6000
1672 V. QVARTO.....	175	700	6000	1676 OCCTAVO.............	200	750	6500
1673 V. QVARTO		*Extremely rare*		1677 V. NONO..............	175	700	6000
1673 V. QVINTO	175	700	6000	1677/6 V. NONO............	175	700	6000
1673 B/R in BR.........	250	875	—	1678/7 TRICESIMO......	225	900	7000
1673/2 V. QVINTO...	185	750	6250	1679 T. PRIMO..............	175	700	6000
1674 V. SEXTO..............		*Extremely rare*		1680/79 T. SECVNDO.......	220	800	6750
1675/3 V. SEPTIMO .	675	2250	—	1680 T. SECVNDO	200	750	6500

3359
Fourth bust Crown

3359 Crown. Fourth dr. bust r. still larger, with older features and more pointed nose. From end of tie to tip of nose is 21mm. R.Similar die axis ↑↓

	F	VF	EF		F	VF	EF
1679 T. PRIMO.........	200	700	6000	1682/1 T. QVARTO	200	700	6000
1679 HIBR·EX..........	375	1500	—	1682 T. QVARTO...........	225	800	6500
1680 T. SECVNDO...	200	700	6000	1682/1 QVRRTO error.....	225	800	6500
1680/79 T. SECVNDO .	250	850	6750	1683 T. QVINTO	325	1250	8500
1681 T. TERTIO........	200	700	6000	1684 T. SEXTO..............	250	850	6750

3360 Crown. — elephant and castle below bust, die axis ↑↓

	F	VF	EF
1681 T. TERTIO.......	5000	13500	—

3361 - First bust Halfcrown

3362 - Second bust Halfcrown

	F £	VF £	EF £		F £	VF £	EF £

3361 Halfcrown. First dr. bust r. R. Crowned cruciform shields, interlinked C's in angles, regnal year on edge in Roman figures die axis ↑↓

	F	VF	EF
1663 XV	200	900	4500
1663 XV V/S in CAROLVS	250	1000	4750
1663 XV A/T in GRATIA	275	1050	5000
1663 XV no stops on obverse	250	1000	4750
3362 Halfcrown. Second dr. bust r., similar die axis ↑↓ 1664 XVI	350	1250	6000
3363 Halfcrown. Third dr. bust r., similar die axis ↑↓ 1666/4 XVIII	950	3750	—

3364 - Third bust, elephant below Halfcrown

3364 Halfcrown. Third bust elephant below, die axis ↑↓ 1666 XVIII 900   3500   —

3365 - 1670 Halfcrown, third bust   MRG for MAG var

3365 Halfcrown. Third dr. bust r. regnal date on edge in words (eg. 1667=DECIMO NONO) ↑↓

1667/4 D. NONO	4000	—	—	1670 V. SECVNDO	150	575	3750
1668/4 VICESIMO	375	1350	—	1670 – MRG for MAG	300	1000	—
1669/4 V. PRIMO	250	1000	—	1670 V/S CAROLVS	250	900	—
1669 V. PRIMO	375	1350	—	1670 E/R in ET	250	925	—
1669 – R/I in PRIMO	400	1450	—			

3366
1671 Halfcrown third bust variety

	F	VF	EF		F	VF	EF
	£	£	£		£	£	£

3366 Halfcrown. Third bust variety r. R. Similar die axis ↑↓

	F	VF	EF		F	VF	EF
1671 V. TERTIO	150	575	3750	1672 V. TERTIO	*Extremely rare*		
1671 A/R in MAG	250	900	—	1672 V. QVARTO	160	575	3750
1671/0 V. TERTIO	165	650	4000				

3367
Fourth bust Halfcrown

3367 Halfcrown. Fourth dr. bust r. R. Similar die axis ↑↓

	F	VF	EF		F	VF	EF
1672 V. QVARTO	160	550	3500	1678 TRICESIMO	225	900	5000
1673 V. QVINTO	160	550	3500	1679 T. PRIMO	150	525	3250
1673 —A/R in FRA	185	700	—	1679 — DECNS error	185	700	—
1673 — B/R in BR	185	700	—	1679 — DNCVS error	175	650	—
1673 — FR/M in FRA	185	700	—	1679 — PRICESIMO	160	550	3500
1674 V. SEXTO	160	575	3750	1680 T. SECVNDO	160	550	3500
1674/3 V. SEXTO	200	750	—	1680 T. SECVNCIO error	175	600	3750
1675 V. SEPTIMO	160	550	3500	1681 T. TERTIO	200	750	4500
1675 — Retrograde 1	165	575	3750	1681/0 —	250	900	—
1676 V. OCTAVO	150	525	3250	1682 T. QVARTO	160	575	3750
1676 R/T in BR	200	800	—	1682/79 T. QVARTO	200	800	—
1676 — Retrograde 1	160	550	3500	1683 T. QVINTO	150	525	3250
1676 F/H in FRA	185	700	—	1684/3 T. SEXTO	250	950	—
1677 V. NONO	150	525	3250				
1677 F/H in FRA	200	800	—				

3369 - Plume in centre

	F £	VF £	EF £		F £	VF £	EF £
3368 Halfcrown. Fourth bust plume below, R. Similar die axis ↑↓							
1673 V. QVINTO	6500	18500	—	1683 T. QVINTO	7500	22500	—
3369 Halfcrown. — plume below bust and in centre of *rev.*, die axis ↑↓							
1673 V. QVINTO					8500	24000	—

3370 - Elephant and Castle below bust

3370 Halfcrown. — elephant and castle below bust, die axis ↑↓

	F	VF	EF
1681 T. TERTIO	4000	12500	32500

SHILLINGS

First bust   First bust variety   Second bust   Third bust

First bust   First bust variety   First and first bust   Second bust
                                          variety, double top leaf   single top leaf

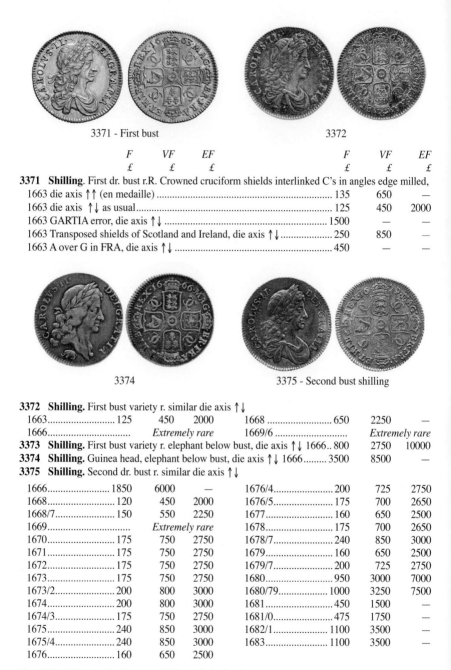

3371 - First bust   3372

	F	VF	EF		F	VF	EF
	£	£	£		£	£	£

3371 Shilling. First dr. bust r.R. Crowned cruciform shields interlinked C's in angles edge milled,

1663 die axis ↑↑ (en medaille) 135   650   —

1663 die axis ↑↓ as usual.. 125   450   2000

1663 GARTIA error, die axis ↑↓ 1500   —   —

1663 Transposed shields of Scotland and Ireland, die axis ↑↓ 250   850   —

1663 A over G in FRA, die axis ↑↓ 450   —   —

3374   3375 - Second bust shilling

3372 Shilling. First bust variety r. similar die axis ↑↓

1663	125	450	2000	1668	650	2250	—
1666		*Extremely rare*		1669/6		*Extremely rare*	

3373 Shilling. First bust variety r. elephant below bust, die axis ↑↓ 1666.. 800   2750   10000

3374 Shilling. Guinea head, elephant below bust, die axis ↑↓ 1666......... 3500   8500   —

3375 Shilling. Second dr. bust r. similar die axis ↑↓

1666	1850	6000	—	1676/4	200	725	2750
1668	120	450	2000	1676/5	175	700	2650
1668/7	150	550	2250	1677	160	650	2500
1669		*Extremely rare*		1678	175	700	2650
1670	175	750	2750	1678/7	240	850	3000
1671	175	750	2750	1679	160	650	2500
1672	175	750	2750	1679/7	200	725	2750
1673	175	750	2750	1680	950	3000	7000
1673/2	200	800	3000	1680/79	1000	3250	7500
1674	200	800	3000	1681	450	1500	—
1674/3	175	750	2750	1681/0	475	1750	—
1675	240	850	3000	1682/1	1100	3500	—
1675/4	240	850	3000	1683	1100	3500	—
1676	160	650	2500				

The 1668 shilling is also known with large 6's in the date

3376 - Plume both sides shilling of 1671

	F £	VF £	EF £		F £	VF £	EF £

3376 Shilling. Second Bust — plume below bust and in centre of *rev.* similar die axis ↑↓

1671	500	1750	4500	1676	550	1850	5000
1673	550	1850	5000	1679	525	1800	4750
1674	500	1750	4500	1680/79	1350	3750	9000
1675	550	1850	5000				

3378
1679 Shilling - plume on obverse only

3377 Shilling. — Plume *rev.* only, similar die axis ↑↓ 1674 1250   3500   8500
3378 Shilling. — Plume *obv.* only similar die axis ↑↓

| 1677 | 1250 | 3500 | 8500 | 1679 | 1100 | 3250 | 8000 |

3379 Shilling. — elephant and castle below bust, die axis ↑↓ 1681/0 3750   11500   —

3380   3381
Third bust Shilling   1684 Shilling - fourth bust

3380 Shilling. Third dr. (large) bust r. similar die axis ↑↓

| 1674 | 575 | 2000 | 6000 | 1675/3 | 425 | 1500 | 4250 |

3381 Shilling. Fourth dr. (large) bust r., older features, similar die axis ↑↓

| 1683 | 225 | 800 | 2750 | 1684 | 225 | 800 | 2750 |

3382
1677 Sixpence

	F	VF	EF		F	VF	EF
	£	£	£		£	£	£

3382 Sixpence. Dr. bust r. R. Crowned cruciform shields, interlinked C's in angles die axis ↑↓

	F	VF	EF		F	VF	EF
1674	75	250	750	1679	85	300	850
1675	80	275	800	1680	85	300	850
1675/4	80	275	800	1681	75	250	750
1676	90	300	900	1682	95	325	900
1676/5	90	300	900	1682/1	90	300	850
1677	75	250	750	1683	75	250	750
1678/7	80	275	800	1684	80	275	800

3383
Undated Fourpence

3384 -
1678 Fourpence

3383 Fourpence. Undated. Crowned dr. bust l. to edge of coin, value
behind. R. Shield, die axis ↑↓ 20 50 120

3384 Fourpence. Dated. Dr. bust r. R. Crowned four interlinked Cs quartered emblems die axis ↑↓

	F	VF	EF		F	VF	EF
1670	20	45	125	1678	18	45	120
1671	18	40	110	1678/6	18	40	100
1672/1	22	48	125	1678/7	18	40	100
1673	18	40	100	1679	10	20	70
1674	18	40	100	1680	12	22	80
1674/4 sideways	20	40	150	1681	15	40	95
1674 7 over 6	18	40	100	1681 B/R in HIB	18	38	150
1675	18	40	100	1681/0	15	32	115
1675/4	18	45	120	1682	18	40	110
1676	18	40	100	1682/1	18	40	115
1676 7 over 6	18	45	135	1683	18	40	110
1676/5	18	45	120	1684	20	40	120
1677	15	32	95	1684/3	20	40	110

3386 - 1678 Threepence

	F £	VF £	EF £		F £	VF £	EF £
3385 Threepence. Undated. As 3383, die axis ↑↓					14	35	110
3386 Threepence. Dated. Dr. bust r. R. Crowned three interlinked C's, die axis ↑↓							
1670	12	25	90	1678	12	25	100
1671	10	22	80	1678 on 4d flan	12	25	125
1671 GRⱯTIA	18	38	150	1679	10	20	60
1671 GRATIA	12	28	100	1679 O/A in CAROLVS	15	38	150
1672/1	10	22	90	1680	12	25	85
1673	10	22	80	1681	14	22	90
1674	12	25	90	1681/0	12	30	100
1675	15	30	95	1682	15	30	105
1676	10	22	85	1682/1	15	32	95
1676/5	12	28	100	1683	15	30	105
1676 ERA for FRA	12	38	175	1684	15	30	105
1677	15	30	100	1684/3	15	32	95

3388 - 1678 Twopence

	F £	VF £	EF £		F £	VF £	EF £
3387 Twopence. Undated. As 3383 (double arch crown) die axis ↑↓					12	30	90
3388 Twopence. Dated. Dr. bust r. R. Crowned pair of linked C's, die axis ↑↓							
1668 die axis ↑↑	15	30	100	1678/6	13	28	100
1670	10	22	75	1679	10	20	65
1671	10	20	65	1679 HIB over FRA	13	38	150
1672/1	10	20	65	1680	10	20	70
1672/1 GRATIA	13	38	165	1680/79	13	28	85
1673	12	25	80	1681	10	20	70
1674	10	20	65	1682/1	13	28	80
1675	12	25	80	1682/1 ERA for FRA	13	38	150
1676	10	20	75	1683	10	22	70
1677	12	25	75	1683/2	13	28	70
1678	15	35	95	1684	13	28	75

COINS OF BRITAIN
PO BOX 2, MONMOUTH, NP25 3YR, UK

BNTA

E-mail: lloydbennett@coinsofbritain.com   +44(0)7714 284 939

3390 - 1678 Penny

	F £	VF £	EF £		F £	VF £	EF £
3389 Penny. Undated. As 3383 (double arch crown) die axis ↑↓ 12		35	110				
3390 Penny. Dated. Dr. bust r. R. Crowned C die axis ↑↓							
1670........................... 12		30	105	1678 24		55	145
1671........................... 12		30	105	1678 RATIA error ... 12		50	185
1672/1....................... 12		30	105	1679 24		55	145
1673........................... 12		30	105	1680 12		30	105
1674........................... 14		35	120	1680 on 2d flan		*Extremely rare*	
1674 ƆRATIA error... 18		40	175	1681 22		65	170
1675........................... 12		30	105	1682 22		50	140
1675 ƆRATIA error... 18		40	175	1682/1 18		40	145
1676........................... 22		50	145	1682 ERA for FRA 18		40	150
1676 ƆRATIA error... 15		40	175	1683/1 13		35	110
1677........................... 12		30	105	1684 24		50	145
1677 ƆRATIA error... 15		40	175	1684/3 24		50	150
3391 Maundy Set. Undated. The four coins... 100		225	575				
3392 Maundy Set. Dated. The four denominations. Uniform dates							
1670........................... 100		275	650	1678 115		300	800
1671........................... 90		200	550	1679 90		225	650
1672........................... 95		250	600	1680 85		200	600
1673........................... 80		200	550	1681 100		300	650
1674........................... 90		210	600	1682 90		250	725
1675........................... 90		225	600	1683 80		200	750
1676........................... 100		250	700	1684 100		275	775
1677........................... 90		225	675				

TimeLine Auctions
Inc. Gregory's **Est.1858**

www.timelineauctions.com

+44 [0]1277 815121; enquiries@timelineauctions.com

COPPER AND TIN

3393 - 1675 Halfpenny

	F	VF	EF		F	VF	EF
	£	£	£		£	£	£

3393 Copper **Halfpenny** Cuir. bust l. R. Britannia seated l. date in ex., die axis ↑↓

	F	VF	EF		F	VF	EF
1672.............................60	350	1400		1673 no rev. stop........90	500	—
1672 CRAOLVS error....	*Extremely rare*			1675 60	350	1400
1673.............................50	330	1200		1675 no stops on obv. 90	500	—
1673 CRAOLVS error .225	—	—		1675/3 165	600	—
1673 no stops on obv......	*Extremely rare*					

3394 - 1672 Farthing

3394 Copper **Farthing.** Cuir. bust l. R. Britannia sealed l. date in ex., die axis ↑↓

	F	VF	EF		F	VF	EF
1672.............................45	265	825		1673 no stops on obv.165	—	—
1672 Rev.				1673 no rev. stop 165	—	—
loose drapery 65	325	1000		1674............................55	300	900
1672 no stops on obv.. 65	325	1000		1674 'O' for 'C' in		
1672 RO/OL on obv. .. 90	450	—		CAROLVS...... 100	500	—
1672 die axis ↑↑.........65	325	1000		1675............................50	275	825
1673............................50	275	825		1675 no stop after		
1673 CAROLA error 150	550	—		CAROLVS........ 165	—	—
1673 O/sideways O 75	325	1100		1679............................55	300	900
1673 BRITINNIA error225	—	—		1679 no rev. stop 65	325	1100

3395 - Tin Farthing

Prices for tin coinage based on corrosion free examples, and in the top grades with some lustre

3395 Tin **Farthing.** Somewhat similar, but with copper plug, edge inscribed NUMMORVM FAMVLVS, and date on edge only die axis ↑↓

1684 various varieties of edge 55	250	900	3600
1685		*Extremely rare*	

JAMES II, 1685-88

James II, brother of Charles II, was born on 14th October 1633, he married Anne Hyde with whom he produced 8 children. He lost control of his subjects when the loyalist Tories moved against him over his many Catholic appointments. Parliament invited his protestant daughter Mary with husband William of Orange to be joint rulers. James II abdicated and died in exile in France.

During this reign the dies continued to be engraved by John Roettier (1631-1700), the only major difference in the silver coinage being the ommission of the interlinked C's in the angles of the shields on the reverses. The only provenance marked silver coin of this reign is the extremely rare plume on reverse 1685 Shilling. The elephant and castle provenance mark continues to appear on some of the gold coins of this reign. Tin halfpence and farthings provided the only base metal coinage during this short reign. All genuine tin coins of this period have a copper plug.

GOLD

	F	VF	EF		F	VF	EF
	£	£	£		£	£	£

3396 Five Guineas. First laur. bust l., R. Crowned cruciform shields sceptres misplaced in angles smaller crowns date on edge in words (e.g. 1686 = SECVNDO)
die axis ↑↓ 1686 SECVNDO 4750   14500   60000

3397 Five Guineas. First laur bust l. R. similar bust sceptres normal. die axis ↑↓
1687 TERTIO 4250   13500   55000   1688 QVARTO....... 4250   13500   55000

3397A
1687 Five Guineas, second bust

3397A Five Guineas. Second laur. bust l. R. similar die axis ↑↓
1687 TERTIO 4000   12500   50000   1688 QVARTO....... 4000   12500   50000

3398
1687 Five Guineas, first bust, elephant and castle below

3398 Five Guineas. First laur. bust l. Elephant and castle below R. Similar die axis ↑↓
1687 TERTIO 4250   13500   55000   1688 QVARTO....... 4250   13500   55000

3399 - Two Guineas

	F	VF	EF		F	VF	EF
	£	£	£		£	£	£

3399 Two Guineas. Laur. bust l. R. Crowned cruciform shields, sceptres in angles, edge milled, die axis ↑↓

1687 2500	7000	24000	1688/7 2750	7500	25000

3400 Guinea. First laur. bust l. R. Crowned cruciform shields, sceptres in angles, edge milled, die axis ↑↓

1685 800	2750	11000	1686 B/I in HIB 850	2850	11500
1686 800	2750	11000	1686/5 second 6 over S 875	3000	12000

3401 Guinea. First bust elephant and castle below R. similar die axis ↑↓

1685 900	3750	13500	1686 1500	—	—

3402   3403

1688 Guinea, second bust

3402 Guinea. Second laur. bust l. R. similar die axis ↑↓

1686 750	2500	9750	1687/6 800	2750	10000
1687 750	2500	9750	1688 750	2500	9750

3404

3403 Guinea. Second bust elephant and castle below R. similar die axis ↑↓

1686 900	3500	12500	1688 875	3250	12000
1687 900	3500	12500			

3404 Half-Guinea. Laur. bust l. R. Crowned cruciform shields sceptres in angles, edge milled die axis ↑↓

1686 525	1750	5000	1687 525	1750	5500
1686 OBV/BVS 550	1800	6000	1688 525	1750	5500

3405 Half-Guinea. Laur bust with elephant and castle below, R. similar die axis ↑↓

1686 850	3000	9000			

SILVER

3406
1686 Crown, first bust

	F	VF	EF		F	VF	EF
	£	£	£		£	£	£

3406 Crown. First dr. bust, l. regnal year on edge in words (e.g. 1686 = SECVNDO) die axis ↑↓

1686 SECVNDO	300	1250	6500
1686 — No stops on obverse	325	1350	7000

3407
1687 Crown, second bust

3407 Crown. Second dr. bust l. narrower than first bust. R. Crowned cruciform shields edge inscribed in raised letters

die axis ↑↓

1687 TERTIO	250	750	5250	1688/7 QVARTO	300	900	6000
1688 QVARTO	275	800	5500				

ARTHUR BRYANT COINS

Dealers in British coins and medals

www.bryantcoins.com
abcoins@live.co.uk
07768 645 686

| 3408 | | | 1st bust | 2nd bust |
| 1686 Halfcrown, first bust | | | Halfcrown hair ties | |

3408 Halfcrown. First laur and dr. bust, l. regnal year on edge in words (e.g. 1685 = PRIMO) die axis ↑↓

	F £	VF £	EF £		F £	VF £	EF £
1685 PRIMO	200	700	5000	1686 TERTIO	225	725	4750
1686 SECVNDO	185	675	4500	1687 TERTIO	200	700	4500
1686/5 —	240	775	5000	1687/6 —	250	825	5000
1686 TERTIO V over S or B in JACOBVS	240	775	4250	1687 — 6 over 8	300	975	—
				1687 A/R in GRATIA	250	825	5000

3409 Halfcrown. Second laur and dr. bust l. R. Crowned cruciform shields edge inscribed in raised letters die axis ↑↓

1687 TERTIO	225	775	5000	1688 QVARTO	225	775	5000

3410
1687 Shilling

3410 Shilling. Laur and Dr. bust l. R. Crowned cruciform shields die axis ↑↓

1685	240	675	2750	1687	260	750	3100
1685 no stops on rev.	250	725	3000	1687 G/A in MAG	275	800	3250
1686	240	700	2850	1687/6	240	700	2850
1686/5	275	800	3250	1687/6 G/A in MAG	250	725	3000
1686 V/S in JACOBVS	260	750	3100	1688	275	800	3250
1686 G/A in MAG	260	750	3100	1688/7	260	750	3100

3411 Shilling. Similar, plume in centre of *rev.*, die axis ↑↓ 1685 .... 9500 20000 —

3412
1686 Sixpence, early shileds, indented tops

3412 Sixpence. Laur and dr. bust l. R. Early type crowned cruciform shields die axis ↑↓

1686	150	450	1350	1687/6	175	500	1500
1687	175	525	1600				

3413
1687 Sixpence, later shields

	F £	VF £	EF £		F £	VF £	EF £
3413 Sixpence. Similar R. Late type shields die axis ↑↓							
1687	150	450	1400	1687 Later/early shields	175	525	1600
1687/6	200	550	1650	1688	150	450	1400

3414	3415	3416	3417
Fourpence	Threepence	Twopence	Penny

	F £	VF £	EF £		F £	VF £	EF £
3414 Fourpence. Laur. head l. R. IIII Crowned die axis ↑↓							
1686	15	30	100	1688	22	45	145
1686 Date over crown	18	30	110	1688 1 over 8	25	55	150
1687/6	15	25	100	1688/7	22	45	140
1687 8 over 7	18	30	110				
3415 Threepence. Laur. head l. R. III Crowned die axis-↑↓							
1685	12	30	95	1687	12	32	100
1685 Groat flan	35	80	165	1687/6	12	32	100
1686	12	35	100	1688	22	55	145
1686 4d obv. die	18	40	120	1688/7	25	55	140
3416 Twopence. Laur. head l. R. II Crowned die axis ↑↓							
1686	15	35	90	1687 ERA for FRA	25	45	150
1686 IΛCOBVS	18	35	115	1688	18	40	130
1687	12	32	85	1688/7	18	40	120
3417 Penny. Laur. head l. R. I Crowned die axis ↑↓							
1685	15	30	100	1687/8	25	50	130
1686	20	40	110	1688	25	55	140
1687	20	40	110	1688/7	25	55	130
1687/6	20	40	110				
3418 Maundy Set. As last four. Uniform dates							
1686	100	300	575	1688	175	350	750
1687	100	300	575				

TIN

3419 Tin Halfpenny

	Fair £	F £	VF £	EF £

Prices for tin coinage based on corrosion free examples, and in the top grades with some lustre

3419 Halfpenny. Laur. and dr. bust r. R. Britannia seated l. date on edge die axis ↑↓

	Fair	F	VF	EF
1685 various varieties of edge	100	250	775	3850
1686	110	275	825	4200
1687	90	300	775	3850

3420
Cuirassed bust Tin Farthing

3420 Farthing. Laur. and Cuir. bust r. R. Britannia seated l. date on edge die axis ↑↓

	Fair	F	VF	EF
1684			*Extremely rare*	
1685 various varieties of edge	65	195	700	3000
1686 two varieties of edge	80	225	775	3250
1687			*Extremely rare*	

3421 Farthing. Dr. bust r.; date on edge, 1687 various varieties of edge ↑↓

	Fair	F	VF	EF
	100	250	875	3750

timeline
Auctions
Inc. Gregory's **Est.1858**

We are accepting single entries and collections
of antiquities & milled coins

Sold for:
£5,082

www.timelineauctions.com

Mary Stuart was born on 30 April 1662, and married William of Orange as part of Charles II's foreign policy. She eventually became William's loyal servant but bore him no children. The Bill and the Claim of Rights were both passed in 1689 and curbed the Royal and Prerogative rights of Monarchs. Mary died from smallpox on 28 December 1694.

Due to the poor state of the silver coinage, much of it worn hammered coin, the Guinea, which was valued at 21s. 6d. at the beginning of the reign, circulated for as much as 30s. by 1694. The elephant and elephant and castle provenance marks continue on some gold coin. The tin Halfpennies and Farthings were replaced by copper coins in 1694. The rampant Lion of Nassau is now placed as an inescutcheon on the centre of the royal arms. The WM monogram appears in the angles of the silver coins of this reign.

Engravers and designers: George Bower (d.1689), Henry Harris (d.1704), John Roettier (1631-1700), James Roettier (1663-1698), Norbert Roettier (b.1665)

GOLD

3422
Five Guineas

	F £	VF £	EF £		F £	VF £	EF £
3422 Five Guineas. Conjoined busts r. regnal year on edge in words (e.g. 1691 = TERTIO) ↑↓						
1691 TERTIO	3500	11000	45000	1693 QVINTO	3500	11000	45000
1692 QVARTO	3500	11000	45000	1694/2 SEXTO	3750	11500	47500
1692 QVINTO	4000	13000	52500	1694 SEXTO	3500	11000	45000

3423
Elephant and castle below busts

3423 Five Guineas. Conjoined busts, elephant and castle below, R. Crowned shield of arms die axis ↑↓

1691 TERTIO	3500	11000	45000	1694/2 SEXTO	4000	12000	50000
1692 QVARTO	3500	11000	45000	1694 SEXTO	3750	11500	47500
1693 QVINTO	3750	11500	47500				

3424
1694 Two Guineas

	F	VF	EF		F	VF	EF
	£	£	£		£	£	£

3424 Two Guineas. Conjoined busts r. R. Crowned shield of arms, Lion of Nassau at centre die axis ↑↓

1693 1750	5250	18500	1694/3 1650	5000	17500

3425 Two Guineas. Conjoined busts, elephant and castle below, R. similar die axis ↑↓

1691	*Extremely rare*		1694/3 1750	5250	18500
1693 2000	6500	22500			

3426   3427
1689 Guinea   1689 Elephant and castle below busts

3426 Guinea. Conjoined busts r. R. Crowned shield of arms Lion of Nassau at centre die axis ↑↓

1689 Early slanting harp			1690 D of		
with base of harp in line			DEI over G 850	2850	10500
with X of REX 750	2500	9500	1690 GVLIFLMVS.. 850	2850	10500
1689 Later upright harp			1691 800	2750	10000
with base of harp in line			1692 800	2750	10000
with R of REX.......... 750	2500	9500	1693 800	2750	10000
1689 MVS over EL . 800	2650	9750	1694......................... 800	2750	10000
1690 800	2750	10000	1694/3...................... 800	2750	10000
1690 FT for ET exists . 850	2850	10500			

3427 Guinea. Conjoined busts elephant and castle below R. Similar die axis ↑↓

1689 775	2500	9750	1692 850	2850	10500
1689 G of REGINA			1693 950	3250	11500
over E 800	2750	10000	1694 850	2850	10500
1690 950	3250	11500	1694/3....................... 875	3000	11000
1691 850	2850	10500			

3428 Guinea. Conjoined busts elephant only below, R. Similar die axis ↑↓

1692 950	3000	11000	1693 1000	3250	11500

3429
1689 Half-Guniea, first busts, first shield

3430
1690 Half-Guinea, second busts, second shield

	F £	VF £	EF £		F £	VF £	EF £
3429 Half-Guinea. First busts r. R. First Crowned shield of arms die axis ↑↓							
1689	625	1850	5750				
3430 Half-Guinea. Second busts r. R. Second Crowned shield of arms die axis ↑↓							
1690	600	1750	5250	1693	675	2100	6250
1691	600	1750	5250	1693/2	650	2000	6000
1692	625	1850	5750	1694	600	1750	5250
3431 Half-Guinea. Second busts elephant and castle below, R. Second shield of arms die axis ↑↓							
1691	650	2000	6000	1692	650	2000	6000
3432 Half-Guinea. Second busts elephant only below, R. Second shield of arms die axis ↑↓							
1692..........................	750	2250	6500				

SILVER

3433
Crown

3433 Crown. Conjoined busts r. regnal year on edge in words (e.g. 1691 = TERTIO) die axis ↑↓							
1691 TERTIO...........	575	1850	7500	1692 QVARTO..........	575	1850	7500
1691 I/E in legend	650	2000	7750	1692/ᘕ QVARTO	600	2000	7750
1691 TERTTIO	650	2000	8000	1692/ᘕ QVINTO.......	575	1850	7500

AMR Coins
Dealers in Quality British Coins

BNTA

British Coins Bought and Sold

www.amrcoins.com

email: info@amrcoins.com
tel: +44 (0)7527 569308

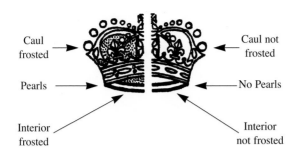

Caul frosted → ← Caul not frosted

Pearls → ← No Pearls

Interior frosted ← Interior not frosted

3434
1689 Halfcrown - first reverse

3435
1689 Halfcrown - second reverse

	F £	VF £	EF £		F £	VF £	EF £

3434 Halfcrown. First busts, r. R. First crowned shield, 1689 PRIMO Ꝛ. Crown with caul and interior frosted, with pearls edge inscribed die axis ↑↓ 130 350 2750
1689 — 2nd L/M in GVLIELMVS 135 375 3000
1689 — 1st V/A in GVLIELMVS, only caul frosted 135 375 3000
1689 — — interior also frosted, no pearls 135 375 3000
1689 Caul only frosted, pearls 130 350 2750
1689 — no pearls 135 375 3000
1689 No frosting, pearls 130 350 2750
1689 No stops on obverse 200 575 3500
1689 FRA for FR 175 525 3250

3435 Halfcrown. First busts r. R. Second crowned shield die axis ↑↓
1689 PRIMO Ꝛ. Caul 120 350 2750 and interior frosted with pearls
1689 — — no pearls 130 375 3000
1689 Caul only frosted pearls 120 350 2750
1689 interior frosted, no pearls 130 375 3000
1689 Caul only frosted, no pearls 130 375 3000
1689 no frosting, pearls 120 350 2750
1689 no frosting, no pearls 120 350 2750
1690 SECVNDO — 175 525 3250
1690 — GRETIA error with second V of GVLIELMVS struck over S 300 800 3750
1690 TERTIO 185 525 3250

3436

Halfcrown, second busts, third reverse

	F	VF	EF		F	VF	EF
	£	£	£		£	£	£

3436 Halfcrown. Second busts r. ℞. Crowned cruciform shields, WM monogram in angles
die axis ↑↓

1691 TERTIO	150	525	3250	1692 QVINTO	275	750	3500
1692 QVARTO	150	525	3250	1693 QVINTO	150	475	2850
1692 R/G in REGINA also				1693 3/inverted 3	160	525	3000
showing H/B in HI	175	550	3400	1693 inverted 3	325	900	4000

3437 - Shilling   3438 - Sixpence

3437 Shilling. Conjoined busts r. ℞. Crowned cruciform shields, WM monogram in angles die axis ↑↓

1692	200	600	2750	1693 9/0	225	650	2850
1692 inverted 1	225	650	2850	1693	200	600	2750
1692 RE/ET on R	225	650	2850				
1692 A of GRATIA							
over T and T over I	250	725	3000				

3438 Sixpence. Conjoined busts r. R. Crowned cruciform shields, WM monogram in angles die axis ↑↓

1693	135	425	1250	1694	145	475	1400
1693 inverted 3	225	575	1650				

3439 - Groat, first busts

3439 Fourpence. First busts, r. no tie to wreath. R. Crowned 4 die axis ↑↓

1689 GV below bust	15	30	80	1690	20	50	110
1689 G below bust	15	30	80	1690 6 over 5	20	55	120
1689 stop befor G	15	30	80	1691	20	45	130
1689 berries in wreath	15	30	80	1691/0	20	40	120
1689 GVLEELMVS	65	200	–	1694	20	60	160
1689 I over first E in GVLEELMVS							
corrected die for above	65	200	–				

3440
Groat, Second busts

	F £	VF £	EF £		F £	VF £	EF £
3440 Fourpence. Second busts r. tie to wreath. R. Crowned 4 die axis ↑↓							
1692 30		90	180	1693/2 35	100	280	
1692/1........................... 25		65	165	1694 30	95	200	
1692 MAR•IA..................		*Extremely rare*		1694 small lettering 30	95	200	
1693 35		100	280				
3441 Threepence. First busts, r. no tie to wreath. R. Crowned 3 die axis ↑↓							
1689 15		30	75	1690 6 over 5 20	50	105	
1689 No stops on rev.... 20		40	110	1690 Large lettering..... 20	50	105	
1689 LMV over MVS .. 20		40	110	1690 9 over 6 20	50	105	
1689 Hyphen stops on rev. 20		40	100	1691 100	220	450	
1690 20		50	105				
3442 Threepence. Second busts, r. tie to wreath R. Crowned 3 die axis ↑↓							
1691 40		130	220	1693 GV below bust 20	55	140	
1692 G below bust........ 25		65	140	1694 G below bust....... 20	55	140	
1692 GV below bust..... 25		65	140	1694 — MARIΛ error . 24	60	170	
1692 GVL below bust... 25		65	140	1694 GV below bust 20	55	140	
1693 G below bust........ 20		55	140	1694 GVL below bust.. 20	55	140	
1693/2 G below bust 20		55	140				
3443 Twopence. Conjoined busts r. R. Crowned 2 die axis ↑↓							
1689 18		40	90	1694/3 18	45	120	
1691 18		45	110	1694/3 no stop after DG 18	45	120	
1692 20		45	120	1694 MARLA error 35	65	275	
1693 15		42	115	1694 HI for HIB........... 20	45	120	
1693/2........................... 18		42	115	1694 GVLI below bust.. 20	45	120	
1693 GV below bust 18		42	115	1694 GVL below bust.. 20	45	120	
1694 20		45	120				

3444 - Penny   3445 - Legend intruded

	F £	VF £	EF £		F £	VF £	EF £
3444 Penny. Legend continuous over busts, R. Crowned 1 die axis ↑↓							
1689 225		425	800	1689 MARIΛ 250	450	850	
1689 GVIELMVS error 250		525	1000				
3445 Penny. Legend broken by busts, R. Crowned 1 die axis ↑↓							
1690 28		55	125	1694 date spread 22	50	120	
1691/0........................... 35		60	135	1694 no stops on obv.... 22	55	120	
1692 45		85	200	1694 HI for HIB........... 28	60	190	
1692/1........................... 35		80	180	1694 — 9/6 25	55	135	
1693 35		60	130				

3446 - Maundy Set

	F £	VF £	EF £		F £	VF £	EF £

3446 Maundy Set. The four denominations. Uniform dates

1689	375	750	1500	1693	180	475	1100
1691	175	425	1000	1694	145	375	950
1692	160	400	975				

TIN AND COPPER

3447
Tin Halfpenny first busts

	Fair £	F £	VF £	EF £

Prices for tin coinage based on corrosion free examples, and in the top grades with some lustre

3447 Tin **Halfpenny.** Small dr. busts r.; date on edge ↑↓ 1689 925   1800   —   —

— — — obv. with star stops 1689 ....   *Extremely rare*

3448
Tin Halfpenny cuirassed busts

3448 Tin **Halfpenny.** — Large cuir. busts r.; R. Britannia seated L. date only on edge, die axis ↑↓

1690 various edge varieties 80   190   800   3250

3449 Tin **Halfpenny.** Similar date in ex. and on edge die axis ↑↓

1691 various edge varieties 70   175   700   2750

1691 in ex. 1692 on edge..   *Extremely rare*

1692 70   175   700   2750

3450 Tin **Farthing.** Small dr. busts r. R. Britannia seated l. die axis ↑↓

1689 275   700   2250   —

1689, in ex. 1690 on edge..   *Extremely rare*

3451
Tin Farthing

	Fair	F £	VF £	EF £

3451 Tin **Farthing.** Large cuir. busts r. R. Britannia seated l.die axis ↑↓

1690, in ex. 1689 on edge			*Extremely rare*	
1690 various edge varieties	55	175	700	3000
1691 various edge varieties	55	175	700	3000
1692	70	190	750	3000

3452
1694 Halfpenny

3452 Copper **Halfpenny,** Conjoined busts r. R. Britannia die axis ↑↓

1694	75	275	1150
1694 GVLIEMVS error	200	600	–
1694 MVRIA error	225	650	–
1694 MΛRIΛ error	150	525	–
1694 BRITΛNNI/Λ	175	550	–
1694 no rev. stop	150	525	–
1694 GVLEELMVS	250	625	–

3453
1694 Farthing

3453 Copper **Farthing,** Conjoined busts r. R. Britannia die axis ↑↓

1694	65	275	1000
1694 MΛRIΛ error	175	500	–
1694 no stop after MΛRIΛ	100	415	–
1694 — BRITΛNNIΛ	125	415	–
1694 no stop on rev.	100	350	–
1694 no stop on obv.	100	350	–
1694 GVLIELMS, BRITΛNNIΛ errors	225	525	–
1694 BRITΛNNIΛ	150	475	–
1694 Broad heavier flan 25.5mm	200	500	–

William of Orange was born on 4th November 1650. He married Mary Stuart under Charles II's foreign policy and was invited to England by Parliament, where he proceeded to supress the Jacobites. The Bank of England was founded during this reign, and William ruled alone and without issue after Mary's death until his own demise on 8th March 1702 following a serious fall from his horse.

In 1696 a great re-coinage was undertaken to replace the hammered silver that made up most of the coinage in circulation, much of it being clipped and badly worn. Branch mints were set up at Bristol, Chester, Exeter, Norwich and York to help with the re-coinage. For a short time before they were finally demonetized, unclipped hammered coins were allowed to circulate freely provided they were officially pierced in the centre. Silver coins with roses between the coats of arms were made from silver obtained from the West of England mines. The elephant and castle provenance mark continues on some guineas and half-guineas.

Engravers and designers: Samuel Bull (d.c.1720), John Croker (1670-1740), Henry Harris (d.1704), John Roettier (1663-1698).

GOLD

3454
1699 Five Guineas, first bust

	F	VF	EF			F	VF	EF
	£	£	£			£	£	£

3454　Five Guineas. First laur. bust r. regnal year on edge in words (e.g. 1699 = UNDECIMO) ↑↓

1699 UNDECIMO .. 4000　　12000　　50000　　　1700 DVODECIMO ...... 4000　12000　50000

3455
Elephant and castle below first bust

3455　Five Guineas. First bust elephant and castle below, 1699 UNDECIMO ...... 4750　14500　60000

3456
1701 Five Guineas 'Fine Work'

	F	VF	EF		F	VF	EF
	£	£	£		£	£	£

3456 Five Guineas. Second laur. bust r. ('fine work'), R. Crowned cruciform shields Plain or ornamental
sceptres DECIMO TERTIO die axis ↑↓ 1701*......................................3750 11500 47500

3457
'Fine work' Two Guineas

3457 Two Guineas. ('fine work'), Laur. bust r. similar die axis ↑↓ 1701 ....2000 5250 17500

3458
1695 Guinea, first bust

3458 Guinea. First laur. bust r. R. Crowned cruciform shields, sceptres in angles die axis ↑↓
1695 large and small   1696 ....700 3000 9250
lis in French arms.....675 2750 8250   1697 ....700 3000 9250

3459 Guinea. First bust elephant and castle below R. Similar die axis ↑↓
1695 ....1250 5250 15000 1696 ....*Extremely rare*

* Beware of low grade counterfeits

3460
Guinea, second bust

3463
Narrow crowns

	F £	VF £	EF £		F £	VF £	EF £

3460 **Guinea.** Second laur. bust r. R. Similar with human-headed harp in Irish arms. die axis ↑↓

1697	700	2750	9000	1700 large or small lions			
1698	675	2400	8000	in arms	675	2400	8000
1699	700	2500	8750				

3461 **Guinea.** Second bust elephant and castle below. R. Similar die axis ↑↓

| 1697 | 1350 | 5000 | — | 1699 | | | *Extremely rare* |
| 1698 | 1250 | 4500 | 13500 | 1700 | 1300 | 4750 | — |

3462 **Guinea.** Second laur. bust. r. R. Similar with Human headed harp. Large lettering and large date, die axis ↑↓ 1698 675   2500   8500

3463 **Guinea.** — R. Narrow crowns, plain or ornamented sceptres, axis ↑↓ 1701 675   2500   8250

3464 **Guinea.** Second bust elephant and castle below, die axis ↑↓ 1701 .... *Extremely rare*

3465 **Guinea.** Third laur. bust r. ('fine work'), R. Similar die axis ↑↓ 1701 1250   4500   14000

3466
1695 Half-Guinea, early harp

3468
Later harp

3466 **Half-Guinea.** Laur. bust r. R. With early harp, die axis ↑↓ 1695 400   1050   4000

3467 **Half-Guinea.** Laur. bust elephant and castle below. R. With early harp, die axis ↑↓

| 1695 | 675 | 2000 | 6250 | 1696 | 550 | 1500 | 5000 |

3468 **Half-Guinea.** Laur. bust r. R. Crowned cruciform shields, sceptres in angles with late harp, die axis ↑↓

1697	650	1850	6000	1700	450	1250	4250
1698	400	1050	4000	1701	400	1100	4000
1699		*Extremely rare*					

3469 **Half-Guinea.** Laur. bust elephant and castle below, die axis ↑↓ 1698 625   1750   5750

SILVER

First harp

3470
Crown - first bust - round collar

	F £	VF £	EF £		F £	VF £	EF £

3470 Crown. First dr. bust, r. with curved breast plate or drapery. R.First harp, regnal year on edge in words (e.g. 1696 = OCTAVO) ↑↓

1695 SEPTIMO..........110	375	3000		1696 G/D IN GRA 210	600	3250
1695 SEPTIMO cinquefoils				1696 — no stops........ 200	550	3100
for crosses on edge.... 200	575	—		1696/5.........................200	550	3100
1695 OCTAVO...........110	375	3000		1696 GEI for DEI.......350	1250	—
1695 TVTA·EN error 175	525	—		1696 — no stops........ 375	1350	—
1695 plain edge proof *FDC* £13500				1696 plain edge proof *FDC* £15000		
1696 OCTAVO.......... 100	325	2750				
1696 No stops on						
obverse...............225	625	3500				

Second harp

3471
1696 Crown, second bust - hair across breast

3471 Crown. Second dr. bust r. with two locks of hair across the bust and no hair below the truncation. R. Second harp (hair across breast), 1696 (two varieties) die axis ↑↓
OCTAVO .... *Each unique*

3472
Third bust, straight breastplate

	F £	VF £	EF £

3472 **Crown**. Third dr. bust, r. Easily distinguished by the straight breast plate or drapery. ℞. First harp, die axis ↑↓ 1696 OCTAVO...100 325 2750
1696 TRICESIMO... *Extremely rare*
1696 plain edge proof *FDC* £14000

3473 **Crown**. Similar, ℞. Second harp, die axis ↑↓ 1697 NONO 2750 10000 47500

Third harp

3474
1700 Crown, third bust variety

3474 **Crown**. Third bust variety r. of same general style but dies have been recut and hair varied a little. Tie is slightly longer and thinner than normal third bust. ℞. Third harp with scroll front and back, ↑↓ 1700 DVODECIMO 110 375 3000
1700 DECIMO. TERTIO...135 450 3500

3475 **Halfcrown.** First bust r. ℞. Small shields, 1696 die axis ↑↓ OCTAVO 80 275 2000
— — 1696 DECⱯS error 90 325 2500

3476 **Halfcrown.** B (*Bristol*) below First bust, die axis ↑↓ 1696 OCTAVO.......90 300 2250
— 1696 B Similar proof *FDC* £16500

3477
Chester Mint

3478
Exeter Mint

3477 **Halfcrown.** C (*Chester*) below first bust, die axis ↑↓ 1696 OCTAVO....200 625 3000
3478 **Halfcrown.** E (*Exeter*) below first bust, die axis ↑↓ 1696 OCTAVO 200 625 3000

	F	VF	EF
	£	£	£

3479 **Halfcrown.** N (*Norwich*) below first bust, die axis ↑↓ 1696 OCTAVO 175 525 2500
3480 **Halfcrown.** y (*York*) below first bust, die axis ↑↓ 1696 OCTAVO 175 525 2500

3480
1696 Halfcrown - York Mint

3481
1696 Halfcrown, large shield
reverse with early harp

3481 **Halfcrown.** First bust r. ℞. Large shield, early harp,
die axis ↑↓ 1696 OCTAVO...80 275 2000
1696 Proof plain edge *FDC* .... — — 13500
3482 **Halfcrown.** — B (*Bristol*) below bust, die axis ↑↓ 1696 OCTAVO 90 325 2250
3483 **Halfcrown.** — C (*Chester*) below bust, die axis ↑↓ 1696 OCTAVO 200 625 3000
3484 **Halfcrown.** — E (*Exeter*) below bust, die axis ↑↓ 1696 OCTAVO...........150 525 2500
3485 **Halfcrown.** — N (*Norwich*) below bust, die axis ↑↓ 1696 OCTAVO...........350 1200 —
3486 **Halfcrown.** — y (*York*) below bust, die axis ↑↓ 1696 OCTAVO 110 350 2250
— — die axis ↑↓ 1696 y (*York*), Scots Arms at date.............................. 1000 — —
— die axis ↑↓ y over E 1696 .... 250 850 —

3487
Large shields, ordinary harp

	F	VF	EF		F	VF	EF
	£	£	£		£	£	£

3487 **Halfcrown.** First bust r. ℞. Large shields, ordinary harp die axis ↑↓

	F	VF	EF		F	VF	EF
1696 OCTAVO	175	575	2750	1697 G/A in MAG	350	—	—
1697 NONO	75	250	1750	1697/6 —	150	500	2500
1697 — GRR for GRA	400	—	—	1697 Proof plain edge *FDC* £12000			

3488 **Halfcrown.** — B (*Bristol*) below first bust, die axis ↑↓ 1697 NONO........90 325 2250
1697 proof on thick flan *FDC*.. *Extremely rare*
1697 — no stops on reverse... 135 525 2500

3489
Chester Mint Halfcrown, large shields

	F £	VF £	EF £		F £	VF £	EF £
3489 Halfcrown. — C *(Chester)* below first bust, similar die axis ↑↓							
1696 OCTAVO 200		625	3000	1697 NONO 135		525	2500

3490
Exeter Mint Halfcrown, large shields

3490 Halfcrown. — E *(Exeter)* below first bust, similar die axis ↑↓							
1696 OCTAVO 150		500	2500	1697 NONO 80		275	2000
1696 NONO 450		—	—	1697 E over C or B			
1697 OCTAVO 475		—	—	under bust 200		800	—

3491
Norwich Mint Halfcrown, large shields

3491 Halfcrown. — N *(Norwich)* below first bust, similar die axis ↑↓							
1696 OCTAVO 375		1350	—	1697 NONO 125		500	2500
1697 OCTAVO 250		950	—	1697 — Scots Arms at date £1000			
3492 Halfcrown. — — y *(York)* below first bust, similar die axis ↑↓							
1697 NONO 85		275	2000	1697 OCTAVO 350		—	—
3493 Halfcrown. Second dr. bust r. (hair across breast), die axis ↑↓ 1696 OCTAVO					*Unique*		

3494

1700 Halfcrown, modified large shields

| | F | VF | EF | | F | VF | EF |
| | £ | £ | £ | | £ | £ | £ |

3494   Halfcrown. First dr. bust R. Modified large shields die axis ↑↓

1698 OCTAVO	400	1300	—	1699 — Lion of			
1698 DECIMO	70	225	1350	Nassau inverted	525	1500	—
1698/7 —	250	800	—	1700 DVODECIMO	80	250	1500
1698 UNDECIMO	350	1000	—	1700 D. TERTIO	90	275	1600
1699 UNDECIMO	150	525	2500	1700 — DECⱯS error	90	275	1600
1699 — Inverted A's for				1701 D. TERTIO	80	250	1750
V's on edge	175	600	—	1701 — no stops			
1699 — Scots Arms at				on reverse	120	350	2250
date	900	—	—				

3495

1701 Halfcrown, elephant and castle below bust

3495   Halfcrown. – elephant and castle below bust, die axis ↑↓

1701 D. TERTIO.. 3250   9500   —

3496

1701 Halfcrown, plumes on reverse

3496   Halfcrown. – R. Plumes in angles, die axis ↑↓ 1701 D. TERTIO 275   950   5500

SHILLINGS

First bust	Third bust	Third bust variety,
This bust is distinctive in having the hair turned outwards above and below the crown of the head	This is rather like the first bust but the hair at the back all turns downwards and inwards	tie thicker, more hair below bust, more aquiline profile and coarser features

3498	3499
Bristol Mint	1696 Chester Mint Shilling

	F	VF	EF		F	VF	EF
	£	£	£		£	£	£

3497 Shilling. First dr. bust r. R. Crowned cruciform shields edge milled die axis ↑↓

	F	VF	EF		F	VF	EF
1695 35	100	575	1696 GVLELMVS........575	—	—	
1695 E of ET over H 50	150	750	1696 2nd L over M........125	400	—	
1696 30	85	500	1696-1669 error date 800	2250	—	
1696/5 and GVLICLMVS 45	135	600	1697 30	85	500	
1696 no stops on reverse..100	350	—	1697 E/A in DEI............135	475	—	
1696 MAB for MAG			1697 GRI for GRA error . 225	650	2500	
error......................600	—	—	1697 Arms of Scot/Ireland			
1696 GVLIEMVS			transposed 650	—	—	
error......................575	—	—	1697 Irish Arms at date .750	—	—	
1696 GVLIELMVS			1697 no stops on reverse .110	375	—	
error..........................85	300	—	1697 GVLELMVS error. 525	—	—	
1696 GⱯLIELMVS			1697 GVLIELMⱯS error.100	350	—	
error......................110	375	—	1697 L/M in legend.......125	400	—	

3498 Shilling. Similar B (*Bristol*) below bust die axis ↑↓

	F	VF	EF		F	VF	EF
1696 65	210	900	1696 small x in REX................ *Scarce variety*			
1696 GⱯLIELMVS error and			1697 65	210	900	
large G in MAG 70	225	950				

3499 Shilling. Similar C (*Chester*) below bust die axis ↑↓

	F	VF	EF		F	VF	EF
1696 85	275	1200	1696 thick flan proof *FDC*... *Extremely rare*			
1696 R/V in GRA..........110	325	1250	1697....................................80	250	1100	

3500

| | F | VF | EF | | F | VF | EF |
| | £ | £ | £ | | £ | £ | £ |

3500 Shilling. Similar E (*Exeter*) below bust die axis ↑↓

| 1696 | 80 | 250 | 1100 | 1697 | 90 | 300 | 1200 |
| 1697 E over N | 120 | 350 | 1350 | | | | |

3501 Shilling. Similar N (*Norwich*) below bust die axis ↑↓

| 1696 | 100 | 325 | 1250 | 1697 | 100 | 325 | 1250 |
| 1697 no stops on obv. | 120 | 375 | 1350 | | | | |

3502 Shilling. Similar y (*York*) below bust die axis ↑↓

1696	70	225	950	1697 Arms of France/Ireland			
Also known with no stop after GVLIELMVS				transposed	1000	—	—
1696	80	250	975	1697 Arms of Scotland/Ireland			
1697	70	225	950	transposed	1000	—	—

3503 Shilling. Similar Y (*York*) below bust die axis ↑↓

| 1696 | 100 | 325 | 1200 | 1697 | 135 | 500 | — |
| 1697 Y over Λ | 250 | 900 | — | | | | |

3504 Shilling. Second dr. bust r. (hair across breast), similar die axis ↑↓ 1696   *Unique*

3505 - Third bust   3513 - Chester Mint, Third bust variety

3505 Shilling. Third dr. bust r., similar die axis ↑↓ 1697 40   125   600

3506 Shilling. Similar B (*Bristol*) below bust, die axis ↑↓ 1697 110   350   1350

3507 Shilling. Similar C (*Chester*) below bust die axis ↑↓

1696	135	400	1450	1697 no stops on reverse	100	325	1350
1697 small or large				1697 Arms of Scotland			
lettering	80	250	1000	at date	1000	—	—
1697 FR.A error	100	325	1350				

3508 Shilling. Similar E (*Exeter*) below bust, die axis ↑↓

| 1696 | 2000 | — | — | 1697 | 100 | 325 | 1200 |

3509 Shilling. Similar N (*Norwich*) below bust, die axis ↑↓ 1697 110   350   1350

3510 Shilling. Similar y (*York*) below bust die axis ↑↓

| 1696 | 900 | — | — | 1697 | 80 | 275 | 1000 |

3511 Shilling. Third bust variety r. similar die axis ↑↓

1697 GVLIELMVS				1697 GVLIELMVS error	80	300	—
error	80	300	—	1698	90	300	1100
1697	40	125	600	1698 plain edge proof *FDC* £6500			

	F	VF	EF		F	VF	EF
	£	£	£		£	£	£

3512 Shilling. Similar B (*Bristol*) below bust, die axis ↑↓ 1697 110   350   1350
3513 Shilling. Similar C (*Chester*) below bust, die axis ↑↓ 1697 135   450   1600
— — 1697 thick flan .... *Extremely rare*
3514 Shilling. Similar R. Plumes in angles, die axis ↑↓ 1698 225   725   2400

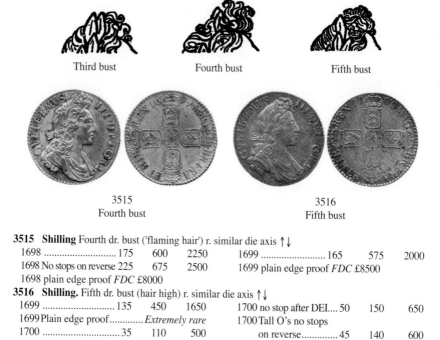

Third bust   Fourth bust   Fifth bust

3515
Fourth bust

3516
Fifth bust

3515 Shilling Fourth dr. bust ('flaming hair') r. similar die axis ↑↓
1698 175   600   2250   1699 165   575   2000
1698 No stops on reverse 225   675   2500   1699 plain edge proof *FDC* £8500
1698 plain edge proof *FDC* £8000

3516 Shilling. Fifth dr. bust (hair high) r. similar die axis ↑↓
1699 135   450   1650   1700 no stop after DEI.... 50   150   650
1699 Plain edge proof .... *Extremely rare*   1700 Tall O's no stops
1700 35   110   500   on reverse............... 45   140   600
1700 no stops on rev, also   1701 small or large lions..90   325   1200
     with larger O's........ 45 140   600   1701 DEI/GRA 300   —   —
1700 Circular small
     O's in date 35   110   500

3517
1701 Shilling, plumes on reverse

3517 Shilling. Similar R. Plumes in angles die axis ↑↓
1699 175   525   1850   1701 175   525   1850

3518
1699 Shilling, roses on reverse

3520
First bust Sixpence, French arms at date

	F	VF	EF		F	VF	EF
	£	£	£		£	£	£
3518 **Shilling.** Similar R. Roses in angles, die axis ↑↓ 1699	225	750	2250
3519 **Shilling.** Similar plume below bust, die axis ↑↓ 1700	3000	10500	—

SIXPENCES

First bust   Third bust   Early harp. large crown.   Later harp, small crown.

3520 **Sixpence.** First dr. bust r. R. Crowned cruciform shields, large crowns, edge milled, early
harp, die axis ↑↓

1695	30	80	275	1696 Scots Arms		
1696	25	60	225	at date	450	—	—
1696 Heavy flan	850	—	—	1696/5	40	110	425
1696 French Arms				1696 no stops on		
at date	550	—	—	obverse	50	125	500
1696 GVLIELMⱯS	40	110	425	1696 DFI for DEI	125	—	—

	F	VF	EF
3521 **Sixpence.** Similar B *(Bristol)* below bust, die axis ↑↓ 1696	30	90	375
— — 1696 B over E	50	135	475
3522 **Sixpence.** Similar C *(Chester)* below bust, die axis ↑↓ 1696	30	90	375

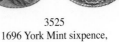

3523

3525
1696 York Mint sixpence,
early harp, first bust

	F	VF	EF
3523 **Sixpence.** Similar E *(Exeter)* below bust, die axis ↑↓ 1696	45	125	450
3524 **Sixpence.** Similar N *(Norwich)* below bust, die axis ↑↓ 1696	45	125	450
3525 **Sixpence.** Similar y *(York)* below bust, die axis ↑↓ 1696	30	90	375

	F	VF	EF		F	VF	EF
	£	£	£		£	£	£

3526 Sixpence. Similar Y *(York)* below bust, die axis ↑↓ 1696.................30 | 90 | 375
— — — 1696 no stops on obverse...50 | 135 | 450

3527 Sixpence. Similar R. Later harp, large crowns, die axis ↑↓ 1696 ....50 | 135 | 475
— — — 1696 no stops on obverse...90 | 250 | —

3528 Sixpence. — — — B *(Bristol)* below bust, similar die axis ↑↓
1696 ....70 | 175 | 575 | 1697 ....45 | 125 | 450
1696 no stops on
obv. ....90 | 225 | 650

3529 Sixpence. — — — C *(Chester)* below bust, similar die axis ↑↓ 1697 ....100 | 250 | 700

3530 Sixpence. — — — E *(Exeter)* below bust, similar die axis ↑↓ 1697 ....60 | 150 | 500

3531 Sixpence. — — R. small crowns, similar die axis ↑↓
1696 .... 60 | 150 | 475 | 1697 Arms of France/Ireland
1697 .... 30 | 80 | 325 | transposed ....400 | — | —
1697 GVLIELMⱯS .... 65 | 165 | —

3532
Bristol Mint Sixpence, small crowns

3532 Sixpence. — — — B *(Bristol)* below bust, similar die axis ↑↓
1696 ....70 | 175 | 575 | 1697 ....30 | 80 | 325
1696 no stops on O ... 100 | 250 | 700 | 1697 B over E ....45 | 110 | 400

3533 Sixpence. — — — C *(Chester)* below bust, similar die axis ↑↓
1696 ....90 | 225 | 625 | 1697 Irish shield
1697 ....40 | 95 | 325 | at date.......................375 | 1000 | —
  | | | 1697 Plain edge ....150 | 350 | 1000

3534 Sixpence. — — — E *(Exeter)* below bust, similar die axis ↑↓
1697 ....50 | 125 | 450 | 1697 E over B ....100 | 250 | 675

3535 Sixpence. — — — N *(Norwich)* below bust, similar die axis ↑↓
1696 ....80 | 200 | 600 | 1697 ....45 | 110 | 375
1697 GVLIEMVS ..150 | 500 | —

3536 Sixpence. — — — y *(York)* below bust, similar die axis ↑↓
1697 ....50 | 125 | 450 | 1697 Irish shield at date .....250 | 700 | —

SPINK
founded 1666

COINS OF ENGLAND 2017

E-book available on Amazon, iBookstore,
Google, Kobo, OverDrive
and across most other platforms

For more information or enquiries please contact
Tel: +44 (0)20 7563 4000 | Email: books@spink.com
69 Southampton Row, Bloomsbury, London WC1B 4ET

WWW.SPINKBOOKS.COM

3537
Second bust Sixpence

3538
Sixpence, third bust,
later harp, large crowns

	F	VF	EF		F	VF	EF
	£	£	£		£	£	£

3537 Sixpence. Second dr. bust r. R. Similar die axis ↑↓

1696	275	850	2250	1697 GVLIEMVS	275	850	2250
1696 hair across breast				1696 GVLELMVS	325	950	2500
(as 3471) Three known examples				1697	175	675	2000
1697 GVLIELMVⱯ	200	750	2100	1697 GR/DE in GRA	200	700	2250
1697 G/I in GRA	175	675	2000				

3537A Sixpence. Third dr. bust, r. early harp, large crowns. E *(Exeter)* below

bust, 1696	525	1750	—

3537B Sixpence. — — — Y *(York)* below bust, similar die axis ↑↓ 1696..... 325 1000 —

3538 Sixpence. Third dr. bust, r., R. Later harp, large crowns, similar die axis ↑↓

1697 GVLIEIMVS	30	85	300	1699	90	225	600
1697	25	70	275	1700	35	90	325
1697 GⱯLIELMVS	35	90	350	1701	65	175	525
1698	40	100	375				

3539 Sixpence. — — B *(Bristol)* below bust, similar die axis ↑↓

1697	50	135	475	1697 IRA for FRA	90	250	—

3540
Chester Mint Sixpence, third bust

3540 Sixpence. — — C *(Chester)* below bust, similar die axis ↑↓ 1697	90	225	575
3541 Sixpence. — — E *(Exeter)* below bust, similar die axis ↑↓ 1697	100	250	625

3542 Sixpence. Third dr. bust, r. R. Small crowns, similar die axis ↑↓

1697	35	85	325	1697 G/D in GRA	100	250	650
1697 D/F in DEI	110	275	675				

3543 Sixpence. — — C *(Chester)* below bust, similar die axis ↑↓ 1697	70	175	575
3544 Sixpence. — — E *(Exeter)* below bust, similar die axis ↑↓ 1697	70	175	575

3545
York Mint Sixpence - Y provenance mark

3547
Sixpence, roses on reverse

	F £	VF £	EF £		F £	VF £	EF £
3545 **Sixpence.**— — Y *(York)* below bust, similar die axis ↑↓ 1697					50	135	475
3546 **Sixpence.**— — R̟. Plumes in angles, similar die axis ↑↓							
1698	90	225	675	1699	90	225	675
3547 **Sixpence.**— R̟. Roses in angles, similar die axis ↑↓							
1699	110	275	775	1699 GⱯLIELMVS	125	325	—

3548
1700 Sixpence, plume below bust

3549
1699 Groat or Fourpence

	F	VF	EF		F	VF	EF
3548 **Sixpence.**— plume below bust, R. Similar die axis ↑↓ 1700	2000	—	—				
3549 **Fourpence.** Laur. and dr. bust r. R̟. 4 Crowned die axis ↑↓							
1697		*Unique*		1700	25	50	165
1698	28	60	190	1701	30	65	190
1699	25	50	145	1702	20	45	90
3550 **Threepence.** Laur. and dr. bust r. R̟. 3 Crowned die axis ↑↓							
1698	20	40	110	1701 GBA for GRA	24	45	150
1699	25	50	140	1701 small lettering	20	40	110
1700	22	45	130	1701 large lettering	20	40	110
3551 **Twopence.** Laur. and dr. bust r. R̟. Crown to edge of coin, large figure 2 die axis ↑↓							
1698	25	50	135				
3551A **Twopence.** Laur. and dr. bust r. R̟ Crown within inner circle of legend, smaller figure 2, die axis ↑↓							
1698	25	45	125	1700	18	30	95
1699	18	30	95	1701	18	30	95
3552 **Penny.** Laur. and dr. bust r. R̟. 1 Crowned die axis ↑↓							
1698	25	45	135	1699	40	80	225
1698 IRA for FRA error	25	45	125	1700	35	70	165
1698 HI.BREX error	25	45	125	1701	25	45	120

3553 - 1701 Maundy Set

	F	VF	EF		F	VF	EF
	£	£	£		£	£	£

3553 Maundy Set. The four denominations. Uniform dates

1698	125	300	775	1700	165	375	825
1699	175	400	925	1701	125	300	750

COPPER

3554 - Halfpenny

3554 Halfpenny. First issue. Laur. and cuir. bust r. Ɽ. Britannia with r. hand raised die axis ↑↓

1695	45	210	1150	1697	35	175	950
1695 BRITANNIΛ error	200	—	—	1697 all stops omitted	225	—	—
1695 no stop on rev.	60	275	—	1697 I/E in TERTIVS	225	—	—
1695 no stops on obv.	60	275	—	1697 GVLILMVS,			
1696	35	175	1000	no rev. stop	300	—	—
1696 GVLIEMVS,				1697 no stop			
no rev. stop	300	—	—	after TERTIVS	50	275	—
1696 TERTVS error	275	—	—	1698	45	210	1150

3555 Halfpenny. Second issue. Laur. and cuir. bust r. Ɽ. Britannia, date in legend die axis ↑↓

1698 Stop after date	35	200	1050	1699 GVLIEMVS error	225	—	—
1699 no stop after date	30	165	1000	1699 BRITAN IA error	225	—	—
1699 BRITANNIΛ error	225	—	—				

3556 Halfpenny. Third issue. Laur. and cuir. bust r. Ɽ. Britannia, date in exergue, die axis ↑↓

1699	35	175	950	1700 BRITANNIΛ error	40	175	950
1699 stop after date	225	—	—	1700 BRTTANNIA error	50	180	1000
1699 BRITANNIΛ error	380	—	—	1700 — no stop after	45	195	1000
1699 GVILELMVS error	275	—	—	1700 GVLIELMS	100	350	—
1699 TERTVS error	275	—	—	1700 GVLIEEMVS	65	250	1200
1699 — no rev. stop	150	—	—	1700 GVLIEEMVS	65	250	1200
1699 no stops on obv.	85	380	—	1700 TER TIVS	45	195	1000
1699 no stop after				1700 I/V in TERTIVS	225	—	—
GVLIELMVS	85	325	—	1701	40	175	950
1700	35	175	950	1701 BRITANNIΛ	50	225	1050
1700 no stops on obv.	100	350	—	1701 — no stops on obv.	225	—	—
1700 no stop after				1701 — inverted A's			
GVLIELMVS	100	350	—	for V's	60	250	1050

3557
1696 Farthing date in exergue

3558
1699 Farthing date in legend

	F £	VF £	EF £		F £	VF £	EF £
3557	**Farthing.** First issue Laur. and cuir. bust r. R. Britannia l. die axis ↑↓						
1695 40		250	950	1698 200		625	—
1695 GVLIELMV error. 200		—	—	1698 B/G on rev. 325		—	—
1696 35		210	900	1699 35		240	900
1697 30		175	825	1699 GVLILEMVS•..... 175		450	—
1697 GVLIELMS error......250		—	—	1700 30		155	775
1697 TERTIV error....... 250		—	—	1700 RRITANNIA........ 225		—	—
3558	**Farthing.** Second issue. Laur. and cuir. bust r. R. Britannia date at end of legend die axis ↑↓						
1698 Stop after date 45		275	1000	1699 — No stop before or after *Extremely rare*			
1699 no stop after date.... 50		300	1050	1699 BRITΛNNIΛ........ 225		—	—
1699 no stop after GVLIELMVS 125		—	—	1699 BRITANNIΛ........ 225		—	—

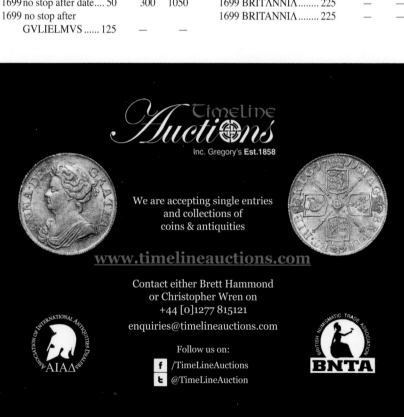

TimeLine
Auctions
Inc. Gregory's Est.1858

We are accepting single entries
and collections of
coins & antiquities

www.timelineauctions.com

Contact either Brett Hammond
or Christopher Wren on
+44 [0]1277 815121
enquiries@timelineauctions.com

Follow us on:

f /TimeLineAuctions
t @TimeLineAuction

ASSOCIATION OF INTERNATIONAL ANTIQUITIES DEALERS
AIAΔ

BRITISH NUMISMATIC TRADE ASSOCIATION
BNTA

Anne, the second daughter of James II, was born on 6th February 1665 and as a protestant succeeded to the throne on William III's death. Anne married Prince George of Denmark and produced 17 children, sadly none surviving to succeed to the throne. Anne died on 1st August 1714.

The Act of Union of 1707, which effected the unification of the ancient kingdoms of England and Scotland into a single realm, resulted in a change in the royal arms—on the Post-Union coinage the English lions and Scottish lion are emblazoned per pale on the top and bottom shields. After the Union the rose in the centre of the reverse of the gold coins is replaced by the Garter star.

Following a successful Anglo-Dutch expedition against Spain, bullion seized in Vigo Bay was sent to be minted into coin, and the coins made from this metal had the word VIGO placed below the Queen's bust. The elephant and castle provenance mark continues on some guineas in the Post-Union period.

Engravers and designers: Samuel Bull (d.c1720), Joseph Cave (d.c1760), James Clerk, John Croker (1670-1741), Godfrey Kneller (1646-1723)

GOLD

PRE-UNION WITH SCOTLAND 1702-07

3560
1705 Pre-Union Five Guineas

The shields on the reverse are Pre-Union type.

	F	VF	EF		F	VF	EF
	£	£	£		£	£	£

3560 **Five Guineas.** Dr. bust l, regnal year on edge in words (e.g. 1705 = QVARTO) die axis ↑↓

1705 QVARTO 6500	22500	75000	1706 QVINTO 6000	20000	72500

3561 **Five Guineas.** Similar VIGO below bust, die axis ↑↓ 1703 (Three varieties)

SECVNDO 45000 115000 375000

3562	3563
1705 Pre-Union Guinea	1703 VIGO Guinea

3562 **Guinea.** Dr. bust l. R. Crowned cruciform shields sceptres in angles die axis ↑↓

1702 1250	4250	1400	1706 1250	4250	14000
1702 plain edge proof... —	—	20000	1707 1250	4250	14000
1705 1350	4500	15000			

3563 **Guinea.** Similar with VIGO below bust, die axis ↑↓ 1703 .... 15000 42500 110000

3564
Pre-Union Half-Guinea

3565
VIGO Half-Guinea

	F £	VF £	EF £		F £	VF £	EF £

3564 Half-Guinea. Dr bust l. R. Crowned cruciform shields sceptres in angles die axis ↑↓
1702 950   3000   9250   1705 900   2750   9000
3565 Half-Guinea. Similar with VIGO below bust, 1703 6500   17500   45000

POST UNION WITH SCOTLAND 1707-14

3566
1706 Post-Union Five Guineas

The shields on the reverse are changed to Post-Union type die axis ↑↓
3566 Five Guineas. Dr. bust l., regnal year on edge in words 1706 QVINTO 4000   13000   52500

3567
1709 - Narrow shields

3568
1711 - Broad shields

3567 Five Guineas. Similar R. Narrower shields, tall narrow crowns, larger rev. lettering, die axis ↑↓
1709 OCTAVO 4250   13500   55000
3568 Five Guineas. New bust l. R. Broader shields edge inscribed die axis ↑↓
1711 DECIMO 4250   13500   55000   1714/3 D. TERTIO 4750   14500   60000
1713 DVODECIMO 4500   14000   57500   1714 D. TERTIO 4500   14000   57500

3569 - 1713 Two Guineas

	F £	VF £	EF £		F £	VF £	EF £

3569 Two Guineas. Dr. bust l.R. Crowned cruciform shields sceptres in angles edge milled die axis ↑↓

	F	VF	EF		F	VF	EF
1709	1500	4250	16000	1713	1450	4000	15000
1711	1450	4000	15000	1714/3	1500	4250	16500

3570 Guinea. First dr. bust l. R. Crowned cruciform shields sceptres in angles edge milled die axis↑↓

1707	800	3250	11000	1708	800	3250	11000

3571	3574
1708 Guinea, first bust, elephant and castle below	1713 Guinea, third bust

3571 Guinea. First dr. bust l. elephant and castle below, R. Similar die axis ↑↓

1707	1250	5000	15000	1708		*Extremely rare*	

3572 Guinea. Second* dr. bust l. R. Similar die axis ↑↓

1707	750	3000	10000	1709	650	2500	8250
1708	650	2500	8250				

3573 Guinea. Second bust elephant and castle below R. Similar die axis ↑↓

1708	1100	4250	13500	1709	950	3750	12500

3574 Guinea. Third* dr. bust l. R. Similar die axis ↑↓

1710	575	1650	6000	1713	525	1500	5500
1711	625	1750	6000	1714	525	1500	5000
1712	625	1850	6500	1714 GRATIA	550	1600	5250
1713/1	550	1600	5750				

3575 - 1710 Half-Guinea

3575 Half-Guinea. Dr. bust l. R. Crowned cruciform shields, sceptres in angles, edge milled die axis ↑↓

1707	350	900	3750	1711	325	825	3250
1708	375	1050	4000	1712	350	900	3750
1709	350	900	3750	1713	325	825	3250
1710	325	850	3500	1714	325	825	3250

* If there exists any difference between the 2nd and 3rd busts, it is miniscule.

SILVER

PRE UNION WITH SCOTLAND

3576
1703 VIGO Crown

	F	VF	EF		F	VF	EF
	£	£	£		£	£	£

The shields on the reverse are Pre-Union type.

3576 Crown. VIGO below dr. bust, l., regnal year on edge in words (e.g. 1703 = TERTIO) die axis↑↓
1703 TERTIO.................. 350   1350   6000

3577
1705 Crown, plumes on reverse

3578
1707 Pre-Union crown, roses and plumes

3577 Crown. Dr bust l. R. Plumes in angles, die axis ↑↓ 1705 QVINTO ..550   2250   8500
3578 Crown. R. Similar Crowned cruciform shields Roses and plumes in angles die axis ↑↓
1706 QVINTO 275   750   4250   1707 SEXTO 250   675   4000

3579
1703 Halfcrown, plain below bust

3579 Halfcrown . Dr. bust l. R. Similar Regnal year on edge in words die axis ↑↓
1703 TERTIO 750   2500   9500

3580
1703 VIGO Halfcrown

	F	VF	EF		F	VF	EF
	£	£	£		£	£	£
3580 **Halfcrown.** Similar VIGO below bust, die axis ↑↓ 1703 TERTIO....	150	525	2750				

3581
Halfcrown, plumes on reverse

3581 **Halfcrown.** Dr. bust l. R. Plumes in angles, similar die axis ↑↓

1704 TERTIO	200	750	4000	1705 QVINTO	200	750	4000

3582
Halfcrown, Pre-Union,
roses and plumes

3583
Shilling

3582 **Halfcrown.** Dr. bust l. R. Roses and plumes in angles, similar die axis ↑↓

1706 QVINTO	135	400	2500	1707 SEXTO............	125	375	2250

First bust   Second bust

3583 **Shilling.** First dr. bust l. R. Similar die axis ↑↓ 1702 90   350   1250

	F	VF	EF		F	VF	EF
	£	£	£		£	£	£

3584 **Shilling.** Similar R. Plumes in angles, die axis ↑↓ 1702 .... 100 | 375 | 1600

3585 **Shilling.** First dr. bust VIGO below , die axis ↑↓
1702 .... 80 | 275 | 1000 | 1702 :ANNA .... 135 | 475 | 2000

3586
1703 VIGO Shilling

3587
'Plain' Shilling

3586 **Shilling.** Second dr. bust, l. VIGO below R. Similar, die axis ↑↓ 1703 .... 80 | 275 | 1000

3587 **Shilling.** Similar R. Crowned cruciform shields, angles plain, die axis ↑↓
1704 .... 375 | 1350 | — | 1705 .... 200 | 675 | 2250

3588 **Shilling.** Second dr. bust l. R. Plumes in angles die axis ↑↓
1704 .... 125 | 450 | 1750 | 1705 .... 100 | 400 | 1500

3589 **Shilling.** Second dr. bust l. R. Roses and plumes in angles die axis ↑↓
1705 .... 110 | 425 | 1600 | 1707 .... 110 | 450 | 1650

3590 **Sixpence.** Dr. bust l. VIGO below dr. bust, l. die axis ↑↓ 1703 .... 35 | 125 | 475

3591 **Sixpence.** Dr bust l., R. Angles plain, die axis ↑↓ 1705 .... 60 | 200 | 650

3592 **Sixpence.** Similar R. Early shields, plumes in angles, die axis ↑↓ 1705 .... 40 | 150 | 500

3593
1705 Plumes Sixpence

Early Shield

Late Shield

3593 **Sixpence.** Similar R. Late shields, plumes in angles, die axis ↑↓ 1705 .... 50 | 185 | 600

3594 **Sixpence.** Similar R. Crowned cruciform shields Roses and plumes in angles die axis ↑↓
1705 .... 45 | 175 | 575 | 1707 .... 45 | 175 | 575

3595
Groat or fourpence, first bust

3595 **Fourpence.** First dr. bust l. small face, curls at back of head point downwards.
R Small crown above the figure 4 die axis ↑↓
1703 .... 20 | 50 | 150 | 1704 .... 15 | 30 | 75

3595C
Groat or Fourpence, second bust

	F	VF	EF		F	VF	EF
	£	£	£		£	£	£

3595A Fourpence. Second dr. bust l. larger face, curls at back of head point upwards die axis ↑↓

1705	40	95	200	1709	15	40	100
1706	15	30	85	1710	12	25	70
1708	18	38	95

3595B –Fourpence. Similar ℞ Large crown with pearls on arch, larger serifs on the figure 4 die axis ↑↓

| 1710 | 12 | 25 | 75 | 1713 | 15 | 30 | 80 |

3595C Fourpence. Second dr. bust l., but with re-engraved hair R. Crowned 4 die axis ↑↓

| 1710 | 12 | 25 | 75 | 1713 | 15 | 30 | 80 |

3596 Threepence. First dr. bust l., broader, tie riband pointing outwards. ℞. Crowned 3 die axis ↑↓

| 1703 7 above crown | 18 | 45 | 130 | 1703 7 not above crown | 18 | 45 | 130 |

3596A Threepence. Second dr. bust l., taller and narrow, tie riband pointing inwards die axis ↑↓

| 1704 | 18 | 40 | 100 | 1706 | 15 | 35 | 105 |
| 1705 | 18 | 45 | 130 |

3596B
Threepence, third bust

3596B Threepence. Third larger more finely engraved dr. bust l. R. Crowned 3, die axis ↑↓

1707	15	30	75	1710	12	28	85
1708	15	35	105	1713	15	35	100
1708/7	15	35	105	1713 mule with 4d obv.			
1709	15	35	105	die	20	42	150

3597 Twopence. First dr. bust l., as fourpence, ℞. Crown to edge of coin, small figure 2 die axis ↑↓

1703	22	50	130	1705	25	55	125
1704	20	40	80	1706	20	40	95
1704 No stops on obv.	22	50	110	1707	20	40	80

3597A Twopence. Second dr. bust l., as fourpence, ℞ Crown within inner circle of legend, large figure 2 die axis ↑↓

| 1708 | 20 | 40 | 85 | 1710 | 18 | 35 | 80 |
| 1709 | 25 | 50 | 115 | 1713 | 20 | 40 | 85 |

3598 Penny. Dr. bust l. R. Crowned 1 die axis ↑↓

1703	25	50	125	1709	20	40	90
1705	22	45	105	1710	60	120	230
1706	22	45	105	1713/0	30	55	135
1708	200	300	450

3599
1713 Maundy Set

	F £	VF £	EF £		F £	VF £	EF £
3599 Maundy Set. The four denominations. Uniform dates							
1703	125	300	750	1709	125	250	650
1705	150	300	750	1710	150	300	750
1706	125	250	650	1713	125	250	650
1708	300	450	950				

POST UNION WITH SCOTLAND, 1707-14

The shields on the reverse are changed to the Post-Union types. The Edinburgh coins have been included here as they are now coins of Great Britain.

3600 Crown. Second dr. bust, l. E (Edinburgh) below, R. Crowned cruciform shields regnal year on edge in words, die axis ↑↓ (e.g. 1708 = SEPTIMO)

	F	VF	EF		F	VF	EF
1707 SEXTO	185	575	3750	1708 SEPTIMO	200	625	4000
1707 SEPTIMO	1850	—	—	1708/7 SEPTIMO	210	650	4000

3601
Crown, second bust, plain reverse

3601 Crown. Second dr. bust l. R. Crowned cruciform shields, angles plain die axis ↑↓

	F	VF	EF		F	VF	EF
1707 SEPTIMO	185	575	3750	1708 SEPTIMO	185	575	3750

3602 Crown. Similar R. Plumes in angles, die axis ↑↓

	F	VF	EF		
1708 SEPTIMO	210	650	4000	1708 — BR for BRI	*Extremely rare*

3603
1713 Crown, third bust, roses and plumes

	F £	VF £	EF £		F £	VF £	EF £
3603 **Crown.** Third dr. bust. l. R. Roses and plumes, 1713 DVODECIMO.....					200	625	4000

3604
1708 Halfcrown, Post-Union

3604 Halfcrown. Dr. bust R. Plain, regnal year on edge in words (e.g. 1709 = OCTAVO), die axis ↑↓

	F	VF	EF		F	VF	EF
1707 SEPTIMO	100	325	2250	1709 OCTAVO..............	100	325	2250
1707 no stops on reverse ..	150	550	—	1713 DVODECIMO	110	375	2400
1708 SEPTIMO............	100	325	2250				

3605

3605 Halfcrown. Dr. bust E below R. Crowned cruciform shields die axis ↑↓

	F	VF	EF		F	VF	EF
1707 SEXTO	100	325	2250	1708 SEPTIMO	100	325	2250
1707 SEPTIMO	475	2500	8500	1709 OCTAVO..............	275	1000	—

	3606				3607		
1708 Halfcrown, plumes on reverse				1714 Halfcrown, roses and plumes			
	F	VF	EF		F	VF	EF
	£	£	£		£	£	£

3606 Halfcrown. Similar R. Plumes in angles, die axis ↑↓ 1708 SEPTIMO .. 120   400   2400

3607 Halfcrown. Similar R. Roses and plumes in angles die axis ↑↓

1710 NONO 95	325	2100	1714 D. TERTIO 95	325	2100
1712 UNDECIMO 90	300	2000	1714/3 D. TERTIO 110	350	2250
1713 DVODECIMO 90	300	2000			

| | 3608 | | 3609 |
| 1707 Edinburgh Mint Shilling, second bust | | 1708 E* Shilling |

3608 Shilling. Second dr. bust, l. E *(Edinburgh)* below, R. Crowned cruciform shields die axis ↑↓

1707 110	425	1500	1707 Plain edge proof *FDC* £12500
1707 no stops on			1708 175	650	2250
reverse 250	800	—			

3609 Shilling. Similar E* *(Edinburgh)* below bust die axis ↑↓

1707 150	500	2000	1708 no rays to
1708 150	500	2000	garter star 500	—	—
1708/7 350	—	—			

3609A Shilling. Similar E* *(Edinburgh)* local dies die axis ↑↓

| 1707 .... 325 | 1000 | — | 1708 .... 400 | 1500 | — |

ARTHUR BRYANT COINS

Dealers in British coins and medals

www.bryantcoins.com
abcoins@live.co.uk
07768 645 686

Third bust

Fourth bust

3610
Shilling, third bust

3611
Shilling, plumes on reverse

	F	VF	EF		F	VF	EF
	£	£	£		£	£	£

3610 Shilling Third dr. bust. l. ℞. Crowned cruciform shields, angles Plain, die axis ↑↓

1707	30	120	575	1709	30	110	525
1708	30	110	525	1711	90	300	1000

3611 Shilling. Third dr. bust. l. ℞. Plumes in angles die axis ↑↓

1707	90	300	1000	1708	90	300	1000

3612 Shilling. Third dr. bust. E below ℞. angles plain die axis ↑↓

1707	90	300	1000	1708/7	125	375	1250
1708	100	325	1100				

3613 Shilling. Second dr. bust l. ℞. Roses and plumes, die axis ↑↓ 1708... 135 | 475 | 1600

3614
1708 Shilling, roses and plumes

3614 Shilling. Third dr. bust l. ℞. Crowned cruciform shields Roses and plumes die axis ↑↓

1708	100	325	1100	1710	90	300	1000

COINS OF ENGLAND
& THE UNITED KINGDOM

SPINK
founded 1666

COINS OF ENGLAND 2017
E-book available on Amazon, iBookstore,
Google, Kobo, OverDrive
and across most other platforms

For more information or enquiries please contact
Tel: +44 (0)20 7563 4000 | Email: books@spink.com
69 Southampton Row, Bloomsbury, London WC1B 4ET
WWW.SPINKBOOKS.COM

3615	3620	3623
Edinburgh bust – E* Shilling	Edinburgh Mint Sixpence	1707 Sixpence, plumes on reverse

	F	VF	EF		F	VF	EF
	£	£	£		£	£	£

3615 Shilling. 'Edinburgh' bust, E* below, R. Crowned cruciform shields die axis ↑↓

1707	550	—	—	1709	200	700	2250
1708	225	750	2500				

3616 Shilling. — E below, R. Similar die axis ↑↓ 1709 325   1100   —

3617 Shilling. Fourth dr. bust. l. R. Roses and plumes die axis ↑↓

1710	80	225	875	1713/2	80	225	875
1710 plain edge proof *FDC*	*Extremely rare*			1714	75	185	800
1712	70	175	750	1714/3	85	250	925

3618 Shilling. Similar, R. angles plain, die axis ↑↓

| 1711 | 30 | 125 | 500 | 1711 plain edge proof *FDC* | *Extremely rare* |

3619 Sixpence. Normal dr. bust. l. R. angles plain die axis ↑↓

1707	35	125	450	1711	25	70	300
1707 BR. FRA error	450	—	—	1711 Large Lis	30	75	325
1708	40	135	475				

3620 Sixpence. Normal dr. bust E *(Edinburgh)* below R. Similar die axis ↑↓

1707	45	165	525	1708/7	70	200	700
1707 Proof FDC £6000				1708	55	175	575

3621 Sixpence. Normal dr. bust E* *(Edinburgh)* below, R. Similar die axis ↑↓

1708	60	185	625	1708/7	70	200	700

3622 Sixpence. 'Edinburgh' bust, l. E* below, R. Similar die axis ↑↓ 1708.. 65   185   650

3623 Sixpence. Normal dr. bust. l. R. Plumes in angles die axis ↑↓

1707	40	125	475	1708	45	135	500

3624 Sixpence. Similar R. Roses and plumes in angles, die axis ↑↓ 1710 ... 50   175   600

COPPER

3625
1714 Pattern Farthing

3625 Farthing. Dr. bust l. R. Britannia 1714 pattern only, die axis ↑↓ 325   650   1350

GEORGE I, 1714-27

George I was born on 28th May 1660 son of Ernest, Elector of Hanover and Sophia grandaughter of James I, and inherited the English Throne as Parliament considered him a better alternative than James Edward Stuart – Anne's half-brother. He was however, thoroughly German, did not want to learn English and spent over half his reign in Germany. He brought two mistresses with him to England while his wife ironically languished in a German prison on a charge of adultery. His reign created a government that could run independently of the King. The office of Prime Minister was created in 1721. He also kept England out of war for his entire reign, and he died on 11 June 1727.

The coins of the first of the Hanoverian kings have the arms of the Duchy of Brunswick and Luneberg on one of the four shields, the object in the centre of the shield being the Crown of Charlemagne. The King's German titles also appear, in abbreviated form, and name him 'Duke of Brunswick and Luneberg. Arch-treasurer of the Holy Roman Empire, and Elector', and on the Guinea of 1714, 'Prince Elector'. A Quarter-Guinea was struck for the first time in 1718, but it was of an inconvenient size, and the issue was discontinued. The elephant and castle provenance mark continues on some guineas and half-guineas, but today are rarely seen.

Silver coined from bullion supplied to the mint by the South Sea Company in 1723 shows the Company's initials S.S.C.; similarly Welsh Copper Company bullion has the letters W.C.C. below the King's bust; and plumes and an interlinked CC in the reverse angles. Roses and plumes together on the reverse indicate silver supplied by the Company for Smelting Pit Coale and Sea Coale.

Engravers and Designers: Samuel Bull (d.c.1720), John Croker (1670-1741), John Rudulf Ochs Snr, (1673-c.1748), Norbert Roettier (b.1665)

Prime Minister: Sir Robert Walpole (1676 – 1745) –Whig, 1721-42

GOLD

3626
1717 Five Guineas

	F	VF	EF		F	VF	EF
	£	£	£		£	£	£

3626 Five Guineas. Laur. head r. regnal year on edge in words (e.g. 1717 = TERTIO) die axis↑↓

	F	VF	EF		F	VF	EF
1716 SECVNDO	4750	15000	60000	1720 SEXTO..........	5000	16000	65000
1717 TERTIO	5000	16000	65000	1726 D. TERTIO....	4750	15000	60000
Variety O for D on edge exits				Variety И for N on edge exists			

3627
Two Guineas

	F £	VF £	EF £			F £	VF £	EF £

3627 Two Guineas. Laur. head r. R. Crowned cruciform shields, sceptres in angles, edge milled, die axis ↑↓

1717	1400	3750	12500	1720/17	1500	4000	13000
1720	1400	3750	12500	1726	1350	3500	11500

3628
1714 'Prince Elector' Guinea

3630
Third bust

3631
Fourth bust

3628 Guinea. First laur. head r. R. Legend ends ET PR . EL (Prince Elector), die axis ↑↓

1714						1500	4000	13500

3629 Guinea. Second laur. head, r. tie with two ends, R. Crowned cruciform shields, sceptres in angles normal legend ↑↓ 1715 .... 800 2000 7500

3630 Guinea. Third laur. head, r. no hair below truncation R. Similar die axis ↑↓

1715	550	1500	5500	1716	600	1650	5750

3631 Guinea. Fourth laur. head, r. tie with loop at one end R. Similar die axis ↑↓

1716	575	1500	5000	1720 large or small			
1717	600	1600	5250	20 in date	575	1500	5000
1718		*Extremely rare*		1721	600	1600	5250
1718/7		*Extremely rare*		1722	575	1500	5000
1719	575	1500	5000	1722/0	600	1600	5250
1719/6	650	1600	5250	1723	600	1600	5250

3632 Guinea. Fourth Laur. head, elephant and castle below R. Similar die axis ↑↓

1721		*Extremely rare*		1722		*Extremely rare*	

3633
Guinea, fifth bust

	F £	VF £	EF £		F £	VF £	EF £

3633 Guinea. Fifth (older) laur. head, r. tie with two ends R. Similar die axis ↑↓

1723	575	1500	5000	1725	600	1500	5250
1723 II for H in TH	600	1600	5250	1725 large 5 in date	600	1400	5000
1724	575	1500	5000	1726	550	1350	4750
1724 R/I in				1727	650	1750	5750
GEORGIVS	600	1600	5250				

3634 Guinea. Fifth laur. head, elephant and castle below, die axis ↑↓ 1726 1750   6250   18500

3635 Half-Guinea. First laur. head r. R. Crowned cruciform shields, sceptres in angles die axis ↑↓

1715	575	1500	4500	1721			*Extremely rare*
1717	350	800	3500	1722	350	800	3500
1718	325	750	3250	1722/0	375	825	3650
1718/7	350	800	3500	1723	375	850	3750
1719	325	750	3250	1724	400	900	4000
1720	350	800	3500				

3636 Half-Guinea. First laur. head elephant and castle below, die axis ↑↓ 1721   *Extremely rare*

3637   3638
Half-Guinea, second bust   Quarter Guinea

3637 Half-Guinea. Second (older) laur. head r. R. Crowned cruciform shields, sceptres in angles die axis ↑↓

1725	300	700	3250	1727	350	800	3500
1726	325	700	3250				

3638 Quarter-Guinea. Laur. head R. Similar die axis ↑↓ 1718 150   300   750

COINS OF BRITAIN
PO BOX 2, MONMOUTH, NP25 3YR, UK

BNTA

E-mail: lloydbennett@coinsofbritain.com   +44(0)7714 284 939

SILVER

3639A - 1726 Crown - small roses and plumes

	F £	VF £	EF £		F £	VF £	EF £

3639 Crown. Laur and dr. bust r. R. Roses and plumes in angles, regnal year on edge in words
(e.g. 1716 = SECVNDO) die axis ↑↓

	F	VF	EF		F	VF	EF
1716 SECVNDO	525	1500	6000	1720/18 SEXTO...........	525	1500	6000
1718/6 QUINTO	550	1650	6250				

3639A Crown. Similar R. small roses and plumes in angles

1720 SEXTO...........	625	2000	7000	1726 D. TERTIO..........	550	1650	6250

3640 Crown. Similar R. SSC (South Sea Company) in angles, die axis ↑↓

1723 DECIMO					525	1500	6000

3641 - 1715 Pattern Halfcrown

3641 Halfcrown. Laur and dr. bust r. R. Angles plain (pattern only), die axis ↑↓ 1715 *FDC* £15000

3642 - Halfcrown, roses and plumes

3642 Halfcrown. — R. Roses and plumes in angles, regnal year on edge in words
(e.g. 1717 = TIRTIO)

	F	VF	EF		F	VF	EF
1715 SECVNDO	325	850	4000	1717 TIRTIO...............	325	850	4000
1715 Edge wording out...				1720/17 SEXTO..........	325	850	4000
of order.............	375	1100	4500	1720 SEXTO...............	375	900	4250
1715 Plain edge	500	1600	—				

3643 - 1723 SSC Halfcrown

	F	VF	EF		F	VF	EF
	£	£	£		£	£	£

3643 Halfcrown. Similar R. SSC in angles, die axis ↑↓ 1723 DECIMO .... 300 | 750 | 3750

3644 - 1726 Halfcrown small roses and plumes

3644 Halfcrown. — R. Small roses and plumes, die axis ↑↓ 1726 D.TERTIO ... 4750 | 13500 | 27500

3645	3646
Shilling, roses and plumes	1721 Shilling, plain reverse

3645 Shilling. First laur. and dr. bust. r. R. Roses and plumes in angles, die axis ↑↓

1715	 80	275	950	1721	 150	500	1650
1716	 150	500	1600	1721/0	 100	350	1350
1717	 135	375	1350	1721/19	 135	450	1500
1718	 75	225	800	1721/18 plumes and			
1719	 150	500	1600	roses error 375	1600	—
1720	 110	350	1350	1722	 100	350	1350
1720/18	 175	525	1750	1723	 110	375	1400

3646 Shilling. First laur. and dr. bust r. R. angles plain (i.e. no marks either side) die axis ↑↓

1720	 45	150	700	1721	 150	500	1650
1720 large O	 50	160	725	1721 O of GEORGIVS over zero			

LETTERING ERRORS:
3645 1716 V of GEORGIVS over L   1720 Large O in date
      1717 Large lettering on obverse

3647
1723 SSC Shilling, first bust

3649
1727 Shilling, second bust

	F	VF	EF		F	VF	EF
	£	£	£		£	£	£

3647 Shilling. First laur. and dr. bust r. R̃. SSC in angles, die axis ↑↓

1723 30	85	350	1723 C/SS in 3rd			
1723 French Arms at			quarter 40	100	400	
date 100	350	1100				

LETTERING VARIETIES:

B·RVN on Rev., Large N in BRVN and stop between E.T. after BRVN.

3648 Shilling. Second dr. bust, r. bow to tie. R̃. Similar, die axis ↑↓ 1723 ... 50   135   500

3649 Shilling. Similar R̃. Roses and plumes in angles die axis ↑↓

1723 110	375	1300	1726 no stops on obv. 700	2100	—
1724 120	400	1450	1727 550	1600	—
1725 110	375	1300	1727 no stops on obv. 500	1450	3750
1725 no stops on obv. 120	400	1450	1727 no stops on rev 600	1750	—
1725 no stops on rev 135	475	1600			

3650 - 1726 WCC Shilling

3650 Shilling. Second laur. and dr. bust r. W.C.C. (Welsh Copper Company) below bust die axis ↑↓

1723 750	2250	7000	1725 800	2500	7500
1724 750	2250	7000	1726 800	2500	7500

3651 Sixpence. Laur. and dr. bust r. R̃. Roses and plumes in angles, die axis ↑↓

1717 100	350	900	1720/17 90	300	800
1717 Plain edge...............	*Extremely rare*				

3652 - 1723 SSC Sixpence

3653 - 1726 Sixpence, small roses and plumes

3652 Sixpence. Laur. and dr. bust r. R̃. SSC in angles, die axis ↑↓

1723 25	90	350	1723 larger lettering... 30	95	375

3653 Sixpence. Similar R̃. Small roses and plumes, die axis ↑↓ 1726.......... 85   275   750

	F £	VF £	EF £		F £	VF £	EF £

3654 Fourpence. Laur. and dr. bust r. R. Crowned 4, die axis ↑↓

| 1717 | 15 | 40 | 100 | 1723 | 20 | 50 | 160 |
| 1721 | 15 | 40 | 100 | 1727 | 22 | 55 | 160 |

3655 Threepence. Laur. and dr. bust r. R. Crowned 3, die axis ↑↓

| 1717 | 20 | 45 | 95 | 1723 | 20 | 55 | 160 |
| 1721 | 25 | 48 | 95 | 1727 small lettering | 20 | 50 | 150 |

3656 Twopence. Laur. and dr. bust r. R. Crowned 2, die axis ↑↓

1717	12	32	65	1726	12	25	60
1721	12	25	60	1727 small lettering	15	32	85
1723	15	40	110				

3657 Penny. Laur. and dr. bust r. R. Crowned 1, die axis ↑↓

1716	12	32	65	1723	15	30	80
1718	12	32	65	1725	12	32	65
1720	12	32	65	1726	15	40	70
1720 HIPEX error	20	85	150	1727 BRI·FR	20	50	110

3658

3658 Maundy Set. As last four. Uniform dates

| 1723 | 150 | 275 | 800 | 1727 | 125 | 250 | 700 |

COPPER

3659

3659 Halfpenny. 'Dump' issue obv. legend continuous over bust, plain edge, die axis ↑↓

1717	40	250	800	1718 no stops on obv	150	500	—
1717 no stops on obv.	100	525	—	1719	1000	—	—
1718	30	225	725	1719 grained edge	1000	—	—
1718 R/B on rev.	50	250	900	*(1719 is an extremely rare date, perhaps only 2 or 3 known to exist of each type)*			

3660

	F £	VF £	EF £		F £	VF £	EF £

3660 Halfpenny. Second issue, second obverse, plain left shoulder strap, less hair to the right of tie knot, R. Britannia plain edge, die axis ↑↓

	F	VF	EF		F	VF	EF
1719	40	210	900	1722	30	155	700
1719 grained edge	1000	—	—	1722 ∀ for V on obv.	100	500	—
1720	30	175	825	1723	30	155	750
1721	30	165	725	1723 Thin Flan		*Extremely rare*	
1721 stop after date	40	200	800	1723 no stop on rev.	100	525	—
1721/0	40	200	800	1724	30	155	700

3660A Halfpenny. Second issue, second obverse, ornate shoulder straps, die axis ↑↓

	F	VF	EF
1719	40	195	900

3661

3662

3661 Farthing. 'Dump' issue, Similar die axis ↑↓

	F	VF	EF		
1717	200	675	1250	1718	*Unique*

3662 Farthing. Second issue laur. and cuir. bust r. R. Britannia, date in ex. die axis ↑↓

	F	VF	EF		F	VF	EF
1719 small letters	60	330	775	1720 obv. large letters	80	350	—
1719 no stop on rev.	70	380	—	1721	25	135	650
1719 large lettering on obv.	30	165	650	1721/0	40	165	675
1719 — no stops on obv.	70	410	—	1721 stop after date	35	165	625
1719 — no stops on rev.	90	450	—	1722	30	155	625
1719 last A/I on rev.	80	350	—	1722 obv. large letters	40	210	725
1720	30	165	600	1723 R/≃ in REX	100	330	900
1720 milled edge	150	500	1150	1723	30	165	600
				1724	30	165	625

George II was born on 30 October 1683 and was raised in Hanover, but upon his succession to the throne as George I's only son, he adapted himself to English society. His passions were the military, music and his wife – Caroline of Anspach, though he despised his eldest son Frederick as his own father despised him. George declared war on Spain in 1739 and he was the last King to have personally led his troops at the battle of Dettingen on 17 June 1743. Upon his death on 25 October 1760 the throne passed to his grandson George as Frederick had already died.

Silver was coined only spasmodically by the Mint during this reign; and no copper was struck after 1754. Gold coins made from bullion supplied by the East India Company bear the Company's E.I.C. initials. Some of the treasure seized by Admiral Anson during his circumnavigation of the globe, 1740-4, and by other privateers, was made into coin, which had the word LIMA below the king's bust to celebrate the expedition's successful harassment of the Spanish Colonies in the New World. Hammered gold was finally demonetized in 1733.

Engravers and designers: John Croker (1670-1741), John Rudolf Ochs Snr (1673-1748) and jnr (1704-88), Johann Sigismund Tanner (c.1706-75)

Prime Ministers: Sir Robert Walpole (1676-1745) Whig, 1721-43; Spencer Compton (1673-1743) Whig 1742-3; Henry Pelham (c.1695-1754) Whig 1743-54; William Cavendish (1720-1764) Whig 1756-7; Thomas Pelham-Holles (1693-1768) Whig 1754-6; 1757-62.

GOLD

3663A
1741 Five Guineas - revised shield

	F	VF	EF		F	VF	EF
	£	£	£		£	£	£

3663 Five Guineas. Young laur. head l. R. Crowned shield of arms, die axis ↑↓ regnal year
on edge in words (e.g. 1729 = TERTIO)

| 1729 TERTIO | 3250 | 10500 | 42500 | 1729 Plain edge proof *FDC* £100000 | | | |

3663A Five Guineas. Similar R. Revised shield garnish die axis ↑↓

1731 QVARTO	4000	13000	52500	1738 DVODECIMO	3750	11500	47500
1731 QVARTO proof *FDC* £115000				1741/38 D. QVARTO	3500	11000	45000
1735 NONO	4000	13000	52500	1741 D. QVARTO	3250	10500	42500

3664 Five Guineas. Young laur. head, E.I.C. (East India Company) below, die axis ↑↓

| 1729 TERTIO | | | | | 3250 | 10500 | 42500 |

3665
1746 LIMA Five Guineas

	F	VF	EF		F	VF	EF
	£	£	£		£	£	£

3665 Five Guineas. Old laur. head, l. LIMA below, ↑↓1746 D. NONO... 3500   11000   45000

3666 Five Guineas. Old laur. head plain below, R. Crowned shield, edge inscribed die axis ↑↓

  1748 V. SECVNDO 3500   11000   45000   1753 V. SEXTO 3500   11000   45000

3667 Two Guineas. Young laur. head l. R Crowned shield with rounded arches, die axis ↑↓

  1733 Proof *FDC* £45000   1734/3 1850   5000   15000

3667A
1735 Two Guineas - new reverse

3667A Two Guineas. – R. Crown with pointed arches, new type of shield garnishing die axis ↑↓

  1735 1250   2750   9000

3667B Two Guineas. Repositioned legend on obverse R. Similar

  1738*........................ 800   1750   5000   1739 825   1850   5250

3668
1740 Two Guineas - Intermediate head

3668 Two Guineas. Intermediate laur. head l. R. Crowned shield of arms die axis ↑↓

  1739*........................ 800   1750   5000   1740 900   2250   6000

  1740/39.................... 850   2250   6250

3669 Two Guineas. Old laur. head l. R. Crowned shield of arms die axis ↑↓ ..

  1748 900   2500   6750   1753 950   2750   7500

Beware recent forgeries.

	F	VF	EF		F	VF	EF
	£	£	£		£	£	£

3670 Guinea. First young laur. head, l. small lettering, die axis ↑↓ 1727. 1000 3500 12000

3671   3676

1727 Guinea - small reverse shield

3671 Guinea. Similar larger lettering, smaller shield, die axis ↑↓

1727 1150	3750	12500	1728 1150	3750	12500

3672 Guinea. Second (narrower) young laur. head l. die axis ↑↓

| 1729 Proof *FDC* £22500 | | | 1731 .... 625 | 2000 | 7000 |
| 1730 .... 700 | 2250 | 7500 | 1732 .... 650 | 2000 | 7250 |

3673 Guinea. Second young laur. head, E.I.C. below R. Crowned shield of arms die axis ↑↓

| 1729 .... 1200 | 4000 | 13500 | 1732 .... 1100 | 3500 | 11000 |
| 1731 .... 1150 | 3750 | 12500 | | | |

3674 Guinea. Second young laur. head l. larger lettering R. Crowned shield of arms die axis ↑↓

1732 625	1850	6000	1736 575	1650	5250
1733 550	1500	5000	1737 575	1650	5250
1734 550	1500	5000	1738 575	1650	5250
1735 575	1650	5250			

3675 Guinea. — — E.I.C. below, die axis ↑↓ 1732................................. 1250 3500 11000

Note: All 1739-45 Guineas read GEORGIUS

3676 Guinea. Intermediate laur. head l. r. Crowned shield of arms die axis ↑↓

| 1739 .... 550 | 1500 | 5000 | 1741/39 .... 750 | 2500 | 7500 |
| 1740 .... 575 | 1600 | 5250 | 1743 .... 750 | 2500 | 7500 |

3677 Guinea. Similar E.I.C. below, R. Similar die axis ↑↓ 1739.............. 1000 3250 11500

3678 Guinea. Similar larger lettering on *obv.*, GEORGIUS die axis ↑↓

1745 (also exists with small S in date) 550 1500 4500

3678A   3679

1746 Guinea - GEORGIVS legend   LIMA below bust Guinea

3678A Guinea. Similar as last but reads GEORGIVS die axis ↑↓

1746 .... 575 1650 5000

3679 Guinea. Intermediate laur. head LIMA below, GEORGIUS die

axis ↑↓ 1745 .... 1750 5750 17500

3680

Old head Guinea

	F £	VF £	EF £		F £	VF £	EF £

3680 Guinea. Old laur. head l. R. Crowned shield of arms die axis ↑↓

1747	500	1200	4750	1753	500	1200	4750
1748	500	1200	4750	1755	500	1200	4750
1749	500	1200	4750	1756	500	1200	4750
1750	500	1200	4750	1758	450	1100	4000
1751	475	1150	4500	1759	425	1000	3750
1752	475	1150	4500	1760	450	1100	4000

3681 Half-Guinea. Young laur. head. l. R First shield of arms, die axis ↑↓

1728	475	1200	4000	1729	450	1200	4000

1728 Proof *FDC* £12500

3681A

1731 Half-Guinea - modified shield

3681A Half-Guinea. Young laur. head l. R. Modified garnished shield die axis ↑↓

1730	425	1000	3750	1736	325	850	3250
1731	300	850	3250	1737	350	900	3500
1732	325	900	3500	1738	300	850	3250
1734	300	850	3250	1739	300	850	3250

3682 Half-Guinea. Young laur. head l. E.I.C. below R. Similar die axis ↑↓

1729	650	1600	5250	1732		*Extremely rare*	
1730	750	1750	6000	1739		*Extremely rare*	
1731		*Extremely rare*					

3683A

Half-guinea - GEORGIVS legend

3683 Half-Guinea. Intermediate laur. head l. R. Similar die axis ↑↓

1740	300	850	3250	1745	300	900	3500
1743		*Extremely rare*					

3683A Half-Guinea. Similar, but reads GEORGIVS, die axis ↑↓ 1746 275   700   2750

3684
LIMA Half-Guinea

3685
Half-Guinea, old head

	F	VF	EF		F	VF	EF
	£	£	£		£	£	£

3684 Half-Guinea. Intermediate laur. head LIMA below, die axis ↑↓ 1745 .. 1250   3250   10500

3685 Half-Guinea. Old laur. head l. R. Similar die axis ↑↓

1747	300	750	2850	1753	275	650	2650
1748	300	750	2850	1755	260	600	2500
1749	325	850	3250	1756	250	550	2250
1750	300	750	2850	1758	275	650	2650
1751	285	725	2750	1759	240	550	2400
1751/0	300	750	2850	1759/8	250	575	2500
1752	275	650	2650	1760	250	575	2500

SILVER

3686
Crown, young head

3686 Crown. Young laur. and dr. bust. l. R. Crowned cruciform shields Roses and plumes
in angles, regnal year on edge in words (e.g. 1736 = NONO), die axis ↑↓

1732 SEXTO	350	1100	4500	1735 OCTAVO	325	1000	4000
1732 Proof, plain edge *FDC* £17500				1736 NONO	325	1000	4000
1734 SEPTIMO	350	1100	4500				

3687

3687 Crown. Similar R. Roses in angles die axis ↑↓

1739 DVODECIMO	325	900	3500	1741 D. QVARTO	325	900	3500

3688
Crown, old head

	F	VF	EF			F	VF	EF
	£	£	£			£	£	£

3688 **Crown.** Old laur. and dr. bust l. ℞. Crowned cruciform shields Roses in angles, die axis ↑↓
1743 D. SEPTIMO 300   800   3250
3689 **Crown.** — LIMA below, die axis ↑↓ 1746 D. NONO 300   850   3500

3690
Plain reverse

3691
1731 Pattern Halfcrown

3690 **Crown.** Old laur. and dr. bust l. ℞. angles Plain (i.e. no marks either side) die axis ↑↓
1746 Proof only, VICESIMO *FDC* £12500
1750 V. QVARTO 325   1000   4250   1751 V. QVARTO 350   1100   45000
3691 **Halfcrown.** Young dr. bust l. ℞. angles plain (pattern only), 1731 *FDC* £7000

Follow us on:

f /TimeLineAuctions
t @TimeLineAuction

TimeLine Auctions
Inc. Gregory's Est.1858

We are accepting single entries
and collections of milled coins

www.timelineauctions.com

3692
1736 Halfcrown, roses and plumes

3693
1741 Halfcrown, roses on reverse

	F £	VF £	EF £		F £	VF £	EF £

3692 Halfcrown. Young laur. and dr. bust l. R. Roses and plumes, regnal year on edge in words (e.g. 1732 = SEXTO), die axis ↑↓

1731 QVINTO	150	450	2250	1735 OCTAVO	165	475	2500
1732 SEXTO	150	450	2250	1736 NONO	165	475	2500
1734 SEPTIMO	165	475	2500				

3693 Halfcrown. Young laur. and dr. bust l. R. Roses in angles die axis ↑↓

1739 DVODECIMO	140	450	2250	1741 Large *obv.* letters	150	475	2350
1741 D. QVARTO	140	450	2250	1741/39 D. QVARTO	165	500	2400

3694 Halfcrown. Old dr. bust. l. GEORGIUS R. Roses in angles die axis ↑↓

1743 D. SEPTIMO	110	325	2000	1745/3 D. NONO	120	350	2100
1745 D. NONO	110	325	2000				

3695 Halfcrown. Old laur. and dr. bust LIMA below die axis ↑↓

1745 D. NONO	70	175	800	1745/3	85	225	1000

3695A Halfcrown. Old laur. and dr. bust as last LIMA below but reads GEORGIVS die axis ↑↓

1746 D. NONO	65	170	750	1746/5 D. NONO	70	175	800

3696
1751 Halfcrown

3697
1727 Plumes Shilling

3696 Halfcrown. Old laur. and dr. bust l. R. Plain angles die axis ↑↓

1746 proof only VICESIMO *FDC* £5750				1751 V. QVARTO	225	625	3000
1750 V. QVARTO	200	575	2850				

3697 Shilling. Young laur. dr. bust. l. R. Plumes in angles, die axis ↑↓

1727	135	525	1850	1731	175	625	2250

3698
Shilling, young bust, small letters

3699
Young bust Shilling, large letters

	F £	VF £	EF £		F £	VF £	EF £

3698 Shilling. Young laur. and dr. bust l. R. Roses and plumes in angles, die axis ↑↓

1727	90	325	1250	1731	100	350	1350
1728	110	375	1500	1732	100	350	1400
1729	110	375	1500				

3699 Shilling. Young laur. and dr. bust l. R. Plain, die axis ↑↓ 1728 90   300   1100

3700 - Shilling, plain reverse

3701 - Shilling, roses reverse

3700 Shilling. Similar larger lettering. R. Roses and plumes in angles die axis ↑↓

1734	65	250	950	1737	65	250	950
1735	70	275	1000	1737 known with GRATIΛ error			
1736	65	250	950	1737 with 3/5 exists			
1736/5	70	275	1000				

3701 Shilling. Young laur. and dr. bust l. R. Roses in angles die axis ↑↓

1739 normal garter				1739 smaller garter star	65	250	900
star	50	200	750	1741	50	200	750
1739/7	100	325	1300	1741/39	100	350	1250

3702
Shilling, old bust, roses

3703
LIMA Shilling

3702 Shilling. Old laur. and dr. bust, l. R. Roses in angles die axis ↑↓

1743	35	125	550	1745/3	65	175	750
1743/1	50	150	675	1747 only known with GEORGIVS			
1745	60	165	725	on obv	40	135	650

3703 Shilling. Old laur. and dr. bust LIMA below die axis ↑↓

| 1745 | 30 | 120 | 575 | 1746/5 | 90 | 300 | 1100 |
| 1746 | 90 | 300 | 1100 | | | | |

N.B. In and after 1746 the 'U' was changed to 'V' on old Head Shillings.

3704
1758 Shilling

	F £	VF £	EF £		F £	VF £	EF £

3704 Shilling. Old laur. and dr. bust R. plain angles die axis ↑↓

1746 Proof only *FDC* £3250				1751 110	350	1350
1750 40	135	700	1758 also known with small		
1750/46........................ 45	150	750	58 in date............ 20	45	225
1750 Wide O 45	150	750			

3705	3706	3707
1728 Sixpence, young bust	1728 Sixpence, plumes on reverse	1728 Sixpence, roses and plumes

3705 Sixpence. Young laur. and dr. bust. l. R. Angles plain, die axis ↑↓ 1728... 50   175   600
1728 Proof *FDC* £4250
3706 Sixpence. Similar R. Plumes in angles die axis ↑↓ 1728..................... 45   150   575
3707 Sixpence. Young laur. and dr. bust l. R. Roses and plumes in angles die axis ↑↓

1728 35	125	475	1735 40	135	550
1731 35	125	500	1735/4 45	150	575
1732 35	125	500	1736 50	175	600
1734 40	135	550			

3708	3709
Sixpence, roses	Sixpence, old bust, roses

3708 Sixpence. Young laur. and dr. bust l., R. Roses in angles, die axis ↑↓

1739 30	110	450	1741 30	120	475
1739 O/R in legend..... 35	125	500			

3709 Sixpence. Old laur. and dr. bust. l. R. Roses in angles die axis ↑↓

1743 25	90	375	1745/3 30	100	400
1745 25	90	375			

	F	VF	EF			F	VF	EF
	£	£	£			£	£	£

3710 Sixpence. Old laur. and dr. bust LIMA below bust R. angle plain die axis ↑↓
1745 .... 25 — 80 — 325

3710A Sixpence. Similar as last but reads GEORGIVS die axis ↑↓
1746 .... 20 — 70 — 300 — 1746/5 .... 35 — 110 — 350

3711
Proof Sixpence

3711 Sixpence. Old laur. and dr. bust l. R. angles plain die axis ↑↓
1746 *proof only FDC* £1750

1750 25	65	300	1758 10	30	125
1751 30	85	375	1758 ĐEI error 20	40	175
1757 10	30	125	1758/7 15	35	150

3712 Fourpence. Young laur. and dr. bust l. R. Small dome-shaped crown without pearls on arch, figure 4

1729 22	48	120	1731 20	45	110

3712A Fourpence. Similar R.Double arched crown with pearls, large figure 4, die axis ↑↓

1732 22	48	120	1740 18	35	100
1735 22	48	125	1743 35	80	250
1737 22	48	125	1743/0 35	80	250
1739 20	45	110	1746 15	30	85
			1760 22	45	130

3713 Threepence. Young laur. and dr. bust l. R. Crowned 3, pearls on arch, die axis ↑↓
1729 .... 18 — 38 — 90

3713A Threepence. Similar R. Ornate arch die axis ↑↓
1731 Smaller lettering 18 — 38 — 90 — 1731 .... 18 — 38 — 90

3713B Threepence. Similar R. Double arched crown with pearls, die axis ↑↓

1732 18	38	85	1743 Large lettering... 15	30	80
1732 with stop over head 18	38	85	1743 Small lettering... 15	30	80
1735 18	38	90	1743 — stop over head 18	35	85
1737 15	35	80	1746 12	25	75
1739 15	30	80	1746/3 14	30	75
1740 15	30	80	1760 18	38	85

3714 Twopence. Young laur. and dr. bust l. R. Small crown and figure 2, die axis ↑↓
1729 .... 15 — 25 — 70 — 1731 .... 15 — 25 — 65

3714A Twopence. Young laur. and dr. bust l. R. Large crown and figure 2 die axis ↑↓

1732 15	25	70	1743/0 15	28	70
1735 15	25	65	1746 12	22	60
1737 15	25	70	1756 12	25	50
1739 15	25	70	1759 12	25	45
1740 22	35	90	1760 18	30	75
1743 15	28	70			

3715 Penny. Young laur. and dr. bust l. head. R. Date over small crown and figure 1, die axis ↑↓
1729 .... 12 — 25 — 70 — 1731 .... 12 — 25 — 70

	F	VF	EF		F	VF	EF
	£	£	£		£	£	£

3715A Penny. Young laur. and dr. bust l. R. Large crown dividing date die axis ↑↓

1732	12	25	65
1735	15	30	60
1737	15	30	65
1739	12	25	60
1740	12	25	60
1743	10	22	60
1746	10	20	60
1746/3	12	32	65
1750	10	20	40
1752	10	20	40
1752/0	10	30	60
1753/2	10	25	45
1753	10	20	40
1754	10	25	45
1755	10	20	45
1756	10	20	45
1757	10	20	50
1757 GRATIA:	12	35	70
1758	10	20	45
1759	10	20	50
1760	18	30	75

3716

3716 Maundy Set. The four denominations. Uniform dates

1729	80	225	500
1731	80	225	500
1732	80	200	450
1735	80	200	450
1737	80	200	450
1739	75	165	425
1740	75	165	425
1743	100	250	550
1746	70	150	400
1760	85	225	500

COPPER

3717

3717 Halfpenny. Young laur. and cuir. bust l. R. Britannia, date in ex. die axis ↑↓

1729	15	100	380
1729 rev. no stop	20	110	410
1730	10	100	360
1730 GEOGIVS error	20	150	470
1730 stop after date	20	110	380
1730 no stop after REX on obv	25	160	470
1731	10	90	360
1731 rev. no stop	20	150	440
1732	10	100	360
1732 rev. no stop	20	150	440
1733	10	90	370
1734	10	90	370
1734 R/O on obv	20	145	450
1734/3	30	210	—
1734 no stops on obv.	30	210	—
1735	10	90	370
1736	15	110	400
1736/0	20	130	450
1737	15	100	400
1738	10	75	370
1738 V/S on obv	20	145	450
1739	10	75	370

	F	VF	EF			F	VF	EF
	£	£	£			£	£	£

3718 Halfpenny. Old laur. and cuir. bust l., GEORGIVS R. Britannia, date in ex. die axis ↑↓

1740	10	70	300	1743	10	70	300
1742	10	70	300	1744	10	70	300
1742/0	20	130	425	1745	10	70	300

3719
1746 Halfpenny

3719 Halfpenny. Old laur. and cuir. bust l. GEORGIVS, R. Britannia, date in ex. die axis ↑↓

1746	10	65	300	1751	10	65	300
1747	10	70	320	1752	10	65	300
1748	10	70	320	1753	10	65	300
1749	10	70	300	1754	10	70	320
1750	10	70	320				

3720

3720 Farthing. Young laur. and cuir. bust l. R. Britannia, date in ex. die axis ↑↓

1730	10	70	330	1735 3 over 5	20	130	425
1731	10	70	330	1736	10	70	330
1732	15	75	365	1736 triple tie ribands	30	130	425
1732/1	20	110	385	1737 small date	10	65	300
1733	10	70	330	1737 large date	15	80	375
1734	15	75	365	1739	10	65	300
1734 no stop on obv.	30	120	385	1739/5	25	100	300
1735	10	65	300				

3721 Farthing. Old laur. and cuir. bust. GEORGIVS R. Britannia, date in ex. die axis ↑↓

1741	15	80	300	1744	10	65	275

3722 Farthing. Similar R. Britannia, date in ex. die axis ↑↓

1746	8	65	240	1750	15	75	275
1746 V over U	90	250	—	1754	5	45	135
1749	15	75	275	1754/0	25	130	300

George III, grandson of George II was born on 4 June 1738. He married Charlotte of Mecklenburg and they had nine sons and six daughters. The French Revolution and the American War of Independence both happened in his long reign, the longest yet of any King. The naval battle of Trafalgar and the Battle of Waterloo also took place during his reign. Later in his reign, he was affected by what seems to be the mental disease porphyria, and the future George IV was appointed as regent. George III died at Windsor Castle on 29 January 1820.

During the second half of the 18th century very little silver or copper was minted. In 1797 Matthew Boulton's 'cartwheels', the first copper Pennies and Twopences, demonstrated the improvement gleaned from the application of steam power to the coining press.

During the Napoleonic Wars bank notes came into general use when the issue of Guineas was stopped between 1799 and 1813, but gold 7s. pieces, Third-Guineas; were minted to relieve the shortage of smaller money. As an emergency measure Spanish 'Dollars' were put into circulation for a short period after being countermarked, and in 1804 Spanish Eight Reales were overstruck and issued as Bank of England Dollars.

The transition to a 'token' silver coinage began in 1811 when the Bank of England had 3s and 1s. 6d. tokens made for general circulation. Private issues of token money in the years 1788-95 and 1811-15 helped to alleviate the shortage of regal coinage. A change over to a gold standard and a regular 'token' silver coinage came in 1816 when the Mint, which was moved from its old quarters in the Tower of London to a new site on Tower Hill, began a complete re-coinage. The Guinea was replaced by a 20s. Sovereign, and silver coins were made which had an intrinsic value lower than their face value. The St. George design used on the Sovereign and Crown was the work of Benedetto Pistrucci.

Engravers and Designers:– Conrad Heinrich Kuchler (c.1740-1810), Nathaniel Marchant (1739-1816), John Rudulf Ochs Jnr. (1704-88), Lewis Pingo (1743-1830), Thomas Pingo (d.1776) Benedetto Pistrucci (1784-1855), Johann Sigismond Tanner (c.1706-75), Thomas Wyon (1792-1817), William Wyon (1795-1851), Richard Yeo (d.1779).

GOLD

EARLY COINAGES

3723
1770 Pattern Five Guineas

3723 Five Guineas. Pattern only, young long haired bust r. R. crowned shield of arms, die axis ↑↑ (en medaille)
1770 *FDC* £330,000   1773 *FDC* £320,000
3723A Five Guineas. Pattern only, young bust right, hair extends under bust similar
1777 *FDC* £300,000

3724
1768 Pattern Two Guineas

3724A
1777 Pattern Two Guineas

3724 Two Guineas. Pattern only, young long haired bust r. R. crowned shield of arms, die axis ↑↑
(en medaille)
1768 *FDC* £90,000   1773 *FDC* £80,000
3724A Two Guineas. Pattern only, thinner young bust right, hair extends under bust similar
1777 *FDC* £70,000
There are six different bust varieties for 3723 and 3724, for further details see Wilson & Rasmussen

3725
1761 Guinea first head, two leaf wreath

3726
1763 Guinea second head

	F	VF	EF		F	VF	EF
	£	£	£		£	£	£

3725 Guinea. First laur. head r., 1761 (varieties with two or three leaves at top
of wreath). R. Crowned shield of arms die axis ↑↓ 2000   5750   13000
3726 Guinea. Second laur. head r. R. Crowned shield of arms die axis ↑↓
1763 1300   4500   11500   1764 no stop
1764 1300   4000   11000   over head........ 2250   5250   11500
Plain edge patterns exist of 1761 Guinea by John Tanner and 1763 by Richard Yeo. Both are
extremely rare and trade too infrequently to price.

3727	3728	3729
Guinea, third head	Guinea, fourth head	Guinea, fifth head, 'spade' type

	F	VF	EF		F	VF	EF
	£	£	£		£	£	£

3727 Guinea. Third laur. head r. R. Crowned shield of arms die axis ↑↓

1765	375	750	2100	1770	1350	2850	7500
1766	375	800	2350	1771	375	700	2000
1767	475	1100	2950	1772	375	700	2100
1768	375	750	2100	1773	375	700	1900
1769	400	800	2500	1773 first 7 over 1	475	1100	—

3728 Guinea. Fourth laur. head r. Crowned shield of arms die axis ↑↓

1774	350	650	1500	1779 9/7 error *exists*			
1774 Proof *FDC* £13000				1781	350	650	1600
1775	350	650	1500	1782	350	650	1600
1776	350	850	2000	1783	350	700	1700
1777	425	650	1600	1784	350	650	1500
1778	425	1000	2850	1785	350	650	1500
1778 E over C in REX *exists*				1786	350	650	1500
1779	350	800	1850				

3729 Guinea. Fifth laur. head r. R. 'Spade'-shaped shield, die axis ↑↑

1787	300	525	1200	1794	300	575	1300
1787 Proof *FDC* £12000				1795	300	575	1300
1788	300	575	1300	1796	300	700	1600
1788 second 8/7 *exists*				1797	300	675	1650
1789	300	600	1350	1798*	300	500	1200
1790	300	625	1500	1798/2 error *exists*			
1791	300	575	1300	1798/7	300	700	1700
1792	300	575	1350	1799	350	750	1950
1793	300	600	1350	* *Beware counterfeits*			

3730	3731
1813 Guinea "Military type"	Half-Guinea, first head

3730 Guinea. Sixth laur. head. r. R. Shield in Garter, known as the Military guinea, die axis ↑↑

1813		800	2250	5000

3731 Half-Guinea. First laur. head r. R. Crowned shield of arms die axis ↑↓

1762	700	2000	5500	1763	800	2650	6500

Note: All figure 1's are Roman style I's for Guineas from 1781-1799.

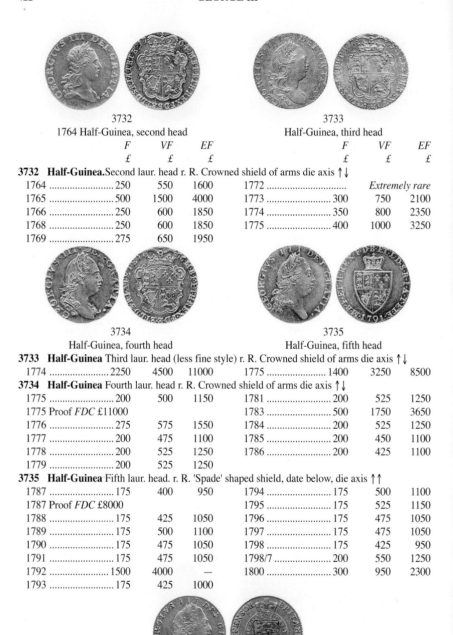

| | 3732 | | | | 3733 | |
| 1764 Half-Guinea, second head | | | | Half-Guinea, third head | | |

| | F | VF | EF | | F | VF | EF |
| | £ | £ | £ | | £ | £ | £ |

3732 Half-Guinea. Second laur. head r. R. Crowned shield of arms die axis ↑↓

1764	250	550	1600	1772		*Extremely rare*	
1765	500	1500	4000	1773	300	750	2100
1766	250	600	1850	1774	350	800	2350
1768	250	600	1850	1775	400	1000	3250
1769	275	650	1950				

| 3734 | 3735 |
| Half-Guinea, fourth head | Half-Guinea, fifth head |

3733 Half-Guinea Third laur. head (less fine style) r. R. Crowned shield of arms die axis ↑↓

| 1774 | 2250 | 4500 | 11000 | 1775 | 1400 | 3250 | 8500 |

3734 Half-Guinea Fourth laur. head r. R. Crowned shield of arms die axis ↑↓

1775	200	500	1150	1781	200	525	1250
1775 Proof *FDC* £11000				1783	500	1750	3650
1776	275	575	1550	1784	200	525	1250
1777	200	475	1100	1785	200	450	1100
1778	200	525	1250	1786	200	425	1100
1779	200	525	1250				

3735 Half-Guinea Fifth laur. head. r. R. 'Spade' shaped shield, date below, die axis ↑↑

1787	175	400	950	1794	175	500	1100
1787 Proof *FDC* £8000				1795	175	525	1150
1788	175	425	1050	1796	175	475	1050
1789	175	500	1100	1797	175	475	1050
1790	175	475	1050	1798	175	425	950
1791	175	475	1050	1798/7	200	550	1250
1792	1500	4000	—	1800	300	950	2300
1793	175	425	1000				

| 3736 |
| Half-Guinea, sixth head |

3736 Half-Guinea Sixth laur. head. r. R. Shield in Garter, date below die axis ↑↑

| 1801 | 175 | 350 | 800 | 1803 | 225 | 425 | 900 |
| 1802 | 200 | 375 | 850 | | | | |

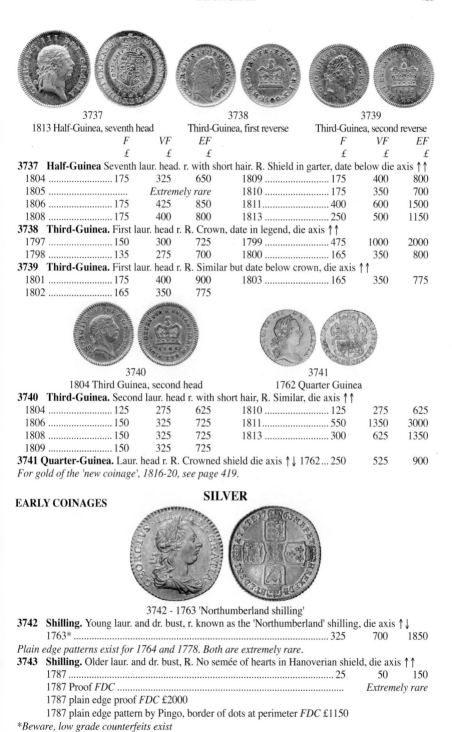

3737
1813 Half-Guinea, seventh head

3738
Third-Guinea, first reverse

3739
Third-Guinea, second reverse

	F	VF	EF		F	VF	EF
	£	£	£		£	£	£

3737 Half-Guinea Seventh laur. head. r. with short hair. ℞. Shield in garter, date below die axis ↑↑

1804	 175	325	650	1809	 175	400	800
1805	....	*Extremely rare*		1810	 175	350	700
1806	 175	425	850	1811	 400	600	1500
1808	 175	400	800	1813	 250	500	1150

3738 Third-Guinea. First laur. head r. ℞. Crown, date in legend, die axis ↑↑

1797	 150	300	725	1799	 475	1000	2000
1798	 135	275	700	1800	 165	350	800

3739 Third-Guinea. First laur. head r. ℞. Similar but date below crown, die axis ↑↑

1801	 175	400	900	1803	 165	350	775
1802	 165	350	775				

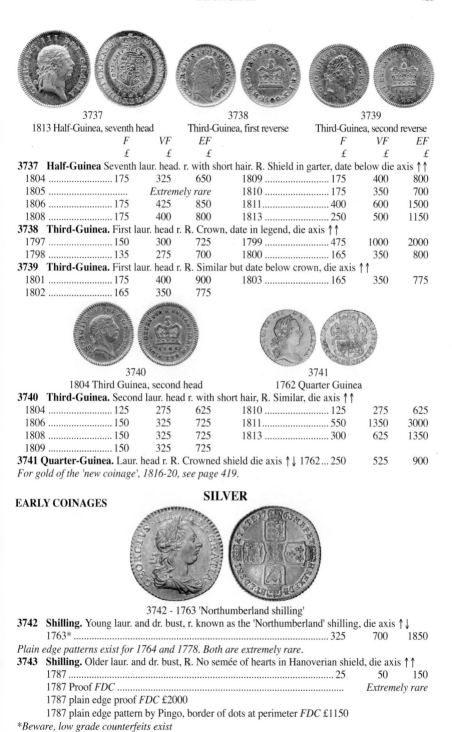

3740
1804 Third Guinea, second head

3741
1762 Quarter Guinea

3740 Third-Guinea. Second laur. head r. with short hair, ℞. Similar, die axis ↑↑

1804	 125	275	625	1810	 125	275	625
1806	 150	325	725	1811	 550	1350	3000
1808	 150	325	725	1813	 300	625	1350
1809	 150	325	725				

3741 Quarter-Guinea. Laur. head r. ℞. Crowned shield die axis ↑↓ 1762 ... 250   525   900

For gold of the 'new coinage', 1816-20, see page 419.

EARLY COINAGES   # SILVER

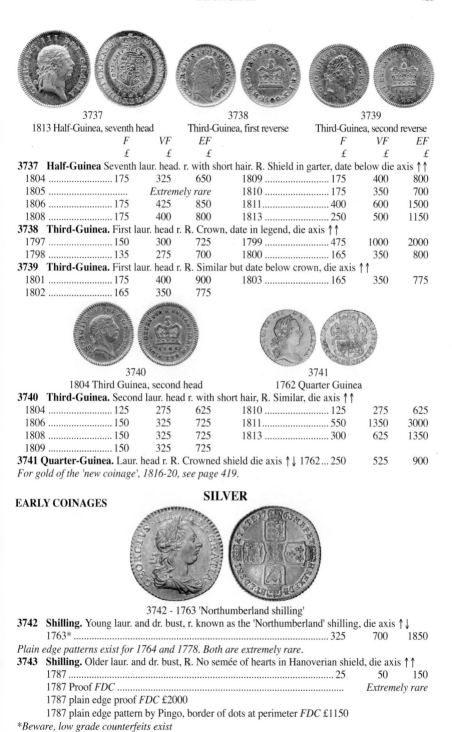

3742 - 1763 'Northumberland shilling'

3742 Shilling. Young laur. and dr. bust, r. known as the 'Northumberland' shilling, die axis ↑↓

1763* 325   700   1850

Plain edge patterns exist for 1764 and 1778. Both are extremely rare.

3743 Shilling. Older laur. and dr. bust, ℞. No semée of hearts in Hanoverian shield, die axis ↑↑

1787 25   50   150

1787 Proof *FDC* .... *Extremely rare*

1787 plain edge proof *FDC* £2000

1787 plain edge pattern by Pingo, border of dots at perimeter *FDC* £1150

*Beware, low grade counterfeits exist

	F £	VF £	EF £		F £	VF £	EF £
3744 **Shilling.** — No stop over head, die axis ↑↑ 1787	40	85	300				

3745
1781 No stops at date Shilling

3745 **Shilling.** — No stops at date, die axis ↑↑ 1787	65	125	475				
3745A **Shilling.** — No stops on *obv.*, die axis ↑↑ 1787	450	1000	2750				
3746 **Shilling.** — R. With semée of hearts, die axis ↑↑ 1787	20	55	135				
1787 1/1 retrograde	55	150	400				
1787 plain edge proof *FDC (Also known on large 27mm flan.)* £1950							

Hanoverian Arms

No semée of hearts　　With semée of hearts　　　3747 - 1798 Shilling

3747 **Shilling.** No stop over head, 1798: known as the 'Dorrien and Magens' shilling *UNC* £27500

3748 **Sixpence.** Laur. and dr. bust r. R. Without semée of hearts, die axis ↑↑

1787	15	45	115	1787 Proof *FDC*	*Extremely rare*		

3749 **Sixpence.** Similar R. With semée of hearts, die axis ↑↑ 1787 .... 15　　45　　115

3749　　　　　　　　　　　　　　　　3750
1787 Sixpence, with hearts　　　　　　1772 Fourpence

3750 **Fourpence**. Young laur. and dr. bust r. R. Crowned 4, die axis ↑↓

1763	12	25	75	1772/0	8	25	95
1763 Proof *FDC of highest rarity*				1776	12	25	75
1765	200	425	1100	1780	12	25	75
1766	12	25	75	1784	15	30	90
1770	10	25	55	1786	18	35	95
1772	15	30	80				

	3751			3753			3755		
	'Wire Money' Fourpence			Young bust Threepence			Older bust Threepence		
	F	VF	EF				F	VF	EF
	£	£	£				£	£	£

3751 Fourpence. Older laur. and dr. bust. R. Thin 4 ('Wire Money'), die axis ↑↑
1792 ....18 50 125

3752 Fourpence. Older laur. and dr. bust r. R. Normal Crowned 4, die axis ↑↑
1795 ....8 25 75 1800 .... 10 20 65

3753 Threepence. Young laur. dr. bust r. R. Crowned 3, die axis ↑↓
1762 ....5 15 50 1772 small III............. 10 25 70
1763 ....5 15 50 1772 very large III 8 20 70
1763 Proof *FDC of highest rarity* 1780 .... 10 20 70
1765 ....250 500 1150 1784 .... 12 30 75
1766 .... 10 30 70 1786 .... 10 20 65
1770 .... 10 25 65

3754 Threepence. Older laur. dr. bust. r. R. Thin 3 ('Wire Money'), die axis ↑↑
1792 ....18 55 150

3755 Threepence. Older laur. and dr. bust r. R. Normal Crowned 3, die axis ↑↑
1795 .... 10 25 65 1800 ....8 20 45

3756 Twopence. Young laur. and dr. bust r. R. Crowned 2, die axis ↑↓
1763 .... 15 30 60 1776 .... 10 20 60
1763 Proof *FDC of highest rarity* 1780 .... 12 20 60
1765 .... 125 350 625 1784 ....8 20 60
1766 ....8 20 45 1786 ....8 20 60
1772 ....8 20 45 1786 large obv. lettering . 5 20 60
1772 second 7/6............ 6 25 70

3756
Young bust Twopence

3757 Twopence. Older laur. and dr. bust. r. R. Thin 2 ('Wire Money'), die axis ↑↑
1792 .... 18 50 115

3758 Twopence. Older laur. and dr. bust r. R. Normal Crowned 2, die axis ↑↑
1795 ....6 15 45 1800 ....6 15 45

3759 Penny. Young laur. and dr. bust r. R. Crowned 1, die axis ↑↓
1763 .... 15 25 60 1779 ....8 15 60
1763 Proof *FDC* .... *Extremely rare* 1780 .... 10 20 60
1766 .... 10 20 60 1781 .... 10 18 60
1770 ....8 15 60 1784 .... 10 18 55
1772 ....8 20 60 1786 ....8 15 45
1776 ....8 15 60

3760 Penny. Older laur. and dr. bust. r. R. Thin 1 ('Wire Money'), die axis ↑↑
1792 .... 10 30 95

	F	VF	EF		F	VF	EF
	£	£	£		£	£	£

3761 Penny. Older laur. and dr. bust r. Ŗ. Normal Crowned 1, die axis ↑↑

| 1795 | 8 | 18 | 50 | 1800 | 6 | 18 | 50 |

3762 Maundy Set. Young laur. and dr. bust. r. Uniform dates

1763	115	200	425	1780	115	200	425
1763 Proof set *FDC* £10000				1784	115	200	425
1766	115	200	425	1786	115	200	425
1772	115	200	425				

3763 Maundy Set. — Older laur. and dr. bust. r. Ŗ. Thin numerals ('Wire Money'),

| 1792 | 150 | 300 | 750 |

3764 Maundy Set. Older laur. and dr. bust r. Ŗ. Normal numerals. Uniform dates

| 1795 | 60 | 150 | 400 | 1800 | 60 | 130 | 375 |

N.B. Set prices are for matched sets, condition, toning etc.

EMERGENCY ISSUES, die axis ↑↑

3765 Dollar. Pillar type (current for 4s 9d). Spanish American 8 Reales, oval countermark with head of George III.

Mexico City Mint — m̥ mint mark in reverse legend	1250	3000	—
Bolivia, Potosi Mint – PTS monogram in reverse legend	1500	3750	—
Peru, Lima Mint – LIMÆ monogram in reverse legend	1650	4000	—

two initials of mint master

denomination

mint mark

3765A

Peru Mint Portrait type Dollar with oval countermark

3765A Dollar. Portrait type, oval countermark.

Mexico City Mint — m̥ mint mark in reverse legend	120	350	850
Bolivia, Potosi Mint — PTS monogram in reverse legend	175	625	1300
Chile, Santiago Mint — s̥ mint mark in reverse legend	700	1850	—
Guatemala Mint — NG mint mark in reverse legend	850	2250	—
Spain, Madrid Mint mint mark in reverse left field	400	1500	3250
Spain, Seville Mint mint mark in reverse left field	400	1350	2750
Peru, Lima Mint — LIMÆ monogram in reverse legend	250	775	1500

3765B Dollar. — Oval countermark on silver French Ecu of crown size .... 3750 | 10500 | —

3765C Dollar. — Oval countermark on USA Dollar.. *Of highest rarity*

3765D Dollar. — Oval countermark on silver Italian crown size coins .... *Of highest rarity*

mint mark S   Mint Master
Initials

3766   3766B

Seville Mint Portrait Dollar with octagonal countermark

	F	VF	EF
	£	£	£
3766 Dollar octagonal countermarks with head of George III			
Mexico City Mint — m̊	400	900	2250
Bolivia, Potosi Mint — PTS monogram	850	2000	4250
Guatamala Mint — NG	1200	3250	—
Peru, Lima Mint — LIME monogram	550	1500	3750
Spain, Madrid Mint M to left of reverse shield	1000	2500	—
Spain, Seville Mint S to left of reverse shield	1100	3000	—
3766A Dollar. — Octagonal countermark on French Ecu or Italian Scudi		*Of highest rarity*	
3766B Dollar. — Octagonal countermark on USA Dollar	18500	50000	—

3767
Half-Dollar with oval countermark, Madrid Mint

3767 Half-Dollar. With similar oval countermark of George III,			
Bolivia, Potosi Mint — PTS monogram	300	700	1500
Chile, Santiago Mint — s̊ mint mark	450	1100	—
Spain, Madrid Mint — Crowned M to left of shield	175	450	1000
Spain, Seville Mint — Crowned S to left of shield	175	450	1000
3767A Half Dollar. With Octagonal countermark. Similar .... *from* 800	800	1500	—

BANK OF ENGLAND ISSUE, 1804-16

3768

	F £	VF £	EF £		F £	VF £	EF £

3768 Dollar. (current for 5s. until 1811, revalued at 5s. 6d. until withdrawn from circulation in 1817). laur. and dr. bust of king. r. ℞.

Britannia seated l., several varieties occur, die axis ↑↑

		F	VF	EF
1804 O. Top leaf to left side of E, R. Upright K to left of shield	....	125	300	775
1804 — —no stops in CHK on truncation	....	175	400	950
1804 O. Top leaf to centre of E R. Similar	....	150	350	850
1804 — —no stop after REX	....	125	300	800
1804 —R. K inverted and incuse	....	175	475	1100
1804 O. Top leaf to right side of E, R. normal K	....		*Extremely rare*	
1804 —R. K inverted to left of shield	....	175	450	1000

Various 1804 Proof strikings of varieties above *FDC from* £1950 to £4750

These dollars were re-struck from Spanish-American 8-Reales until at least 1811. Dollars that still show dates and Mint marks of original coin beneath are worth up to 25% more.

3769
1811 Three Shillings, first bust

3770
Three Shillings, second head

3769 Three Shillings. Dr and laur. bust in armour r. ℞. BANK / TOKEN / 3 SHILL. / date (in oak wreath), die axis ↑↑

1811	 20	75	275	1812	 20	75	300

1811 Proof *FDC* £1750

3770 Three Shillings. — Laureate head r. Top leaf between I/G ℞. As before but wreath of oak and olive, die axis ↑↑

1812	 20	75	275	1813	 20	75	325
1812 Proof *FDC* £1800				1814	 20	75	325
1812 Proof in gold *FDC*	.........*Extremely rare*			1815	 20	75	325
1812 Proof in platinum *FDC* £25000				1816*	 375	800	2750

*Beware of counterfeits

3771
Eighteenpence, first bust

3772
Eighteenpence, second head

	F	VF	EF			F	VF	EF
	£	£	£			£	£	£

3771 Eighteenpence. Dr. and laur. bust r. in armour ℞ BANK/TOKEN/ls. 6D./date (in oak wreath) ↑↑

1811 .... 12 40 225   1812 .... 15 45 250

1811 Proof *FDC* £1400

3772 Eighteenpence. Laureate head r. die axis ↑↑

1812 .... 12 40 225   1813 Platinum proof *FDC of the highest rarity*

1812 Proof *FDC* £1400   1814 .... 12 45 275

1812 Platinum proof *FDC* £25000   1815 .... 12 45 275

1812 Proof R. Small letters *FDC* £3500   1816 .... 12 45 275

1813 .... 12 45 250

3773
1812 Pattern Ninepence, 9D type

3773 Ninepence. Similar, Laur. head 1812, ℞. 9D type (pattern only) die axis ↑↑ *FDC* £2750

3773A Ninepence. — — 1812, ℞. 9 pence type (pattern only) die axis ↑↑ FDC £4500

timeline
Auctions
Inc. Gregory's **Est.1858**

We are accepting single entries
and collections of milled coins

www.timelineauctions.com

+44 [0]1277 815121

enquiries@timelineauctions.com

Follow us on:

f /TimeLineAuctions

t @TimeLineAuction

COPPER

First Issue — Tower Mint, London

3774   3775

Rev. C, leaves point between A and N

	F	VF	EF		F	VF	EF
	£	£	£		£	£	£

3774 Halfpenny. Laur. and Cuir. bust r. R. Britannia l. date in ex., die axis ↑↓

	F	VF	EF
1770 10	60	350	
1770 Proof die axis ↑↑ *FDC* £1950			
1770 Proof in silver *FDC*		*Extremely rare*	
1770 no stop on rev. 15	65	425	
1771 10	50	325	
1771 no stop on rev.........15	65	400	
1771 ball below			
spear blade 10	50	300	
1772 incuse hair coil			
on rev. 10	55	350	
1772 GEORIVS error 50	150	550	

	F	VF	EF
1772 ball below			
spear blade 10	50	275	
1772 no incuse			
hair coil 10	55	325	
1772 — no stop on rev....15	65	375	
1773 12	55	350	
1773 no stop after REX 20	65	425	
1773 no stop on rev. 20	65	425	
1774 different obv.			
profile...................20	80	475	
1775 — 12	75	475	

3775 Farthing. Laur. and cuir. bust r. R. Britannia l. date in ex., die axis ↑↓

	F	VF	EF
1771 Rev A. leaf to r.of N.18	65	350	
1771 Rev B. leaf to N....18	60	325	
1771 Rev C....................18	60	300	
1771 1st 7/1 25	185	575	
1773 10	50	200	
1773 no stop on rev........12	65	375	

	F	VF	EF
1773 no stop after REX . 25	75	400	
1774 12	50	275	
1775 12	50	300	
1775 struck en			
medaille ↑↑ 25	75	375	
1775 GEORGIVS.........35	250	750	

Note: 1771 varieties refer to the direction the top leaf of olive branch points in Britannia's hand

Second Issue—Soho Mint. Birmingham 'Cartwheel' coinage, die axis ↑↓

3776

3776 Twopence. Legends incuse on raised rim,

1797 Copper proof *FDC* £2250
1797 Bronzed proof *FDC* £2000
1797 Silver proof *FDC*.......... *Extremely rare*

	F	VF	EF
1797 30	75	375	
1797 Gold proof *FDC* ....*Extremely rare*			
1797 Gilt copper *FDC* £3250			

Prices for UNCIRCULATED copper coins are no longer quoted. Truly uncirculated copper coins of this period are too seldom traded on the market to fix a meaningful price. As a guide a truly uncirculated coin with full lustre or bloom should fetch 3-4 times the EF price.

3777

	F	VF	EF
	£	£	£
3777 Penny. 1797. Similar, 10 leaves in wreath on obv.	12	60	175
1797 11 leaves in wreath on obv.	15	95	700
1797 Gilt copper proof *FDC* £2250			
1797 Copper proof *FDC* £1500			
1797 Bronzed proof *FDC* £1250			
1797 Silver proof *FDC*			*Extremely rare*
1797 Gold proof *FDC*			*Extremely rare*

Halfpence and Farthings of this issue are patterns.

Third Issue—Soho Mint, Birmingham, die axis ↑↓

| 3778 | | 3779 | |

	VF	EF		VF	EF
	£	£		£	£

3778 Halfpenny. Laur. and dr. bust r., R. Britannia l. date below

1799 Ship on rev. with 5 incuse gunports	10	60	1799 Ship with plain hull	12	135
1799 Ship with 6 relief gunports	10	120	1799 — raised line on hull	15	150
1799 Ship with 9 relief gunports	15	150	1799 Copper proof *FDC* £650		
			1799 Bronzed proof *FDC* £600		
			1799 Gilt copper proof *FDC* £1100		

3779 Farthing. Laur. and dr. bust r. date below R. Britannia l.

1799 Obv. with 3 berries in wreath	5	55	1799 Obv. with 4 berries in wreath	5	80
1799 Copper *FDC* £500			1799 Gold proof *FDC of the highest rarity*		
1799 Bronzed proof *FDC* £450			1799 Silver proof *FDC Extremely rare*		
1799 Copper gilt proof *FDC* £900					

Fourth Issue—Soho Mint, Birmingham, die axis ↑↓

3780

	VF	EF		VF	EF
	£	£		£	£

3780 Penny. Shorter haired, laur. and dr. bust r. date below. R. Britannia l. date below

	VF	EF		
1806 incuse hair curl			1807 Copper proof *FDC* £750	
by tie knot 12		75	1807 Bronzed proof *FDC* £700	
1806 no incuse hair curl.............. 12		110	1807 Gilt copper proof *FDC* £2000	
1806 Copper proof *FDC* £650			1807 Silver proof *FDC* .... *Extremely rare*	
1806 Bronzed proof *FDC* £600			1807 Gold proof *FDC* .... *Extremely rare*	
1806 Gilt copper proof *FDC* £1250			1807 Platinum proof *FDC* .... *Extremely rare*	
1806 Silver proof *FDC* £5750			1808 Proof *FDC*................................. *Unique*	
1807 20		95		

3781   3782

3781 Halfpenny. Shorter haired laur. and dr. bust r. date below, R. Britannia l.

1806 rev. no berries....................... 8		40	1807 10		65
1806 rev. 3 berries........................ 8		85	1807 Copper proof *FDC* £500		
1806 Copper proof *FDC* £500			1807 Bronzed proof *FDC* £450		
1806 Bronzed proof *FDC* £450			1807 Silver proof *FDC* £4000		
1806 Gilt proof *FDC* £850			1807 Gold proof *FDC*............ *Extremely rare*		
1806 Silver proof *FDC* .... *Extremely rare*					

3782 Farthing. Shorter haired laur. and dr. bust r. date below, R. Britannia l.

1806 K. on tr. 10		60	1806 Gold proof *FDC*............ *Extremely rare*		
1806 incuse dot on tr................... 30		150	1807 10		100
1806 Copper proof *FDC* £500........			1807 Copper proof *FDC* £550		
1806 Bronzed proof *FDC* £450			1807 Bronzed proof *FDC* £500		
1806 Gilt copper proof *FDC* £850			1807 Silver proof *FDC* .... *Extremely rare*		
1806 Silver proof *FDC* .... *Extremely rare*			1807 Gold proof *FDC*............ *Extremely rare*		

Prices for UNCIRCULATED copper coins are no longer quoted. Truly uncirculated copper coins of this period are too seldom traded on the market to fix a meaningful price. As a guide a truly uncirculated coin with full lustre or bloom should fetch 3-4 times the EF price.

LAST OR NEW COINAGE, 1816-20

The year 1816 is a landmark in the history of our coinage. For some years at the beginning of the 19th century Mint production was virtually confined to small gold denominations, regular full production being resumed only after the Mint had been moved from the Tower of London to a new site on Tower Hill. Steam powered minting machinery made by Boulton and Watt replaced the old hand-operated presses and these produced coins which were technically much superior to the older milled coins.

In 1816 for the first time British silver coins were produced with an intrinsic value somewhat below their face value, the first official token coinage. The old Guinea was replaced by a Sovereign of twenty shillings in 1817, the standard of 22 carat (0.916) fineness still being retained.

Mint Master or Engraver's and/or designer's initials:

B.P. (Benedetto Pistrucci 1784-1855)   WWP (William Wellesley Pole)

GOLD

3783

3783 Five Pounds. 1820 LX (Pattern only) laur. head r. date below R. St George and dragon, edge inscribed die axis ↑↓ *FDC* £385000

1820 Similar plain edge proof *FDC (*only two struck) *Of highest rarity*

3784

3784 Two Pounds. 1820 LX (Pattern only) laur. head r. date below R. St George and dragon, edge inscribed die axis ↑↓ *FDC* £62500

1820 Similar plain edge proof *FDC Extremely rare*

COINS OF ENGLAND
& THE UNITED KINGDOM

SPINK
founded 1666

COINS OF ENGLAND 2017

E-book available on Amazon, iBookstore,
Google, Kobo, OverDrive
and across most other platforms

For more information or enquiries please contact
Tel: +44 (0)20 7563 4000 | Email: books@spink.com
69 Southampton Row, Bloomsbury, London WC1B 4ET

WWW.SPINKBOOKS.COM

3785   3785A

	F £	VF £	EF £	UNC £		F £	VF £	EF £	UNC £

3785 Sovereign. laur. head r. coarse hair, legend type A (Descending colon after BRITANNIAR, no space between REX and F:D:). R̥. St. George and dragon, die axis ↑↓

1817 500   900 1750 5000   1818 800   1600 4500 8750

1817 Proof *FDC* £27500   1819 .... 50000 110000 250000   −

1817 ↑↑ die axis . 1250   −   −   −

3785A Sovereign. Similar legend type B (Ascending colon after BRITANNIAR, space between REX and F:D:) ↑↓

1818 ....700 1400 4000 7500   1818 Proof *FDC* £35000

3785B Sovereign. laur head r. hair with tighter curls, legend type A. R. Similar die axis ↑↓

1818 ....   *Extremely rare*

3785C
Large date, open 2 variety

3785C Sovereign. Similar legend type B. (as above) die axis ↑↓

1818 ....   *Extremely rare*   1820 short date height, alignment

1820 Roman I in date .   *Extremely rare*   varies...........450   950 2000 4750

1820 open 2, alignment of date   1820 closed 2 alignment of date

    varies...........350   700 1300 4750   varies............400   800 1600 4500

1820 thin date, smaller 0 Proof *FDC* £19500

The above 1820 entries are the main variations, there do exist other subtle differences which are merely sub-varieties and therefore are not included.

3786
1817 Half-Sovereign

3786 Half-Sovereign. laur head r. date below R. Crowned shield, edge milled die axis ↑↓

1817 175   350   700 2050   1818 Proof *FDC* £12500

1817 Proof *FDC* £10000   1818 250   400   800 2500

1818/7....................425   900 2150   −   1820 200   375   700 2250

SILVER

3787

1818 George III Crown

	F	VF	EF	UNC		F	VF	EF	UNC
	£	£	£	£		£	£	£	£

3787 **Crown.** Laur. head r. R̸. Pistrucci's St. George and dragon within Garter edge inscribed, die axis ↑↓

1818	LVIII, edge	45	125	800	1500
1818	LVIII error edge inscription			*Extremely rare*	
1818	LVIII Proof *FDC*			*Extremely rare*	
1818	LIX	45	125	825	1650
1818	LIX TUTΛMEN error	80	350	—	—
1819	LIX	40	110	725	1400
1819	LIX no stops on edge	65	225	950	2000
1819	LIX R. Thicker ruled garter	60	135	850	—
1819/8	LIX	70	275	1000	—
1819	LX	50	135	750	1500
1819	LX no stop after TUTAMEN	60	150	850	—
1820	LX	45	125	750	1600
1820	LX R. S/T in SOIT	65	250	950	—
1820/19	LX	80	300	1150	—

3788

1817 Halfcrown, large bust

3788 **Halfcrown.** Large laur. bust or 'bull' head r. date below R. Crowned garter and shield die axis ↑↑

1816	30	85	500	750	1817 E/R in DEI			*Extremely rare*	
1816 Proof *FDC* £4500					1817 S/I in PENSE	55	275	850	—
1816 Plain edge proof *FDC* £6000					1817 Proof *FDC* £4500				
1817	25	80	475	700	1817 Plain edge proof *FDC* £5500				
1817 D/T in DEI	75	350	950	—					

3789
1817 Halfcrown, small head

	F £	VF £	EF £	UNC £		F £	VF £	EF £	UNC £

3789 Halfcrown. Small laur. head r. date below, R. Crowned garter and shield die axis ↑↑

1817*	30	90	375	800
1817 Proof *FDC* £4500				
1817 Plain edge proof *FDC* £5500				
1817 Reversed s's in garter	*Extremely rare*			
1818 Reversed s's in garter	*Extremely rare*			
1818**	40	110	525	900

1818 Proof *FDC* £5000				
1819 Proof *FDC* £4750				
1819	30	90	475	800
1819/8		*Extremely rare*		
1820	40	110	550	900
1820 Proof *FDC* £4500				
1820 Plain edge proof *FDC* £5000				

* Beware recent low grade forgeries
** Beware of silvered base metal contemporary forgeries

3790
1819 Shilling

3790 Shilling. laur head r. date below R. Crowned Shield in Garter edge milled, die axis ↑↑

1816	10	20	85	175
1816 Proof *FDC* £1500				
1816 Plain edge proof *FDC* £1650				
1816 Proof in gold *FDC*	*Extremely rare*			
1817	10	20	95	200
1817 RRITT flaw	20	35	160	350
1817 Plain edge proof *FDC* £1550				
1817 GEOE error	65	225	600	1100
1817 E over R in GEOR *exists*				

1818	25	65	225	550
1818 High 8	30	75	250	525
1819/8	15	35	150	400
1819	15	30	110	225
1819 9/6 exists				
1820	15	30	110	225
1820 I/S in HONI	35	75	275	575
1820 Proof *FDC* £1550				

3791
1817 Sixpence

	F	VF	EF	UNC		F	VF	EF	UNC
	£	£	£	£		£	£	£	£

3791 Sixpence. laur head r. date below R. Crowned Shield in Garter edge milled, die axis ↑↑

	F	VF	EF	UNC		F	VF	EF	UNC
1816	8	15	70	150	1819/8	15	25	100	200
1816 Proof plain edge FDC £1300					1819	12	20	95	165
1816 Proof in gold FDC			Extremely rare		1819 small 8	12	20	85	160
1817	10	18	80	165	1820	12	20	85	150
1817 Proof plain edge FDC £1300					1820 inverted 1	80	325	650	—
1817 Proof milled edge FDC £1600					1820 I/S in HONI	75	300	575	—
1818	12	20	90	175	1820 obv. no colons	125	400	750	—
1818 Proof milled edge FDC £1750					1820 milled edge Proof FDC £1600				

3792

3792 Maundy Set. (4d., 3d., 2d. and 1d.) laur. head, date below die axis ↑↑

		F	VF	EF	UNC			F	VF	EF	UNC
1817			80	175	400	1820			75	150	375
1818			75	150	375						
3793	**— Fourpence.** 1817, 1818, 1820 ....*from*	12	25	65	100
3794	**— Threepence.** 1817, 1818, 1820 ....*from*	10	20	55	80
3795	**— Twopence.** 1817, 1818, 1820 ....*from*	10	18	35	65
3796	**— Penny.** 1817, 1818, 1820 ....*from*	8	15	35	65

Maundy pennies are always the most requested oddment, it is the smallest coin in the set and is therefore the easiest to lose. Penny collectors also dictate supply and demand for this coin.

Timeline Auctions
Inc. Gregory's Est.1858
We are accepting single entries
and collections of coins & antiquities

www.timelineauctions.com

Sold for:
£3,993

George IV, eldest son of George III, was born on 12 August 1762 and was almost a complete opposite to his father. He was very extravagant and lived in the height of luxury. He especially influenced fashion of the time which became known as the 'Regency' style. He had numerous mistresses, and had an arranged marriage with Caroline of Brunswick. She later left England and travelled Southern Europe, North Africa and the Holy Land basing herself in Naples but returned to claim her place as Queen upon George's accession. George banned her from ever being crowned, and he died without ever conceiving a son on 26 June 1830, when his younger brother William ascended the throne.

The Mint resumed the coinage of copper farthings in 1821, and pennies and halfpennies in 1825. A gold Two Pound piece was first issued for general circulation in 1823. A full cased proof set of the new bare head coinage was issued in limited quantities in 1826.

Engraver's and/or designer's initials on the coins:
B. P. (Benedetto Pistrucci)   W. W. P. (William Wellesley Pole) – Master of the Mint
J. B. M. (Jean Baptiste Merlen)

Engravers and Designers:– Francis Legett Chantrey (1781-1842) Jean Baptiste Merlen (1769-c.1850) Benedetto Pistrucci (1784-1855) William Wyon (1795-1851)

GOLD

3797
3797 Five Pounds. 1826 Bare head l. date below ℞. Crowned shield and mantle, inscribed edge, die axis ↑↓   Proof *FDC* £48500
1826 Piedfort proof *FDC* ....   *Extremely rare*

www.1stSovereign.co.uk
Coins Bought and Sold
ADRIAN GORKA BOND
Email: sales@1stsovereign.co.uk
Tel: 0044(0) 7500772080

3798

3799

	F	VF	EF	UNC
	£	£	£	£

3798 Two Pounds. 1823 Proof *FDC* £10000

1823 Proof no JBM below truncation *FDC* .... *Extremely rare*

1823 Large bare head. l. R. St. George, inscribed edge ↑↓ 700   1100   2500   4500

3799 Two Pounds. Bare head l. date below R. Crowned shield and mantle inscribed edge

    die axis ↑↓

1824 Proof *FDC*   *Extremely rare*   1826. Piedfort proof *FDC*   *Extremely rare*

1825 Proof plain edge *FDC* £18500   1826. Proof *FDC* £13500

3801   3803

Sovereign, second type   Half-Sovereign, second reverse

	F	VF	EF	UNC		F	VF	EF	UNC
	£	£	£	£		£	£	£	£

3800 Sovereign. Laur. head. l. R. St. George and dragon date in ex., die axis ↑↓

1821 400   700   1750   3750   1823 900   2600   7750   —

1821 Proof *FDC* £10500   1824 500   900   2100   4250

1822* 400   750   1800   4250   1825 750   2000   5750   9250

3801 Sovereign. Bare head. date below l. R. Crowned shield, die axis ↑↓

1825 400   750   1600   3500   1827* 425   750   1600   4000

1825 Proof 8 heart semée *FDC* £12500   1828 6000   15000   29500   —

1825 Plain edge proof 7 heart   1829 500   800   2250   4250

    semée *FDC* £13500   1830 500   800   2250   4250

1826 400   700   1500   3750   1830 die axis ↑↑ *Extremely rare*

1826 Proof *FDC* £8500   1830 Milled edge proof *FDC* £40000

3802 Half-Sovereign. Laur. head. l. R. Ornately garnished Crowned shield. die axis ↑↓

1821 950   1800   3250   6250

1821 Proof *FDC* £8500

3803 Half-Sovereign. Laur. head l. R. Plain Crowned shield die axis ↑↓

1823 225   400   900   2350   1825 200   300   650   1800

1824 200   350   750   2000

*Beware counterfeits

3804 -1825 Half Sovereign, bare head

	F	VF	EF	UNC		F	VF	EF	UNC
	£	£	£	£		£	£	£	£

3804 Half-Sovereign. Bare head. date below l. R. Crowned garnished shield die axis ↑↓

1826	200	325	850	1850	1827	200	350	900	2100
1826 Proof *FDC* £5000					1828	200	300	850	2000

3804A Half-Sovereign. Similar with extra tuft of hair to l. ear, much heavier border, die axis ↑↓

1826	200	300	800	1850	1827	200	350	850	2100
1826 Proof *FDC* £5000					1828	200	325	800	2000

SILVER

WWP   B.P.

3805 - 1821 Laureate bust Crown

3805   Crown. Laur. head. l. R. St. George, date in exergue, B.P. to upper right, tiny italic WWP under lance, die axis ↑↓

1821*, edge SECUNDO	50	150	675	1500
1821 SECUNDO WWP inverted under lance	75	450	1000	2250
1821 SECUNDO Proof *FDC* £5000				
1821 SECUNDO Proof in copper *FDC* £10000				
1821 TERTIO Proof *FDC* £9750				
1822 SECUNDO	60	225	1150	2750
1822 TERTIO	55	200	900	2000

3806 - 1826 Proof Crown, bare head

3806 Crown. Bare head. l. R. Shield with crest inscribed edge, die axis ↑↓

1825 Proof *FDC* £25000	1826 Proof *FDC* £21500

* Beware of recent counterfeits in high grade

3807

3807

Halfcrown, lightly garnished shield,
right thistle leaf further from stem

Heavy garnishing, right thistle leaf closer,
more parallel to its stem

	F	VF	EF	UNC		F	VF	EF	UNC
	£	£	£	£		£	£	£	£

3807 Halfcrown. Laur. head. l. R. Crowned Garnished shield, die axis ↑↓

1820 25	85	450	750		1821 Heavier shield garnishing				
1820 Proof *FDC* £2750					40	90	550	1100	
1820 Plain edge proof *FDC* £3750					1823 — 1250	4500	16500	—	
1821 25	85	450	750		1821 Proof *FDC* £2250				

3808

3809

Halfcrown, second reverse

1826 Halfcrown, bare head, third reverse

3808 Halfcrown. Laur. head l. R. Crowned Shield in garter and collar die axis ↑↓

1823 30	90	500	950	1824 40	110	550	1000
1823 Proof *FDC* £5250				1824 Proof *FDC* £5750			

3809 Halfcrown. Bare head. date below l. R. Crowned Shield with crest die axis ↑↓

1824	*Extremely rare*			1826 35	85	425	800
1824 Proof *FDC* £9000				1826 Proof *FDC* £2750			
1825 30	80	400	750	1828 110	300	1100	2750
1825 Proof *FDC* £3250				1829 75	150	600	1100
1825 Plain edge proof *FDC* £3500							

3810 - First reverse

3811 - Second reverse

3810 Shilling. Laur. head. l. R. Crowned garnished shield, die axis ↑↓

1821	12	60	225	600	1821 Milled edge Proof *FDC* £1500			

3811 Shilling. Laur. head l. R. Crowned shield in Garter die axis ↑↓

1823 45	125	350	950	1825 15	60	275	700
1823 Proof *FDC* £3500				1825 Milled edge Proof *FDC* £3250			
1824 8	50	250	675	1825/3	*Extremely rare*		
1824 Milled edge Proof *FDC* £3500							

3812 - Third reverse

	F	VF	EF	UNC		F	VF	EF	UNC
	£	£	£	£		£	£	£	£

3812 Shilling. Bare head l. date below R. Lion on crown die axis ↑↓

1825 8	50	175	500	1826/2			*Extremely rare*	
1825 Roman I 150	450	1100	2200	1827 45	130	450	1100
1825 Milled edge Proof *FDC* £1350				1829 25	65	350	875
1826 5	35	125	425	1829 Milled edge Proof *FDC* £3250			
1826 Proof *FDC* £1100							

3813 - First reverse   3814 - Second reverse   3815 - Third reverse

3813 Sixpence. Laur. head. l. R. Crowned Garnished shield, die axis ↑↓

| 1821 ....8 | 30 | 165 | 500 | 1821 BBITANNIAR. 100 | 350 | 1000 | — |
| 1821 Proof *FDC* £1000 | | | | | | | |

3814 Sixpence. Laur. head l. R. Crowned Shield in Garter die axis ↑↓

1824 8	30	200	550	1825 Proof *FDC* £1500			
1824 Proof *FDC* £1500				1826 35	120	350	850
1825 8	25	190	525	1826 Proof *FDC* £2500			

3815 Sixpence. Bare head. l. with or without tuft of hair to l. of ear date below R. Lion on crown die axis ↑↓

1826 8	35	120	500	1828 12	65	275	725
1826 Proof *FDC* £1000				1829 12	40	175	550
1827 55	150	350	850	1829 Proof *FDC* £1650			

3816 - 1822 Maundy Set

	EF	FDC		EF	FDC
	£	£		£	£

3816 Maundy Set. (4d., 3d., 2d. and 1d.) laur head l. die axis ↑↓

1822	250	450	1827	175	400
1822 Proof set *FDC*	*Extremely rare*		1828	175	400
1823	175	400	1828 Proof set *FDC*	*Extremely rare*	
1824	200	450	1829	175	400
1825	175	400	1830	165	400
1826	175	400			

3817	**Maundy Fourpence.** 1822-30 ....*from*	18	55
3818	**— Threepence**. small head, 1822	35	85
3819	**— Threepence**. normal head, 1823-30 ....*from*	15	50
3820	**— Twopence**. 1822-30 ....*from*	15	45
3821	**— Penny**. 1822-30..*from*	22	60

See note on p. 429 (under 3796)

COPPER

3822 - First Issue Farthing

	F	VF	EF	UNC			F	VF	EF	UNC
	£	£	£	£			£	£	£	£

First Issue, 1821-6. Obv. reads GEORGIUS IIII

3822 Farthing. Laur. and dr. bust l. R. Britannia r. date in ex. die axis ↑↓

1821	3	12	60	175
1822 leaf ribs incuse	2	10	50	150
1822 — inv. A's legend	30	95	375	—
1822 leaf ribs raised	2	10	50	150
1822 Proof *FDC* £1100
1822 Proof die axis ↑↑ *FDC* £1350
1823 —	3	12	60	175

1823 — I for 1 in date	25	85	300	—
1825 —	3	12	60	175
1825 — D/U in DEI	20	85	325	—
1825 leaf ribs raised	5	15	65	200
1825 gold proof *FDC*		*Extremely rare*
1826 —	5	18	75	225
1826 R/E in GRATIA	20	80	300	—

See 3825 for Second Issue farthings of 1826 which have die axis ↑↑

3823 - 1826 Penny - plain saltire

Second issue, 1825-30. Obv. reads GEORGIUS IV

3823 Penny. Laur. head. l. R. Britannia, with shield bearing saltire of arms die axis ↑↑

| 1825 | 10 | 50 | 300 | 875 |
| 1825 Proof *FDC* £1650 |
| 1826 plain saltire on rev. | 8 | 45 | 250 | 775 |
| 1826 Proof *FDC* £1000 |
| 1826 thin line on saltire | 8 | 50 | 300 | 875 |

| 1826-Proof *FDC* £850 |
| 1826 thick line on saltire | 12 | 70 | 325 | 975 |
| 1826-Proof *FDC* £900 |
| 1827 plain saltire | 225 | 950 | 4000 | 17500 |

3824 - 1827 Halfpenny

3825 - 1830 Farthing

	F £	VF £	EF £	UNC £		F £	VF £	EF £	UNC £

3824 Halfpenny.die axis ↑↑ Laur. head. l. R. Britannia, with shield bearing saltire of arms

1825 10	40	225	450	1826 rev. raised line on saltire.......... 8	30	190	400
1826 rev. two incuse lines on saltire .. 5	15	110	350	1827 rev. two incuse lines on saltire 8	20	165	375
1826 Proof *FDC* £750							

3825 Farthing. die axis ↑↑ Laur. head. l. R. Britannia, with shield bearing saltire of arms

1826 2	8	65	175	1828 2	8	80	185
1826 Proof *FDC* £675				1829 3	12	90	275
1826 Roman I 15	55	375	700	1830 2	8	80	185
1827 3	8	75	200				

3826 - 1828 Half-Farthing

3827 - 1827 Third-Farthing

3826 Half-Farthing. (for use in Ceylon). Laur. head. l. date below R.Britannia die axis ↑↑

1828 rev. helmet intrudes legend............. 10	25	150	350	1830 rev. helmet to base of legend 22	70	325	—
1828 rev. helmet to base of legend 10	30	175	450	1830 rev. helmet intrudes legend............ 10	30	165	425

3827 Third-Farthing. (for use in Malta). Laur. head. l. date below R.Britannia die axis ↑↑

1827		12	65	275
1827 Proof *FDC* £750				

Copper coins graded in this catalogue as UNC have full mint lustre.

PROOF SET
PS1 new issue, 1826. Five pounds to Farthing (11 coins) *FDC* £110000

Timeline
Auctions
Inc. Gregory's Est.1858

We are accepting single entries
and collections of coins & antiquities

www.timelineauctions.com

William IV was born on 21 August 1765, and ascended the throne on his elder brother's death. From c.1791-1811 while Duke of Clarence, he was cohabiting with the actress Dorothea Jordan (1762-1816) who bore him ten illegitimate children. After the death of George IV's daughter, William was coerced into a legitimate marriage with Adelaide of Saxe-Coburg and Saxe-Meinigen. She bore him two daughters who both died in childhood. His reign was most notable for the introduction of the Reform bill and abolition of slavery. William was the last House of Hanover King of Britain, and died on 20 June 1837 when the throne passed to his niece Victoria.

In order to prevent confusion between the Sixpence and Half-Sovereign the size of the latter was reduced in 1834, although the weight remained the same. The smaller gold piece was not acceptable to the public and in the following year it was made to the normal size. In 1836 the silver Groat was again issued for general circulation: it is the only British silver coin which has a seated Britannia as the type and was revised upon the suggestion of Mr Joseph Hume thus rendering the nickname "Joey". Crowns were not struck during this reign for general circulation; but proofs or patterns of this denomination were made and are greatly sought after. Silver Threepences and Three-Halfpence were minted for use in the Colonies.

Engraver's and/or designer's initials on the coins:
   W. W. (William Wyon)
Engravers and Designers:– Francis Legett Chantry (1781-1842) Jean Baptiste Merlen (1769-c.1850) William Wyon (1795-1851).

GOLD

3828	3829B
1831 Proof Two Pounds	Second bust with broad ear top

	F	VF	EF	UNC		F	VF	EF	UNC
	£	£	£	£		£	£	£	£

3828 Two Pounds. bare head r. R. crowned shield and mantle, date below, edge plain. die axis ↑↓
1831 (proof only) *FDC* £16500

3829 Sovereign. First bust. r. top of ear narrow and rounded, nose to 2nd N of BRITANNIAR, fine obv. beading. R. Crowned shield. Die axis ↑↓

						F	VF	EF	UNC
1830 Proof plain edge FDC *Extremely rare*					1832	800	1600	3750	7500
1831	600	1000	2750	5500	1832 Proof *FDC* £25000				

3829ASovereign. Similar, WW without stops die axis ↑↓

						F	VF	EF	UNC
1831						900	1800	3750	8000

3829BSovereign. Second bust. r. top of ear broad and flat, nose to 2nd I in BRITANNIAR, coarser obv. beading.↑↓

						F	VF	EF	UNC
1830 plain edge proof *FDC* 20000					1836	450	850	1850	4250
1831	6000	12500	—	—	1836 N of ANNO struck				
1831 Proof plain edge *FDC* £9750					in shield	4000	9500	19500	—
1832*	475	800	2000	4000	1837	500	900	2000	4500
1833	550	950	2250	4500	1837 Tailed 8	550	1000	2750	—
1835	550	950	2250	5000					

* Beware of counterfeits

3830
1834 Half-sovereign

3831
Large size Half-Sovereign

	F	VF	EF	UNC		F	VF	EF	UNC
	£	£	£	£		£	£	£	£

3830 Half-Sovereign. Small size (17.9mm), bare head r.R. Crowned shield and mantle. die axis ↑↓

1831 Proof plain edge *FDC* £5000   1834 350   675   1500   3250

1831 Proof milled edge *FDC* £11500

3831 Half-Sovereign. Large size (19.4mm), bare head r.R. Crowned shield and mantle.die axis ↑↓

1835 250   425   975   2150   1837 250   475   1100   2400

1836 300   500   1250   2500

3832 Half-Sovereign. *Obv.* struck from Sixpence die (19.4mm) in error,

1836 1850   4000   10000   —

SILVER

3833 - 1831 Crown. W.W. on truncation

3833 Crown. R. Shield on mantle, 1831 Proof only incuse W.W. on trun. struck ↑↓ *FDC* £25000

1831 Proof struck in gold of five pounds weight *FDC* £333500

1831 Bare head r. raised W. WYON on trun. struck ↑↑ en medaille (medal die axis) *FDC* £35000

1831 Bare head r. similar die axis ↑↓ *FDC* £28500

1831 Bare head r. incuse WW over W. WYON on trun. *FDC Extremely rare*

1834 Bare head r. W.W. on trun. struck die axis ↑↓ *FDC* £52500

WW script

3834

3834 Halfcrown. Bare head.WW in script on trun. R. Shield on mantle, die axis ↑↓

	F	VF	EF	UNC
	£	£	£	£
1831 Plain edge proof *FDC* £2950				
1831 Milled edge proof *FDC* £3250				
1834	25	75	475	900
1834 Plain edge proof *FDC* £4000				
1834 Milled edge proof *FDC* £2750				

	F	VF	EF	UNC
	£	£	£	£
1835	35	125	575	1400
1836/5	45	125	850	1500
1836	25	75	475	975
1836 Proof *FDC* £3250				
1837	45	175	750	1600

WW block

3834A

3834A Halfcrown. Bare head r. block WW on trun. R. Similar. die axis ↑↓

1831 Proof *FDC* £3000				
1834	45	165	775	1600

3835 - 1831 Shilling   3836 - 1834 Sixpence

3835 Shilling. Bare head r. R. Value in wreath, date below. die axis ↑↓

1831 Plain edge Proof *FDC* £1250				
1831 Milled edge proof *FDC* £3150				
1834	12	45	300	700
1834 Milled edge Proof *FDC* £2150				
1835	18	50	325	725

1835 Proof *FDC* Extremely rare				
1836	18	45	325	750
1836 Proof *FDC* Extremely rare				
1837	25	75	375	875
1837 Proof *FDC* £2350				

3836 Sixpence. Bare head r. R. Value in wreath, date below. die axis ↑↓

1831	12	25	160	450
— Proof *FDC* die axis ↑↓ or ↑↑ £875				
1831 Proof milled edge *FDC* £1150				
1834	12	25	185	450
1834 large date	18	35	220	500
1834 Proof *FDC* £1350				
1835	12	25	160	450

1835 Proof *FDC* Extremely rare				
1836	20	45	325	625
1836 Proof *FDC* Extremely rare				
1837	25	60	325	625
1837 Proof *FDC* Extremely rare				
1837 B/RRITANNIAR	Extremely rare			

3837 - 1836 Groat

3839 - 1835 Three-Halfpence

	F £	VF £	EF £	UNC £		F £	VF £	EF £	UNC £

3837 Groat. Bare head r. ℞. Britannia seated, date in ex. die axis ↑↑

1836	5	18	70	150
1836 Proof *FDC* £1100				
1836 Plain edge proof *FDC* £1000				
1836 Proof in gold *FDC* £16500				

1837	8	22	90	200
1837 Type 2 obv. 'more wiry hair' *values as above*				
1837 Proof *FDC* £1200				
1837 Plain edge proof *FDC* £1450				

3838 Threepence. Obverse 1, small head, low hair (for use in the West Indies). As Maundy threepence but with a dull surface, ↑↓

| 1834 | 12 | 25 | 115 | 275 |
| 1835 | 5 | 18 | 85 | 225 |

| 1836 | 5 | 18 | 95 | 250 |
| 1837 | 12 | 25 | 125 | 250 |

3838A — Obverse 2, large head, high hair

| 1834 | 8 | 20 | 95 | 250 |
| 1835 | 7 | 15 | 80 | 195 |

| 1836 | 5 | 12 | 65 | 150 |
| 1837 | 100 | 175 | 300 | 600 |

3839 Three-Halfpence (for Colonial use). Bare head r. ℞. Value, Crowned in wreath, die axis ↑↓

1834	4	10	50	110
1835/4	5	15	55	130
1835 unconfirmed without 5/4				

1836	5	15	55	130
1837	12	40	150	375
1837 Proof *FDC* £1100				

3840 - 1831 Maundy Set

	EF £	FDC £		EF £	FDC £

3840 Maundy Set (4d., 3d., 2d. and 1d.). Bare head r. Die axis ↑↓

1831	200	475	1834	165	425
— Proof *FDC* £950			1835	165	425
1831 Proof struck in gold *FDC* £27500			1836	200	450
1832	175	450	1837	200	450
1833	165	425			

3841 — **Fourpence**, 1831-7	*from*	15	40
3842 — **Threepence**, 1831-7	*from*	25	60
3843 — **Twopence**, 1831-7	*from*	12	40
3844 — **Penny**, 1831-7	*from*	22	50

See note on p. 423 (under 3796)

COPPER

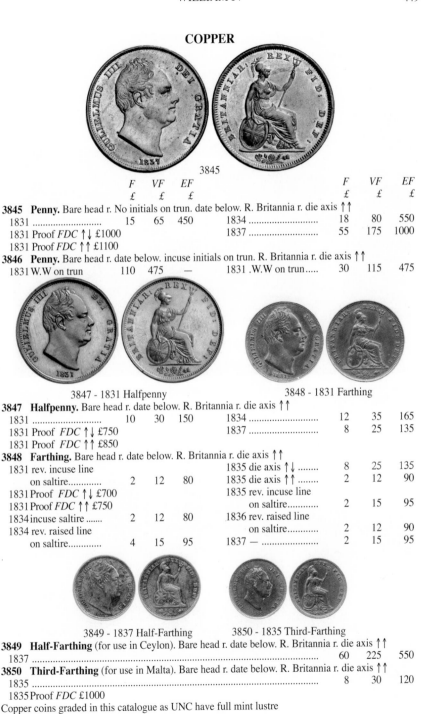

3845

	F £	VF £	EF £		F £	VF £	EF £

3845 Penny. Bare head r. No initials on trun. date below. R. Britannia r. die axis ↑↑

1831	15	65	450	1834	18	80	550
1831 Proof *FDC* ↑↓ £1000				1837	55	175	1000
1831 Proof *FDC* ↑↑ £1100							

3846 Penny. Bare head r. date below. incuse initials on trun. R. Britannia r. die axis ↑↑

1831 W.W on trun	110	475	—	1831 .W.W on trun.....	30	115	475

3847 - 1831 Halfpenny   3848 - 1831 Farthing

3847 Halfpenny. Bare head r. date below. R. Britannia r. die axis ↑↑

1831	10	30	150	1834	12	35	165
1831 Proof *FDC* ↑↓ £750				1837	8	25	135
1831 Proof *FDC* ↑↑ £850							

3848 Farthing. Bare head r. date below. R. Britannia r. die axis ↑↑

1831 rev. incuse line				1835 die axis ↑↓	8	25	135
on saltire.............	2	12	80	1835 die axis ↑↑	2	12	90
1831 Proof *FDC* ↑↓ £700				1835 rev. incuse line			
1831 Proof *FDC* ↑↑ £750				on saltire............	2	15	95
1834 incuse saltire	2	12	80	1836 rev. raised line			
1834 rev. raised line				on saltire............	2	12	90
on saltire.............	4	15	95	1837 —	2	15	95

3849 - 1837 Half-Farthing   3850 - 1835 Third-Farthing

3849 Half-Farthing (for use in Ceylon). Bare head r. date below. R. Britannia r. die axis ↑↑

1837	60	225	550

3850 Third-Farthing (for use in Malta). Bare head r. date below. R. Britannia r. die axis ↑↑

1835	8	30	120
1835 Proof *FDC* £1000			

Copper coins graded in this catalogue as UNC have full mint lustre

PROOF SET.
PS2 Coronation, 1831. Two pounds to farthing (14 coins). *FDC* £80000

SPINK

LONDON
1666

DEFACING THE PAST
Damnation and Desecration
in Imperial Rome

DARIO CALOMINO

ALSO AVAILABLE FROM SPINK
DEFACING THE PAST
DAMNATION AND DESECRATION IN IMPERIAL ROME
by Dario Calomino

Price: £25 + postage

To order your copy, please contact the Spink Books Department:
Tel: +44 (0)20 7563 4046 | Email: books@spink.com
SPINK LONDON | 69 Southampton Row | London | WC1B4ET

#SPINK_AUCTIONS   WWW.SPINKBOOKS.COM

PAUL DAVIES

–BUYING AND SELLING–

WE SPECIALISE IN
MODERN BRITISH GOLD & SILVER PROOF COINS
ALSO BUYING ALL BRITISH & WORLD GOLD COINS

PAUL DAVIES
PO BOX 17, ILKLEY, WEST YORKSHIRE
LS29 8TZ, ENGLAND
PHONE: 01943 603116 FAX: 01943 816326

EMAIL: paul@pauldaviesltd.co.uk

GANA
LIFE MEMBER

BNTA

Victoria was born on 24 May 1819, and enjoyed the longest reign of any Monarch so far. She marrried the German, Prince Albert with whom she enjoyed 21 years of Marriage. Upon Albert's death she descended into a lengthy period of mourning, her ecessive melancholy leading her to be nick-named 'the widow of Windsor'. She skillfully avoided conflict with other European powers, and produced connections with many Royal houses all over Europe. Victoria died on 22 January 1901 at the age of 81.

In 1849, as a first step towards decimalization, a silver Florin (1/10th pound) was introduced, but the coins of 1849 omitted the usual *Dei Gratia* and these so-called 'Godless' Florins were replaced in 1851 by the 'Gothic' issue. The Halfcrown was temporarily discontinued but was minted again from 1874 onwards. Between 1863 and 1880 reverse dies of the gold and silver coins were numbered in the course of Mint experiments into the wear of dies. The exception was the Florin where the die number is on the obverse below the bust.

The gold and silver coins were redesigned for the Queen's Golden Jubilee in 1887. The Double-Florin which was then issued was abandoned after only four years; the Jubilee Sixpence of 1887, known as the 'withdrawn' type, was changed to avoid confusion with the Half-Sovereign. Gold and silver were again redesigned in 1893 with an older portrait of the Queen, but the 'old head' was not used on the bronze coinage until 1895. The heavy copper Penny had been replaced by the lighter bronze 'bun' Penny in 1860. In 1874-6 and 1881-2 some of the bronze was made by Heaton in Birmingham, and these have a letter H below the date. From 1897 Farthings were issued with a dark surface.

Early Sovereigns had a shield-type reverse, but Pistrucci's St. George design was used again from 1871. In order to increase the output of gold coinage, branches of the Royal Mint were set up in Australia at Sydney and Melbourne and, later, at Perth for coining gold of imperial type.

Engraver's and/or designer's initials on the coins:

W. W. (William Wyon 1795-1851)   T. B. (Thomas Brock 1847-1922)
L. C. W. (Leonard Charles Wyon 1826-91)   B. P. (Benedetto Pistrucci, 1784-1855)
J. E. B. (Joseph Edgar Boehm 1834-90)

Engravers and Designers: George William De Saulle, (1862-1903) William Dyce (1806-64), Jean Baptiste Merlen (1769-c.1850) Edward Poynter (1836-1919)

GOLD

YOUNG HEAD COINAGE, 1838-87

3851
1839 Five Pounds - DIRIGIT reverse

3851 Five Pounds. 1839. Young filleted bust l. plain rear fillet R. 'Una and the lion' (proof only)

DIRIGIT legend, inscribed edge, die axis ↑↑	*FDC* £160,000
– 1839 Similar – DIRIGIT legend, struck on thick flan	*FDC* £175,000
– 1839 Similar – DIRIGIT legend, plain edge die axis ↑↑	*FDC* £150,000
– 1839 –13 leaves to rear fillet, R. DIRIGE legend–proof	*FDC* £130,000
– 1839 Similar – DIRIGE legend edge plain proof	*FDC* £135,000
– 1839 –9 leaves to rear fillet, DIRIGE legend	*FDC* £125,000
– 1839 Similar – DIRIGE legend edge plain	*FDC* £140,000
– 1839 Similar – DIRIGIT legend edge plain proof	*FDC* £160,000

Truly FDC 1839 Five Pound coins are hardly ever encountered.

3852
Sovereign - first smaller young head

3852C
Second large head

	F £	VF £	EF £	UNC £

3852 Sovereign. First (small) young head. l. date below. R. First shield. London mint, die axis ↑↓

Left column	F £	VF £	EF £	UNC £	Right column	F £	VF £	EF £	UNC £
1838	875	1500	3500	6750	1843/2 or ℧	450	700	1400	2900
1838 Proof *FDC*		*Extremely rare*			1844 wider date	275	450	900	2000
1838 Plain edge proof *FDC* £25000					1844 closer date	275	450	950	2000
1839	1250	2500	4000	9500	1844 first 4/Ƀ	750	1500	2250	—
1839 die axis ↑↓ Proof *FDC* £10500					1845 wider date	225	450	900	2000
1839 die axis ↑↑ Proof *FDC* £10500					1845 closer date	300	475	925	2000
1839 Milled edge proof *FDC* £22500					1845 4/Ƀ	750	1500	2250	—
1841	5000	10000	22500	—	1845 Roman I	725	1400	—	—
1841 GRATIΛ	4500	9500	21000	—	1846	300	500	950	2000
1842	350	550	975	2000	1846 4/Ƀ	750	1500	—	—
1842 Open 2	600	1000	—		1846 Roman I	675	1250	—	—
1842 GRATIΛ	550	950	—		1847	300	500	950	2000
1843	275	450	925	2000	1847 Roman I	700	1450	—	—
1843 Roman I	675	1250	—	—	1848	1000	2250	7000	—

3852A Sovereign. Similar R similar but leaves of the wreath arranged differently with tops of leaves closer to crown.

	F	VF	EF	UNC
1838	6000	11500	25000	—

3852B Sovereign. Similar narrower shield. Considerably modified floral emblems, different leaf arrangement ↑↓

	F	VF	EF	UNC
1843	5500	10500	22500	—

3852C Sovereign. Second (large) head. l. W W still in relief. date below R. Shield with repositioned legend die axis ↑↓

Left column	F £	VF £	EF £	UNC £	Right column	F £	VF £	EF £	UNC £
1848	300	425	900	2500	1852 Roman I	675	1250	—	—
1849	300	425	900	2600	1852	BV	325	775	2250
1849 Roman I	675	1250	—	—	1853	BV	325	700	1950
1850	325	500	950	2400	1853 F over E in DEF	750	1650	—	—
1850 Roman I	675	1250	—	—	1853 ∇ICTORIA.	1250	—	—	—
1850 ∇ICTORIA.	1250	—	—	—	1854	BV	475	1350	3100
1850 8/5		*Extremely rare*			1855	BV	375	1000	—
1851	BV	375	675	1750					

BV= Bullion value only (if gold price over £1030 an ounce)
NB Truly UNCIRCULATED Victorian sovereigns without any surface marks or hairlines are very rarely encountered.

JON BLYTH
QUALITY COINS
WWW.JONBLYTH.COM
JONBLYTH@HOTMAIL.COM
BNTA +44 (0) 7919 307645 ebay

PAUL DAVIES

—BUYING AND SELLING—

WE SPECIALISE IN
MODERN BRITISH GOLD & SILVER PROOF COINS
ALSO BUYING ALL BRITISH & WORLD GOLD COINS

PAUL DAVIES
PO BOX 17, ILKLEY, WEST YORKSHIRE
LS29 8TZ, ENGLAND
PHONE: 01943 603116 FAX: 01943 816326

EMAIL: paul@pauldaviesltd.co.uk

LIFE MEMBER
BNTA

SPINK
LONDON
1666

BY APPOINTMENT TO
HER MAJESTY THE QUEEN
MEDALLISTS & PHILATELISTS
SPINK & SON LTD. LONDON

BY APPOINTMENT TO
H.R.H. THE DUKE OF EDINBURGH
MEDALLISTS
SPINK & SON LTD. LONDON

ALSO AVAILABLE FROM SPINK
ENGLISH COINS 1180-1551
by Lord Stewartby

This book is an indispensable point of reference for students,
curators, dealers and collectors. It is also a ready source of
information for historians and others with a more general interest in
English medieval coins.

Price: £45 + postage

To order your copy, please contact the Spink Books Department:
Tel: +44 (0)20 7563 4046 | Email: books@spink.com
SPINK LONDON | 69 Southampton Row | Bloomsbury | London | WC1B4ET

ENGLISH
COINS
1180-1551

LORD STEWARTBY

SPINK

⌐SPINK_AUCTIONS   WWW.SPINK.COM   WWW.SPINKBOOKS.COM

3852D
WW Incuse on truncation

3852E
Extra line in ribbon - 'Ansell' named
after Royal Mint Chemist G.F. Ansell

	F £	VF £	EF £	UNC £		F £	VF £	EF £	UNC £
3852D Sovereign. Similar — WW incuse on trun. die axis ↑↓									
1853	300	575	1000	2300	1860	BV	275	500	1150
1853 Roman I	675	1250	—	—	1860 large 0	BV	375	625	1300
1853 Proof *FDC* £20000					1861	BV	300	575	1200
1854	BV	375	725	1500	1861 Roman I	500	750	3250	3250
1854 C over					1861 C over rotated C in				
rotated C	750	1650	—	—	obv. leg	750	1650	—	—
1855 Roman I	650	1450	—	—	1861 T over V in				
1855	BV	375	725	1500	VICTORIA	400	750	—	—
1856	BV	375	725	1500	1861 F/V in DEF				
1857	BV	375	725	1500	narrow date	500	1250	—	—
1857 ⱯICTORIA	1250	—	—	—	1861 E over				
1857/5			*Variety exists*		rotated E	750	1650	—	—
1858 small date	BV	375	725	1600	1862 R/E in BRIT	750	1650		
1858 large date	BV	400	775	1600	1862 Roman I	500	975	—	—
1858 8/7	750	—	—	—	1862 wide date	BV	275	550	1300
1859	BV	375	725	1500	1862 R/ Я in				
1860 O over C in					VICTORIA	1000	2500	—	—
obv. leg	450	1100	—	—	1862 F/Ɐ in DEF	500	1250	—	—
1860 Roman I	650	1450	—	—	1862 narrow date	BV	275	550	1300
1860 ⱯICTORIA	1250	2750	—	—	1863	BV	275	550	1300
1860 DEI GRⱯ	650	1500	—	—	1863 Roman I	500	975	—	—

3852E Sovereign. Similar — As 3852D 'Ansell' ribbon. Additional raised line on the lower part of the ribbon ↑↓

					F	VF	EF	UNC
1859					750	1850	8000	14500

3852F Sovereign. Similar — As 3852D with die number 827 on trun. die axis ↑↓

					F	VF	EF	UNC
1863					4750	10000	18500	—

3853 - Die number location

3853 Sovereign. Similar As 3852D R. die number in space below wreath, above floral emblem, die axis ↑↓

		F	VF	EF	UNC			F	VF	EF	UNC
1863	BV	300	550	1250		1866/5 DIE 17 only	325	500	750	1500	
1864	BV	300	550	1250		1868	BV	300	525	1250	
1865	BV	300	575	1350		1869	BV	300	525	1250	
1866	BV	300	550	1250		1870	BV	300	550	1350	

3853A Sovereign. Similar — As 3853 with die number 827 on trun. R. die number is always no. 22 die axis ↑↓

					F	VF	EF	UNC
1863					3750	7000	15000	—

3853B Sovereign. Similar — WW in relief on trun. R. die number below wreath, above floral emblem die axis ↑↓

		F	VF	EF	UNC			F	VF	EF	UNC
1870	BV	325	500	1150		1872 no die number	BV	300	500	1050	
1871	BV	275	400	1000		1873	BV	375	575	1150	
1872	BV	275	400	1000		1874	2150	4500	10000	—	

BV= Bullion value only (if gold price over £1030 an ounce)

3854 - 'M' Melbourne Mint mark

3855 - 'S' Sydney Mint mark

	F	VF	EF	UNC		F	VF	EF	UNC
	£	£	£	£		£	£	£	£

3854 Sovereign. Second (large) head. l. WW in relief date below R. M below wreath for
Melbourne Mint, Australia ↑↓

	F	VF	EF	UNC		F	VF	EF	UNC
1872 M	BV	BV	275	850	1874 M	BV	BV	325	1100
1872/1 M	200	325	850	2500	1880 M	450	1250	3000	7000

3854A Sovereign. Third young head. Similar but different hair arrangement.

	F	VF	EF	UNC		F	VF	EF	UNC
1881 M	BV	BV	325	1500	1885 M	BV	BV	300	1250
1882 M	BV	BV	325	1250	1886 M	1500	4000	6000	15000
1883 M	BV	200	500	2250	1887 M	600	1100	3000	7500
1884 M	BV	BV	325	1250					

3855 Sovereign. Similar — As 3854. R. with S below wreath for Sydney Mint, Australia die axis ↑↓

	F	VF	EF	UNC		F	VF	EF	UNC
1871 S	BV	BV	325	850	1878 S	BV	BV	300	850
1872 S	BV	BV	325	1100	1879 S	BV	BV	300	850
1873 S	BV	BV	325	1100	1880 S	BV	BV	325	1100
1875 S	BV	BV	325	1100	1880 S VICTORIA	450	1500	3000	7500
1877 S	BV	BV	300	850					

3855A Sovereign. Second (large) head WW incuse on trun. date below R. with S below wreath
for Sydney Mint die axis ↑↓

	F	VF	EF	UNC
1871 S	BV	BV	325	1400

3855B (Previously listed under 3855) as 3854A. Third head with different hair arrangements

	F	VF	EF	UNC		F	VF	EF	UNC
1881 S	BV	BV	325	1000	1885 S	BV	BV	275	1000
1882 S	BV	BV	325	1000	1886 S	BV	BV	275	1000
1883 S	BV	BV	325	1000	1887 S	BV	BV	325	1400
1884 S	BV	BV	325	1000					

*Note: The prices for Australian mint sovereigns are led by current trends in the Australian numismatic
market place (which moved sharply downwards in 2014) and this trend has continued, although less
sharply, in 2015. Being very condition conscious, it is truly UNC coins which command the highest
price, any detraction from a true UNC coin should be taken at the EF guide price. The exchange rate
of the Pound Sterling versus Australian Dollar also has an influence on price.*

3856A

Horse with long tail, small BP in exergue

3857

Melbourne Mint, WW buried in truncation

3856 Sovereign. First young head. l. WW buried in narrow trun. R. St. George. London mint.
Horse with short tail. Large BP and date in ex. die axis ↑↓

	F	VF	EF	UNC
1871	—	BV	325	950

1871 Proof milled edge *FDC* £17500   1871 Plain edge proof *FDC* £12500

3856A Sovereign. — — As 3856 R. Horse with long tail. Small BP and date in ex.die axis ↑↓

	F	VF	EF	UNC		F	VF	EF	UNC
1871	—	BV	300	950	1876	—	BV	300	950
1871 Proof *FDC* plain edge £11000					1878	—	BV	300	950
1872	—	BV	300	950	1879	600	1350	4750	—
1873	—	BV	300	950	1880	—	BV	300	950
1874	—	BV	300	950					

BV= Bullion value only. At the time of going to press the spot price for gold was £1030 per oz.

Horse tails - three variations in tail length exist across Melbourne and Sydney, all are defined more accurately by the number of spurs of extra hair, or not, at tail indent on left side.

Short tail - two spurs of hair in left indent. **Medium tail** - no spurs of hair in left indent. **Long tail** - one spur of hair in left indent.

	F £	VF £	EF £	UNC £		F £	VF £	EF £	UNC £

3856B Sovereign. — — As 3856 R. Horse with short tail, small BP and date in ex.die axis ↑↓

	F	VF	EF	UNC		F	VF	EF	UNC
1880	—	BV	300	950	1884	—	BV	300	950
1880 Second 8/7	BV	250	425	1100	1885	—	BV	300	950

3856C Sovereign. — — As 3856 R. Horse with short tail, date but no BP in ex.die axis ↑↓

	F	VF	EF	UNC		F	VF	EF	UNC
1880	BV	BV	300	850	1880 Second 8/7	BV	250	450	950

3856D Sovereign. Second head. l. WW complete, on broad trun. R. Horse with long tail, small BP and date in ex.die axis ↑↓

	F	VF	EF	UNC		F	VF	EF	UNC
1880 Second 8/7	BV	250	425	950	1880	BV	250	400	850

3856E Sovereign. — — As 3856D R. Horse with short tail. Date but no BP in ex. die axis ↑↓

	F	VF	EF	UNC
1880	BV	250	425	850

3856F Sovereign. — — As 3856E R. Horse with short tail, small BP and date in ex. die axis ↑↓

	F	VF	EF	UNC		F	VF	EF	UNC
1880	BV	BV	300	950	1885	BV	250	400	850
1884	BV	BV	300	950	1887 Proof *FDC* £27500				

3857 Sovereign. — — First head. l. WW buried in trun. M below head for Melbourne Mint, Australia. R. Horse with long tail, small BP and date in ex. die axis ↑↓

	F	VF	EF	UNC		F	VF	EF	UNC
1872 M	BV	BV	400	2500	1877 M	BV	BV	225	650
1873 M	BV	BV	225	800	1878 M	BV	BV	225	650
1874 M	BV	BV	225	800	1879 M	BV	BV	225	500
1875 M	BV	BV	225	650	1880 M	BV	BV	225	600
1876 M	BV	BV	225	650	1881 M	BV	BV	225	600

3857A Sovereign. — — As 3857 R. horse with short tail, date but no BP in ex die axis ↑↓

	F	VF	EF	UNC		F	VF	EF	UNC
1881 M	BV	200	225	650	1883 M	BV	BV	275	1000
1882 M	BV	BV	200	500	1885 M	BV	BV	250	800

3857B Sovereign. First head l. WW buried in trun. M below head for Melbourne Mint, Australia R. Horse with short tail, small BP and date in ex. die axis ↑↓

	F	VF	EF	UNC		F	VF	EF	UNC
1882 M	BV	BV	200	500	1884 M	BV	BV	200	450
1883 M	BV	BV	200	500	1885 M	BV	BV	225	650

3857C Sovereign. — — Second head. l. WW complete on broad truncation. R. Horse with short tail, small BP in ex.

	F	VF	EF	UNC		F	VF	EF	UNC
1882 M	BV	BV	225	750	1885 M	BV	BV	200	450
1883 M	BV	BV	225	500	1886 M	BV	BV	200	450
1884 M	BV	200	225	450	1887 M	BV	BV	225	800

3857D Sovereign. First head. l. WW buried in trun. M below R. Horse with medium tail, small BP

	F	VF	EF	UNC		F	VF	EF	UNC
1879 M	BV	BV	250	800	1881 M	BV	BV	275	1000
1880 M	BV	BV	250	800	1882 M	BV	BV	275	1000

3857E Sovereign. Second head. l. WW complete on trun. M below R. Horse with short tail, no BP in ex.

	F	VF	EF	UNC		F	VF	EF	UNC
1884 M				*Extremely rare*	1885 M	BV	BV	225	600

3858 Sovereign First head. l. WW buried in narrow trun. S below head for Sydney Mint, Australia, R. Horse with short tail, large BP and date in ex. die axis ↑↓

	F	VF	EF	UNC		F	VF	EF	UNC
1871 S						BV	BV	550	2000

3858A Sovereign. — — As 3858 R. Horse with long tail, small BP and date in ex. die axis ↑↓

	F	VF	EF	UNC		F	VF	EF	UNC
1871 S	BV	BV	375	2250	1875 S	BV	BV	250	800
1872 S	BV	BV	250	1000	1876 S	BV	BV	250	800
1873 S	BV	BV	250	1750	1879 S	BV	BV	850	2250
1874 S	BV	BV	250	1250	1880 S	BV	BV	250	800

BV = Bullion value only. At the time of going to press the spot price for gold was £1030 per oz.

3859 - Type A1   3859A - Type A2

	F	VF	EF	UNC		F	VF	EF	UNC
	£	£	£	£		£	£	£	£

3858B Sovereign. First head. As 3858 R. Horse with short tail, date but no BP in ex. die axis ↑↓

	F	VF	EF	UNC		F	VF	EF	UNC
1880 S	BV	BV	300	1100	1881 S	BV	BV	250	750

3858C Sovereign. Second head. l. WW complete on broad trun. R.
Horse with long tail, small BP and date in ex. die axis ↑↓

						F	VF	EF	UNC
1880 S						BV	BV	300	800

3858D Sovereign. — — As 3858C R. Horse with short tail, date but no BP in ex. die axis ↑↓

	F	VF	EF	UNC		F	VF	EF	UNC
1881 S	BV	BV	275	650	1882 S	BV	BV	250	450

3858E Sovereign. — — As 3858D R. Horse with short tail small BP and date in ex. die axis ↑↓

	F	VF	EF	UNC		F	VF	EF	UNC
1882 S	BV	BV	200	450	1885 S	BV	BV	250	450
1883 S	BV	BV	300	1100	1886 S	BV	BV	250	450
1884 S	BV	BV	275	500	1887 S	BV	BV	250	450

3858F Sovereign. Second head. Horse with long tail, no BP in ex.

	F	VF	EF	UNC
1880 S	BV	200	400	850

3859 Half-Sovereign. Type A1. First (smallest) young head. date below l. R. First shield, die axis ↑↓

	F	VF	EF	UNC		F	VF	EF	UNC
1838	185	325	1000	1950	1849	175	300	850	1700
1839 die axis ↑↓ or ↑↑ Proof only *FDC* £5000					1850	250	600	2000	—
1839 Milled edge proof *FDC Extremely rare*					1851	175	300	750	1500
1841	200	325	1100	2750	1852	175	300	800	1600
1842	175	300	800	1600	1853	175	300	750	1450
1843	175	325	850	1850	1853 Proof small date *FDC* £11500				
1844	175	325	800	1700	1853 Proof large date *FDC* £15000				
1845	300	800	3000	—	1855	175	300	750	1550
1846	175	325	800	1700	1856	175	300	725	1450
1847	175	325	800	1700	1856/5	225	350	850	1650
1848 Close date	175	325	800	1700	1857	175	300	750	1500
1848/7	250	500	1100	2350	1858	175	300	750	1500
1848 Wide date	200	325	1000	2000					

3859A Half-Sovereign. Type A2, Second (larger) young head. date below. R. First shield die axis ↑↓

	F	VF	EF	UNC		F	VF	EF	UNC
1858	175	300	625	1300	1861	175	300	700	1250
1859	175	300	625	1300	1862	850	2500	9000	—
1860	175	300	600	1250	1863	175	300	575	1200

3860   3860D   3860E   3860F
Die number location   Type A3   Type A4   Type A5

3860 Half-Sovereign. Type A2, second head, date below R. die number below shield, die axis ↑↓

	F	VF	EF	UNC		F	VF	EF	UNC
1863	175	250	725	1450	1867	BV	200	600	1200
1864	BV	200	600	1200	1869	BV	200	600	1200
1865	BV	200	600	1200	1870	BV	175	575	1100
1866	BV	200	600	1200	1871	BV	175	575	1150

BV= Bullion value only. At the time of going to press the spot price for gold was £1030 per oz.

	F	VF	EF	UNC		F	VF	EF	UNC
	£	£	£	£		£	£	£	£

3860A Half-Sovereign. Second head, date below R. Re-engraved shield legend and rosettes closer to border, coarse boarder teeth both sides, with die number below shield die axis ↑↓

1870	275	675	1500	–	1871	225	575	1350	–

3860B Half-Sovereign. Second head, date below R. As last but with normal border teeth and no die number below shield die axis ↑↓

1871						300	750	1900	–

3860C Half-Sovereign. Second head, date below obv. with repositioned legend, nose now points to T in VICTORIA. R Similar to last but with die number below shield die axis ↑↓

1871	300	875	1800	–	1872	225	575	1350	–

3860D Half-Sovereign. Type A3, Third (larger still) young head l, date below. R. As 3860A, with die number below shield die axis ↑↓

1872	BV	185	500	1100	1875	BV	175	475	1000
1873	BV	185	500	1100	1876	BV	175	475	1000
1874	BV	200	525	1100	1877	BV	175	475	1000

3860E - Half Sovereign   3861 - Type A5

3860E Half-Sovereign. Type A4. Fourth young head l. hair ribbon now narrow, date below. R. As last with die number below shield die axis ↑↓

1876	BV	175	475	1000	1878	BV	175	475	1000
1877	BV	175	475	1000	1879		175	225	675	1250

3860F Half-Sovereign. Type A5. Fifth young head l. in very low relief, date below. R. As last with die number below shield die axis ↑↓

1880						175	225	675	1350

3860G Half-Sovereign. Type A4. Fourth young head, without die number below shield.

1876									*Extremely rare*

3861 Half-Sovereign. Fifth head, date below. R. Cross on crown buried in border. Legend and rosettes very close to heavy border, no die number below shield die axis ↑↓

1880	BV	185	500	1100	1885	BV	175	450	800
1883	BV	175	450	900	1885/3		175	275	850	1500
1884	BV	175	450	900					

3862 Half-Sovereign. Type A2, Second (larger) young head l. nose points between T and O. Date below R. First crowned shield cross clear of border with S below shield for Sydney Mint, Australia, die axis ↑↓

1871 S	125	200	800	8000	1871 S Proof				*Extremely rare*

3862A Half-Sovereign. Similar obv. with repositioned legend, nose now points to T in VICTORIA. Date below R Re-engraved shield cross touches border, S below shield die axis ↑↓

1872 S						125	200	800	8000

3862B Half-Sovereign. Type A3. Third (larger still) young head l. I of DEI points to rear fillet. Date below R. As last die axis ↑↓

1875 S						125	200	800	8000

3862C Half-Sovereign. Type A4. Fourth young head l. front hair fillet now narrow. R. As last, die axis ↑↓

1879 S						125	200	850	7500

3862D Half-Sovereign. Type A5. Fifth young head l. in low relief wider tr. no front ear lobe. Date below R as last. die axis ↑↓

1880 S	125	175	850	1250	1882 S				*Extremely rare*
1880 S Proof				*Extremely rare*	1883 S	125	225	500	10000
1881 S	125	300	1200	14500					

* Beware recent forgeries

BV= Bullion value only. At the time of going to press the spot price for gold was £1030 per oz.

	F	VF	EF	UNC			F	VF	EF	UNC
	£	£	£	£			£	£	£	£

3862E Half-Sovereign. Fifth head, date below Ŗ. Cross on crown buried in border. Legend and rosettes very close to heavy border, S below shield die axis ↑↓

1880 S	125	200	500	11500	1883 S Proof	*Extremely rare*
1881 S	125	225	900	10000	1886 S	125	200	650	4750
1882 S	175	600	2250	14000	1887 S	125	200	550	3750
1883 S	125	200	650	4500					

3863 Half-Sovereign. Type A3. Third (larger still) young head l. Date below Ŗ. Re-engraved shield with M below shield for Melbourne Mint, Australia die axis ↑↓

1873 M	125	200	1100	8000	1877 M	125	250	2750	9500

3863A Half-Sovereign. Type A4, fourth young head l. hair ribbon now narrow. R. As last die axis ↑↓

1877 M	125	200	850	8000	1882 M	125	200	2250	9500

3863B Half-Sovereign. Type A5. Fifth young head l. in low relief. Date below Ŗ. As last die axis ↑↓

1881 M	125	600	4000	12000	1885 M	150	550	5000	11000
1882 M	125	200	750	4500	1886 M	125	400	7000	12000
1884 M	125	250	2750	10000	1886 M Proof	*Extremely rare*
1884 M Proof	*Extremely rare*	1887 M	125	1250	10000	16500

JUBILEE COINAGE, 1887-93, die axis ↑↑

3864 - 1887 Five Pounds

3864* Five Pounds. Jubilee bust 1. Ŗ. St. George date in ex. 1887 .... 1350 2000 2750 3500
— Proof *FDC* £12500
— Proof no B.P. in exergue £18500

3864A* Five Pounds. Jubilee bust 1. Ŗ. St George, S on ground for Sydney Mint, Australia
1887 S .... *Extremely rare*

3865* Two Pounds. Jubilee bust 1. Ŗ. St George die axis ↑↑ 1887 .... 650 875 1250 1750
1887 Proof *FDC* £3000
1887 Proof no BP in exergue FDC *Extremely rare*

3865A* Two Pounds. Ŗ. St George, S on ground for Sydney Mint, Australia ↑↑
1887 S .... *Extremely rare*

3866 - 1887 Sovereign

3866* Sovereign. Normal JEB (ángled J) designer's initials fully on trun. R. St. George. die axis ↑↑

1887	BV	300	475	1890	350	600	1000
1888	325	750	1250	2000			

* Beware recent forgeries

BV= Bullion value only. At the time of going to press the spot price for gold was £1030 per oz.
(See note on page 449 re. horse tails.)
For a detailed variety synopsis of Jubilee Head Sovereigns see publication 'The Jubilee Head Gold Sovereign' by David Iverson.

	VF	EF	UNC			F	VF	EF	UNC
	£	£	£			£	£	£	£

3866A Sovereign. Similar with tiny JEB (hooked J) closer designer's initials at base of truncation; stops in an arc, die axis ↑↑

1887.. 325   750   1250   2000

3866B Sovereign. Similar repositioned legend. G: of D:G: now closer to crown. Normal JEB (angled J) designer's initials at base of trun. ↑↑

1887 Proof *FDC* £2750				1890	BV	325	475
1888...................................BV	325	550		1891 600	1200	2000	—
1889...................................BV	325	475					

3866C Sovereign. Similar obv. as last. R. Horse with longer tail die axis ↑↑

| 1891...................................BV | 325 | 475 | | 1892 .... | BV | 325 | 475 |
| 1891 Proof *FDC* £17500 | | | | | | | |

3866D Sovereign. First legend with tiny JEB (hooked J) with initials more spread across truncation; stops all in line ↑↑

1887.. 350   750   1250   2000

3866E Sovereign. Second legend, normal JEB. R. Horse with medium tail die axis ↑↑

1891 .... *Exists?*

3867

"M' Melbourne Mint on groundline above 8's in date

3867 Sovereign. Similar with small spread JEB (hooked J) designer's initials fully on trun. R. M on ground for Melbourne Mint, Australia, die axis ↑↑

1887 M 275   650   1000   1850

3867A Sovereign. Similar with normal JEB designer's initials on trun. (angled J) die axis ↑↑

1887 M	BV	325	550
1888 M 300	600	1100	2000
1889 M 200	600	1850	
1890 M			*Exists?*

3867B Sovereign. Similar repositioned legend. G: of D: G: now closer to crown. Normal JEB (angled J) initials at base of trun. die axis ↑↑

1887 M 250	500	800		1889 M	BV	325	550
1888 M ....BV	300	550		1890 M	BV	325	550
1888 Proof *FDC* ....*Extremely rare*			1891 M 300	600	1100	2000

3867C Sovereign. Similar obv. as last. R. Horse with longer tail die axis ↑↑

| 1891 M ....BV | 400 | 650 | | 1893 M .... | BV | 325 | 600 |
| 1892 M ....BV | 300 | 500 | | | | | |

3867D Sovereign. Second legend as last. R. Horse with medium tail die axis ↑↑

1893 M .... *Exists?*

3868 Sovereign. First legend with closer JEB (angled J) stops in arc on trun. R. S on ground for Sydney Mint, Australia die axis ↑↑

| 1888 S ....BV | 375 | 675 | | 1890S .... | 300 | 600 | 1350 |
| 1889S ....BV | 375 | 700 | | | | | |

3868A Sovereign. Similar with spread JEB designer's initials stop level on left side of trun.(hooked J) die axis ↑↑

1887 S 400	750	1500	3000
1887 S Proof...	*Extremely rare*		
1888 S 300	600	1100	2000

BV= Bullion value only. At the time of going to press the spot price for gold was £1030 per oz.

	F	VF	EF	UNC		F	VF	EF	UNC
	£	£	£	£		£	£	£	£

3868B Sovereign. Similar repositioned legend. G: of D:G: now closer to crown. Normal JEB (angled J) initials on trun. die axis ↑↑

| 1888 S | .... BV | 300 | 550 | | 1890S | .... | BV | 325 | 600 |
| 1889 S | .... BV | 325 | 600 |

3868C Sovereign. Similar obv. as last. R. Horse with longer tail die axis ↑↑

| 1891 S | .... BV | 300 | 500 | | 1893S | .... | BV | 375 | 650 |
| 1892 S | .... BV | 325 | 600 |

3868D Sovereign. First legend with spread JEB initials ending at right side of trun. (hooked J) ↑↑

| 1887 S | .... 400 | 800 | 1500 | 3000 |

3869
higher shield, cross blends into border

3869D
Plain trun., lower shield, cross clear of border

3869 Half-Sovereign. Similar obv. normal JEB designer's initials. on trun. R. High shield die axis ↑↑

| 1887 | .... BV | 125 | 225 | 375 | | 1890 | .... BV | 175 | 500 | — |

— Proof *FDC* £1750

3869A Half-Sovereign. Similar small close JEB intitials. on trun. R. High shield die axis ↑↑

| 1887 | .... BV | 150 | 450 | — |

3869B Half-Sovereign. Similar normal JEB initials. on trun. R. Lower shield, date therefore spread apart, complete cross at top, die axis ↑↑

| 1890 | .... BV | 150 | 475 | — | | 1892 | .... BV | 150 | 475 | — |

3869C Half-Sovereign. Similar no JEB initials on trun. R. High Shield die axis ↑↑

| 1887 | .... BV | 150 | 450 | — | | 1891 | .... BV | 150 | 450 | — |
| 1890 | .... BV | 240 | 400 | | 1892 | .... BV | 150 | 450 | — |

3869D Half-Sovereign. Jubilee bust 1. R. Lower shield, date therefore spread apart die axis ↑↑

| 1890 | .... BV | 240 | 400 | | 1892 | .... BV | 240 | 400 |
| 1891 | .... BV | 275 | 425 | | 1893 | .... BV | 275 | 425 |

3870

3870 Half-Sovereign. Similar small very spread JEB initials on trun. R. High shield, M below for Melbourne Mint, Australia, die axis ↑↑

| 1887 M | .... 125 | 200 | 400 | 1600 | | 1887 M Proof | .... *Extremely rare* |

3870A Half-Sovereign. Similar small close JEB initials on trun. R. As last die axis ↑↑

| 1887 M | .... 125 | 200 | 350 | 1400 | | 1887 M Proof | .... *Extremely rare* |

3870B Half-Sovereign. Similar normal JEB initials on trun. R. Lower shield, date therefore spread part die axis ↑↑

| 1893 M | .... 125 | 250 | 500 | 2250 |

3871 Half-Sovereign. Similar small very spread JEB initials on trun. (hooked J) R. High shield S below for Sydney Mint, Australia ↑↑

| 1887 S | .... 125 | 200 | 400 | 1200 |

3871A Half-Sovereign. Similar small close JEB initials on trun. R As last. die axis ↑↑

| 1887 S | .... 125 | 200 | 325 | 1100 | | 1887 S Proof | .... *Extremely rare* |

BV= Bullion value only. At the time of going to press the spot price for gold was £1030 per oz.

C.o.R
2003

COINS OF THE REALM
Dealers in Precious & Historical Coinage

Freephone: 0800 169 1066

email: **admin@coinsoftherealm.org**
COR LTD, PO Box 12131, Harlow, CM20 9LY

www.coinsoftherealm.com

Available for sale or purchase by Freephone/Website/Mail order

	EF	UNC			F	VF	EF	UNC
	£	£			£	£	£	£

3871B Half-Sovereign. Jubilee bust 1. Normal JEB initials on trun. R. Lower shield, date therefore
spread apart, S below for Sydney Mint, Australia die axis ↑↑

1889 S 125   250   1400   4500

3871C Half-Sovereign. Jubilee bust 1. Normal JEB initials on trun. R. High shield, S below for
Sydney Mint, Australia die axis ↑↑

1891 S 125   300   1100   3750

3871D Half-Sovereign. Jubilee bust 1. No JEB initials on trun. R. As last die axis ↑↑

1891 S 125   250   700   3000

OLD HEAD COINAGE, 1893-1901, die axis ↑↑

3872
1893 Five Pounds

3872* Five Pounds. Old veiled bust 1. R. St. George and dragon, date and BP in ex.

1893.. 1950   2750   4500   7250

1893 Proof *FDC* £15000

3873   3874
1893 Two Pounds   1893 Sovereign

3873* Two Pounds. Old veiled bust 1. R. St. George and dragon, date and BP in ex. die axis ↑↑

1893.. 750   1000   1950   2750

1893 Proof *FDC* £4750

3874 Sovereign. Old veiled bust 1. R. St. George, London Mint die axis ↑↑

1893	BV	400	1898	BV	400
1893 Proof *FDC* £3000			1899	BV	400
1894	BV	400	1900	BV	400
1895	BV	400	1901	BV	400
1896	BV	400			

3875 Sovereign. Similar R. St. George. M on ground for Melbourne Mint, Australia die axis ↑↑

1893 M	BV	500	1898 M	BV	450
1894 M	BV	450	1899 M	BV	425
1895 M	BV	450	1900 M	BV	425
1896 M	BV	425	1901 M	BV	425
1897 M	BV	425			

* Beware recent forgeries

BV= Bullion value only. At the time of going to press the spot price for gold was £1030 per oz.

*NB Truly UNCIRCULATED old bust sovereigns are very scarce. Any surface defects will cause the
value to drop significantly.*

3876
Perth Mint mark

3878
1893 Half -Sovereign

	F £	VF £	EF £	UNC £		F £	VF £	EF £	UNC £
3876 Sovereign. Similar — P on ground for Perth Mint, Australia die axis ↑↑									
1899 P	BV	250	475	2250	1901 P	BV	250	500	
1900 P	BV	250	500						
3877 Sovereign. Similar — S on ground for Sydney Mint, Australia die axis ↑↑									
1893 S	BV		450		1898 S	BV	250	500	
1894 S	BV		450		1899 S	BV		450	
1895 S	BV		450		1900 S	BV		450	
1896 S	BV	250	500		1901 S	BV		450	
1897 S	BV	250	500						

3878 Half-Sovereign. Old veiled bust 1.R. St. George. Date in ex. (no B.P. on this issue in exergue) London Mint die axis ↑↑

	F £	VF £	EF £		F £	VF £	EF £
1893	BV	150	300	1897	BV	150	300
— Proof *FDC* £2000				1898	BV	150	300
1894	BV	150	300	1899	BV	150	300
1895	BV	150	300	1900	BV	150	300
1896	BV	150	300	1901	BV	150	300

3879 Half-Sovereign. Similar — M on ground for Melbourne Mint, Australia die axis ↑↑

	F £	VF £	EF £	UNC £		F £	VF £	EF £	UNC £
1893 M			*Extremely rare*		1900 M	125	250	650	2000
1896 M	125	250	400	2250	1900 M Proof			*Extremely rare*	
1899 M	125	250	600	2500	1896 M Proof			*Extremely rare*	
1899 M Proof			*Extremely rare*						

3880 Half-Sovereign. Similar — P on ground for Perth Mint, Australia die axis ↑↑

	F £	VF £	EF £	UNC £		F £	VF £	EF £	UNC £
1899 P		Proof only *unique*			1900 P	150	300	750	4000

3881 Half-Sovereign. Similar — S on ground for Sydney Mint, Australia die axis ↑↑

	F £	VF £	EF £	UNC £		F £	VF £	EF £	UNC £
1893 S	125	250	500	1650	1897 S	125	250	425	2000
1893 S Proof			*Extremely rare*		1900 S	125	300	375	1200

BV= Bullion value only. At the time of going to press the spot price for gold was £1030 per oz.
NB Truly UNCIRCULATED old bust sovereigns are very scarce. Any surface defects will cause the value to drop significantly.

BucksCoins

M. 07825 44 00 85   T. 01603 92 70 20
buckscoins1@aol.co.uk
www.stores.ebay.co.uk/BucksCoins

Specialists in Celtic, hammered, milled and world coins. Investment gold, tokens, commemorative medals and banknotes.

St Mary's House
Duke Street • Norwich
Norfolk NR3 1QA

SILVER

YOUNG HEAD COINAGE, 1838-87, die axis ↑↓

Cinquefoil

Star

3882 - 1844 Crown

	F £	VF £	EF £	UNC £		F £	VF £	EF £	UNC £

†**3882 Crown.** Young head. l. R. Crowned shield, regnal year on edge in Roman figures (eg 1847 = XI)

	F	VF	EF	UNC
1839 Proof only *FDC* £25000				
1844 Star stops	60	200	1750	4000
1844 Cinquefoil stops	125	475	3000	5500
1844 Mistruck edge lettering	150	500	3500	–
1845 Star stops	65	275	2000	4500
1845 Cinquefoil stops	65	250	1750	4000
1847 XI Cinquefoil stops	125	400	2750	5000

3883
1847 Gothic Crown

3883*Crown. 'Gothic' type, bust 1. R. Crowned cruciform Shields, emblems in angles. inscribed edge,
mdcccxlvii=1847 Undecimo on edge die axis ↑↓ 800   1350   3000   6250

   1847 Septimo on edge of highest rarity.   1847 Proof, Plain edge die axis ↑↑ *FDC* £10000

   1847 Proof in gold plain edge *FDC* of highest rarity   1847 Proof in white metal plain edge *FDC* £20000

3884 Crown. Similar mdcccliii=1853. Septimo on edge die axis ↑↑ Proof *FDC* £30000

   1853 plain edge proof *FDC* £40000

3885 Halfcrown. Type A¹. Young head l. with one ornate and one plain fillet binding hair. WW in
   relief on trun. R. Crowned shield of arms, edge milled. Die axis ↑↓

   1839 Milled edge Proof *FDC Extremely rare*   1839 Proof plain edge *FDC* £4000

3886 Halfcrown. Type A² Similar, but two ornate fillets binding hair.die axis ↑↓

   1839 Proof only *FDC* £5750

3886A Halfcrown. Type A²ᐟ³ Similar, Two plain fillets, WW relief, die axis ↑↓ plain edge

   1839 Proof *FDC* £6750

*Beware of recent forgeries.

*†The Victorian young head Crowns are notoriously hard to grade. A truly UNC coin must show all
design elements clearly expecially on hair fillets and the reverse shield. All facial features and hair
must also be present.*

	F £	VF £	EF £	UNC £		F £	VF £	EF £	UNC £

3887 Halfcrown. Type A³. Similar two plain fillets. WW incuse on trun. die axis ↑↓

1839	1250	3500	10000	—	1839 Milled edge Proof *FDC* £5750

1839 Plain edge Proof *FDC* £5750

| | | | | | 1840 | 60 | 200 | 1100 | 2750 |

3888 Halfcrown. Type A⁴. Similar but no initials on trun. die axis ↑↓

1841	1000	2250	5250	9000	1849 large date	65	225	1100	2500
1842	50	175	900	2150	1849/7			*Extremely rare*	
1843	125	450	1750	4250	1849 small date	100	350	1250	3000
1844	45	150	850	2000	1850	65	325	1100	2650
1844 not in edge collar		*Extremely rare*			1850 Proof *FDC* £9500				
1845	45	150	850	2000	1853 Proof *FDC* £6750				
1845 5/3			*Extremely rare*		1862 Proof *FDC* £11000				
1846	45	150	850	2000	1862 Plain edge Proof *FDC* £9000				
1848/6	200	600	1950	4000	1864 Proof *FDC* £9500				
1848/7			*Extremely rare*		1864 Plain edge Proof *FDC* £9000				
1848	200	650	2000	4750					

3889
Type A5 Halfcrown

3890
1849 'Godless' Florin

3889 Halfcrown. Similar Type A⁵. As last but design of inferior workmanship R. Crowned shield die axis ↑↓

1874	20	70	375	1000	1881	18	65	375	1100
1874 Proof *FDC* £6500					1881 Proof *FDC* £6750				
1875	20	70	450	1100	1881 Plain edge proof *FDC* £8500				
1875 Proof *FDC* £6000					1882	20	70	400	1150
1876	20	70	425	1150	1883	12	55	300	975
1876/5	30	80	500	1300	1883 Plain edge proof *FDC* £8500				
1877	20	65	375	1100	1884	15	65	375	1100
1878	25	65	375	1100	1885	15	65	375	1100
1878 Proof *FDC* £6750					1885 Proof *FDC* £6750				
1879	25	70	450	1150	1886	15	65	375	1100
1879 Proof *FDC* £6750					1886 Plain edge proof *FDC* £7750				
1880	18	65	400	1100	1887	20	75	425	1150
1880 Proof *FDC* £7250					1887 Proof *FDC* £7000				

3890 Florin. 'Godless' type A (i.e. without D.G.), WW behind bust within linear circle, die axis ↑↓

1848 Plain edge (Pattern) *FDC* £3000

| 1848 Milled edge ↑↑ or ↑↓ Proof *FDC* £4500 | | | | | 1849 WW obliterated | 45 | 90 | 450 | 900 |
| | | | | | 1849 | 20 | 60 | 300 | 650 |

3891 Florin. 'Gothic' type B¹. Reads brit:, WW below bust, date at end of obverse legend in gothic numerals (1851 to 1863) Crowned cruciform Shields, emblems in angles, edge milled. die axis ↑↓

mdccccli Proof only *FDC* £29500					mdccclvii Proof *FDC* £5500				
mdccclii	15	50	350	900	mdccclviii	15	50	350	950
mdccclii Proof *FDC* £4750					mdccclviii Proof *FDC* £5500				
mdccclii, ii/i	20	60	375	1000	mdccclix	15	50	350	950
mdcccliii	15	50	350	925	mdccclx	20	50	375	1000
mdcccliii Proof *FDC* £6000					mdccclxii	225	650	1750	4750
mdcccliv	850	1950	7000	—	mdccclxii Plain edge Proof *FDC* £7000				
mdccclv	25	80	350	1000	mdccclxiii	900	2000	5500	11000
mdccclvi	25	80	350	1000	mdccclxiii Plain edge Proof *FDC* £7250				
mdccclvii	20	60	375	950					

3891

3893

1853 Florin Type B1

	F	VF	EF	UNC		F	VF	EF	UNC
	£	£	£	£		£	£	£	£

3892 Florin. Type B². Similar as last but die number below bust (1864 to 1867) die axis ↑↓

	F	VF	EF	UNC		F	VF	EF	UNC
mdccclxiv	20	65	400	950	mdccclxv	40	110	575	1150
mdccclxiv heavy flan	350	800	1750	5250	mdccclxvi	35	85	425	950
mdccclxiv heavy flan Proof *FDC* £8500					mdccclxvii	30	75	425	950
mdccclxvii Proof *FDC* £5500									

3893 Florin. Type B³. Similar reads britt:, die number below bust (1868 to 1879) die axis

	F	VF	EF	UNC		F	VF	EF	UNC
mdccclxviii	30	100	450	1100	mdccclxxiii	20	60	275	850
mdccclxix	25	85	450	1050	mdccclxxiii Proof *FDC* £4500				
mdccclxix Proof *FDC* £5750					mdccclxxiv	25	70	400	950
mdccclxx	20	60	350	950	mdccclxxiv iv/iii	35	85	350	1050
mdccclxx Proof *FDC* £5750					mdccclxxv	20	55	325	925
mdccclxxi	20	60	350	950	mdccclxxvi	20	55	325	900
mdccclxxi Proof *FDC* £5000					mdccclxxvii	25	55	325	950
mdccclxxii	15	45	275	850	mdccclxxix				*Extremely rare*

3894 Florin. Type B⁴. Similar as last but with border of 48 arcs and no WW below bust die axis ↑↓

1877 mdccclxxvii .... *Extremely rare*

3895 Florin. Type B⁵. Similar but border of 42 arcs (1867, 1877 and 1878) die axis ↑↓

mdccclxvii	2850	—	—	—	mdccclxxviii	20	55	325	850
mdccclxxvii	25	65	400	1000	mdccclxxviii Proof *FDC*				*Extremely rare*

3896 Florin. Type B⁵/⁶. Similar as last but no die number below bust (1877, 1879) die axis ↑↓

mdccclxxvii	125	300	675	1550	mdccclxxix	110	300	800	1800

3897 Florin. Type B⁶. Similar reads britt:, WW; Border of 48 arcs (1879) die axis ↑↓

mdccclxxviii .... *Known to exist*

mdccclxxix						20	55	325	900

3898 Florin. Type B⁷. Similar as last but no WW, Border of 38 arcs (1879) die axis ↑↓

mdccclxxix						20	55	325	900

mdccclxxix Proof *FDC* £5000

3899 Florin. Type B³/⁸. Similar as next but younger portrait (1880) die axis ↑↓

mdccclxxx .... *Extremely rare*

3900 Florin. Type B⁸. Similar but border of 34 arcs (1880 to 1887) die axis ↑↓

mdccclxxx	15	45	325	850	mdccclxxxiii Proof *FDC* £4000				
mdccclxxx Proof *FDC* £5000					mdccclxxxiv	15	55	325	800
mdccclxxxi	15	45	325	850	mdccclxxxv	20	65	325	800
mdccclxxxi Proof *FDC* £4750					mdccclxxxv Proof *FDC* £5000				
mdccclxxxi/xxri	30	85	375	950	mdccclxxxvi	15	55	325	800
mdccclxxxiii	15	45	325	850	mdccclxxxvi Proof *FDC* £5250				

3901 Florin. Type B⁹. Similar but border of 46 arcs die axis ↑↓

1887 mdccclxxxvii						30	80	425	1000

mdccclxxxvii Proof *FDC* .... *Extremely rare*

3902 Shilling. Type A¹. First head l., WW on trun. R. crowned mark of value within wreath, date below, die axis ↑↓

1838	15	55	325	775	1839	45	110	425	1000
1838 Proof *FDC* £3750					1839 Proof *FDC* £3000				

3903 Shilling Type A². Second head, l. WW on trun. (proof only), 1839 die axis ↑↑ *FDC* £1750

3904 - Type A3 Shilling

3904 Shilling Type A³. Second head, l. no initials on trun. R. Similar die axis ↑↓

	F £	VF £	EF £	UNC £		F £	VF £	EF £	UNC £
1839	20	50	325	700	1852	10	30	275	625
1839 Proof plain edge *FDC* £1500					1853	10	25	250	625
1839 Proof plain edge en medaille ↑↑ *FDC* £2750					1853 Milled edge Proof *FDC* £2150				
1839 Proof milled edge *FDC Extremely rare*					1854	250	600	1950	4500
1840	25	70	375	800	1854/1	300	875	3750	—
1840 Proof *FDC* £4000					1855	10	25	225	625
1841	25	75	400	825	1856	10	25	225	625
1842	20	45	275	700	1857	10	25	225	625
1842 Proof *FDC* £4000					1857 REG F: Ɔ:error	215	600	1750	—
1843	25	70	375	825	1858	10	25	225	625
1844	20	40	275	675	1859	10	25	225	625
1845	30	55	325	725	1859 9/8 *exists*				
1846	20	40	275	675	1859 Proof *FDC* £4250				
1848 over 6	65	225	825	1750	1860	12	35	275	700
1849	25	50	300	725	1861	12	35	275	700
1850	800	1750	5000	—	1861 D/B in FD	125	325	900	—
1850/49	875	2000	5250	—	1862	45	75	350	775
1851	55	125	600	1600	1863	100	225	600	1500
1851 Proof *FDC* £5250					1863/1	120	315	950	—

3905 Shilling Type A⁴. Similar as last, R. Die number above date die axis ↑↓

	F	VF	EF	UNC		F	VF	EF	UNC
1864	10	30	225	625	1866 BBITANNIAR..	60	300	1100	—
1865	10	30	225	625	1867	15	35	225	625
1866	10	30	225						

3906 Shilling Type A⁵. Third head, l. R. Similar no die number above date die axis ↑↓

1867 Proof £4250

1867 Proof plain edge £4500

1879 .... 225 500 1250 2200

1879 Proof, milled edge, *FDC* £4250

3906A - Type A6 Shilling

Die number location above date

3906A Shilling Type A⁶. Third head, l. R. Similar die number above date die axis ↑↓

	F	VF	EF	UNC		F	VF	EF	UNC
1867	200	500	1500	3250	1873	10	20	200	575
1868	10	25	200	575	1874	10	20	200	575
1869	20	40	300	625	1875	10	20	200	575
1870	15	35	275	600	1876	15	30	225	600
1871	10	20	200	575	1877	10	20	200	575
1871 Plain edge proof *FDC* £4000					1878	20	40	300	650
1871 Milled edge proof *FDC* £3750					1878 Milled edge Proof *FDC* £4000				
1872	10	20	200	575	1879 uncertain to exist as normal coin or proof?				

	F £	VF £	EF £	UNC £		F £	VF £	EF £	UNC £

3907 Shilling Type A⁷. Fourth head, l. R. Similar no die number above date die axis ↑↓

	F	VF	EF	UNC		F	VF	EF	UNC
1879	10	20	200	550	1883 plain edge Proof *FDC* £4500				
1879 Proof *FDC* £4000					1884	10	20	175	450
1880	10	20	175	500	1884 Proof *FDC* £3500				
1880 Proof plain edge £3750					1885	10	15	165	425
1880 Proof milled edge £3250					1885 Proof *FDC* £3500				
1881	10	20	175	450	1886	10	15	165	425
1881 Proof plain edge £4000					1886 Proof *FDC* £3500				
1881 Proof milled edge £3000					1887	10	25	200	525
1882	10	35	225	525	1887 Proof *FDC* £3000				
1883	10	20	175	450					

3907A Shilling. Type A7. Fourth head, R. Similar die number above date die axis ↑↓

	F	VF	EF	UNC		F	VF	EF	UNC
1878	10	20	175	450	1879	10	35	225	525
1878 Milled edge Proof *FDC* £3750									

3908

Type A1 Sixpence

3908 Sixpence. Type A¹. First head l. R. Crowned mark of value within wreath, date below die axis ↑↓

	F	VF	EF	UNC		F	VF	EF	UNC
1838	10	25	175	525	1851	10	20	175	550
1838 Proof *FDC* £2500					1852	8	20	175	525
1839	10	25	175	525	1853	8	20	165	475
1839 Proof *FDC* £1250					1853 Proof *FDC* £1400				
1840	10	25	175	550	1854	200	500	1100	3150
1841	15	30	200	600	1855	8	20	175	575
1842	10	25	175	550	1855/3	10	25	200	600
1843	10	25	175	550	1855 Proof *FDC*		*Extremely rare*		
1844 Small 44	10	20	175	550	1856	8	20	175	575
1844 Large 44	15	30	200	575	1857	8	20	175	575
1845	10	20	175	550	1858	8	20	175	575
1846	10	20	170	575	1858 Proof *FDC*		*Extremely rare*		
1847 An example in fair condition sold at DNW,					1859	8	20	175	575
29/9/10, lot 1773 for £850 + premium					1859/8	10	20	175	575
1848	45	110	600	1950	1860	10	20	175	575
1848/6 or 7	45	110	575	1400	1862	100	250	700	1700
1850	10	20	160	525	1863	65	150	500	1300
1850/3	15	30	215	475	1866		*Extremely rare*		

3909

Die number location above date

3912

Type 'A5' Sixpence

3909 Sixpence. Type A². First head, R. Similar die number above date die axis ↑↓

	F	VF	EF	UNC		F	VF	EF	UNC
1864	8	20	175	575	1866	8	15	175	575
1865	8	25	200	550	1867	10	25	200	600

	F	VF	EF	UNC		F	VF	EF	UNC
	£	£	£	£		£	£	£	£

3910 Sixpence. Type A³. Second head, l. R. Similar die number above date, die axis ↑↓

	F	VF	EF	UNC		F	VF	EF	UNC
1867	10	20	175	550	1873	8	15	150	450
1867 Proof FDC £2650					1874	8	15	150	450
1868	10	20	175	550	1875	8	15	150	450
1869	10	20	225	625	1876	10	20	175	600
1869 Proof FDC £2850					1877	8	15	150	450
1870	10	20	225	625	1878	8	15	150	450
1870 plain edge Proof FDC £2850					1878 DRITANNIAR	150	420	1100	—
1871	8	15	150	475	1878 Proof FDC £2350				
1871 plain edge Proof FDC £2850					1878/7	35	175	800	—
1872	8	15	150	475	1879	10	20	175	500

3911 Sixpence. Type A⁴. Second head, l. R. Similar No die number, die axis ↑↓

	F	VF	EF	UNC		F	VF	EF	UNC
1871	8	15	150	500	1879 milled edge Proof FDC £2350				
1871 Proof FDC £2100					1879 plain edge Proof FDC £2850				
1877	8	15	150	475	1880	8	15	150	400
1879	8	15	150	475					

3912 Sixpence. Type A⁵. Third head l. R. Similar, die axis ↑↓

	F	VF	EF	UNC		F	VF	EF	UNC
1880	8	15	125	300	1883 plain edge Proof FDC Extremely rare				
1880 Proof FDC £2650					1884	8	15	115	300
1881	8	15	100	275	1885	8	15	115	300
1881 plain edge Proof FDC Extremely rare					1885 Proof FDC £2350				
1881 milled edge Proof FDC Extremely rare					1886	8	15	115	300
1882	10	30	150	500	1886 Proof FDC £2350				
1883	8	15	100	275	1887	8	15	100	275
1883 Small R legend	15	40	175	500	1887 Proof FDC £2150				

3913 Groat (4d.). Young head 1.R. Britannia seated r. date in ex, edge milled, die axis ↑↑

	F	VF	EF	UNC		F	VF	EF	UNC
1837 Plain edge Proof £12500					1846	8	15	80	200
1837 Milled edge Proof £11500					1847/6 (or 8)	30	125	450	875
1838	5	12	75	200	1848/6	10	35	115	250
1838 plain edge Proof FDC £1350					1848	6	15	80	200
1838 Milled edge Proof £1250					1848/7/6	10	30	135	400
1838/∞	8	20	100	225	1849	5	15	80	200
1839	7	15	85	225	1849/8	8	15	90	200
1839 die axis ↑↑ Proof plain edge FDC £650					1851	20	80	300	725
1839 die axis ↑↓ Proof plain edge FDC £700					1852	40	125	450	975
1840	7	15	80	200	1853	100	300	775	1750
1840 small round o	10	20	80	225	1853 Proof FDC milled edge £1350				
1841	10	25	125	300	1853 Proof FDC plain edge £1500				
1842	8	15	80	225	1854	5	15	75	200
1842 Proof FDC £1350					1855	5	15	75	200
1842/1	10	20	85	275	1855/3	10	25	90	215
1843	8	15	80	200	1857 Milled or plain edge proof FDC £2000				
1843 4 over 5	10	25	90	300	1857 Plain edge pattern £2500				
1844	7	15	85	200	1862 Plain or milled edge Proof FDC £2500				
1845	8	15	80	200	1862 Plain edge pattern FDC £3250				

	F	VF	EF	UNC		F	VF	EF	UNC
	£	£	£	£		£	£	£	£

3914 Threepence. Type A[1]. First bust, young head, high relief, ear fully visible, die axis ↑↓
R Crowned 3; as Maundy threepence but with a less prooflike surface.

	F	VF	EF	UNC		F	VF	EF	UNC
1838*......................8	25	90	225		1851 reads 1551 £650				
1838 BRITANNIAB ...	*Extremely rare*				1851 5 over 8 15	40	175	325
1839*......................10	40	125	275		1852* 75	200	600	950
1839 Proof (see Maundy)					1853 25	100	295	550
1840*......................10	35	100	275		1854 8	20	100	250
1841*......................10	40	115	275		1855 10	35	120	275
1842*......................10	40	135	300		1856 8	20	100	225
1843*......................8	25	90	225		1857 8	30	110	275
1844*......................10	35	105	225		1858 8	15	90	225
1845......................8	15	75	200		1858 BRITANNIAB ..	*Extremely rare*			
1846......................30	100	295	600		1858/6 15	35	200	—
1847*......................45	175	365	950		1858/5 10	30	150	—
1848*......................40	150	395	900		1859 8	15	85	225
1849......................10	40	125	275		1860 8	30	110	275
1850......................8	20	75	175		1861 8	15	85	225
1851......................8	25	95	250						

*Issued for Colonial use only.

3914A - Type A2

3914C - Type A4

3914A Threepence. Type A[2]. First bust variety, slightly older portrait with aquiline nose ↑↓

	F	VF	EF	UNC		F	VF	EF	UNC
1859......................8	15	85	200		1865 8	20	115	225
1860......................8	15	85	200		1866 8	15	85	200
1861......................8	15	85	200		1867 8	15	85	200
1862......................10	25	95	200		1868 8	15	85	200
1863......................15	35	115	225		1868 RRITANNIAR ..	*Extremely rare*			
1864......................8	15	85	200						

3914B Threepence. Type A[3]. Second Bust, slightly larger, lower relief, mouth fuller,
nose more pronounced, rounded truncation, die axis ↑↓

	F	VF	EF	UNC
1867...8	25	115	250

3914C Threepence. Type A[4]. Obv. as last. R. Tie ribbon further from tooth border, cross on
crown nearer to tooth border die axis ↑↓

	F	VF	EF	UNC		F	VF	EF	UNC
1866	*Extremely rare*				1874 5	15	60	125
1867......................8	30	95	225		1875 5	15	60	125
1868......................8	30	95	225		1876 5	15	60	125
1869......................10	30	110	300		1877 5	15	70	135
1870......................5	15	80	165		1878 5	15	70	135
1871......................8	20	85	200		1879 5	15	70	135
1872......................8	20	85	200		1879 Proof *FDC*.........	*Extremely rare*			
1873......................5	15	60	135		1884 5	8	60	110

3914D Threepence. Type A[5]. Third bust, older features, mouth closed, hair strands
leading from 'bun' vary, die axis ↑↓

	F	VF	EF	UNC		F	VF	EF	UNC
1880......................5	10	65	125		1885 5	8	50	110
1881......................5	10	50	110		1885 Proof *FDC*.........	*Extremely rare*			
1882......................5	10	75	185		1886 5	8	50	110
1883......................5	10	50	110		1887 5	10	65	125

3914E Twopence. Young head 1. R Date divided by a crowned 2 within a wreath, die axis ↑↓

	F	VF	EF	UNC		F	VF	EF	UNC
1838......................5	10	35	85		1848 5	10	45	90

3915 - Three-Halfpence

	F	VF	EF	UNC		F	VF	EF	UNC
	£	£	£	£		£	£	£	£

3915 Three-Halfpence. (for Colonial use). Young head 1. R. Crowned value and date, die axis ↑↓

1838	5	10	50	125	1843 Proof *FDC* £900				
1838 Proof *FDC* £900					1843/34	5	20	80	175
1839	5	10	45	110	1843/34 Proof *FDC* £850				
1840	8	25	95	225	1860	5	20	75	180
1841	5	15	55	135	1862	5	20	75	180
1842	5	15	55	135	1862 Proof *FDC* £1100				
1843	5	8	40	125	1870 Proof only £1350				

3916 - 1880 Maundy Set

3916 Maundy Set. (4d., 3d., 2d. and 1.) Young head 1., die axis ↑↓

1838	225	650	1864	150	450
1838 Proof *FDC* £1750			1865	150	450
1838 Proof in gold *FDC* £27500			1866	140	425
1839	200	625	1867	140	425
1839 Proof die axis ↑↑ *FDC* £1250			1867 Proof set *FDC* £1600		
1840	250	650	1868	140	425
1841	300	750	1869	150	475
1842	250	600	1870	140	425
1843	200	575	1871	125	400
1844	230	650	1871 Proof set *FDC* £1600		
1845	200	550	1872	125	400
1846	300	775	1873	125	400
1847	300	700	1874	125	400
1848	300	700	1875	125	400
1849	250	650	1876	125	400
1850	180	600	1877	125	400
1851	180	575	1878	135	425
1852	175	350	850	1878 Proof set *FDC* £1600		
1853	235	675	1879	125	400
1853 Proof *FDC* £1400			1880	125	400
1854	185	575	1881	125	400
1855	200	575	1881 Proof set *FDC* £1600		
1856	150	450	1882	125	400
1857	200	525	1882 Proof set *FDC* £1600		
1858	150	425	1883	125	400
1859	150	425	1884	125	400
1860	150	425	1885	125	400
1861	165	425	1886	125	400
1862	180	500	1887	135	425
1863	180	500			

				EF	UNC
3917 — Fourpence, 1838-87			*from*	10	35
3918 — Threepence, 1838-87			*from*	15	55
3919 — Twopence, 1838-87			*from*	10	35
3920 — Penny, 1838-87			*from*	15	50

Maundy Sets in good quality original cases are worth approximately £40 more than the prices quoted.
Refer to footnote after 3796.

JUBILEE COINAGE 1887-93, die axis ↑↑

3921
1887 Crown

	F	VF	EF	UNC		F	VF	EF	UNC
	£	£	£	£		£	£	£	£

3921 Crown. Jubilee bust 1. ℞. St. George and dragon, date in ex, edge milled, die axis ↑↑

1887	25	40	100	225	1889	25	40	125	350
1887 Proof *FDC* £2000					1890	25	50	165	400
1888 narrow date	25	45	165	375	1891	25	60	200	475
1888 wide date	120	325	675	1350	1892	35	65	250	550

3922 Double-Florin (4s.). Jubilee bust 1. ℞. (As Florin) Crowned cruciform shields. Sceptre in angles. Roman I in date, die axis ↑↑

1887						20	40	95	200
1887 Proof *FDC* £1000									

3923
1887 Double-Florin
Arabic 1 in date

3924
1887 Halfcrown

3923 Double-Florin Jubilee bust l. ℞. Similar but Arabic 1 in date, die axis ↑↑

1887	20	35	75	175	1889	20	40	100	250
1887 Proof *FDC* £950					1889 inverted 1 for I in				
1888	20	40	100	250	VICTORIA	45	85	325	675
1888 inverted 1 for I in					1890	20	50	125	300
VICTORIA	40	90	250	650					

3924 Halfcrown. Jubilee bust 1. ℞. Crowned shield in garter and collar, die axis ↑↑

1887	15	20	45	100	1890	15	30	125	275
1887 Proof *FDC* £600					1891	15	30	135	375
1888	15	25	90	250	1892	15	35	150	300
1889	15	30	90	250					

3925
1890 Florin reverse

	F	VF	EF	UNC			F	VF	EF	UNC
	£	£	£	£			£	£	£	£

3925 Florin. Jubilee bust 1. ℞. Crowned cruciform shields, sceptres in angles, die axis ↑↑

	F	VF	EF	UNC		F	VF	EF	UNC
1887......................... 10	15	40	85	1890......................... 15	45	225	600
1887 Proof *FDC* £425				1891......................... 30	80	375	800
1888 obverse die of 1887 . 15	45	120	250	1892......................... 35	90	425	1100
1888......................... 12	30	80	200	1892 Proof *FDC* £10000			
1889......................... 12	35	100	250				

3926
small head Shilling

3926 Shilling. Small Jubilee head. ℞. Crowned shield in Garter, die axis ↑↑

	F	VF	EF	UNC		F	VF	EF	UNC
1887..........................5	15	25	50	1888/7 8	15	60	150
1887 Proof *FDC* £400				1889 50	150	500	950
1888........................50	100	225	400				

3927 Shilling. Large Jubilee head. ℞. Similar as before, die axis ↑↑

	F	VF	EF	UNC		F	VF	EF	UNC
1889..........................8	18	65	150	1891 12	20	85	200
1889 Proof *FDC* £2200				1891 Proof *FDC* £2200			
1890........................10	20	75	175	1892 12	20	85	200

3928
1887 'withdrawn type' Sixpence

3928 Sixpence. JEB designer's initials below trun. ℞. Shield in Garter (withdrawn type), die axis ↑↑

	F	VF	EF	UNC		F	VF	EF	UNC
1887..........................5	10	20	40	1887 JEB on trun. ..30	75	175	425
1887 Proof *FDC* £250				1887 R/V in			
				VICTORIA....25	55	135	300

3929

Crowned value Sixpence

3930

1888 Groat

	F	VF	EF	UNC		F	VF	EF	UNC
	£	£	£	£		£	£	£	£

3929 Sixpence. R. Jubilee bust 1. Crowned, value in wreath, die axis ↑↑

	F	VF	EF	UNC		F	VF	EF	UNC
1887	5	10	20	50	1890	8	15	50	135
1887 Proof *FDC* £1100					1890 Proof *FDC*		*Extremely rare*		
1888	7	15	40	125	1891	10	20	55	150
1888 Proof *FDC* £1750					1892	12	25	60	165
1889	7	15	40	125	1893	550	1100	3250	6500

3930 Groat (for use in British Guiana). Jubilee Bust 1. R. Britannia seated r. date in axis, die axis ↑↑

						F	VF	EF	UNC
1888 Milled edge Proof *FDC* £1350					1888	12	35	85	200

3931 Threepence. As Maundy but less prooflike surface, die axis ↑↑

	F	VF	EF	UNC		F	VF	EF	UNC
1887	—	3	12	30	1890	3	5	15	50
1887 Proof *FDC* £200					1891	3	5	18	55
1888	4	6	20	60	1892	4	6	20	60
1889	3	5	15	50	1893	20	65	200	500

3932

1889 Maundy Set

	EF	FDC		EF	FDC
	£	£		£	£

3932 Maundy Set. (4d., 3d., 2d. and 1d.) Jubilee bust 1. die axis ↑↑

	EF	FDC		EF	FDC
1888	135	250	1890	135	250
1888 Proof set *FDC*	*Extremely rare*		1891	135	250
1889	135	250	1892	135	250
3933 — **Fourpence**, 1888-92	*from*			12	35
3934 — **Threepence**, 1888-92	*from*			18	40
3935 — **Twopence**, 1888-92	*from*			10	30
3936 — **Penny**, 1888-92	*from*			15	45

Maundy Sets in the original undamaged cases are worth approximately £25 more than the prices quoted.

See footnote after 3796.

Timeline Auctions

Inc. Gregory's **Est.1858**

We are accepting single entries
and collections of gold Sovereigns etc.

www.timelineauctions.com

OLD HEAD COINAGE 1893-1901, die axis ↑↑

3937
1893 Old Head Crown

	F	VF	EF	UNC
	£	£	£	£

3937 Crown. Old veiled bust l. R. St. George. date in ex. Regnal date on edge, die axis ↑↑

	F	VF	EF	UNC
1893 edge LVI	20	30	210	500
1893 Proof *FDC* £2750				
1893 LVII	30	90	475	900
1894 LVII	20	45	325	750
1894 LVIII	20	45	325	750
1895 LVIII	20	40	275	700
1895 LIX	20	40	250	675
1896 LIX	22	70	425	850
1896 LX	20	45	275	700
1897 LX	20	40	250	650
1897 LXI	20	40	250	650
1898 LXI	30	90	525	1000
1898 LXII	20	40	325	725
1899 LXII	20	40	250	700
1899 LXIII	20	40	275	750
1900 LXIII	20	40	250	700
1900 LXIV	20	40	225	650

3938
Halfcrown

3938 Halfcrown. Old veiled bust l. R. Shield in collar, edge milled, die axis ↑↑

	F	VF	EF	UNC		F	VF	EF	UNC
	£	£	£	£		£	£	£	£
1893	12	30	65	175	1897	12	30	75	225
1893 Proof *FDC* £1000					1898	15	40	100	300
1894	15	45	150	400	1899	15	35	90	275
1895	12	40	125	325	1900	15	30	75	225
1896	12	40	125	325	1901	15	30	80	250

3938A Small reverse design with long border teeth

	F	VF	EF	UNC
1896	18	40	165	350

3939
Old Head Florin

	F	VF	EF	UNC		F	VF	EF	UNC
	£	£	£	£		£	£	£	£

3939 Florin. Old veiled bust l. R. Three shields within garter, die axis ↑↑

1893	10	20	75	150	1897	10	20	80	175
1893 Proof *FDC* £600					1898	10	25	95	250
1894	12	30	135	350	1899	10	20	90	225
1895	10	25	110	275	1900	10	20	80	175
1896	10	25	110	275	1901	10	20	85	200

3940A
1901 Shilling

3941
1897 Sixpence

3940 Shilling. Old veiled bust l. R. Three shields within Garter, small rose, die axis ↑↑

1893	10	20	60	120	1894	10	20	75	175
1893 small lettering	10	15	55	110	1895	12	25	85	200
1893 Proof *FDC* £450					1896	10	20	75	175

3940A Shilling. Old veiled bust l. R. Second reverse, larger rose, die axis ↑↑

1895	10	18	65	150	1899	10	18	65	150
1896	10	15	60	150	1900	10	15	55	125
1897	10	15	50	125	1901	10	15	55	125
1898	10	15	60	150					

3941 Sixpence. Old veiled bust l. R. Value in wreath, die axis ↑↑

1893	7	12	40	100	1897	8	15	45	100
1893 Proof *FDC* £325					1898	8	15	50	115
1894	10	15	60	150	1899	8	15	50	115
1895	8	15	55	125	1900	8	15	50	115
1896	8	15	50	110	1901	7	12	45	100

3942 Threepence. Old veiled bust l. R. Crowned 3. As Maundy but less prooflike surface, die axis ↑↑

1893	3	7	15	60	1897	3	5	15	45
1893 Proof *FDC* £200					1898	3	5	15	50
1894	3	8	22	70	1899	3	5	15	50
1895	3	8	20	60	1900	3	5	12	45
1896	3	7	20	60	1901	3	5	15	45

3943

1901 Maundy Set

	EF	FDC			EF	FDC
	£	£			£	£

3943 Maundy Set. (4d., 3d., 2d. and 1d.) Old veiled bust l., die axis ↑↑

	EF	FDC			EF	FDC
1893	120	200	1898		125	210
1894	125	215	1899		125	210
1895	125	210	1900		125	210
1896	125	210	1901		125	200
1897	125	210				

		EF	FDC
3944 — Fourpence. 1893-1901 ....*from*		8	30
3945 — Threepence. 1893-1901 ....*from*		15	40
3946 — Twopence. 1893-1901 ....*from*		8	30
3947 — Penny. 1893-1901 ....*from*		15	40

Maundy Sets in the original undamaged cases are worth approximately £25 more than the prices quoted.
See footnote after 3796.

COPPER AND BRONZE

YOUNG HEAD COPPER COINAGE, 1838-60, die axis ↑↑

3948

Penny

Rev. with ornamental trident prongs (OT)

	F	VF	EF	UNC		F	VF	EF	UNC
	£	£	£	£		£	£	£	£

3948 Penny. Young head l. date below R. Britannia seated r.

	F	VF	EF	UNC		F	VF	EF	UNC
1839 Bronzed proof *FDC* £3000					1845 OT 12		35	275	825
1841 Rev. OT 10		55	275	900	1846 OT 10		25	225	725
1841 Proof *FDC* £3750					1846 OT colon close .				
1841 Silver Proof *FDC* £8500					to DEF 12		30	250	775
1841 OT. no colon					1847 — — 7		20	200	600
after REG 5		20	120	525	1847 OT DEF—:...... 7		20	200	600
1843 OT. — 70		275	1750	4250	1848/7 OT 5		20	170	625
1843 OT REG: 80		400	2250	4750	1848 OT 5		20	200	625
1844 OT 10		20	200	625	1848/6 OT 20		140	725	—
1844 Proof *FDC* £3500					1849 OT 225		600	2250	4250

Copper coins graded in this catalogue as UNC have full mint lustre.

	F	VF	EF	UNC
	£	£	£	£

3948 Penny. (Continued)

	F	VF	EF	UNC
1851 OT 15	30	225	800
1851 OT DEF:......... 10	25	200	725
1853 OT DEF—:....... 5	15	110	475
1853 Proof *FDC* £3250			
1853 Plain trident, (PT)			
DEF:............... 15	35	165	625
1854 PT 5	15	135	475
1854/3 PT............... 10	65	250	725
1854 OT DEF—:....... 7	20	120	500
1855 OT — 5	15	120	475
1855 PT DEF: 5	15	130	475
1856 PT DEF: 115	300	800	2750

	F	VF	EF	UNC
1856 Proof *FDC* £3250			
1856 OT DEF—:..... 115	400	1150	3150
1857 OT DEF—:......... 7	20	130	550
1857 PT DEF: 5	15	120	525
1858 OT DEF—:......... 5	12	110	450
1858/7 — — 5	15	120	525
1858/3 7	30	140	525
1858 no ww on trun 5	18	110	525
1859 5	20	130	550
1859 Proof *FDC* £3500			
1860/59 850	1950	3750	6750

3949

1845 Halfpenny

3949 Halfpenny. Young head l. date below R. Britannia seated r., die axis ↑↑   1853 Rev. incuse dots

	F	VF	EF	UNC		F	VF	EF	UNC
1838............................ 5	15	90	325	1852 Rev. normal shield . 10	20	110	350
1839 Bronzed proof FDC £850				1853 dots on shield........ 3	7	55	175
1841 5	12	65	275	1853 — Proof FDC £1250			
1841 — Proof FDC £1500				1853/2 — 15	40	165	400
1841 Silver proof FDC		*Extremely rare*		1854 — 4	7	45	175
1843 25	50	225	750	1855 — 4	7	45	185
1844 12	35	175	375	1856 — 5	12	80	275
1845 250	500	2000	—	1857 — 4	10	60	215
1846 12	35	175	375	1857 Rev. normal			
1847 12	35	175	375	shield 4	10	55	200
1848 25	70	225	600	1858 — 5	10	55	225
1848/7 10	30	175	375	1858/7 — 5	10	55	225
1851 5	15	90	325	1858/6 — 5	10	70	225
1851 Rev. incuse dots ..				1859 — 5	10	70	225
on shield............. 5	15	100	350	1859/8 — 10	20	110	350
1852 Similar................ 7	15	95	325	1860* — 1850	3500	7000	12500

Overstruck dates are listed only if commoner than normal date, or if no normal date is known.

*These 1860 large copper pieces are not to be confused with the smaller and commoner bronze issue with date on reverse (nos. 3954, 3956 and 3958).

Copper coins graded in this catalogue as UNC have full mint lustre.

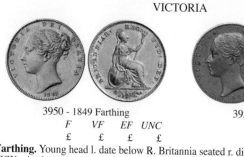

3950 - 1849 Farthing　　　　　3950 - 1864 Proof

3950 Farthing. Young head l. date below R. Britannia seated r. die axis ↑↑

	F £	VF £	EF £	UNC £		F £	VF £	EF £	UNC £
1838 WW raised on trun.	5	10	70	225	1850 5/4	10	30	110	385
1839	4	7	65	175	1851	10	20	90	285
1839 Bronzed Proof FDC £750					1851 D/Ɔ in DEI	80	175	525	950
1839 Silver Proof FDC Extremely rare					1852	10	20	90	285
1839 Copper Proof FDC £1150					1853	5	10	50	185
1840	4	7	70	185	1853 WW incuse on trun	10	30	150	425
1841	4	7	70	185	1853 Proof FDC £1150				
1841 Proof FDC Extremely rare					1854	5	10	50	165
1842	12	45	165	425	1855	5	12	85	200
1843/2	10	30	120	375	1855 WW raised	7	12	85	200
1843	4	7	45	175	1856 WW incuse	7	20	90	285
1843 I for 1 in date	85	375	825	2000	1856 R/E in VICTORIA	15	50	250	550
1844	70	225	775	2000	1857	5	10	55	185
1845	7	10	65	175	1858	5	10	55	185
1846	7	15	85	210	1859	10	20	90	315
1847	5	10	65	175	1860*	1600	3500	6250	12500
1848	5	10	65	175	1864 IWW on truncation proof FDC £25000				
1849	40	100	400	900					
1850	5	10	65	175					

3951 - Half-Farthing　　　3952 - Third-Farthing　　　3953 - Quarter-Farthing

3951 Half-Farthing. Young head l. R. Crowned Value and date, die axis ↑↑

	F	VF	EF	UNC		F	VF	EF	UNC
1839	5	10	65	175	1852	3	10	70	165
1839 Bronzed proof FDC £750					1853	5	15	75	215
1842	5	10	65	175	1853 Proof FDC £750				
1843		5	30	125	1854	7	25	125	350
1844		3	25	110	1856	7	25	125	350
1844 E/N in REGINA	10	20	95	315	1856 Large date	55	150	375	825
1847	3	7	55	175	1868 Proof FDC £1000				
1851 5/0	10	20	115	300	1868 Cupro nickel Proof FDC £1450				
1851	5	10	70	165					

3952 Third-Farthing (for use in Malta). Young head l. date below R. Britannia seated r. die axis ↑↑

	F	VF	EF	UNC		F	VF	EF	UNC
1844	20	45	125	375	1844 RE for REG	30	75	450	950

3953 Quarter-Farthing (for use in Ceylon). Young head l. R. Crowned Value and date, die axis ↑↑

	F	VF	EF	UNC		F	VF	EF	UNC
1839	20	30	90	300	1853	25	45	125	375
1851	15	25	85	275	1853 Proof FDC £1500				
1852	15	25	80	225	1868 Proof FDC £1000				
1852 Proof FDC £1450					1868 Cupro-nickel Proof FDC £1450				

Copper coins graded in this catalogue as UNC have full mint lustre.

*These 1860 large copper pieces are not to be confused with the smaller and commoner bronze issue with date on reverse (nos. 3954, 3956 and 3958).

BRONZE COINAGE, "BUN HEAD" ISSUE, 1860-95, die axis ↑↑

When studying an example of the bronze coinage, if the minutiae of the variety is not evident due to wear from circulation, then the coin will not be of any individual significance. Proofs exist of most years and are generally extremely rare for all denominations.

3954 The Bronze Penny. The bronze coinage is the most complicated of the milled series from the point of view of the large number of different varieties of obverse and reverse and their combinations. Below are set out illustrations with explanations of all the varieties. The obverse and reverse types listed below reflect those as listed originally by C W Peck in his British Museum Catalogue of Copper, Tin and Bronze Coinage 1558-1958, and later in "The Bronze Coinage of Great Britain" by Michael J Freeman which gives much fuller and detailed explanations of the types. Reference can also be compared to "The British Bronze Penny" by Michael Gouby.

OBVERSES

Obverse 1 (1860) - laureate and draped bust facing left, hair tied in bun, wreath of 15 leaves and 4 berries, L C WYON raised on base of bust, **beaded border** and thin linear circle.

Obverse 1* (1860) - laureate and draped bust facing left, **more bulging lowered eye with more rounded forehead**, wreath of **15 leaves and 4 berries**, which are weaker in part, L C WYON raised on base of bust, **beaded border** and thin linear circle.

Obverse 3 (1860-61) - laureate and draped bust facing left, hair tied in bun, **complete rose to drapery**, wreath of 15 leaves and 4 berries, **two leaves have incuse outlines**, L C WYON raised on base of bust **nearly touches border**, toothed border and thin linear circle both sides.

Obverse 2 (1860-62) - laureate and draped bust facing left, hair tied in bun, wreath of 15 leaves and 4 berries, **L C WYON** raised **lower on base of bust** and clear of border, **toothed border** and thin linear circle both sides.

Obverse 4 (1860-61) - laureate and draped bust facing left, hair tied in bun, **finer hair strands at nape of neck**, wreath of 15 leaves and 4 berries, two leaves have incuse outlines, **L C WYON below bust, nearly touches border, toothed border of shorter teeth**, and thin linear circle both sides.

OBVERSES (*continued*)

Obverse 7 (1874) - laureate and draped bust facing left, hair tied in bun, finer hair strands at nape of neck, **wreath of 17 leaves, leaf veins raised, 6 berries**, no signature, toothed border and thin linear circle both sides.

Obverse 5 (1860-61) - laureate and draped bust facing left, hair tied in bun, **finer hair strands at nape of neck**, wreath of 15 leaves and 4 berries, **leaf veins incuse**, two leaves have incuse outlines, **no signature below bust**, toothed border and thin linear circle both sides.

Obverse 8 (1874-79) - laureate and draped bust facing left, hair tied in bun, with **close thicker ties to ribbons**, wreath of 17 leaves, leaf veins raised, 6 berries, no signature, toothed border and thin linear circle both sides.

Obverse 6 (1860-74) - laureate and draped bust facing left, hair tied in bun, finer hair strands at nape of neck, **wreath of 16 leaves, leaf veins raised, no signature**, toothed border and thin linear circle both sides. There is a **prominent flaw** on the **top stop of the colon after D at the end of the legend**.

Obverse 9 (1879-81) - laureate and draped bust facing left, hair tied in bun, with close thicker ties, wreath of 17 leaves, **double leaf veins incuse**, 6 berries, no signature, toothed border and thin linear circle both sides.

OBVERSES *(continued)*

Obverse 10 (1880-81) - laureate and draped bust facing left, hair tied in bun, with close thicker ties, **wreath of 15 leaves, leaf veins raised and recessed, 4 berries**, no signature, toothed border and thin linear circle both sides.

Obverse 12 (1881-94) - laureate and draped bust facing left, hair tied in bun, with close thicker ties, **no curls at nape of neck**, nose more hooked, wreath of 15 leaves, leaf veins raised, 4 berries, no signature, **toothed border, more numerous teeth**, and thin linear circle both sides, weak on obverse, **larger lettering**.

Obverse 11 (1881-83) - laureate and draped bust facing left, more **hooked nose**, hair tied in bun, with close thicker ties, nose more hooked, wreath of 15 leaves, **leaf veins raised**, 4 berries, no signature, toothed border and thin linear circle both sides, **weak circle on obverse**.

Obverse 13 (1889) - laureate and draped bust facing left, hair tied in bun, with close thicker ties, no curls at nape of neck, nose more hooked, **wreath of 14 leaves, leaf veins raised**, no signature, toothed border and thin linear circle both sides, larger lettering.

TimeLine Auctions
Inc. Gregory's Est.1858
We are accepting single entries
and collections of coins & antiquities
www.timelineauctions.com

REVERSES

Reverse A (1860) - Britannia seated right on rocks with shield and trident, **crosses on shield outlined with double raised lines**, L.C.W. incuse below shield, date below in exergue, lighthouse with 4 windows to left, ship sailing to right, **beaded border** and linear circle.

Reverse C (1860) - Britannia seated right on rocks with shield and trident, **crosses on shield outlined with wider spaced thinner double raised lines, thumb touches St. George Cross**, L.C.W. incuse below shield, date below in exergue, lighthouse with 4 windows to left, rocks touch linear circle, ship sailing to right, **beaded border** and linear circle.

Reverse B (1860) - Britannia with **one incuse hemline**, seated right on rocks with shield and trident, **crosses on shield outlined with treble incuse lines**, L.C.W. incuse below shield, date below in exergue, lighthouse with 4 windows to left, ship sailing to right, **beaded border** and linear circle.

Reverse D (1860-61) - Britannia seated right on rocks with shield and trident, crosses on shield outlined with wider spaced thinner double raised lines, thumb touches St. George Cross, L.C.W. incuse below shield, date below in exergue, lighthouse with 4 windows to left, rocks touch linear circle, ship sailing to right, **toothed border**.

REVERSES *(continued)*

Reverse E (1860) - Britannia seated right on rocks with **thick rimmed shield and trident**, crosses on shield outlined with wider spaced thinner double raised lines, thumb touches St. George Cross, **L.C.W. incuse below foot**, date below in exergue, lighthouse with **sharper masonry** to left, **rocks touch linear circle**, ship sailing to right, toothed border.

Reverse G (1861-75) - Britannia seated right on rocks with **convex shield and trident**, no signature, date below in exergue, bell-topped lighthouse to left, **lamp area depicted with five vertical lines, no rocks to left, sea crosses linear circle**, ship sailing to right, toothed border.

Reverse F (1861) - Britannia seated right on rocks with thick rimmed shield and trident, **incuse lines on breastplate**, crosses on shield outlined with wider spaced thinner double raised lines, thumb touches St. George Cross, **no L.C.W. extra rocks**, date below in exergue, **lighthouse with rounded top** and sharp masonry, **three horizontal lines** between masonry and top, rocks touch linear circle, ship sailing to right, toothed border.

Reverse H (1874-75, 1877) - Britannia seated right on rocks, **smaller head, thinner neck,** with convex shield and trident, no signature, **narrow date** below in exergue, **tall thin lighthouse** to left with **6 windows, lamp area of four vertical lines,** close date numerals, **tiny rock to left, sea touches linear circle,** ship sailing to right, toothed border.

REVERSES *(continued)*

Reverse I (1874) - Britannia seated right on rocks with convex shield and trident, **thick trident shaft**, no signature, **narrow date** below in exergue, **thicker lighthouse** to left with **4 windows**, lamp area of four vertical lines, close date numerals, tiny rock to left, sea touches linear circle, ship sailing to right, toothed border.

Reverse L (1880) - Britannia seated right on rocks with shield and trident, **extra feather to helmet plume, trident with three rings above hand**, date below in exergue, lighthouse with **cluster of rocks to left**, ship sailing to right, toothed border.

Reverse J (1875-81) - **larger Britannia** seated right on rocks with shield and trident, **left leg more visible, wider date** below in deeper exergue, lighthouse to left, ship sailing to right, **sea does not meet linear circle either side**, toothed border.

Reverse M (1881-82) - larger Britannia seated right on rocks with shield and trident, **flatter shield heraldically coloured**, date and **H below in exergue**, lighthouse to left with faint masonry, ship sailing to right, **sea does not meet linear circle**, toothed border.

Reverse K (1876, 1879) - Britannia with **larger head** seated right on rocks with convex shield and trident, **thicker helmet**, no signature, **narrow date** and in exergue, **tall thin lighthouse** to left, tiny rock to left, **sea touches linear circle**, ship sailing to right, toothed border.

REVERSES *(continued)*

Reverse O (1882 - proof only) – larger Britannia seated right on rocks with shield and trident, flatter shield heraldically coloured, date and **H in exergue**, lighthouse to left with faint masonry, ship sailing to right, **sea meets linear circle**, toothed border with more teeth.

Reverse N (1881-94) - **thinner Britannia** seated right on rocks with shield and thinner trident, **helmet plume ends in a single strand**, shield heraldically coloured with different thickness crosses, date in exergue, thinner lighthouse to left, ship sailing to right, sea meets linear circle, toothed border with more teeth.

Beaded border

Toothed border

Shield outlined with double raised lines

Shield outlined with treble incuse lines

Normal nose

More hooked nose

Penny Crown Coins

An extensive catalogue mostly comprised of English and United Kingdom milled issues prior to 1971, all illustrated online using high-quality photographs at:

PennyCrownCoins

P.O. Box 831, Amersham HP6 9GF
Tel. No. 01494-776141
E-mail: info@pennycrowncoins.co.uk

www.pennycrowncoins.co.uk

3954

	F £	VF £	EF £	UNC £
3954 Penny. Laur. bust l. R. Britannia seated r. date in ex. lighthouse l. ship to r., die axis ↑↑				
1860 obv 1, rev A..... 70	135	650	1700
1860 obv 1, rev B..... 15	55	350	1100
1860 obv 1*, rev A. 150	500	1350	2500
1860 obv 1, rev C 65	125	650	2150
1860 obv 1*, rev C. 125	475	1150	2350
1860 obv 1, rev D ..400	850	2400	4000
1860 obv 2, rev B . 425	875	2750	4500
1860 obv 2, rev D.......3	15	85	375
1860 — heavy flan. 2750	—	—	—
1860 N/Z in ONE, 2+D 90	300	825	1850
1860 obv 3, rev D.......3	15	95	425
1860 obv 3, rev E... 125	375	975	2150
1860 obv 4, rev D 2	10	95	550
1860 obv 5, rev D.......7	45	250	850
1860 obv 6, rev D.....35	135	450	1000
1861 obv 2, rev D.....75	175	525	1400
1861 obv 2, rev F... 125	250	950	1950
1861 obv 2, rev G.....30	110	400	1100
1861 obv 3, rev D ..250	600	1650	3000
1861 obv 4, rev D.......2	15	100	550
1861 — — heavy flan....2750	—	—	—
1861 obv 4, rev F ... 110	350	1250	3000
1861 obv 4, rev G.....40	175	600	1850
1861 obv 5, rev D.......2	10	95	500
1861 obv 5, rev F ...950	—	—	—
1861 obv 5, rev G... 110	400	1200	2500
1861 obv 6, rev D 2	10	95	375
1861 — — 6 over 8 450	2150	—	—
1861 obv 6, rev F ..150	600	1600	—
1861 obv 6, rev G.......2	10	95	425
1861 — 8 over 6.....450	2150	—	—
1862 obv 2, rev G... 500	1350	2950	3850
1862 obv 6, rev G.......2	10	75	300
1862 — 8 over 6.....600	2150	—	—
1862 — Halfpenny numerals........950	3000	4750	—
1863 obv 6, rev G.......2	10	75	325
1863 Die number below1350	4000	—	—
1863 slender 3......1100	2750	—	—
1863/1 obv 6, rev G 1000	2650	—	—
1864 Upper serif 20	110	925	3500

	F £	VF £	EF £	UNC £
1864 Crosslet 4 25	150	1100	4000
1865 obv 6, rev G...........7	20	215	875
1865/3 obv 6, rev G 45	125	600	1700
1866 obv 6, rev G...........3	15	125	600
1867 obv 6, rev G...........7	30	250	1100
1868 obv 6, rev G.........10	40	300	1150
1869 obv 6, rev G...... 110	450	1850	4500
1870 obv 6, rev G.........10	25	200	750
1871 obv 6, rev G.........40	150	825	2150
1872 obv 6, rev G...........3	15	100	500
1873 obv 6, rev G...........3	15	100	500
1874 obv 6, rev G...........3	15	150	725
1874 obv 7, rev G...........7	35	165	600
1874 obv 6, rev G.........20	55	225	950
1874 obv 8 rev H.........15	50	200	850
1874 obv 6, rev H.........30	85	425	975
1874 obv 7, rev H...........7	35	165	600
1875 obv 8, rev G.........15	60	300	675
1875 obv 8, rev H...........2	10	85	425
1875 obv 8, rev J............3	15	100	475
1877 obv 8, rev J............2	10	95	425
1877 obv 8, rev H..... 3250	—	—	—
1878 obv 8, rev J............2	15	135	700
1879 obv 8, rev J...........7	20	165	850
1879 obv 9, rev J............1	7	85	325
1879 obv 9, rev K.........25	90	400	1500
1880 obv 9, rev J............2	15	165	600
1880 obv 9, rev L............2	15	165	600
1881 obv 9, rev J............2	15	135	700
1881 obv 10, rev J........30	90	400	1000
1881 obv 11, rev J........60	150	600	1300
1882† obv 11, rev N. 1000	3500	—	—
1883 obv 12, rev N.........2	10	95	400
1883 obv11, rev N..........2	10	95	450
1884 obv 12, rev N.........2	7	85	300
1885 obv 12, rev N.........2	7	85	300
1886 obv 12, rev N.........2	10	85	325
1887 obv 12, rev N.........2	7	85	300
1888 obv 12, rev N.........2	10	85	325
1889 obv 12, rev N.........3	15	110	500

† *not to be confused with Heaton Mint - H - the mint letter is the first device to disappear on worn specimens*
Bronze coins graded in this catalogue as UNC have full mint lustre

	F £	VF £	EF £	UNC £		F £	VF £	EF £	UNC £

3954 Penny. (Continued)

1889 obv 13, rev N	2	7	75	300
1890 obv 12, rev N	2	7	75	300
1891 obv 12, rev N	2	7	70	300
1892 obv 12, rev N	2	7	75	300
1893 obv 12, rev N	2	7	65	300
1893 obv 12, rev N 3 over 2	150	400	700	1500
1894 obv 12, rev N	2	15	100	375

3955 Penny. Similar R. Britannia, H Mint mark below date – (struck by Ralph Heaton & Sons, Birmingham)

1874 H obv 6, rev G	5	20	135	500
1874 H obv 6, rev H	10	30	190	600
1874 H obv 6, rev I	175	1000	2500	–
1874 H obv 7, rev G	10	30	165	550
1874 H obv 7, rev H	5	20	135	475
1874 H obv 7, rev I	150	480	2250	–
1875 H obv 8, rev J	35	100	1100	2500
1876 H obv 8, rev K	2	15	100	400
1876 H obv 8, rev J	10	30	190	600
1881 H obv 11, rev M	3	15	95	450
1881 H obv 9, rev M	475	1250	2750	–
1882 H obv 12, rev M	10	25	165	700
1882 H obv 12, rev N	2	10	85	325
1882/1 H obv 11, rev M	10	25	135	875

3955
H Mint mark location

3956
1860 Halfpenny Beaded border

3956 Halfpenny. Laur. bust l. R. Britannia seated r. date in ex. lighthouse l. ship to r., die axis ↑↑

1860 Beaded border	1	5	40	160
1860 no tie to wreath	5	15	120	425
1860 Toothed border	2	10	110	350
1860 round top light house	15	120	425
1860 5 berries in wreath	3	10	110	400
1860 – 15 leaves, 4 berries	1	10	100	325
1860 – rounded lighthouse	2	10	130	400
1860 – Double incuse . leaf veins	3	12	125	425
1860 – 16 leaves wreath	10	30	175	550
1860 TB/BBmule	700	1400	2700	–
1861 5 berries in wreath	10	30	165	500
1861 15 leaves in wreath	5	20	120	450
1861 – R. no hemline . to drapery	10	30	165	500
1861 – R. Door on lighthouse	3	12	125	450
1861 4 leaves double incuse veins	1	10	95	325
1861 16 leaves wreath	3	12	120	450
1861 – R. LCW incuse on rock	10	30	165	500
1861 – R. no hemline to drapery	2	10	110	400
1861 – R. door on lighthouse	–	5	85	275
1861 HALP error	300	850	–	–
1861 6 over 8	275	800	–	–
1862	–	4	50	190
1862 Die letter to left of lighthouse				
A	600	1400	2650	4000
B	900	2250	–	–
C	1000	2750	–	–
1863 small 3	–	5	80	300
1863 large 3	–	5	80	290
1864	1	10	110	400
1865	2	12	150	600
1865/3	45	100	400	1200
1866	1	10	110	400
1867	1	12	120	500
1868	–	8	110	425
1869	25	85	500	1450
1870	1	7	100	375
1871	25	90	500	1450
1872	1	7	95	300
1873	1	10	110	375
1873 R. hemline to drapery	1	10	110	400
1874	4	25	185	625
1874 narrow date	12	60	425	950

Bronze coins graded in this catalogue as UNC have full mint lustre

	F £	VF £	EF £	UNC £		F £	VF £	EF £	UNC £

3956 Halfpenny.

1874 older features	5	25	185	625
1875	—	5	95	300
1877	—	5	95	300
1878	4	20	160	600
1878 wide date	90	200	525	1150
1879	—	5	85	250
1880	1	7	95	300
1881	1	7	95	300
1883	—	7	95	300
1883 rose for brooch obv.	25	65	185	375
1884	—	4	65	225
1885	—	4	60	210
1886	—	4	60	210
1887	—	4	50	190
1888	—	4	85	250
1889	—	4	85	250
1889/8	25	60	265	600
1890	—	4	50	190
1891	—	4	50	190
1892	1	5	95	300
1893	—	4	85	235
1894	1	6	95	285

3957 Halfpenny. Similar R. Britannia, H Mint mark below date (struck by Ralph Heaton & Sons, Birmingham)

1874 H	—	4	95	300
1875 H	1	5	100	325
1876 H	—	4	95	300
1881 H	—	4	95	300
1882 H	—	4	95	300

3958
1860 Farthing

3960
1868 Third-Farthing

3958 Farthing. Laur bust l. R. Britannia seated r. date in ex. lighthouse l. ship to r. die axis ↑↑

1860 Beaded border		3	30	110
1860 Toothed border		5	40	130
1860 — 5 berries		3	40	130
1860 TB/BB mule	175	475	1100	—
1861 5 berries		3	50	145
1861 4 berries		3	35	140
1862		3	35	130
1862 large 8	55	175	425	—
1863	20	50	300	650
1864 4 no serif		5	60	170
1864 4 with serif		7	65	185
1865		3	50	145
1865/2		10	60	200
1866		3	45	145
1867		3	55	160
1868		4	55	160
1869		10	65	200
1872		3	50	145
1873		2	35	110
1875 large date	2	10	65	215
1875 small date	10	25	175	525
1875 — older features	7	20	120	385
1877 Proof only £10000				
1878		3	30	120
1879 large 9		4	45	145
1879 normal 9		3	40	130
1880		4	55	160
1881		3	40	140
1883	—	10	65	185
1884		2	25	80
1885		2	25	80
1886		2	25	80
1887		3	35	130
1888		3	35	120
1890		3	30	100
1891		2	25	100
1892	—	10	65	200
1893		2	25	100
1894		3	35	125
1895	7	25	110	335

Bronze coins graded in this catalogue as UNC have full mint lustre

	F	VF	EF	UNC		F	VF	EF	UNC
	£	£	£	£		£	£	£	£

3959 Farthing. Similar R. Britannia. H Mint mark below date (struck by Ralph Heaton & Sons, Birmingham)

	F	VF	EF	UNC		F	VF	EF	UNC
1874 H older features....3		10	65	175	1876 H large 6..........7		30	100	250
1874 H, both Gs over sideways G					1876 H normal 6.....3		10	65	185
on obv. 125		350	900	—	1881 H....................—		5	25	110
1875 H younger features .80		250	475	1000	1882 H....................—		5	25	110
1875 H older features......		2	20	110					

3960 Third-Farthing (for use in Malta). Laur. head l. R. Crowned date and Value die axis ↑↑

	F	VF	EF	UNC		F	VF	EF	UNC
1866..............................—		4	35	110	1881 ....—		5	40	120
1868..............................—		4	35	100	1884 ....—		4	35	110
1876..............................—		5	40	120	1885 ....—		4	35	110
1878..............................—		4	35	110					

Old Head Issue, 1895-1901, die axis ↑↑

Proofs exist of most years and are generally extremely rare for all denominations

3961
1897 Penny

	VF	EF	UNC		VF	EF	UNC
	£	£	£		£	£	£

3961 Penny. Old veiled bust l. R. Britannia seated r. date in ex., die axis ↑↑

	VF	EF	UNC		VF	EF	UNC
1895..............................	1	30	110	1898	7	40	115
1896..............................	3	30	95	1899	3	30	85
1897..............................	3	30	95	1900	5	20	70
1897 O'NE flawed	100	500	1600	1901	1	12	50

3961 'Normal Tide'
Horizon is level with folds in robe

3961A 'Low Tide'
Horizon is level with hem line of robe

3961A Penny. Similar As last but 'Low tide' and 'P' 2mm from trident, 1895...45 | 100 | 425 | 1650
3961B Penny. Similar, higher tide level above two folds of robe, 1897.......20 | 75 | 400 | 1500

3962 Halfpenny. Old veiled bust l. R. Britannia seated r. date in ex., die axis ↑↑

	VF	EF	UNC		VF	EF	UNC
1895..............................	3	12	80	1898	3	12	80
1896..............................	2	10	75	1899	2	10	75
1897..............................	2	10	75	1900	2	10	70
1897 Higher tide level.	5	15	80	1901	—	7	60

	VF £	EF £	UNC £		VF £	EF £	UNC £
3963 Farthing. Old veiled bust l. R. Britannia seated r. date in ex. Bright finish, die axis ↑↑							
1895..........................	—	7	50	1897	3	12	55
1896..........................	1	10	55				

3962 - Old Head Halfpenny   3964 - Old Head Farthing

	VF £	EF £	UNC £		VF £	EF £	UNC £
3964 Farthing. Similar Dark finish, die axis ↑↑							
1897..........................	—	7	35	1899	1	10	35
1897 Higher tide level.	3	12	55	1900	—	7	30
1898..........................	1	10	45	1901		4	25

PROOF SETS

PS3 Young head, **1839.** 'Una and the Lion' Five Pounds, and Sovereign to Farthing (15 coins) *FDC* £250000

PS4 — **1853.** Sovereign to Half-Farthing, including Gothic type Crown (16 coins) *FDC* £110000

PS5 Jubilee head. Golden Jubilee, **1887.** Five pounds to Threepence (11 coins)*FDC* £32500

PS6 — — **1887.** Crown to Threepence (7 coins) *FDC* £5750

PS7 Old head, **1893.** Five Pounds to Threepence (10 coins) *FDC* £42500

PS8 — — **1893.** Crown to Threepence (6 coins) *FDC* £6750

† *NB Truly 'FDC' proof sets are hardly ever encountered. Component coins showing any surface marks, hairlines or nicks will be worth less than the prices quoted above.*

Inc. Gregory's **Est.1858**

+44 [0]1277 815121
enquiries@timelineauctions.com

We are accepting single
entries and collections of
coins and antiquities

Follow us on:

 /TimeLineAuctions
@TimeLineAuction

www.timelineauctions.com

AIAD

THE ART LOSS REGISTER

LIVE AUCTIONEERS

the-saleroom.com
live auctions

BNTA

THE HOUSE OF SAXE-COBURG-GOTHA, 1901-1917
EDWARD VII, 1901-10

'Edward the Peacemaker' was born on 9 November 1841, and married Princess Alexandra of Denmark. He indulged himself in every decadent luxury, while his wife tried to ignore his extra-marital activities. Edward travelled extensively and was crucial in negotiating alliances with Russia and France. Edward VII died on 6 May 1910.

Five Pound pieces, Two Pound pieces and Crowns were only issued in 1902. A branch of the Royal Mint was opened in Canada at Ottawa and coined Sovereigns of imperial type from 1908.

Unlike the coins in most other proof sets, the proofs issued for the Coronation in 1902 have a matt surface in place of the more usual brilliant finish.

Designer's initials: De S. (G. W. De Saulles 1862-1903)
B. P. (Benedetto Pistrucci, d. 1855)
Engravers and Designers: WHJ Blakemore, George William De Saulles (1862-1903), Benedetto Pistrucci (1784-1855)

GOLD

Die axis: ↑↑

3966 - Matt Proof Five Pounds 1902

	VF	EF	UNC		F	VF	EF	UNC
	£	£	£		£	£	£	£

3965 Five Pounds. Bare head r. R. St. George and dragon, date in ex.
1902 .... 1350 1900 2600 3850
3966 Five Pounds. Similar Proof. 1902. *Matt surface FDC £3000*
3966A Five Pounds. Similar Proof 1902S. S on ground for Sydney Mint, Australia   *Extremely rare*

3967 - 1902 Two Pounds   3969 - 1902 Sovereign

3967 Two Pounds. Bare head r. R. St George and dragon, date in ex.
1902.. 750 950 1350 2200
3968 Two Pounds. Similar Proof. 1902. *Matt surface FDC £1950*
3968A Two Pounds. Similar Proof 1902S. S on ground for Sydney Mint, Australia   *Extremely rare*
3969 Sovereign. Bare head r. R . St. George and dragon, date in ex. London mint, die axis ↑↑

1902 Matt proof *FDC £750*				1906	—	BV	400
1902.....................	—	BV	350	1907	—	BV	400
1903.....................	—	BV	400	1908	—	BV	400
1904.....................	—	BV	400	1909	—	BV	400
1905.....................	—	BV	400	1910	—	BV	400

3970 Sovereign. Similar R. C on ground for Ottawa Mint, Canada
1908 C (Satin proof only) *FDC £11500*   1909 C Satin finish
1909 C......................... 275 450 800   specimen *FDC* ....*Extremely rare*
                                                          1910 C......................... 250 425 700

BV= Bullion value only. At the time of going to press the spot price for gold was £1030 per oz.

	EF £	UNC £			EF £	UNC £

3971 Sovereign. Similar R. St. George M on ground for Melbourne Mint, Australia, die axis ↑↑

1902 M	.... BV	425	1906 M	.... BV	450
1902 M Proof	..........*Extremely rare*		1907 M	.... BV	450
1903 M	.... BV	450	1908 M	.... BV	450
1904 M	.... BV	450	1909 M	.... BV	450
1904 M Proof	..........*Extremely rare*		1910 M	.... BV	450
1905 M	.... BV	450	1910 M Proof	..........*Extremely rare*	

3972 Sovereign. Similar R. P on ground for Perth Mint, Australia die axis ↑↑

1902 P	.... BV	450	1907 P	.... BV	425
1903 P	.... BV	475	1908 P	.... BV	425
1904 P	.... BV	475	1909 P	.... BV	425
1905 P	.... BV	425	1910 P	.... BV	450
1906 P	.... BV	425			

3973 Sovereign. Similar R. S on ground for Sydney Mint, Australia die axis ↑↑

1902 S	.... BV	425	1906 S	....	425
1902 S Proof	..........*Extremely rare*		1907 S	....	425
1903 S	.... BV	425	1908 S	....	425
1904 S	.... BV	425	1909 S	....	425
1905 S	.... BV	425	1910 S	....	425

3974A - 1902 Half-Sovereign, no BP in exergue

	F £	VF £	EF £	UNC £		F £	VF £	EF £	UNC £

3974 A Half-Sovereign. Bare head r. R. St. George. London Mint no BP in exergue, die axis ↑↑

| 1902 Matt proof *FDC* £675 | | | | | 1903 | .... BV | | 125 | 235 |
| 1902 | .... BV | 125 | 235 | | 1904 | .... BV | | 125 | 235 |

3974 B Half-Sovereign. R. Similar with BP in exergue

1904	.... BV	125	235		1908	.... BV		125	235
1905	.... BV	125	235		1909	.... BV		125	235
1906	.... BV	125	235		1910	.... BV		125	235
1907	.... BV	125	235						

3975 Half-Sovereign. Similar R. M on ground for Melbourne Mint, Australia, die axis ↑↑

| 1906 M | .... BV | 250 | 850 | 2250 | 1908 M | .... BV | 125 | 250 | 500 |
| 1907 M | .... BV | 125 | 225 | 750 | 1909 M | .... BV | 125 | 275 | 700 |

3976 A Half-Sovereign. — P on ground for Perth Mint, Australia R. no BP in exergue, die axis ↑↑

| 1904 P | .... BV | 275 | 1250 | 5500 | | | | | |

3976 B Half-Sovereign. Similar R. P on ground for Perth Mint, Australia R. with BP in exergue, die axis ↑↑

| 1904 P | ....*Extremely rare* | | | | 1909 P | .... BV | 225 | 550 | 2000 |
| 1908 P | .... BV | 225 | 1100 | 4500 | | | | | |

3977 A Half-Sovereign. Similar R. S on ground for Sydney Mint, Australia R. No BP in exergue, die axis ↑↑

| 1902 S | .... BV | 125 | 225 | 425 | 1903 S | .... BV | 125 | 200 | 600 |
| 1902 S Proof | ....*Extremely rare* | | | | | | | | |

3977 B Half-Sovereign. — S on ground for Sydney Mint, Australia R. with BP in exergue, die axis ↑↑

| 1906 S | .... BV | 125 | 500 | | 1910 S | .... BV | 125 | 325 | |
| 1908 S | .... BV | 125 | 350 | | | | | | |

BV= Bullion value only. At the time of going to press the spot price for gold was £1030 per oz.

SILVER

3978
1902 Crown

	F	VF	EF	UNC		F	VF	EF	UNC

3978 Crown. Bare head r. ℞. St. George and dragon date in ex. die axis ↑↑
1902........................80   140   225   350   1902 error edge inscription.... *Extremely rare*
3979 Crown. Similar Matt proof *FDC* £350

3980   3981
1904 Halfcrown   Florin

3980 Halfcrown. Bare head r. ℞. Crowned Shield in Garter, die axis ↑↑

1902	15	40	120	275	1906	15	60	350	1000
1902 Matt proof *FDC* £250					1907	15	55	315	950
1903	175	575	2650	5250	1908	20	55	525	1300
1904	60	300	1050	3000	1909	15	50	425	1100
1905*	550	1750	5250	10500	1910	15	40	285	750

3981 Florin. Bare head r. ℞. Britannia standing on ship's bow die axis ↑↑

1902	7	20	80	150	1906	10	30	185	525
1902 Matt proof *FDC* £175					1907	10	40	215	550
1903	10	30	185	475	1908	15	50	350	800
1904	15	45	265	600	1909	15	50	325	750
1905	65	200	850	1850	1910	10	25	145	400

*Beware of 1970's forgeries.

3982
1902 Shilling

3983
1902 Sixpence

	F £	VF £	EF £	UNC £		F £	VF £	EF £	UNC £

3982 Shilling. Bare head r. R. Lion passant on crown die axis ↑↑

	F	VF	EF	UNC		F	VF	EF	UNC
1902	5	12	70	125	1906	5	10	85	275
1902 Matt proof *FDC* £150					1907	5	10	90	300
1903	7	20	185	525	1908	12	25	200	550
1904	7	15	165	450	1909	12	25	200	550
1905	110	350	1650	3500	1910	5	10	80	175

3983 Sixpence. Bare head r. R. Value in wreath die axis ↑↑

	F	VF	EF	UNC		F	VF	EF	UNC
1902	5	10	55	100	1906	4	10	60	150
1902 Matt proof *FDC* £125					1907	5	10	65	165
1903	4	10	60	150	1908	5	12	70	175
1904	7	25	125	325	1909	4	10	65	150
1905	5	20	90	250	1910	4	7	50	100

3984 Threepence. As Maundy but dull finish die axis ↑↑

	F	VF	EF	UNC		F	VF	EF	UNC
1902	2	5	15	40	1906	3	7	50	140
1902 Matt proof *FDC* £50					1907	3	7	30	65
1903	3	7	30	65	1908	2	5	15	55
1904	4	10	40	115	1909	3	7	30	65
1905	3	7	30	90	1910	2	5	15	55

3985
1903 Maundy Set

	EF £	FDC £		EF £	FDC £

3985 Maundy Set (4d., 3d., 2d. and 1d.) Bare head r. die axis ↑↑

	EF	FDC		EF	FDC
1902	110	185	1906	110	195
1902 Matt proof *FDC* £195			1907	110	195
1903	110	195	1908	110	195
1904	110	195	1909	160	300
1905	110	195	1910	160	300

		EF £	FDC £
3986 — **Fourpence.** 1902-10 ....*from*		7	30
3987 — **Threepence.** 1902-10 ....*from*		10	30
3988 — **Twopence.** 1902-10 ....*from*		7	30
3989 — **Penny.** 1902-10...*from*		12	35

Maundy sets in the original undamaged cases are worth approximately £25 more than the prices quoted.
See foontnote after 3796.

BRONZE

3990
1902 Penny

3990 Normal Tide

'3990A 'Low Tide'

	VG £	F £	VF £	EF £	UNC £		F £	VF £	EF £	UNC £
3990 Penny. Bare head r. ℞. Britannia seated r. date in ex. die axis ↑↑										
1902....................			1	15	60	1906...................		4	30	120
1903 Normal 3 ...			2	25	110	1907...................		1	35	130
1903 Open 3...60		125	500	—	—	1908...................		4	30	120
1904....................			7	55	160	1909...................		5	35	130
1905....................			5	50	150	1910...................		2	20	100
3990A Penny. Similar R. As last but 'Low tide', 1902,'2' has wavy base line							7	50	150	300

3991
Halfpenny

	VF	EF	UNC		F	VF	EF	UNC
	£	£	£		£	£	£	£

3991 Halfpenny. Bare head r. ℞. Britannia seated r. date in ex. die axis ↑↑

1902	1	12	45	1907		1	20	90
1903	2	20	85	1908		1	20	90
1904	2	28	125	1909		2	25	100
1905	2	25	100	1910		2	20	90
1906	2	25	95					

3991A Halfpenny. Similar ℞. As last but 'Low tide', 1902......................15　85　165　410

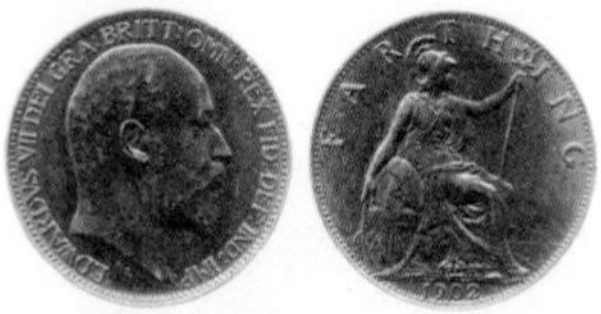

3992
Farthing

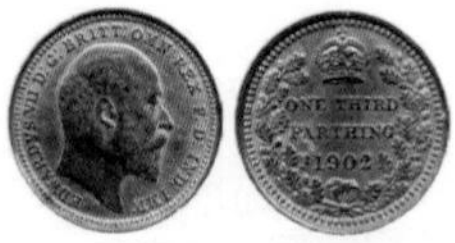

3993
1902 Third-Farthing

3992 Farthing. Bare head r. ℞. Britannia seated r. date in ex. Dark finish die axis ↑↑

1902	—	8	30	1907		1	12	40
1903	1	12	35	1908		1	12	40
1904	2	15	40	1909		1	10	35
1905	1	12	40	1910		2	22	45
1906	1	12	40					

3993 Third-Farthing (for use in Malta) Bare head r. ℞. Crowned date and value die axis ↑↑.
1902 .... 7　22　55
No proofs of the bronze coins were issued in 1902

PROOF SETS
PS9　Coronation, **1902.** Five Pounds to Maundy Penny, matt surface, (13 coins) *FDC*　£7500
PS10 — **1902.** Sovereign to Maundy Penny, matt surface, (11 coins)................... *FDC*　£2350

† *NB Truly 'FDC' proof sets are hardly ever encountered. Component coins showing any surface marks, hairlines or nicks will be worth less than the prices quoted above.*

George V, the second son of Edward VII, was born on 3 June 1865 and married Mary of Teck who bore him five sons and a daughter. He was King through World War I and visited the front on several occassions. He suffered a fall breaking his pelvis on one of these visits, an injury that would pain him for the rest of his life. He watched the Empire divide; Ireland, Canada, Australia, New Zealand and India all went through changes. He died on 20th January 1936 only months after his Silver Jubilee.

Paper money issued by the Treasury during the First World War replaced gold for internal use after 1915 but the branch mints in Australia and South Africa (the main Commonwealth gold producing countries) continued striking Sovereigns until 1930-2. Owing to the steep rise in the price of silver in 1919/20 the issue of standard (.925) silver was discontinued and coins of .500 silver were minted.

In 1912, 1918 and 1919 some Pennies were made under contract by private mints in Birmingham. In 1918, as Half-Sovereigns were no longer being minted, Farthings were again issued with the ordinary bright bronze finish. Crown pieces had not been issued for general circulation but they were struck in small numbers about Christmas time for people to give as presents in the years 1927-36, and in 1935 a special commemorative Crown was issued in celebration of the Silver Jubilee.

As George V died on 20 January, it is likely that all coins dated 1936 were struck during the reign of Edward VIII.

Engravers and Designers:– George Kuger Gray (1880-1943), Bertram MacKennal (1863-1931), Benedetto Pistrucci (1784-1855) Percy Metcalfe (1895-1970)

Designer's initials:
  B. M. (Bertram Mackennal)   P. M. (Percy Metcalfe)
  K. G. (G. Kruger Gray)   B. P. (Benedetto Pistrucci; d. 1855)

Die axis: ↑↑

GOLD

£
3994 Five Pounds.* Bare head l. R. St. George and dragon, date in ex., 1911 (Proof only)..... 7000
3995 Two Pounds.* Bare head l. R. St. George and dragon, date in ex., 1911 (Proof only)..... 2750

3996

	VF	EF	UNC		VF	EF	UNC
	£	£	£		£	£	£

3996 Sovereign. Bare head l. R. St. George and dragon. London Mint die axis: ↑↑

	VF	EF	UNC		VF	EF	UNC
1911	BV	BV	450	1914	BV	BV	400
1911 Proof *FDC* £1450				1915	BV	BV	400
1911 Matt Proof *FDC of highest rarity*				1916	BV	350	650
1912	BV	BV	400	1917*	5500	15000	—
1913	BV	BV	400	1925	BV	BV	365

*Forgeries exist of these and of most other dates and mints.

BV= Bullion value only. At the time of going to press the spot price for gold was £1030 per oz.

	F £	VF £	EF £	UNC £		F £	VF £	EF £	UNC £

3997 Sovereign. Bare head l. R. St George, C on ground for the Ottawa Mint, Canada die axis: ↑↑

1911 C	BV	250	550	1917 C	BV	250	450
1913 C	350	1500	—	1918 C	BV	250	450
1914 C	275	800	—	1919 C	BV	250	450
1916 C*	6500	17000	—				

* Beware of recent forgeries

3997
Canada 'c' Mint mark

3998 Sovereign. Similar R. I on ground for Bombay Mint, India 1918 ....BV   335   550

3999 Sovereign. Similar R. M on ground for Melbourne Mint, Australia die axis: ↑↑

1911 M	BV	400	1920 M	800	1750	3000	5500
1912 M	BV	400	1921 M	2750	5000	7500	17000
1913 M	BV	400	1922 M	1750	4000	6500	13500
1914 M	BV	400	1923 M	BV	250	425
1915 M	BV	400	1924 M	BV	250	425
1916 M	BV	400	1925 M	BV	400
1917 M	BV	400	1926 M	BV	275	425
1918 M	BV	400	1928 M	600	1000	1750	2850
1919 M	225	450				

4000 Sovereign. Similar small bare head l. die axis: ↑↑

1929 M	375	850	1750	3000	1930 M		BV	225	375
1929 M Proof *FDC*			*Extremely rare*	1931 M	BV	350	550	700

4000	4001
1930 M Sovereign, small head	Perth Mint Sovereign

4001 Sovereign. Similar R. P on ground for Perth Mint, Australia die axis: ↑↑

1911 P	BV	350	1920 P	BV	350
1912 P	BV	350	1921 P	BV	350
1913 P	BV	350	1922 P	BV	350
1914 P	BV	350	1923 P	BV	350
1915 P	BV	350	1924 P	—	BV	225	425
1916 P	BV	350	1925 P	BV	BV	325	600
1917 P	BV	350	1926 P	400	675	1100	2500
1918 P	BV	350	1927 P	BV	BV	375	600
1919 P	BV	350	1928 P	—	BV	225	425

BV= Bullion value only. At the time of going to press the spot price for gold was £1030 per oz.

	VF	EF	UNC		F	VF	EF	UNC
	£	£	£		£	£	£	£

4002 Sovereign. Similar — small bare head l. die axis: ↑↑

		VF	EF/UNC			UNC
1929 P	BV	225	425	1931 P	BV	350
1930 P	BV	225	425			

4003 Sovereign. Similar R. S on ground for Sydney Mint, Australia die axis: ↑↑

		UNC			F	VF	EF	UNC
1911 S	BV	350	1919 S	BV				400
1912 S	BV	350	†1920 S					*Of highest rarity*
1913 S	BV	350	1921 S	500		800	1700	2500
1914 S	BV	350	1922 S	5000		9500	14000	27500
1915 S	BV	350	1923 S	3500		6500	10000	25000
1916 S	BV	350	1924 S	400		800	1500	2750
1917 S	BV	350	1925 S	BV				400
1918 S	BV	350	1926 S	6000		12500	20000	31500

4004 Sovereign. Similar R. SA on ground for Pretoria Mint, South Africa die axis: ↑↑

	VF	EF	UNC				EF	UNC
1923 SA	1250	3000	7500	1926 SA			BV	350
1923 SA Proof *FDC* £1750				1927 SA			BV	350
1924 SA	2250	5000	11000	1928 SA			BV	350
1925 SA		BV	350					

4005 Sovereign. Similar — small head die axis: ↑↑

		EF	UNC			EF	UNC
1929 SA	BV		350	1931 SA	BV		350
1930 SA	BV		350	1932 SA	BV		350

† *An example of the proof 1920 S sold at a uk auction in May 2012 for £780,000*

4003
1921 Sydney 's' Sovereign

4006
1914 Half-sovereign

4006 Half-Sovereign. Bare head l. R. St. George and dragon date in ex. London Mint die axis: ↑↑

		EF	UNC			EF	UNC
1911	BV	125	235	1913	BV	125	235
1911 Proof *FDC* £950				1914	BV	125	235
1911 Matt Proof *FDC of highest rarity*				1915	BV	125	235
1912	BV	125	235				

4007 Half-Sovereign. Similar R. M on ground for Melbourne Mint, Australia die axis: ↑↑

	VF	EF	UNC
1915 M	BV	BV	235

4008 Half-Sovereign. Similar R. P on ground for Perth Mint, Australia die axis: ↑↑

		EF	UNC		F	VF	EF	UNC
1911 P	BV	125	350	1918 P	200	600	2000	3750
1915 P	BV	125	325					

4009 Half-Sovereign. Similar R. S on ground for Sydney Mint, Australia die axis: ↑↑

	VF	EF	UNC		VF	EF	UNC
1911 S	BV	BV	185	1915 S	BV	BV	185
1912 S	BV	BV	185	1916 S	BV	BV	185
1914 S	BV	BV	185				

4010 Half-Sovereign. Similar R. SA on ground for Pretoria Mint, South Africa die axis: ↑↑

	VF	EF	UNC		VF	EF	UNC
1923 SA Proof *FDC* £1250				1926 SA	BV	BV	195
1925 SA	BV	BV	195				

BV= Bullion value only. At the time of going to press the spot price for gold was £1030 per oz.

SILVER

FIRST COINAGE, 1911-19 Sterling silver (.925 fine)

4011
1911 Halfcrown

	F £	VF £	EF £	UNC £		F £	VF £	EF £	UNC £

4011 Halfcrown. Bare head l. R. Crowned shield in Garter die axis: ↑↑

1911	8	25	85	225	1915	8	12	40	100
1911 Proof *FDC* £300					1916	8	12	40	100
1912	8	25	75	275	1917	8	15	60	150
1913	8	30	85	275	1918	8	12	45	125
1914	8	12	45	125	1919	8	15	55	150

4012
1912 Florin

4013
1911 Proof

4012 Florin. Bare head l. R. Crowned Cruciform shields sceptres in angles die axis: ↑↑

1911	6	12	60	165	1915	6	20	65	200
1911 Proof *FDC* £200					1916	6	12	50	115
1912	6	15	70	225	1917	6	15	55	150
1913	8	25	85	250	1918	6	12	45	110
1914	6	12	50	115	1919	6	15	55	150

4013 Shilling. Bare head l. R. Lion passant on crown, within circle die axis: ↑↑

1911	3	10	40	85	1915		2	30	75
1911 Proof *FDC* £135					1916		2	30	75
1912	3	12	45	115	1917		3	40	125
1913	6	15	75	225	1918		2	35	85
1914	3	10	40	90	1919	2	8	45	100

4014
1911 Sixpence

	F £	VF £	EF £	UNC £		F £	VF £	EF £	UNC £

4014 Sixpence. Bare head l. R. Lion passant on crown, within circle die axis: ↑↑

	F	VF	EF	UNC		F	VF	EF	UNC
1911	1	7	30	60	1916	1	7	30	60
1911 Proof *FDC* £100					1917	4	15	55	160
1912	3	10	40	80	1918	1	7	30	65
1913	6	12	45	85	1919	3	10	35	75
1914	1	7	30	65	1920	4	12	45	90
1915	1	7	30	75					

4015 Threepence. As Maundy but dull finish die axis: ↑↑

	F	EF	UNC		F	EF	UNC
1911	1	5	30	1916	1	5	25
1911 Proof *FDC* £50				1917	1	5	25
1912	1	5	30	1918	1	5	25
1913	1	5	30	1919	1	5	25
1914	1	5	30	1920	2	10	35
1915	1	5	35				

4016
1915 Maundy Set

	EF £	FDC £		EF £	FDC £

4016 Maundy Set (4d., 3d., 2d. and 1d.) die axis: ↑↑

	EF	FDC		EF	FDC
1911	125	225	1916	125	225
1911 Proof *FDC* £250			1917	125	225
1912	125	225	1918	125	225
1913	125	225	1919	125	225
1914	125	225	1920	155	275
1915	125	225			

		EF	FDC
4017 — Fourpence. 1911-20	*from*	10	30
4018 — Threepence. 1911-20	*from*	12	32
4019 — Twopence. 1911-20	*from*	8	25
4020 — Penny. 1911-20	*from*	10	35

See footnote after 3796

SECOND COINAGE, 1920-27 Debased silver (.500 fine). Types as before.

	F £	VF £	EF £	UNC £		F £	VF £	EF £	UNC £

4021 Halfcrown. Deeply engraved. Bare head l. R. Crowned shield in garter die axis: ↑↑

	F	VF	EF	UNC
1920......................3	12	60	185	

4021A — recut shallow portrait

	F	VF	EF	UNC		F	VF	EF	UNC
1920......................5	15	75	215		1924 Specimen Finish £4250				
1921......................3	12	60	160		1925....................25	75	375	1000
1922......................3	10	60	160		1926......................3	18	85	195
1923......................2	6	40	95		1926 No colon			
1924......................3	10	60	160		after OMN.15	45	175	395

4022 Florin. Deeply engraved. Bare head l. R. Crowned cruciform shields, sceptres in angles die axis: ↑↑

	F	VF	EF	UNC
1920......................3	12	60	160	

4022A — recut shallow portrait

	F	VF	EF	UNC		F	VF	EF	UNC
1920......................5	18	75	175		1924......................2	12	65	150
1921......................2	7	55	120		1924 Specimen Finish £3250			
1922......................2	6	50	110		1925....................25	55	275	650
1922 Proof in gold *FDC of highest rarity*					1926......................2	12	65	150
1923......................2	6	40	85					

4023 Shilling. Deeply engraved. Bare head l. R. Lion passant on crown within circle die axis: ↑↑

	F	VF	EF	UNC		F	VF	EF	UNC
1920......................3	12	45	100		1921 nose to S....12	30	90	225

4023A — recut shallow portrait

	F	VF	EF	UNC		F	VF	EF	UNC
1920 4	15	65	160		1924......................1	10	55	100
1921 nose to SV...3	15	65	160		1925......................3	12	65	160
1922......................1	4	45	95		1926......................1	7	35	90
1923......................1	3	35	90					

Note: 1923 and 1924 Shillings exist struck in nickel and are valued at £3500 each FDC.

4024 Sixpence. Bare head l. R. Lion passant on crown within circle die axis: ↑↑

	F	VF	EF	UNC		F	VF	EF	UNC
1920......................1	5	30	85		1924......................1	2	20	65
1921......................1	2	25	80		1924 Specimen Finish *FDC* £3000			
1922......................1	3	25	80		1924 Proof in gold *FDC* £27500			
1923......................1	4	30	90		1925......................1	2	30	70

4025 - George V Sixpence   4026 - Threepence

4025 Sixpence. Similar new beading and broader rim die axis: ↑↑

	F	VF	EF	UNC		F	VF	EF	UNC
1925......................1	2	30	60		1926......................1	4	30	60

4026 Threepence. Bare head l. R. Crowned 3 die axis: ↑↑

	F	VF	EF	UNC		F	VF	EF	UNC
1920......................	1	4	28		1924 Proof in gold *FDC* £12500			
1921......................	1	4	28		1925.................BV	2	22	75
1922......................	1	20	90		1926......................1	8	45	150
1924 Specimen Finish £3000								

	EF £	FDC £		EF £	FDC £

4027 Maundy Set. (4d., 3d., 2d. and 1d.) die axis: ↑↑

	EF	FDC		EF	FDC
1921...................................	120	225	1925...................................	120	225
1922...................................	120	225	1926...................................	120	225
1923...................................	120	225	1927...................................	120	225
1924...................................	120	225			

		EF	FDC
4028 — Fourpence. 1921-7 ....*from*		15	35
4029 — Threepence. 1921-7 ....*from*		12	30
4030 — Twopence. 1921-7 ....*from*		10	25
4031 — Penny. 1921-7...*from*		15	40

2nd coinage
BM more central on tr.

3rd coinage
Modified Effigy
BM to right of tr.

THIRD COINAGE, 1926-27. As before but modified effigy, with details of head more clearly defined. The BM on truncation is nearer to the back of the neck and without stops; beading is more pronounced.

	F	VF	EF	UNC		F	VF	EF	UNC
	£	£	£	£		£	£	£	£

4032 Halfcrown. Modified effigy l. R. Crowned Shield in Garter die axis: ↑↑

| 1926 | 4 | 20 | 85 | 225 | 1927 Proof in gold *FDC of highest rarity* |
| 1927 | 3 | 7 | 45 | 110 |

4033 Shilling. Modified effigy l. R. Lion passant on crown, within circle die axis: ↑↑

| 1926 | 1 | 2 | 30 | 65 | 1927 | 1 | 5 | 40 | 75 |

4034 Sixpence. Modified effigy l. R. Lion passant on crown, within circle die axis: ↑↑

| 1926 | | 3 | 20 | 50 | 1927 | 1 | 3 | 25 | 55 |

4035 Threepence. Modified effigy l. R. Crowned 3 die axis: ↑↑

| 1926 | | | | | | 1 | 12 | 55 |

FOURTH COINAGE, 1927-36

4036
1927 'Wreath' Crown proof

4036 Crown. Modified Bare head l. R. Crown and date in wreath die axis: ↑↑

1927 –15,030 struck Proof only† *FDC* £300				1931 –4056 struck ... 95	225	475	775
1927 Matt Proof *FDC Extremely rare*				1932 –2395 struck . 150	325	725	1100
1928* –9034 struck . 90	185	400	750	1933* –7132 struck . 90	175	425	750
1929 –4994 struck . 100	225	500	850	1934 –932 struck . 1350	2250	4000	6000
1930 –4847 struck ... 90	200	450	800	1936 –2473 struck . 150	325	750	1200

†N.B. Proofs of other dates from 1927also exist, but are extremely rare as they were for V.I.P. issue
* Beware recent counterfeits

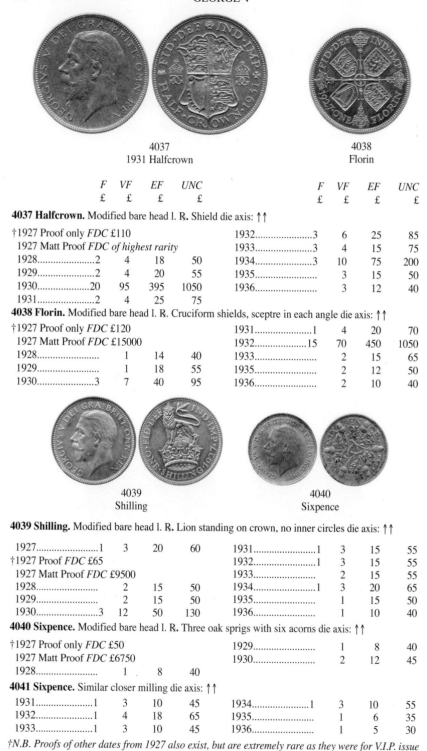

4037
1931 Halfcrown

4038
Florin

	F £	VF £	EF £	UNC £		F £	VF £	EF £	UNC £

4037 Halfcrown. Modified bare head l. R. Shield die axis: ↑↑

†1927 Proof only *FDC* £110					1932	3	6	25	85
1927 Matt Proof *FDC of highest rarity*					1933	3	4	15	75
1928	2	4	18	50	1934	3	10	75	200
1929	2	4	20	55	1935		3	15	50
1930	20	95	395	1050	1936		3	12	40
1931	2	4	25	75					

4038 Florin. Modified bare head l. R. Cruciform shields, sceptre in each angle die axis: ↑↑

†1927 Proof only *FDC* £120					1931	1	4	20	70
1927 Matt Proof *FDC* £15000					1932	15	70	450	1050
1928		1	14	40	1933		2	15	65
1929		1	18	55	1935		2	12	50
1930	3	7	40	95	1936		2	10	40

4039
Shilling

4040
Sixpence

4039 Shilling. Modified bare head l. R. Lion standing on crown, no inner circles die axis: ↑↑

1927	1	3	20	60	1931	1	3	15	55
†1927 Proof *FDC* £65					1932	1	3	15	55
1927 Matt Proof *FDC* £9500					1933		2	15	55
1928		2	15	50	1934	1	3	20	65
1929		2	15	50	1935		1	15	50
1930	3	12	50	130	1936		1	10	40

4040 Sixpence. Modified bare head l. R. Three oak sprigs with six acorns die axis: ↑↑

†1927 Proof only *FDC* £50					1929		1	8	40
1927 Matt Proof *FDC* £6750					1930		2	12	45
1928		1	8	40					

4041 Sixpence. Similar closer milling die axis: ↑↑

1931	1	3	10	45	1934	1	3	10	55
1932	1	4	18	65	1935		1	6	35
1933	1	3	10	45	1936		1	5	30

†N.B. Proofs of other dates from 1927 also exist, but are extremely rare as they were for V.I.P. issue

SILVER

4042
Threepence

4043
George V Maundy Set

	F	VF	EF	UNC		EF	UNC
	£	£	£	£		£	£

4042 Threepence. Modified Bare head l. R. Three oak sprigs with three acorns die axis: ↑↑

	F	VF	EF	UNC		EF	UNC
†1927 Proof only *FDC* £110					1932.......................	1	20
1927 Matt Proof *FDC* £5500					1933.......................	1	20
1928........................	1	3	15	55	1934.......................	1	18
1930........................	1	5	20	65	1935.......................	1	20
1931........................			1	20	1936.......................	1	15

	EF	FDC		EF	FDC
	£	£		£	£
4043 Maundy Set. As earlier sets die axis: ↑↑			1933.................................	135	225
1928.................................	120	225	1934.................................	135	225
1929.................................	120	225	1935.................................	135	225
1930.................................	150	250	1936.................................	145	325
1931.................................	120	225			
1932.................................	120	225			

The 1936 Maundy was distributed by King Edward VIII

		EF	FDC
4044 — Fourpence. 1928-36 ....*from*		10	30
4045 — Threepence. 1928-36 ....*from*		10	30
4046 — Twopence. 1928-36 ....*from*		10	30
4047 — Penny. 1928-36..*from*		15	40

Silver Jubilee Commemorative issue, die axis: ↑↑

4048
1935 'Jubilee' Crown

	VF	EF	UNC
	£	£	£
4048 Crown. 1935. R. St. George, incuse lettering on edge –714,769 struck ..	15	30	45
1935 — error edge		*Extremely rare*	
4049 Crown. Similar Specimen striking issued in box			75
4050 Crown. Similar raised lettering on edge 2,500 struck. Proof (.925 Æ) *FDC* £850			
— error edge inscription Proof *FDC* £4500			
— Proof in gold –28 struck £50000			

†*N.B. Proofs of other dates from 1927 also exist, but are extremely rare as they were for V.I.P. issue*

GEORGE V
BRONZE

H Mint mark location – 4052

4052
1912 H Penny

KN Mint mark location
as above – 4053

	F £	VF £	EF £	UNC £		F £	VF £	EF £	UNC £

4051 Penny. Bare head l. R. Britannia seated right die axis: ↑↑

1911	1	15	60
1912	1	20	70
1913	3	30	95
1914	1	22	75
1915	1	25	80
1916	1	22	75
1917	1	15	65
1918	1	15	65

1919	1	18	65
1920	1	18	70
1921	1	18	65
1922	3	35	135
1922 Rev. of 1927 . 2750	10000	—	—
1922 Specimen finish..	*Extremely rare*		
1926	4	40	140

4052 Penny. Bare head l. R. Britannia, H (Heaton Mint, Birmingham, Ltd.) to l. of date die axis: ↑↑

| 1912 H | 1 | 15 | 115 | 350 |
| 1918 H | 2 | 30 | 325 | 800 |

| 1919 H | 1 | 25 | 375 | 1150 |

4053 Penny. Bare head l. R. Britannia KN (King's Norton Metal Co.) to l. of date die axis: ↑↑

| 1918 KN | 3 | 75 | 450 | 1450 |
| 1918KN Cupro-nickel . *Of the highest rarity* | | | | |

| 1919 KN | 7 | 90 | 1000 | 2500 |

4054 Penny. Modified effigy l. R. as 4051

| 1926 | 35 | 350 | 1650 | 4000 |

4054A Penny. Modified effigy. R. Britannia seated r. Shorter index finger date in ex. die axis ↑↑

| 1922 | *Of the highest rarity* |
| 1926 | *Of the highest rarity* |

| 1927 | 1 | 18 | 60 |

4055 Penny. Small bare head l. R. Britannia Seated r. date in ex. die axis: ↑↑

1928	1	12	55
1929	1	12	65
1930	3	20	85
1931	1	18	70
1932	5	45	185

1933	*Extremely rare*		
1934*	3	25	85
1935	1	10	30
1936	1	7	25

†*N.B. Proofs of other dates from 1927also exist, but are extremely rare as they were for V.I.P. issue.*
Matt proofs also exist of some dates for most denominations and are all extremely rare.
* Most 1934 pennies were mint darkened. Coins with original lustre are rare.

4056
Halfpenny

4058
Small head

	VF £	EF £	UNC £		VF £	EF £	UNC £

4056 Halfpenny. Bare head l. R. Britannia Seated r. date in ex. die axis: ↑↑

1911	1	8	50	1919	2	12	55
1912	2	12	55	1920	2	22	65
1913	2	12	55	1921	2	12	55
1914	2	15	60	1922	2	25	100
1915	2	20	65	1923	2	12	55
1916	2	20	65	1924	2	12	55
1917	2	12	55	1924 Specimen finish.. *Extremely rare*			
1918	2	12	55	1925	2	12	55

4057 Halfpenny. Modified effigy l. R. Britannia Seated r. date in ex. die axis: ↑↑

1925	3	20	75	1927	2	8	50
1926	2	12	55				

4058 Halfpenny. Small bare head l. R. Britannia Seated r. date in ex. die axis: ↑↑

1928	1	8	40	1933	1	8	45
1929	1	8	40	1934	1	12	40
1930	4	12	50	1935	1	8	35
1931	1	8	45	1936	1	6	25
1932	1	8	45				

4059
Farthing

4059 Farthing. Bare head l. R. Britannia Seated r. date in ex. Dark finish die axis: ↑↑

1911	4	25	1915	5	30
1912	3	20	1916	3	20
1913	3	20	1917	3	15
1914	3	20	1918	10	45

	EF	UNC		VF	EF	UNC
	£	£		£	£	£

4060 Farthing. Similar Bright finish, die axis: ↑↑

1918	3	20	1922		4	28
1919	3	20	1923		5	25
1920	4	25	1924		5	25
1921	4	25	1925		4	25

4061 Farthing. Modified effigy l. R. Britannia Seated r. date in ex. die axis: ↑↑

1926	2	20	1932		2	15
1927	2	20	1933		2	20
1928	2	15	1934		2	20
1929	2	20	1935		5	35
1930	3	25	1936		2	15
1931	2	20				

4062
Third-Farthing

4062 Third-Farthing (for use in Malta). Bare head l. R̵. Crowned date and Value die axis: ↑↑

1913..3   25   55

PROOF SETS

PS11 Coronation, **1911.** Five pounds to Maundy Penny (12 coins) .... *FDC*   £15000
PS12 — **1911.** Sovereign to Maundy Penny (10 coins) .... *FDC*   £3250
PS13 — **1911.** Half crown to Maundy Penny (8 coins) .... *FDC*   £1150
PS14 New type, **1927.** Wreath type Crown to Threepence (6 coins) .... *FDC*   £650

† *NB Truly 'FDC' proof sets are hardly ever encountered. Component coins showing any surface marks, hairlines or nicks will be worth less than the prices quoted above.*

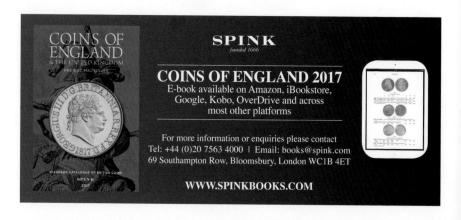

COINS OF ENGLAND
& THE UNITED KINGDOM
PRE-DECIMAL ISSUES

STANDARD CATALOGUE OF BRITISH COINS
SPINK
2017

SPINK
founded 1666

COINS OF ENGLAND 2017
E-book available on Amazon, iBookstore,
Google, Kobo, OverDrive and across
most other platforms

For more information or enquiries please contact
Tel: +44 (0)20 7563 4000 | Email: books@spink.com
69 Southampton Row, Bloomsbury, London WC1B 4ET

WWW.SPINKBOOKS.COM

Succeeded his father on 20 January 1936. Abdicated 10 December. Edward VIII was born 23 June 1894, and was very popular as Prince of Wales. He ruled only for a short time before announcing his intended marriage to the American divorcee Wallis Simpson; a potential religious and political scandal. Edward was not a traditionalist, as evidenced on the proposed coinage, where he insisted against all advice on having his effigy face the same way as his father's, instead of opposite. He abdicated in favour of his brother, and became Edward, Duke of Windsor, marrying Mrs Simpson in France, where they lived in exile. He governed the Bahamas from 1940-45 and died on 28 May 1972.

No coins of Edward VIII were issued for currency within the United Kingdom bearing his name and portrait. The Mint had commenced work on a new coinage prior to the Abdication, and various patterns were made. No Proof Sets were issued for sale and only a small number of sets were struck.

Coins bearing Edward's name, but not his portrait, were issued for the colonial territories of British East Africa, British West Africa, Fiji and New Guinea. The projected U.K. coins were to include a Shilling of essentially 'Scottish' type and a nickel brass Threepence with twelve sides which might supplement and possibly supersede the inconveniently small silver Threepence.

Engravers and Designers:– George Kruger Gray (1880-1943), Thomas Humphrey Paget (1893-1974), Benedicto Pistucci (1784-1855) Frances Madge Kitchener, Percy Metcalfe (1895-1970), H Wilson Parker (1896-1980)

Designer's initials: H. P. (T. Humphrey Paget)   B.P. (Benedetto Pistrucci, d. 1855)
                            K. G. (G. Kruger Gray)   M. K. (Madge Kitchener)
                            W. P. (H. Wilson Parker)

Die axis ↑↑

GOLD

4063
Edward VIII Proof Five Pounds

4063 Proof Set

Gold, Five Pounds, Two Pounds and Sovereign, Silver Crown, Halfcrown, Florin, Scottish Shilling, Sixpence and Threepence, Brass Threepence, Penny, Halfpenny and Farthing, 1937 *FDC. Only one complete set known in private hands..*

Five Pounds, Bare head 1. R St George and dragon, date in ex 600000
Two Pounds, Bare head 1. R St George and dragon, date in ex 275000
Sovereign, Bare head l. R. St George and dragon date in ex 600000
Crown, Bare head l. R. Crowned Shield of arms and supporters....................... 250000
Halfcrown, Bare head l. R. Quartered Standard of arms 125000
Florin, Bare head l. R. Crowned rose and emblems 97500
Shilling, Bare head l. R. Lion seated facing on crown 77500
Sixpence, Bare head l. R. Six interlinked rings.. 51500
Threepence, Bare head l. R. three interlinked rings 39500

4064A

4064A Nickel brass. **Threepence,** 1937 Bare head l. R. Thrift plant below.......		51500
Bronze. **Penny,** 1937		77500
Halfpenny, 1937..		41500
Farthing, 1937..		36500

Note: Matt proofs exist of most denominations

Pattern

Edward VIII Brass Threepence

UNC
£

4064B Nickel brass dodecagonal **Threepence,** 1937. Bare head l. R. Thrift plant of more
   naturalistic style than the modified proof coin. A small number of these coins were
   produced of differing thickness for experimental purposes and a few did get into
   circulation.. 52500

SPINK
founded 1666

COINS OF ENGLAND 2017
E-book available on Amazon, iBookstore,
Google, Kobo, OverDrive
and across most other platforms

For more information or enquiries please contact
Tel: +44 (0)20 7563 4000 | Email: books@spink.com
69 Southampton Row, Bloomsbury, London WC1B 4ET

WWW.SPINKBOOKS.COM

George VI was born on 14 December 1895 and never expected to be King. He suffered ill-health through much of his life and had a stammer. He married Elizabeth Bowes Lyon and together they became very popular especially through the ravages of World War II, when Buckingham Palace was bombed. The war took its toll on George, and ever a heavy smoker he succumbed to lung cancer on 6th February 1952. Elizabeth, known after his death as 'Queen Elizabeth the Queen Mother', lived on to the age of 101 dying on 30 March 2002.

Though they were at first issued concurrently, the twelve-sided nickel-brass Threepence superseded the small silver Threepence in 1942. Those dated 1943-4 were not issued for circulation in the U.K. In addition to the usual English 'lion' Shilling, a Shilling of Scottish type was issued concurrently. This depicts the Scottish lion and crown flanked by the shield of St. Andrew and a thistle. In 1947, as silver was needed to repay the bullion lent by the U.S.A. during the war, silver coins were replaced by coins of the same type and weight made of cupro-nickel. In 1949, after India had attained independence, the title IND:IMP (Indiae Imperator) was dropped from the coinage. Commemorative Crown pieces were issued for the Coronation and the 1951 Festival of Britain.

Engravers and Designers:– Frances Madge Kitchener, George Kruger Gray (1880-1943), Percy Metcalfe (1895-1970) Thomas Humphrey Paget (1893-1974), H Wilson Parker (1896-1980), Benedetto Pistrucci (1784-1855)

Designer's initials: K. G. (G. Kruger Gray)   B. P. (Benedetto Pistrucci, d. 1855)
                     H. P. (T. Humphrey Paget)   W. P. (Wilson Parker)

Die axis ↑↑

GOLD

4074
1937 Proof Five Pounds

4076
1937 Proof Sovereign

	FDC £
4074 Five Pounds. Bare head l. R. St. George, 1937. Proof plain edge only (5001 struck)..	6500
4074-4077 Proof Struck to Matt finish *FDC of highest rarity*	
4075 Two Pounds. Similar, 1937. Proof plain edge only (5001 struck)	2850
4076 Sovereign. Similar, 1937. Proof plain edge only (5001 struck)	3500
4077 Half-Sovereign. Similar, 1937. Proof plain edge only (5001 struck)	1000

SILVER

FIRST COINAGE, 1937-46 Silver, .500 fine, with title IND:IMP

4078
1937 Crown

	VF £	EF £	UNC £
4078 Crown. Coronation commemorative, 1937. R. Arms and supporters	12	30	45

4079 Crown. Similar 1937 Proof *FDC* £85
      Similar 1937 Frosted 'VIP' Proof £1150

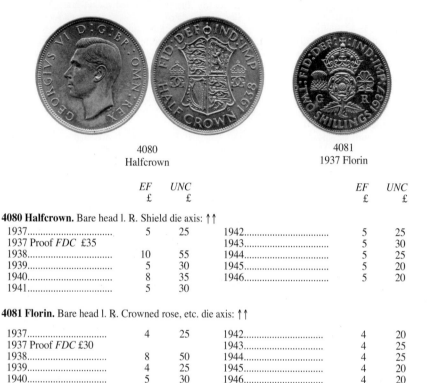

4080
Halfcrown

4081
1937 Florin

	EF £	UNC £		EF £	UNC £
4080 Halfcrown. Bare head l. R. Shield die axis: ↑↑					
1937	5	25	1942	5	25
1937 Proof *FDC* £35			1943	5	30
1938	10	55	1944	5	25
1939	5	30	1945	5	20
1940	8	35	1946	5	20
1941	5	30			

	EF £	UNC £		EF £	UNC £
4081 Florin. Bare head l. R. Crowned rose, etc. die axis: ↑↑					
1937	4	25	1942	4	20
1937 Proof *FDC* £30			1943	4	25
1938	8	50	1944	4	25
1939	4	25	1945	4	20
1940	5	30	1946	4	20
1941	4	25			

4082
1942 'English' Shilling

4083
1945 'Scottish' Shilling

4082 Shilling. 'English' reverse. Bare head l. R. Lion standing on large crown die axis: ↑↑

	EF	UNC		EF	UNC
1937	3	25	1942	3	25
1937 Proof *FDC* £25			1943	3	25
1938	8	50	1944	3	25
1939	3	25	1945	3	18
1940	5	30	1946	3	18
1941	3	25			

	EF	UNC		VF	EF	UNC
	£	£		£	£	£

4083 Shilling. 'Scottish' reverse. Bare head l. R. Lion seated facing on crown die axis: ↑↑

	EF	UNC		VF	EF	UNC
1937............................	3	20	1942............................		4	30
1937 Proof *FDC* £25			1943............................		3	25
1938............................	8	45	1944............................		3	25
1939............................	3	25	1945............................		3	18
1940............................	5	30	1946............................		3	18
1941............................	4	30				

4084
1945 Sixpence

4085
1944 Threepence

4084 Sixpence. Bare head l. R. GRI crowned die axis: ↑↑

	EF	UNC			EF	UNC
1937............................	2	15	1942............................		2	20
1937 Proof *FDC* £20			1943............................		2	20
1938............................	6	30	1944............................		2	20
1939............................	2	25	1945............................		2	15
1940............................	5	30	1946............................		2	15
1941............................	2	25				

4085 Threepence. Bare head l. R. Shield on rose die axis: ↑↑

	EF	UNC		VF	EF	UNC
1937............................	2	15	1942*............................	8	20	45
1937 Proof *FDC* £18			1943*............................	8	25	55
1938............................	2	20	1944*............................	15	40	110
1939............................	6	35	1945*............................		*Extremely rare*	
1940............................	5	30	* *issued for Colonial use only*			
1941............................	4	30				

4086
1937 Maundy Set

	EF	FDC		EF	FDC
	£	£		£	£

4086 Maundy Set. Silver, .500 fine. Uniform dates die axis: ↑↑

	EF	FDC		EF	FDC
1937............................	100	175	1942............................	120	225
1937 Proof *FDC* £175			1943............................	120	225
1938............................	120	225	1944............................	120	225
1939............................	120	225	1945............................	120	225
1940............................	135	250	1946............................	120	225
1941............................	120	225			

	EF £	FDC £		EF £	FDC £
4087 — **Fourpence.** 1937-46 .... *from*		20			
4088 — **Threepence.** 1937-46 .... *from*		22			
4089 — **Twopence.** 1937-46 .... *from*		20			
4090 — **Penny.** 1937-46 .... *from*		30			

SECOND COINAGE, 1947-48, Silver, .925 fine, with title IND:IMP (Maundy only)
4091 Maundy Set (4d., 3d., 2d. and 1d.). Uniform dates die axis: ↑↑

1947 120	225	1948 120	225

4092 — **Fourpence,** 1947-8	20
4093 — **Threepence,** 1947-8	22
4094 — **Twopence,** 1947-8	20
4095 — **Penny,** 1947-8	30

THIRD COINAGE, 1949-52, Silver, .925 fine, but omitting IND:IMP. (Maundy only)
4096 Maundy Set (4d., 3d., 2d. and 1d.). Uniform dates die axis: ↑↑

1949 120	225	1952 160	275
1950 135	250	1952 Proof in copper *FDC* £7500	
1951 135	250		

The 1952 Maundy was distributed by Queen Elizabeth II.

4097 — **Fourpence,** 1949-52 .... *from*	20
4098 — **Threepence,** 1949-52 .... *from*	22
4099 — **Twopence,** 1949-52 .... *from*	20
4100 — **Penny,** 1949-52 .... *from*	30

See footnote re Maundy Pennies after 3796.

CUPRO-NICKEL

SECOND COINAGE, 1947-48, Types as first (silver) coinage, IND:IMP.

	EF £	UNC £		EF £	UNC £
4101 Halfcrown. Bare head l. R. Shield die axis: ↑↑					
1947	2	15	1948	2	12
4102 Florin. Bare head l. R. Crowned rose die axis: ↑↑					
1947	2	15	1948	2	15
4103 Shilling. 'English' reverse. Bare head l. die axis: ↑↑					
1947	2	15	1948	2	15
4104 Shilling. 'Scottish' reverse. Bare head l. die axis: ↑↑					
1947	2	15	1948	2	15
4105 Sixpence. Bare head l. R. GRI crowned die axis: ↑↑					
1947	2	12	1948	2	12

THIRD COINAGE, 1949-52, Types as before but title IND:IMP. omitted

4106
1949 Halfcrown

	VF £	EF £	UNC £		VF £	EF £	UNC £

4106 Halfcrown. Bare head l. R. Shield die axis: ↑↑

	VF	EF	UNC		VF	EF	UNC
1949		3	30	1951 Proof *FDC* £40			
1950		8	40	1952			*Unique*
1950 Proof *FDC* £40				1952 Proof *FDC* £80000			
1951	1	8	40				

4107 Florin. Bare head l. R. Crowned rose die axis: ↑↑

	VF	EF	UNC		VF	EF	UNC
1949		5	35	1951		8	40
1950		8	35	1951 Proof *FDC* £40			
1950 Proof *FDC* £40							

4108 Shilling. 'English' reverse. Bare head l. die axis: ↑↑

	VF	EF	UNC		VF	EF	UNC
1949		5	35	1951		6	35
1950		8	35	1951 Proof *FDC* £30			
1950 Proof *FDC* £35				1952 Proof *FDC* £35000			

4109 Shilling. 'Scottish' reverse. Bare head l. die axis: ↑↑

	VF	EF	UNC		VF	EF	UNC
1949		5	35	1951		6	35
1950		8	35	1951 Proof *FDC* £28			
1950 Proof *FDC* £35							

4110
1952 Sixpence

4110 Sixpence. Bare head l. R. Crowned cypher die axis: ↑↑

	VF	EF	UNC		VF	EF	UNC
1949		1	15	1951 Proof *FDC* £25			
1950		3	20	1951 Matt Proof *FDC* £1500			
1950 Proof *FDC* £25				1952	5	45	135
1951		5	25				

Festival of Britain issue die axis: ↑↑

4111
Festival of Britain Crown

	EF £	UNC £
4111 Crown. Bare head l. R. St. George and dragon, date in ex, 1951. *Proof-like.*		
Two reverse types exist	5	15
Similar — 1951 Frosted 'VIP' Proof £1000, narrow edge lettering		
Similar — 1951 Matt Proof *FDC* £4750		
Similar — 1951 Plain edge Proof *FDC* £1450		

NICKEL BRASS

FIRST ISSUE, 1937-48, with title IND:IMP.

4112	4113
1941 Brass Threepence	Second issue obverse

4112 Threepence (dodecagonal). Bare head l. R. Thrift plant die axis: ↑↑

	VF £	EF £	UNC £		VF £	EF £	UNC £
1937..............................		2	15	1942..............................		2	15
1937 Proof *FDC* £20				1943..............................		2	15
1938..............................		6	30	1944..............................		2	20
1939..............................		10	50	1945..............................		5	20
1940..............................		6	30	1946.............	30	250	950
1941..............................		3	20	1948..............................		10	65

SECOND ISSUE, 1949-52, omitting IND:IMP.
4113 Threepence. Bare head l. R. Similar die axis: ↑↑

1949	30	200	750	1951 Proof *FDC* £50			
1950		25	150	1951 Matt Proof *FDC* £1000			
1950 Proof *FDC* £45				1952..............................		5	25
1951..............................3		30	150				

BRONZE

FIRST ISSUE, 1937-48, with title IND:IMP.

4114
1938 Penny

	EF £	UNC £		EF £	UNC £
4114 Penny. Bare head l. R. Britannia Seated r. date in ex die axis: ↑↑					
1937..............................	1	10	1944* —......................	6	30
1937 Proof *FDC* £25			1945* —......................	5	25
1938..............................	3	12	1946* —......................	2	12
1939..............................	4	20	1947 —.........................	1	10
1940..............................	10	60	1948 —.........................	1	10
1940 Double exergue line	4	25	1946 ONE' die flaw 75		225

most pennies of these date were darkened at the mint.

4115
1937 Halfpenny

4116
1943 Farthing

	EF	UNC		EF	UNC
4115 Halfpenny. Bare head l. R. Ship sailing l. date below die axis: ↑↑					
1937..............................	1	10	1943..............................	1	10
1937 Proof *FDC* £20			1944..............................	1	10
1938..............................	2	15	1945..............................	1	10
1939..............................	3	30	1946..............................	3	25
1940..............................	3	30	1947..............................	1	12
1941..............................	2	12	1948..............................	1	12
1942..............................	1	10			

	EF	UNC		EF	UNC
4116 Farthing. Bare head l. R. Wren l. date above die axis: ↑↑					
1937..............................	1	7	1943..............................	1	7
1937 Proof *FDC* £15			1944..............................	1	7
1938..............................	2	15	1945..............................	1	7
1939..............................	1	8	1946..............................	1	7
1940..............................	1	8	1947..............................	1	7
1941..............................	1	8	1948..............................	1	7
1942..............................	1	7			

SECOND ISSUE, 1949-52

	VF £	EF £	UNC £		VF £	EF £	UNC £

4117 Penny. Bare head l. R. Britannia Seated r. date in ex. die axis: ↑↑

	VF £	EF £	UNC £		VF £	EF £	UNC £
1949............................		1	10	1951...................... 12		35	60
1950........................ 8		20	75	1951 Proof *FDC* £50			
1950 Proof *FDC* £35				1952 Proof only *FDC* £77500			

4118
Second issue Halfpenny

4119
Second issue Farthing

4118 Halfpenny. Bare head l. R. Ship Sailing l. date below die axis: ↑↑

	EF £	UNC £		EF £	UNC £
1949..............................	4	20	1951..............................	5	30
1950..............................	3	15	1951 Proof *FDC* £20		
1950 Proof *FDC* £18			1952..............................	2	10

4119 Farthing. Bare head l. R. Wren l. date above die axis: ↑↑

	EF £	UNC £		EF £	UNC £
1949.........................	1	8	1951..............................	2	9
1950.........................	1	7	1951 Proof *FDC* £20		
1950 Proof *FDC* £18			1952..............................	1	7

The coins dated 1952 were issued during the reign of Elizabeth II.

PROOF SETS

PS15 Coronation, **1937.** Five pounds to Half-sovereign (4 coins).........................*FDC*   £14500
PS16 — **1937.** Crown to Farthing, including Maundy Set (15 coins)...................*FDC*   £375
PS17 Mid-Century, **1950.** Halfcrown to Farthing (9 coins) ....*FDC*   £185
PS18 Festival of Britain, **1951.** Crown to Farthing (10 coins) ....*FDC*   £225

Elizabeth II was born on 21 April 1926. Our current Monarch has lived a long and glorious reign celebrating her Golden Jubilee in 2002. She married Philip a distant cousin in 1947 and has four children, Charles, Anne, Andrew and Edward. Significantly she is the first Monarch to pay taxes and her coinage has been an interesting one with the change to decimal coinage and the numerous bust changes since 1953.

The earliest coins of this reign have the title BRITT:OMN, but in 1954 this was omitted from the Queen's titles owing to the changing status of so many Commonwealth territories. The minting of 'English' and 'Scottish' shillings was continued. A Coronation commemorative crown was issued in 1953, another crown was struck on the occasion of the 1960 British Exhibition in New York and a third was issued in honour of Sir Winston Churchill in 1965. A very small number of proof gold coins were struck in 1953 for the national museum collections, but between 1957 and 1968 gold sovereigns were minted again in quantity for sale in the international bullion market and to counteract the activities of counterfeiters.

Owing to inflation the farthing had now become practically valueless; production of these coins ceased after 1956 and the coins were demonetized at the end of 1960. In 1965 it was decided to change to a decimal system of coinage in the year 1971. As part of the transition to decimal coinage the halfpenny was demonetized in August 1969 and the halfcrown in January 1970. (See also introduction to Decimal Coinage.

Designer's initials:
A. V. (Avril Vaughan)
B. P. (Benedetto Pistrucci, 1784-1855)
B. R. (Bruce Rushin)
C.D. (Clive Duncan)
C. T. (Cecil Thomas)
D. C. (David Cornell)
E. F. (Edgar Fuller)
G. L. (Gilbert Ledward)
I. R. B. (Ian Rank-Broadley)
J. B. (James Butler)
J. M. (Jeffrey Matthews)
J. M. M. (John Mills)
M. B. (Matthew Bonaccorsi)

M. G. (Mary Gillick)
M. M. D. (Mary Milner Dickens)
M. N. (Michael Noakes)
M. R. (Michael Rizzello)
N. S. (Norman Sillman)
P. N. (Philip Nathan)
R. D. (Ron Dutton)
R. D. M. (Raphael David Maklouf)
R. E. (Robert Elderton)
r. e. (Robert Evans)
R. L. (Robert Lowe)
T. N. (Timothy Noad)
W. G. (William Gardner)
W. P. (Wilson Parker 1896-1980)

Other designers whose initials do not appear on the coins:
Christopher Ironside (1913-1992)
Arnold Machin (1911-1999)
David Wynne
Professor Richard Guyatt
Eric Sewell
Oscar Nemon

Leslie Durbin
Derek Gorringe
Bernard Sindall
Tom Phillips
Edwina Ellis
David Gentleman
Matthew Dent

PRE-DECIMAL ISSUES, 1952-71
Die axis ↑↑

GOLD

First coinage, with title BRITT.OMN, 1953. *Proof only. Originally produced for institutional collecting.*

4120 Five Pounds. Young laur. head r. R. St. George 1953............		*of the highest rarity*
4121 Two Pounds. Young laur. head r. R. St. George 1953............		*of the highest rarity*
4122 Sovereign. Young laur. head r. R. St. George 1953...............		£400000
4123 Half-Sovereign. Young laur. head r. R. St. George 1953.........		*of the highest rarity*

SECOND ISSUE, BRITT.OMN omitted

4125
1958 Sovereign

	EF	UNC			EF	UNC
	£	£			£	£

4124 Sovereign. Young laur head r. ℞. St. George, fine graining on edge

1957					BV	275

1957 Proof *FDC* £12500

4125 Sovereign. Similar, but coarser graining on edge

1958	BV	275	1963 Proof *FDC* £11500			
1958 Proof *FDC* £11000			1964		BV	275
1959	BV	275	1965		BV	275
1959 Proof *FDC* £11000			1966		BV	275
1962	BV	275	1967		BV	275
1963	BV	275	1968		BV	275

SILVER

The Queen's Maundy are now the only coins struck regularly in silver.
The location of the Maundy ceremony is given for each year.

FIRST ISSUE, with title BRITT:OMN:

4126
Maundy Set

	EF	FDC		EF	FDC
	£	£		£	£
4126 Maundy Set (4d., 3d., 2d. and 1d.), 1953. *St Paul's Cathedral*	600	1150			

1953 Proof struck in gold *FDC Extremely rare*
1953 Proof struck in nickel bronze *FDC Extremely rare*

	EF	FDC
4127 — Fourpence. 1953		250
4128 — Threepence. 1953		225
4129 — Twopence. 1953		225
4130 — Penny. 1953		375

SECOND ISSUE, with BRITT:OMN: omitted

4131 Maundy Set (4d., 3d., 2d. and 1d.). Uniform dates

1954 *Westminster*	120	250	1956 *Westminster*	120	250
1955 *Southwark*	120	250	1957 *St. Albans*	120	250

BV= Bullion value only. At the time of going to press the spot price for gold was £1030 per oz.

	EF	FDC		EF	FDC
	£	£		£	£

4131 Maundy Set

1958 *Westminster*	120	250	1965 Canterbury	120	250
1959 *Windsor*	120	250	1966 Westminster	120	250
1960 *Westminster*	120	250	1967 Durham	120	250
1961 *Rochester*	120	250	1968 Westminster	120	250
1962 *Westminster*	125	250	1969 Selby	120	250
1963 *Chelmsford*	120	250	1970 Westminster	120	250
1964 Westminster	120	250			

For a continuation of these issues see 'Coins of England, Decimal Issues'.

4132 — Fourpence. 1954-70 ....*from*	20
4133 — Threepence. 1954-70 ....*from*	25
4134 — Twopence. 1954-70 ....*from*	20
4135 — Penny. 1954-70..*from*	35

See footnote after 3796

CUPRO-NICKEL

FIRST ISSUE, 1953, with title BRITT.OMN.

4136 - 1953 Coronation Crown

			Proof
	EF	UNC	FDC
	£	£	£

4136 Crown. Queen on horseback. R. Crown in centre of emblematical cross,
shield of Arms in each angle, 1953 .... 3 | 8 | 35

Similar 1953 Frosted 'VIP' proof with more fine detail apparent £1250

4137A - 1953 Halfcrown - 2nd obverse die   4138 - 1953 Florin

4137 Halfcrown. First obverse die, I of DEI points to a space between beads . | 5 | 1700 |

4137A Halfcrown. Second obverse die, I of DEI points to a bead, with title
BRITT:OMN: Young laur. head r. R. Arms, 1953..................................... | 5 | 20 |

4138 Florin. Young laur. head r. R. Double rose, 1953..................................... | 4 | 12 |

4139	4140	4141
1953 'English' Shilling - 1st obv. die	'Scottish' reverse	1953 Sixpence - 2nd obv. die

	UNC	Proof FDC
	£	£
4139 Shilling. 'English' reverse. Young laur. head r. R. Three lions, 1953........	2	10
4140 Shilling. '—' 'Scottish' reverse. Young laur. head r. R. Lion rampant in shield, 1953	2	10
4141 Sixpence. Young laur. head r. R. Interlaced rose, thistle, shamrock and leek, 1953	1	8
4142 Set of 9 uncirculated cu-ni, ni-br and Æ coins (2/6 to 1/4d.) in Royal Mint plastic envelope	30	—

SECOND ISSUE, similar types but omitting BRITT.OMN.

4143	4144
1960 Crown	1965 Churchill Crown

	EF	UNC
	£	£
4143 Crown, 1960. Young laur. head r. R. As 4136	5	12
— — Similar, from polished dies (New York Exhibition issue)	10	35
— — 'VIP' *Proof,* frosted design *FDC* £850		
4144 Crown, Churchill commemorative, 1965. As illustration. R. Bust of Sir Winston Churchill r.		2
— — Similar, "Satin-Finish". VIP *Specimen*		1750
— — —, with 'ON' designer's initials on reverse...		3000

	EF	UNC		EF	UNC		EF	UNC
	£	£		£	£		£	£
4145 Halfcrown. Young laur. head r. R. As 4137								
1954...................... 8		45	1960......................		20	1965......................		5
1955......................		12	1961......................		6	1966......................		3
1956......................		18	1961 Polished die..		25	1967......................		3
1957......................		8	1962......................		6	1970 Proof *FDC* £12		
1958...................... 8		40	1963......................		6			
1959...................... 8		45	1964......................		8			

4146
1957 Florin

	EF £	UNC £		UNC £
4146 Florin. Young laur. head r. R. As 4138				
1954	8	50	1962	5
1955		12	1963	4
1956		12	1964	4
1957	8	45	1965	4
1958	10	50	1966	3
1959	10	60	1967	3
1960		12	1970 Proof *FDC* £8	
1961		12		

	EF £	UNC £		UNC £
4147 Shilling. 'English' reverse. Young laur. head r. R. As 4139				
1954		6	1961	3
1955		6	1962	2
1956		12	1963	2
1957		5	1964	2
1958	8	65	1965	2
1959		5	1966	2
1960		8	1970 Proof *FDC* £8	

	EF £	UNC £		UNC £
4148 Shilling. 'Scottish' reverse. Young laur. head r. R. As 4140				
1954		6	1961	20
1955		8	1962	5
1956		12	1963	2
1957	5	35	1964	2
1958		4	1965	2
1959	10	110	1966	2
1960		8	1970 Proof *FDC* £8	

	EF £	UNC £		UNC £
4149 Sixpence. Young laur. head r. R. As 4141				
1954		8	1962	2
1955		4	1963	2
1956		5	1964	2
1957		4	1965	1
1958		10	1966	1
1959		3	1967	1
1960		7	1970 Proof *FDC* £7	
1961		6		

NICKEL BRASS
FIRST ISSUE, with title BRITT.OMN.

4152	4153
1953 Brass Threepence - 2nd obv. die Proof	Second issue

	UNC		*UNC*
	£		£

4152 Threepence (dodecagonal). Young laur. head r. R. Crowned portcullis, 1953 4
— Proof *FDC* £12

SECOND ISSUE (omitting BRIT.OMN)
4153 Threepence Similar type

1954	8	1962	2
1955	10	1963	2
1956	10	1964	2
1957	6	1965	2
1958	15	1966	1
1959	6	1967	1
1960	7	1970 Proof *FDC* £6	
1961	3		

BRONZE
FIRST ISSUE, with title BRITT.OMN.

4154	4155	4156
1953 Penny - 1st obv. die	1953 Halfpenny 2nd obv. die	1953 Farthing

			Proof
VF	*EF*	*UNC*	*FDC*
£	£	£	£

4154 Penny. Young laur. head r. R. Britannia (only issued with Royal Mint set in plastic envelope)
1953 Beaded border 1   3   10   25
1953 Toothed border *FDC* £2950
4155 Halfpenny. Young laur. head r. R. Ship, 1953 3   12
4156 Farthing. Young laur. head r. R. Wren, 1953 2   10

	UNC		EF	UNC
	£		£	£

SECOND ISSUE, omitting BRITT.OMN.
4157 Penny. Young laur. head r. R. Britannia (1954-60 *not issued*)

1954 *Unique*	77500	1965	1
1961	3	1966	1
1962	1	1967	1
1963	1	1970 Proof *FDC* £7	
1964	1		

4158 Halfpenny. Young laur. head r. R. Ship (1961 *not issued*)

1954	8	1960	2
1954 larger border teeth	10	1962	1
1955	6	1963	1
1956	8	1964	1
1957	4	1965	1
1957 calm sea	50	1966	1
1958	3	1967	1
1959	2	1970 Proof *FDC* £4	

4159 Farthing. Young laur. head r. R. Wren

1954	6	1956	3	10
1955	6			

PROOF SETS
PS19 Coronation, **1953.** Crown to Farthing (10 coins) .... *FDC*   150
PS20 'Last Sterling', **1970.** Halfcrown to Halfpenny plus medallion .... *FDC*   30

PRE-DECIMAL PROOF SETS

All prices quoted assume coins are in their original case. Issued by the Royal Mint in official case from 1887 onwards, but earlier sets were issued privately by the engraver. All pieces have a superior finish to that of the current coins.

		No. of coins	FDC £
PS1	**George IV, 1826.** New issue, Five Pounds to Farthing	(11)	110000
PS2	**William IV, 1831.** Coronation, Two Pounds to Farthing	(14)	80000
PS3	**Victoria, 1839.** Young head. "Una and the Lion" Five Pounds and Sovereign to Farthing	(15)	250000
PS4	— **1853.** Sovereign to Half-Farthing, including Gothic type Crown	(16)	110000
PS5	— **1887.** Jubilee bust for Golden Jubilee, Five Pounds to Threepence	(11)	32500
PS6	— **1887.** Silver Crown to Threepence	(7)	5750
PS7	— **1893.** Old bust, Five Pounds to Threepence	(10)	42500
PS8	— **1893.** Silver Crown to Threepence	(6)	6750
PS9	**Edward VII, 1902.** Coronation, Five Pounds to Maundy Penny. Matt finish to surfaces	(13)	7500
PS10	— **1902.** Sovereign to Maundy Penny. Matt finish	(11)	2350
PS11	**George V, 1911.** Coronation, Five Pounds to Maundy Penny	(12)	15000
PS12	— **1911.** Sovereign to Maundy Penny	(10)	3250
PS13	— **1911.** Silver Halfcrown to Maundy Penny	(8)	1150
PS14	— **1927.** New Coinage. Wreath type Crown to Threepence	(6)	650
PS15	**George VI, 1937.** Coronation. Five Pounds to Half-Sovereign	(4)	14500
PS16	— **1937.** Coronation. Crown to Farthing, including Maundy Set	(15)	375
PS17	— **1950.** Mid-Century, Halfcrown to Farthing	(9)	185
PS18	— **1951.** Festival of Britain, Crown to Farthing	(10)	225
PS19	**Elizabeth II, 1953.** Coronation. Crown to Farthing	(10)	140
PS20	— **1970.** "Last Sterling" set. Halfcrown to Halfpenny plus medallion	(8)	25

Truly flawless FDC sets of the earlier period are commanding prices in excess of catalogue values'

COINS OF ENGLAND

Decimal Issues

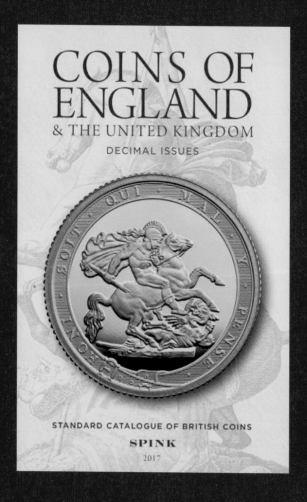

COINS OF ENGLAND & THE UNITED KINGDOM

DECIMAL ISSUES

STANDARD CATALOGUE OF BRITISH COINS

SPINK

2017

The Decimal Coinage
published in a separate volume

A SELECT NUMISMATIC BIBLIOGRAPHY

Listed below is a selection of general books on British numismatics and other works that the specialist collector will need to consult.

General Books:

BROOKE, G. C. *English Coins*. 3rd ed., 1966.

CHALLIS, C. E. (ed.) *A New History of the Royal Mint*. 1992

GRUEBER, H. A. *Handbook of the Coins of Great Britain and Ireland*. Revised 1970

KENYON, R. Ll. *Gold Coins of England*. 1884

NORTH, J. J. *English Hammered Coinage*, Vol. I, c. 650-1272. 1994; Vol. II, 1272-1662. 1991

STEWARTBY, Lord. *English Coins 1180-1551*. 2009

SUTHERLAND, C. H. V. *English Coinage, 600-1900*. 1972

Specialist Works:

ABRAMSON, T. Sceattas, *An Illustrated Guide*. 2006

ALLEN, D. *The Origins of Coinage in Britain: A Reappraisal*. Reprint 1978

ALLEN, D. F. *The Coins of the Coritani*. (SCBI no. 3) 1963

ALLEN, D. F. *English Coins in the British Museum: The Cross-and-Crosslets ('Tealby') type of Henry II*. 1951

ALLEN, M. *The Durham Mint*. 2003

ARCHIBALD, M. M. and BLUNT, C. E. *British Museum. Anglo-Saxon Coins. Athelstan to the reform of Edgar*. 924-c.973. 1986

ASKEW, G. *The Coinage of Roman Britain*. (1951) Reprinted 1980.

BESLY, E. M. *Coins and Medals of the English Civil War*. 1990

BLACKBURN, M. A. S. *Anglo-Saxon Monetary History*. 1986

— — *Viking Coinage and Currency in the British Isles*. 2011

BLUNT, C. E. and WHITTON, C. A. *The Coinages of Edward IV and of Henry VI (Restored)*.

BLUNT, C. E., STEWART, B.H.I.H. and LYON, C.S.S. *Coinage in Tenth-Century England. From Edward the Elder to Edgar's Reform*. 1989

BOON, G. C. *Coins of the Anarchy. 1135-54*. 1988

BRAND, J. D. *The English Coinage 1180-1247: Money, Mints and Exchanges* 1994

BROOKE, G. C. *English Coins in the British Museum: The Norman Kings*. 1916

BROWN, I. D., COMBER, C. H. & WILKINSON, W. *The Hammered Silver coins produced at the Tower Mint during the reign of Elizabeth I*. 2006

BROWN, I. D. and DOLLEY, M. *Bibliography of Coin Hoards of Great Britain and Ireland 1500-1967*. 1971

BUCK, I. *Medieval English Groats*. 2000

CARSON, R. A. G. *Mints, Dies and Currency. Essays in Memory of Albert Baldwin*. 1971

CHICK, D. *The Coinage of Offa and his Contemporaries*. 2010

CHURCHILL, R. *Mints and Moneyers during the reign of Henry III*. 2012

CHURCHILL, R. and THOMAS B. *The Brussels Hoard of 1908. The Long Cross Coinage of Henry III*. 2012

DAVIES, P. J. *British Silver Coins Since 1816 with Engravers' Patterns and Proofs and Unofficial Pieces*. 1982

DE JERSEY, P. *Coinage in Iron Age Armorica.* 1994

DOLLEY, R. H. M. (ed.). *Anglo-Saxon Coins; studies presented to Sir Frank Stenton.* 1964

EAGLEN, R. J. *The Abbey and Mint of Bury St. Edmunds to 1279.* 2006

EVERSON, T. *The Galata Guide to The Farthing Tokens of James I & Charles I.* 2007

FREEMAN, M. J. *The Bronze Coinage of Great Britain.* 2006

GRIERSON, P. and BLACKBURN, M. A. S. *Medieval European Coinage, vol. 1, The Early Middle Ages.* 1986

HOBBS, R. *British Iron Age Coins in the British Museum.* 1996

KEARY, C. and GREUBER, H. *English Coins in the British Museum: Anglo-Saxon Series.* 1887, reprinted, 1970, 2 volumes.

LAKER, A. J. *The portrait Groats of Henry VIII.* 1978

LAWRENCE, L. A. *The Coinage of Edward III from 1351.*

LINECAR, H. W. A. *The Crown Pieces of Great Britain and the British Commonwealth.* 1962
— — *English Proof and Pattern Crown-Size Pieces.* 1968

MACK, R. P. *The R. P. Mack Collection, Ancient British, Anglo-Saxon and Norman Coins.* (SCBI no. 20) 1973

MANVILLE, H. E. *Encyclopedia of British Numismatics. Numismatic Guide to British and Irish Periodicals 1731-1991.* 1993

MANVILLE, H. E. and ROBERTSON, T. J. *An Annotated Bibliography of British Numismatic Auction Catalogues from 1710 to the Present.* 1986

MARSH, M. A. *The Gold Half Sovereign.* 2nd Edition, revised 2004

MARSH, M. A. *The Gold Sovereign.* 2nd Edition 1999

MASS, J. P. *The J. P. Mass collection of English Short Cross Coins 1180-1247. (SCBI 56).* 2001

NAISMITH, R. *The Coinage of Southern England, 796-c.865.* 2011

NORTH, J. J. *Edwardian English Silver Coins 1279-1351. (SCBI 39)* 1989

NORTH, J. J. and PRESTON-MORLEY, P. J. *The John G. Brooker Collection: Coins of Charles I. (SCBI 33)* 1984

PECK, C. W. *English Copper, Tin and Bronze Coins in the British Museum, 1558-1958.* 1970

RAYNER, P.A. *The English Silver Coinage from 1649.* 5th ed. 1992

REECE, R. *Coinage in Roman Britain,* 1987

ROBINSON, Dr. B. *The Royal Maundy.* 1992

RUDD, C. *Ancient British Coins (ABC).* 2009

RUDING, REV. R. *Annals of the Coinage of Great Britain.* 3rd Edition 1840

SEAR, D. R. *Roman Coins and their Values.* 4th Edition (1999) Reprinted 2000

SILLS, J. *Gaulish and Early British Gold Coinage.* 2003

THOMPSON, J. D. A. *Inventory of British Coin Hoards, A.D. 600-1500.* 1956

VAN ARSDELL, R. *Celtic Coinage of Britain.* 1989

VAN ARSDELL, R. D. *The Coinage of the Dobunni.* 1994

WHITTON, C. A. *The Heavy Coinage of Henry VI.*

WILSON, A. and RASMUSSEN, M. *English Patten, Trial and Proof Coin in Gold, 1547-1968.* 2000

WITHERS, P. & B. R. *The Galata Guide to the Pennies of Edward I and II and the Coins of the mint of Berwick-upon-Tweed.* 2006

WOODHEAD, P. *English Gold Coins 1257-1603. The Herbert Schneider Collection, vol. 1 (SCBI 47)* 1996
— — *English Gold Coins 1603-20th Century. The Herbert Schneider Collection, vol. 2 (SCBI 57)* 2002

WREN, C. R. *The Short-cross coinage 1180-1247. Henry II to Henry III. An illustrated Guide to Identification.* 1992

— — *The Voided Long-Cross Coinage 1247-1279. Henry III and Edward I.* 1993

— — *The English Long-Cross Pennies 1279-1489. Edward I-Henry VII.* 1995

For further references to British hammered coinage see *Sylloge of Coins of the British Isles,* a serial publication now comprising 66 volumes cataloguing collections in private hands and institutions. For a full list of the volumes published to date in this series, please contact Spink at the address below.

Other authoritative papers are published in the *Numismatic Chronicle, British Numismatic Journal and Spink's Numismatic Circular.* A complete book list is available from Spink & Son Ltd., 69 Southampton Row, Bloomsbury, London WC1B 4ET. Tel: 020 7563 4046 Fax: 020 7563 4068. Email: Books@spink.com

Further information regarding membership of the British Numismatic Society can be found at www.britnumsoc.org

Inc. Gregory's Est.1858

Books
by our CEO Brett Hammond

**British Artefacts
Volume 1
Early Anglo-Saxon**

**British Artefacts
Volume 2
Middle Saxon
& Viking**

**British Artefacts
Volume 3
Late Saxon, Late
Viking & Norman**

enquiries@timelineauctions.com
+44 [0]1277 815121

LATIN OR FOREIGN LEGENDS ON ENGLISH COINS

A DOMINO FACTUM EST ISTUD ET EST MIRABILE IN OCULIS NOSTRIS. (This is the Lord's doing and it is marvellous in our eyes: *Psalm 118.23.*) First used on 'fine' sovereign of Mary.

AMOR POPULI PRAESIDIUM REGIS. (The love of the people is the King's protection.) Reverse legend on angels of Charles I.

ANNO REGNI PRIMO, etc. (In the first year of the reign, etc.) Used around the edge of many of the larger milled denominations.

CHRISTO AUSPICE REGNO. (I reign under the auspice of Christ.) Used extensively in the reign of Charles I.

CIVIUM INDUSTRIA FLORET CIVITAS. (By the industry of its people the State flourishes.) On the 1951 Festival Crown of George VI.

CULTORES SUI DEUS PROTEGIT. (God protects His worshippers.) On gold double crowns and crowns of Charles I.

DECUS ET TUTAMEN. (An ornament and a safeguard: Virgil, *Aenid,* v.262.) This inscription on the edge of all early large milled silver was suggested by Evelyn, he having seen it on the vignette in Cardinal Richelieu's Greek Testament, and of course refers to the device as a means to prevent clipping. This legend also appears on the edge of U.K. and Northern Ireland one pound coins.

DIEU ET MON DROIT. (God and my right.) On halfcrowns of George IV and later monarchs

DIRIGE DEUS GRESSUS MEOS. (May God direct my steps: *Psalm 118.133.*) On the 'Una' Five pounds of Queen Victoria.

DOMINE NE IN FURORE TUO ARGUAS ME. (O Lord, rebuke me not in Thine anger: *Psalm 6, 1.).* First used on the half-florin of Edward III and then on all half-nobles.

DomiNus Deus Omnipotens REX. (Lord God, Almighty King.) Viking coins.

DUM SPIRO SPERO. (Whilst I live, I hope.) On the coins struck at Pontefract Castle during the Civil War after Charles I had been imprisoned.

EXALTABITUR IN GLORIA. (He shall be exalted in glory: *Psalm 111.9.*) On all quarter-nobles.

EXURGAT DEUS ET DISSIPENTUR INIMICI EIUS. (Let God arise and let His enemies be scattered: *Psalm* 68, 1.) On the Scottish ducat and early English coins of James I (VI) and was chosen by the King himself. Also on Charles I, civil war, and Declaration coins,

FACIAM EOS IN GENTEM UNAM. (I will make them one nation: *Ezekiel, 37, 22.)* On unites and laurels of James I.

FLORENT CONCORDIA REGNA. (Through concord kingdoms flourish.) On gold unite of Charles I and broad of Charles II.

HANC DEUS DEDIT. (God has given this, i.e. the crown .) On siege-pieces of Pontefract struck in the name of Charles II.

HAS NISI PERITURUS MIHI ADIMAT NEMO. (Let no one remove these [letters] from me under penalty of death.) On the edge of crowns and half-crowns of Cromwell.

HENRICUS ROSAS REGNA JACOBUS. (Henry united the roses, James the kingdoms.) On English and Scottish gold coins of James I (VI).

HONI SOIT QUI MAL Y PENSE. (Evil to him who evil thinks.) The Motto of the Order of the Garter, first used on the Hereford (?) halfcrowns of Charles I. It also occurs on the Garter Star in the centre of the reverse of the silver coins of Charles II, but being so small it is usually illegible; it is more prominent on the coinage of George III.

ICH DIEN. (I serve.) Aberystwyth Furnace 2d, and Decimal 2p. The motto of The Prince of Wales.

INIMICOS EJUS INDUAM CONFUSIONE. (As for his enemies I shall clothe them with shame: *Psalm* 132, 18.) On shillings of Edward VI struck at Durham House, Strand.

JESUS AUTEM TRANSIENS PER MEDIUM ILLORUM IBAT. (But Jesus, passing through the midst of them, went His way: *Luke iv. 30.)* The usual reverse legend on English nobles, ryals and hammered sovereigns before James I; also on the very rare Scottish noble of David II of Scotland and the unique Anglo-Gallic noble of Edward the Black Prince.

JUSTITIA THRONUM FIRMAT. (Justice strengthens the throne.) On Charles I half-groats and pennies and Scottish twenty-penny pieces.

LUCERNA PEDIBUS MEIS VERBUM EST. (Thy word is a lamp unto my feet: *Psalm 119, 105.)* Obverse legend on a rare half-sovereign of Edward VI struck at Durham House, Strand.

MIRABILIA FECIT. (He made marvellously: *Psalm 97.1.*) On the Viking coins of (?) York.

NEMO ME IMPUNE LACESSIT. (No-one provokes me with impunity.) On the 1984 Scottish one pound. Motto of The Order of the Thistle.

NUMMORUM FAMULUS. (The servant of the coinage.) The legend on the edge of the English tin coinage at the end of the seventeenth century.

O CRUX AVE SPES UNICA. (Hail! O Cross, our only hope.) On the reverse of all half-angels.

PAX MISSA PER ORBEM. (Peace sent throughout the world.) The reverse legend of a pattern farthing of Anne.

PAX QUÆRITUR BELLO. (Peace is sought by war.) The reverse legend of the Cromwell broad.

PER CRUCEM TUAM SALVA NOS CHRISTE REDEMPTOR. (By Thy cross, save us, O Christ, our Redeemer.) The normal reverse of English angels.

PLEIDIOL WYF I'M GWLAD. (True am I to my country.) Used on the 1985 Welsh one pound. Taken from the Welsh National Anthem.

POST MORTEM PATRIS PRO FILIO. (After the death of the father for the son.) On siege-pieces struck at Pontefract in 1648 (old style) after the execution of Charles I.

POSUI DEUM ADJUTOREM MEUM. (I have made God my Helper: *comp. Psalm* 54, 4.) Used on many English and Irish silver coins from Edward III until 1603. Altered to POSUIMUS and NOSTRUM on the coins of Philip and Mary.

PROTECTOR LITERIS LITERÆ NUMMIS CORONA ET SALUS. (A protection to the letters [on the face of the coin], the letters [on the edge] are a garland and a safeguard to the coinage.) On the edge of the rare fifty-shilling piece of Cromwell.

QUÆ DEUS CONJUNXIT NEMO SEPARET. (What God hath joined together let no man put asunder: *Matthew* 19, 6.) On the larger silver English and Scottish coins of James I after he succeeded to the English throne.

REDDE CUIQUE QUOD SUUM EST. (Render to each that which is his own.) On a Henry VIII type groat of Edward VI struck by Sir Martin Bowes at Durham House, Strand.

RELIGIO PROTESTANTIVM LEGES ANGLIÆ LIBERTAS PARLIAMENTI. (The religion of the Protestants, the laws of England, the liberty of the Parliament.) This is known as the 'Declaration' and refers to Charles I's declaration to the Privy Council at Wellington, 19 September, 1642; it is found on many of his coins struck at the provincial mints during the Civil War. Usually abbreviated to REL:PROT:LEG: ANG:LIB:PAR:

ROSA SINE SPINA. (A rose without a thorn.) Found on some gold and small coins of Henry VIII and later reigns.

RUTILANS ROSA SINE SPINA. (A dazzling rose without a thorn.) As last but on small gold only.

SCUTUM FIDEI PROTEGET EUM or EAM. (The shield of faith shall protect him, or her.) On much of the gold of Edward VI and Elizabeth.

SIC VOS NON VOBIS (Thus we labour but not for ourselves). 1994 £2 Bank of England.

TALI DICATA SIGNO MENS FLUCTUARI NEQUIT. (Consecrated by such a sign the mind cannot waver: from a hymn by Prudentius written in the fourth century, entitled 'Hymnus ante Somnum'.) Only on the gold 'George noble' of Henry VIII.

TIMOR DOMINI FONS VITÆ. (The fear of the Lord is a fountain of life: *Proverbs, 14, 27.)* On many shillings of Edward VI.

TVAETVR VNITA DEVS. (May God guard these united, i.e. kingdoms.) On many English Scottish and Irish coins of James I.

VERITAS TEMPORIS FILIA. (Truth, the daughter of Time.) On English and Irish coins of Mary Tudor.

Some Royal Titles:

REX ANGL*orum*—King of the English.

REX SAXONIORVM OCCIDENTALIVM —King of the West Saxons.

DEI GR*Atia* REX *ANGLiae* ET FRANC*iae DomiNus* HYB*erniae ET AQVITaniae*—By the Grace of God, King of England and France, Lord of Ireland and Aquitaine.

D*ei GRAtia Magnae Britanniae, FRanciae ET Hiberniae REX Fidei Defensor BRunsviciensis ET Luneburgen-sis Dux, Sacri Romani Imperii Archi-THesaurarius ET ELector*=By the Grace of God, King of Great Britain, France and Ireland, Defender of the Faith, Duke of Brunswick and Luneburg, High Treasurer and Elector of the Holy Roman Empire.

BRITANNIARUM REX —King of the Britains (i.e. Britain and British territories overseas).

BRITT:OMN:REX:FID:DEF:IND:IMP: —King of all the Britains, Defender of the Faith, Emperor of India.

VIVAT REGINA ELIZABETHA — Long live Queen Elizabeth. On the 1996 £5 Queen's 70th birthday £5 crown.

APPENDIX III

NUMISMATIC CLUBS AND SOCIETIES

Coin News, The Searcher and *Treasure Hunting*, are the major monthly magazines covering numismatics. Many local numismatic societies and clubs in the British Isles are affiliated to the British Association of Numismatic Societies (BANS) which holds an annual Congress and an annual Conference (weekend meetings) with a range of speakers in convivial surroundings. Details and contacts for a club or society near can be found online, www.coinclubs.org.uk or by contacting the Hon. Secretary, Phyllis Stoddart, British Association of Numismatic Societies, c/o Dept. of Numismatics, Manchester Museum, Oxford Road, Manchester M13 9PL email: phyllis.stoddart@manchester.ac.uk.

The two principal learned societies are the Royal Numismatic Society (RNS), c/o Department of Coins and Medals, the British Museum, Great Russell Street, Bloomsbury, London WC1B 3DG, and the British Numismatic Society (BNS), c/o The Secretary, Peter Preston-Morley, c/o Dix, Noonan, Webb, 16 Bolton Street, London, W1J 8BQ, email: ppm@dnw.co.uk. Both these societies publish an annual journal. To find out more about membership, meetings and publications, for the RNS go to www.numismatics.org.uk and for the BNS, go to www.britnumsoc.org.uk

MINTMARKS AND OTHER SYMBOLS ON ENGLISH COINS

A Mintmark (*mm.*), is a term borrowed from Roman and Greek numismatics where it showed the place of mintage; it was generally used on English coins to show where the legend began (a religious age preferred a cross for the purpose). Later, this mark, since the dating of coins was not usual, had a periodic significance, changing from time to time. Hence it was of a secret or 'privy' nature; other privy marks on a coin might be the code-mark of a particular workshop or workman. Thus a privy mark (including the *mintmark.*) might show when a coin was made, or who made it. In the use of precious metals this knowledge was necessary to guard against fraud and counterfeiting.

Mintmarks are sometimes termed 'initial marks' as they are normally placed at the commencement of the inscription. Some of the symbols chosen were personal badges of the ruling monarch, such as the rose and sun of York, or the boar's head of Richard III, the dragon of Henry Tudor or the thistle of James I; others are heraldic symbols or may allude to the mint master responsible for the coinage, e.g. the *mm.* bow used on the Durham House coins struck under John Bowes and the WS mark of William Sharrington of Bristol.

A table of mintmarks is given overleaf. Where mintmarks appear in the catalogue they are sometimes referred to only by the reference number, in order to save space, i.e. *mm. 28* (=mintmark Sun), *mm.28/74* (=*mm.* Sun on obverse, *mm.* Coronet on reverse), *mm. 28/-* (=*mm.* Sun on obverse only).

Timeline **Auctions**
Inc. Gregory's **Est.1858**

We are accepting single entries and collections
of coins & antiquities

www.timelineauctions.com

Contact either Brett Hammond
or Christopher Wren on
+44 [0]1277 815121
enquiries@timelineauctions.com

Follow us on:

f /TimeLineAuctions
t @TimeLineAuction

AIAΔ

BNTA

1	Edward III, Cross 1 (Class B+C).	
2	Edward III, broken Cross 1 (Class D).	
3	Edward III, Cross 2 (Class E)	
4	Edward III, Cross 3 (Class G)	
5	Cross Potent (Edw. III Treaty)	
6	Cross Pattée (Edw. III Post Treaty Rich. III).	
7	(a) Plain of Greek Cross. (b) Cross Moline.	
8	Cross Patonce.	
9	Cross Fleuree.	
10	Cross Calvary (Cross on steps).	
11	Long Cross Fitchée.	
12	Short Cross Fitchée.	
13	Restoration Cross (Hen. VI).	
14	Latin Cross.	
15	Voided Cross (Henry VI).	
16	Saltire Cross.	
17	Cross and 4 pellets.	
18	Pierced Cross.	
19	Pierced Cross & pellet.	
20	Pierced Cross & central pellet.	
21	Cross Crosslet.	
22	Curved Star (rayant).	
23	Star.	
24	Spur Rowel.	
25	Mullet.	
26	Pierced Mullet.	
27	Eglantine.	
28	Sun (Edw. IV).	
29	Mullet (Henry V).	
30	Pansy.	
31	Heraldic Cinquefoil (Edw. IV).	
32	Heraldic Cinquefoil (James I).	
33	Rose (Edw. IV).	
34	Rosette (Edw. IV).	
35	Rose (Chas. I).	
36	Catherine Wheel.	
37	Cross in circle.	
38	Halved Sun (6 rays) & Rose.	
39	Halved Sun (4 rays) & Rose.	
40	Lis-upon-Half-Rose.	
41	Lis-upon-Sun & Rose.	
42	Lis-Rose dimidiated.	
43	Lis-issuant-from-Rose.	
44	Trefoil.	

45	Slipped Trefoil, James I (1).	
46	Slipped Trefoil, James I (2).	
47	Quatrefoil.	
48	Saltire.	
49	Pinecone.	
50	Leaf (-mascle, Hen. VI).	
51	Leaf (-trefoil, Hen. VI).	
52	Arrow.	
53	Pheon.	
54	A.	
55	Annulet.	
56	Annulet-with-pellet.	
57	Anchor.	
58	Anchor & B.	
59	Flower & B.	
60	Bell.	
61	Book.	
62	Boar's Head (early Richard III).	
63	Boar's Head (later Richard III).	
64	Boar's Head, Charles I.	
65	Acorn	(a) Hen. VIII
		(b) Elizabeth.
66	Bow.	
67	Br. (Bristol, Chas. I).	
68	Cardinal's Hat.	
69	Castle (Henry VIII).	
70	Castle with H.	
71	Castle (Chas. I).	
72	Crescent	(a) Henry VIII
		(b) Elizabeth.
73	Pomegranate. (Mary; Henry VIII's is broader).	
74	Coronet.	
75	Crown.	
76	Crozier	(a) Edw. III
		(b) Hen. VIII.
77	Ermine.	
78	Escallop (Hen. VII).	
79	Escallop (James I).	
80	Eye (in legend Edw. IV).	
81	Eye (Parliament).	
82	Radiate Eye (Hen. VII).	
83	Gerb.	
84	Grapes.	
85	Greyhound's Head.	
86	Hand.	
87	Harp.	
88	Heart.	
89	Helmet.	
90	Key.	
91	Leopard's Head.	

91A	Crowned Leopard's Head with collar (Edw. VI).
92	Lion.
93	Lion rampant.
94	Martlet.
95	Mascle.
96	Negro's Head.
97	Ostrich's Head.
98	P in brackets.
99	Pall.
100	Pear.
101	Plume.
102	Plume. Aberystwyth and Bristol.
103	Plume. Oxford.
104	Plume. Shrewsbury.
105	Lis.
106	Lis.
107	Portcullis.
108	Portcullis, Crowned.
109	Sceptre.
110	Sunburst.
111	Swan.
112	R in brackets.
113	Sword.
114	T (Henry VIII).
115	TC monogram.
116	WS monogram.
117	y or Y.
118	Dragon (Henry VII).
119	(a) Triangle (b) Triangle in Circle.
120	Sun (Parliament).
121	Uncertain mark.
122	Grapple.
123	Tun.
124	Woolpack.
125	Thistle.
126	Figure 6 (Edw. VI).
127	Floriated cross.
128	Lozenge.
129	Billet.
130	Plume. Bridgnorth or late declaration
131	Two lions.
132	Clasped book.
133	Cross pommée.
134	Bugle.
135	Crowned T (Tournai, Hen VIII)
136	An incurved pierced cross

The reign listed after a mintmark indicates that from which the drawing is taken. A similar mm. may have been used in another reign and will be found in the chronological list at the beginning of each reign.

1	2	3	4	5	6	7a	7b	8 / 9 / 37
10	11	12	13	14	15	16	17	18 / 19
20	21	22	23	24	25	26	27	28 / 29
30	31	32	33	34	35	36	37	38 / 39
40	41	42	43	44	45	46	47	48 / 49
50	51	52	53	54	55	56	57	58 / 59 B
60	61	62	63	64	65a	65b	66	67 / 68
69	70	71	72a	72b	73	74	75	76 / 77
78	79	80	81	82	83	84	85	86 / 87
88	89	90 a	90b	90c.	91	92	93	94 / 95
96	97	98 (P)	99	100	101	102	103	104 / 105
106	107	108	109	110	111	112 (R)	113	114 / 115
116	117a.	117b.	118	119 a.	119 b.	120	121	122 / 123
124	125	126	127	128	129	130	131	132 / 133
134	135	136						

Page

'Aedic Sia', Iceni 45
'Aesu', Iceni 44
'Agr', Trinovantes and Catuvellauni 30
'Ale Sca', Iceni 44
'Anted', Dobunni 34
'Anted', Iceni 43
'Avn Cost', Corieltauvi 38
'Bodvoc', Dobunni 36
'Can Dvro', Iceni 43
'Cat', Corieltauvi 40
'Catti', Dobunni 35
'Comux', Dobunni 35
'Corio', Dobunni 35
'Crab', Durotriges 33
'Dias', Catuvellauni 24
'Diras', Trinovantes 20
'Dvmno Tigir Seno', Corieltauvi 39
'Ece', Iceni 44
'Ecen', Iceni 44
'Edn', Iceni 44
'Eisv', Dobunni 35
'Esvp Rasv', Corieltauvi 38
'Iat Iso E', Corieltauvi 40
'Inam', Dobunni 35
'Lat Ison', Corieltauvi 40
'Rues', Catuvellauni 25
'Saenu', Iceni 44
'Sam', Cantii 18
'Sego', Catuvellauni 23
'Solidv', Trinovantes and Catuvellauni 30
'Vep Corf', Corieltauvi 39
'Vep', Corieltauvi 38
'Volisios Cartivel', Corieltauvi 48
'Volisios Dvmnocoveros', Corieltauvi 39
'Volisios Dvmnovellaunos', Corieltauvi 40
Addedomaros, Trinovantes 19
Aelfwald I, King of Northumbria 102
Aelfwald II, King of Northumbria 103
Aethelberht, King of East Anglia 114
Aethelberht, King of Wessex 123
Aethelheard, Archbishop of Canterbury 107
Aethelred I, King of Danish East Anglia 115
Aethelred I, King of Northumbria 102
Aethelred I, King of Wessex 124
Aethelred II 134
Aethelred II, King of Northumbria 104
Aethelstan 127
Aethelstan I, King of East Anglia 115
Aethelstan II, King of Danish East Anglia... 115
Aethelwald Moll, King of Northumbria 102
Aethelweard, King of East Anglia 115

Page

Aethelwulf, King of Wessex 122
Aethelred, Archbishop of Canterbury 108
Alberht, King of East Anglia 114
Alchred, King of Northumbia 102
Aldfrith, King of Northumbria 101
Alfred, imitations, Danish East Anglia 116
Alfred, King of Wessex 124
Allectus, Roman Britain 74
Amminus, Cantii 18
Andoco, Catuvellauni 24
Anlaf Guthfrithsson, Hiberno-Norse King
of York 120
Anlaf Sihtricsson, Hiberno-Norse King
of York 120
Anne 387
Anonymous coinage, Kings of Kent 106
Baldred, King of Kent 107
Beonna, King of East Anglia 114
Beorhtric, King of Wessex 121
Beornwulf, King of Mercia 111
Berhtwulf, King of Mercia 112
Brian Fitzcount, Angevin issued 159
Burgred 112
Caratacus, Trinovantes and Catuvellauni 32
Carausius, Roman Britain 72
Ceolnoth, Archbishop of Canterbury 108
Ceolwulf I, King of Mercia 111
Ceolwulf II, King of Mercia 114
Charles I 282
Charles II 330
Cnut 136
Cnut, Viking coinage of York 118
Coenwulf, King of Mercia 110
Commius, Atrebates and Regni 9
Commonwealth 325
Cromwell 328
Cunobelin, Trinovantes and Catuvellauni 25
Cuthred, King of Kent 106
Cynethryth, Wife of Offa 110
David I, King of Scotland 156
Dubnovellaunus, Cantii 17
Dubnovellaunus, Trinovantes 20
Eadberht Praen, King of Kent 106
Eadberht, Bishop of London 110
Eadberht, King of Northumbria 102
Eadgar 130
Eadmund 128
Eadred 129
Eadwald, King of East Anglia 114
Eadwig 129
Eanbald II, Archbishop of York 104

Page

Eanred, King of Northumbia...... 104
Eardwulf...... 103
Ecgberht, Archbishop of York...... 102
Ecgberht, King of Kent...... 106
Ecgberht, King of Wessex...... 121
Edmund, King of East Anglia...... 115
Edward I...... 173
Edward II...... 180
Edward III...... 182
Edward IV or V...... 224
Edward IV, First Reign...... 213
Edward IV, Second Reign...... 221
Edward the Confessor...... 138
Edward the Elder, King of Wessex...... 125
Edward the Martyr...... 132
Edward VI...... 246
Edward VII...... 493
Edward VIII...... 511
Elizabeth I...... 259
Elizabeth II...... 521
Epaticcus, Trinovantes and Catuvellauni...... 31
Eppillus, Atrebates and Regni...... 12
Eric Blood-axe, Hiberno-Norse King of York. 121
Eustace Fitzjohn, Baronial Issue...... 157
George I...... 399
George II...... 407
George III...... 419
George IV...... 438
George V...... 499
George VI...... 513
Guthfrith, Viking Coinage of York...... 117
Harold I...... 137
Harold II...... 142
Harthacnut...... 137
Heaberht, King of Kent...... 106
Henry of Neubourg, Angevin issue...... 158
Henry I...... 151
Henry II...... 162
Henry III...... 165
Henry IV...... 197
Henry V...... 200
Henry VI...... 203
Henry VI Restored...... 220
Henry VII...... 227
Henry VIII...... 234
Henry, Bishop of Winchester, Baronial issue.. 157
Henry, Earl of Northumberland, Baronial issue...... 156
Henry Murdac, Archbishop of York...... 157
Howel Dda, King of Dyfed...... 129
Jaenberht, Archbishop of Canterbury...... 107

Page

James I...... 272
James II...... 356
John...... 164
Ludica, King of Mercia...... 111
Mary...... 255
Matilda, Empress...... 158
Offa, King of Mercia...... 109
Olaf Sihtricsson, Hiberno-Norse, King of York...... 121
Osberht, King of Northumbria...... 104
Oswald, King of Danish East Anglia...... 115
Patrick, Earl of Salisbury?, Angevin issue... 159
Philip and Mary...... 257
Plegmund, Archbishop of Canterbury...... 108
Plegmund, imitation, Danish East Anglia.... 117
Prasutagus, Iceni...... 45
Redwulf, King of Northumbria...... 104
Regnald Guthfrithsson, Hiberno-Norse King of York...... 121
Regnald I, Hiberno-Norse, King of York..... 119
Richard I...... 163
Richard II...... 193
Richard III...... 225
Robert, Earl of Gloucester, Angevin issue... 159
Robert, Earl of Leicester?, Baronial issue ... 157
Rodbert de Stuteville, Baronial issue...... 157
Sceattas, 'Aethiliraed'...... 87
Sceattas, 'Animal mask' group...... 99
Sceattas, 'Archer' type...... 99
Sceattas, 'Carip' group...... 97
Sceattas, 'Hexagon type'...... 91
Sceattas, 'Interlace Cross' type...... 91
Sceattas, 'Monita Scorum' type...... 98
Sceattas, 'Pada'...... 86
Sceattas, 'Saltire Standard' type...... 100
Sceattas, 'Saroaldo' type...... 88
Sceattas, 'SEDE' type...... 89
Sceattas, 'Triquetras' eclectic' group...... 98
Sceattas, 'Vanimundus'...... 86
Sceattas, 'Vernus' type...... 88
Sceattas, Series A...... 87
Sceattas, Series B...... 87
Sceattas, Series C...... 87
Sceattas, Series D...... 90
Sceattas, Series E...... 89
Sceattas, Series F...... 88
Sceattas, Series G...... 91
Sceattas, Series H...... 92
Sceattas, Series J...... 92
Sceattas, Series K...... 92
Sceattas, Series L...... 93

	Page
Sceattas, Series M	94
Sceattas, Series N	94
Sceattas, Series O	94
Sceattas, Series Q	95
Sceattas, Series R	96
Sceattas, Series S	97
Sceattas, Series T	97
Sceattas, Series U	97
Sceattas, Series V	97
Sceattas, Series W	89
Sceattas, Series X	91
Sceattas, Series Z	88
Sceattas, Type 8	91
Sceattas, Type 10	91
Sceattas, Type 22, 'Victory'	99
Sceattas, Type 23e	94
Sceattas, Type 30	100
Sceattas, Type 53 'Stepped Cross'	89
Sceattas, Type 70	100
Siefred, Viking Coinage of York	117
Sihtric I, Hiberno-Norse, King of York	120
Sihtric Sihtricsson, Hiberno-Norse, King of York	121
Sihtric, Earl, Danish East Anglia	117

	Page
St. Martin of Lincoln, Danish East Anglia	116
St. Peter coinage, Hiberno-Norse Kings of York	119
St. Edmund, memorial coinage, Danish East Anglia	116
Stephen	153
Tasciovanus, Catuvellauni	21
Thrymsas, Crondall types	85
Thrymsas, Post-Crondall types	86
Thrymsas, Ultra-Crondall types	85
Tincomarus, Atrebates and Regni	10
Verica, Atrebates and Regni	14
Victoria	451
Vosenos, Cantii	18
Wiglaf, King of Mercia	111
Wigmund, Archbishop of York	105
William and Mary	362
William I	149
William II	150
William III	370
William IV	445
William, Earl of Gloucester, Angevin issue	159
Wulfhere, Archbishop of York	105
Wulfred, Archbishop of Canterbury	108

Timeline Originals

TimeLine Originals is pleased to offer for sale many fine coins and antiquities. Prime English, ancient and classical coins are always available. Visit our website to discover what we have to offer:

TimeLine Originals is one of the world's leading web-based coin galleries. Our stock changes constantly – please check back regularly.

www.time-lines.co.uk

Single items or entire collections for sale? Our friendly, professional team can provide free, confidential appraisals without obligation.

TimeLine Originals
The Court House
363 Main Road
Harwich, Essex
CO12 4DN, UK
+44 [0]1277 815121
sales@time-lines.co.uk
Belgravia Developments UK Ltd.

NOTES

NOTES

NOTES

NOTES

SPINK

LONDON
1666

OUTSTANDING GLOBAL SERVICE
FOR COLLECTORS AND NUMISMATISTS

MARKET LEADING SPECIALISTS
AND AUCTIONEERS FOR:

COINS | HISTORICAL MEDALS
NUMISMATIC BOOKS | ACCESSORIES

AVAILABLE FOR SALE OR
PUCHASE BY PRIVATE TREATY

NOW ACCEPTING CONSIGNMENTS
FOR OUR FORTHCOMING SALES IN
LONDON | NEW YORK | HONG KONG

For more information about Spink's auctions around the world, please contact

RICHARD BISHOP | **Tel:** +44 (0)20 7563 4053 | **Email:** rbishop@spink.com
SPINK LONDON | 69 Southampton Row | Bloomsbury | London | WC1B 4ET

GREGORY COLE | **Tel:** +1 212 262 8400 | **Email:** gcole@spink.com
SPINK USA | 145 W. 57th St. | 18th Floor | New York, NY | 10019

DR KELVIN CHEUNG | **Tel:** +852 3952 3000 | **Email:** kcheung@spink.com
SPINK CHINA | 4/F & 5/F | Hua Fu Commercial Building | 111 Queen's Road West | Hong Kong

WWW.SPINK.COM

LONDON
1666

SPINK BOOKS

STAMPS | COINS | BANKNOTES | MEDALS | BONDS & SHARES | AUTOGRAPHS | BOOKS | WINES

Spink has been a leading publisher of Numismatic Books for over
100 years.

Offering a wide range of important works on British coins, medals
and tokens, all publications, including those of the
British Numismatic Society and the Royal Numismatic Society,

Available for order on our website:

WWW.SPINKBOOKS.COM

For more information or enquiries, please contact the **Spink Book Department:**
Tel: +44 (0)20 7563 4000 | **Fax:** +44 (0)20 7563 40785 | **Email:** books@spink.com

SPINK | 69 Southampton Row | Bloomsbury | London | WC1B 4ET
WWW.SPINKBOOKS.COM

LONDON | NEW YORK | HONG KONG | SINGAPORE | LUGANO